*THE GUN COLLECTOR'S HANDBOOK OF VALUES*

A page from an early Colt advertisement, showing markings on the cylinders of the Dragoon, Navy and Pocket models, made at Hartford. *Courtesy Albert Foster, Jr.*

# THE
# Gun Collector's
# Handbook
# of Values

*THIRTEENTH REVISED EDITION*

## by *Charles Edward Chapel*

FIRST LIEUTENANT, U.S. MARINE CORPS, RETIRED

*Revised by Mrs. Charles Edward Chapel*

COWARD, McCANN & GEOGHEGAN, INC.
NEW YORK

*Dedicated to my wife,*
*Dorothy M. Chapel*

**Thirteenth Revised Edition**

*Statements in this book are the personal opinions of the author. They are not to be construed as necessarily reflecting the official opinions of the Navy Department or the naval service at large. (Required by U.S. Navy Regulations.)*

**Library of Congress Cataloging in Publication Data**

Chapel, Charles Edward, 1904-1967.
    The gun collector's handbook of values.

    Bibliograph: p.
    Includes index.
    1.   Firearms—Collectors and collecting.      2.   Firearms—Catalogs.
    I.   Chapel, Charles Edward, Mrs.
II.   Title.
TS532.4.C47        1979        683'.4'0075        79-16182
ISBN 0-698-11011-0 cloth
ISBN 0-698-11010-2 paper

# CONTENTS

# ILLUSTRATIONS

# INTRODUCTION

THIS BOOK describes about 3,000 American and foreign firearms, both ancient and semi-modern, and assigns values for these pieces in "good" and "fine" condition according to the author's definitions of these terms, which coincide with the condition standards of the National Rifle Association of America.

The firearms described and illustrated have been selected on the basis of the interest in them demonstrated by collectors since 1940. In this text are descriptions of the majority of arms found in a typical American collection and those proudly displayed by museums and advanced specialists. Also, the space devoted to weapons, in both description and chapter organization, reflects the preferences of the majority of collectors in the United States. No attempt has been made to include every firearm ever made. No single volume, however large, could include adequate descriptions of all firearms.

In the practical use of this book by collectors, dealers, museum curators, and historians, the following suggestions are offered:

First, reading a book is not a substitute for practical experience. In case of doubt, consult an expert before buying or selling a firearm unless you want to run the risk of losing money. Beware of fakes!

Second, many guns in this book have high values, but there are many firearms in this text within the financial reach of the average collector. The guns that have fairly low values now will have high values eventually because the number of antique and semi-modern guns theoretically remains fixed while the population and the demand for old guns increase. The phrase "theoretically remains fixed" assumes that old guns are not destroyed by fire, the perils of the sea, or other destruction.

Third, it is advisable to buy antique and semi-modern guns in the best possible condition. Avoid buying guns in a condition less than "good" except as a means of temporarily filling a vacant place in a specialized collection.

Fourth, although it is carefully explained in more detail in the chapters on gun values and condition, a gun in a condition better than "fine" may be worth anywhere from 25% to 100% more, depending upon the law of supply and demand and the desire of the owner to sell.

Fifth, the advanced collectors, the men and women who specialize in the more desirable weapons and have devoted many years to their hobby, agree with the author of this text that the beginner should subscribe to several gun magazines, including those on shooting, as well as the periodicals devoted entirely to gun collecting. The novice should write to all dealers in antique arms for their price lists and catalogues. Many dealers charge for their publications, but the beginner cannot lose because even the price lists and catalogues of dealers are collected and increase in value. In reading the catalogues and price lists, look for the description and the price assigned each item. In case of doubt, write to the National Rifle Association of America, publishers of *The American Rifleman*, 1600 Rhode Island Avenue, N.W., Washington, D.C. 20036, and ask if it publishes advertisements for any dealer whose catalogue or price list attracts your attention. If the reply is negative, beware!

Sixth, beginners should read the author's book *The Complete Book of Gun Collecting* to learn how to plan the organization of a gun collection. In order to care for firearms properly, the next book to read is *The Complete Guide to Gunsmithing*. Although that book was written for amateur and professional gunsmiths, the text and illustrations enable a gun collector to understand how firearms are made, repaired, cleaned, and ethically restored. Then, as his collection grows, the beginner may find that many desirable weapons presently valued within his means are described and illustrated in *Guns of the Old West,* together with the true stories of the men and women whose lives and liberties depended on those old guns. Those interested in the early martial history of the United States, including the Confederate States of America, will find material in *U.S. Martial and Semi-Martial Single-Shot Pistols* that will help them collect old firearms for both fun and profit.

References to the author's own books in this text are made simply because these books have been the product of a lifetime of research, adventure, and travel—the latter consisting principally of what might be referred to politely as "guided tours by the U.S. Navy and U.S. Marine Corps." The reader does not need to buy these books. He can borrow them from any public library. The only problem there is that many librarians are ladies who hate snakes, firearms, and possibly males; hence, they are not enthusiastic about stocking books on guns unless they receive several specific requests. This statement should not be misinterpreted. Some of our best friends are librarians.

Finally, we must frankly admit the possibility of error exists. From the first edition of this text to the current edition, the book has gone through many changes, all intended to approach accuracy in classification, description, and evaluation.

The first edition of this book was privately published by the author in 1940 in response to a demand from people who had read *Gun Collecting,* now titled *The Complete Book of Gun Collecting,* and wanted both detailed descriptions and values of firearms found in typical American collections. There were 2,000 clothbound and 1,000 paperbound copies of the first edition of *The Gun Collector's Handbook of Values.* Most of the copies were sold in advance of publication, and all were sold within less than a year after publication. Today it is a collector's item.

The first revised edition and all subsequent editions were published by Coward, McCann & Geoghegan, Inc. The first revised edition was produced in 1947. It was a complete revision and amplification of the original, in both text and values, with many added photographs.

The second revised edition, produced in 1951, was substantially the same as the 1947 edition except that value increases were indicated for each chapter on a percentage basis, based on the theory that all items in a particular, specialized category go up and down in value according to the same ratio. The author tried this method in response to suggestions from many experienced collectors and dealers, even though he personally questioned the validity of the theory.

The third revised edition, produced in 1955, was a thorough revision of all values for good and fine condition and included numerous changes in the descriptions of firearms.

The fourth revised edition, produced in 1958, included many changes in the detailed descriptions of firearms and an adjustment of all values to reflect the market at that time.

The fifth revised edition, produced late in 1960, also included changes in descriptions of many weapons. Values were given for the 1961–1962 market. The values were based on the reports of hundreds of collectors, dealers, and museum curators and were projected scientifically to remain valid through the year 1962. This was done with the help of economists and statisticians whose regular duties are the preparation of budgets for business, industry, and government. Fortunately, they also are gun collectors and realize that the values of antique firearms do not rise and fall with other commodities in the same ratio.

The sixth revised edition was revised more thoroughly than any previous revised edition because the author learned many new facts about antique firearms from the original sources during the many years he spent in writing *Guns of the Old West* and *U.S. Martial and Semi-Martial Single-Shot Pistols*. The publication of both of these books preceded the publication of the sixth revised edition of this text. The seventh edition could be called the eighth edition, counting the original edition as the first in a series.

In subsequent revised editions, the chapters on gun values and condition were revised thoroughly. All values were individually adjusted to reflect the market through the years. The salable quantity of genuine antique firearms decreases constantly. The demand for antique firearms increases as the population increases; hence, values increase steadily, regardless of such variables as the purchasing power of the dollar.

On February 20, 1967, while serving in the California legislature, Charles Edward Chapel died suddenly of a heart attack.

At that time he was engaged in the preparation of a revised edition of *The Gun Collector's Handbook of Values*. The publisher of this book, Coward, McCann & Geoghegan, Inc., asked me to complete the revision inasmuch as I had worked with my husband throughout previous editions.

For the past thirty-two years, the frequent revisions of this book have been the cooperative effort of gun experts throughout the United States. It is our plan to continue his work in maintaining *The Gun Collector's Handbook of Values* as a current and valuable reference for gun collectors all over the world. Constructive suggestions for changes, deletions, or additions in future editions are cordially and respectfully invited.

MRS. CHARLES EDWARD CHAPEL

# Chapter 1

## GUN VALUES

### Dictionary Definitions of Value

66 "VALUE," according to *Webster's New International Dictionary of the English Language*, Second Edition, Unabridged, is: "A fair return in money, goods, services, etc., for something exchanged; that which is considered an equivalent in worth, as to get the *value* of one's money in a purchase; to recover the *value* of lost merchandise."

The same dictionary has many other definitions. One says in part: "The value of an article depends, not upon its *total* utility, but upon its *marginal* utility, diminishing as the supply increases." This definition has a definite relationship to firearms for collectors.

Still another definition from the same source defines value as: "The estimate which an individual places upon some of his possessions as compared with others, independently of any intent to sell—sometimes called *subjective* value, or less correctly, *value in use*, and employed in a loose sense as nearly equivalent to *utility*." This third definition applies to a gun collector who places a value on each weapon in his collection even when he has no present intention of selling his arms. He may list such values in an inventory of his gun collection, but if it is stolen, destroyed by fire, or on his death passes to his heirs, the collector's subjective values have doubtful weight unless they have been confirmed by an expert appraiser of antique arms. In the latter case, the subjective values become objective values and may be what the lawyers refer to as fair market values.

### Legal Definitions of Value

Fair market value is the value a willing purchaser will pay to a willing seller in an open market. This definition is found in a California case cited by the lawyers as Kaiser Co. v. Reid (1947), 30 C2d, 184 P2d 879. It can be found in any large law library and also in *California Words, Phrases and Maxims,* published by the Bancroft-Whitney Co., San Francisco, 1960. Almost all experienced real estate brokers and salesmen throughout the United States of America are familiar with this definition, although it is phrased slightly differently in the various states.

Actually, we could drop the word "fair" and simply say market value without altering the meaning of the above definition. However, to avoid quibbling about the meaning of the word "fair," we can quote another California court decision which certainly applies to gun values, thus:

"Fair," as used in the definition of market value, means "honest" rather than "average" or "middling." This definition is condensed from the California case of East Bay Municipal Utility District v. Kieffer (1929), 99 CA 240, 278 P 476, 279 P 178. The significance of the definition of "fair" in the court case cited here is that anyone who compiles a list of prices for which antique firearms have sold in any arbitrary period and then strikes an arithmetical average, without knowing anything about the *condition* of the guns he has listed, is merely presenting to the public an unrealistic, misleading "average" or "middling" set of prices. Therefore, such lists, whether published in magazines or books, are not compilations of fair market values, market values, or any other kind of values. As price lists, they are interesting to experts, but misleading to beginners, regardless of the sincerity and honesty of the compilers.

## Price as Contrasted with Value

Oscar Wilde said: "A cynic is a man who knows the *price* of everything and the *value* of nothing."

Having explored the dictionary and legal definitions of value, market value, and fair market value, it is not necessary to belabor the subject much further, but it is important to understand clearly that in economics and in the common language of the people, price is the amount of money given, or set as the amount that will be given or received, in exchange for anything. Even if no money changes hands, as in the case of one collector trading an antique gun for an old firearm owned by another collector, both collectors may be thinking in terms of price instead of value.

## Auction Prices Are Not Necessarily Values

Prices of firearms auctioned by the creditors of a gun collector to satisfy his debts as the result of a court order, or of firearms auctioned to settle the estate of a deceased collector, are not necessarily values. In most auctions, the prices for which antique firearms are sold to the highest bidder definitely are prices and not values in any sense of the word. Arms collectors are scattered all over the world. Most of them have neither the time nor the money to attend gun auctions. Those attending and bidding sometimes are wealthy collectors, but usually they are arms dealers buying for resale. Therefore, auction prices are generally quite low, far below the retail prices for which the arms will be sold by the dealers.

Furthermore, auction prices are unreliable because many owners set a "reserve price" on all or some of the guns. The auctioneer receives his commission whether the arms are sold or not, and in his list of prices obtained, if he published such a list, he often lists the unsold arms as "sold" at the reserve prices. He does this for two reasons: first, it will help the owner to obtain that price or a higher price at a future auction; second, it helps the auctioneer to obtain higher prices on that particular lot of weapons, or on other gun collections, thus giving him a bigger commission. It should be obvious that the auctioneer depends on obtaining the highest possible prices as his source of income.

The use of reserve prices is perfectly legal, to the best of the knowledge and belief of the author of this text. However, some auctioneers advertise in magazines and newspapers that they do not use reserve prices. The mere fact that they publicly mention the existence of reserve prices confirms what we have said, that they are used and do exist. Sometimes the auctioneer who most blatantly announces that he does not use reserve prices is a liar. This is a case of what Shakespeare had in mind when he said: "Methinks the lady doth protest too much!"

## Dealers' Catalogues and Price Lists

Dealers and collectors who publish and distribute price lists and catalogues are frequently perfectly honest and ethical in all respects, but there are enough exceptions to warrant an examination of their practices. There are several factors to be weighed in examining price lists and catalogues, such as: (1) Is the designation of the gun accurate or vague? In other words, are the make, model, caliber, barrel length, markings, and other important details set forth sufficiently for the prospective buyer to know what he is ordering? (2) Is the condition of the gun stated accurately? (3) Is the price a firm price or is it an asking price below which the dealer will drop if he does not make a sale quickly?

Chapter 2 of this text, "Condition," has been completely revised and is in accordance with the recommendations of the National Rifle Association of America. Those dealers who abide by the condition standards of the National Rifle Association of America deserve the support of the gun-collecting fraternity. Since condition is an essential factor in determining value, it cannot be emphasized too much.

Assuming that a collector accumulates price lists and catalogues from many dealers and collector-dealers, and assuming that such price lists and catalogues do set forth in detail gun designation, description, condition, and other vital facts accurately, it is impossible to strike an average of such price lists and catalogues and obtain an accurate set of values because of certain underlying reasons for the prices set by dealers and collector-dealers. Incidentally, the term "collector-dealer" is a popular phrase for an advanced collector who is primarily a collector but wants to get rid of duplicate items or close out part of a general collection in order to raise money for the purchase of guns in a fairly narrow field of specialization, such as U.S. martial flintlock pistols, for example.

Dealers and collector-dealers often base their prices on what they paid for their guns. For example, antique dealers in general, and gun dealers in particular, pay no more for a firearm than necessary. They are not philanthropists. Frequently they buy arms for as low as 10% of their fair market value if the seller seems to be anxious to raise cash quickly, or if he or she does not know gun values. On the other hand, if a dealer knows that the prospective seller can "shop around" and not sell until he gets the highest offer in a city where there are several dealers in antique arms, the dealer may pay as high as 50% of fair market value, especially if he knows a collector who is anxious to buy the particular gun offered to the dealer for sale. This is based upon ordinary, honest, cold business practice.

Regardless of what he paid for a gun, the dealer or collector-dealer realizes that if he sets the price too high, buyers will patronize another dealer if two or more are offering the same item in substantially the same condition. Therefore, the dealer sets a price somewhere near what he believes his competitors will charge, and he often sells at that figure.

If the dealer lists a gun at too high a price, he may lower the price in his next list or catalogue. Also, if he is overloaded with slow-moving items, he may set prices well below the prevailing prices of his competitors in order to make a profit, raise cash for the purchase of other guns, and clear his shelves and cases to make room for new acquisitions.

In Europe, for many years it was the custom of antique dealers, including merchants selling antique guns, to raise the retail price about 5% each year, hoping to eventually sell the slow-moving guns at a handsome profit plus enough additional money to pay all or part of what they would receive if they had their money invested in stocks, bonds, or some other commodity. Whether or not this is the custom today, the author does not know, but it is worth considering.

In Shanghai, China, when the author was serving there with the Fourth Regiment U.S. Marine Corps, a dealer in genuine works of art (including highly decorated firearms) from the old Imperial Palaces of Peking, found that his stock was not moving fast enough to warrant the continuance of his business. The author suggested that he double all his prices, act haughty when customers entered his shop, and see what happened. In less than a year, the dealer sold out all his stock at a tremendous profit and complained to the author of this text that, having followed the advice, he had no more valuable merchandise to sell! Since that incident, the author has refrained from telling dealers how to run their businesses.

The discussion above applies generally to dealers stocking the comparatively common antique firearms, but does not apply to those extremely rare antique guns which are worth anywhere from a few hundred to several thousand dollars, if genuine and in good condition or better. Here is an example: Early in 1940, a dealer bought a beautifully ornamented wheel-lock pistol in fine condition for $100, which was a bargain even for a dealer. The wheel-lock pistol was marked with the name of a famous Italian pistol maker and the date of manufacture. Since the dealer was not an expert on genuine early wheel-lock pistols, he asked the advice of several experts and then listed the pistol at a retail price of $350. He sent a photograph and a complete description of the pistol to several wealthy collectors who had told him they wanted a genuine wheel-lock pistol in good condition or better. One of the collectors bought it with a written agreement that he could return it and obtain a full refund if not satisfied. On receiving the pistol, the collector wrote the dealer that he did not want to pay more the $250 for the pistol, that the dealer could send him $100, or the collector would return the pistol and ask for the return of his $350.

When the dealer received this counteroffer of $250, he was negotiating for the purchase of a whole collection of valuable arms and needed every cent he could get to buy the collection immediately or lose it to a rival dealer, hence the dealer sent the collector $100, thus closing that transaction.

Three months later, the collector sold the pistol for more than $250 to a second dealer who then listed it and sold it for $375. In 1946, the same pistol was sold three times, first for $480, then for $500, and finally for $520. In later years, the same pistol sold for as much as $2000.

In case any reader of this text thinks that the author is criticizing dealers, he should clearly understand that for every unethical or dishonest dealer in the United States of America, there are hundreds of unethical or dishonest collectors who are trying to swindle one another and also endeavoring to defraud dealers. All the good men are not on one side of the counter and all the bad men on the other side.

Before turning away from the subject of dealers, the reader should know that the price lists and catalogues of both dealers and collector-dealers are worth every cent they charge. Some enthusiasts do not collect antique guns but collect price lists and catalogues of old guns. The values of old price lists and catalogues increase astronomically as the years go on because many collectors who buy price lists and catalogues throw them away when dealers and collector-dealers issue new publications.

Curiously enough, one dealer in antique firearms and war surplus items told the author more than thirty years ago that his big catalogue, for which he obtained a reasonably high price in both paperbound and clothbound editions, contained many items which had been sold years before and that he made more money from selling the catalogues than he gained from selling antique arms and war surplus! His heirs not only sell a partially revised catalogue but are

publishing and successfully retailing reprints of their ancestor's early catalogues. This statement is not made in derogation of the family
which has been so financially successful in selling catalogues containing items not available for sale. Advanced and experienced collectors and dealers know all about this, continue to buy the catalogues,
laugh at the story behind the catalogues, and have nothing but
praise for the canny Scots who can keep generations of Americans
entertained. Glory be to the Scot of old who founded the business!
May his descendants forever copy his example bold!

From this examination of price lists and catalogues, it is apparent
that even the most complete, frank, accurate reports from many ethical dealers would not provide more than a good index to fair market values.

## How Some People Misinterpret This Text

The author once visited the shop of a dealer in antique firearms.
A customer entered, examined a pistol, complained about the price
being too high, and was shown the latest edition of *The Gun Collector's Handbook of Values.* The customer took the pistol apart with the
help and consent of the dealer, agreed that the condition of the pistol was such that the dealer's price was correct according to the
*Handbook,* and bought the pistol. One-half hour later, another man
entered the shop with the same make, model, type, caliber, barrel
length, and condition as the one sold to the customer. This man
wanted to sell his pistol to the dealer. The dealer then reached under the counter, showed the prospective seller a very old edition of
*The Gun Collector's Handbook of Values,* listing much lower values
than those in the latest edition, and offered the man 25% of the listed value for that pistol. The man sold his pistol to the dealer and left
the shop, apparently satisfied! Some readers may wonder why the
author did not intervene, but the answer is that the incident oc-
curred long after the author had learned in Shanghai that he should
not attempt to tell dealers how to run their businesses. If any moral
is needed, it is obvious that obsolete editions of this text are now collectors' items, but are not reliable guides to the purchase or sale of
firearms on today's market.

## Demand and Supply

Gun collectors have many motivations. Some are interested in the patriotic and historic background and use of firearms. Others are intrigued by the mechanical improvement of firearms from the primitive hand cannon to the modern automatic weapons. Still others collect antique arms for the same reason that some people collect stamps, coins, first editions of books, or old musical instruments. A surprisingly large number collect firearms for exhibition purposes. They want something to show their relatives, neighbors, and friends that is different from what everyone in town has in his home. Subconsciously, some gun collectors are seeking status, prestige, and public recognition through the accumulation of obsolete firearms, especially if the metal parts are beautifully engraved, the wooden portions are of excellent material and skillfully carved; and the firearms as a group invoke admiration and provoke discussion. Regardless of the motive for collecting old guns, there is a steadily growing demand. This demand increases but the supply of genuine antique weapons in presentable condition remains fixed. In theory, the supply is fixed, but in practice museums acquire collections, some are destroyed by fire, and others simply disappear through the years.

It is perfectly obvious that the theoretically fixed supply and the steadily increasing demand combine to force up the values of genuine antique firearms. This creates a vacuum into which men move who make money by manufacturing fake, counterfeit, false reproductions. This phase of the gun-collecting hobby is covered in Chapter 2, but it must be recognized before proceeding to other phases of the interaction of demand and supply.

## Five Major Factors of Demand

All collectors do not want to specialize in the same firearms. A study of the collecting trends for the last fifty years shows that there are at least five major trends in demand. First, a collector usually prefers arms made in his own nation. Second, he may favor a particular ignition period, such as flintlock, percussion, or cartridge. Third, he then tends to specialize within some classification, such as martial handguns (pistols and revolvers); non-martial handguns; martial shoulder arms (muskets, musketoons, rifles, and carbines); non-martial shoulder arms, such as hunting or marksmanship weapons. Fourth, there is a strong preference for handguns, probably because pistols and revolvers are easier to store, exhibit, and transport than shoulder arms. Fifth, but by no means least, the collector may specialize in one particular make, such as Colt, Remington, Smith & Wesson, Winchester, or some other manufacturer.

There are many other trends in specialization. For example, until recently there was little demand for shotguns, even the primitive scatter guns that preceded the percussion and cartridge shotguns, but with the increasing demand for antique firearms and the theoretically fixed (practically diminishing) supply of genuine pieces for the collector, people are beginning to specialize in firearms that have been ignored by most collectors for centuries. The various trends in specialization are so numerous that they are beyond the scope of this text. Such trends are treated in great detail in the author's other gun books.

## Scarcity in Itself Does Not Create Demand or Raise Values

One of the most important things for every collector to remember is that scarcity in itself does not create demand or raise values. For example, the Collier flintlock revolver is one of the rarest of all firearms and yet many variations of the percussion revolvers made by Samuel Colt at Paterson, New Jersey, are sold for far greater prices even when the condition of the Paterson Colt percussion revolvers is below that of the few Collier flintlock revolvers on the market. The reason is that during his lifetime Samuel Colt was one of the greatest promoters and public relations experts in the world. He started the public demand for Colt weapons and his remarkable accomplishment in obtaining free advertising for firearms bearing the Colt name continues in our generation and probably will last as long as men and women collect firearms.

In Western fiction and non-fiction, the name Colt is used as a synonym for a revolver, even if the hero or villain carries a Remington revolver, or a revolver of some other make. This is similar to the fact that the name Winchester means a rifle to almost everyone. Actually, both Colt and Winchester made weapons other than revolvers and rifles, but tradition is often stronger and more enduring than fact.

Returning to the preference for handguns over shoulder weapons, Colt shoulder arms made at Paterson, New Jersey, are probably rarer than the Colt Paterson percussion revolvers, but the values of the Colt Paterson shoulder arms are normally far less than those of

Colt Paterson percussion revolvers of the same period, caliber, and design.

These are only a few of the many concrete examples of the fact that in the absence of demand, scarcity means little or nothing in creating values.

## The Identification and Classification of New Types Raises Values

Before 1940, Kentucky pistols, both flintlock and percussion, were classified by collectors, dealers, historians, and gun authors as "horsemen's pistols," "great cloak pistols," "U.S. martial pistols," and "U.S. secondary martial pistols," especially when they were of large caliber with long barrels and comparatively great overall size and shape. This is explained in detail in the author's other gun books, but the fact that the identification and classification of new models and types raise values is demonstrated by the fact that after the publication of the first edition of *The Gun Collector's Handbook of Values* in 1940, which identified and classified Kentucky pistols as a distinct type or model, the values and the prices of Kentucky pistols shot up astronomically.

## Reclassification Raises Values

The publication of *U.S. Martial and Semi-Martial Single-Shot Pistols* materially increased the value of many single-shot pistols because the reports of historical research in that book made it necessary to move some pistols from the U.S. secondary martial classification into the U.S. martial classification. Before these pistols were reclassified, they were regarded by collectors as less desirable, hence the values were smaller than they became after the pistols were correctly classified.

These references by the author to his own books are necessary because the identification and classification of firearms is best understood by the person who does the work, although it must be admitted that this was not the sole work of the author but reflected years of research and cooperation by more than one hundred experts on antique firearms. Personally, the author hurts himself each time the values of firearms increase because it makes it more and more difficult to obtain desirable specimens for his own collection.

## How Values Were Determined for This Edition

As soon as the twelfth completely revised edition of *The Gun Collector's Handbook of Values* came on the market, copies were sent to more than one hundred experts. Some were experts in only one or two of the specialized fields. Others were experts in the broad field of gun values with years of experience. All of them began to make notes for the present revision and revised their notes right up until press time for the current edition. They then went through the twelfth completely revised edition, wrote new values for both "good" and "fine" conditions, keeping in mind the reclassification of U.S. martial and semi-martial single-shot pistols which was presented in the author's book on that subject. Furthermore, each of these experts had his own ideas about values, identification, and classification, and they expressed them freely in correspondence with one another and with the author, thus supplementing their value determinations.

The result is before you. This is a completely revised edition and it offers you not only descriptions and classifications but also what many of us believe to be values for both "good" and "fine" condition of the firearms most popular with American collectors and dealers, brought up to the years 1979 and 1980. Furthermore, the values were rechecked by statisticians and economists who also are gun experts. This is not the final work on the subject because the identification, classification, and evaluation of firearms for the collector is a continuing process. In a dynamic world, change is the only certainty. In future editions of this work, the author and his many friends of the gun-collecting fraternity will look back on this edition with the same lofty detachment with which we now regard the humble little first edition of 1940.

The Civil War Centennial celebrations held all over the United States of America, during the years 1961 to 1965, created a demand for uniforms and firearms of the 1861 to 1865 period. Obviously, the supply of Civil War firearms was very limited, hence reproductions were made in great quantities. There is nothing illegal or unethical about producing reproductions and selling them as reproductions, but the sale of reproductions as authentic, original firearms is fraudulent.

When the manufacturers of imitation Civil War firearms discovered that they had a lucrative and expanding market, they did not limit their activities to Civil War weapons but went into the business of producing imitations of Kentucky (Pennsylvania) pistols and rifles, as well as other items for collectors.

Making and selling counterfeit firearms for collectors is nothing new and it is not confined to the United States of America. It is an industry as old as the hobby of collecting arms.

In this, the thirteenth revised edition, which is actually the four-teenth edition, all values are for genuine, original specimens.

# Chapter 2

## CONDITION

### Past Condition Descriptions

CONDITION is extremely important because it is one of the principal factors in the appraisal of firearms. In each of the editions of *The Gun Collector's Handbook of Values* preceding the sixth completely revised edition, the author explained and defined various degrees of condition, but the sixth edition contained a uniform set of condition designations which can be accepted by the overwhelming majority of all antique firearm collectors and dealers. Before proceeding to set forth a uniform standard, it is necessary to review briefly past condition descriptions.

In the 1940, 1947, 1951, 1955, 1958, and 1960 editions of *The Gun Collector's Handbook of Values,* condition descriptions went through a slow evolution based upon the recommendations of hundreds of collectors and dealers. Finally, in the fifth completely revised edition, copyrighted in 1960, the author presented the following descriptions for "fine," "good," and "fair" condition:

FINE: At least 50% of the original factory finish. Markings distinct. All parts original. Perfect working order. The amount of original finish should be given.

GOOD: Little or no original factory finish. Markings absent or indistinct. Barrel may be rusted or pitted slightly. Stock may be scratched, bruised, or cracked but sound and complete. Shows wear but no abuse. Good working order. The amount of rusting and pitting should be carefully stated.

FAIR: No finish on parts. Barrel rusted or pitted slightly or shows signs of cleaning. Markings absent. Fair working order. Shows much use. Stock scratched, bruised, cracked, or repaired.

Major parts must be original, but minor parts may be replacements.

The author added an explanation that many collectors and dealers advised him that almost nobody uses the word "fair" because if a weapon is in "fair" condition, it is almost always called "good," "about good," or "almost good." In some instances, a firearm in "fair" condition is listed in a catalogue without any accurate condition description. This also applies to correspondence between collectors and between collectors and dealers. Therefore, the author has always given two values, the higher one being for the weapon in "fine" condition and the lower value for one in "good" condition.

## National Rifle Association of America Condition Standards

The National Rifle Association of America, publishers of *The American Rifleman,* 1600 Rhode Island Avenue, N.W., Washington, D.C. 20036, has given the author official permission to include its condition standards for antique firearms with the restriction that these standards must be used in their entirety and must not be edited, as follows:

FACTORY NEW—All original parts; 100% original finish; in perfect condition in every respect, inside and out.

EXCELLENT—All original parts; over 80% original finish; sharp lettering, numerals, and design on metal and wood; unmarred wood; fine bore.

FINE—All original parts; over 30% original finish; sharp lettering, numerals, and design on metal and wood; minor marks in wood; good bore.

VERY GOOD—All original parts; none to 30% original finish; original metal surfaces smooth with all edges sharp; clear lettering, numerals, and design on metal; wood slightly scratched or bruised; bore disregarded for collector's firearms.

GOOD—Some minor replacement parts; metal smoothly rusted or lightly pitted in places, cleaned or reblued; principal lettering, numerals, and design on metal legible; wood refinished, scratched, bruised, or minor cracks repaired; in good working order.

FAIR—Some major parts replaced; minor replacement parts may be required; metal rusted, may be lightly pitted all over, vigorously cleaned or reblued; rounded edges of metal and wood; principal lettering, numerals, and design on metal partly obliterated; wood scratched, bruised, cracked, or repaired where broken; in fair working order or can be easily repaired and placed in working order.

POOR—Major and minor parts replaced; major replacement parts required and extensive restoration needed; metal deeply pitted; principal lettering, numerals, and design obliterated; wood badly scratched, bruised, cracked, or broken; mechanically inoperative; generally undesirable as a collector's firearm.

## National Rifle Association of America Code of Ethics for Gun Collectors and Dealers

The National Rifle Association of America has given the author official permission to present its Code of Ethics with the restriction that it must be used in its entirety and must not be edited, as follows:

"A listing of practices considered unethical and injurious to the best interests of the collecting fraternity."

1. The manufacture or sale of a spurious copy of a valuable firearm. This shall include the production of full-scale replicas of historic models and accessories, regardless of easily effaced modern markings, and it also shall include the rebuilding of any authentic weapon into a rarer and more valuable model. It shall not include the manufacture or sale of firearms or accessories which cannot be easily confused with the rare models of famous makers. Such items are: plastic or pottery products, miniatures, firearms of original design, or other examples of individual skill, plainly stamped with the maker's name and date, made up as examples of utility and craftsmanship and not representative of the design or models of any old-time arms maker.

2. The alteration of any marking or serial number, or the assembling and artificially aging of unrelated parts for the purpose of creating a more valuable or unique weapon, with or without immediate intent to defraud. This shall not include the legitimate restoration or completion of missing parts with those of original type, provided that such completions or restorations are indicated to a prospective buyer.

3. The refinishing (bluing, browning, or plating) or engraving

of any collector's weapons, unless the weapons may be clearly marked under the stocks or elsewhere to indicate the date and nature of the work, and provided the seller unequivocally shall describe such non-original treatment to a buyer.

4. The direct or indirect efforts of a seller to attach a spurious historical association to a firearm in an effort to inflate its fair value; efforts to "plant" a firearm under circumstances which are designed to inflate the fair value.

5. The employment of unfair or shady practices in buying, selling, or trading at the expense of young and inexperienced collectors or anyone else; the devious use of false appraisals, collusion, and other sharp practices for personal gain.

6. The use of inaccurate, misleading, or falsified representations in direct sales or a selling by sales list, catalogues, periodical advertisement, and other media; the failure to make prompt refunds, adjustments, or other proper restitution on all just claims which may arise from arms sales, direct or by mail.

## Value Designations in This Text

In the sixth, seventh, eighth, ninth, tenth, eleventh, twelfth and this thirteenth revised editions of *The Gun Collector's Handbook of Values,* the author abandoned all condition descriptions in earlier editions of this text and has based the revised values on the National Rifle Association of America condition standards for two conditions, "good" and "fine." The value for a weapon in "good" condition appears first, followed by the value of a weapon in "fine" condition. In general, but not always, the value of a weapon in "fine" condition is about 50% greater than it is for one in "good" condition. This differential is based upon long years of research and the advice of hundreds of expert collectors and dealers, but it does not necessarily mean that the National Rifle Association of America agrees or disagrees with these values.

All editions of *The Gun Collector's Handbook of Values* from the first edition to the current edition have set forth values for only "fine" and "good" condition because these two condition standards represent the condition of most arms bought, sold, and traded by collectors and dealers.

Obviously, any book on values of items for a collector is only a guide. Using the values given herein for "good" and "fine" condition, any reasonable person can determine what he or she believes to be the value of a weapon in any other condition.

## Beware of Superficial Condition Descriptions

The values in this book are for antique firearms which are genuine. Notice that the National Rifle Association condition standards for "fine" condition require all original parts; and that for "good" condition, some *minor* replacement parts are permitted under the definition, but this means exactly what it says. Such replacement parts must be inferior in bulk, degree, kind, importance, etc.

The number of genuine antique firearms in a condition from "good" to "factory new" is limited. The number of antique firearm collectors increases each year, hence the demand increases but the supply remains fixed. This increases the values and in turn tempts many dishonest, unethical people to meet the increasing demand and the rising values by misrepresenting the classification, identification, and condition of firearms for the purpose of making money.

In addition, there is a brazen and widespread business of making counterfeit, false parts, subassemblies, and even complete weapons. The manufacturers of these parts, subassemblies, and complete weapons openly advertise their wares in several magazines and many newspapers.

Some manufacturers of counterfeit, false, allegedly antique firearms sell them in conditions that the National Rifle Association of America describes as "factory new." Others artificially age counterfeit firearms because even experienced collectors are sometimes deceived unless they are able to completely disassemble a weapon and examine it carefully before buying it.

## Precautions in Purchasing Antique Firearms

The following precautions in purchasing antique firearms are those advocated by the author for more than thirty years in magazine articles and books he has written. In addition, they are very similar to the recommendations of the National Rifle Association of America.

1. Investigate the person offering to sell or trade an antique weapon, especially if the value is more than ten dollars. This is an

arbitrary amount. In actual practice, unless you can afford to waste your money, always investigate before you buy, whether the person offering to sell or trade is a dealer or a private collector. Regard the person offering to sell or trade an antique gun with the same caution that your grandfather exercised in trading or selling horses. Use the same common sense that your father followed in buying a used automobile.

2. Unless you, yourself, are an expert, find an expert and pay him for an appraisal. Incidentally, the author normally does not appraise, classify, or identify firearms for love, money, friendship, or any other consideration. Write to the National Rifle Association of America for the names and addresses of competent firearm appraisers in your area.

3. If you buy or accept an antique weapon in trade for something of value, demand a bill of sale, describing the gun in minute detail, and signed in ink by the person transferring title to you. Also, have a witness present who signs the bill of sale as a witness and be sure the bill of sale is dated. If the value of the firearm is sufficiently great to warrant the cost, find and hire an honest lawyer to handle the transaction.

The National Rifle Association of America will mail you, free, a copy of their "Bill of Sale for Antique Firearms," but you should send them a stamped, addressed reply envelope. Even when you obtain their bill of sale, all of the above precautions still apply.

Finally, remember the old Latin legal phrase: *Caveat Emptor.* This means: Let the buyer take care. It can be more fully translated by saying that the purchaser of anything of value should examine, judge, and test it for himself, being bound to discover any obvious defects or imperfections. However, under modern laws, fools are protected from their own folly to some extent. The author's concluding advice is: If in doubt, do not buy!

# Chapter 3

## U.S. MARTIAL FLINTLOCK PISTOLS

FLINTLOCK pistols made in the United States armories at Harpers Ferry, Virginia, and Springfield, Massachusetts, or by private individuals and companies under contract with the United States, for use by the federal military and naval forces, or for distribution to state forces under federal jurisdiction, can be classified as U.S. martial flintlock pistols.

The Congress of the United States passed a resolution in 1777 that all arms belonging to the United States be stamped or marked with the words "United States." This resolution was obeyed in general, but there were many arms not marked, some were marked "U. States," and some were merely marked "U.S." The absence of the "U.S." mark raises doubt regarding the federal status of the weapon unless overcome by other facts. The presence of the "U.S." mark is not, in itself, sufficient to classify an arm as a federal weapon.

In this book, U.S. martial firearms are presented in the chronological order of their model years. The model year is the year in which the weapon became officially recognized for the first time. It is usually the year in which the contract or order for its manufacture became official, but in some cases it is the year in which the gun was first made. When a year is given in parentheses, it is the model year erroneously used in the past by authors, collectors, and dealers, presented here to avoid confusion.

All important firearms, and many which are not important, are cross-indexed in the index. For example, U.S. Pistol, Model 1799, North & Cheney, is so indexed, and also under North & Cheney.

**U.S. PISTOL, MODEL 1799, NORTH & CHENEY**, cal. .69; smoothbore,

8.5-inch barrel, which originally was marked "US," "P," and "V." Stock 5.75 inches long. Total length 14.5 inches. Weight 3 lbs. 4 oz. Lock plate 3.313 inches long. Brass trigger guard 4.85 inches long with round ends. Brass frame may be marked either "North & Cheney Berlin" or "S. North and E. Cheney Berlin." Brass pan made as part of frame. Brass butt cap. Steel ramrod. Double-neck hammer. Resembles Model 1777 French Army Pistol but has longer barrel and other variations. $10,000–$17,500.

U.S. PISTOL, MODEL 1805 (1806), HARPERS FERRY, cal. .54; smoothbore, 10.625-inch, round barrel, key-fastened with projecting rib. Lock plate 4.875 inches long and 1 inch wide, marked with spread eagle, "US," and "Harpers Ferry," with date, which may be 1806, 1807, or 1808. Walnut half-stock 11.75 inches long. Total length 16 inches. Trigger guard 5.75 inches long with round rear end. Weight 2 lbs. 9 oz. Flat double-neck hammer. Steel ramrod on most specimens, but original may have been hickory. Small brass front sight, but original may have been made without sight. Brass-mounted. The manufacture was authorized Nov. 13, 1805, hence the correct model date is 1805. Most specimens were made in 1807. Plate 1, Fig. 1.

| | |
|---|---|
| Dated 1806 | $1,850–$2,400 |
| Dated 1807 | $1,250–$1,650 |
| Dated 1808 | $1,450–$1,950 |

U.S. PISTOL, MODEL 1807, SPRINGFIELD. This is a debatable model. Cal. .69; 10.813-inch barrel marked with year; 15.313-inch stock. Total length 17.313 inches. Lock plate 5.125 inches long and 1.06 inches wide, marked with an eagle, "U.S.," "Springfield," and "1818." Gooseneck hammer. Trigger guard 6.188 inches long with round ends. One band. Full stock, walnut. Iron pan forged as part of lock plate. Iron trigger guard, butt cap, and back strap. Lock plate has sharp teat-shaped rear end and resembles that on French Charleville musket. Frizzen has turned-up toe and resembles that of Charleville musket. It is possible that although authorized in 1807, this pistol may not have been assembled before 1818, and it may not have been used in the field by troops. If it is dated 1818, has an ordinary frizzen, a lock plate with a blunt rear end, and a double-necked hammer, it is not a Model 1807, but a U.S. Pistol, Model 1817 (1818), Springfield. $1,850–$2,775.

SAME, but with lock plate marked "1815." $2,050–$2,950.

U.S. PISTOL, MODEL 1807–1808, made by contractors, sometimes called an officer's pistol and also called a militia pistol, but used by regular enlisted men of the federal forces, and possibly carried by officers as well as enlisted militiamen; resembles U.S. Pistol, Model 1805 (1806), Harpers Ferry, except that it was usually pin-fastened and often full-stocked, somewhat resembling a Kentucky pistol. It was made under contracts in 1807 and 1808 with several gunmakers, probably including the following: William Calderwood; Jacob Cooke; A. & J. Ansted; O. & E. Evans; Abraham Henry; Joseph Henry; Henry Pickel; De Huff, Gonter & Dickert; Adam Leitner; John Shuler; Winner, Nippes & Steinman; John Miles; Martin Frye; Wm. & Hugh Shannon; and I. Guest. Values vary greatly according to the contractor and his workmanship. It is possible that contractors other than those mentioned here made this type of pistol. There is a strong argument in favor of classing this as a U.S. martial flintlock pistol; hence it is described here in general terms, but similar specimens of this general type are described under the names of their makers in Chapter 4 on U.S. Secondary Martial Flintlock Pistols. Plate 1, Fig. 2, made by I. Guest. $2,850–$3,500.

In addition to pistols of the type described above, O. & E. Evans made a pistol at Evansburg, Pa., in 1814 resembling the French Model Year IX (1800–1801) Cavalry Pistol; cal. .689, 7.87-inch barrel, total length 14.564 inches. Brass butt cap, band, side plate, and separate trigger bow. Lock plate may or may not be marked "Evans" and has a rounded face at the rear end. Plate 1, Fig. 3. $2,250–$2,850.

**U.S. PISTOL, MODEL 1808, S. NORTH, NAVY,** cal. .64; 10.125-inch round, smoothbore, pin-fastened, browned, unmarked barrel. Walnut stock to 2 inch from muzzle. Total length 16.25 inches. Weight 2 lbs. 14 oz. No sights. Brass-mounted. Double-necked hammer. Horizontal brass pan with fence. Brass mountings. Hickory ramrod. Iron belt hook on left. Lock plate marked "U. States" between hammer and frizzen spring, with an eagle, and "S. North Berlin Con." in 3 lines behind hammer. Plate 1, Fig. 4. $1,400–$2,250.

**U.S. PISTOL, MODEL 1811 (1810), S. NORTH, ARMY,** cal. .69; 8.625-inch round, smoothbore, pin-fastened barrel marked with "V," and eagle head with letters "CT" within the same oval. Walnut stock extends to 2 inch from muzzle. Total length 15 inches. Weight 2 lbs. 11 oz. Lock plate 5.188 inches long and 1.05 inches wide. Brass trigger guard 6.25 inches long with pointed ends. Double-necked hammer. Brass pan with fence. Umbrella-shaped brass butt cap. Lock plate marked with eagle and "U. States" between hammer and frizzen spring, and "S. North Berlin Con." in 3 lines behind hammer. Usually listed as either Model 1810 or S. North, Berlin. 1st Contract. Plate 1, Fig. 5. $1,475–$2,500.

SAME, but made with 1 band, whereas standard model is pin-fastened. Barrel slightly longer. Stock nearly 2 inches shorter. Trigger guard very slightly longer with round instead of pointed ends. $1,525–$2,600.

**U.S. PISTOL, MODEL 1813, S. NORTH, ARMY,** cal. .69; 9-inch, smoothbore, round barrel with semi-octagonal breech, banded to stock with double straps, the forward one of which is not fluted, marked "P" and "US." Walnut stock, about 12.69 inches long, ends at forward edge of barrel band. Total length 15.3 inches. Weight 3 lbs. 6 oz. Trigger guard 5.56 inches long with round ends. Brass pan without fence. Double-necked hammer. Lock plate marked "S. North," followed by an eagle and "US MIDln Con." but sometimes marked only "S. North US." Plate 1, Fig. 6. $1,275–$2,000.

SAME, but Navy model, with belt hook on left. $1,475–$1,900.

U.S. PISTOL, MODEL 1816, S. NORTH, ARMY, cal. .54; 9-inch, round, smoothbore barrel marked with "P," "US" and initials of either proof tester or barrel maker. Stock 13.25 inches long. Total length 15.3 inches. Lock plate 5.25 inches long, 1.125 inches wide, flat, beveled in front, rounded at rear, and marked "S. North," with an eagle, "US," and "MIDLn Con." between the pan and the hammer. Weight 3 lbs. 3 oz. Trigger guard 5.56 inches long with round ends. Iron-mounted. Double-strap barrel band. Iron butt strap. Brass front sight. Brass pan without fence. Hickory ramrod. Double-necked hammer. Plate 1, Fig. 7. $485–$725.

SAME, but lock plate marked "S. North," an eagle, "US," and "MIDLtn Conn." Note the extra "t" in the abbreviation for the town and the extra "n" in the abbreviation for the state. $485–$725.

U.S. PISTOL, MODEL 1817 (1818), SPRINGFIELD, cal. .69; 11.06-inch, round, smoothbore barrel held by a double-strap iron band with a brass sight on front strap, and marked over the breech plug "1818," and also marked on some specimens with an eagle head between "P" and "V." Lock plate marked "Springfield 1818" in 3 lines behind hammer, and "US" under an eagle between the frizzen spring and the hammer. To be a Model 1817 (1818), Springfield, it should have an ordinary frizzen, a lock plate with a blunt rear end, and a double-necked hammer in addition to the markings described. If it has a frizzen resembling that of the French Charleville musket, with a turned-up toe, and a lock plate resembling that of the Charleville, with a sharp teat-shaped rear end, it may be classified as a U.S. Pistol, Model 1807, Springfield. There is doubt whether the Model 1817 (1818) was issued to the army for service use. Plate 1, Fig. 8. $1,750–$2,800.

---

PLATE 1. U.S. Martial Flintlock Pistols

*Figure*

1. U.S. Pistol, Model 1805 (1806), Harpers Ferry.
2. U.S. Pistol, Model 1807–1808, Contract Type, made by I. Guest.
3. U.S. Pistol, Model 1814, Contract Type, made by O. & E. Evans.
4. U.S. Pistol, Model 1808, S. North, Navy.
5. U.S. Pistol, Model 1811 (1810), S. North, Army.
6. U.S. Pistol, Model 1813, S. North, Army.
7. U.S. Pistol, Model 1816, S. North, Army.
8. U.S. Pistol, Model 1817 (1818), Springfield.

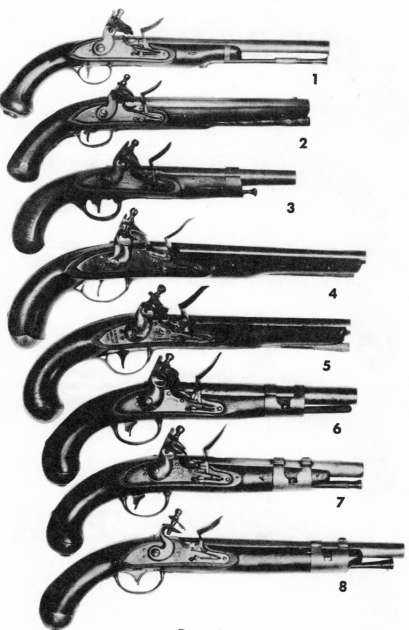

1

2

3

4

5

6

7

8

PLATE 1

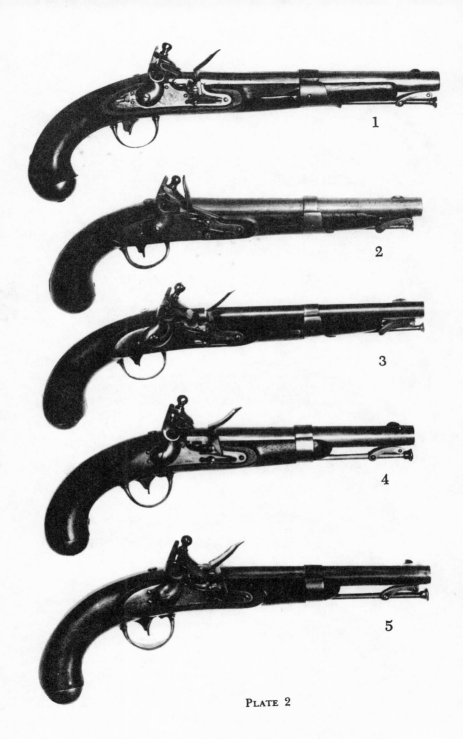

PLATE 2

U.S. PISTOL, MODEL 1819, S. NORTH, ARMY, cal. .54; 10-inch, round, smoothbore, browned barrel with brass sight on muzzle, held by a single spring-fastened band, and marked "P," "US," and the initial of the proof tester. Full stock, walnut, 13.75 inches long. Total length 15.5 inches. Weight 2 lbs. 10 oz. Lock plate 4.625 inches long and 1 inch wide, marked "S. North," eagle, "US," and "Midltn Conn." with date, either 1821, or 1822. Trigger guard 5.25 inches long with round ends. Iron-mounted. Brass pan without fence. Double-necked hammer. Sliding safety bolt on outside of lock near hammer. Peculiar catch behind cock on lock plate. Rear sight. Plate 2, Fig. 1. $625–$950.

SAME, but bears additional marks, such as "S.N.Y." for State of New York. $625–$950.

U.S. PISTOL, MODEL 1826, S. NORTH, ARMY, cal. .54; 8.625-inch round, smoothbore, browned barrel held by single spring-fastened band, with brass sight on muzzle, and marked "P," "US," and initials. Total length 13.25 inches. Weight 2 lbs. 4 oz. Full stock, walnut. Iron-mounted. Swivel ramrod. No safety bolt. Double-necked hammer. Brass pan without fence. Lock plate marked "US" and "S. North" with date, 1827 or 1828. Belt hook on left side. $925–$1,475.

SAME, Navy model, but with tinned barrel. $950–$1,500.

U.S. PISTOL, MODEL 1826, W. L. EVANS, NAVY, cal. .54; 8.625-inch round, smoothbore, browned barrel held by a single spring-fastened band, with brass sight on muzzle, marked "P." Rear sight. Full stock, walnut. Total length 13.375 inches. Weight 2 lbs. 4 oz. Brass pan without fence. Swivel ramrod. Double-necked hammer. Lock plate marked "U.S.N." behind hammer, and "W. L. Evans" and "V. Forge" between hammer and frizzen spring, with the date. Some specimens do not have the "V. Forge" marking, and some lack the N in "U.S.N." Steel belt hook on left, held by separate screw and a pin. Some specimens have a few parts tinned. $1,250–$1,800.

SAME, but made at Evansburg and marked "E. Burg." $1,550–$1,975.

---

## PLATE 2. U.S. Martial Flintlock Pistols

*Figure*

1. U.S. Pistol, Model 1819, S. North, Army.
2. U.S. Pistol, Model 1826, S. North, Navy.
3. U.S. Pistol, Model 1826, S. North, Navy.
4. U.S. Pistol, Model 1836, R. Johnson, Army.
5. U.S. Pistol, Model 1836, A. Waters, Army.

U.S. PISTOL, MODEL 1836, R. JOHNSON, ARMY, cal. .54; 8.5-inch, round, smoothbore, bright barrel held on stock by single branch-band, and marked "US," "P," and initials. Three-quarter, walnut stock 11.125 inches long. Total length 14.25 inches. Weight 2 lbs. 10 oz. Flat, beveled lock plate 4.65 inches long and 1 inch wide, marked "US," "R. Johnson Middn Conn." and date. Rear sight. Brass front sight on barrel. Trigger guard 5 inches long with round ends. Polished iron mountings. Swivel ramrod. Double-necked hammer. Brass pan with fence. Plate 2, Fig. 4. $425–$700.

SAME, but A. Waters, army, marked on lock plate with eagle head and "A. Waters, Milbury, Ms." with date. Plate 2, Fig. 5. $425–$675.

SAME, but A. H. Waters & Co., army, marked on lock plate "A. H. Waters & Co. Milbury, Mass." with date. $450–$785.

# Chapter 4

## U.S. SECONDARY MARTIAL FLINTLOCK PISTOLS

THE collective term "U.S. secondary martial flintlock pistols" is applied by collectors, and by dealers who are accurate in their descriptions, to those single-barrel flintlock pistols which are of large caliber and size and fall into one of the following groups:

1. Made by official contractors who also made U.S. martial flintlock pistols. In this group are placed those arms which are not known for sure to have been strictly federal weapons; that is, they may have been issued to or used by federal forces, but the present state of historical firearms research assigns them to the secondary classification. An example is the U.S. Pistol, Model 1807–1808, made by contractors, sometimes called an officer's pistol, and also called a militia pistol. Because there is some argument about the proper classification of this particular pistol, and doubt about its absolute identification in each case, it has been described in general in Chapter 3 on U.S. martial flintlock pistols, but individual specimens have been described in detail under the "secondary" classification of this chapter.

2. Made by private contractors who were not official contractors to the United States but were contractors to the states, or contractors to semi-official military or naval organizations or activities.

3. Made by private enterprise for sale to individuals, such as officers of the federal or state forces, or enlisted men, or anyone who had the price and the opportunity to buy.

4. Made by private enterprise for sale to the owners, officers, and crew of privateers which were vessels of war armed and equipped by private individuals and furnished with a commission or license, known as a letter of marque, from the government, to cruise against the shipping of the enemy.

43

5. Made by private enterprise as experimental, speculative, trial, or sample weapons in the hope of obtaining a contract from the United States or one of the states.

## General Comments

1. The presence of the "U.S." mark on a weapon does not mean that it is necessarily a United States martial pistol, nor does its absence necessarily mean that it is a United States secondary martial pistol. Each specimen must be judged on its own merits.

2. The arms listed in this chapter are those generally accepted in the "U.S. secondary martial" classification by experienced collectors and dealers, but there are doubtless many others which we have not described here that belong in this group. For example, Kentucky flintlock pistols were carried in battle during the Revolutionary War, and many of them answer all the technical requirements of secondary martial pistols of that period, such as size, caliber, etc., but we have placed them in a classification of their own because of their distinct features of construction and their historical background. Likewise, flintlock dueling pistols were sometimes carried in battle, and they could be placed in the secondary martial classification, even though most of them were highly decorated, expensively constructed, and in general not intended for the rough usage of warfare. However, there must be some reasonable limit to each classification, hence they are listed elsewhere.

3. Some of the arms described in this chapter were used by the Confederates in the Civil War, either in their original flintlock condition, or converted to percussion; hence such arms can be classified as Confederate as well as U.S. secondary martial. It is obvious that there is bound to be overlapping in any system of classification where the human factor enters. The presence of Confederate marks would transfer a weapon from the U.S. secondary martial to the Confederate group if such marks were definitely recognized as genuine, but it is too easy to fake these marks to justify giving such arms values materially above those assigned to them in their original state.

## Dueling Pistols

Dueling pistols during the last half of the eighteenth century were standardized as single-barrel flintlocks with a smoothbore 0.5 inch in diameter, or caliber .50, as we would term it today. The barrel could not exceed 10.5 inches or be less than 9 inches in length. The sights had to be fixed and the trigger pull could not exceed three pounds. Otherwise, the grip, safety, and trigger system could be of any design and construction. Dueling pistols of the period were usually stocked to the muzzle, although later models often had half-stocks. The barrel was almost always octagonal in shape. Sights were provided for target practice, but the code of dueling prohibited taking deliberate aim; that is, the opponents were to aim and fire on signal, or on command, as determined by their seconds.

Hair triggers were invented so that it would be possible to fire the pistol by a slight pressure on the trigger, so light that it would not disturb the aim. A small, powerful spring was first compressed or "set" by pressing the trigger forward. Years later, set triggers were made so that they could be "set" by means of a button.

The unfortunate custom of classifying an unknown pistol as a "dueler" can be avoided if the above facts are remembered. Dueling pistols were not the property of poor men, hence they were usually carefully made, with checkering, engraving, inlay work, and other forms of ornamentation, although some were entirely lacking in decoration but unmistakably showed the skill of the maker.

Dueling pistols were usually provided in pairs, in a case which itself was in keeping with the quality of the arms. Finally, certain gunmakers, both in Europe and in the United States, were famous for producing superb dueling pistols, but they did not always mark their products for fear of prosecution after laws were passed which made dueling a crime.

Dueling pistols were not martial pistols, either primarily or secondarily, hence they do not belong in this chapter in the strict sense of its purpose. However, this is the most convenient place in the book to explain the limitations on the dueling classification of firearms.

In spite of the fact that dueling pistols were never intended to be used as martial weapons, here is another case of overlapping. Officers frequently carried their dueling pistols with them on campaigns. If their regular martial pistols became damaged or lost, they would use their dueling pistols; hence it is historically possible for a dueling pistol to have been carried in battle, although this does not excuse collectors and dealers from the necessity for classifying their weapons honestly.

*Note: Cross references in this chapter to other entries all refer to Chapter 3, on U.S. martial flintlock pistols, unless otherwise specified.*

A. & J. ANSTED PISTOL, cal. .54; 8.625-inch, round-octagon, pin-fastened, smoothbore barrel marked "Ansted." Apparently there were many Pennsylvania gunmakers of similar names, such as Ansted, Anstadt, Angstad, etc.; hence there is great confusion as to who did what to which. Also, they were largely unlettered men who might spell their own names differently at various times. See U.S. Pistol, Model 1807–1808, made by contractors, where A. & J. Ansted are listed as contractors. Total length 13.5 inches. Brass trigger guard and front sight. No rear sight. No back strap. Iron pan with fence. Flat gooseneck hammer. Hickory ramrod. Full stock of curly maple. $1,875–$2,500.

BIRD & CO. PISTOL, cal. .58; 12-inch, half-octagon, smoothbore, pin-fastened barrel. Total length 17 inches. Weight 2 lbs. 5 oz. Iron pan with fence, iron trigger guard, and other iron mountings. Gooseneck hammer. Lock plate marked "C. Bird & Co. Philada. Warranted." Full stock, walnut. Hickory ramrod. Plate 3, Fig. 1. $1,350–$1,825.

BOOTH PISTOL, cal. .58; 8-inch, round, tapering, smoothbore, pin-fastened brass barrel marked "Philadelphia." Total length 13.5 inches. Weight 2 lbs. 5 oz. Brass-mounted. Iron pan with fence. Brass trigger guard. Full stock, walnut. Hickory ramrod. Lock plate marked "Booth." Plate 3, Fig. 2. $1,475–$1,950.

CHERINGTON PISTOL, cal. .45; 12.25-inch, octagon, smoothbore barrel marked "T. P. Cherington." Total length 17.75 inches. Weight 3 lbs. 1 oz. Full-length walnut stock. Brass end-cap, thimbles, front sight, and pan with fence. Iron trigger guard. Flat gooseneck hammer. Hickory ramrod. Lock plate also marked "T. P. Cherington." $1,450–$1,850.

COLLIER FLINTLOCK REVOLVER, cal. .34, 5-shot; 9-inch octagon barrel. Total length 17.5 inches. One specimen has a 4-inch barrel and a total length of 11.5 inches. Another specimen has a 6.125-inch barrel and a total length of 14 inches. Patented in 1818 by Elisha Haydon Collier, of Boston, Mass., an American citizen living in London. Plain metal finish. Brass-bead front sight. Raised-notch rear sight. Cylinder rotated by hand, although some had a spring arrangement for rotation. Collier returned to the United States. His patents were granted in England, France, and the United States; and although the known specimens in collections were apparently made in England, this rare and interesting weapon is listed here to provide for the occurrence of American-made specimens. Plate 3, Fig. 3. $9,500–$16,500.

CONSTABLE PISTOL, cal. .50; 10-inch, pin-fastened, round barrel marked "Philadelphia." Total length 15.5 inches. Brown metal finish. Brass-mounted. Walnut stock to within 1 inch from muzzle. Gooseneck hammer. Lock marked "R. Constable." Most of the parts were made in England, imported to Philadelphia, and there assembled. $950–$1,475.

JACOB COOKE PISTOL—See U.S. Pistol, Model 1807–1808.

COUTTY PISTOL, cal. .58; 7.75-inch, tapering, brass, pin-fastened, smoothbore barrel marked "Philadelphia," with proof marks. Total length 13.5 inches. Weight 1 lb. 12 oz. Full stock, walnut. Iron pan with fence. Gooseneck hammer. Brass trigger guard. Hickory ramrod. Lock plate marked "Coutty." Plate 3, Fig. 4. $1,350–$2,100.

DE HUFF, GONTER & DICKERT—See U.S. Pistol, Model 1807–1808.

DERINGER U.S. PISTOL, MODEL 1814–1815, cal. .52; 10-inch, round, pin-fastened barrel. Total length 16.5 inches. Weight 2 lbs. 10 oz. Full stock, walnut. Brass trigger guard, butt cap, and thimbles. Iron pan with fence. Flat double-necked hammer. Bevel-edged flat lock plate. Hickory ramrod. Lock marked "H. Deringer Phila." Barrel marked "M." Also see U.S. Pistol, Model 1807–1808. Plate 3, Fig. 5. $2,750–$3,600.

O. & E. EVANS U.S. PISTOL, CONTRACT OF 1814, FRENCH MARTIAL TYPE, cal. .69; 8.875-inch, round, smoothbore barrel fastened to stock with brass band, marked "PM" with date and "P." Total length 15 inches. Weight 2 lbs. 13 oz. Double-necked hammer. Oval brass trigger guard. Brass pan without fence. Steel ramrod. Iron back strap. Flat lock plate marked "Evans." This is supposed to have been patterned after the French Model Year IX (1800–1801) cavalry pistol, cal. .69, 7.9-inch barrel; total length 14.567 inches, with a round-faced, reinforced hammer; brass pan without fence; brass band, butt cap, side plate, and separate trigger bow; lock plate with rounded face at rear end. However, the usual specimen found in collections follows the description given. (This is merely a more complete description of the same pistol listed in Chapter 3.) These contract-made pistols are classified sometimes as U.S. martial and sometimes as U.S. secondary martial. Plate 3, Fig. 6. $2,250–$2,850.

EVANS MODEL 1826 NAVY PISTOL—See U.S. Pistol, Model 1826, W. L. Evans, Navy (Chapter 3).

T. FRENCH, MODEL 1807–1808 PISTOL, cal. .64; 10.625-inch, round, smoothbore, pin-fastened barrel marked "P.M.," "P.C." and date. Total length 16.75 inches. Full stock, walnut. Brass-mounted. Flat gooseneck hammer. Iron pan without fence. Brass trigger guard. Lock plate marked with eagle, "U.S.," "T. French," and "Canton." See U.S. Pistol Model 1807–1808. $2,100–$3,400.

MARTIN FRYE PISTOL—See U.S. Pistol, Model 1807–1808.

GOLCHER FOUR-SHOT SINGLE-BARREL PISTOL, cal. .44; 10-inch octagon, smoothbore barrel sometimes found marked "Golcher," but often not marked. Total length 15 inches. Lock marked "Golcher." Blued trigger guard and lock. Powder is automatically sprinkled into the pan and into four touchholes in a horizontal row. A complicated mechanism provides for firing four successive shots after one loading. Made by one of several Pennsylvania gunsmiths named Golcher. $2,650–$3,400.

GRUBB PISTOL, cal. .44; 8.75-inch, brass, round, smoothbore, key-fastened barrel marked "T. Grubb." Total length 14.375 inches. Horn-tipped walnut stock extends almost to muzzle. Silver-mounted. Flat gooseneck hammer. Iron pan with fence. Horn-tipped hickory ramrod. Bird's-head butt. $1,975–$2,575.

HALBACH & SONS PISTOL, cal. .50; 6.75-inch, rifled, bronze barrel, part octagonal and part round, with cannon muzzle, pin-fastened. Total length 12 inches. Bronze-mounted with butt cap ornamented with the American eagle, shield, and 13 stars. Flat gooseneck hammer. Iron pan with fence. Specimen illustrated is not marked, but some specimens are stamped on the lock plate "Halbach & Sons." Plate 5, Fig. 4. $965–$1,400.

HALL BREECH-LOADING BRONZE-BARREL PISTOL, cal. .50; single-shot; 5.562-inch, bronze, octagon, smoothbore, pin-fastened barrel. Weight 2 lbs. 13 oz. Full-length walnut stock. Checked butt. Brass, oval, pin-fastened trigger guard. Pan is part of bronze breechblock. Steel hammer, frizzen, and side plates. Bronze latch frame. No marks except what appears to be a serial number on right of breechblock, but this piece was undoubtedly made by John H. Hall, since it is similar in design to the U.S. Rifle, Model 1819, John H. Hall Breechloader (see Chapter 21 on U.S. Martial Shoulder Arms). Plate 3, Fig. 7. $7,850–$11,000.

HALL BREECH-LOADING IRON-BARREL PISTOL, cal. .50, single-shot; 7.125-inch, iron, octagon, rifled, key-fastened barrel. Total length 16.25 inches. Weight 2 lbs. 15 oz. Full stock, walnut. Silver-mounted. Flat-bottomed, oval, checked butt. Iron pan is part of iron breechblock. Steel hammer and frizzen. Resembles the design of the U.S. Rifle, Model 1819,

---

PLATE 3. U.S. Secondary Martial Flintlock Pistols

*Figure*

1. Bird & Co. Pistol.
2. Booth Pistol.
3. Collier Flintlock Revolver.
4. Coutty Pistol.
5. Deringer    U.S.    Pistol,    Model 1807–1808.

6. O. & E. Evans U.S. Pistol, Contract of 1814, French Martial Type.
7. Hall Breech-loading Bronze-Barrel Pistol.

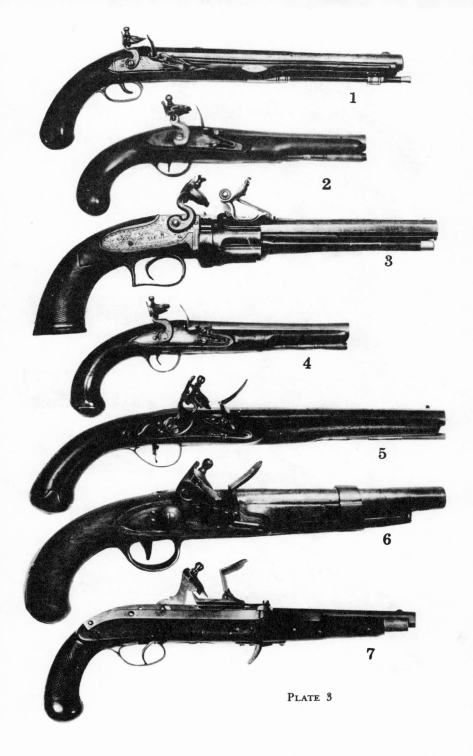

1

2

3

4

5

6

7

PLATE 3

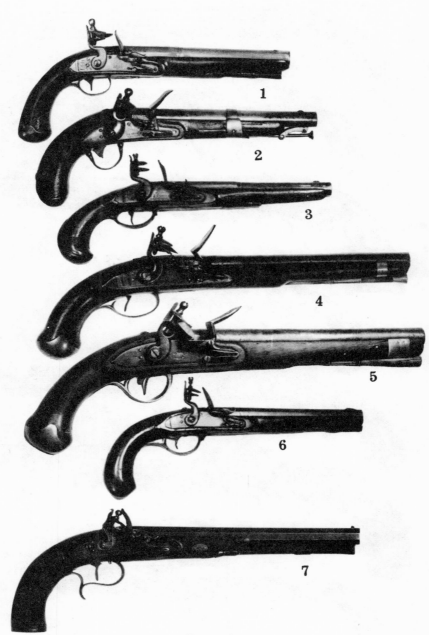

1

2

3

4

5

6

7

PLATE 4

John H. Hall Breechloader (U.S. Martial Shoulder Arms). Breechblock marked "John H. Hall Patent" and on one specimen "RB40." $8,500–$12,750.

HARPERS FERRY—See U.S. Pistol, Model 1805.

ABRAHAM HENRY—See U.S. Pistol, Model 1807–1808.

HENRY (J. PHILA.) U.S. PISTOL MODEL 1807–1808, cal. .54; 10-inch, round, smoothbore, pin-fastened barrel marked "J. Henry Phila" with "P" and an eagle head within the same oval. Lock plate marked "US" and "J. Henry Phila." Total length 16 inches. Full stock, walnut. Brass-mounted. Flat double-necked hammer. Iron pan with fence. Hickory ramrod. Brass trigger guard. $1,650–$2,400.

HENRY (J.) PISTOL, cal. .62; 10-inch, octagon, smoothbore, key-fastened barrel. Total length 15.75 inches. Full-length walnut stock. Brass-mounted. Brass front sight, butt cap, and trigger guard. Flat gooseneck hammer. Iron pan with fence. Hickory ramrod. Lock plate marked "J. Henry" with two vertical slashes near rear end of plate. $1,350–$1,650.

HENRY (J. BOULTON) PISTOL, cal. .60; 8.875-inch, round, smoothbore, pin-fastened barrel. Total length 14.25 inches. Full stock, walnut. Brass-mounted. Flat gooseneck hammer. Iron pan with fence. Brass butt cap and trigger guard. Hickory ramrod. Lock plate marked "J. Henry Boulton." Plate 4, Fig. 1. $1,150–$1,750.

HENRY (J. J. BOULTON) U.S. PISTOL, MODEL 1826, cal. .54; 8.5-inch, round, smoothbore barrel held by single band. Total length 13.5 inches. Full-length walnut stock. Swivel, steel ramrod. Brass pan without fence. Double-neck hammer. Lock plate marked "J. J. Henry Boulton." Plate 4, Fig. 2. $1,150–$1,750.

R. JOHNSON PISTOL—See U.S. Pistol, Model 1836.

KENTUCKY FLINTLOCK PISTOLS—See Chapter 5.

KETLAND—See McCormick below, and also Kuntz.

---

PLATE 4. U.S. Secondary Martial Flintlock Pistols

Figure

1. Henry (J. Boulton) Pistol.
2. Henry (J. J. Boulton) U.S. Pistol, Model 1826.
3. Kuntz Pistol.
4. McCormick U.S. Pistol.
5. Miles Pistol, U.S. Model 1807–1808.
6. Moll Pistol.
7. North Dueling Pistol.

KLINE PISTOL, cal. .48; 9.25-inch, round, smoothbore, pin-fastened barrel. Total length 16 inches. Full stock, walnut. Flat gooseneck hammer. Iron pan with fence. Hickory ramrod. Brass-mounted. Lock plate marked "C. Kline." $950–$1,300.

KUNTZ PISTOL, cal. .44; 9-inch, round, smoothbore, pin-fastened barrel marked "Kuntz Philad." Total length 12.75 inches. Full-length walnut stock. Bird's-head butt. Flat gooseneck hammer. Iron pan with fence. Brass trigger guard. Lock plate marked "J.K. Philad." Plate 4, Fig. 3. $2,350–$3,100.

LAWRENCE PISTOL, cal. .62; 9-inch, round, iron, smoothbore, pin-fastened barrel. Total length 15 inches. Flat gooseneck hammer. Brass-mounted. Marked "Lawrence" on the lock plate and "Philada" on the barrel. Lawrence was listed in the Philadelphia city directory as a gunsmith from 1821 to 1829. Plate 5, Fig. 6. $1,100–$1,850.

ADAM LEITNER—See U.S. Pistol, Model 1807–1808.

McCORMICK U.S. PISTOL, cal. .64; 10.25-inch, round barrel marked "U.S." with eagle head over "P" in an oval. Brass trigger guard, butt cap, and side plate. One brass thimble. Full-length walnut stock with brass band partly around barrel. Brass-tipped hickory ramrod. Flat lock plate marked "Ketland & Co." in front of hammer and "United States" in two curved lines behind hammer. Iron pan with fence. Flat gooseneck hammer. Stock marked "U.S." on left and "McCormick," the name of the U.S. contractor. The lock, of course, was made by Ketland in England. Plate 4, Fig. 4. $3,400–$5,500.

McK BROS. PISTOL, cal. .54; 10-inch, smoothbore, pin-fastened, part round and part fluted barrel, which is round for first third of distance from muzzle and fluted with two flutes, one on each side of barrel, to the breech. Two brass thimbles. No back strap. Marked "McK Bros. Baltimore" on lock. This was made by McKim Brothers, Baltimore, Md., gunmakers who also made a single-shot percussion pistol listed on page 72. Total length about 15.5 inches. $1,000–$1,450.

MEACHAM & POND PISTOL, cal. .54; 8.5-inch, round, smoothbore, pin-fastened barrel. Total length 13.25 inches. Full stock, walnut. Brass-mounted. Iron pan with fence. Lock plate marked "Meacham & Pond Warranted." $775–$960.

MILES PISTOL, U.S. MODEL 1807–1808, cal. .58; 9.75-inch, round, smoothbore, pin-fastened barrel marked "Miles Philada P." Total length 15.5 inches. Full-length walnut stock. Brass-mounted. Flat double-neck hammer. Iron pan with fence. Hickory ramrod. Flat lock plate marked "Miles Phila" within an oval. Plate 4, Fig. 5. $1,950–$2,750.

MILES PISTOL, cal. .69; 10.5-inch, round, smoothbore, pin-fastened barrel marked "C.P." Full stock, walnut. No sights. Total length 16 inches. Lock plate marked "Miles" and, behind the hammer, "C.P." Brass-mounted. Bludgeon-type handle. Double gooseneck hammer. $1,490–$1,950.

MILES PISTOL, cal. .64; 9.375-inch, round, smoothbore, pin-fastened barrel. Total length 15.25 inches. Full-length walnut stock. Brass-mounted. Gooseneck hammer. Iron pan with fence. No sights. Hickory ramrod. Flat lock plate marked "Miles" and "C.P." with two vertical slashes. This C.P. stands for "Commonwealth of Pennsylvania" and not for "Continental Property" as collectors and historians once believed. $1,490–$1,950.

MOLL PISTOL, cal. .38; 8.375-inch, brass, octagon, rifled, pin-fastened barrel marked "P. & D. Moll Hellerstown." Total length 14 inches. Full-length tiger-striped maple stock. Gooseneck hammer. Iron pan with fence, forged as part of lock plate. Brass trigger guard. Brass knife-blade front sight. Open rear sight, of iron. Hickory ramrod. Flat imported lock plate marked "London Warranted." Supposedly used by cavalry in War of 1812. Plate 4, Fig. 6. $2,200–$2,950.

NORTH DUELING PISTOL, cal. .50; smoothbore, 10.25-inch, octagon, browned barrel with a countersunk gold seal having "S. North Middletown Conn." in raised letters, and the word "Connecticut" engraved in Old English letters on the barrel itself. Single set trigger. Two iron thimbles. Engraved double-neck hammer. Safety lock. Gold-lined vent. Engraved tang. Horn-tipped walnut half-stock. Checkered grip. Square butt. Rib under barrel for horn-tipped hickory ramrod. Silver wedge escutcheons. Parts other than barrel are casehardened. Specimen described was one of a matched pair, each of which was numbered 11. This was not a martial weapon and is included here only for convenience in listing. Plate 4, Fig. 7; per matched pair. $8,250–$10,500.

NORTH U.S. MARTIAL PISTOLS—See U.S. Pistol, Models 1808, 1811, 1813, 1816, 1819, 1826.

NORTH & CHENEY PISTOLS—See U.S. Pistol Model 1799.

PERKIN PISTOL, cal. .69, single-shot; 8.25-inch, round, brass, pin-fastened barrel marked "I. Perkin." Total length 14.5 inches. Brass trimmings. No sights. Full-length walnut stock. Gooseneck hammer. $2,450–$3,200.

PERKIN PISTOL, cal. .62; 8.875-inch, round, brass, smoothbore, pin-fastened barrel marked "I. Perkin." Total length 14.125 inches. Full stock, walnut. Brass-mounted. Flat gooseneck hammer. Iron pan with fence. Brass trigger guard. Hickory ramrod. Lock plate marked "I. Perkin." $2,450–$3,200.

PICKEL PISTOL—See U.S. Pistol, Model 1807–1808.

POND PISTOL, cal. .56; 9-inch, octagon, smoothbore, brass, key-fastened barrel marked "Albany." Total length 15 inches. Full-length apple stock. Gooseneck hammer. Iron pan with fence. Brass butt cap, trigger guard, and front sight. No rear sight. Hickory ramrod. Lock plate marked "Pond & Co." $800–$1,050.

RAPPAHANNOCK FORGE PISTOL, cal. .69; 9-inch, smoothbore, pin-fastened barrel. Total length 15.125 inches. Brass trigger guard. Full stock. No sights. Double-neck, flat, beveled hammer. Iron pan with flat beveled edges and fence to rear. Hickory ramrod held by brass thimble. Brass mountings. Lock plate marked "RAPaFORGE." Made at Rappahannock Forge, which was part of the Hunter Iron Works, Falmouth, Va., founded before the American Revolution and dismantled in 1781 on the approach of a British force. Butt marked "3RGT."

*Caveat emptor!* Do not buy a pistol of this description at any price unless three experts of national reputation examine it and pronounce it genuine! $9,500–$15,500.

RAPPAHANNOCK FORGE PISTOL, cal. .65; 8.75-inch, smoothbore, pin-fastened barrel, sometimes marked "J. Hunter." Total length 13 inches. Brass butt plate, trigger guard, and thimble. Iron ramrod. Lock plate marked "RAPa FORGE." Some specimens marked on side plate with organization designation, such as, for example, "A.L.D." for Albemarle Light Dragoons, followed by the serial number assigned to that particular piece by the organization. Butt plate may bear organization marks, such as "3rd Rgt." (3rd Regiment). This specimen, converted to percussion, is sometimes classified as a Confederate weapon when the marks or record show that it was used by the Confederates. *Beware:* This pistol may be a fake! $9,500–$15,500.

SAME, but converted to percussion. *Beware:* This pistol may be a fake! $6,750–$9,000.

RICHMOND-VIRGINIA PISTOL, cal. .54; 10-inch, round, smoothbore, key-fastened barrel with extending rib. Total length 16.625 inches. Weight

---

PLATE 5. U.S. Secondary Martial Flintlock Pistols

*Figure*

1. Richmond-Virginia Pistol, marked "Richmond, Virginia."
2. Richmond-Virginia Pistol, marked "Richmond."
3. Walsh Pistol.
4. Halbach & Sons Pistol.
5. Smith & Hyslop Pistol.
6. Lawrence Pistol.

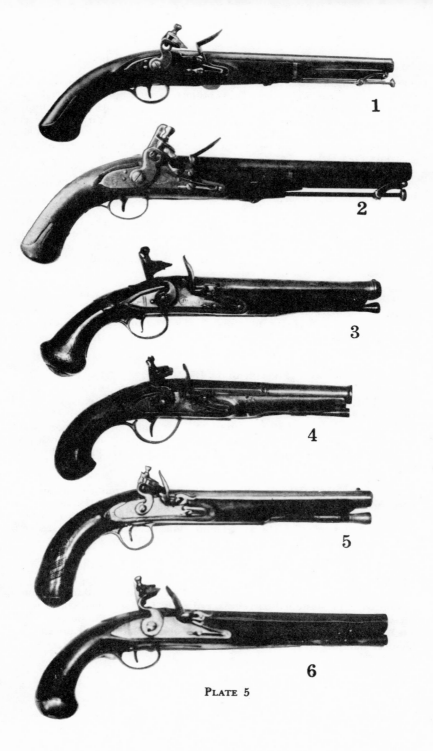

1

2

3

4

5

6

PLATE 5

2 lbs. 13 oz. Walnut half-stock. Swivel ramrod. Brass-mounted. Double-neck hammer. Iron pan with fence. Brass butt cap, trigger guard, ramrod thimble, and barrel reinforcing band. Lock plate usually marked "Richmond" with the date (somewhere between 1812 and 1816), and "Virginia." Resembles U.S. Pistol, Model 1805 (1806), Harpers Ferry except for the swivel ramrod design. Made for the Militia by the State of Virginia. Plate 5, Fig. 1. $2,100–$2,900.

SAME, but marked "Richmond" and the date, without the "Virginia." Plate 5, Fig. 2. $2,250–$2,975.

ROGERS & BROTHERS PISTOL, cal. .54; 8.5-inch, half octagon, smoothbore, key-fastened barrel. Total length 14 inches. Full stock, striped maple. Brass-mounted. Gooseneck hammer. Iron pan with fence. Hickory ramrod. Lock plate marked "Rogers & Brothers" and "Warranted." $1,200–$1,650.

RUPP PISTOL, cal. .47; 8.5-inch, round-octagon, smoothbore, key-fastened barrel marked "John Rupp." Total length 13.75 inches. Full stock, maple, finished red. Silver-mounted. Bird's-head butt. Silver butt cap and trigger guard. Gooseneck hammer. Iron pan with fence. Hickory ramrod. $1,900–$2,400.

SHANNON—See U.S. Pistol, Model 1807–1808.

SHULER PISTOL, U.S. MODEL 1807–1808, cal. .54; 9.625-inch, round, smoothbore, pin-fastened barrel marked "Shuler." Total length 16 inches. Full-length walnut stock. Brass-mounted. Brass butt cap and trigger guard. Iron pan with fence. Double-neck hammer. Hickory ramrod. Lock plate marked "U.S." Some unmarked. Resembles Henry (J. Phila.) pistol, described before. $2,800–$3,500.

SMITH & HYSLOP PISTOL, cal. .58; 8.75-inch, round, iron, smoothbore, pin-fastened barrel. Total length 14 inches. Late type gooseneck hammer. Brass-mounted. Lock plate marked "Smith & Hyslop New York Warranted." Full stock with checkered butt. The manufacturer was active in New York City in the 1820's. Plate 5, Fig. 5. $885–$1,150.

SPRINGFIELD PISTOLS—See U.S. Pistol, Models 1807 and 1817.

SWEITZER PISTOL, U.S. MODEL 1807–1808, cal. .54; 10.5-inch round, smoothbore, pin-fastened barrel marked with "CT" and eagle head within the same oval. Total length 16 inches. Weight 2 lbs. 6 oz. Full-length walnut stock. Brass-mounted. Brass front sight, butt cap, and trigger guard. Double-neck hammer. Iron pan with fence. Lock plate marked "Sweitzer & Co." $2,800–$3,500.

TRYON PISTOL, cal. .69; smoothbore, 9.25 inch round iron or bronze barrel. Lock stamped "Tryon" and barrel marked "Tryon Philadelphia" with English proof marks. Contract assembly in U.S. arsenal in Philadelphia in 1814 and 1815. Full stock. $925–$1,260.

U.S. MARTIAL FLINTLOCK PISTOLS—See Chapter 3.

VIRGINIA MANUFACTORY PISTOL, cal. .69; 12.062-inch, round, smoothbore barrel. Total length 17 inches. Weight 3 lbs. 6 oz. Full stock, walnut. Barrel held with double band. Iron mountings, back strap, and butt cap. Steel ramrod. Brass front sight. No rear sight. Gooseneck hammer. Iron pan with fence forged as part of lock plate. Lock plate marked "Virginia Manufactory" and "Richmond," with the date, usually from 1805 to 1811. The marks "Richmond" and the date may be within a circle or in two curved lines. $2,600–$3,500.

VIRGINIA-RICHMOND PISTOL—See above, Richmond-Virginia Pistol.

WALSH PISTOL, cal. .54; 8-inch, brass, tapering, cannon-shaped, smoothbore, pin-fastened barrel marked "J. Walsh Philad" inside an engraved panel. Total length 14 inches. Weight 1 lb. 15 oz. Full-length walnut stock. Gooseneck hammer. Brass pan and fence cast as part of lock plate. Brass mountings, lock plate, trigger guard, and name plate. Hickory ramrod. Lock plate marked "J. Walsh" inside an engraved panel. Plate 5, Fig. 3. $2,950–$3,800.

WATERS PISTOL—See U.S. Pistol, Model 1836, A. Waters.

WINNER, NIPPES & STEINMAN—See U.S. Pistol, Model 1807–1808.

# Chapter 5

## *KENTUCKY FLINTLOCK PISTOLS*

THE discovery of the Kentucky (Pennsylvania) pistol as a distinct type of firearm was the most important event in the firearm-collecting field during the past forty-five years. The honor of this discovery belongs to Mr. Calvin Hetrick, of New Enterprise, Pennsylvania, who was the first to recognize the Kentucky pistol as a separate type, the first to acquire a collection of representative pieces, and the first to announce his discovery to the hobby world, which he did in the pages of the first edition of this book.

Mr. Joe Kindig, Jr., of York, Pennsylvania, an outstanding authority on Kentucky (Pennsylvania) rifles, and Mr. Richard D. Steuart, of Baltimore, Maryland, the great authority on Confederate arms, were among the many experts who confirmed Mr. Hetrick's classification of the Kentucky pistol as an individual type. Later, all of the original Hetrick specimens, plus many more important pieces, became the property of Mr. Herman P. Dean, of Huntington, West Virginia, and later to the famous J. W. Desserich collection in Maineville, Ohio.

The true Kentucky pistol is the short arm that was made by the same gunsmiths who made the well-known Kentucky rifle. These pistols are really miniature Kentucky rifles, with their slender stocks and "furniture" like the rifles—trigger guards, ramrod thimbles, muzzle caps, etc. They are full-stocked; a half-stocked pistol is regarded as a hybrid type, and not as a true Kentucky type. In design, these pistols are characterized by their individuality; they are as individual as the pioneer Americans who made them. Each maker scorned foreign patterns and in his constant seeking for perfection never made two pieces exactly alike except in the case of matched pairs.

One of the striking features of the Kentucky pistol is that it is usually found unmarked, especially if it was made during the Revolutionary period. The probable explanation is that during the Revolution the gunmakers were afraid of reprisals from the British if they were known to be supplying arms for the American forces. Since it is known that matched pairs were made for and carried by officers of the Revolutionary army, this is a reasonable explanation.

Another theory for the lack of marks is based on the small number of Kentucky pistols fabricated. Few of the early gunsmiths made more than from three to six in their entire lives, although they may have turned out hundreds of Kentucky rifles. Even if we discard the theory of leaving off marks to avoid reprisals from the British, we can believe that since the Kentucky pistol was usually made only for a special order, the maker did not have the same incentive to mark it with his name as he would in the case of a Kentucky rifle, for making rifles was his main business, while pistols were probably only a sideline.

It is believed that most of these pistols were made in eastern Pennsylvania, although a few were made in the neighboring states of New York, New Jersey, and Ohio. As to the total number made, no definite statement can be made at present, and it remains for the collectors, curators, and dealers of America to add to our knowledge regarding this colorful and interesting firearm. Interestingly enough, the percentage of pieces in original flintlock condition is much larger than in the case of the Kentucky rifle. The relative number of original flintlock pistols in the Hetrick collection, and in the collections of a few others who have followed Hetrick's lead, show that about 50% of the existing specimens are in original flintlock condition, 37½% are conversions from flintlock to percussion, and that 12½% are pieces which were made for percussion fire.

This distribution of percentages was almost in inverse proportion to the number of Kentucky rifles in the three forms. Mr. Hetrick believed that many of these pistols made before 1800, and some made thereafter, were carried by officers of the American army, and that their use by civilians was limited. After the introduction of percussion revolvers, these pistols were laid away as souvenirs of the Revolution, or the War of 1812, or they were treasured as ancestral possessions. Just the opposite was true of the Kentucky rifles, since they were in constant use as hunting weapons and target arms, and were converted to percussion in large numbers.

By keeping the facts about the Kentucky pistol to himself, Mr. Hetrick could have acquired more pieces at less cost than he could after the first edition of this book was printed, but he was a true collector at heart and unselfishly shared his newly acquired knowledge with his brothers of the arms fraternity. It is interesting to note, however, that in the first edition we described seven flintlock Kentucky pistols and two converted to percussion about the time that all flintlocks were beginning to be converted. In addition, we listed one that was probably made as a percussion piece. The average value, as given by Mr. Hetrick at that time, was $75 in good condition and $95 in fine condition for the flintlocks. The percussion pistols were given an average value of $30 in good condition and $40 in fine condition. The author of this text was severely criticized by some collectors and dealers for listing these values.

As soon as collectors began to hear about the new type, they started searching for specimens for their collections, with the result that the values began to soar. Today, Kentucky flintlock pistols without any special ornamentation often sell for about $2,500 in good condition and $3,700 in fine condition and Kentucky percussion pistols frequently sell for $1,100 in good condition and $1,450 in fine condition, although there are many sales where Kentucky percussion pistols are sold for almost as much as Kentucky flintlock pistols. The specimens described and valued in this chapter are presented to indicate the Kentucky type, but no two Kentucky pistols are alike. Even the same gunsmith never made two exactly alike.

KENTUCKY FLINTLOCK PISTOL, Revolutionary period; cal. .36, rifled, with eight deep grooves; 9.5-inch octagon barrel; 14.875 inches over

---

PLATE 6. Kentucky (Pennsylvania) Pistols

*Figure*

1. Flintlock Pistol, Revolutionary Period.
2. Flintlock Pistol, Colonial Period, Early Type.
3. Flintlock Pistol, Pre-Revolutionary.
4. Flintlock Pistol, Revolutionary Period.
5. Flintlock Pistol, 1812 or Later.
6. Percussion Pistol, Converted from Flintlock about 1800.
7. Percussion Pocket Pistol Used by River Steamer Captains.

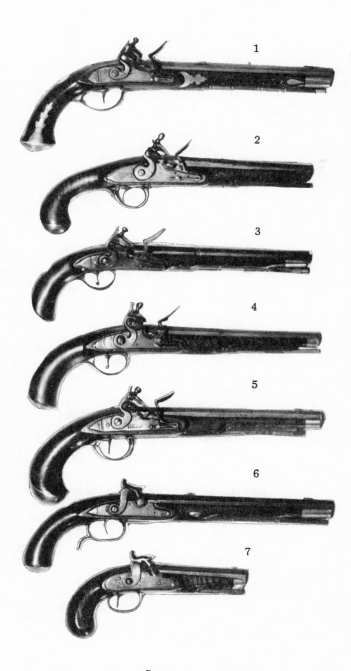

1

2

3

4

5

6

7

PLATE 6

all. Kentucky-rifle-type front and rear sights. Engraved lock, 4.125 inches. Iron pan with fence. High-quality full-burl maple stock fastened to barrel with dart-shaped silver pins. Silver butt cap, finely engraved silver inlays on each side of grip, silver barrel pin escutcheons and name plate. Brass trigger guard, engraved brass lockpin escutcheons, ramrod thimbles, and muzzle cap. Silver-tipped hickory ramrod. Weight 2 lbs. This is the only early rifled Kentucky flintlock pistol in the Hetrick collection. It is extremely rare. It is unsigned, but it is known that this particular piece was the personal arm of Captain William Cowan, of Chester County, Pa., who carried it at the Battle of Yorktown in the Revolutionary War. Plate 6, Fig. 1. $3,600–$4,950.

KENTUCKY FLINTLOCK PISTOL, Colonial period, about 1740; cal. .48, smoothbore; 7.5-inch, brass, half octagon, half round barrel; 13.375 inches over all. No sights. Engraved lock, 4.875 inches; iron pan with fence; no bridle over tumbler or frizzen pin; pan and plate separately forged and pinned together. Full stock, curly maple, round-pin-fastened; engraved brass butt cap and trigger guard, brass ramrod thimbles. No muzzle cap. Note very early type of grip. Ramrod and trigger not original. Unsigned. Probably one of the first pistols of the Kentucky type made in America. Extremely rare. Weight 1 lb. 12 oz. Plate 6, Fig. 2. $2,375–$3,000.

KENTUCKY FLINTLOCK PISTOL, probably pre-Revolutionary period; cal. .44, smoothbore; 9.125-inch, part octagon, part round barrel: 13.625 inches over all. No sights. Four-and-one-fourth-inch lock, severely plain with single vertical slash across tail. Marked on inside of plate "HVF." No frizzen spring. Iron pan and plate separately forged and fastened together with screws. Round-pin-fastened to stock. Full stock with bird's-head grip; brass butt cap extending toward tang; brass trigger guard, side plate, ramrod thimbles, muzzle cap. Simple, neat engraving on butt cap, guard, and side plate. Ramrod not original. Early, wide trigger with curl to rear. The stock is exceptionally slender for a pistol of this size, and of walnut. Unsigned except as noted. Weight 1 lb. 11 oz. Plate 6, Fig. 3. $2,490–$3,225.

KENTUCKY FLINTLOCK PISTOL, Revolutionary period; cal. .44, smoothbore; 10-inch octagon barrel; 15.5 inches over all. Kentucky-type sights. Five-inch lock, severely plain with slash across tail of plate. No roller on frizzen. Pan and plate separately forged. Iron pan with fence. Round-pin-fastened. Full stock, curly maple with attractive red violin finish. Brass butt cap with extension toward tang; brass trigger guard, ramrod, thimbles, barrel-pin escutcheons, muzzle cap. Early-type trigger with curl to rear. Silver name plate. Not signed on lock or barrel, but has peculiar-type lockpin escutcheons exactly like the .38-caliber example below, and the same style finish. Original striped hickory ramrod with worm. Weight 2 lbs. This was one of a pair carried by Captain Samuel Russell, of Pennsylvania, in the Revolution, with Sullivan's expedition. $2,625–$3,360.

**KENTUCKY FLINTLOCK PISTOL**, Revolutionary period; cal. .44, smoothbore; 8.75-inch, brass, part octagon, part round barrel; 14.25 inches over all. No sights. Plain lock, 4.25 inches, with curved slash across tail of plate; roller on frizzen; pan separately forged; iron pan with high fence. Full stock, maple, dark finish, with silver butt cap extending toward tang; silver trigger guard; silver name plate with monogram; silver ramrod thimbles, muzzle cap, side plate. Butt cap, guard, side plate, barrel, and tang simply but tastefully engraved. Fine relief carving on stock at rear of tang; incised carving on fore stock. Excellent workmanship. Ramrod not original. Not signed on barrel or lock, but inside of plate is marked with a large, curiously curved "H." Early-type trigger guard. Plate 6, Fig. 4. $2,750–$3,355.

**KENTUCKY FLINTLOCK PISTOL**, period of 1812 or later; cal. .48, smoothbore; 9-inch octagon barrel; 14.5 inches over all. Barrel is round-pin-fastened. Kentucky-type front sight; no rear sight. Plain lock, 4.25 inches, with vertical slash across tail of plate. Iron pan with fence. Lock marked "J. J. Henry Boulton." Full stock, maple, red violin finish with heavy brass furniture; butt cap extends upward toward tang at rear; trigger guard, ramrod, thimbles, side plate, muzzle cap. Not marked on barrel. Hickory ramrod, Kentucky rifle type. Weight 2 lbs. 1 oz. Plate 6, Fig. 5. $2,490–$3,135.

**KENTUCKY PISTOL**, converted from flintlock to percussion, Revolutionary period originally; cal. .38, smoothbore; 10-inch octagon barrel; 15.5 inches over all. Original browning still on barrel, fully equal to that of Hall rifles. Barrel marked, in script, "S.M.," which probably stands for Simon Miller, Hamburg, Pa., the maker. Kentucky-rifle front and rear sights. Lock, 4.5 inches, marked on plate "T. Ketland & Co." Full stock, curly maple, beautiful red violin finish with incised carving around tang. Silver inlays around muzzle of barrel; silver butt cap, name plate; silver escutcheons for dart-shaped barrel pins. Brass trigger guard, ramrod thimbles, muzzle cap. Early-type trigger. Hickory ramrod. Weight 1 lb. 6 oz. This was one of a pair carried by Col. Nathan Dennison, a Pennsylvania officer at the Battle of Wyoming, July 3, 1778. $2,275–$3,000.

**KENTUCKY PISTOL**, converted from flintlock to percussion, period about 1800; cal. .34, smoothbore; 9.75-inch octagon barrel; 15.375 inches over all. Plain, handmade lock, originally flint, with vertical slash across tail of plate, marked, in script, "A.J." Attractive dark-finished curly maple full stock with brass butt cap, trigger guard with spur, ramrod thimbles, long muzzle cap. Barrel is flat-pin-fastened. Silver name plate. Kentucky front and rear sights. Very slender and graceful in design. Barrel not signed. Kentucky-type hickory ramrod. Weight 2 lbs. Plate 6, Fig. 6. $2,200–$2,800.

**KENTUCKY PERCUSSION POCKET PISTOL**, probably pre-Civil War period; about cal. .32, 4.875-inch octagon barrel, rifled with 7 grooves; 8.75

inches over all. Front and rear sights. Lock, 3.25 inches long, marked "T. Howell Philadelphia." Barrel marked "J. Fleeger, Allegheny." (This was the John Fleeger who was proprietor of the Allegheny Iron Works, Pittsburgh.) Tang extends well toward butt, which has no cap. Fine, natural stripe, full curly maple stock. Brass trigger guard and ramrod thimbles. Silver muzzle cap. Flat-pin-fastened. Weight 1 lb. 3 oz. According to tradition, a few of this type were made for captains of steamboats plying between Pittsburgh and New Orleans, to keep order among the passengers and crew. Plate 6, Fig. 7. $1,200–$1,585.

## Special Caution

Genuine Kentucky flintlock pistols are extremely rare and seldom come on the market. This also is true of genuine Kentucky percussion pistols, but pistols of the "Kentucky" type are even more rare when originally made with percussion ignition. The values given in this chapter are conservative. This means that a genuine Kentucky pistol is worth whatever the buyer wants to pay for it. There are many imitation, counterfeit pistols on the market. The buyer should be extremely wary.

# Chapter 6

## U.S. MARTIAL PERCUSSION PISTOLS

THE U.S. martial percussions pistols, as classified by arms historians and collectors, are those single-shot percussion pistols made in the United States armories at Harpers Ferry, Virginia, and Springfield, Massachusetts, and by the following private contractors: Henry Aston, Middletown, Connecticut; the reorganized firm of H. Aston & Co., also of Middletown; Ira N. Johnson, Middletown; William Glaze & Co., Columbia, South Carolina, operating as the Palmetto Armory; N. P. Ames, Springfield, Massachusetts; and Henry Deringer, Philadelphia, Pennsylvania. These weapons bear the model years of 1842, 1843, and 1855.

ELGIN CUTLASS PISTOL, C. B. ALLEN, Springfield, Mass., cal. .54; 5-inch, smoothbore, octagon barrel bearing iron-blade front sight, and marked "Elgin's Patent PM CBA 1837," with a serial number, such as 149, as on the specimen illustrated, on the left side. No rear sight. Total length 15.57 inches. Weight 2 lbs. 7 oz. Left side of iron frame marked "C. B. Allen Springfield Mass." with same serial number as on barrel. Side hammer. Iron back strap. Walnut grips. Iron trigger guard loops at rear to the butt to serve as a hilt when the blade is used. Knife or cutlass blade is 11.5 inches long and 2.063 inches wide, fastened in front of trigger guard under the barrel. Leather scabbard. This was formerly regarded as a U.S. martial secondary percussion pistol, but recent information shows that it belongs in the U.S. martial classification. The United States contracted to purchase 150 of these pistols on September 8, 1837. Plate 7, Fig. 5. $3,850–$6,000.

GEDNEY CONVERSION OF MODEL 1836, flintlock pistol to percussion. Usual Johnson or Waters lock markings and barrel stamps. Conversion accomplished by use of George Gedney patented hammer marked "Pat. March 15, 1859" containing tube of fulminate, with cutter and carrier enclosed in hammer. $875–$1,250.

U.S. PISTOL, MODEL 1842, ARMY, H. ASTON, cal. .54; 8.5-inch, smoothbore, round barrel marked "US," "P," with initials, and the date on the tang, bearing a brass-blade front sight. Three-quarter-length black walnut stock, 11 inches long. Total length 14 inches. Flat beveled lock plate 4.8 inches long and 1.125 inches wide, marked "U.S. H ASTON" in front of hammer, and "MIDDtn CONN." with date behind hammer. Trigger guard 5 inches long with round ends. Barrel held to stock by single branch-band. Weight 2 lbs. 12 oz. Swivel ramrod. Brass mountings. All bright steel parts except trigger, which is blued. $295–$500.

SAME, but Navy-marked with anchor stamped at rear of barrel. $335–$550.

SAME, but marked "H. Aston and Co." on lock plate. $310–$525.

U.S. PISTOL, MODEL 1842, I. N. JOHNSON, cal. .54; same as U.S. Pistol, Model 1842, Army, H. Aston, described above, but barrel marked "US," "P," and with initials. Lock plate marked "US" and "I. N. JOHNSON" in front of hammer, and "MIDDtn CONN." with date behind hammer. $300–$510.

U.S. PISTOL, MODEL 1842, PALMETTO ARMORY, cal. .54; 8.5-inch, smoothbore, round barrel marked "Wm. GLAZE & Co.," "P," "V," with a palmetto tree and the date on the breech. Lockplate marked "COLUMBIA S.C." and the date. Except for the marks, this pistol is almost exactly like the U.S. Pistol, Model 1842, Army, H. Aston, and the same model made by I. N. Johnson, described above. Plate 7, Figs. 1 and 6. $760–$1,250.

U.S. PISTOL, MODEL 1843, NAVY, N.P. AMES, cal. .54; 6-inch, smoothbore, round, browned barrel without sights, marked "USR" (United States Revenue), "RP," and "P," with the date. Three-quarter, 10.625-inch walnut stock extending to the swivel ramrod. Total length 11.625 inches.

---

PLATE 7. U.S. Martial Percussion Pistols

*Figure*

1. U.S. Pistol, Model 1842, Palmetto Armory.
2. U.S. Pistol, Model 1843, Deringer, Army.
3. U.S. Pistol-Carbine, Model 1855, Springfield.
4. U.S. Pistol, Model 1843, Army, N.P. Ames.
5. Elgin Cutlass Pistol, C.B. Allen, Springfield, Mass., with scabbard.
6. Another view of the U.S. Pistol, Model 1842, Palmetto Armory, identical to Fig. 1 but photographed larger.
7. U.S. Breech-loading Percussion Martial Pistol bearing the stamp of the inspector in two places, possibly made by Simeon North, and probably unique.
8. U.S. Army Signal Pistol, 1862.
9. U.S. Army Signal Pistol, 1862.

PLATE 7

Brass mountings. Casehardened box lock, with hammer inside lock plate. Rounded, countersunk, brass butt plate. Flat lock plate 4.3 inches long and 1.25 inches wide, marked "N. P. AMES," "Springfield Mass." and "USR," with the date. Trigger guard 4.75 inches wide with square ends. One band. Brass-blade front sight. No rear sight. Plate 7, Fig. 4. $530–$850.

SAME, but navy model, marked "USN" in place of "USR." $440–$695.

U.S. PISTOL, MODEL 1843, DERINGER, ARMY, cal. .54; smoothbore, identical with U.S. Pistol Model 1843, N. P. Ames, except that lock plate is marked "US DERINGER PHILADELa." Notice that the last letter in "PHILADELa" is in lower case. Barrel may be unmarked, it may be marked "RP," or it may be marked "DERINGER PHILADELa RP." Brass-blade front sight. No rear sight. Plate 7, Fig. 2. $590–$900.

SAME, but rifled, with both front and rear sights. $665–$1,200.

SAME, but Navy model, smoothbore, marked "USN," with date 1847 behind hammer. $785–$1,350.

U.S. PISTOL-CARBINE, MODEL 1855, SPRINGFIELD, cal. .58; Maynard tape lock, 12-inch, round, rifled barrel having a low-blade front sight, a triple-leaf rear sight, marked "P," "V," with an eagle head and the model year, 1855, on the tang. Total length of pistol without detachable stock 17.75 inches. Weight of pistol alone 3 lbs. 13 oz. Brass mountings. Trigger guard 5.25 inches long with round ends. One band. Full-length oil-finished walnut stock, with ring in butt. Flat, beveled-edge lock plate marked "U.S: Springfield" in front of hammer and "1855" behind the hammer. Maynard primer recess cover marked with spread eagle. Brass mounted, detachable, oil-finished walnut stock, 26.5 inches long, with sling swivel. Butt plate of stock marked "US." Total length of pistol and detachable stock, when assembled, 28.25 inches. Total assembled weight, 5 lbs. 7 oz. Dragoons carried this weapon in two pieces on the saddle. When they dismounted to fight, they used it as a carbine. This weapon is also listed under U. S. martial percussion shoulder arms (in Chapter 21) for obvious reasons. $1,155–$2,000.

SAME, but without the detachable stock. Plate 7, Fig. 3. $590–$860.

U.S. PISTOL-CARBINE, MODEL 1855, HARPERS FERRY, cal. .58; 12-inch, round, rifled barrel, semi-octagonal at breech, marked "P," "V," and with an eagle head. Length of pistol alone 18 inches. Total length of pistol and detachable stock, when assembled, 28.25 inches. Length of stock alone 11.5 inches. Steel knife-blade front sight on barrel. No rear sight. Brass mountings. Swivel ramrod. Lock plate marked "Pistol Carbine," "Harpers Ferry," and "U.S." The lock plate is not cut away for the Maynard primer magazine recess. In other respects this Harpers Ferry model generally resembles the Springfield model. Very few were made, hence collectors regard this as an experimental model, or as a pattern prepared for the design of the Springfield model. Complete with shoulder stock. $2,500–$4,000.

U.S. SIGNAL PERCUSSION PISTOL, ARMY, MODEL 1861, 9 inches, tapered 1 ⅜-inch barrel, about cal. .74 at muzzle. Grips and frame are brass. Entire left side removable for repairing. Level below barrel operates a toothed arm which holds the wood of the flare in position. All are marked "U.S. Army Signal Pistol 1861 A.J.M." First army model and rare. $600–$850.

U.S. SIGNAL PERCUSSION PISTOL, ARMY, MODEL 1862, 6 inches long, tapered 1⅜-inch barrel, about cal. .74 at muzzle. Two-piece wood grips, brass frame, nickle plated. Butt on all specimens marked "U.S. Army Signal Pistol 1862 A.J.M." In 1861 Major Albert J. Myer was chief army signal officer. Plate 7, Fig. 8, with flare lever closed, Fig. 9 with lever open. $400–$575.

U.S. SIGNAL PERCUSSION PISTOL, NAVY, MODEL 1861, 9 inches long, tapered 1 3/16-inch barrel, about cal. .71 at muzzle. Very similar to 1861 Army but on this model the forward 2⅜ inches of the left side is integral with the right side. Dated 1861 through 1870. Some marked "U.S.O. Y.W.," others "U.S. N.Y.W.," Navy flares were smaller than Army. $425–$600.

UNVERIFIED U.S. BREECH-LOADING PERCUSSION MARTIAL PISTOL, cal. .54; 6.5-inch, smoothbore, round, iron barrel. Total length 14 inches. Center hammer similar to that of percussion carbines of the same period made by Simeon North. Spring catch on the underside allows the barrel to drop for loading. Stamped "NWP" on top of rising breech block and also "NWP" in oval on left side of stock. These are the initials of Nahun W. Patch who was an arms inspector at the armories of Simeon North and Asa Waters from 1831 to the 1850's. The workmanship indicates that it may be a North product. This is a unique specimen, unknown to most of the leading collectors and dealers, and owned by Mr. Sam E. Smith, Markesan, Wisconsin. Because of its unique character the value range is only estimated. Plate 7, Fig. 7. $3,000–$4,500.

# Chapter 7

## AMERICAN SECONDARY
## MARTIAL PERCUSSION PISTOLS

A MERICAN secondary martial percussion pistols are those single-shot percussion pistols which are of large caliber and size, which are not known to have been bought by the United States and issued to United States troops, but which were carried either officially or unofficially by state troops, by semi-official military and naval organizations, and by the officers and crew of privateers, or manufactured by those who sought government contracts.

Many of the Kentucky (Pennsylvania) pistols described in Chapter 5 could be classified as American secondary martial percussion pistols, if they were converted to percussion from flint, or made as percussion arms, and used in military and naval operations.

Since Confederate martial percussion pistols cannot be classified as United States martial arms, they could be classified as American secondary martial percussion pistols, but it is better to give them their own classification and list them in a separate chapter, which we have done (Chapter 10).

It should be obvious to any student of American history that it is possible that any and all American flintlock pistols could have been converted to percussion and used as secondary martial weapons. However, we have limited this chapter to those which are generally accepted under this classification by experienced collectors and dealers.

CONSTABLE, PHILADELPHIA, PISTOL, cal. .54; 6-inch, smoothbore, octagonal, pin-fastened barrel marked "Philadelphia." Total length 10.5 inches. Lock plate marked "Constable." Iron-pin front sight and no rear sight. Full stock. Horn-tipped ramrod. Iron-mounted. Made about 1840 by Richard Constable, famous Philadelphia gunsmith. Plate 8, Fig. 11. $500–$675.

JOHN DERR PISTOL, cal. .54; 10.375-inch, round, smoothbore barrel, octagonal at rear, key-fastened to stock, bearing long brass-blade front sight and open V-notch iron rear sight, and marked "John Derr Warranted." Flat lock plate not marked. Full-length maple stock ends in brass end-cap at muzzle. Brass mountings. Pinned thimbles. No back strap. Hickory ramrod. Bird's-head butt. Brass trigger guard forks at rear end. Made at Lancaster, Pa., by John Derr, and follows generally the lines of a Kentucky pistol. $835–$1,100.

DREPPERD, LANCASTER, PISTOL, cal. .40; 8.875-inch, smoothbore, unmarked, octagonal brass barrel, key-fastened, with brass front sight, and an open rear sight on the tang. Brass mountings. Pin-fastened thimbles. Full-length maple stock with a brass end-cap near the muzzle. No butt strap. Rounded butt with brass cap. Engraved lock plate marked "Drepperd Lancaster" forward of hammer. Brass trigger guard. Drepperd was another Lancaster, Pa., gunmaker who carried much of the beauty of the Kentucky pistols into the percussion period. $850–$1,175.

ELGIN CUTLASS PISTOL, MORRILL, MOSMAN & BLAIR, cal. .54; 5-inch round barrel. Cutlass blade 9 inches long marked on both sides with U.S. martial scenes, on left side "Morrill Mosman & Blair Amherst Mass." and on right side "Elgin's Pat." Side hammer. Barrel frame and cutlass of bright metal. Total length 14.5 inches. $2,525–$3,400.

ELGIN CUTLASS PISTOL, MORRILL, MOSMAN & BLAIR, cal. .38; 4-inch, octagonal, rifled barrel bearing brass-blade front sight and open notch rear sight, and usually unmarked. Weight 1 lb. 10 oz. Total length 14.5 inches. Iron frame, maple stock. Side hammer. No ramrod. Leather scabbard with belt hook. Blade 9.5 inches long and 1.5 inches wide, marked "Elgin's Patent" on right side and "Morrill, Mosman & Blair Amherst Mass" on left side, mounted under barrel with rear end of blade forming a trigger guard. $2,435–$3,300.

ELGIN CUTLASS PISTOL OR BOWIE-KNIFE PISTOL, MORRILL BLAIR, cal. .36; 3-inch round barrel. Iron frame. Side hammer. Knife blade 7 inches long, 1 inch wide, etched with "Horn of Plenty" on right side and "Morrill Blair Amherst Mass." on left side and serial number, such as 8 on specimen illustrated. Plate 8, Fig. 1. $2,600–$3,500.

*Note on Elgin Cutlass Pistols: All of these are rare and valuable. Those made by Morrill, Mosman & Blair, and by Morrill & Blair, are even more rare than the famous Paterson and Walker Colts, but they are less well known to collectors. Eventual-*

*ly all of these Elgin cutlass pistols will be worth $5,000–$7,500 apiece. When they climb to those values, the counterfeiters will get busy and we shall see as many fakes as there are of the more valuable Colts. See Chapter 6 for Elgin Cutlass Pistol, C.B. Allen, U.S. Contract of 1837.*

LINDSAY 2-SHOT SINGLE-BARREL PISTOL, cal. .45; 8.25-inch, half octagonal, smoothbore barrel bearing brass-blade front sight, marked in front of cones "Lindsay's Young America Patented Oct. 9, 1860." Rear sight is a notch in the brass frame. Total length 12 inches. Walnut grips. Spur trigger. Simple trigger operates two centrally hung hammers. Right hammer falls on right cone to discharge forward load, and then, if trigger is pressed, left hammer falls on left cone to discharge rear load, since loads are placed one in front of the other in the single barrel. No ramrod, about 110 pistols made. Plate 8, Fig. 2. $1,000–$1,550.

LINDSAY 2-SHOT SINGLE-BARREL PISTOL, cal. .41; 4-inch, part square, part octagonal barrel. Walnut grips, brass frame, spur trigger. Hammers like those on the .45-caliber model. Blade front sight. Groove rear sight. Marked "Lindsay's Young America. Man'f'd by J.P. Lindsay-Man'f'g Co. New York" on right side of barrel, and "Patent'd Feb. 8, 1859. Patent'd Oct. 9, 1860" on under side of barrel. Frame engraved with deer and dog. Left side of barrel engraved with lion, flags, etc, about 1250 pistols made. Plate 8, Fig. 3. $385–$725.

LINDSAY 2-SHOT SINGLE-BARREL PISTOL, cal. .40; 4.875-inch, tapered, octagonal barrel marked "Lindsay's Young America" on top and "Patent Apd. For" on right side, at the breech. Walnut grips, engraved brass frame, and double spur triggers. Brass-blade front sight and no rear sight. This model with 2 separate triggers, 1 for each hammer, is the first type of Lindsay made, and less than 200 were produced. Plate 8, Fig. 4. $975–1,450.

---

PLATE 8. American Secondary Martial Percussion Pistols

*Figure*

1. Elgin Cutlass Pistol or Bowie-Knife Pistol, Morrill & Blair, Amherst, Mass.
2. Lindsay 2-Shot Single-Barrel Pistol, cal. .45, 8.25-inch barrel.
3. Lindsay 2-Shot Single-Barrel Pistol, cal. .41, 4-inch barrel.
4. Lindsay 2-Shot Single-Barrel Pistol, cal. .40, 4.875-inch barrel.
5. Marston Breech-loading Pistol.
6. Perry Breech-loading Pistol, with Automatic Capping Device.
7. Perry Breech-loading Pistol, without Automatic Capping Device
8. Sharps Breech-loading Pistol, with 6.5-inch barrel.
9. Sharps Breech-loading Pistol, with 5-inch barrel and different marking.
10. A.H. Waters & Co. Pistol.
11. Constable, Philadelphia, Pistol.
12. Tryon, Philadelphia, Pistol

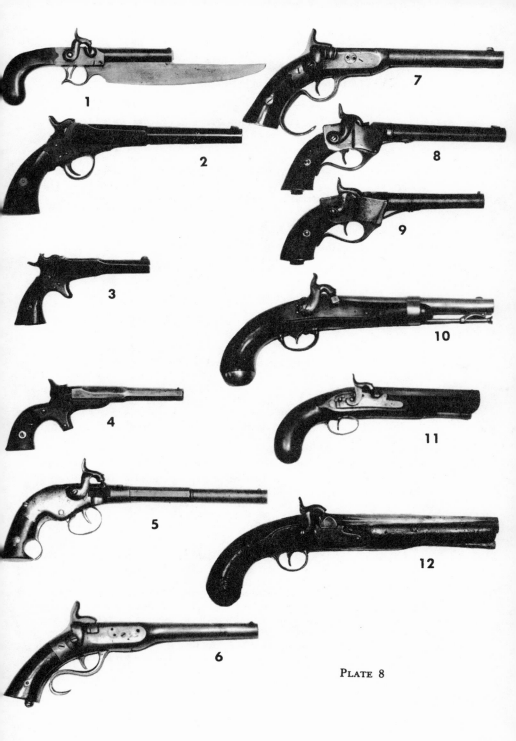

PLATE 8

74

Lindsay data furnished by Samuel E. Smith.

MARSTON BREECH-LOADING PISTOL, cal. .36; 5.75-inch, rifled, blued barrel, round at front and octagonal at rear, bearing brass-blade front sight and V-notch iron rear sight, and marked "W.W. Marston Patented New York" on top and "Cast Steel" on right. Total length 10.75 inches. Weight 1 lb. 12 oz. Walnut grips. Oval iron trigger guard. Engraved side hammer and engraved silver-plated bronze frame. Blued barrel, casehardened hammer, trigger, and lever for operating sliding breechblock. This pistol fired a peculiar cartridge having a cardboard case with a leather base. The earlier, bronze-frame specimens are worth more than the later ones having iron frames. $590–$910.

SAME, but with 6-inch barrel. $600–$925.

SAME, but with 7-inch barrel. $635–$950.

SAME, but with 8-inch barrel. $660–$975.

SAME, but with 8.5-inch barrel. Plate 8, Fig. 5. $685–$1,025.

McK BROTHERS PISTOL, cal. .60; 10.375-inch, smoothbore, part round, part fluted, pin-fastened, unmarked barrel. Total length 16 inches. Full-length walnut stock ends .375-inch behind muzzle. Hickory ramrod. Brass mountings. Two pin-fastened split brass thimbles. Small butt cap. Oval trigger guard. No back strap. Flat lock plate marked "McK Brothers Baltimore." Bird's-head handles. The cone set into a cylindrical side lug indicates that this was originally a flintlock. Made by McKim Brothers of Baltimore, Md. $600–$825.

B. MILLS, HARRODSBURG, KY., PISTOL, cal. .75; 10.75-inch, smoothbore, round, key-fastened barrel with rib extension from muzzle to end of stock. Half-stock tipped with German silver end-cap. Brass-tipped hickory ramrod. German silver mountings. Iron trigger guard. Rounded butt. No back strap or butt cap. Bolster-type cone seat. Apparently converted from flintlock. $610–$835.

PERRY BREECH-LOADING PISTOL, cal. .52; 6.188-inch, round, rifled barrel with brass-blade front sight and V-notch rear sight grooved in barrel over breach. Total length 12.75 inches. Weight 2 lbs. 15 oz. Walnut grips. No forearm. Side hammer. Breechblock marked "A.D. Perry Patented" and "Perry Patent Fire Arms Co. Newark, N.J." Blued finish. To load, the trigger guard is lowered, thus tilting the breech up and the barrel down, and permitting the loading of the pistol with loose powder and ball or with a paper cartridge. A projecting beveled ring fits into the chamber and forms a gas-tight joint which is an improvement on the Sharps breech-loading pistol, which the Perry otherwise resembles. When the breechblock is closed, a percussion cap is fed to the nipple by an automatic capping magazine extending through the butt. This is the model usually listed. Plate 8, Fig. 6. $1,200–$1,850.

SAME, but without the automatic capping device. Plate 8, Fig. 7. $1,000–$1,350.

SAME, but cal. .56, and 20.25-inch, round, smoothbore steel barrel. Total length 26.5 inches. Breechblock marked "Perry Patent Arms Co. Newark, N.J." and "Patented 1855." Without capping device. $790–$1,075.

SAME, 16-inch barrel, etc., but without capping device. $760–$1,010.

SAME, but army model, cal. .44; 6.2-inch barrel, with capping device. $1,200–$1,850.

*Note on Perry values: The Perry was made in various calibers and barrel lengths, but the greater values are for the short barrel holster types.*

SHARPS BREECH-LOADING PISTOL, cal. .38; 6.5-inch, rifled, round, tapered barrel with brass-blade front sight. Total length 11 inches. Weight 2 lbs. V-notch rear sight in frame. Walnut grips. No fore end. Steel back strap and frame. Side hammer. Frame marked on left "C. Sharps & Co. Rifle Works Phila. Pa. C. Sharps Patent 1848." Lawrence pellet priming device is a tube in the frame which automatically feeds priming pellets to the cone when the hammer is cocked. Trigger guard serves a breechblock lever. Plate 8, Fig. 8. $810–$1,200.

SAME, but cal. .31; 5-inch round barrel marked "Sharp's Patent Arms Manufacturing Co., Fairmount, Philadelphia, Pa." Total length 12 inches. Plate 8, Fig. 9. $800–$1,135.

*Note on Sharps Pistols: These pistols vary in caliber, barrel length, marking, and in minor structural details, such as the presence or absence of fore ends, wood or metal grips, etc. Many specimens give the impression of having been made by hand, which may explain the variations.*

TRYON, PHILADELPHIA, PISTOL, converted from flintlock to percussion, cal. .64; 9.25-inch, smoothbore, round iron, pin-fastened barrel marked "Tryon Philadelphia" with English proof marks. Lock plate marked "Tryon." Total length 14.5 inches. Tryon imported the barrel from England, probably because it was often cheaper to import barrels and locks than it was to make them here, but he apparently made the rest and assembled the pistol. Plate 8, Fig. 12. $675–$900.

A.H. WATERS & CO. PISTOL, cal. .54; 8.15-inch round, smoothbore, bright, finished barrel with usual military sights, knife-blade front and open rear. Total length 14 inches. Weight 2 lbs. 6 oz. Three-quarter-length black walnut stock with swivel ramrod. Iron-mounted but some specimens have strange variety of brass mounts, including brass trigger, trigger guard, or even sideplate. Three models are known: First model stamped on lock with eagle head and marked "A.H. Waters & Co., Milbury, Mass." and no date. Nipple sent into top of barrel like a conversion, which this pistol is not. Second model marked same on lock with date "1844" added, and the nipple is set on a squared side lug. Third model has a pointed rear to the flat, flush lock plate found on all these pistols, whereas first and second models have rounded rear to lock plates. Third model marked on lock same as second, but dated "1849." All the three models of the pistol, known as the Flat Lockplate Waters are original percussion, secondary martials, and not to be confused with converted-to-percussion Waters' 1836 models which were originally flintlock. Values for all three models the same. Plate 8, Fig. 10. $400–$525.

A.H. WATERS & CO. "ALL-METAL" PISTOL, cal. .54; 8-inch, round, smoothbore barrel, total length 12.625 inches. The martial-type, steel swivel is held in an iron tube, 2.5 inches long, fastened to the lower surface of the barrel. There is a rounded iron frame instead of the three-quarter-length black walnut stock of the A.H. Waters & Co. This "all-metal" pistol has no stock. The only wooden parts are the two walnut grips fastened to the butt portion of the frame. $750–$1,100.

# Chapter 8

## AMERICAN MARTIAL
## PERCUSSION REVOLVERS

D URING the Civil War, the United States purchased for its forces Allen & Wheelock, Colt, Joslyn, Pettengill, Remington (cal. .44 and cal. .36), Remington-Beals (cal. .44), Rogers & Spencer, Savage Navy, Starr (ca. .44), and Whitney Navy revolvers. Revolvers were also imported from Europe and issued to the Union army. All of these revolvers, including the imported arms, can be classified as United States martial revolvers.

Individuals, militiamen, volunteers, and others who were not originally federal forces often purchased martial-type percussion revolvers and still carried them after they became federalized. Officers were supposed to use the revolvers issued to them, but many carried their own in addition.

In the war between Texas and Mexico, the Mexican War, and the Indian campaigns before and after the Civil War, martial percussion revolvers other than those bought by the United States were in use. Therefore, although we can state definitely in many cases whether or not arms were bought and issued by the United States, there are many percussion revolvers of a martial type which cannot be accurately classified as martial, secondary martial, or non-martial arms. For all of these reasons we have classified most of the martial-type percussion revolvers made in the United States as American martial percussion revolvers. Certain martial-type revolvers whose martial use was extremely doubtful have been included in Chapter 9 on American Percussion Pistols and Revolvers. Colt arms are treated separately because collectors and dealers normally classify them in a group by themselves.

ADAMS ARMY REVOLVER—See below, Mass. Arms Co.—Adams and Kerr Patents Army Revolver.

ADAMS NAVY REVOLVER—See below, Mass. Arms Co.—Adams and Kerr Patents Navy Revolver.

ALLEN & WHEELOCK ARMY REVOLVER, cal. .44, 6-shot, S.A.; 7.5-inch, rifled, round barrel, octagonal near breech, marked on left "Allen & Wheelock Worcester Mass. U.S. Allen's Pt's. Jan. 13, Dec. 15, 1857. Sept. 7, 1858." Total length 13.25 inches. Weight 2 lbs. 14 oz. Brass front sight on barrel. V-notch in lip of center hammer serves as rear sight. Cylinder, 1.94 inches long, removed by pressing spring catch at front of frame and removing cylinder pin to front. Walnut grips. Blued barrel, cylinder, and frame. Hammer and trigger guard casehardened in mottled colors. Trigger guard serves as rammer when dropped by pressing spring catch. Called "Last Model." Plate 9, Fig. 1. $375–$725.

ALLEN & WHEELOCK NAVY REVOLVER, cal. .36, 6-shot, S.A.; 8-inch, octagonal, rifled barrel marked "Allen & Wheelock Worcester Mass. U.S. Allen's Pts. Jan. 13, Dec. 15, 1857, Sept. 7, 1858." Total length 13.5 inches. Weight 2 lbs. 6 oz. Cylinder, 1.845 inches long, is engraved with scene of animals in forest. German-silver-blade front sight on barrel. V-notch rear sight grooved in frame. Blued barrel, cylinder, and frame. Casehardened hammer and trigger guard. Side hammer on right. Trigger guard serves as loading lever and operates hammer. Cylinder removed by pulling cylinder pin from rear. Plate 9, Fig. 2. $400–$660.

SAME, but with 7.25-inch barrel. $395–$590.

SAME, but with 6-inch barrel. $360–$510.

SAME, but with 4-inch barrel. $305–$380.

SAME, but with 8-inch barrel and center hammer. $435–$700.

SAME, but with 7.25-inch barrel and center hammer. $325–$490.

SAME, but with 6-inch barrel and center hammer. $325–$480.

SAME, but with 5-inch barrel and center hammer. $310–$430.

ALSOP NAVY REVOLVER, cal. .36, 5-shot, S.A.; 4.5-inch, octagon, rifled barrel marked "C.R. Alsop Middletown Conn. Patented July 17th, August 7th 1860, May 14th, 1861." Total length 9.875 inches. Weight 1 lb. 4 oz. Round cylinder marked "C.R. Alsop Patented Nov. 26th, 1861." Spur trigger. Brass cone front sight on barrel. V-notch rear sight grooved in frame. Blued cylinder and frame. Casehardened hammer and loading lever. Walnut grips. Made with loading lever. Cocking hammer revolves cylinder and forces it against barrel. This is the description of the standard Navy model. Plate 9, Fig. 3. $575–$810.

SAME, but with 5.375-inch barrel. Total length 10.75 inches. Either fluted or round cylinders. $635–$875.

BEALS ARMY REVOLVER—See below, Remington-Beals.

BEALS NAVY REVOLVER—See below, Remington-Beals.

BUTTERFIELD ARMY REVOLVER, cal. .41, 5-shot, S.A.; 7-inch, octagonal, blued, rifled barrel. Total length 13.75 inches. Weight 2 lbs. 10 oz. Brass knife-blade front sight set in barrel. Grooved rear sight in frame. Bronze oval trigger guard. Bronze frame marked on top "Butterfield's Patent Dec. 11, 1855 Philada." although many specimens are found unmarked except for a serial number on the barrel, cylinder, cylinder lock, loading lever, hammer block, and the inside of the frame side plates, which number is usually above 560. Disk primer magazine in front of trigger guard. Cocking the hammer feeds primers to cones from magazine tube. Blued cylinder, 1.69 inches long. Plate 9, Fig. 5. $800–$1,250.

SAME, but unmarked except for serial number, as described above. $750–$950.

*Note: Collectors and dealers sometimes erroneously list this Butterfield as caliber .44, probably because the chamber diameter is .44-inch, but the groove diameter of the bore is only .411. There is at least one specimen in existence made in caliber .50, with a 6.625-inch barrel, a total length of 14.5 inches, and a weight of 5 lbs. 2 oz., but a value cannot be accurately assigned.*

CALDERWOOD PISTOL, cal. .54; 10-inch, round, smoothbore barrel marked "P" with an eagle head. Total length 16 inches. Brass butt cap, trigger guard, front sight, pan, and mountings. No rear sight. Gooseneck hammer. Hickory ramrod. Lock plate marked "Calderwood Phila," "U.S.," and date. Also see U.S. Pistol, Model 1807–1808. This is a U.S. martial pistol. $2,850–$3,500.

COCHRAN PATENT MONITOR OR TURRET PISTOL, cal. .40, 7-shot, S.A.; 5-inch, rifled barrel, round except for 1 inch at the breech which is octagonal. The strap at the top lifts to remove the turret-line cylinder for loading and priming. Underhammer. No trigger guard. Total length 10 inches. Top strap marked "Cochran's Patent C.B. Allen Springfield, Mass." The specimen illustrated bears serial number 106 on the barrel, frame, top, strap, and cylinder. This is one of the rarest of all American revolving weapons and was patented by J.W. Cochran of New York City on April 29, 1837, with C. B. Allen as the maker. Plate 9, Fig. 4. $2,850–$3,900.

COLT MARTIAL REVOLVERS—See Chapters 11, 12, and 13 on Colts.

COOPER NAVY REVOLVER, cal. .36, 5-shot, D.A.; 5.875-inch, octagonal, rifled, blued barrel marked "Cooper Firearms Mfg. Co. Frankford Phila Pa. Pat. Jan. 7, 1851, Apr. 25, 1854, Sep 4 1860, Sep. 1 1863, Sep. 22, 1863." Total length 10.75 inches. Weight 1 lb. 12 oz. Brass-cone front sight. V-notch rear sight in hammer lip. Blued cylinder, 1,625 inches long, rebated like Colt Army Model 1860 Revolver. Silver-plated, bronze back strap and oval trigger guard. Frame, trigger, and part of loading lever casehardened in mottled colors. Black walnut grips. By removing a wedge from the left, the barrel and cylinder can be removed. Except for the cylinder this revolver superficially resembles the Colt Model 1851 Navy Revolver. $300–$550.

FREEMAN'S PATENT-HOARD'S ARMORY ARMY REVOLVER, cal. .44, 6-shot, S.A.; 7.5-inch, round, rifled barrel. Total length 12.5 inches. Weight 2 lbs. 13 oz. Steel-blade front sight. Rear sight grooved in frame. Blued barrel, cylinder, and frame. Casehardened hammer and loading lever. Walnut grips. Frame marked "Freeman's Pat. Decr. 9, 1862, Hoard's Armory, Watertown, N.Y." Loading lever operates rammer. To remove the cylinder and cylinder pin, a slide in front of the cylinder is pushed forward. Plate 9, Fig. 6. $525–$750.

JOSLYN ARMY REVOLVER, cal. .44, 5-shot, S.A.; 8-inch, octagonal, rifled barrel marked on top "B.F. Joslyn Patd May 4th 1858," or it may be marked "B.F. Joslyn, Stonington, Conn." or "B.F. Joslyn Worcester Mass." Total length 14.375 inches, and weight 3 pounds, but the total length and the weight vary with the barrel length, which in some specimens is either more or less than the standard 8 inches. Steel knife-blade front sight set in barrel. Grooved-frame rear sight. Partly checkered walnut grips. Blued finish. Made with loading lever which operates hammer. Side hammer is

---

PLATE 9. American Martial Percussion Revolvers

Figure

1. Allen & Wheelock Army Revolver.
2. Allen & Wheelock Navy Revolver.
3. Alsop Navy Revolver.
4. Cochran Patent Turret Pistol, C. B. Allen.
5. Butterfield Army Revolver.
6. Freeman's Patent-Hoard's Armory Army Revolver.
7. Joslyn Army Revolver.

8. Mass. Arms Co.-Wesson's & Leavitt's Patent Army Revolver, cal. .40.
9. Mass. Arms Co.-Adams and Kerr Patent Navy Revolver, cal. .36.
10. Pettingill's Patent Army Revolver.
11. Remington Army Revolver, Model 1861 (Old Model) Revolver.
12. Remington Army Revolver, Model 1861, with Ivory Grips

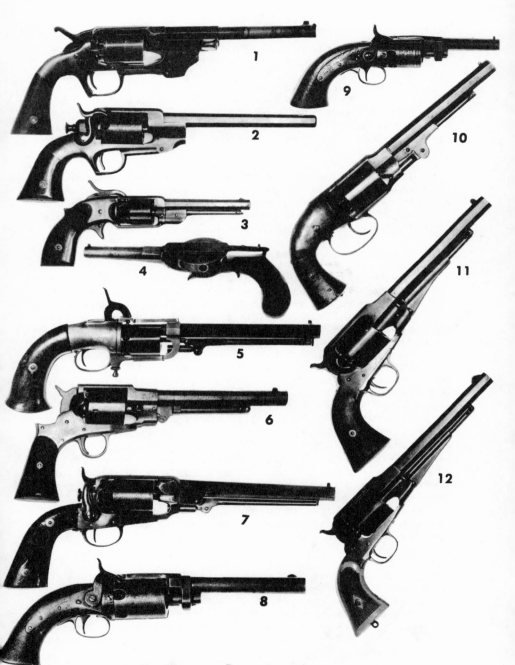

PLATE 9

curved to strike through the center of the frame, not to one side. Iron trigger guard and frame. Plate 9, Fig. 7. $530–$775.

LEAVITT REVOLVER, cal. .40, 6-shot, S.A.; 6.75-inch round barrel. Total length 13.875 inches. Walnut grips. Cylinder turns by hand. Tip-up action released by pressing a lever inside the front end of the trigger guard. Marked "Leavitt's Patent Manufactured by Wesson, Stephens & Miller Hartford Ct." Manufactured under Patent No. 182, issued April 29, 1837, to Daniel Leavitt. $975–$1,650.

MANHATTAN NAVY REVOLVER, cal. .36, 5-shot, S.A.; 6.5-inch octagon barrel marked "Manhattan Fire Arms Co. Newark N.J. Patented March 8, 1864." Cylinder marked "Patented Dec. 27, 1859." Total length 11.5 inches. Weight 2 lbs. The hammer strikes a spring plate which strikes the primers to fire. Walnut stock. Resembles Colt Model 1851 Navy. $310–$525.

SAME, but with 4- or 5-inch barrel. $280–$495.

MASS. ARMS CO.-ADAMS AND KERR PATENT NAVY REVOLVER, cal. .36, 5-shot, D.A.; 6-inch, octagonal, rifled barrel. Total length 11.5 inches. Weight 2 lbs. 9 oz. Oval iron trigger guard. Checkered walnut grip with hole for lanyard. Steel-blade front sight on barrel. V-notch rear sight on frame. Loading lever on left side of barrel. Safety lock on right side of barrel. Frame marked on top "Manufactured by Mass. Arms Co. Chicopee Falls," on right "Patent June 3, 1856," and on left side "Adam's Patent May 3, 1858." Loading lever marked "Kerr's Patent April 14, 1857." This arm is sometimes listed as Adams Navy Revolver and also as Kerr's Patent Revolver. $360–$550.

MASS. ARMS CO.-WESSON'S & LEAVITT'S PATENT ARMY REVOLVER, cal. .40, 6-shot, S.A.; 7.125-inch, round, rifled barrel marked on top of barrel extension "Mass. Arms Co. Chicopee Falls," and on the barrel locking device "Patented Nov. 26, 1850." Frame marked "Wesson's & Leavitt's Patent." Total length 15 inches. Weight 4 lbs. 6 oz. Brass-blade front sight on barrel and V-notch rear sight on barrel extension. Walnut grips. Brass oval trigger guard. Cylinder, 2.25 inches long, is removed by first turning a catch in front of the cylinder and then raising the barrel. Blued back strap and barrel. Cylinder, frame, and hammer may be either case-hardened or finished in a gray color. Cylinder is revolved by cocking hammer. Plate 9, Fig. 8. $800–$1,475.

MASS. ARMS CO.-WESSON'S & LEAVITT'S PATENT REVOLVER, cal. .40, 6-shot, S.A.; 6.25-inch, round, rifled barrel marked on barrel extension "Mass. Arms Co. Chicopee Falls." Total length 13.75 inches. Weight 3 lbs. 10 oz. Brass-blade front sight. No rear sight. Brass oval trigger guard. Walnut grips. Cylinder, 2.25 inches long, is revolved by cocking hammer, and is removed by first turning a locking catch on the barrel, raising barrel, and then sliding cylinder from shaft. Lock frame marked "Wesson's & Leavitt's Patent." $775–$1,400.

**METROPOLITAN ARMS CO. NAVY REVOLVER**, cal. .36, 6-shot, S.A.; 7.5-inch, octagonal, rifled barrel marked "Metropolitan Arms Co. New York." Total length 13 inches. Weight 2 lbs. 8.5 oz. Brass-cone front sight. V-notch rear sight in hammer lip. Silver-plated brass back strap and oval trigger guard. Blued barrel, cylinder, frame, and trigger. Casehardened hammer and loading lever. Walnut grip. Cylinder is 1.688 inches long, engraved with scene of United States ships firing on Confederate shore defenses, marked "New Orleans April 1862 W. L. Ormsby Sc." This arm is an imitation of the Colt Model 1851 Navy Revolver but made from 1864–66. $390–$600.

**METROPOLITAN ARMS CO. POCKET NAVY REVOLVER**, cal. .36, 5-shot, S.A.; 5.5-inch, round, rifled barrel marked on top "Metropolitan Arms Co. New York." Total length 10.625 inches. Weight 1 lb. 10 oz. Brass-cone front sight. Rear sight grooved in hammer lip. Silver-plated brass back strap and trigger guard. Blued barrel and cylinder. Casehardened frame, hammer, loading lever, and trigger. Walnut grip. Rebated, semi-fluted cylinder with hammer-rest notches between cones. This arm was a close imitation of the Colt Model 1862 Police Revolver. $400–$625.

SAME, but with 6.5-inch barrel. $425–$650.

SAME, but with 4.5-inch barrel. $400–$625.

**PETTENGILL'S PATENT ARMY REVOLVER**, cal. .44, 6-shot, D.A.; hammerless; 7.5-inch, rifled, octagon barrel sometimes marked "Pettengill's Patent." Frame marked on top "Pettengill's Patent 1856" and "Raymond & Robitaille Patented 1858," and sometimes with only the latter phrase when the former phrase, minus the patent date, appears on the barrel. Total length 14 inches. Weight 3 lbs. Brass-cone front sight. Rear sight grooved in frame. Walnut grips. Hammer concealed in frame. Blued barrel and either blued or browned frame. Made with loading lever. Made by Rogers & Spencer, Willowdale, New York. Squeezing trigger cocks, revolves cylinder, and fires. Plate 9, Fig. 10. $485–$750.

**PETTENGILL'S PATENT NAVY REVOLVER**, cal. .36, 6-shot, D.A.; 4.625-inch, rifled, octagonal barrel. Total length 10.5 inches. Weight 1.5 lbs. Made with loading lever. $500–$745.

**PLANT'S MFG. CO. ARMY REVOLVER**, cal. .42, 6-shot, S.A.; 6-inch, octagonal, rifled barrel marked on left side "Merwin & Bray, New York" and "Plant's Mfg. Co., New Haven Ct." on barrel rib. Total length 10.75 inches. Weight 2 lbs. Cylinder marked "Patented July 12, 1859 & July 21, 1863." Silver-plated bronze frame. Spur trigger. Either walnut or rosewood grips. White brass front sight. Rear sight grooved in frame. Percussion cylinder has recessed primer cones, but is interchangeable with cylinder for cup primer, hence this revolver is also listed elsewhere in this text as a cartridge revolver, which is what it was primarily. This is not a martial weapon. $390–$510.

REMINGTON ARMY REVOLVER, MODEL 1861 (OLD MODEL) REVOLVER, cal. .44, 6-shot, S.A.; 8-inch, octagonal, rifled barrel, marked on top "Patented Dec. 17, 1861 Manufactured by Remington's Ilion N.Y." Total length 13.75 inches. Weight 2 lbs. 14 oz. German silver cone front sight. Rear sight grooved in frame. Brass oval trigger guard. Blued throughout except for casehardened hammer. Walnut stocks. Made with loading lever, cut away on top to permit removal of cylinder without dropping lever. Manufactured in 1862. Numbered 1 to over 5,000. Plate 9, Fig. 11. $340–$595.

SAME, but with ivory grips. Plate 9, Fig. 12. $440–$725.

SAME, but Navy model 1861 (old model), cal. .36; 7.375-inch, octagonal, rifled barrel. Total length 13.125 inches. Weight 2 lbs. 8 oz. Walnut grips. Made in 1862. Numbered 1 to over 5,000. $350–$600.

REMINGTON-BEALS ARMY REVOLVER, also called Remington-Beals Old-Model Army Revolver, cal. .44, 6-shot, S.A.; 8-inch, octagonal, rifled barrel marked "Beals Patent Sept. 14, 1858. Manufactured by Remington's Ilion New York." Total length 13.875 inches. Weight 2 lbs. 14 oz. Low-blade brass front sight set in barrel. Rear sight grooved in frame. Brass oval trigger guard. Walnut grips. Blued finish. Cylinder, 2 inches long, is removed by lowering loading lever and pulling cylinder pin to front. No hammer-rest indentations in cylinder. Made from 1860 to 1862. Numbered 1 to about 3,000. Plate 10, Fig. 1. $450–$800.

REMINGTON-BEALS NAVY REVOLVER, also called Remington-Beals Old Model Navy Revolver, cal. .36, 6-shot, S.A.; 7.5-inch, octagonal, rifled barrel. Total length 13.375 inches. Weight 2 lbs. 10 oz. Otherwise identical with Army Model. Made from 1860 to 1862. Numbered 1 to over 8,000. $395–$570.

REMINGTON NEW MODEL ARMY REVOLVER, cal. .44, 6-shot, S.A.; 8-inch, octagonal, rifled barrel marked "Patented Sept. 14, 1858. E. Remington & Son, Ilion, New York, U.S.A." and "New Model." Total length 13.75 inches. Weight 2 lbs. 14 oz. Barrel threads where barrel joins cylinder are exposed. Brass oval trigger guard. Walnut grips. Blued finish except for casehardened hammer. Blade front sight. Grooved-frame rear sight. Loading lever is lowered and cylinder pin is withdrawn to front to remove cylinder. Cylinder has hammer-rest notches, sometimes called intermediate recesses, between the cones. Made from 1863 to 1888. Numbered 1 to over 5,000. $345–$555.

REMINGTON NEW MODEL NAVY REVOLVER, cal. .36, 6-shot, S.A.; 7.375-inch, octagonal, rifled, blued barrel. Total length 13.375 inches. Weight 2 lbs. 8 oz. Made from 1863 to 1875. Numbered 1 to over 5,000. $375–$595.

REMINGTON-RIDER'S PT. NAVY REVOLVER, cal. .36, 6-shot, D.A.; 6.5-inch, octagonal, blued, rifled barrel marked on top "Manufactured by Remington's Ilion N.Y. Rider's Pt. Aug. 17, 1858, May 3, 1859." Brass-cone front sight. Rear sight is V-notch in frame. Blued cylinder, barrel and frame. Brass oval trigger guard. Casehardened hammer. Walnut grips. Total length 11.5 inches. Weight 2 lbs. 1 oz. Full fluted cylinder. Made in 1863 to 1888. Numbered 1 to over 5,000. Plate 10, Fig. 2. $450–$600.

ROGERS & SPENCER ARMY REVOLVER, cal. .44, 6-shot, S.A.; 7.5-inch, octagonal, rifled barrel. Total length 13.375 inches. Weight 3 lbs. 2 oz. Brass-cone front sight. Grooved-frame rear sight. Frame marked on top "Rogers & Spencer Utica N.Y." Blued cylinder, barrel, and frame. Hammer and loading lever casehardened in mottled colors. Bell-shaped, square-bottom, black walnut grips. Plate 10, Fig. 3. $385–$600.

E. SAVAGE-H. S. NORTH NAVY REVOLVER, also called Savage First Model Navy Revolver, cal. .36, 6-shot, S.A.; 7.2-inch, octagonal, rifled barrel marked "E. Savage Middletown Ct. H. S. North Patented June 17, 1856." Total length 14 inches. Weight 3 lbs. 7 oz. Made without trigger guard. Brass-cone front sight. V-notch rear sight set in frame. Blued barrel and cylinder. Casehardened hammer and loading lever. Walnut grips. Trigger is large and shaped like figure 8, hence this revolver is sometimes called the Figure 8 Model. This trigger cocks the hammer and operates the cylinder, but the piece is fired by another trigger which is inside the upper circle of the figure 8. Made with loading lever. Bronze frame. Plate 10, Fig. 5. $1,720–$2,850.

SAME, but made with iron instead of bronze frame. Plate 10, Fig. 4. $2,010–$3,035.

E. SAVAGE-H. S. NORTH FIRST MODEL NAVY REVOLVER, cal. .36; 6-shot, S.A.; 6.75-inch, octagonal, rifled barrel marked "E. Savage Middletown, Ct. H. S. North Patented June 17, 1856." Total length 13.5 inches. Made without trigger guard. This type is the rarest of all the rare so-called figure-eight models and is distinguished by its flat iron frame and the very slight spur on the back strap as compared with the round iron frame and more pronounced back strap spur on the other models. Plate 10, Fig. 6. $2,625–$3,750.

E. SAVAGE-H. S. NORTH NAVY REVOLVER, also called Savage Second Model Navy Revolver, cal. .36, 6-shot, S.A.; 7.125-inch, octagonal, rifled barrel marked "Savage R.F.A. Co. Middletown, Ct. H. S. North Patented June 17, 1856. Jan. 18, 1859, May 15, 1860." Total length 14.25 inches. Weight 3 lbs. 6 oz. Brass-cone front sight. V-notch rear sight set in frame. Walnut grips. Blued barrel, cylinder, and frame. Hammer, loading lever, trigger guard, and triggers are casehardened in mottled colors. Steel frame. Instead of the trigger design of the first model, this second model has a large loop trigger guard containing two triggers. The lower trigger is a ring trigger for cocking the hammer and working the cylinder; the upper trigger is a conventional trigger for firing. Made with loading lever. $400–$550.

STARR DOUBLE-ACTION ARMY REVOLVER, cal. 44, 6-shot, D.A.; 6-inch, round, rifled barrel. Total length 11.625 inches. Weight 2 lbs. 15 oz. Steel-blade front sight set in barrel. V-notch rear sight in hammer lip. Blued barrel, cylinder, and frame. Loading lever and trigger casehardened in mottled colors. Frame marked "Starr's Patent Jan. 15, 1856" on right side and "Starr Arms Co. New York" on left side. Walnut grips. $385–$625.

STARR DOUBLE-ACTION NAVY REVOLVER, cal. .36, 6-shot, D.A.; 6-inch, round, rifled barrel. Total length 12 inches. Weight 3 lbs. 3 oz. Barrel tips down to permit cylinder removal for loading, Martial markings bring top value. Marks on both D.A. models are the same. The cylinder on this Navy Model is 0.375-inch longer than the cylinder on the Army Model. Also, the curve of the frame at the grip is different, thus making this Navy Model 0.375-inch longer in total length. Plate 10, Fig. 7. $390–$700.

STARR SINGLE-ACTION ARMY REVOLVER, cal. .44, 6-shot, S.A.; 8-inch, round, rifled barrel. Total length 13.75 inches. Weight 3 lbs. 1 oz. Otherwise the same as the Starr Double-Action Army Revolver. Plate 10, Fig. 8. $395–$650.

SAME, but presentation engraved. $1,600–$2,200.

UNION ARMS CO. NAVY REVOLVER, cal. .36, 6-shot, S.A.; 7.875-

PLATE 10. American Martial Percussion Revolvers

*Figure*

1. Remington-Beals Army Revolver.
2. Remington-Rider's Pt. Navy Revolver.
3. Rogers & Spencer Army Revolver.
4. E. Savage-H. S. North Navy Revolver, also called Savage First Model Navy Revolver.
5. E. Savage-H. S. North Navy Revolver, with iron instead of bronze frame.
6. E. Savage-H.S. North First Model Navy Revolver with flat frame.
7. Starr Double-Action Navy Revolver.
8. Starr Single-Action Army Revolver.
9. Walch 12-Shot Navy Revolver.
10. Warner Patent, Springfield Arms Co. First Model .36 Navy Revolver.

PLATE 10

inch, rifled, octagonal barrel marked "Union Arms Co." Total length 13.5 inches. Weight 2 lbs. 8 oz. Brass-cone front sight. V-notch rear sight in frame. Blued barrel, cylinder, frame, loading lever, and hammer. Walnut grips. Brass oval trigger guard. Made with loading lever. $320–$495.

WALCH 12-SHOT NAVY REVOLVER, cal. .36, 12-shot, S.A.; 6-inch, octagonal, rifled barrel marked "Walch Firearms Co. New York Pat. Feb. 8, 1859." Total length 12.25 inches. Weight 2 lbs. 4 oz. Brass front sight. No rear sight. Blued barrel, cylinder, and frame. Casehardened hammers and triggers. Walnut grips, partly checkered. Made with a loading lever which operated a rammer. Two hammers, two triggers, and twelve cones, since it was loaded with two loads, one on top of the other, in each of the six chambers, and each load was fired from its own cone. $2,000–$3,000.

SAME, but not marked. Plate 10, Fig. 9. $1,500–$2,200.

WALCH 10-SHOT POCKET REVOLVER, cal. .31, S.A.; 3.25-inch, round, rifled barrel marked "Walch Firearms Co., New York." Total length 10 inches. Stud trigger. Bead front sight. Brass lock and butt frame. Polished walnut grips. $420–$675.

WALCH 10-SHOT REVOLVER, cal. .31; 3.25-inch, octagon, rifled barrel, marked as previous models. Made without loading lever. Iron frame. $465–$700.

WARNER-SPRINGFIELD ARMS CO. SECOND MODEL NAVY REVOLVER, cal. .36, 6-shot, S.A.; 6-inch, round, rifled barrel marked "Springfield Arms Co." Total length 12.5 inches. Weight 2 lbs. 2 oz. Iron frame and trigger guard. Side hammer. Walnut grip. Blued. Cylinder shaft forms lower part of frame. Made with loading lever which operates rammer. Brass-cone front sight set in barrel. V-notch rear sight on barrel extension. Two triggers. The front trigger turns the cylinder; the rear trigger releases the hammer. Frame marked "Warner's Patent Jan. 7, 1851." $495–$650.

SAME, but single-trigger, first model. There is only one trigger and there is a center hammer on all models. Plate 10, Fig. 10. $475–$625.

WARNER ARMY REVOLVER, cal. .44, 6-shot, S.A.; 6-inch, round, rifled barrel. Total length 12.5 inches. Iron handle. Side hammer. Cones covered by a shield. Frame marked "Springfield Arms Co., Warner's Patent." $1,910–$2,350.

WESTERN ARMS CO. REVOLVER, cal. .36, 6-shot, S.A.; 7.75-inch octagon barrel marked on top "Western Arms Co. N.Y.," total length 13.5 inches. Solid frame, plain round cylinder, brass trigger guard and front sight. $435–$600.

WHITNEY NAVY REVOLVER, cal. .36, 6-shot, S.A.; 7.625-inch, octagonal, rifled barrel marked on top "E. Whitney New Haven." Total length 13.125 inches. Weight 2 lbs. 9 oz. Small brass front sight on barrel. V-notch rear sight on frame. Hammer lip has groove in line of sight. Cylinder, 1.75 inches long, marked "Whitneyville," together with a naval battle scene and a coat of arms. Blued barrel, frame, and cylinder. Casehardened hammer and loading lever. Bronze trigger guard. Polished walnut grips. Sometimes called the Whitney Colt. To remove cylinder, pull out screw-held lug on left of frame, and then remove loading lever and cylinder to front. Early variations bring top figure. $365–$700.

# Chapter 9

## AMERICAN PERCUSSION PISTOLS AND REVOLVERS

I N THIS chapter are described all types, makes, and models of percussion short arms made in the United States of America, except those classified as U.S. martial, U.S. secondary martial, Colt, and Confederate percussion pistols and revolvers, all of which are described in chapters under those headings. The word pistol has several meanings. In general it has been applied to any firearm fired from the hand. In the restricted sense, it may mean a single-shot pistol; or on the other hand, it may refer to an "automatic" (actually semiautomatic) handgun.

Henry Deringer, designer and manufacturer of the famous weapon named for him, also called a "derringer," described it thus: "It is a single-barrel pistol with a back-action percussion lock, patent breech, wide bore, and a walnut stock. It varies in length of barrel from 1½ to 6 inches for the ordinary, and from 6 to 9 inches for the dueling pistol. It is commonly mounted with German silver. The barrels used are all rifled. The locks vary in proportion to the length of the barrels. On the lock plates and breech of such pistol the words DERINGER PHILADEL[A] are stamped, the stamps being the same which have been used from the first manufacture of these pistols and by which they are known everywhere."

A revolver is a short arm, or handgun, or a special kind of pistol, having a cylinder containing chambers for holding cartridges. The cylinder revolves and successively presents the chambers holding the cartridges in line with a single barrel. A pepperbox does not have a cylinder containing chambers and a single barrel. Instead, it has several barrels revolving about a common axis.

Lewis Winant, author of *Pepperbox Firearms,* defines a pepperbox as "any hand firearm with three or more barrels encircling a central axis, firing shots successively with only one striker. A pepperbox differs from a revolver in that it has no one directing barrel for the shots. In a modern revolver, all shots pass through a single barrel; a pepperbox has a separate barrel for each shot."

Incidentally, without detracting from the honor due to Samuel Colt, it should be clearly understood that he did not invent the revolver in the strict sense of the term. The principle of the revolver was known in Asia and Europe in the matchlock period, as shown by the many specimens of matchlock revolving pistols and muskets. It was also known and applied in the flintlock period. What Colt did was to improve the design mechanically to make it practical, develop assembly-line production methods, and, most important, sell his product. In other words, Colt did for the firearm business what Henry Ford did for the automobile business.

ADAMS—See below, Massachusetts Arms Co. and also Ames Arms Co.

ALLEN CUTLASS PISTOL—See American Secondary Martial Percussion Pistols, Elgin Cutlass Pistol, C. B. Allen model, in Chapter 6.

ALLEN MONITOR OR TURRET ALL-METAL PISTOL—See below, Cochran Monitor or Turret All-Metal Pistol.

ALLEN'S PATENT PISTOL, Sash or Gambler's Model, cal. .31, D.A.; single-shot, made without sights. Barrel marked on left "Cast Steel." Top of hammer marked "Allen's Patent." Caliber varies from .31 to .44 and barrel length varies from 2 to 8 inches. Value depends partly on caliber and barrel length. Sometimes marked "Patented 1837." $90–$145.

E. ALLEN POCKET RIFLE, cal. .31; 7-inch, part round, part octagon barrel. Walnut saw-handle grip. Made without trigger guard. Underhammer. Frame slightly engraved and marked on top. "E. Allen Grafton Mass. Pocket Rifle Cast Steel Warranted." Small-bead front sight. Open rear sight. Small silver oval inlaid on sides of grip. Resembles the so-called bootleg pistols in shape and size. Few were made. Plate 11, Fig. 1. $150–$270.

ALLEN PEPPERBOX, cal. .36, 6-shot, D.A.; 5.25-inch, round, ribbed barrels. Bar hammer. Belt hook on left side of frame. Spur on guard. Engraved. Hammer marked "Allen's patent." Plate 11, Fig. 2. $295–$625.

ALLEN PEPPERBOX, cal. .31, 6-shot; 3.25-inch, round, ribbed barrels. Ring trigger. Walnut grips. Engraved. Plate 11, Fig. 3. $225–$430.

ALLEN & THURBER (GRAFTON, MASS.) PEPPERBOXES, hammer marked "Allen & Thurber, Grafton, Mass.":

Cal. .36, 6-shot, 5.25-inch, round, ribbed barrels. Iron guard and frame, engraved. Walnut grips. Plate 11, Fig. 4. $395–$645.

Cal. .31, 6-shot, D.A.; 3.5-inch barrels. Total length 6.5 inches. Weight 1 lb. 3 oz. $395–$585.

ALLEN & THURBER (GRAFTON, MASS.) SINGLE-SHOT PISTOLS:

Cal. .36, 4-inch half-octagon barrel. Total length 7.25 inches. Weight 10 oz. Underhammer. Marked "Allen & Thurber, Grafton, Mass." $240–$355.

Cal. .36, D.A.; 2.625-inch, part round, part octagon barrel. Underhammer made without spur. Marked "Cast Steel Warranted. Pocket Rifle. Allen & Thurber, Grafton, Mass. PM EA 1837" on barrel. $255–$365.

Cal. .36, D.A.; 3.5-inch barrel. Total length 5.75 inches. Weight 1 lb. 3 oz. Flat-top hammer. Marked "Allen & Thurber, Grafton Mass." $245–$385.

SAME, but with rounded hammer instead of flat-top hammer. $265–$385.

ALLEN & THURBER (NORWICH, CONN.) PEPPERBOXES:

Cal. .31, 6-shot, D.A.; 3.25-inch, round, ribbed barrels. Ring trigger. Engraved frame. Marked "Allen & Thurber Norwich C-T." Plate 11, Fig. 5. $250–$385.

---

PLATE 11. American Percussion Pistols and Revolvers

*Figure*

1. E. Allen Pocket Rifle.
2. Allen Pepperbox, cal. .36.
3. Allen Pepperbox, cal. .31.
4. Allen & Thurber (Grafton, Mass.) Pepperbox, cal. .36.
5. Allen & Thurber (Norwich, Conn.) Pepperbox, cal. .31.
6. Allen & Thurber (Worcester, Mass.) Pepperbox, cal. .34.
7. Allen & Thurber (Worcester, Mass.) Pepperbox, cal. .34.
8. Allen & Thurber (Worcester, Mass.) Pepperbox, cal. .34.
9. Allen & Wheelock Pepperbox, cal. .36.
10. Allen & Wheelock Pepperbox, cal. .31.
11. Allen & Wheelock Cased Pocket Revolver.
12. Andrus & Osborn Bootleg Pistol, cal. .31.
13. Bacon & Co., Single-Shot Pistol, cal. .36.
14. Armstrong Pistol.

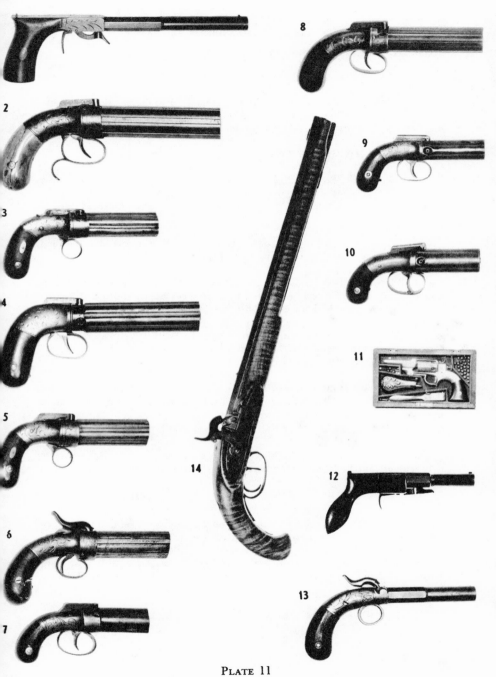

PLATE 11

Cal. .31, same as above but with plain frame. $205–$335.

Cal. .28, same as above. $230–$350.

ALLEN & THURBER (NORWICH, CONN.) PISTOL, cal. .31, single-shot, D.A.; 3.5-inch barrel. Total length 6 inches. Weight 8 oz. Flat-top hammer. Marked "Allen & Thurber, Norwich, Conn." $145–$220.

ALLEN & THURBER (WORCESTER, MASS.) PEPPERBOXES:

Cal. .34, 6-shot, S.A.; 3.25-inch round, ribbed barrels. Engraved iron guard and frame. Walnut grips. Center-hung hammer with spur. Barrels marked "Allen & Thurber Worcester Mass. Cast Steel." Plate 11, Fig. 6. $235–$370.

Cal. .34, 5-shot, 2.25-inch round barrels. Walnut grips. Iron guard. Marked as above. Engraved frame. Plate 11, Fig. 7. $205–$335.

Cal. .34, 6-shot, D.A.; 4.5-inch, round, ribbed barrels. Bar hammer. Iron guard. Engraved. Marked "Allen & Thurber Worcester Patented 1837 Cast Steel." Hammer marked "Allen & Thurber." Plate 11, Fig. 8. $185–$325.

Cal. .36, 6-shot; 5-inch, round, rifled barrels. Walnut grips. Iron guard, with spur. Hammer marked "Allen & Thurber, Worcester. Patented 1837 Cast Steel." $325–$565.

Cal. .31, 6-shot; barrel 3,4 or 5.5 inches long, total length from 6.5 to 7.5 inches, and weight from 1 lb. 2 oz. to 2 lbs. 6 oz., with either a thumb hammer or a flat-top hammer, and with a ring trigger. Marked "Allen & Thurber, Worcester, Mass." $230–$360.

Cal. .31, 6-shot, 3-inch barrel, 6.5 inches long, weight 1 lb. Hammerless; ring trigger. Marked "Allen Thurber & Co., Worcester, Mass." $220–$350.

ALLEN & THURBER (WORCESTER, MASS.) PISTOLS:

TARGET PISTOL, cal. .38; 10-inch, part octagon barrel marked on top "Allen & Thurber, Worcester" and on left side "Cast Steel." Total length 14.75 inches. Solid frame. Round hardwood handles. Large hammer. Brass-tipped ramrod under barrel. Brass-blade front sight. Adjustable rear sight. Sometimes listed by dealers as a "Pocket Rifle," but this is wrong classification. $195–$285.

TARGET PISTOL, cal. .36; 10-inch, part octagon barrel marked "Allen, Thurber & Co. Target Pistol." Total length 14 inches. Weight 1.5 lbs. $195–$285.

DOUBLE-BARREL PISTOL, cal. .34; 2.75-inch, round, rifled steel barrels cast in one piece. Single trigger operates two superposed hammers. Front sight, but no ramrod or rear sight. Marked "Allen & Thurber." $200–$325.

## ALLEN & WHEELOCK PEPPERBOXES:

Cal. .36, D.A.; 4-shot; 2.875-inch, round, fluted barrels marked "Allen & Wheelock." Walnut grips. Iron guard. Engraved iron frame. Hammer marked "Allen's Patent Jan. 13, 1857." Plate 11, Fig. 9. $190–$315.

Cal. .31, D.A.; 5-shot, 2.875-inch round barrels. Walnut grips. Iron guard and frame. Marked as above. Plate 11, Fig. 10. $185–$305.

Cal. .28 or .31; 4-, 5-, or 6-shot; barrel from 2.5 to 3.75 inches; total length from 6 to 7.5 inches; and marked either "Allen & Wheelock, Worcester, Mass." or "Allen & Wheelock, Allen's Patent 1845," and with a weight from 12 oz. to 1 lb. 4 oz. with little change in value for variations. $180–$260.

Cal. .28, 3-shot, 2.5-inch barrel, 6 inches long, weight 12 oz. Flat-top hammer. Marked "Allen & Wheelock, Worcester, Mass." $200–$290.

## ALLEN & WHEELOCK POCKET REVOLVERS:

EARLY POCKET MODEL, cal. .36, 5-shot, S.A.; 4-inch octagon barrel marked "Allen & Wheelock Worcester Mass. U.S. Allen's Pts. Jan. 13 Dec. 15, 1857." Stud trigger. Outside hammer. Blade front sight. Notched-frame rear sight. Cylinder locks in front and can be removed for loading. Also made in cal. .31, 6-shot, with barrel lengths from 4 to 7.5 inches, with small changes in value for variations. $190–$275.

POCKET REVOLVER, cal. .32, 5-shot, D.A.; 5.75-inch octagon barrel, total length 10.75 inches. Cylinder engraved with scenes of animals in woods. Otherwise, plain metal finish. Polished hardwood handles. Frame marked on top "Allen & Wheelock." Hammer marked "Patented April 16, 1845." Also made in calibers from .25 to .41, with small changes in value. This model must not be confused with the same model made in England by J.W. Laird, and marked with English proof marks. $160–$295.

POCKET REVOLVER, FLAT-TOP HAMMER, cal. .28 or cal. .31, 5-shot, with either 2.375-inch or 4-inch octagon barrel; total length either 5.75 inches or 9 inches; and weight either 9 oz. or 1 lb. 2 oz.; marked "Allen & Wheelock, Worcester, Mass." $175–$250.

POCKET REVOLVER, SIDE HAMMER, cal. .28, or cal. .31; 5-shot; 2.375-inch or 4-inch octagon barrel. Trigger guard acts as loading lever. $175–$250.

CASED POCKET REVOLVER, cal. .28, 5-shot, 2.875-inch octagon barrel. Walnut grips. Trigger guard acts as loading lever when unlatched. Side hammer. Cylinder engraved with animals in forest. Casehardened trigger guard. Blued frame and barrel. Blade front sight. V-notch rear sight. Barrel marked "Allen & Wheelock Worcester Mass., U.S. Allens Pts. Jan. 13, Dec. 15, 1857." Mahogany case, red-plush-lined. Accessories of lacquered flask and iron mold with sprue cutter. There are compartments in the case for bullets and primers ("caps"). Plate 11, Fig. 11. $500–$700.

ALLEN & WHEELOCK POCKET PISTOL, cal. .28, 5-inch octagon barrel. Usually unmarked, called "Providence Police." Spur trigger, iron frame, center-hung hammer, walnut grips. $200–$385.

ALLEN & WHEELOCK ARMY AND NAVY REVOLVERS—See Chapter 8.

ALSOP NAVY REVOLVER—See Chapter 8.

ALSOP POCKET REVOLVER, cal. .31, 6-shot, S.A.; 4-inch octagon barrel. Total length 9.5 inches. Weight 1 lb. 6 oz. Marked "C.R. Alsop, Middletown, Conn." with patent dates similar to those on Alsop Navy model. $500–$725.

AMERICAN STANDARD TOOL CO.—See below, Hero Pistol.

N.P. AMES—See Chapter 6.

ANDRUS & OSBORN BOOTLEG PISTOL, cal. .31; 4-inch, part round, part octagon barrel marked "Andrus & Osborn, Canton, Conn." Underhammer. Made without trigger guard. Maple grip, brass-bound. Plate 11, Fig. 12. $175–$290.

SAME, but cal. .30; part round, part octagon barrel marked with American eagle in addition to above marks. $180–$295.

ARMSTRONG PISTOL, cal. .34; 15-inch, octagon, rifled barrel. Total length 20 inches. Iron trigger guard. Double set triggers. Full-length fiddleback maple stock. Originally made as a flintlock and later converted to percussion. Original lock plate retained. Percussion hammer added. Lock marked "A. Armstrong. Warranted." Plate 11, Fig. 14. $1,050–$1,250.

H. ASTON, U.S. PISTOL—See Chapter 6.

W. ASTON UNDERHAMMER PISTOL, cal. .31; 4.5-inch, half octagon barrel. Total length 9 inches. Weight 12 oz. Saw-handle grip. Marked "W. Aston, Middletown, Conn." $180–$295.

W. ASTON UNDERHAMMER PISTOL, cal. .36; 4.5-inch, half octagon barrel. Total length 8.5 inches. Weight 12 oz. Marked "W. A. Middletown, Conn." $180–$295.

BACON & CO. SINGLE-SHOT PISTOL, cal. .36; 4-inch, part round, part octagon barrel marked "Bacon & Co. Norwich C-T. Cast Steel." Ring trigger, made without guard. Inside-hung hammer. Engraved iron frame. Plate 11, Fig. 13. $130–$185.

BACON & CO. SINGLE-SHOT PISTOL, cal. .34; 4-inch, part round, part octagon barrel, marked as previous pistol. Underhammer, made without trigger guard. Engraved iron frame. Walnut grips. Also made with 5-inch barrel, without value change. Plate 12, Fig. 1. $115–$175.

BACON & CO. UNDERHAMMER PEPPERBOX, cal. .31, 6-shot, S.A.; 3.25-inch, round, ribbed barrels, marked as above models. $195–$325.

BACON MFG. CO. REVOLVER, cal. .31, 5-shot; 4-inch round barrel marked "Bacon Mfg. Co., Norwich, Conn." $190–$260.

SAME, but 6-inch barrel. $210–$290.

SAME, but 4-inch barrel, strapped frame, and sheathed trigger. $260–$370.

W. BILLINGHURST MUZZLE-LOADING TARGET PISTOL, cal. .30; 10.5-inch, rifled, octagon barrel marked "W. Billinghurst Rochester N.Y." Fitted with detachable stock. Underhammer. Made without trigger guard. Saw-handle grip. This is of the bootleg type. Plate 12, Fig. 15. $800–$1,000.

SAME, but cal. .38; 12-inch, rifled, octagon barrel. Weight with shoulder stock 7.5 lbs. Otherwise the same as above. $825–$1,050.

C. BIRD & CO. UNDERHAMMER PISTOL, cal. .36, D.A.; 9-inch octagon barrel marked "C. Bird & Co. Philadelphia, Pa." Total length 16 inches. Bead front sight. Trigger guard serves as main spring. $325–$510.

F. R. J. BITTERLICH & CO. DERRINGER, cal. .42; rifled, 2.875-inch, octagon barrel marked "F. R. J. Bitterlich & Co. Nashville, Tenn." Back-action lock marked like barrel. Walnut stock. Square butt with German silver inlay. Checkered grip. German silver guard. Plate 12, Fig. 2. $400–$585.

F. R. J. BITTERLICH & CO. DERRINGER, cal. .44 or .45; 4.25-inch round barrel with octagon breech, marked as above. Walnut stock extending nearly the full length. Back-action lock, engraved, and marked as above on some specimens. Spur trigger. Made without trigger guard. Plate 12, Fig. 3 and Plate 13, Fig. 4. $430–$635.

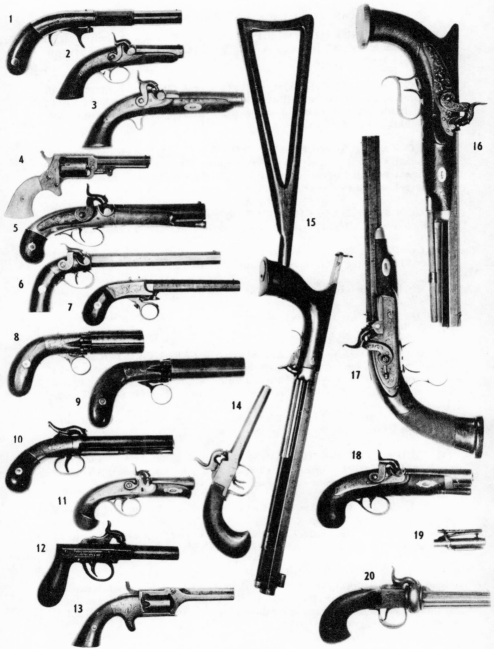

PLATE 12

BLISS & GOODYEAR REVOLVER, cal. .28, 6-shot; 3-inch octagon barrel marked "Bliss & Goodyear New Haven Ct." Spur trigger. Ivory grips. Engraved frame. Plate 12, Fig. 4. $265–$350.

BLISS & GOODYEAR REVOLVER, cal. .31, 6-shot, S.A.; 6-inch round barrel marked "F. D. Bliss Patent, New Haven, Conn." Total length 10 inches. Stud-type trigger. Loading lever. Center hammer. Blued finish. $215–$310.

BLUNT & SYMS SINGLE-SHOT PISTOL, cal. .42; 4-inch, round, flattop barrel marked "B & S, New York, Cast Steel." Total length 8 inches. Weight about 1 lb. 2 oz. Back-action lock. Hickory ramrod. Some specimens are found without marks. Plate 12, Fig. 5. $185–$250.

SAME, but with ring trigger. $200–$275.

BLUNT & SYMS SINGLE-SHOT PISTOL, cal. .36; 6-inch octagon barrel marked "B & S New York Cast Steel." Walnut grips. Iron guard and frame, engraved. Outside hammer. Plate 12, Fig. 6. $220–$300.

BLUNT & SYMS DOUBLE-BARREL PISTOL, cal. .44; 7.375-inch, octagon, rifled barrels marked as above. Front and rear sights. Wooden ramrod. $250–$350.

BLUNT & SYMS DOUBLE-BARREL PISTOL, cal. .34; 4-inch octagon barrels marked as above. Walnut grips. Ring trigger. Underhammer strikes

---

PLATE 12. American Percussion Pistols and Revolvers

*Figure*

1. Bacon & Co. Single-Shot Pistol, cal. .34.
2. F. R. J. Bitterlich & Co. Derringer, cal. .42.
3. F. R. J. Bitterlich & Co. Derringer, cal. .44 or .45.
4. Bliss & Goodyear Revolver, cal. .28.
5. Blunt & Syms Single-Shot Pistol, cal. .42.
6. Blunt & Syms Single-Shot Pistol, cal. .36.
7. Blunt & Syms Single-Shot Pistol.
8. Blunt & Syms Pepperbox.
9. Blunt & Syms Pepperbox.
10. Bruce & Davis Double-Barrel Pistol, cal. .35.
11. Bruff Derringer.
12. Butler All-Metal Single-Shot Pistol.
13. Bryce Revolver.
14. Swedish (Darling) 2-Shot Brass-Barrel Pistol
15. W. Billinghurst Muzzle-loading Target Pistol, cal. .30.
16. H. T. Cooper Pistol.
17. Constable Dueling Pistol, cal. .47.
18. R. Constable Derringer.
19. S. Coon Alarm or Trap Pistol, cal. .25
20. Swedish (Darling) 4-Shot Brass Pepperbox, cal. .30.

both nipples at same time. Blued barrels. Engraved frame. Plate 12, Fig. 7. $200–$300.

BLUNT & SYMS SINGLE-SHOT POCKET PISTOL, cal. .34; 5-inch, part round, part octagon barrel. Double action. Barrel marked as above. $160–$245.

BLUNT & SYMS DUELING PISTOL, cal. .53; 9-inch, octagon, smooth-bore barrel marked "Blunt & Syms Cast Steel." $430–$585.

BLUNT & SYMS PEPPERBOX, cal. .31; 6-shot; 2.5-inch, round, ribbed barrels. Ring trigger. Shovel-shaped hammer. Engraved. Walnut grips. Frame marked "Blunt & Syms New York." Plate 12, Fig. 8. $350–$485.

BLUNT & SYMS PEPPERBOX, cal. .31, 6-shot; 3.25-inch round barrels marked "Blunt & Syms New York." Walnut grips. Ring trigger. Scoop-shaped underhammer. Engraved iron frame. Total length 7 inches. Weight 1.25 lbs. Made in various barrel lengths. Plate 12, Fig. 9. $350–$485.

BOLEN PEPPERBOX, cal. .31, 6-shot; 3-inch, round, ribbed barrels marked "Patented 1837. Cast Steel." Iron guard and frame. Hammer marked "J.G. Bolen, N.Y." $340–$465.

BOSWORTH BOOTLEG PISTOL, cal. .37; 6-inch, part round, part octagon barrel. Bronze frame and grip. Trigger and underhammer, but made without trigger guard. Frame marked "B. M. Bosworth." $230–$310.

BRUCE & DAVIS DOUBLE-BARREL PISTOL, cal. .35; 4-inch round barrels, side by side, marked "Bruce & Davis." Iron guard and frame. Single trigger works both hammers. Total length 7.25 inches. Plate 12, Fig. 10. $200–$295.

SAME, but cal. .31. $200–$295.

BRUFF DERRINGER, cal. .41; 2.5-inch, flat-top, round barrel marked "R. P. Bruff N.Y. Cast Steel." Back-action lock. Full-length walnut stock. Plate 12, Fig. 11. $355–$505.

BRYCE REVOLVER, cal. .28, 6-shot; 3-inch, octagon, ribbed barrel. Spur trigger. Engraved iron frame. Barrel swings up to remove cylinder for loading. Walnut grips. Marked, but made by Sharps & Co., Phila, Pa., 1858. Plate 12, Fig. 13. $395–$625.

BUTLER ALL-METAL SINGLE-SHOT PISTOL, cal. .35, 2.25-inch round barrel. Center-hung hammer. Entire pistol of cast iron, with no other material used. Right side of frame is removable, and marked "Wm. S. Butler's Patent. Patented Feb. 3, 1857." Plate 12, Fig. 12. $225-$350.

BUTTERFIELD ARMY REVOLVERS—See Chapter 8.

CARLETON UNDERHAMMER PISTOL, cal. .31; 3.5-inch barrel. Total length 8.5 inches. Trigger guard serves as mainspring. Marked "M. Carleton & Co. Patent 1860." $155-$240.

SAME, but cal. .36; 4.125-inch, part round, part octagon barrel, and marked "Patent. M. Carleton & Co." $170-$250.

CASE WILLARD & CO. BOOTLEG PISTOL, cal. .35; 6-inch, part round, part octagon barrel marked "Case Willard & Co. Hartford, Conn." Underhammer. Made without trigger guard. $175-$260.

COCHRAN MONITOR OR TURRET ALL-METAL PISTOL, cal. .36, 7-shot; 4.75-inch barrel. Total length 10.75 inches. Weight 2.5 lbs. Cylinder is in same horizontal plane as barrel, and resembles the turret of a battleship. Marked "C. B. Allen, Springfield, Mass.," but listed here because it is probably better known as the Cochran. $3,000-$4,050.

COCHRAN REVOLVER, cal. .31, 5-shot; 7-inch barrel. Total length 13.25 inches. Cylinder works like Cochran Monitor Pistol. Top strap lifts to remove cylinder. Hammer serves as trigger guard. Marked "W. Berry, Maker, Poughkeepsie, Cochran's Patent." $2,850-$3,950.

COLT PERCUSSION REVOLVERS—See Chapters 11 and 12 on this subject, as well as Chapter 8.

R. CONSTABLE DERRINGER, cal. .43; 3.5-inch, round, wedge-fastened, flat-top barrel marked "R. Constable." Hickory ramrod. Walnut stock. German silver tip. Back-action engraved lock. Engraved iron guard. Short rib under barrel for hickory ramrod. Plate 12, Fig. 18. $375-$565.

CONSTABLE DUELING PISTOL, cal. .47, smoothbore; 10-inch octagon barrel marked "Constable Philadelphia." Total length 16 inches. Sawhandle walnut half-stock. German silver tip. Back-action lock with sliding safety lock. Iron trigger guard with spur. Lock, hammer, and guard engraved. Single set trigger. Engraved silver band around butt and silver inlay in butt. Two iron thimbles and iron rib under barrel. Brass-tipped wooden ramrod. Lock marked "Constable." Blade front sight; open rear sight. Plate 12, Fig. 17. $550-$800.

SAME, but cal. .69, with barrel marked "Constable Phila Pa." $550-$800.

SAME, but cal. .50; 9.625-inch octagon barrel marked "R. Constable, Philadelphia." Converted from flint to percussion, and lacking several of the refinements of the above duelers. $550–$800.

L. COON SINGLE-SHOT PISTOL, cal. .40; 8-inch, octagon, rifled barrel marked "L. Coon Warranted." $200–$325.

S. COON ALARM OR TRAP PISTOL, cal. .25, 2.5-inch round barrel. Spring on top of barrel acts as hammer, striking primer to fire. Barrel has long screw for fastening to window or door, which, when opened, causes pistol to fire. Not marked but unquestionably made under Coon's American patent of Sept. 22, 1857. Plate 12, Fig. 19. $215–$265.

S. COON ALARM OR TRAP PISTOL (sometimes called a Door-Jamb Pistol), cal. .28; 4-inch round barrel marked "Made for M. Patch, Springfield, Ill. Pat. Sept. 22, 1857, S. Coon, Pat." Blued finish. Total length the same as that of the barrel, 4 inches. Operates the same as the above alarm pistol. $215–$265.

H. T. COOPER PISTOL, cal. .50, smoothbore; 9.5-inch, octagon, twist-steel barrel marked "Henry T. Cooper New York." Engraved steel trigger guard has spur. Single set trigger. Made without ramrod. Lock marked "Henry T. Cooper." Plate 12, Fig. 16. $550–$800.

J. M. COOPER & CO. DOUBLE-ACTION REVOLVER, cal. .31, 5-shot; 5-inch, octagon, rifled barrel. Total length 10 inches. Iron guard and ramrod. Marked "Manf'd by J. M. Cooper & Co., Pittsburgh, Pa." with patent dates. $375–$480.

COOPER FIREARMS MFG. CO. DOUBLE-ACTION REVOLVER, cal. .31, 6-shot; 4-inch, octagon, rifled barrel marked "Cooper Firearms Mfg. Co., Frankford, Phila., Pa.," followed by patent dates. Brass back strap and trigger guard. Total length 7 inches. Weight 1 lb. 6 oz. $225–$365.

COOPER FIREARMS MFG. CO. DOUBLE-ACTION NAVY REVOLVER—See Chapter 8.

DARLING. It is now known that the brass-frame percussion pepperboxes in 4- and 6-shot sizes and the single-barrel and double-barrel brass pocket pistols that were formerly thought to be made by the Darling Bros. in the United States were actually made in Sweden and brought to the U.S. by emigrants. Plate 12, Figs. 14 and 20, and Plate 13, Figs. 1 and 2. This information was first publicized by Mr. Samuel E. Smith in his talk entitled "Probing the Questionable, The Swedish Darling," which he presented at a meeting of the American Society of Arms Collectors on Oct. 3, 1965. His information was later published in the Bulletin of the American Society of Arms Collectors, Issue 13, in the Spring of 1966. Additional information later appeared in an article in the June, 1966, issue of Gun Report magazine by H. J. Dunlap, as a result of Mr. Smith's initial disclosure.

DARLING PEPPERBOX. The true American-made Darling pepperbox is a six-shot, iron frame, and iron barrel piece. All but one of those known are stamped "B. & B.M. Darling Patent" and a number believed to be the serial number. The one exception is marked "W. Glaze Columbia, S.C. Patent 4." Caliber from .28 to .30 smoothbore. All were made by the Darling Brothers in Woonsocket, Rhode Island, in 1836 and 1837 and are among the rarest of American percussion pepperboxes. $985–$1,450.

DERINGER DERRINGERS, sometimes called Philadelphia Deringers:

Cal. .48; 3.5-inch round, flat-top barrel marked "Deringer Philadel," with short rib underneath for brass-tipped hickory ramrod. Total length 7.625 inches. Walnut stock with German silver tip. Engraved German silver guard. Cap box in butt. Back-action lock, engraved, and marked like barrel. Plate 13, Fig. 3. $495–$700.

Cal. .41; 4-inch, round barrel marked "Mand. for F. H. Clarke & Co. Memphis Tenn. Agents." Lock marked "Deringer Philadel." Plate 13, Fig. 20. $535–$730.

Cal. .47; 2.75-inch, round, flat-top barrel. Lock marked "Deringer Philadel." $475–$675.

Cal. .46; 4.25-inch round barrel with octagon breech. Back-action lock. Walnut stock, checkered grip. German silver mounting. Spur trigger enclosed in a German silver housing. Usual marks. $460–$700.

Cal. .48; 3.25-inch, round, flat-top barrel marked "Phila." Walnut stock, checkered grip. German silver stock tip, trigger guard, inlay in butt, side plate, and wedge escutcheon. Trigger guard and butt inlay engraved. Back-action lock, engraved. Walnut ramrod. German silver tip, with slotted steel ferrule on small end. Short iron rib under barrel. Lock marked "Derringer" (with two r's). Browned finish. Plate 13, Fig. 5. $500–$665.

SAME, but a matched pair. $1,150–$1,800.

Cal. .44; 2.5-inch, round, flat-top barrel marked "Deringer Philadel." and "Made for A. J. Plate San Francisco." Back-action lock, engraved and marked "Deringer Philadel." Walnut stock. German silver guard and mountings. Plate 13, Fig. 6. $600–$800.

Cal. .43; 3.5-inch, round, flat-top barrel marked "Deringer Philadela. Manud. for Hyde & Goodrich Agents N. Orleans." Lock marked "Deringer Philadela." Walnut stock with German silver tip. German silver guard and escutcheons. Back-action lock, engraved. Cap box in butt. Short iron rib under barrel for brass-tipped hickory ramrod. Two gold bands inlaid at breech. Plate 13, Fig. 7. $625–$825.

Cal. .43; 4-inch, flat-top, round, barrel marked "Mand for Hyde & Goodrich Agents N.O." Lock marked "Deringer Philadela." Walnut stock. Checkered grip. German silver tip. German silver mountings; engraved guard. Short iron rib under barrel for ebony ramrod. Plate 13, Fig. 8. $625–$825.

Cal. .41; 2.5-inch, round, flat-top barrel marked "Deringer Philadela. Mand. for A. J. Taylor & Co. San Franco. Cala." Walnut stock. German silver tip. Back-action lock marked "Deringer Philadela." Guard and all mountings German silver, engraved. Hickory ramrod under barrel. Cap box butt. Plate 13, Fig. 9. $600–$800.

Cal. .41; 1.75-inch, round, flat-top barrel marked "Deringer Philadel." and "N. Curry & Bro. San Franco. Cala. Agents." Total length 4.25 inches. Walnut stock. Cap box in butt. German silver guard and mounts. Back-action lock marked "Deringer Philadel." Plate 13, Fig. 10. $605–$805.

Cal. .41; 2.125-inch, round, flat-top barrel marked "Deringer Philadel. C. Curry San Franco. Cala." Engraved back-action lock marked "Deringer Philadel." German silver guard and mountings. Plate 13, Fig. 11. $600–$800.

Cal. .41; 1.75-inch, round, flat-top barrel marked "Deringer Philadel." Back-action lock marked like barrel. Total length 4.375 inches. Walnut stock. German silver guard and mountings. Cap box in butt. Plate 13, Fig. 12. $520–$715.

Cal. .41; 4-inch flat-top barrel marked "Deringer Philadel. Mand for F. H. Clarke & Co. Memphis Tenn." Total length 8 inches. Walnut stock, checkered grip, and German silver tip. All mountings, engraved German silver. Cap box in butt. Wooden ramrod. Lock marked "Deringer Philadel." Plate 13, Fig. 13. $550–$750.

Cal. .40; 1.75-inch, round, flat-top barrel marked "Deringer Philadela." Engraved, back-action lock marked the same. Full-length walnut stock, checkered grip. German silver guard and mountings. Plate 13, Fig. 14. $500–$685.

Cal. .40; 2-inch, round, flat-top barrel marked "Deringer Philadel. N. Curry & Bro. San Franco. Cala. Agents." Walnut stock. German silver mountings. Lock marked "Deringer Philadel." Plate 13, Figs. 15 and 17. $605–$805.

Cal. .36; 2-inch flat-top barrel marked "Made for A. J. Plate San Francisco." Full-length walnut stock, plain grip. German silver mountings, engraved. Barrel and lock both marked "Deringer Philadel." Front and rear sights. Not usually found in this small caliber. $600–$800.

DERINGER VEST-POCKET PISTOL, cal. .28, single-shot; 1.5-inch round barrel marked by letter "P" within a wreath, which was Henry Deringer's registered mark. Blued metal finish. Fancy engraving on trigger guard, lock, and hammer. Brass-post front sight. Indented rear sight. Total length 4 inches. Polished hardwood stock to within ¼ inch of muzzle. Bird's-head handles. Barrel fastened to stock with a pin. Probably intended for a gambler or for a lady to carry in a muff or purse. Such small calibers are rare in this type and make. $525-$750.

DERINGER POCKET PISTOL, Lincoln Murder Model. The Deringer pistol with which John Wilkes Booth murdered President Abraham Lincoln is in the possession of the U.S. Government, and it will stay there. About five hundred fools and liars claim they have the identical pistol used to kill one of the three greatest presidents in our history. Quite often dealers advertise that they have this pistol. The reader is advised to be careful in dealing with such persons, and it is recommended that they refer the matter to the nearest district attorney for prosecution under both the civil and the criminal statutes. The genuine pistol is caliber .44, with a 2.5-inch barrel marked "Deringer, Philadelphia." The total length is 6 inches. It has a polished hardwood stock and forearm. The butt is of the bird's-head shape. The wood is checkered. However, many were made exactly like this. The value indicated is for one of the same make, model, and type, *not* for the murder pistol. $525–$715.

DICTATOR REVOLVER, cal. .36, 5-shot; 4-inch round barrel marked "Dictator." Walnut grips. Iron guard, frame. Cylinder engraved. Made by Hopkins & Allen. Plate 13, Fig. 16. $245–$385.

DIMICK DERRINGER, cal. .47; 3-inch, round, flat-top barrel marked "H.E. Dimick & Co. St. Louis Mo." Engraved back-action lock marked "H.E. Dimick & Co." Fine burl walnut stock, silver tipped. Engraved iron guard. $505–$720.

DIMICK DERRINGER, cal. .47; 3-inch, round, flat-top barrel marked "H.E. Dimick." Back-action lock engraved with American eagle. Walnut stock, checkered grip. German silver guard and wedge escutcheons, engraved. Browned. $500–$720.

DREPPERD PISTOL—See Chapter 7.

ELGIN—See Chapter 7.

ELLS REVOLVER, cal. .36, 6-shot, D.A.; 5-inch octagon barrel marked on top "Josiah Ells, Pittsburgh, Pa." Right side of bar-type hammer marked

"Ells Patent Aug. 1, 1854, April 24, 1857." Blued barrel and cylinder. Fancy engraving on frame and hammer. Large trigger guard. Brass-bead front sight. Cylinder removed for loading. No rear sight. Polished hardwood handles. Total length 13.5 inches. $265–$350.

ELLS REVOLVER, cal. .36, both S.A. and D.A. at will of shooter; 6-inch octagon barrel marked "Ells Patent 1857." Center hammer. Blued barrel and cylinder. Hardwood handles. Total length 12 inches. $265–$350.

ELLS REVOLVER, cal. .31, 5-shot; 3-inch octagon barrel. Walnut grips. Iron guard and frame. Hammer resembles that in a typical pepperbox, and is engraved "Ells Patent Aug 1, 1854, April 28, 1857." Engraved frame and cylinder. Plate 13, Fig. 18. $210–$300.

ELLS REVOLVER, cal. .28 or .31, D.A.; 5-shot; 3.75-inch octagon barrel. Walnut grips. Iron guard and frame. Engraved frame and cylinder. Hammer resembles that in pepperbox, and is engraved "Ells Patent Aug. 1, 1854." Plate 13, Fig. 19. $220–$315.

ELLS REVOLVER, cal. .31, 5-shot, D.A.; 3.75-inch octagon barrel. Walnut grips. Iron guard and frame, engraved. Pepperbox-type hammer marked "Ells Patent Aug. 1, 1854." Plate 13, Fig. 21. $210–$300.

G. ERICHSON DERRINGER, cal. .41; 3.25-inch flat-top barrel marked "G. ERICHSON HOUSTON." Lock marked like barrel. Full-length walnut stock with white metal tip and checkered grip. Plain German silver mountings. Wooden ramrod. Front and rear sights. This is regarded as a Texan imitation of a Philadelphia-Deringer derringer. Plate 13, Fig. 22. $600–$850.

A. ESCHERICH DOUBLE-BARREL POCKET PISTOL, cal. .52, smoothbore, 4-inch, side-by-side barrels; total length 7.875 inches. Brass-tipped ramrod under barrels. Rib between barrels marked "A. Escherich Baltimore." Steel mounts elaborately chiseled with designs of American Indians, hunter with game, etc. A very rare American pistol. $600–$800.

J.E. EVANS DERRINGER, cal. .50; 2-inch, round, flat-top barrel marked "J. E Evans Philada." Walnut stock, checkered grip. German silver trigger guard, side plate, and shield inlaid in back of grip. Engraved back-action lock. Hammer and lock casehardened in colors. Browned barrel. $385–$535.

SAME, but cal. .36. Plate 13, Fig. 23. $370–$525.

FAIRBANKS ALL-METAL PISTOL, cal. .33, 3-inch, part round, part octagon barrel marked "Fairbanks Boston. Cast Steel." Brass frame. Trigger and hammer in one piece. Belt hook on left of frame. Plate 13, Fig. 24. $260–$345.

FITCH & WALDO REVOLVER, cal. .31, S.A.; 4-inch round barrel marked "Fitch & Waldo, N.Y." Total length 9 inches. Cylinder either plain or fluted. Plainly engraved frame. Polished walnut handles. Collectors and dealers often ascribe Fitch & Waldo arms to Bacon on the grounds that Fitch & Waldo were only distributors. $225–$295.

FOEHL DERRINGER, cal. .44; 2-inch, round flat-top barrel marked "Chas. Foehl Phila." Back-action lock marked like barrel. $425–$600.

FOWLER POCKET PISTOL, cal. .38, S.A., single-shot; 4-inch, half octagon barrel marked "B. Fowler Jr." Brass front sight. Grooved rear sight. Round hardwood handles. Reported to have been made in Connecticut State Prison armory. $195-$300.

FOWLER UNDERHAMMER PISTOL, cal. .31, single-shot; 4-inch half octagon barrel marked "Fowler." Total length 8.5 inches. Hammer is shaped like a woman's leg. Reported to have been made in Connecticut State Prison armory. $180–$275.

FRANCE BOOTLEG PISTOL, cal. .57; 10.625-inch round-octagon barrel marked "J.A. France Cobleskill N.Y." Total length 14 inches. Walnut grips. Iron frame. Center-hung hammer. Spur trigger. Hickory ramrod. $325–$475.

FREEMAN—See Chapter 8.

GIBBS TIFFANY & CO. BOOTLEG PISTOL, cal. .34; 6-inch, round-octagon, rifled barrel marked "Cast Steel." Total length 10 inches. Made without trigger guard. Blade front sight; peep rear sight. Frame marked "Gibbs Tiffany & Co. Sturbridge Mass." Underhammer. $195–$375.

GIBBS & TIFFANY MFG. CO. BOOTLEG PISTOL, cal. .36, S.A.; 3.875-inch, half octagon barrel marked "Gibbs & Tiffany Mfg. Co., Sturbridge, Mass." Total length 7.75 inches. Blued finish. Brass front sight. Notch rear sight. Made without trigger guard. Rounded wooden handle at right angles to barrel. Similar to above. Underhammer. $195–$365.

GEORGE GEDNEY PATENT PRIMER HAMMER was used on Model 1836 flintlock pistols made by either R. Johnson or A. Waters, which had been converted to percussion. Patented March 15, 1859, the hammer contained a tube of fulminate with an enclosed cutter and carrier to place it on the nipple. A slightly different hammer, embodying the same principle,

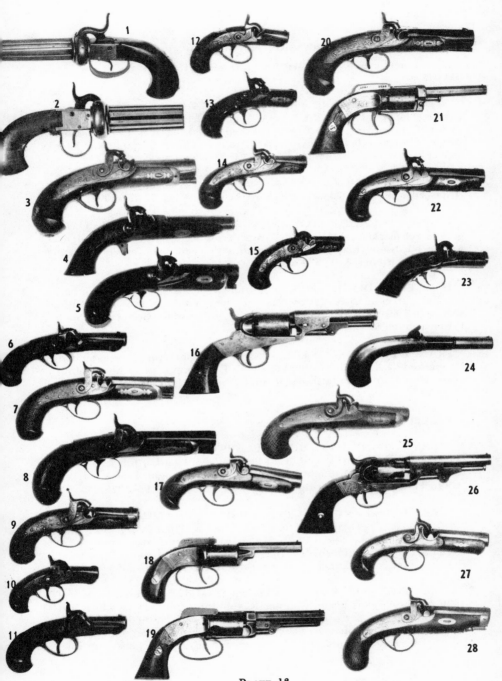

PLATE 13

could be used on the Model 1842 percussion pistols by H. Aston or I. N. Johnson. See Chapter 7. Completely altered pistol. $825–1,250.

GLASSICK DERRINGER, cal. .40; 3.75-inch octagon barrel marked "F. Glassick & Co. Memphis, Tenn." Back-action lock. Sheathed spur trigger. Walnut stock almost to muzzle. $430–$620.

GRUBB DERRINGER, cal. .40, single-shot; 3.5-inch octagon barrel. Walnut stock. Resembles Philadelphia-Deringer derringers but grip more closely approaches a square shape. $465–$625.

GRUBB PISTOL, cal. .36, single-shot; 8-inch round barrel marked "J.C. Grubb." Total length 11 inches. Polished walnut bird's-head handle. Ramrod held by brass insert and thimble. Checkered stock and forearm. $490–$670.

HALE BOOTLEG PISTOL, cal. .36; 6-inch round-octagon barrel marked "H.J. Hale, Worcester, Mass." Total length 9 inches. Underhammer. Made without trigger guard. $185–$325.

---

PLATE 13. American Percussion Pistols and Revolvers

*Figure*

1. (Darling) 6-Shot Pepperbox, frame marked "J. Engh."
2. (Darling) 6-Shot Pepperbox, frame marked "A C S."
3. Deringer, cal. .48, marked "Derringer Philadel."
4. F.R.J. Bitterlich & Co. Derringer, cal. .44 or .45.
5. Deringer, cal. .48, lock marked "Derringer."
6. Deringer, cal. .44, made for A.J. Plate.
7. Deringer, cal. .43, made for Hyde & Goodrich.
8. Deringer, cal. .43, made for Hyde & Goodrich.
9. Deringer, cal. .41, made for A.J. Taylor.
10. Deringer, cal. .41, made for N. Curry & Bro.
11. Deringer, cal. .41, made for C. Curry.
12. Deringer, cal. .41, 1.75-inch barrel.
13. Deringer, cal. .41, made for E.H. Clarke & Co.
14. Deringer, cal. .40, 1.75-inch barrel.
15. Deringer, cal. .40, 2-inch barrel, made for N. Curry.
16. Dictator Revolver, cal. .36, 5-shot.
17. Deringer, cal. .40, 2-inch barrel, made for N. Curry.
18. Ells Revolver, cal. .31, 3-inch barrel.
19. Ells Revolver, cal. .31, 3.75-inch barrel.
20. Deringer, cal. .41, 4-inch barrel.
21. Ells Revolver, cal. .31, 3.75-inch barrel.
22. G. Erichson Derringer.
23. J.E. Evans Derringer, cal. .36.
24. Fairbanks All-Metal Pistol, cal. .33.
25. Deringer, cal. .46, marked "Derringer."
26. B.J. Hart & Bro. Revolver, cal. .31.
27. Hawes & Waggoner Derringer.
28. Krider Derringer, cal. .43.

SAME, but cal. .31, and barrel marked "H.J. Hale, Warranted Cast Steel." $195–$305.

HANKINS POCKET REVOLVER, cal. .28, 5-shot; 3-inch barrel. Total length 7 inches. Weight 8 oz. Marked "Wm. Hankins Phila, Pa." $380–$595.

HARPERS FERRY FLINTLOCK PISTOL, MODEL 1806, converted to percussion, cal. .54; 10-inch, round, smoothbore barrel. Total length 16 inches. Resembles original flintlock except for drum-type percussion conversion. See Chapter 3 for details. $975–$1,450.

HARPERS FERRY PERCUSSION PISTOL-CARBINE—See U.S. Pistol, Model 1805, in Chapter 3.

B.J. HART & BRO. REVOLVER, cal. .31, 5-shot; 4-inch round barrel marked "B.J. Hart & Bro. N.Y." Total length 9 inches. Weight 1 lb. 4 oz. Half fluted cylinder. Plate 13, Fig. 26. $195–$285.

B.J. HART & BRO. SINGLE-SHOT PISTOL, cal. .36. $110–$145.

HAWES & WAGGONER DERRINGER, cal. .41; 3-inch, round, flat-top barrel marked "Hawes & Waggoner." Resembles Philadelphia Deringers. Plate 13, Fig. 27. $535–$675.

HAWKEN PISTOL, cal. .58, smoothbore; 6.75-inch octagon barrel marked "Hawken, St. Louis, Mo." Total length 12.5 inches. Full-length walnut stock. Belt hook on left. Checkered grip. Swivel-type ramrod holder. Jacob Hawken was the maker of famous percussion rifles, especially those classified as the Western Plains type. $1,150–$1,625.

HAZZARD & BLAIR PISTOL, cal. .52; 5.75-inch octagon barrel marked "Imported by Hazzard & Blair." Back-action lock marked "Wm. Chance." Belt hook on left. $155–$220.

HERO PISTOL, cal. .34, 3-inch, round barrel. Brass frame marked "A.S.T. Co. Hero." Spur trigger. Walnut grips. Center-hung hammer. A.S.T. Co. is the abbreviation for the American Standard Tool Co. $75–$100.

HERO PISTOL, cal. .34; 2.5-inch, round, tapering steel barrel attached to bronze body, marked "Hero M.F.A. Co." The abbreviation represents Manhattan Fire Arms Co. $85–$100.

HOPKINS & ALLEN BELT REVOLVER, cal. .31; 4-inch round barrel marked "Hopkins & Allen, Norwich, Ct." Total length 8.875 inches. Weight 1 lb. 3 oz. Walnut grips. Resembles Bacon 5-shot revolver. $200–$285.

SAME, but octagonal barrel. $250–$325.

W. IRVING REVOLVER, cal. .31, 6-shot; 4.5-inch octagon barrel. Iron frame. Iron trigger guard. Total length 9 inches. Weight 1.5 lbs. Marked "W. Irving, 20 Cliff St. N.Y." This percussion Irving was made after the cartridge Irving was discontinued. $200–$275.

JACQUITHS PATENT REVOLVER—See below, Springfield Arms Co.

JENISON UNDERHAMMER PISTOL, cal. .31, single-shot, S.A.; 6.5-inch, part octagon barrel marked "J. Jenison & Co. Southbridge Mass." Total length 10.5 inches. Plain metal finish. Brass front sight. Raised-notch rear sight. No trigger guard. Rounded hardwood handles taper to a point at bottom. $155–$225.

KERR—See Massachusetts Arms Co., Chapter 8.

KRIDER DERRINGER, cal. .43; 3.25-inch, round, flat-top barrel marked "Krider Phila." Back-action lock marked "Krider." German silver mountings. Walnut stock, checkered grip. Plate 13, Fig. 28. $450–$655.

SAME, but cal. .40, 2.25-inch barrel. $445–$645.

KRIDER DERRINGERS, cased presentation pair, cal. .40; 2.187-inch, round, flat-top, rifled barrel marked "Philadelphia." Back-action lock marked "Krider." Gold and silver name plates. Mahogany case with accessories. The specimen illustrated was presented to Governor M.S. Latham, of California, who became a U.S. Senator. Plate 14, Fig. 1. $3,500–$4,500 per pair.

WM. LAWRENCE POCKET RIFLE-PISTOL, cal. .36; rifled, 14-inch, octagon barrel, muzzle turned for bullet starter, marked "Wm. Lawrence Cast Steel." Walnut stock extends one-third of barrel length. Pistol grip resembles that on a dueling pistol. Walnut rifle stock attached to pistol stock by two screws through back strap, and made to be detached when weapon is fired as a pistol. Iron trigger guard with spur. Hooded pinhead front sight. Peep rear sight on back strap. Plate 14, Fig. 2. $415–$650.

LEAVITT REVOLVER—See Chapter 8.

LEONARD PEPPERBOX, cal. .31, D.A.; 5-inch fluted cylinder, ribbed barrels in one block, removable from frame for capping. Walnut grips. Hammerless. Ring trigger for cocking, with another trigger, forward of the cocking trigger, for firing. Firing pin revolves, striking nipples in rotation. Engraved trigger and frame. Marked "G. Leonard, Jr. Charlestown. Patented 1849." Brown finish. Plate 14, Fig. 3. $375–$585.

LIBEAU REVOLVER, cal. .34, S.A.; 4.625-inch, blued, octagon barrel marked "V G Libeau, New Orleans, La.—1847." Blued frame stamped

"New Orleans." Folding trigger. Polished rosewood handles. Total length 11.75 inches. Very rare, but one known. $1,000–$1,350.

LINDSAY 2-SHOT PISTOL—See Chapter 7.

LINS DERRINGER, cal. .50, 2-inch barrel. Total length 5.75 inches. Marked "A. Frederick Lins, Phila. Pa." $365–$585.

SAME, but total length 9.75 inches. $370–$590.

LINS MINIATURE PISTOL, cal. .22, 0.875-inch barrel. Total length 3 inches. Weight 0.5 oz. $360–$450.

J.P. LOWER DERRINGER, cal. .43; rifled, 2-inch, round, flat-top barrel marked "Philada." Back-action lock engraved and marked "J.P. Lower." Walnut stock, checkered grip. German silver guard, engraved. Either made by Lower in Denver or by Deringer of Philadelphia for Lower as distributor. Plate 14, Fig. 5. $460–$620.

MANHATTAN SINGLE-SHOT PISTOL, cal. .31; 2-inch round-octagon barrel. Total length 4.5 inches. Hammer marked "Manhattan F.A. Mfg. Co. New York." Walnut grips. Iron guard. Pepperbox-type hammer. $80–$115.

MANHATTAN PEPPERBOX, cal. .31, D.A., 3-shot; 2.875-inch triangular-shaped barrels which revolve by hand. Walnut grips. Iron guard and frame, engraved. Marked "Manhattan F.A. Mfg. Co. New York." Plate 14, Fig. 6. $225–$415.

---

### PLATE 14. American Percussion Pistols and Revolvers

*Figure*

1. Krider Derringers, Cased Presentation Pair.
2. Wm. Lawrence Pocket Rifle-Pistol.
3. Leonard Pepperbox, cal. .31, 4-shot.
4. Robbins & Lawrence D.A. Pepperbox, cal. .31, 5-shot.
5. J.P. Lower Derringer.
6. Manhattan Pepperbox, cal. .31.
7. Massachusetts Arms Co. Revolver, cal. .31.
8. Massachusetts Arms Co. Revolver, cal. .31.
9. Massachusetts Arms Co. Revolver, cal. .28.
10. Massachusetts Arms Co. Single-Shot Pistol.
11. Massachusetts Arms Co.—Wesson & Leavitt Revolver.
12. Neal Bootleg Pistol.
13. Nepperhan F.A. Co. Revolver.
14. Newbury Arms Co. Revolver, cal. .31.
15. Newbury Arms Co. Revolver, cal. .28.
16. North & Couch Trap or Doorjamb Pistol, cal. .31.
17. North & Couch Trap or Doorjamb Pistol, cal. .28.
18. Parker 4-Shot, Single-Action Pistol.

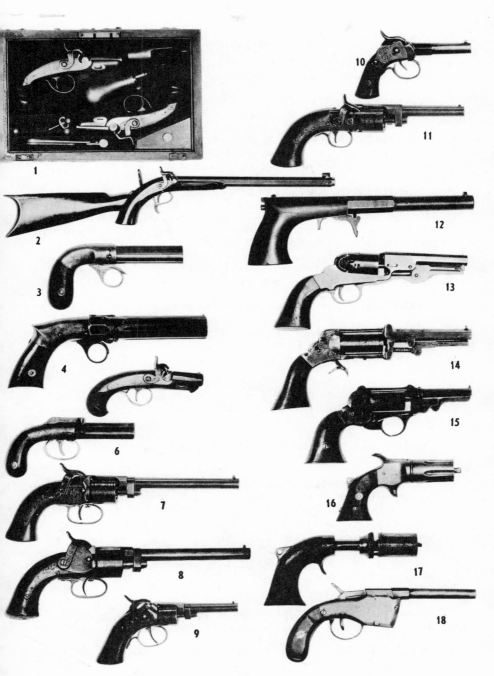

PLATE 14

MANHATTAN PEPPERBOX, cal. .31, 5-shot, 2.25-inch round barrels; otherwise same as before. $240–$425.

MANHATTAN PEPPERBOX, cal. .31, 6-shot, 2.375-inch round barrels; otherwise same as before. $240–$425.

MANHATTAN POCKET REVOLVER, cal. .31, 5-shot; 4-inch octagon barrel, marked like pepperbox. Total length 9 inches. Burl walnut grips. Iron guard and frame, engraved. $175–$240.

MANHATTAN "NAVY" REVOLVER, cal. .36, 5-shot, S.A.; 6.5-inch octagon barrel marked "Manhattan Fire Arms Co. Newark, N.J. Patented March 8, 1864." Cylinder marked "Patented Dec. 27, 1859." Total length 11.5 inches. Weight 2 lbs. Hammer strikes a spring plate which strikes the primers to fire. $310–$485.

SAME, but so-called regular model, lacking the spring-plate primer-striking feature, and constructed in a conventional manner. $300–$375.

SAME, regular model, 5-inch barrel. $290–$345.

SAME, regular model, 4-inch barrel. $290–$345.

MARSTON SINGLE-SHOT, BREECH-LOADING PISTOL—See Chapter 7.

MARSTON PEPPERBOX, cal. .26, 6-shot, 2.75-inch barrels. Total length 6.5 inches. Flat-top hammer, marked "W.W. Marston, New York." $240–$425.

SAME, but cal. .31, 6-shot, 3.5-inch barrel. Total length 8 inches. $240–$425.

MARSTON REVOLVER, cal. .31, 5-shot, 4.5-inch barrel. Total length 10 inches. Marked "W.W. Marston Armory, New York." $275–$450.

SAME, but 4.75-inch barrel. Total length 9.25 inches. Marked "Wm. Marston Phoenix, New York City." $280–$460.

MARSTON REVOLVER, cal. .32, S.A., 5-shot; 5.5-inch octagon, rifled barrel marked "W.W. Marston Phoenix Armory, New York City." $285–$465.

MARSTON & KNOX SINGLE-SHOT PISTOL, cal. .36; 5.5-inch barrel marked on top "W.W. Marston & Knox, New York, 1854." $115–$165.

SAME, but cal. .31, marked on barrel "W.W. Marston & Knox, New

York," and on hammer "W.W. Marston, Patented 1849 New York." $135–$195.

MARSTON & KNOX PEPPERBOX, cal. .26, 6-shot, 2.75-inch barrels, same marks as above. $240–$425.

SAME, but cal. .31, 3.5-inch barrels. $250–$445.

*Note: Similar to Marston, and Marston & Knox, are "Sprague & Marston" marked arms, including pistols, revolvers, and pepperboxes, listed later in this chapter under "S." There are several variations in barrel length not listed here. In general, Sprague & Marston pieces seem to average more in value than the corresponding Marston pieces.*

MASSACHUSETTS ARMS CO.—ADAMS—See Chapter 8.

MASSACHUSETTS ARMS CO. REVOLVER, cal. .31, S.A., 6-shot; 6-inch round barrel marked as above. Maynard tape primer. Total length 11 inches. Maynard priming attachment marked with eagle and "Maynard's Patent, Sept. 22, 1845." Frame marked on left "Mass. Coat of Arms.". Blade front sight. Grooved-frame rear sight. Round hardwood handles. Plate 14, Fig. 7. $350–$575.

MASSACHUSETTS ARMS CO. REVOLVER, cal. .31, 6-shot, S.A.; 6-inch round barrel marked "Mass. Arms Co. Chicopee Falls." Walnut grips. Silver-plated trigger guard. Primer marked as above. Back-action lock. Maynard tape primer. Cylinder revolved by hand. Cylinder stop released by small button in front of trigger. Engraved. Plate 14, Fig. 8. $350–$375.

MASSACHUSETTS ARMS CO. REVOLVER, cal. .28, S.A., 6-shot; 3-inch round barrel marked as above. Maynard tape primer. Iron guard. One nipple serves all chambers. Engraved cylinder and frame. Primer marked as above. Plate 14, Fig. 9. $295–$420.

MASSACHUSETTS ARMS CO. SINGLE-SHOT PISTOL with Maynard tape lock, cal. .31, S.A.; 3.5-inch round-octagon barrel, marked on top "Mass. Arms Co. Chicopee Falls." Primer magazine marked "Maynard's Patent Sept. 22, 1845." Total length 5.5 inches. Made with trigger guard. Walnut grips. Iron guard. $310–$465.

SAME, but with 2.625-inch barrel. Plate 14, Fig. 10. $300–$450.

SAME, but cal. .28, with 3-inch barrel. $310–$465.

MASSACHUSETTS ARMS CO.—WESSON & LEAVITT POCKET REVOLVER, cal. .31, 6-shot, 3.5-inch round barrel. Back-action lock marked

"Wesson & Leavitt's Patent" and "Mass. Arms Co. Chicopee Falls."
$320–$485.

SAME, but cal. .31, 6-shot, S.A.; 4-inch round barrel. Burl walnut grip.
Gold-plated, engraved back strap and trigger guard on some specimens.
Cylinder revolves to left, and is turned by bevel gears. All parts except barrel
engraved. Marked "Mass. Arms Co. Chicopee Falls" and "Wesson & Leavitt's Patent." Plate 14, Fig. 11. $300–$425.

SAME, but 5-inch barrel. $310–$440.

SAME, but 6-inch barrel. $320–$450.

MASSACHUSETTS ARMS CO. ARMY REVOLVER AND NAVY RE-
VOLVER—See Chapter 8.

McK BROTHERS PISTOL—See Chapter 7.

METROPOLITAN REVOLVER, cal. .36, 5-shot, S.A.; 5.5-inch round
barrel marked on top "Metropolitan Arms Co. New York." Total length
10.625 inches. Weight 1 lb. 10 oz. Oval trigger guard, walnut grip. This was
an imitation of the Colt 1862 Police Percussion Revolver. Some specimens
are nickel-plated or silver-plated. $400–$625.

SAME, but 6.5-inch barrel. $425–$650.

METROPOLITAN NAVY REVOLVER—See Chapter 8. This is the 6-
shot model with the 7.5-inch barrel.

MIDNIGHT DUELING PISTOL, cal. .35, 7-inch octagon barrel marked
"L. E. Midnight." Back-action lock. Walnut stock almost to muzzle. Engraved. Silver inlay. Usually found in pairs. Each $475–$610.

MILLS PISTOL, cal. .75; 10.75-inch, round, smoothbore barrel. Total
length 16.75 inches. Half stock. Iron trigger guard. Hickory ramrod. Lock
plate marked "B. Mills Harrodsburg Ky." $610–$835.

MILLS PISTOL, cal. .36, S.A.; 10-inch octagon barrel. Total length 16.5
inches. Lock marked "B. Mills Harrodsburg Ky." Set triggers. Brass-blade
front sight. Raised-notch rear sight. Polished rosewood stock for one-half
barrel length. Saw-handle grip. Ramrod held by metal tubes in forearm.
$465–$645.

NEAL BOOTLEG PISTOL, cal. .35, rifles; 6.25-inch, part round, part
octagon barrel marked "Wm. Neal Bangor Me." Walnut grip shaped something like modern automatic pistol grips. Underhammer. Made without

trigger guard. Blade front sight. V-notch rear sight. Plate 14, Fig. 12. $200–$295.

NEPPERHAN F. A. CO. REVOLVER, cal. .31, 5-shot; 4.25-inch octagon barrel marked "Nepperhan F.A. Co. Yonkers N. Y." Walnut grips. Iron frame and straps in one piece. Brass guard. Resembles Colt Model 1849. Plate 14, Fig. 13. $285–$375.

SAME, but with 5.125-inch barrel. $285–$375.

NEWBURY ARMS CO. REVOLVER, cal. .31, 5-shot, 4.125-inch octagon barrel. Iron frame. One-piece walnut grip. Cylinder primed without removing, through gate. Hammer made without spur and lies flush with back of frame. Loading lever under barrel held in position by tension of coil spring bearing against front of barrel stud. Barrel hinged at top front of frame; locked by spring catch. Made about 1855 in Albany, N. Y. Not marked. Plate 14, Fig. 14. $775–$1,100.

NEWBURY ARMS CO. REVOLVER, cal. .28, 6-shot, S.A.; 3.125-inch octagon barrel marked "Newbury Arms Co. Albany." Iron frame. Walnut grips. Cylinder must be removed for priming. Loading lever under barrel. Cylinder marked "Newbury Arms Co. Albany." Plate 14, Fig. 15. $875–$1,250.

NEWBURY ARMS CO. REVOLVER, cal. .31, 6-shot, S.A.; 3.5-inch round barrel marked "Newbury Arms Co., Albany, N.Y." Total length 9.25 inches. No trigger guard. Crescent-shaped trigger. Hardwood handles. No straps holding barrel to lock or breech. Barrel held only by square head on cylinder axis. Brass frame. $685–$975.

*Note: Newbury Arms Co. weapons are so seldom seen or reported that most collectors and dealers regard them as inventor's models. Complete Newbury revolver story by Samuel E. Smith in* Gun Collector Magazine.

NORTH & COUCH TRAP OR DOORJAMB PISTOL, sometimes erroneously called a pepperbox, cal. .31, S.A., 6-shot; 2.125-inch round, fluted barrels. Walnut grips. Spur trigger. Iron frame. One nipple fires all barrels at once. Hammer enters frame with only spur projecting. Rod runs through center of barrel group and moves in when chamber is cocked. By means of a cord running through the hole in the end of rod, piece can be fired when rod is pulled out. A block on back strap is drilled for fixing cord and attaching pistol to some object, such as a doorjamb. Cord on muzzle rod is then fixed to door and the pistol cocked. When door is opened, pistol fires all barrels into the person entering the room, much to his surprise. The specimen illustrated is marked "North & Couch. Address J. D. Locke 197 Water St. N. Y." Plate 14, Fig. 16. $210–$300.

NORTH & COUCH TRAP OR DOORJAMB PISTOL, cal. .28, S.A., 6-shot; 1.75-inch round cylinder in which are 6 barrels. This cylinder is fixed to the end of a shaft on which slides a heavy steel disk acting as the hammer. The outer rim of the disk is knurled. In the center of the shaft is a driving spring for the disk. Projecting from the front of the barrel block is a rod with a transverse through the end. Steel pistol grip frame with walnut grips. Spur trigger. On back of grip is a lug with a hole through it. According to a pious legend, this trap pistol was made for hunting kangaroos in Australia. The pistol was hung from a tree by a cord through the rear lug. Another cord with a bundle of grass was fixed to the rod at the muzzle. When the kangaroo pulled the tuft of grass, he got his through the head. Plate 14, Fig. 17. $210–$300.

*Note: Some specimens are marked "North & Couch, Middletown, Conn."*

S. NORTH BERLIN MODEL 1810 FLINTLOCK PISTOL, converted to percussion, cal. .72, smoothbore, 9-inch round barrel. Iron-mounted. Walnut stock. Double spring-fastened upper band. Swell-tip hickory ramrod. Lock marked "S. North Berlin Con." and "U. States." $1,050–$1,400.

PALMETTO ARMORY PISTOL—See U.S. Pistol, Model 1842, in Chapter 6; see also Chapter 10.

PARKER 4-SHOT, SINGLE-ACTION PISTOL, cal. .33; 4-inch, round, ribbed barrels enclosed for their full length in a steel tube. Rectangular breechblock has 4 chambers in vertical line, each with a nipple. Pulling hammer past full cock lifts breechblock up one chamber. Chambers loaded through front of frame. Less than 100 are supposed to have been made. Some are marked "Parker" and some are marked "Springfield Mass. 1849." Plate 14, Fig. 18. $600–$875.

PECARE & SMITH PEPPERBOX, cal. .31, 4-shot; 3.25-inch round barrel marked "Pecare & Smith's Patent 1849. New York. Cast Steel." Walnut grips. Brass frame, engraved. Pepperbox-type hammer. Folding trigger. Plate 15, Fig. 1. $600–$825.

PECARE & SMITH PEPPERBOX, cal. .28, D.A., 10-shot; 4-inch, round, smoothbore barrel. Iron guard and frame. Pepperbox-type marked "Pecare & Smith's Pat. 1849. New York." Engraved brass frame. Walnut or bone grips. Concealed trigger with small projection so that it may be unfolded for firing. Hammer is without spur and works in and out of the front of the frame. This weapon is often described as the "rarest and oddest of all American pepperboxes." Plate 15, Fig. 2. $750–$1,100.

PECARE & SMITH PEPPERBOX, cal. .31, 4-shot; 2.75-inch round barrel marked as above. Walnut grips. Concealed trigger. Engraved iron frame. Each barrel has small brass front sight. Plate 15, Fig. 3. $620–$875.

PECARE & SMITH PEPPERBOX, cal. .31, 4-shot; 2.5-inch steel cylinder marked "Pecare and Smith's Patent 1849. New York Cast Steel," containing four smoothbore barrels and revolved by hand. Nipple shield. Top hammer with offset head to make cocking easier. $750–$1,100.

PECARE & SMITH PEPPERBOX, cal. .31, 4-shot; 3.25-inch round barrel marked "Pecare & Smith's Patent 1849. New York. Cast Steel." Walnut grips. Engraved brass frame. Pepperbox-type hammer. Folding trigger. Blued finish. Plate 15, Fig. 4. $600–$825.

PERRY—See Chapter 7.

PETTENGILL POCKET REVOLVER, cal. .31, 6-shot, 4.5-inch octagon barrel; total length 10 inches. Made without loading lever. Top of frame over cylinder marked "Pettengill's Patent 1856." Round cylinder. Engraved iron frame. $550–$700. With rammer $500–$650.

PETTENGILL—See Chapter 8.

PIKE BOOTLEG PISTOL, cal. .31; 6-inch round-octagon barrel marked "Pike's Patent, Troy, N.Y." Underhammer. Maple grip. $180–$275.

PORTER REVOLVER, cal. .35, 8-shot, D.A.; 4-inch, half octagon barrel marked "Porter's Patent, New York." No trigger guard. Plain metal finish. Front sight but no rear sight. Total length 12 inches. Vertical radial chamber holds 8 charges primed with percussion pellets. Hammer strikes on side. Only three or four made. $1,800–$3,250.

SAME, but made with tape primer. $1,700–$3,000.

POST PEPPERBOX, cal. .31, 6-shot, D.A.; 3.75-inch barrels with fluted ribs. Total length 7.25 inches. Weight 1.5 lbs. Hammerless. Ring trigger. Marked "J. Post's Self-Acting Set Patented 1849" or "J. Post Self Acting Pistol Patent 1849." Engraved frame. $450–$725.

PRESCOTT POCKET REVOLVER, cal. .31, 6-shot, brass frame, sheath trigger. 8.75 inches overall with 4.25-inch octagon barrel. Some marked "E. A. Prescott Worcester Ms. Pat'd. Oct. 2, 1860." Some unmarked. Very few made. $510–$650.

QUINNEBAUG UNDERHAMMER PISTOL, cal. .31; 7.75-inch barrel marked as above. Total length 12 inches. Weight 1 lb. $180–$300.

RAYMOND & ROBITAILLE REVOLVER, cal. .44, D.A., 6-shot, hammerless. Brass-cone front sight. Notched rear sight. Bronze frame. Polished hardwood handles. Made by Rogers & Spencer, for Raymond & Robitaille. $1,000–$1,450.

REMINGTON—See the martial models in Chapter 8.

REMINGTON POCKET REVOLVER (New Model), cal. .31, 5-shot, S.A.; 3.5-inch, octagon, rifled barrel. Spur trigger. Nickel-plated. Walnut grips. Otherwise similar to New Model Army and Navy Revolvers described elsewhere. Made from 1863 to 1873. Numbered 1 to over 17,000. Plate 15, Fig. 5. $205–$345.

SAME, but with rare brass frame, 4.5-inch barrel. $280–$480.

REMINGTON DOUBLE-ACTION NAVY REVOLVER, cal. .36, 6-shot, 6.5-inch octagonal barrel. Walnut grips. Brass guard. Round cylinder. Blade front sight. S.A. and D.A. Blued. Made from 1863 to 1873. Numbered 1 to over 5,000. (Not martial.) $340–$495.

REMINGTON FULL-FLUTED-CYLINDER REVOLVER, cal. .36, 6-shot, D.A.; 6.5-inch barrel marked "Manufactured by Remington's Ilion N.Y. Riders Pt. Aug 17, 1858, May 3, 1859." Blued. Full fluted cylinder. Walnut grips. Brass trigger guard. Made from 1863 to 1873. Numbered 1 to over 5,000. Plate 15, Fig. 6. $475–$675.

REMINGTON-BEALS—See also Chapter 8.

---

PLATE 15. American Percussion Pistols and Revolvers

*Figure*

1. Pecare & Smith Pepperbox, cal. .31.
2. Pecare & Smith Pepperbox, cal. .28.
3. Pecare & Smith Pepperbox, cal. .31.
4. Pecare & Smith Pepperbox, cal. .31.
5. Remington Pocket Revolver (New Model).
6. Remington Full-Fluted-Cylinder Revolver.
7. Remington-Beals Pocket Revolver.
8. Remington-Beals Pocket Revolver.
9. Remington New Model Police, cal. .36.
10. Remington-Rider Revolver.
11. Remington-Rider All-Metal, Breech-loading, Single-Shot Pistol.
12. Reuthe's Patent Trap Pistol.
13. Robbins & Lawrence Pepperbox, cal. .31.
14. Sharps Pocket Revolver.
15. Simpson Derringer, cal. .55.
16. Slotter & Co. Derringer, cal. .50.
17. Slotter & Co. Derringer, cal. .46.
18. Slotter & Co. Derringer, cal. .44.
19. Slotter & Co. Derringer, cal. .44.
20. Slotter & Co. Derringer, cal. .41.
21. Spies Pepperbox.
22. Sprague & Marston Pepperbox.
23. Springfield Arms Co.—Jacquith's Patent Revolver.
24. Springfield Arms Co.—Warner's Patent Revolver, cal. .31.
25. Springfield Arms Co.—Warner's Patent Revolver, cal. .31.
26. Springfield Arms Co.—Warner's Patent Revolver, cal. .28.
27. Springfield Arms Co.—Warner's Patent Revolver, cal. .28.
28. Springfield Arms Co.—Warner's Patent Revolver, cal. .28.

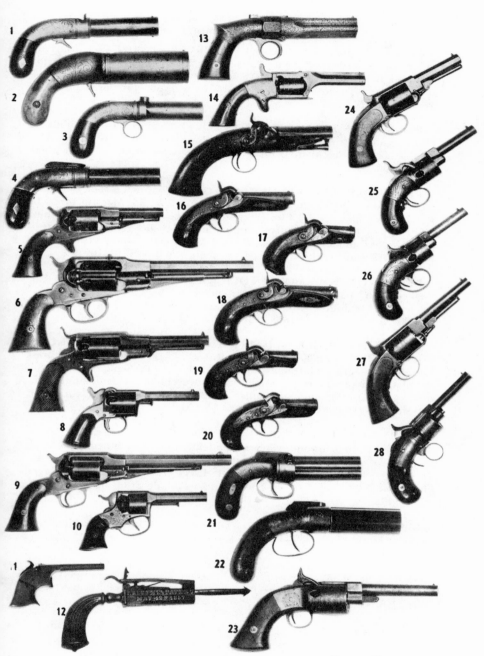

PLATE 15

REMINGTON-BEALS POCKET REVOLVER, cal. .31, 5-shot, 3-inch octagon barrel marked "F. Beal's Patent June 24, '56 and May 26 '57. Manufactured by Remingtons Ilion, N.Y." One-piece hard-rubber grips. No loading lever. First Pocket Model. Made in 1857 and 1858. Numbered 1 to about 4,500. Plate 15, Fig. 8. $245–$460.

REMINGTON-BEALS POCKET REVOLVER, cal. .31, 5-shot. Similar to above, but has spur trigger. Rarest of the three pocket Beals revolvers. This is the second model. Made from 1858 to 1860. Numbered 1 to about 1,000. $525–$900.

REMINGTON-BEALS POCKET REVOLVER, cal. .31, 5-shot, 4-inch octagon barrel marked "Beals' Patent 1856 & '57 & '58. Manufactured by Remingtons Ilion, N.Y." Checkered hard-rubber grips. This is the third model, made with longer barrel and loading lever, but retaining spur trigger of second model. Outside pawl revolves cylinder as in first two models. Made in 1859 and 1860. Numbered 1 to about 1,500. $265–$510.

REMINGTON NEW MODEL POLICE REVOLVER, cal. .36, 5-shot, 6.5-inch octagon barrel, single action. Also made in 3.5-, 4.5-, and 5.5-inch barrel lengths. Walnut grips. Usual trigger guard and loading lever. Over 18,000 made. Made from 1863 to 1888. Plate 15, Fig. 9. $310–$565.

REMINGTON-RIDER ALL-METAL, BREECH-LOADING, SINGLE-SHOT PISTOL, usually listed under Rider; cal. .15; 3-inch, round, brass barrel cast integral with frame and marked "Rider's Pt. Sept. 13, 1859." Silver-plated and engraved. Hammer acts as breechblock. Center-hung hammer, spur trigger. Unique mechanism. Made from 1860 to 1863. Numbered 1 to about 1,000. Plate 15, Fig. 11. $900–$1,250.

REMINGTON-RIDER POCKET REVOLVER, cal. .31, double-action model called "mushroom cylinder" model; 5-shot, 3-inch octagon barrel, marked "Manufactured by Remingtons Ilion, N.Y. Rider's Pt. Aug. 17, 1858, Mar 3, 1859." No loading lever. Large-size German silver trigger guard. Some 115,000 of this model made. Made from 1860 to 1888. $310–$465.

REUTHE'S PATENT TRAP PISTOL, cal. .25, 3.25-inch barrel bored in cast-iron block. Marked "F. Reuthe's Patent May 12, 1857." Plate 15, Fig. 12. $155–$210.

SAME, but cal. .32, with two 3.5-inch, octagon, smoothbore barrels. Similar marks. Hooks on gun were baited. When animal tugged at bait, it received both charges. $165–$225.

RIDER (NATHAN RIDER & CO.) UNDERHAMMER PISTOL, cal. .31,

6-inch barrel marked "Nathan Rider & Co. Southbridge, Mass." Total length 9.5 inches. Weight 12 oz. $180–$240.

ROBBINS & LAWRENCE PEPPERBOX, cal. .31, 5-shot; 4.5-inch, round ribbed barrels marked "Leonards Patent 1849" and "Robbins & Lawrence Co., Windsor Vt." Hammer moves forward and backward and is revolved at the same time it is drawn to rear. Barrels unscrew to load 3.125 inches from muzzle. Short section is loaded with powder and ball, and upper section screwed back into place. Barrels tip down for capping. Engraved iron frame. Plate 14, Fig. 4. $295–$440.

ROBBINS & LAWRENCE PEPPERBOX, cal. .31, 5-shot; 3.5-inch, round, fluted barrels which tip downward to prime. Cylinder marked "Robbins & Lawrence Co. Windsor, Vt." Total length 9 inches. Concealed hammer. Ring trigger. Saw handle. Ring trigger cocks inside hammer and another trigger in front of ring trigger is used to fire. Plate 15, Fig. 13. $310–$465.

SAME, but cal. .28, 3.25-inch barrels. $265–$415.

ROBERTSON DUELING PISTOL, cal. .48; 10-inch octagon barrel marked "Robertson, Philadelphia, Pa." Total length 15.5 inches. Weight 2 lbs. 6 oz. $450–$685.

ROGERS & SPENCER—See Chapter 8.

RUGGLES BOOTLEG OR UNDERHAMMER POCKET PISTOL, cal. .41, single-shot; 4.75-inch, part octagon barrel which may or may not be marked "A. Ruggles Stafford, Conn." Frame marked "A. Ruggles, Stafford, Conn. F. Hutchins Co., Agents, Baltimore, Maryland." Total length 8.75 inches. Brass-blade front sight. Notched rear sight. Polished hardwood handles. Plain metal finish. $190–$275.

RUGGLES BOOTLEG OR UNDERHAMMER POCKET PISTOL, cal. .30, single-shot; 6-inch round-octagon barrel marked "A. Ruggles, Stafford, Conn." Made without trigger guard. Walnut grip with brass strap, front and rear. $190–$275.

SAVAGE—See Chapter 8.

SAVAGE-NORTH—See Chapter 8.

SCHNEIDER & CO. DERRINGER, cal. .40; 3.75-inch octagon barrel marked "Schneider & Co. Memphis, Tenn." Spur trigger. Back-action lock. Walnut stock. Checkered grip. $525–$750.

SCHNEIDER & GLASSICK DERRINGER, cal. .45; 3-inch octagon barrel marked "Schneider & Glassick, Memphis, Tenn." Otherwise like Schneider Derringer above. $500–$725.

SHARPS—See Chapter 7.

SHARPS POCKET REVOLVER, cal. .25, 6-shot; 3-inch, octagon, ribbed barrel marked "C. Sharps & Co. Phila. Pa." Total length 7.5 inches. Weight 10 oz. Iron frame. Spur trigger. Walnut grips. Barrel swings up to remove cylinder for loading. Plate 15, Fig. 14. $465–$750.

SHAW & LEDOYT PISTOL, cal. .31; 2.375-inch round-octagon barrel marked "Shaw & Ledoyt Stafford Ct." Brass-bound maple grip. Underhammer. Made without trigger guard. $165–$250.

SIMPSON DERRINGER, cal. .55; 3.25-inch, round, Damascus steel barrel with grooved top, marked "R.J. Simpson, New York." Steel-mounted. Engraved. Back-action lock. Walnut stock almost to muzzle. Checkered fishtail grip. Steel-tip hickory ramrod. Plate 15, Fig. 15. $345–$475.

SLOTTER & CO. DERRINGER, cal. .50; 3-inch, round, flat-top barrel marked "Slotter & Co. Phila. Steel." Back-action lock marked "Slotter & Co. Phila." Walnut stock nearly to muzzle. German silver guard, escutcheons, butt inlay, and name plate, all engraved. Plate 15, Fig. 16. $390–$535.

SLOTTER & CO. DERRINGER, cal. .46; 2-inch, round, flat-top barrel marked "Slotter & Co. Phila." Back-action lock marked like barrel. Total length 4.5 inches. Full-length walnut stock. German silver guard and mountings. Plate 15, Fig. 17. $395–$555.

SLOTTER & CO. DERRINGER, cal. .44; 3-inch, round, flat-top barrel marked "Slotter & Co. Phila. Made for R. Liddle & Co. San Franco Cala." Back-action lock marked "Slotter & Co. Phila." Walnut stock. German silver guard and mountings, engraved. Cap box in butt. Plate 15, Fig. 18. $405–$570.

SLOTTER & CO. DERRINGER, cal. .44; 2-inch, round, flat-top barrel marked "Slotter & Co. Phila. Made for A. J. Plate San Francisco." Back-action lock marked "Slotter & Co. Phila." Walnut stock. German silver guard and mountings. Engraved. Plate 15, Fig. 19. $405–$570.

SLOTTER & CO. DERRINGER, cal. .41; 2-inch, round, flat-top barrel marked "Slotter & Co. Phila." German silver guard and mountings. Engraved. Back-action lock marked like barrel. Plate 15, Fig. 20. $405–$570.

SLOTTER & CO. LARGE DERRINGER, cal. .40; 5.625-inch, round, flat-top barrel. Total length 10 inches. Usual marks. $415–$585.

*Note: The usual specimens of Slotter & Co. derringers vary from cal. .31 to about cal. .50, with such intermediate calibers as .41, .44, and .46. There is little variation in marking except that some carry the names of the same agents that were marked on Philadelphia-Deringer derringers. The longer barrels and larger calibers usually are valued higher, but a combination of a very short barrel and a very large caliber raises the value.*

SMITH-PERCIVAL MAGAZINE PISTOL, cal. .32, 40-shot, S.A.; 7.5-inch, round barrel marked "H. Smith, Norwich, Conn. 1850." Total length 14.5 inches. Side hammer. No sights. Bludgeon-style hardwood handles. Plain engraving on frame. Semi-cannon-mouth muzzle. Two vertical chambers hold loads. Designed by Orville Percival and made by H. Smith. Beware of a fake! $7,500–$9,000.

SPIES PEPPERBOX, cal. .31, D.A., 6-shot; 3.25-inch, round, ribbed barrels. Iron guard. Walnut grips. Marked "A. W. Spies. Allen's Patent." Plate 15, Fig. 21. $295–$435.

SPILLER & BURR—See Chapter 10.

SPRAGUE & MARSTON PEPPERBOX, cal. .31, 6-shot; 3.25-inch, round, ribbed barrels marked "Sprague & Marston New York. Cast Steel." Hammer marked "W. W. Marston." Iron guard. Walnut grips. Engraved frame. Plate 15, Fig. 22. $245–$355.

SAME, but with 2.5-inch barrels. $245–$355.

SPRAGUE & MARSTON PEPPERBOX, cal. .26, 6-shot, 2.75-inch barrels. $210–$315.

SAME, but cal. .31, 3.5-inch barrels. $225–$325.

SPRAGUE & MARSTON SINGLE-SHOT PISTOL, cal. .36, 5-inch round-octagon barrel. $145–$185.

SAME, but cal. .31. $145–$185.

SPRINGFIELD ARMS CO.—See also Chapter 8.

SPRINGFIELD ARMS CO.—JACQUITH'S PATENT REVOLVER, cal. .31, S.A., 6-shot, 4.25-inch round barrel. Iron guard and frame. Hammer hung inside frame. Barrel strap marked "Springfield Arms Co." Frame marked "1838, Jacquith's Patent." First model of Springfield Arms Co. Plate 15, Fig. 23. $395–$545.

SPRINGFIELD ARMS CO.—WARNER'S PATENT REVOLVER, cal. .28, S.A., 6-shot, 3-inch octagon barrel. Marked "James Warner, Springfield, Mass." Walnut grips. Iron guard, center-hung hammer, and loading lever. Based on Warner's July 28, 1857, patent and were first revolvers marked with his name. Plate 15, Fig. 24. $255–$390.

SPRINGFIELD ARMS CO.—WARNER'S PATENT, cal. .40, Dragoon size, side hammer. Model with loading lever. 7.5-inch round barrel. Walnut grips. Only three known. $2,500–$3,500.

SPRINGFIELD ARMS CO.—WARNER'S PATENT REVOLVER, cal. .31, S.A., 6-shot, 2.5-inch round barrel. Iron guard. Engraved frame. Hammer hung inside frame. Cylinder marked "Warner's Patent." Walnut grips. Plate 15, Fig. 25. $195–$290.

SPRINGFIELD ARMS CO.—WARNER'S PATENT REVOLVER, cal. .28, S.A., 2.625-inch round barrel. Total length 6.375 inches. Two triggers as in First Model Navy Warner Revolver. Usual marks. Plate 15, Fig. 26. $195–$280.

SPRINGFIELD ARMS CO.—WARNER'S PATENT REVOLVER, cal. .28, 6-shot, 3.75-inch round barrel. Center-hung hammer. Walnut grips. Plate 15, Fig. 27. $210–$300.

SPRINGFIELD ARMS CO.—WARNER'S PATENT REVOLVER, cal. .28, 6-shot, S.A., 2.625-inch round barrel. Two triggers, one of which is plain and the other a ring trigger. When the hammer is cocked, the ring trigger is pulled, revolving the cylinder and striking the rear trigger to fire. Walnut grips. Iron guard. Engraved cylinder. Plate 15, Fig. 28. $250–$375.

SPRINGFIELD ARMS CO.—WARNER'S PATENT REVOLVER, cal. .31, 6-shot, S.A., 5-inch round barrel. Total length 10.5 inches. Iron guard. Engraved cylinder, frame, and hammer. $275–$425.

SAME, but 6-inch round barrel. Total length 12 inches. $295–$450.

*Note: James Warner was the manager of the Springfield Arms Co., and he is also reported to have operated as James Warner & Co. His Army and Navy percussion revolvers are normally marked on the barrel "Springfield Arms Company" and on the frame "Warner's Patent Jan. 7, 1851." He also obtained a patent on July 15, 1851. The specimens described above are often listed by authors and dealers under the name Warner.*

STARR—See also Chapter 8.

STARR REVOLVER, cal. .44, stocked, 6-shot, D.A., 6-inch round barrel. Frame marked "Starr's Patent Jan. 15, 1856" on right and "Starr Arms Co. New York" on left. Walnut shoulder stock permanently attached to revolver to form a carbine. Steel butt plate. Rounded walnut block attached to front of trigger guard for a left-hand guard. V-notch rear sight inletted into frame in front of hammer. It is not known whether this piece was stocked in factory or not. Plate 16, Fig. 1. $400–$525.

STOCKING & CO. PEPPERBOX, cal. .31, 6-shot; 4.375-inch, round, ribbed barrels. Iron guard with spur. Walnut grips. Hammer is pepperbox type, with spur added for facility in hand-cocking. Marked "Stocking & Co. Worcester. Warranted Cast Steel." Plate 16, Fig. 2. $270–$420.

SAME, but with 3.5-inch, round, ribbed barrels. $270–$380.

STOCKING & CO. PEPPERBOX, cal. .31, S.A.; 4-inch, round, ribbed barrels. Iron guard with spur. Walnut grips. Engraved. Hammer with spur for hand cocking. Plate 16, Fig. 3. $170–$255.

SAME, but cal. .28, 4.5-inch barrels. $170–$250.

SAME, but cal. .28, 3.5-inch barrels. Plate 16, Fig. 4. $180–$280.

STOCKING & CO. SINGLE-SHOT PISTOL, cal. .36, S.A.; 4-inch, part round, part octagon barrel. Iron guard. Walnut grips. Engraved iron frame. Hammer like pepperbox. Marked "Stocking & Co. Worcester, Warranted Cast Steel." Plate 16, Fig. 5. $140–$185.

SUTHERLAND UNDERHAMMER PISTOL, cal. .36, single-shot; 8.25-inch, part octagon, blued barrel marked "S. Sutherland, Richmond, Va." Total length 12.5 inches. Brass-post front sight. Raised-notch rear sight. No trigger guard. Peculiar maple handles. Samuel Sutherland was an importer, and not a manufacturer, but arms marked with his name are usually classified thus: Made in New England. $400–$525.

TRYON BOOTLEG PISTOL, cal. .31; 4-inch round-octagon barrel marked "Tryon Philada." Underhammer. Open rear sight. Bead front sight. Walnut grip. $240–$395.

TRYON DERRINGER, cal. .47; 4-inch, octagon, twist-steel barrel marked "E. K. Tryon Philada." Walnut stock. Checkered grip. Swivel iron ramrod. Engraved iron guard and thimble. Back-action lock, elaborately engraved. Plate 16, Fig. 6. $395–$500.

TRYON DERRINGER, cal. .41; 4.625-inch, round, flat-top barrel marked "Philadelphia." Back-action lock, engraved, marked "Tryon." Total length 8.625 inches. Walnut stock. German silver tip. Cap box in butt. Engraved iron guard. Rib under barrel with one thimble. Ivory ramrod. Plate 16, Fig. 7. $395–$500.

TRYON PISTOL, cal. .41, single-shot, 5.5-inch round barrel. Total length 10 inches. Lock plate marked "Tryon, Phila." Brass-tip front sight. Notch rear sight. Polished walnut handles. Stocked to one inch behind muzzle. Brass bands, trigger guard, and butt plate. Ramrod held by locking device. $285–$410.

TRYON PISTOL, cal. .52; 7.5-inch octagon barrel. Back-action lock. German silver stock tip, thimble, trigger guard, and wedge ornaments. Hammer and lock engraved. Walnut half-stock, checkered grip. Lock engraved "Tryon." British proof marks on underside of barrel. $285–$400.

TRYON PISTOL, cal. .45; 2.25-inch, round, steel barrel. Engraved brass frame and a smooth oval grip. Left side of frame engraved "Tryon" and right side engraved "Philadelphia." $285–$400.

TRYON PISTOL, cal. .31; 3-inch round barrel marked "Tryon." Center-hung hammer. Spur trigger. Walnut grips. $155–$200.

UNION ARMS CO.—See also Chapter 8.

UNION ARMS CO. REVOLVER, cal. .31, S.A., 5-shot; either round or octagon, 4.25-inch barrel marked "Union Arms Co. N. Y." Cylinder either fluted or plain. Total length 9.5 inches. Iron guard. Walnut grips. Blued. Engraved frame. Plate 16, Fig. 8. $240–$325.

UNION ARMS CO. REVOLVER, cal. .31, 6-shot; 5.5-inch round barrel marked "Union Arms Co. N. Y." Walnut grips. Iron guard and frame, engraved. Half-fluted cylinder. Resembles a Whitney. Plate 16, Fig. 9. $240–$325.

---

PLATE 16. American Percussion Pistols and Revolvers

Figure

1. Starr Revolver, stocked.
2. Stocking & Co. Pepperbox, cal. .31.
3. Stocking & Co. Pepperbox, cal. .31.
4. Stocking & Co. Pepperbox, cal. .28.
5. Stocking & Co. Single-Shot Pistol.
6. Tryon Derringer, cal. .47.
7. Tryon Derringer, cal. .41.
8. Union Arms Co. Revolver.
9. Union Arms Co. Revolver.
10. Union Arms Co. Revolver.
11. Walch 10-Shot Revolver, Iron Frame.
12. Washington Arms Co. Pepperbox.
13. Walch 10-Shot Revolver, Brass Frame.
14. Rollin White Pistol.
15. Whitney-Beal Ring-Trigger Pocket Revolver.
16. Whitney-Beal Ring-Trigger Pocket Revolver.
17. Whitney Hand-Turning 2-Trigger Revolver.
18. Whitney Center-Hammer Revolver.
19. A. Wurfflein Derringer, cal. .44.
20. A. Wurfflein Derringer, cal. .22.

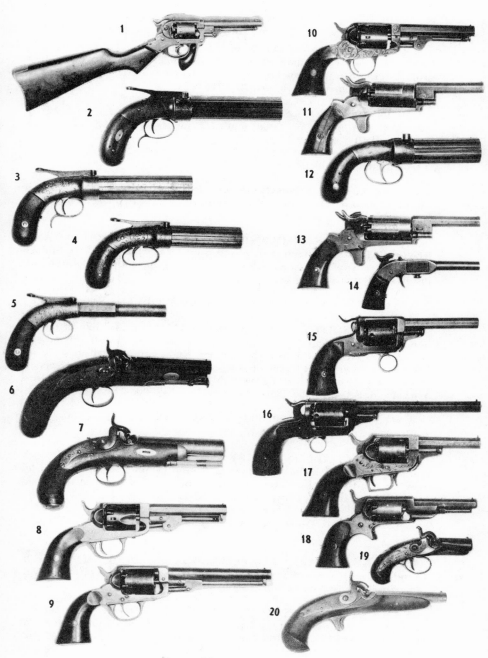

PLATE 16

UNION ARMS CO. REVOLVER, cal. .31, 5-shot; 4.375-inch octagon barrel marked "The Union Arms Co." Resembles a Remington. Walnut grips. Engraved frame. Loading lever casehardened in colors. Blued barrel, cylinder, and frame. Plate 16, Fig. 10. $275–$400.

UNION ARMS CO. 6-SHOT PEPPERBOX, cal. .31; 3.75-inch barrel marked "Union Arms Co." Total length 7.75 inches. Weight 1.5 lbs. Flat-top hammer. $240–$330.

SAME, but with 2-inch barrel. $240–$330.

UNION ARMS CO. SINGLE-SHOT PISTOL, cal. .31, D.A.; 2-inch round-octagon barrel marked "The Union Arms Co." Pepperbox hammer. $150–$195.

UNITED STATES ARMY AND NAVY PERCUSSION PISTOLS AND REVOLVERS—See Chapters 6, 7, and 8 on U. S. Martial and Secondary Martial Percussion Pistols and Revolvers, and Chapter 10 on Confederate Pistols and Revolvers.

WALCH 12-SHOT NAVY PERCUSSION REVOLVER—See Chapter 8.

WALCH 10-SHOT REVOLVER, IRON FRAME, cal. .31, 3.25-inch octagon barrel. Spur trigger. Two hammers. Cylinder is bored with 5 chambers; two charges are loaded into each chamber. Right hammer falls first, firing first charge. On second pull of trigger, left hammer falls, firing second charge. Made without loading lever. Marked "Walch Fire Arms Co. New York. Pat'd. Feb. 8, 1859." Plate 16, Fig. 11. $465–$700.

WALCH 10-SHOT REVOLVER, BRASS FRAME, like that above. 1,500 made. Plate 16, Fig. 13. $420–$675.

WARNER (CHARLES) POCKET REVOLVER, cal. .28, 6-shot, 3-inch round barrel; 7.25 inches total length. Round cylinder stamped "Charles Warner Windsor Locks, Conn." Rammer under barrel. Single-action, solid frame like that on James Warner models. $300–$465.

WARNER (JAMES)—See Springfield Arms Co., above, and also Chapter 8.

WASHINGTON ARMS CO. PEPPERBOX, cal. .31, 6-shot; 3.25-inch, round, ribbed barrels. Hammer marked "The Washington Arms Co." Walnut grips. Plate 16, Fig. 12. $225–$365.

WASHINGTON ARMS CO. PISTOL, cal. .31, 3-inch octagon barrel. Total length 6 inches. Weight 6 oz. Iron frame and guard. Walnut grips. Flat hammer marked "Washington Arms Co." $100–$140.

WASHINGTON ARMS CO. PISTOL, cal. .34, D.A.; 3-inch round-octagon barrel marked "Washington Arms Co." Iron guard. Walnut grips. Pepperbox hammer. $95–$145.

WASHINGTON ARMS CO. TARGET PISTOL, cal. .36; 6-inch round-octagon barrel marked "Washington Arms Co." Total length 10 inches. Weight 1 lb. $115–$165.

WATERS PISTOL—See Chapter 7.

WESSON & LEAVITT—See Massachusetts Arms Co., above.

WESTERN ARMS CO. REVOLVER, cal. .31, 6-shot; 4.5-inch octagon barrel marked "Western Arms Co. N. Y." Solid frame as in Remington. $240–$325.

WESTERN ARMS CO. REVOLVER, cal. .31, 6-shot, 4.25-inch round barrel marked "Western Arms Co. N. Y." made similar to the Bacon revolver, with a semi-fluted cylinder. $240–$325.

WHITE (L. B.) BOOTLEG PISTOL, cal. .31; 4.5-inch round-octagon barrel marked "L. B. White." Underhammer and trigger. Made without trigger guard. Walnut grip with silver inlay. $345–$455.

WHITE (ROLLIN) PISTOL, cal. .28, single-shot; 2.5-inch round barrel. Center-hung hammer. A rectangular block slides into frame from right to left. This block contains the chamber. Held in place by a setscrew under frame. Plate 16, Fig. 14. $240–$400.

WHITNEY-BEALS RING-TRIGGER POCKET REVOLVER, cal. .28, semi-D.A., 6-shot; 3-inch octagon barrel marked "Address E. Whitney, Whitneyville, Ct. F. Beals Patent, June 24, 1856." Total length 7.5 inches. Brass-post front sight. Grooved-framed rear sight. Center hammer. Polished hardwood handles. $390–$525.

WHITNEY-BEALS RING-TRIGGER POCKET REVOLVER, cal. .31, S.A., 7-shot; 3-inch octagon barrel. Total length 7.5 inches. Left side of cylinder has hood containing cylinder-revolving mechanism. Frame marked on side "F. Beals Patent Stp. 1854" and on top of frame "Address E. Whitney Whitneyville Ct." $300–$425.

SAME, but 4-inch barrel. Plate 16, Fig. 15. $300–$425.

SAME, but 6-inch octagon barrel. Plate 16, Fig. 16. $325–$475.

*Note: Above Whitney Revolvers are "Walking Beam" models.*

WHITNEY FIRST MODEL, BRASS-FRAME REVOLVER, cal. .28, 6-shot, with button release on frame to rear of hammer. Barrel marked "E. Whitney N. Haven Ct." Frame stamped "Patent Applied For." Very rare offset center hammer. Cylinder turns by hand. This model also made with a 3-inch barrel. $995–$1,285.

WHITNEY HAND-TURNING 2-TRIGGER REVOLVER, cal. .31, 5-inch octagon barrel. Total length 9.75 inches. Marked "E. Whitney, N. Haven, Ct. Patent Applied For." Square back; brass trigger guard. Cylinder stops are at front end of cylinder. The revolver is cocked, a trigger in front of the guard is pulled and the cylinder is then revolved. $475–$640.

SAME, but with brass frame. Plate 16, Fig. 17. $385–$525.

WHITNEY CENTER-HAMMER REVOLVER, cal. .28, 6-shot; 3.5-inch octagon barrel marked "E. Whitney. N. Haven." Spur trigger. Square grips. Sheathed trigger. Resembles Colt Model 1855. Plate 16, Fig. 18. $295–$440.

WHITNEY 5-SHOT POCKET REVOLVER, cal. .31, 5-inch barrel. Total length 9.875 inches. Weight 1.5 lbs. Marked "E. Whitney, N. Haven." $185–$340.

SAME, but 4-inch, half octagon barrel. Total length 8.75 inches. $185–$340.

SAME, but 6-inch barrel. Total length 10.875 inches. $195–$365.

WHITNEY 6-SHOT NAVY REVOLVER—See Chapter 8.

WINGERT UNDERHAMMER REVOLVER, cal. .44. Marked "Wm. Wingert, Detroit." $365–$525.

A. WURFFLEIN DUELING PISTOL, cal. .50, smoothbore; 9.75-inch, octagon, browned barrel marked "A. Wurfflein, Philad'a." Hair triggers. Total length 17.25 inches. French-style fluted handles. Half-stocked. Bands around barrel, breech and stock are key-fastened. Double sights. Silver name plate. All metal parts, such as hammer, butt plate, trigger guard, etc., are engraved. Each $525–$700.

A. WURFFLEIN DERRINGER, cal. .44; 3-inch, round, flat-top barrel marked "A. Wurfflein, Phila." Back-action lock. Short rib under barrel from stock to muzzle. German silver guard and mountings, engraved. Brass-tipped hickory ramrod. $450–$550.

SAME, but 2.125-inch, round, flat-top barrel. Plate 16, Fig. 19. $425–$630.

*Supplementary Texts*

The American percussion pistols and revolvers described and valued above include many of the most interesting of all firearms that are popular with collectors, but in order to buy and sell these weapons intelligently both collectors and dealers are referred to three other books by the author.

*Guns of the Old West,* published 1961 by Coward-McCann, Inc., contains a vast amount of illustrated material on derringers, dueling pistols, pepperboxes, underhammer pistols, bootleg pistols, alarm pistols, trap pistols, doorjamb pistols, and percussion revolvers.

*U.S. Martial and Semi-Martial Single-Shot Pistols,* published 1962 by Coward-McCann, Inc., also contains copious illustrated material on dueling pistols, percussion Kentucky pistols, and other single-shot percussion pistols.

*The Complete Guide to Gunsmithing,* published 1962 by A.S. Barnes & Co., Inc., is an illustrated text of 479 pages, which contains much technical information necessary for collectors and dealers who want to appraise firearms accurately.

Also the most recent book on the subject, *American Percussion Revolvers,* by Frank M. Sellers and Samuel E. Smith, published in 1971 by The Museum Restoration Service, Ottawa,Canada. It is completely illustrated and describes all known makes.

# Chapter 10

## CONFEDERATE PISTOLS AND REVOLVERS

ONFEDERATE pistols and revolvers, in the broad sense of the phrase, are all those pistols and revolvers made within the borders of the Confederate States of America, imported from foreign countries for Confederate use, bought or captured from the United States forces, or in the possession of Southern organizations or persons prior to the Civil War, and used by the Confederate forces, or by their allied irregular forces, against the armed forces of the United States of America during the Civil War, which tender-minded persons prefer to call the War Between the States.

In their desperation and poverty, the Confederates used any and all makes, models, types, modifications, and variations of every kind of firearm known to man. Therefore, everything from single-shot flintlock pistols and muskets to the latest repeating cartridge firearms were fired at the United States forces. The problem for the collector is not what firearms to include in a Confederate collection but what weapons to exclude. If the Confederates had marked every piece they used with names, initials, numbers, etc., which they did not do, the identification of genuine Confederate arms would still be difficult because any dishonest person could stamp "C.S.A." on any firearm made before 1865 and sell it for a profit as a "Confederate weapon." In fact, many people are doing exactly that today.

Genuine Confederate firearms are rare. Until a few years before the publication of this revised edition of *The Gun Collector's Handbook of Values,* the values of Confederate arms were not in proportion to their rarity because of the demand was comparatively low. The Civil War Centennial of 1961–1965; the publication of many magazine and newspaper articles about the Civil War, and especially the publi-

134

cation of thousands of books about the Civil War, created a demand for all firearms used in the Civil War, including Confederate weapons.

Confederate soldiers, sailors, and marines in many instances owned their own firearms and took them with them when they joined the great migration into the cities and ranches of the then "Far West" at the close of the Civil War. These firearms are described and illustrated in *Guns of the Old West,* by the author of this text.

In the author's book *U.S. Martial and Semi-Martial Single-Shot Pistols,* thirty pages are devoted to strictly Confederate single-shot pistols, both percussion and cartridge.

Since the above books were published in 1961 and in 1962, during the Civil War Centennial, the demand for Confederate firearms has greatly increased. When great demand is coupled with scarcity, values increase materially.

The Confederate pistols and revolvers described and valued in this chapter are what may be called "strictly Confederate" weapons. In other words, these are the ones about which there is no argument among collectors, dealers, and historians.

The armed forces of the Confederacy captured from the armed forces of the United States forts, arsenals, warehouses, ships, and other sources for supplying themselves with every conceivable type, make, and model of weapons, including, of course, pistols, revolvers, carbines, rifles, and shot guns. Therefore, many of the weapons described in this text in the chapters on U.S. Martial Percussion Pistols, American Secondary Martial Percussion Pistols, American Martial Percussion Revolvers, and American Percussion Pistols and Revolvers (Chapters 6, 7, 8, and 9) were used by the Confederacy.

In addition to the firearms captured in wholesale lots, mentioned above, thousands of firearms were captured in battle by the Confederates. For example, the First Battle of Bull Run was a disaster to the Union Army but a bonanza for the Confederates.

Here we run into a very complex job of deciding how to classify, identify, and value the firearms taken by the armed forces of the Confederacy from the armed forces of the United States. This problem is explored in detail in the author's book, *U.S. Martial and Semi-Martial Single-Shot Pistols.* It can be summarized here by briefly stating that a Confederate weapon is a Confederate firearm according

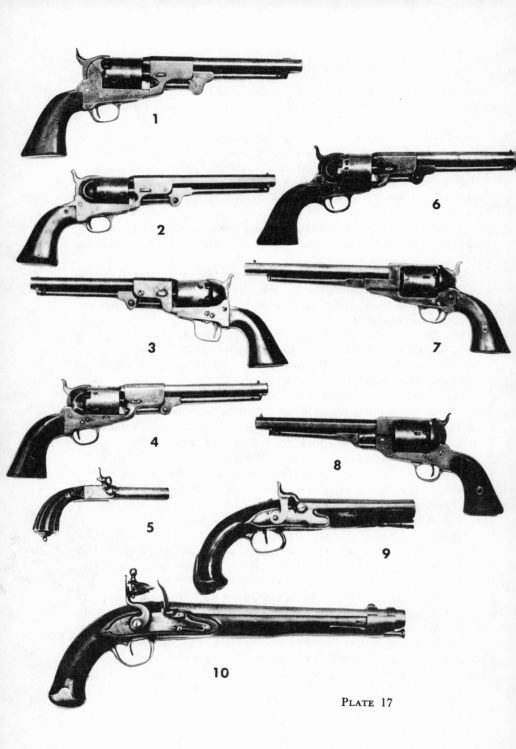

PLATE 17

to its use by the Confederates during the Civil War and not where it was made or how it was obtained. The danger of the collector or dealer acquiring what he believes to be genuine Confederate weapons when they are otherwise genuine, but not Confederate, is one of the reasons for describing and giving values for comparatively few Confederate pistols and revolvers in this chapter. The other reason is that a book on gun *values* cannot include voluminous explanations without defeating the purpose for its publication.

The Civil War marked a transition period in the development of firearms. Muzzle-loading, single-shot, percussion firearms were being displaced by breech-loading, multi-shot, cartridge weapons. This transition was already taking place before the Civil War began, but hostilities hastened the transition.

Many of the Colt revolvers described in Chapters 11, 12, and 13 of this book were used by the Confederates, and the same statement applied to subsequent chapters on hand guns and shoulder weapons, but it is apparent that no firearm made after the close of the Civil War in 1865 can be regarded as Confederate.

T.W. COFER PERCUSSION REVOLVER, cal. .36, 6-shot; 7-inch rifled barrel marked "T.W. Cofer's Patent, Portsmouth, Va." Brass frame stamped "E.B. Georgia." Rifled with 7 grooves, right. The Confederate Patent Office issued a patent for this revolver to Thomas W. Cofer, Aug. 12, 1861. $4,500–$8,500.

COLUMBUS FIRE ARMS MFG. CO. PERCUSSION REVOLVER, cal. .36, 6-shot; 7.5-inch barrel marked "Columbus Fire Arms Manuf. Co., Columbus." Trigger guard plate marked "C.S." Serial number in various places. Brass trigger guard, front sight, and handle strap. Made at Colum-

---

PLATE 17. Confederate Pistols and Revolvers

*Figure*

1. Dance Brothers cal. .44 Percussion Revolver.
2. Dimick-Colt Percussion Revolver.
3. Griswold & Gunnison Percussion Revolver.
4. Leech & Rigdon Percussion Revolver.
5. Radcliffe & Guignard Percussion Pocket Pistol.
6. Rigdon & Ansley Percussion Revolver.
7. Shawk & McLanahan Percussion Revolver.
8. Spiller & Burr Percussion Revolver.
9. Samuel Sutherland Percussion Pistol.
10. Virginia Manufactory Flintlock Pistol.

bus, Ga., by Louis and Elias Haiman. Resembles the Leech & Rigdon revolvers but is of poorer workmanship. However, this company did produce some outstandingly fine revolvers. $3,000–$5,000.

DANCE BROTHERS PERCUSSION REVOLVER, cal. .44; 8-inch, part octagon, rifled barrel. Brass trigger guard, back strap, and blade front sight. Flat frame. No recoil shield. No rear sight. Serial number 89 on various parts of specimen illustrated. Not marked. Made at Columbia, Texas, 1863–64. Exceedingly rare. Plate 17, Fig. 1. $2,115–$3,335.

DANCE BROTHERS NAVY PERCUSSION REVOLVER, cal. .36; 6-inch, part octagon barrel. Flat frame. No recoil shield. Serial number on several parts otherwise not marked. Made at Columbia, Texas, 1863–1864. $2,100–$3,200.

DIMICK-COLT PERCUSSION REVOLVER, cal. .36, 6-shot; 7.5-inch rifled barrel marked "H.E. Dimick, St. Louis." Total length 14 inches. Brass front sight, trigger guard, and strap. Historians believe that this was made for Dimick by the Manhattan Fire Arms Co. Plate 17, Fig. 2. $925–$1,200.

GRISWOLD & GUNNISON PERCUSSION REVOLVER, cal. .36, 6-shot; 7.5-inch barrel, rifled with 6 grooves, right. Brass frame. Unmarked except for serial numbers. Known as Brass-Frame Confederate Colt to some collectors and dealers. Made near Macon, at Griswoldville, Georgia. Confederate newspapers called this a "Colt's Navy Repeater." Plate 17, Fig. 3. $1,250–$1,850.

HAIMAN REVOLVER—See Columbus Fire Arms Mfg. Co., above.

LEECH & RIGDON PERCUSSION REVOLVER, cal. .36, 6-shot; 7.5-inch rifled barrel marked "Leech & Rigdon, C.S.A." Brass front sight, trigger guard, and handle strap. Some specimens marked "Leech & Rigdon" without the C.S.A. The manufacturer made imitation Colt Navy revolvers. The factory was moved from Memphis, Tenn., to Columbus, Miss., and from there to Greensboro, Ga., and finally to Augusta, Ga., because of the approach of the United States Army in each case. Also see Rigdon & Ansley Revolver, below. Plate 17, Fig. 4. $1,575–$2,285.

LEECH & CO. C.S.A. PERCUSSION REVOLVER, cal. .36, 6-shot; 7.5-inch round barrel marked "Leech & Co. CSA." Brass mounted and steel frame. Made by Thomas Leech in Greensboro, Georgia, in 1864 after he and Charles Rigdon dissolved partnership. One of the rarest of all Confederate revolvers. $2,310–$3,185.

PALMETTO ARMORY PERCUSSION PISTOL, cal. .54; 8.5-inch barrel marked "1852." Lock plate marked "Palmetto Armory Columbia S.C." with palmetto tree. Brass hardware. Manufactured by William Glaze & Co., Columbia, S.C., in 1852, under contract with the State of South Carolina. Beware of fakes! $575–$865.

RADCLIFFE & GUIGNARD PERCUSSION POCKET PISTOL, cal. .44, single-shot; 3-inch, round, rifled barrel. Total length 7 inches. Engraved iron mountings. Folding trigger. An example of the type of pocket pistol sold in the Confederacy during the Civil War. Plate 17, Fig. 5. $300–$410.

RAPPAHANNOCK FORGE FLINTLOCK PISTOL, cal. .65; 8.75-inch barrel usually marked "J. Hunter." Total length 13 inches. Brass butt plate, trigger guard, and thimble. Iron ramrod. Lock plate marked "Rapa Forge." Some specimens are marked on lock plate with an organization designation, such as "A.L.D." (Albemarle Light Dragoons), followed by a serial number assigned to the weapon by the organization. The butt plate may bear organization marks, such as "3 Rgt" (3rd Regiment). Also see the description of this pistol in Chapter 4 on U. S. Secondary Martial Flintlock Pistols. $9,500–$15,500.

SAME, but converted to percussion. $6,750–$9,000.

RIGDON & ANSLEY PERCUSSION REVOLVER, cal. .36, 6-shot; 7.5-inch rifled barrel marked on top "Augusta, Ga. C.S.A." There are 12 cylinder stops. Brass trigger guard, front sight, and handle strap. Serial numbers are on the cylinder, trigger guard frame, barrel lug, handle strap, and loading lever. Plate 17, Fig. 6. See also Chapter 11 for description of second type of this revolver. $2,100–$3,150.

SHAWK & McLANAHAN PERCUSSION REVOLVER, cal. .36, 6-shot; 8-inch round barrel. Brass frame. Back strap marked "Shawk & McLanahan, St. Louis, Carondelet, Mo." Manufactured about 1858–1859 at Carondelet, St. Louis, Missouri. Most specimens have a serial number inside the trigger guard frame. Plate 17, Fig. 7. $2,325–$3,250.

SPILLER & BURR PERCUSSION REVOLVER, cal. .36, 6-shot; 7-inch octagon barrel marked "Spiller & Burr." Resembles a Whitney. The letters "C.S." followed by the serial number are usually found on various parts, such as the cylinder, the underside of the barrel, underside of the frame, the loading lever, and the grip strap. Plate 17, Fig. 8. $1,800–$2,250.

SAMUEL SUTHERLAND PERCUSSION PISTOL, cal. .60, single-shot, 6.25-inch, octagon, brass barrel. Lock plate marked "Sutherland Richmond." This was a French flintlock pistol converted to percussion by Sutherland during the Civil War. Plate 17, Fig. 9. $500–$650.

TUCKER & SHERROD PERCUSSION REVOLVER, cal. .44; 7.5-inch, part octagon, rifled barrel. Unmarked except for serial number on various parts. Silver stars and other decorations are set in the grips of some specimens. No loading aperture on right side of frame. Copied from Colt Dragoon Revolver. Made at Lancaster, Texas. $2,800–$4,165.

VIRGINIA MANUFACTORY FLINTLOCK PISTOL, cal. .69, 12.5-inch barrel. Total length 17.5 inches. Iron mountings. Lock plate of specimen illustrated is marked "Richmond 1807" in rear of hammer. See Chapter 4 on U.S. Secondary Martial Flintlock Pistols for a more complete description of this pistol. Plate 17, Fig. 10. $2,600–$3,500.

SAME, but converted to percussion. $1,850–$2,400.

## Warning Regarding Values of Confederate Arms.

The above values are for specimens that are genuine Confederate arms beyond any doubt. Any dishonest person with a slight degree of ability can etch, engrave, chisel, or stamp "C.S.A.," or similar Confederate marks, on metal or wooden parts, or cause the same to be done. Only an expert on Confederate firearms can accurately distinguish a genuine piece from a fake. Unfortunately, there are very few experts on Confederate firearms in the world. Values on most Confederate firearms decreased due to the fact that the Civil War Centennial has passed, and it had a great influence on the demand for these arms. Recently values have again resumed an upward trend like all gun collector specimens.

# Chapter 11

## COLT PERCUSSION REVOLVERS

PATERSON COLT revolvers, sometimes called Paterson pistols, were marked "Patent Arms M'g Co. Paterson, N.J. Colt's Pt." on the barrel, although minor variations, such as "Colt Pt." instead of "Colt's Pt." are found. Those bearing low serial numbers were hand-engraved, but those with higher serial numbers, which were made later, were stamped with a die. The size of the letters is approximately in proportion to the size of the revolver, that is, the letters on the larger revolvers are slightly larger and more spread out than those on the smaller revolvers. A very few genuine specimens have been found which were never marked on the barrel, but the beginner should regard the absence of the barrel marking with caution.

The usual calibers were .28, .31, .34, and .36, but these were nominal calibers, that is, they were the calibers used by Colt in describing his arms, and corresponded to the Colt bullet mold designations for the round-ball bullets for which the Paterson revolvers were made. A ball cast from a cal. .36 Colt mold is almost 0.375-inch in diameter, hence the cal. .36 revolver was actually cal. .375. When it became worn the barrel might have a 0.40-inch bore, hence dealers and collectors have thought that some of the revolvers were made cal. .40, whereas they were probably designated as cal. .36 by Colt. On the other hand, Colt made many special-order revolvers, and it is therefore possible that some revolvers were made cal. .40, or very close to that size. In this text, the calibers given as .40 actually measure 0.40-inch in bore diameter.

Paterson Colt revolvers were *revolvers*. They were made with revolving cylinders, and all cylinders had five chambers, hence they were 5-shot revolvers. The word *pistol* has been applied to revolvers frequently, and also to repeating handguns which were not revolv-

141

ers, therefore there is no harm in using the word pistol, but to some beginners it suggests a single-shot weapon.

Paterson Colt revolvers were described in early Colt advertisements as Pocket Pistols, Belt Pistols, and Holster Pistols.

Pocket pistols are normally .28, .31, or .34 caliber; and their barrel lengths are usually 2.5, 3, 3.5, 4, 4.5, or 4.75 inches, although a few other lengths have been found. The grip and frame are smaller than on the belt and holster models. The original finish was a dark charcoal blue. This pocket model is almost never found with elaborate engraving, and rarely with any engraving other than the standard factory marking. The cylinder is engraved with a centaur scene, and the word "Colt" within a rectangle. Some were made with loading levers and some were made without. It is probable that pocket pistols were made without loading levers before 1840, and that about that year the factory began to make them with loading levers. In general, those with loading levers have only rounded cylinders and those without loading levers have only straight cylinders.

Belt pistols are normally either cal. .31 or cal. .34, and the barrel lengths range between 4 and 6 inches, although a few, especially in cased sets, were made with an extra 12-inch barrel, usually in the case and not on the pistol. Barrel lengths such as 4, 4.25, 4.5, 4.75, 5, and 5.5 inches are comparatively common, but the 6-inch length is relatively rare. The frame may be as small as it is on the larger pocket pistols, but generally it is larger. The cylinder is engraved with a centaur scene, and "Colt" within a rectangle is usually found. The original finish was dark blue steel. These belt pistols are rarely found with elaborate engraving, and very few were made with a loading lever. Those with a loading lever have rounded cylinders.

Holster pistols are all caliber .36. The barrel lengths are 4, 4.5, 5, 5.5, 6, 7.5, 9, and 12 inches, although the majority are either 7.5 or 9 inches. The frame and grip are large. The standard factory grip was plain walnut, made in two pieces, but on special order the grip was often checkered, and some were made of ivory or pearl, carved to meet the requirements of the customer. The cylinder is engraved with a stagecoach holdup scene. The original standard factory finish was a dark charcoal blue, except that the hammer was casehardened in natural colors. On special order, these holster pistols were elaborately engraved, inlaid, and otherwise decorated. The majority were made without loading levers. The cylinder pins are found in large and small sizes. The barrel wedge (key) may have a simple groove or it may have a spring catch. This holster pistol is often called the Texas pistol because of its widespread use there, but this term has been applied rather loosely to all Paterson Colt revolvers of large caliber and size.

All Paterson Colt revolvers generally known to collectors have serial numbers under 1,000, and low serial numbers are found on pocket, belt, and holster models, except that holster pistols made with loading levers have relatively high serial numbers. Many authorities believe that each of the three models or types (pocket, belt, and holster) had its own system of numbers, starting with number 1, and that the total number of Paterson Colt revolvers manufactured was about 2,000. Most authorities doubt that serial numbers were duplicated within a group or type, but a few collectors seem to believe that some were numbered in pairs, with both revolvers in a pair having the same serial number. There is very little evidence to support the latter assumption as a general method of numbering.

The concealed folding trigger, which snaps out when the piece is brought to the full cock, is an outstanding characteristic of the Paterson Colt revolvers, although it was retained after the closing of the factory at Paterson, and was used until 1847 by Colt on later non-Paterson models. The absence of a trigger guard is another characteristic of the revolvers made with a folding trigger.

Although we have attempted to present the characteristics of the pocket, belt, and holster models or types, it must be clearly understood that there was considerable overlapping. Each caliber was made in a variety of barrel lengths, and with handles of different sizes and shapes. There may be round- or square-cornered butts, round-back or straight cylinders, centaur or stagecoach marking on the cylinder, plain or chamfered cylinders, and either an octagonal breech or a round barrel with an octagonal breech. Since the Paterson Colt revolvers were hand-finished, and often made to special order, they were not mechanically standardized in all respects, even though their parts were usually interchangeable.

These Colt percussion revolvers made at Paterson, New Jersey, are described and discussed in the author's books listed in the Bibliography, particularly *The Complete Book of Gun Collecting; U.S. Martial and Semi-Martial Single-Shot Pistols;* and *Guns of the Old West.* These three books also contain descriptions, discussions, and illustrations of other Colt firearms. Books by James E. Serven and other authorities on Colt firearms are in the Bibliography.

The Patent Arms Manufacturing Company of Paterson, New Jersey, was granted a charter on March 5, 1836, and began to manufacture revolving firearms that year. In 1842 the corporation went into bankruptcy. Since it is reasonably certain that no arms were made there after 1841, the Paterson-made models are usually designated as Models 1836–1841.

In certain sizes, calibers, and barrel lengths, some of the revolvers made at Paterson can be classified as U.S. martial and U.S. secondary martial percussion revolvers. The Colt percussion revolvers in this chapter are typical, representative specimens and not those made on special order.

## PATERSON COLT MODELS 1836–1841

Cal. .28, 5-shot, 3-inch octagon barrel. Made with loading lever, which is a rare feature. Walnut grips. Cylinder stops between nipples are rounded and not square. Nipple shields are rounded. Loading lever held in place by a hook-shaped spring as in the Walker model. Cylinder engraved with a centaur scene and "Colt" in a rectangle. Total length about 7 inches. This is supposed to have been the last model and type made by Colt at the original factory. Plate 18, Fig. 2. $3,650–$4,875.

Cal. .28, 5-shot, 4-inch octagon barrel. Made without loading lever. Walnut grips. Rounded cylinder stops. Total length not quite 8 inches. Cylinder engraved with centaur scene and "Colt" in rectangle. This was an earlier model than that described above. Colt specialists made a distinction between two types of this 4-inch-barrel model, but there is apparently no appreciable difference in value. Not illustrated. $3,400–$4,950.

Cal. .28, 5-shot, 4.25-inch barrel, marked "Patent Arms M'g. Co. Paterson N.J. Colt's Pt." Concealed trigger. Walnut grips. Two rounded bands extend around cylinder, formed by the narrow grooves running parallel around the circumference of the cylinder. Between these rounded bands the cylinder is engraved with a scene showing centaurs firing revolvers. The word "Colt" is in a rectangle between the beginning and the end of the centaur scene. Round cylinder stops. Low blade front sight. Rear sight on hammer nose. Shoulders between nipples are rounded. Plate 18, Fig. 3. $3,250–$4,700.

Cal. .31, 5-shot. The barrel length in the usual specimen varies from about 4.25 inches to about 4.75 inches, and the total length is usually from 8 inches to 8.5 inches, approximately. Octagon barrel. Walnut grips. Cylinder engraved with centaur scene and "Colt." Made without loading lever, as were most Paterson models and types except where specifically stated otherwise. Weight of 4.75-inch-barrel revolver is about 1 lb. 4 oz. Nipple separations are square, not rounded. Early specimens of this model were chamfered at the muzzles of the chambers, and later specimens lack the chamfering, but there appears to be no effect on values by reason of chamfering or its lack. Not illustrated. $3,450–$4,625.

Cal. .31, 5-shot, 4.75-inch octagon barrel, same as specimen described above but cased in original Paterson Colt mahogany case with extra cylinder, bullet mold, combination tool, cleaning rod, priming device (capper), and combination bullet and powder flask, all of which are original Paterson products, one or more bearing the Paterson Colt markings. Plate 19, Fig. 2. $6,500–$8,750.

Cal. .34, 5-shot, 4.75-inch barrel, total length 7.6 inches. Chambers are not chamfered. Cylinder engraved with the usual centaur scene. Walnut grips. Weight 1 lb. 3 oz. Not illustrated. $2,750–$3,650.

Cal. .36, 5-shot, 9-inch octagon barrel. Straight cylinder with two grooves, 0.687-inch apart, around the circumference of the cylinder. Between these grooves is an engraved stagecoach holdup scene instead of the usual centaur scene and this holdup scene is different from that which appears on later models. The word "Colt" in Roman-type letters appears in the rectangle outlining the scene. The shoulders between the nipples are rounded and not square as in some specimens. Chambers are chamfered at the front. Concealed trigger. Made without a loading lever. Plate 18, Fig. 1. $5,100–$7,000.

SAME, but made with loading lever. Not illustrated separately, and see below. $6,000–$7,500.

Cal. .36, 5-shot, 9-inch octagon barrel, marked "Patent Arms M'g. Co. Paterson N. J. Colt's Pt." Cased. Concealed trigger. Made with loading lever under barrel, with hook-shaped spring catch as on Walker model. In original Paterson Colt case with Paterson-made accessories, including an extra cylinder, bullet mold, priming device (capper), combination tool, and combination bullet and powder flask. At least two of the items bear Paterson marks. One-piece ivory grips carved with shell design at rounded top section. Plate 19, Fig. 4. $12,500–$19,500.

Cal. .36, 5-shot, 4.75-inch barrel, concealed trigger, and all the other usual Paterson Colt characteristics. Cased with Paterson-made mold, extra cylinder, combination tool, priming device, combination powder and bullet flask, cleaning rod, and an extra 12-inch barrel, all in the original Paterson case. The case is not illustrated. Plate 18, Fig. 4. $14,000–$22,500.

Cal. .40, 5-shot, 9-inch barrel. Total length 14.4 inches. Chambers are not chamfered as in other barrel lengths of this caliber. There is no hole in the nose of the hammer as there is in the case of those of other barrel lengths. Weight 2 lbs. 6.5 oz. Cylinder engraved with stagecoach holdup scene. Not illustrated. $5,875–$8,500.

Cal. .40, 5-shot, 4.7-inch barrel. Total length 10.3 inches. Weight 2 lbs. 3.5 oz. Chambers are chamfered. There is a hole in the nose of the hammer for the safety. Otherwise same as above. Not illustrated. $3,000–$4,500.

Cal. .40, 5-shot, 7.5-inch barrel. Total length 13 inches. Weight 2 lb. 11 oz. Chamfered chambers and hole in hammer for the safety. Otherwise same as the above. Not illustrated. $4,750–$6,750.

## WHITNEYVILLE WALKER MODEL 1847

*Note: This model was made at Whitneyville, Conn.*

COLT ARMY REVOLVER, MODEL 1847, also called Colt-Walker Model 1847, Whitneyville Walker, and Walker Pistol. Made for Colt at Whitneyville, Conn. Cal. .44, 6-shot, S.A.; 9-inch round barrel with octagon breech; total length 15.5 inches. Weight 4 lbs. 9 oz. Straight round cylinder, usually engraved with scene of battle between Indians and dragoons. Oval slots. Hinged-lever ramrod. Spring cramp latch which may be attached to barrel forward of joint. Square-back brass trigger guard. Iron back strap. Frame

---

PLATE 18. Paterson Colt Revolvers

Figure

1. Paterson Colt Revolver, "Texas" Model of 1836, cal. .36, 5-shot, 9-inch octagon barrel, concealed trigger, and straight cylinder engraved with a stagecoach holdup scene instead of the usual centaurs.

2. Paterson Colt Revolver, cal. .28, 5-shot, 3-inch octagon barrel, concealed trigger, and cylinder engraved with the usual centaur scene. Loading lever and rammer are permanently attached to the barrel. Loading lever is held in place by a hook-shaped spring as in the Walker model.

3. Paterson Colt Revolver, cal. .28, 5-shot, 4.25-inch barrel marked "Patent Arms M'g. Co. Paterson N. J. Colt's Pt." Concealed trigger. Cylinder engraved with centaurs firing revolvers.

4. Paterson Colt Revolver, cal. .36, 5-shot, 4.75-inch barrel, concealed trigger, and usual markings. Cased with mold, extra cylinder, combination tool, priming device, combination powder and bullet flask, cleaning rod, and extra 12-inch barrel in original Paterson Colt case (not shown).

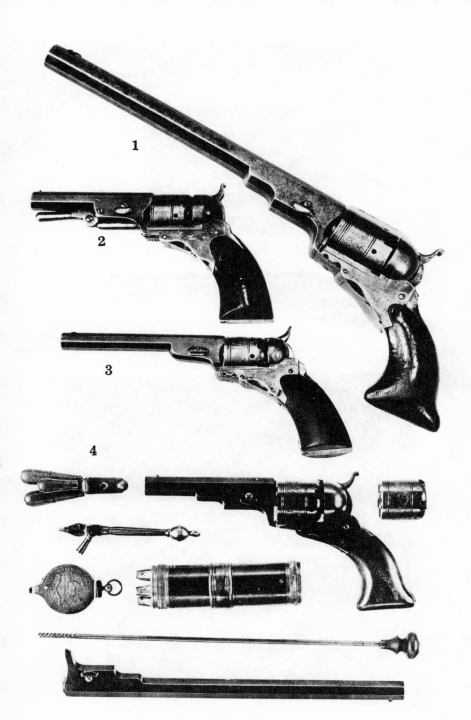

PLATE 18

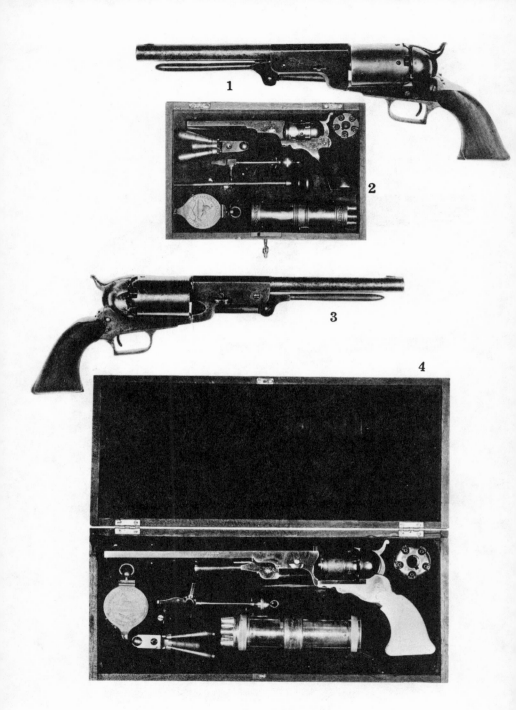

PLATE 19

may be oval where joined by the grips, square at the back, or the Whitney-ville type. Blade and hammer-notch sights. Barrel marked on top "Address Sam'l Colt, New York City," on the right "U.S. 1847," and on most speci-mens marked on left side with designation such as "A Company 53." Cylin-der marked "Colt's Patent Model U.S.M.R." Frame may be marked like left side of barrel, such as "A Company 53." Walnut grips. Cylinder revolves to right. Made with loading lever held up by catch spring under barrel. Be-cause of military use, this weapon is rarely found with much original finish or very clear marks. Collectors usually distinguish between the regular mod-el and the square-frame model, and especially notice whether there is a side-hook latch, a Dragoon latch, or a Navy latch. This weapon may be classified as a U.S. martial percussion revolver. Plate 19, Figs. 1 and 3. $11,000–$21,500.

# HARTFORD COLT MODELS:

*Note: From here to the London-made Colts (below), all Colt arms mentioned, both percussion and cartridge, were made at Hartford, Connecticut.*

---

PLATE 19. Colt Army Model 1847 and Paterson Colt
Revolvers

*Figure*

1. Army Revolver, Model 1847, also called Colt-Walker Model 1847, Whitneyville Walker, and Walker Pistol, with square-back trigger guard.

2. Paterson Revolver, cal. .31, 5-shot, 4.75-inch octagon barrel, one-piece walnut grips, folding trigger, round cylinder stops and cylinder engraved with centaur scene and marked "Colt." The flash shields between the nipples are not rounded. In original Paterson Colt mahogany case with extra cylinder, bullet mold, combina-tion tool, cleaning rod, priming de-vice (capper), combination bullet and powder flask.

3. Army Model 1847, also called Colt-Walker, and Walker Pistol, with square-back trigger guard. The reg-ular rammer catch was removed from this specimen, and a spring fitted into the side of the rammer. This spring bears against the front of the hole through the barrel lug. The specimen illustrated conforms otherwise to the description in the text.

4. Paterson "Texas" Model with Load-ing Lever, cased, cal. .36, 5-shot, 9-inch octagon barrel marked "Patent Arms M'g. Co. Paterson N.J. Colt's Pt." Concealed trigger. Made with loading lever under spring catch as on Walker model. In original Pater-son Colt case with extra cylinder, mold, priming device, combination tool, and combination bullet and powder flask, all original.

COLT ARMY REVOLVER, MODEL 1848, also known as the Improved Holster Pistol, the Old Model Holster Pistol, the Old Model Army Pistol, Model of 1848 Holster Pistol, the Dragoon Colt, and the No. 1 Dragoon. This revolver has more names than the average fellow traveler for the Russian Communists. Cal. .44 6-shot, S.A.; 7.5-inch round barrel, semi-octagon at rear, and rifled with seven grooves. Total length 14 inches. Weight 4 lbs. 1 oz. Cylinder is 2.188 inches long, with round stops. Brass trigger guard is square at the rear. Brass back strap. Low-blade white brass front sight set into the barrel. V-notch rear sight in hammer lip. The frame is straight at its back where it joins the grips. Walnut grips. Not cut for shoulder stock. Loading lever hinged on a screw in front of the wedge, and held to the barrel by a spring snap catch, sometimes called a Dragoon-type latch. Octagon part of barrel marked on top "Address Saml Colt. New York City." Cylinder engraved with a scene of a battle between soldiers and Indians, and it also may bear the name of the engraver and the abbreviation for the word *sculpsit,* thus: "W.L. Ormsby Sc.," although the Sc. may be missing. Cylinder may be marked "Model U.S.M.I. Colt's Patent" instead of the Ormsby name. Frame marked "Colt's Patent" and "U.S." on left side. The same serial number may be found on the cylinder, frame, loading lever, trigger guard, and grip frame. If serial numbers vary, all parts are probably not original parts of that particular revolver. Superficially, this Model 1848 resembles the Model 1847, but this model has a shorter cylinder and barrel, weighs less, and has a better catch spring for the loading lever. Specialists recognize the following three principal variations, modifications, or models as you may be pleased to call them:

1. Square-back trigger guard. Rounded cylinder-stop recesses. Vertical loading-lever latch. Plate 20, Fig. 3. $1,250–$2,700.
2. Trigger guard usually oval but sometimes square-backed, as before. Rectangular cylinder-stop recesses. Loading-lever latch is horizontal instead of vertical. Plate 20, Fig. 4. $1,250–$3,500.
3. Trigger guard oval and rectangular cylinder stops. $1,100–$2,100.

   a. Same, equipped with shoulder stock, with numbers matching. (Walnut, iron butt plate, sling ring, and yoke.) $2,575–$3,325.
   b. Same, equipped with shoulder stock, but numbers not matching. $2,100–$2,850.
   c. Same, equipped with shoulder stock with canteen in the butt, and with numbers on stock and revolver corresponding. $3,500–$4,750.
   d. Shoulder stock only, 17.625 inches long, without canteen. Plate 20, Fig. 6. $665–$950.
   e. Shoulder stock only, with canteen in butt. $1,200–$1,750.

*Note: Cylinders are sometimes engraved "U.S. Dragoons" or "U.S. Navy" instead of "U.S.M.R." The presence of one of these unusual markings adds to the value.*

## Variation from Conventional Construction

Made with oval trigger guard and vertical loading-lever latch. There are English proof marks on the barrel and cylinder in addition to the usual Dragoon markings. Plate 20, Fig. 2. $950–$1,650.

Summing up the details observed by advanced collectors, we find that the cylinder may be round or fluted, the cylinder stops may be round (oval) or rectangular; the barrel is usually 7.5 inches long, but it may be 8 inches long; the trigger guard may be oval or square-backed; there may be no safety pins or hammer roller, or there may be safety pins and a hammer roller; the latch may be either the Dragoon type or the Navy type; the revolver may be either cut for stock or not cut for stock; and the barrel may be round with an octagon breech or both round and octagon in its length. Furthermore, combinations and permutations of any or all of these variations may be found in the same specimen, to the great delight of overgrown boys who should be collecting stamps and not guns. The normal gun collector will be happy if he knows that he has a genuine specimen of this colorful revolver which has played an important part in our American history.

COLT OLD MODEL POCKET PISTOL, also called Model of 1848 Pocket Pistol, Baby Dragoon, Model 1848 Baby Dragoon, and Model 1848 Pocket Revolver. Cal. .31, 5-shot, 3-inch octagon barrel, total length 8 inches, weight about 1 lb. 4 oz. Square-back brass trigger guard. No loading lever or latch. No bearing wheel (roll) on hammer. One safety pin between chambers. Brass back strap. Trigger guard and back strap sometimes found silver-plated. Round or oval cylinder stops. Straight, round cylinder; may be engraved with scene of a stagecoach holdup, although some specimens have battle between Indians and soldiers. Barrel and cylinder were originally blued on some specimens. Brass-pin and hammer-notch sights. Barrel marked "Address Sam'l Colt, New York City." Cylinder marked "Colt's Patent" with the serial number. Frame marked "Colt's Patent." Trigger guard not marked. Usual specimen has walnut grips, although ivory grips were available on special order. $750–$1,165.

SAME, with 4-inch barrel. $710–$1,115.

SAME, but with 5-inch barrel. $725–$1,185.

SAME, but with 6-inch barrel. $810–$1,245.

SAME, but made later, with 3-inch barrel, with a loading lever (ramrod) similar to the Colt Model 1849 Pocket Revolver. $660–$1,025.

SAME, with 4-inch barrel, and loading lever. $665–$1,045.

SAME, with 5-inch barrel, and loading lever. $675–$1,060.

SAME, with 6-inch barrel, and loading lever. $675–$1,115.

The specimen illustrated has a 5-inch octagon barrel, square-back trigger guard, oval cylinder stops and is made without a loading lever. Plate 20, Fig. 1. $735–$1,260.

COLT MODEL 1849 POCKET REVOLVER, also called Improved Pocket Pistol, Old Model Pocket Pistol, and Model of 1849 Pocket Pistol. Details observed by collectors are the regular model, the squareback trigger guard, the round barrel, the stagecoach holdup engraving, and barrel lengths from 4 to 6 inches. Values are indicated below. Square-back model, 1849. $695–$1,080.

MODEL 1849 POCKET REVOLVER, cal. .31, 5-shot, 3-inch octagon barrel. Round trigger guard. Made without loading lever. Silver-plated guard and straps. Rectangular cylinder stops. This type is sometimes called the Wells Fargo Model. Plate 21, Fig. 1. $750–$1,205.

*Note on so-called Wells Fargo Model: Collectors and dealers have often applied the term Wells Fargo to certain Colt models, but both the recognized Colt and the established Wells Fargo historians agree that there was never any single, exclusive Wells Fargo Colt model, type, modification, or variation, and that certain Remington models are just as much entitled to be termed Wells Fargo as any of the Colts.*

SAME, but cal. .31, 5-shot, 6-inch octagon barrel, brass guard and straps. Trigger guard has square back. Plate 21, Fig. 2. $710–$1,185.

SAME, but cal. .31, 5-shot, 6-inch octagon barrel, engraved "Saml. Colt." Silver-plated oval trigger guard and straps. All metal parts elaborately deco-

---

PLATE 20. Colt Old Model Pocket Pistol; Army Revolver,
Model 1848; and Shoulder Stock for Model 1848

*Figure*

1. Old Model Pocket Pistol, also called Baby Dragoon, etc., 5-inch octagon barrel, square-back trigger guard, oval cylinder stops, and made without a loading lever.
2. Army Revolver, Model 1848, also known as the Dragoon Colt, etc.; oval guard, vertical loading-lever latch, usual Dragoon markings, but with English proof marks on barrel and cylinder.

3. Army Revolver, Model 1848, with square-back trigger guard and rounded cylinder-stop recesses.
4. Army Revolver, Model 1848, with square-back trigger guard and vertical loading-lever latch.
5. Army Revolver, Model 1848, with oval trigger guard and rectangular cylinder stops.
6. Shoulder Stock for Army Revolver, Model 1848.

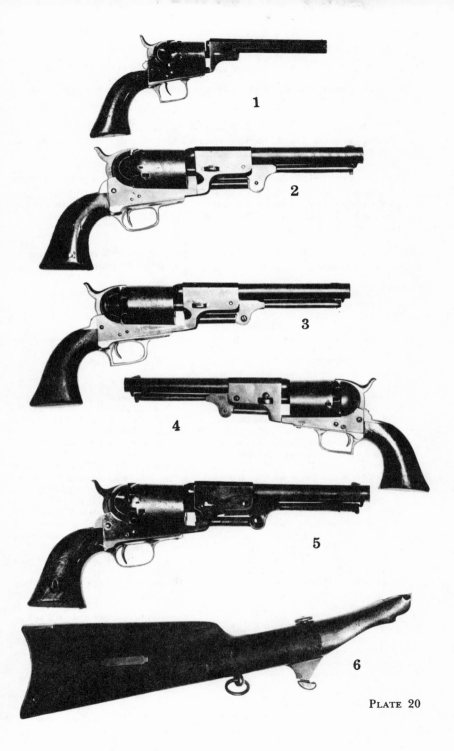

1

2

3

4

5

6

Plate 20

rated. Blued barrel and cylinder. Frame casehardened in natural colors. Plate 21, Fig. 3. $875–$1,565.

SAME, but cal. .31, 5-shot, 6-inch octagon barrel. Silver-plated oval guard and straps. English proof marks on barrel and cylinder. Plate 21, Fig. 4. $315–$510.

SAME, but cal. .31, 5-shot, 6-inch octagon barrel. All metal parts are elaborately engraved and inlaid with gold markings, figures of animals, floral patterns, and borders. The value starts with the revolver itself, but the engraving and gold inlay account for most of the value of this specimen. Plate 21, Fig. 5. $2,000–$3,500.

SAME, but cal. .31, 5-shot, 5-inch octagon barrel, with engraved metal parts and one-piece ivory grips. Plate 21, Fig. 6. $940–$1,950.

SAME, but cal. .31, 5-shot, 4-inch octagon barrel, with one-piece ivory grips and engraved metal parts. Silver-plated guard and straps. Plate 21, Fig. 7. $890–$1,765.

---

## PLATE 21. Colt Model 1849 Pocket Revolver

*Figure*

1. Model 1849 Pocket Revolver, cal. .31, 5-shot, 3-inch octagon barrel, silver-plated guard and straps. Rectangular cylinder stops. Roundback trigger guard. Made without loading lever. Sometimes called the Wells Fargo Model.

2. Model 1849, cal. .31, 5-shot, 6-inch octagon barrel. Brass guard and straps. Trigger guard has square back.

3. Model 1849, cal. .31, 5-shot, 6-inch octagon barrel engraved "Saml. Colt." Silver-plated oval trigger guard and straps. All metal parts elaborately decorated. Blued barrel and cylinder. Frame casehardened in natural colors.

4. Model 1849, cal. .31, 5-shot, 6-inch octagon barrel. Silver-plated oval guard and straps. English proof marks on barrel and cylinder.

5. Model 1849, cal. .31, 5-shot; 6-inch octagon barrel. All metal parts are elaborately engraved and inlaid with gold markings, figures of animals, floral patterns, and borders.

6. Model 1849, cal. .31, 5-shot, 5-inch octagon barrel, one-piece ivory grips, and engraved metal parts.

7. Model 1849, cal. .31, 5-shot, 4-inch octagon barrel, with one-piece ivory grips and engraved metal parts. Guard and straps silver-plated.

8. Model 1849, cal. .31, 5-shot, 5-inch octagon barrel, with one-piece ivory grips. Silver-plated engraved guard and straps. Engraved barrel, cylinder, and frame. Blued finish.

9. Model 1849, cal. .31, 5-shot, 5-inch octagon barrel. Square-back, brass trigger guard. Made with loading lever.

10. Model 1849, cal. .31, 5-shot, 5-inch octagon barrel. Same details as Fig. 8, above.

11. Model 1849, cal. .31, 5-shot, 4-inch octagon barrel. British proof marks. Cased with accessories.

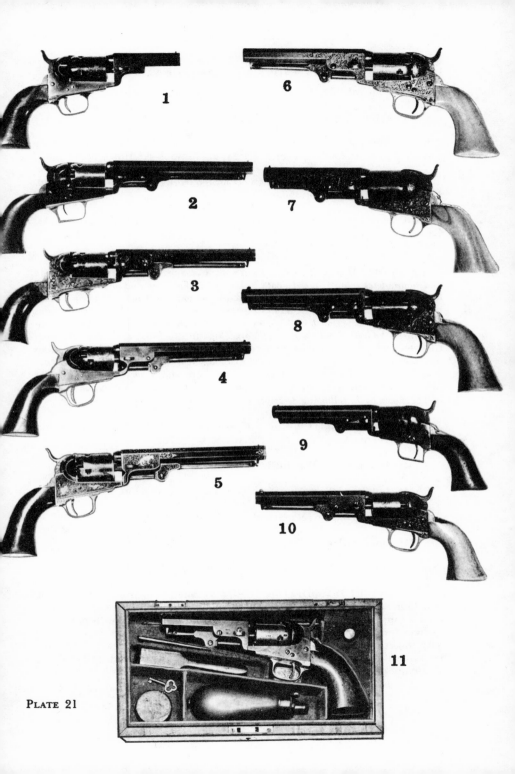

PLATE 21

SAME, but cal. .31, 5-shot, 5-inch octagon barrel, with one-piece ivory grips. Silver-plated engraved guard and straps. Engraved barrel, cylinder, and frame. Blued finish. Plate 21, Fig. 8. $930–$1,550.

SAME, but cal. .31, 5-shot, 5-inch octagon barrel. Square-back trigger guard. Made with loading lever. Plate 21, Fig. 9. $685–$1,100.

SAME, but cal. .31, 5-shot, 5-inch octagon barrel, exactly like Fig. 8 above. Plate 21, Fig. 10. $835–$1,350.

SAME, but cal. 31, 5-shot, 5-inch octagon barrel. British proof marks. Cased with accessories. Iron guard and straps. Plate 21, Fig. 11. $825–$1,295.

*Note on 1849 Models: This model was made in many variations, with both round and square-back trigger guards, both 5-shot and 6-shot, with and without a loading lever. The scene on the cylinders examined was the stagecoach holdup. The presentation models are often marked "Saml Colt" but not always. The ordinary models have a variety of markings, such as "Address Col Saml Colt New York U.S. America" in one line; "Address Saml Colt, New York City" in two lines; and "Address Saml Colt, Hartford, Ct." in either one or two lines. We have indicated value variations for many of the 5-shot variations. In the case of the 6-shot, the Hartford marks are usually considered worth more than the New York marks, other things being the same. However, there is a similar situation in the case of the 5-shot specimens. This will be shown by the following descriptions and values:*

MODEL 1849, cal. .31, 5-shot, round-back guard with loading lever and 4-inch barrel marked "New York." Plain. $210–$375.

SAME, But marked "Hartford." $220–$390.

SAME, but 5-inch barrel marked "New York." $210–$450.

SAME, But 5-inch barrel marked "Hartford." $215–$395.

SAME, but 6-inch barrel marked "New York." $235–$390.

SAME, but 6-inch barrel marked "Hartford." $275–$420.

COLT POCKET MODEL OF 1850, also called Improved Pocket Pistol, and Old Model Pocket Pistol. Cal. .31, 6-shot; octagon barrel from 4 to 6 inches long. Total length for 4-inch barrel, 9 inches; for 5-inch barrel, 10 inches; and for 6-inch barrel, 11 inches. Straight round cylinder, engraved with stagecoach holdup. Rectangular slots. Hinged loading lever. Navy-type latch. Oval brass trigger guard. Brass back strap. Regular frame. Brass-pin and hammer-notch sights. Barrel marked "Address Sam'l Colt, New York,

U.S. America" or it may show the address as "Hartford, Ct." Cylinder marked "Colt's Patent" with the serial number. Trigger guard marked ".31 Cal." It is not known when the manufacture started, but it is assumed to be 1850, and it ended in 1872. Collectors report, in addition to the regular model, the square-back trigger guard, a round barrel, and a fluted cylinder. Collectors and historians often argue that this was not a distinct model but a modification of the 1849 pocket pistol, already described, even though it was originally marketed by the factory as a separate model. For this reason many authorities do not recognize the existence of any 1850 model. Regardless of whether it should be classified as a separate type or not, the values follow those of the 1849 model, already described in detail. Therefore, refer to the descriptions of the 1849 model and obtain values according to those details.

COLT MODEL 1851 NAVY REVOLVER, also called Old Model Belt Pistol, Old Model Navy Pistol, model of 1851 Navy, and Model of 1851 Navy Pistol. Cal. .36, 6-shot, S.A.; 7.5-inch octagon barrel, total length 13 inches, weight 2 lbs. 10 oz. Straight round cylinder, 1.689 inches long, with rectangular notches (slots) and safety pins to keep the capped nipples away from the hammer, sometimes marked "Colt's Patent" with the serial number, and engraved with a scene showing a naval battle, and the words "Engaged 16 May 1843." Small wheel at the base of the hammer. Made with hinged loading lever and Navy-type latch. Square-back brass trigger guard. Brass grip and frame. Barrel, cylinder, and trigger were blued. Walnut grip. Barrel marked "Address Col. Sam'l Colt, New York, U.S. America" on standard model, although specimens are found marked "Address Sam'l Colt, New York City." Frame marked on left "Colt's Patent." The values shown are for the standard model described above. In addition, collectors are interested in variations with a round barrel, cut for shoulder stock, cut for shoulder stock with sling swivel, cut for shoulder stock with frame screw, fluted cylinder, oval iron trigger guard, barrel less than 7.5 inches long, and caliber .34, each of which may occur by itself or in combination with one or more of the variations listed. 1st model—serial number 1200 & under, $1,000–$2,300. 2nd model—square back, $850–$1,425.

SAME, but oval trigger guard and ivory grips, butt stamped "U.S.N." Plate 22, Fig. 1. $665–$925.

SAME, but square-back trigger guard and walnut grips, silver-plated guard and straps. Plate 22, Fig. 2. $860–$1,255.

SAME, but oval trigger guard, walnut grips, and Belgian-made with "Colt Brevete" on the barrel, with Liege proof marks. Plate 22, Fig. 3. $400–$570.

SAME, but frame stamped "U.S.," barrel cylinder, trigger guard, and back strap stamped with inspector's marks and walnut grips stamped with inspector's initials. $515–$975.

SAME, but with square-back trigger guard and the wedge screw under the wedge instead of above. Known to collectors as the first type or model of the Model 1851. Plate 22, Fig. 5. $1,115–$1,680.

SAME, but oval trigger guard and wedge screw above the wedge, barrel marked "Address Col. Colt London," with English proof marks on the barrel and cylinder. Plate 22, Fig. 7. $590–$925.

SAME, but conventional oval-trigger-guard model with one-piece ivory grips carved with the Mexican eagle in high relief on the left grip and silver-plated frame. Not engraved. Plate 22, Fig. 8. $765–$975.

SAME, but a plain specimen made by Confederates during Civil War. Dragoon-type barrel, walnut grips, bronze frame and straps, and bearing serial numbers without other marks. Plate 22, Fig. 9. $1,250–$1,850.

CASED PAIR WITH ENGLISH PROOF MARKS, cal. .36, 6-shot, 7.5-inch octagon barrel, walnut grips, iron guard and straps. British proof marks on barrel and cylinder. These pistols are in a mahogany case with two Colt flasks, two Colt iron bullet molds, two nipple wrenches, and two cases of primers. Plate 22, Fig. 11. $3,550–$6,500.

*Note: The following specimens are not illustrated.*

MODEL 1851, plain with oval trigger guard. $330–$655.

---

### PLATE 22. Colt Model 1851 Navy Revolver and Colt Flasks

*Figure*

1. Model 1851 Navy Revolver with ivory grips, butt stamped "U.S.N."
2. Model 1851 Navy Revolver with walnut grips and square-back trigger guard. Silver-plated trigger guard and straps.
3. Model 1851 Navy Revolver, Belgian-made with "Colt Brevete" on the barrel and Liege proof marks.
4. Colt Rifle Powder Flask.
5. Model 1851 Navy Revolver with square-back trigger guard and the wedge screw under the wedge instead of above. Known to collectors as the first type or model of the Modeld 1851.
6. Colt Pistol Powder Flask.
7. Model 1851 Navy Revolver, London Model. Barrel marked "Address Col. Colt London." English proof marks on barrel and cylinder.
8. Model 1851 Navy Revolver with one-piece ivory grips carved with Mexican eagle in high relief on left grip and silver-plated frame.
9. Model 1851 Navy Revolver, probably made by Confederates during Civil War. Dragoon-type barrel. Bronze frame, guard, and straps.
10. Colt Pistol Powder Flask.
11. Model 1851 Navy Revolver, London Model, cased pair with accessories.

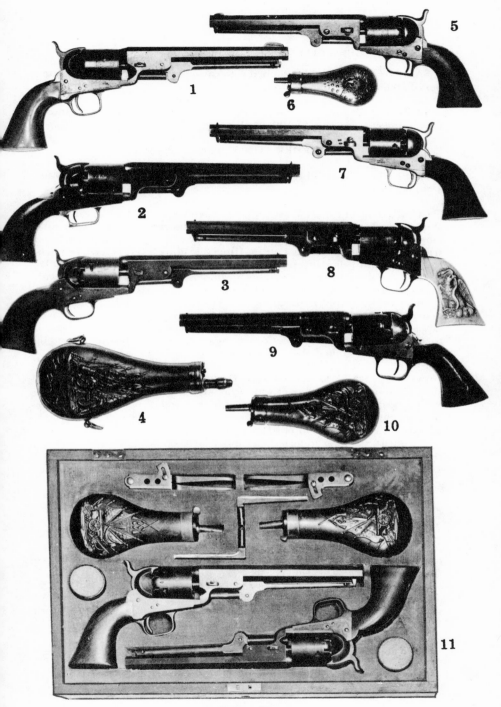

PLATE 22

SAME, but cut for and equipped with carbine stock, with the same numbers on the revolver and the stock. $2,775–$3,525.

SAME, but cut for and equipped with carbine stock, hollow-butt, canteen type, numbers the same. $3,100–$4,125.

SOLID-BUTT SHOULDER STOCK, alone. $625–$800.

HOLLOW,    CANTEEN-BUTT    SHOULDER    STOCK,    alone. $900–$1,475.

CONFEDERATE-COLT MODEL 1851 NAVY REVOLVER, cal. .36, 6-shot, 7.5-inch round barrelbarrel with octagon breech (Dragoon-type), total length 13 inches. Walnut grips. All brass frame of conventional shape, brass trigger guard, and brass back strap. Hinged loading lever. Navy-type latch. Round straight cylinder, engraved with scene of naval battle. Rectangular slots. Pin and hammer-notch sights. Cylinder marked "Colt's Patent" with serial number. Frame marked with serial number. Barrel not marked. The cylinder of this revolver was apparently a genuine Colt product, but the remainder of the revolver was undoubtedly made in 1864 by the the firm of Griswold & Gunnison. This could be classed as a U.S. secondary martial weapon, but not as a U.S. martial arm, since it was not issued to or used by the forces of the United States. Not illustrated. $700–$850.

CONFEDERATE-COLT MODEL 1851 NAVY REVOLVER, cal. .36, 6-shot, 7.375-inch round barrel with octagon breech, total length 13 inches. Walnut grips. Regular Colt frame, oval brass trigger guard, straight cylinder, not engraved but marked with serial number. Twelve rectangular slots. Marked "C.S.A." on the top (flat) portion of the barrel breech. The purpose of having 12 slots was to lock the cylinder between any pair of nipples as a safety measure in the absence of safety pins between the nipples. This is a Leech & Rigdon revolver. Not illustrated. $1,575-$2,285.

(One variation, known as the Rigdon & Ansley Percussion Revolver, when identified as such, may be worth $2,100–$3,150.)

*Note on Confederate Colts: The above two specimens are described in this chapter for the benefit of those who are Colt specialists and who might neglect to read the chapter of this text on Confederate handguns, but it is recommended that the chapters on Confederate arms be read by all collectors.*

COLT MODEL 1851 NAVY REVOLVER with fancy engraving and ivory grips, cal. .36, 7.5-inch octagon barrel, 6-shot, one-piece ivory grips with Mexican eagle in high relief on left grip, silver-plated. $875–$1,850.

SAME, but with one-piece ivory grips carved in high relief with American eagle on left grip; right grip checkered. $960–$1,950.

SAME, but presentation piece. Barrel, frame, and straps elaborately engraved; guard and straps silver-plated. One-piece ivory grips, elaborately carved with Mexican eagle in high relief on left grip and name of original owner "Francisco Vizcaya" in high relief on right. The condition of the gun itself, plus the high quality of engraving and carving, gives a piece like this a value higher than one of average workmanship. $1,500–$3,450.

SIMILAR, but Turkish Model 1851 Navy, cal. .35, not .36; 6-shot; 7.375-inch octagon barrel, not 7.5-inch; cylinder 2 inches long instead of usual 1.75. Barrel of specimen marked "M. N. Aramian & Co. American Liege Constantinople." Frame marked "Patent System" and "Cal. 35." Liege proof mark on cylinder, but other proof marks are: crossed keys under crown, crossed flags. Elaborately engraved, nickel-plated; two-piece plain ivory grips. $600–$850.

COLT POLICE POCKET PISTOL, also called Old Model Police Pistol, and erroneously called Wells Fargo Colt. There is actually no separate, distinct model under these titles. This information is presented here merely to clarify the situation in the minds of collecters and dealers. This so-called "model" is simply the Model 1849 Pocket Pistol without a loading lever (rammer or ramrod), made for express messengers and policemen who could load in advance and were not expected to reload quickly on duty. This variation or modification was probably made between 1851 and 1860, but no one can say for sure. The typical specimen is cal. .31, 5-shot, with a 3-inch octagon barrel marked "Address Samuel Colt New York City"; a straight round cylinder with rectangular slots, engraved with the stagecoach holdup scene, and marked "Colt's Patent" with a serial number; an oval, nickel-plated trigger guard, a nickel-plated brass back strap, pin and hammer-notch sights, and a regular frame marked "Colt's Patent" with the serial number. We have said that there is no loading lever, and of course there is then no latch. The values of this so-called type are found under the description of the Model 1849 Pocket Pistol.

COLT POCKET MODEL 1853, also called by other names. In the first edition of this text we erroneously gave this name to the New Model Pocket Pistol of Navy Caliber, described later in this chapter, simply because we followed the practice of most collectors and dealers without realizing that there is actually no such thing as a Colt Pocket Model 1853.

COLT NEW MODEL POCKET PISTOL, also called Model of 1855 Pocket Pistol, Sidehammer Colt, and Root's Patent Pistol; listed in the first edition of this text as Colt Pocket Model 1855 Side Hammer Revolver. Although called Model 1855, these revolvers were not sold to the public before 1857. They were probably made from 1857 to 1872. Cal. .265, 5-shot; 3.5-inch straight octagon barrel marked "Colt's Pat. 1855—Address Col. Colt, Hartford, Ct. U.S.A." Straight round cylinder engraved with picture of man standing with a Colt revolver in each hand firing at Indians, and marked

"Colt's Patent" with a serial number, and made without slots. The loading lever is of the Model 1855 type and has a latch of the same model year. Made without trigger guard. The back strap is part of the frame. The blued steel frame is not marked. The total length is 8 inches and the weight is 1 lb. 1 oz. Caliber .265 is often listed by collectors and dealers as caliber .28, but cal. .265 is according to the Colt records. $315–$675.

SAME, but with 3.5-inch round barrel with shoulder; Navy-type latch, solid forged frame, pin and grooved-frame sights, with cylinder engraved with the usual stagecoach holdup scene, and with the barrel marked "Address Col. Colt, New York, U.S.A." $315–$575.

SAME, but with 4.5-inch barrel, and fluted straight cylinder without engraving. The fluted cylinder is found on more specimens of this model than it is on other models. Plate 23, Figs. 3 and 5. $350–$675.

SAME, but cal. .31, 5-shot; 4.5-inch round barrel marked "Address Col. Colt Hartford, Conn." Usual spur trigger. Full fluted cylinder. Blued finish. Walnut grips. $350–$675.

SAME, but cal. .31, 5-shot, 3.5 inch round barrel; fluted cylinder and other details as in specimen described immediately above. $295–$575.

SAME, but cal. .31, 5-shot; 3.5-inch, shouldered, round barrel marked "Address Col. Colt, New York"; straight round cylinder without slots, en-

---

PLATE 23. Colt New Model Pocket Pistol of Navy Caliber; New Model Pocket Pistol; and Army Revolver, Model 1860

*Figure*

1. New Model Pocket Pistol of Navy Caliber with 6.5-inch barrel.
2. New Model Pocket Pistol of Navy Caliber with 5.5-inch barrel.
3. New Model Pocket Pistol, also called Model of 1855 Pocket Pistol, etc., with 4.5-inch round barrel and full-fluted cylinder.
4. New Model Pocket Pistol with 3.5-inch round barrel, round cylinder engraved with stagecoach holdup scene, and a screw in the cylinder.
5. New Model Pocket Pistol with 4.5-inch round barrel and a full-fluted cylinder.

6. Army Revolver, Model 1860, with 7.5-inch barrel and full-fluted cylinder.
7. Army Revolver, Model 1860, with 7.5-inch round barrel, full-fluted cylinder, and studs screwed into sides of frame for shoulder stock support. Army Revolver, Model 1860, with 8-inch round barrel, straight cylinder, left ivory grip carved with Mexican eagle in high relief within an oval, all metal parts engraved, except rammer, and nickel-plated.

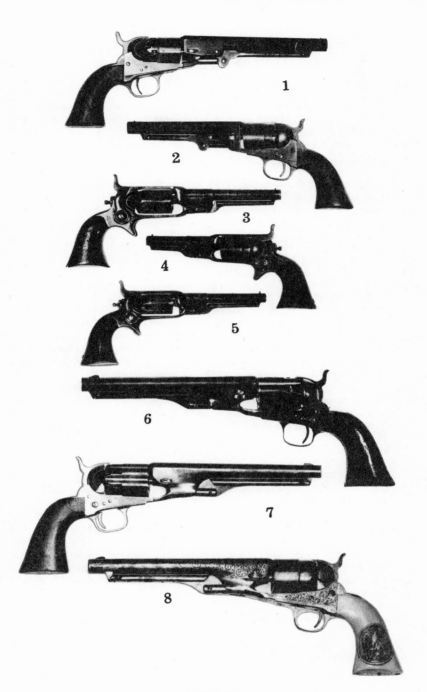

PLATE 23

graved with stagecoach holdup scene and marked "Colt's Patent" with serial number, with screw in the cylinder to hold the center pin in place, instead of the usual cross bolt through the frame. The latter feature is the rarest of the several departures from the standard design. Model-1855-type loading lever with Navy-type latch. Made without trigger guard. Back strap is part of the frame which is one solid forging. Total length 8 inches. Plate 23, Fig. 4. $310–$480.

*Note: Experimental side-hammer models were probably made, but not in quantity and not for for public sale, as follows: Army Model 1855, cal. .44, 6-shot, S.A., 8.5-inch barrel, total length 15.125 inches, weight 4 lbs. 2.5 oz.; Navy Model 1855, cal. .36, 6-shot, S.A., 7.5-inch barrel, total length 13.25 inches, weight 3 lbs. 15 oz.*

COLT ARMY REVOLVER, MODEL 1860, also called New Model Holster Pistol, New Model Army Pistol, and Round-barreled Army Pistol, cal. .44, 6-shot, S.A.; 8-inch round barrel marked "Address Sam'l Colt, Hartford, Ct." or "Address Col. Sam'l Colt, New York, U.S. America." Total length 14 inches. Weight 2 lbs. 11 oz. Round rebated cylinder with rectangular slots, engraved with naval battle scene and words "Engaged 16 May 1843." marked "Colt's Patent" and "Patented Sept. 10th, 1850." Round or oval brass trigger guard. Iron back strap. Creeping loading lever with Navy-type latch. Walnut grip. Blued barrel, cylinder, and trigger. Low-blade brass front sight set into barrel. V-notch rear sight cut in hammer lip. Frame and back strap are notched for attaching the shoulder stock with screws. Hammer has a bearing wheel. Frame, loading lever, and hammer are casehardened. When revolver is attached to shoulder stock, total length is 26.5 inches and the total weight is then 5 lbs. Indicated value here is without stock. This is a U.S. martial revolver. $355–$795.

SAME, but equipped with shoulder stock. Numbers match. $2,250–$3,075.

SAME, but not cut for stock or equipped with stock, called "Civilian Model" by collectors. $360–$745.

SAME, but with fluted instead of rebated cylinder, without stock. Plate 23, Fig. 6. $665–$1,285.

SAME, but presentation type, with elaborate engraving on metal parts and elaborately carved ivory grips, without shoulder stock. Plate 23, Fig. 8. $1,915–$2,900.

Value of shoulder stock (carbine stock) alone: $650–$875.

SAME, but with full-fluted cylinder and studs screwed into the side of the frame to receive the shoulder stock. Plate 23, Fig. 7. $700–$1,400.

COLT MODEL 1861 NAVY REVOLVER, also called New Model Belt Pistol, New Model Navy Pistol, Model of 1861 Navy Pistol, and Round-barreled Navy. Cal. .36, 6-shot, S.A.; 7.5-inch round barrel marked "Address Col. Sam'l Colt, New York, U.S. America." Total length 13 inches. Weight 2 lbs. 9 oz. or 2 lbs. 10 oz. (It weighs 3 lbs. on my butcher's scales.) Straight round cylinder with rectangular slots, engraved with usual naval engagement scene and words, and marked "Colt's Patent" with a serial number. Regular frame but not cut for stock. Brass back strap and brass oval trigger guard. Creeping loading lever and Navy-type latch. Frame marked "Colt's Patent." Trigger guard marked ".36 Cal." This is a U.S. martial weapon. Plate 24, Fig. 1. $500–$975.

SAME, but with inspector's marks on barrel, cylinder, frame, trigger guard, and back strap; walnut grips stamped with inspector's initials. This is a U.S. martial revolver. $575–$1,275.

SAME, but cut for stock. $800–$1,750.

SAME, but with carved ivory grips and elaborate engraving, and silver-plated guard and straps. The exact value depends upon the amount and quality of the engraving as well as the condition of the revolver. Plate 24, Figs. 2, 3, 4, and 5. $1,750–$3,250.

COLT NEW MODEL POLICE PISTOL, also called Model of 1862 Pocket Pistol, Officers' Model Pocket Pistol, 1862 Belt Model, and New Model Police Pistol with Creeping Lever Ramrod. Cal. .36, 5-shot, S.A.; 6.5-inch round barrel marked "Address Sam'l Colt, New York, U.S. America." Total length 12 inches. Weight about 1 lb. 10 oz. Half-fluted rebated cylinder, without engraving or marking. Rectangular cylinder slots. Creeping loading lever. Navy-type latch. Brass back strap and brass oval trigger guard, latter marked ".36 Cal." Regular frame marked "Colt's Patent." Brass-pin and hammer-notch sights. Blued barrel and cylinder. Walnut grip. Barrel may be marked "Address Sam'l Colt Hartford Conn." The exposed brass parts are silver-plated on some specimens. This revolver was carried as a personal weapon by Union officers during the Civil War and hence may be regarded as a U.S. secondary martial arm. In the first edition of this text we erroneously listed this revolver under the heading Colt Model 1862 Navy Revolver. Plate 24, Fig. 6. $285–$720.

SAME, but with elaborate engraving. $900–$1,650.

SAME, plain but with iron trigger guard and back strap. $365–$735.

SAME, but with 5.5-inch barrel, brass trigger guard. $340–$640.

SAME, but with 4.5-inch barrel. $310–$690.

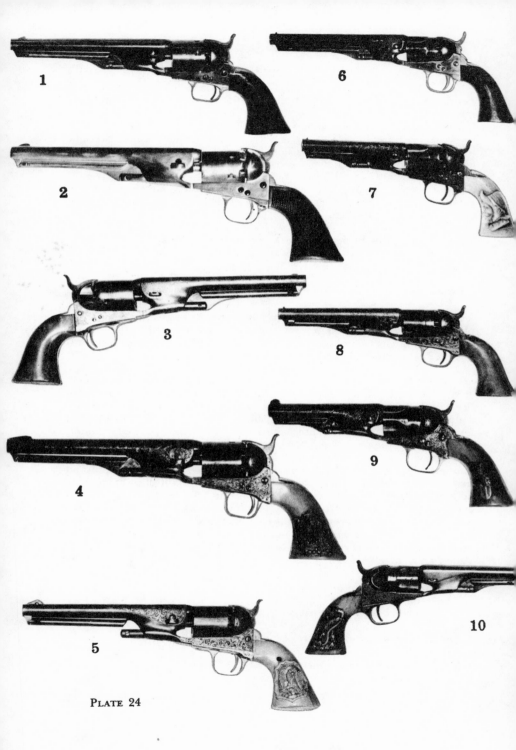

PLATE 24

SAME, but presentation type with elaborately carved ivory grips. Barrel lengths 4.5 or 5.5 inches. Plate 24, Figs. 7, 8, 9, and 10. $1,500–$1,925.

COLT NEW MODEL POCKET PISTOL OF NAVY CALIBER, also called Pocket Navy Revolver, and Pocket Navy Pistol, and erroneously listed in the first edition of this text as Colt Pocket Model 1853, although it was actually made from 1860 or 1861 to 1872. It was made on the grips and frame of the Colt Model 1849 Pocket Revolver, also called the Improved Pocket Pistol, Old Model Pocket Pistol, and Model of 1849 Pocket Pistol, but cutting out the frame to make room for the rebated caliber-.36 cylinder. Cal. .36, 5-shot, S.A.; 4.5-inch octagon barrel marked "Address Col. Sam'l Colt, U.S. America." Total length 9.5 inches, weight 1 lb. 9 oz. in this barrel length. Round rebated cylinder with rectangular slots, engraved with stagecoach holdup scene and marked "Colt's Patent" with the serial number. Regular frame, usually of lighter weight, marked "Colt's Patent, .36 Cal." Hinged

## PLATE 24. Colt Model 1861 Navy Revolver and Colt New Model Police Pistol

*Figure*

1. Model 1861 Navy Revolver, service issue.
2. Model 1861 Navy Revolver with checkered, one-piece ivory grips, and all metal parts silver-plated except screws, which are black.
3. Model 1861 Navy Revolver with ivory grips and silver-plated guard and straps.
4. Model 1861 Navy Revolver with one-piece ivory grips with Mexican eagle carved in high relief on left grip. All metal parts elaborately engraved. Silver-plated guard and straps. Low blade front sight.
5. Model 1861 Navy Revolver with ivory grips with Mexican eagle carved in high relief inside a scalloped border on left grip. Silver-plated guard and straps. All metal parts finely engraved.
6. New Model Police Pistol, also called Model of 1862 Pocket Pistol, Officers' Model Pocket Pistol, 1862 Belt Model, and New Model Police with Creeping-Lever Ramrod. The specimen illustrated conforms to the description in the text.
7. New Model Police Pistol with 4.5-inch round barrel, genuine elephant-ivory grips carved with man's head in high relief on left grip and all metal parts elaborately engraved.
8. New Model Police Pistol with 5.5-inch round barrel, ivory grips, and all metal parts except the cylinder and loading lever engraved. Rear sight removed from hammer; open sight set into barrel in front of cylinder.
9. New Model Police Pistol with 4.5-inch round barrel, one-piece ivory grips carved with American eagle and shield in relief on left grip. Engraved, silver-plated guard and straps. Engraved frame, barrel cylinder, and hammer. Blade front sight.
10. New Model Police Pistol with 4.5-inch round barrel, ivory grips with Mexican eagle carved in high relief on right side, and nickel-plated barrel, frame, and cylinder; hammer polished bright.

loading lever. Navy-type latch. Brass back strap. Brass oval trigger guard. $355–$750.

SAME, but with 5.5-inch barrel. Plate 23, Fig. 2. $385–$825.

SAME, but with 6.5-inch barrel. Plate 23, Fig. 1. $435–$900.

SAME, but with 4.5-inch barrel, in cased set with accessories. $1,075–$1,875.

## COLT POWDER FLASKS FOR PERCUSSION ARMS

COLT RIFLE POWDER FLASK. Copper flask with fixed charger of plunger type. Two triangular carrying rings. On both sides, in high relief, are: a stand of flags in the background; field cannon, shot, mortar, swords, etc., in the foreground. Below are crossed revolving rifles and crossed revolvers with a ribbon lettered "Colts Patent." Swinging cover over compartments in the top of the flask is marked "Colts Patent." Size 9 inches by 3.5 inches. Plate 22, Fig. 4. $275–$500.

COLT PISTOL POWDER FLASK. Copper flask with American eagle, crossed revolvers, 13 stars, and "Colts Patent" in relief on one side, above a ribbon with the motto "E. Pluribus Unum." Size 4.625 inches by 2 inches. Plate 22, Fig. 6. $65–$165.

COLT PISTOL POWDER FLASK. Copper flask with cannon, crossed flags, crossed rifles and revolvers, anchor, etc., in relief on one side, with "Colts Patent" under crossed revolvers. Fixed charger. Size 6.75 inches by 3 inches. Plate 22, Fig. 10. $185–$300.

## COLT LONDON MODELS

Four different Colt percussion revolvers were made at the Colt factory in London, England. These were Model 1849 Pocket Revolver, cal. .31, 5-shot, made in 4-, 5-, and 6-inch barrel lengths; and the Model 1851 Navy Revolver, cal. .36, 6-shot, 7.5-inch barrel.

The usual marking reads "Address Col. Colt London," but on presentation models it sometimes reads "Col. Colt London." British proof marks are usually, but not always, present. It must be understood that all arms marked "Address Col. Colt London," or "Col. Colt London," were not necessarily made in the London factory, since it is known that specimens made in Hartford were thus marked for the British trade, appealing to the strong British inclination to "Buy British" even then.

It should be understood that although Dragoon Models are sometimes found with the London mark, they were never made there, even though they were listed in a price list published and distributed by the London factory. This is an example of the fallacy of relying entirely upon catalogues and old price lists in an effort to reconstruct the history of firearms. Such publications are merely evidence that a piece might have been made as listed; they are definitely not final proof of the existence of the items described.

### Values for Genuine London-made Colt Revolvers

MODEL 1849 POCKET REVOLVER, cal. .31, 5-shot, 4-inch barrel. $305–$515.

SAME, but with 5-inch barrel. $310–$530.

SAME, but with 6-inch barrel. $330–$560.

MODEL 1851 NAVY REVOLVER, cal. .36, 6-shot, 7.5-inch barrel. $525–$885.

## COLT CASES AND ACCESSORIES FOR PERCUSSION REVOLVERS

### Standard Cased Sets

Most Colt percussion revolvers were sold without cases. When sold to civilians, a bullet mold, a powder flask, and a nipple wrench were often delivered with the revolver. On special order, any type or model was delivered in a case with accessories. The standard case was made of either rosewood or mahogany, lined with either velvet or baize, and divided into compartments. In this case were placed one or two revolvers; a powder flask made of lacquered copper, usually beautifully ornamented, and made with a measuring neck for delivering the correct quantity of powder for loading the weapon with which it was cased; a bullet mold, marked "Colt's Patent," marked with the caliber, made of either brass or steel; a combination nipple wrench and screw driver; a box of percussion caps (primers); and a quantity of loose bullets, except that in the latter days of the percussion era a box of paper cartridges was usually supplied instead of the loose bullets. Sometimes a magazine capper was added to the set. The accessories were sometimes supplied in pairs with a matched pair of revolvers.

## London, England, Cased Sets

Cased sets assembled at the Colt factory in London, England, in general resembled the standard cased sets, with a few exceptions. The case was usually made of oak, and the powder flask was made in England, presumably at Sheffield. A few English-made cases were copied from the French dueling-pistol cases of that era, with the result that the baize or velvet was fastened so that it was even with the top of the case. The revolver and its accessories were then lowered into the folds of the cloth, probably on the theory that the finish would be damaged less.

## Presentation Cased Sets

Like the presentation revolvers, presentation cased sets made by Colt defy any attempt at classification or general description. Since the presentation revolvers were usually elaborately engraved, often inlaid, and frequently provided with beautifully carved ivory grips, the case and its accessories were made on a corresponding scale of magnificence. When Samuel Colt wanted to impress foreigners, he sometimes made the case of American light curly maple or American walnut, with a velvet lining of a contrasting color, the purpose being to suggest the superiority of everything American, including, of course, Colt revolvers. When he wanted to impress an American, he often had the case made of imported rosewood or mahogany.

One of the most unusual types of cases was constructed to resemble a book bound in tooled leather, having a title such as "Colt on Law and Order." Another favorite title for the book-like cases was "Colt on the Constitution, Higher Law and Irrepressible Conflict." The author of this text has never seen one of these book-type cases and knows of only one sold during the past thirty years, but their production by Colt has been reported frequently by reliable authorities.

## Miniature Cased Sets

For presentation purposes, and sometimes purely for publicity reasons, Colt had perfect miniatures of his revolvers constructed and placed with miniature accessories in tiny cases. The length of one of the miniature revolvers was one inch, and the largest was probably three inches, yet they were working models and not merely dollhouse ornaments.

## Appraising the Value of Cased Colt Sets

To appraise the value of a cased Colt set, start with the value of the firearm itself. Add at least $100 if it has plain ivory grips, and at least $200 if it has well-carved ivory grips. These ivory grip values apply to the lower-priced Colt revolvers. In appraising the higher-priced Colt revolvers, high-quality carved ivory grips are worth more than the same grips would be on cheaper specimens.

If there is a matched pair of revolvers, add their separate values and then add 50% because they are a matched pair, provided that they are in the upper price range. A bullet mold or a flask may be worth at least $50 and often more. Sometimes there is an extra cylinder or a spare barrel in the case; these add greatly to the value. Add up the estimated value of all accessories, spare parts, cartridges, bullets, etc., and then add the value of the case. A Colt-made case is worth more than one provided by an antique-arms collector or dealer from a modern source. Finally, compare your appraisal with bona fide records of recent sales of similar goods. Prices realized on auction sales are usually too low. Prices charged by large city department stores are usually too high. The retail prices obtained by the regular, established antique-arms dealers in the course of their normal business are the best guides. Remember that guns are not always sold at the prices listed in a catalogue or circular; the higher-priced arms may be sold for something less than the first asking price, although this is by no means a general rule.

In appraising cased sets in general, if the firearms in the cases are not genuine weapons, with all parts original, and in good condition or better, then the case (box) itself is of little value as a firearm collector's item, and the values of the accessories are their values as separate items.

Cased sets of replicas of Colt percussion revolvers, although manufactured by the Colt Corporation itself in the 1960's, are merely interesting souvenirs. They are *not* collectors' items in the strict sense of the term.

# Chapter 12

## COLT PERCUSSION REVOLVERS CONVERTED TO FIRE METALLIC CARTRIDGES

COLT ARMY REVOLVER, Model 1848, also known as Old Model Holster Pistol, and Dragoon Colt, converted to cartridge, cal. .44 r.f.; 6-shot; 7.5-inch round barrel with octagon breech, marked "Address Sam'l Colt, New York City." Total length 14 inches. Straight round cylinder marked and engraved as usual, with rectangular slots. Hinged loading lever. Dragoon-type latch. Brass oval trigger guard. Brass back strap. Straight frame marked with serial number. Regular sights. The conversion was accomplished by cutting off the cylinder and inserting a removable breech plate with slots through which the hammer could reach the cartridge primers. It is possible to remove the converted cylinder and have percussion fire with an ordinary percussion-cap cylinder. This conversion probably took place after the Civil War and is not a factory conversion. $850–$1,075.

SAME, but with 8-inch round barrel. Plate 25, Fig. 1. $865–$1,090.

SAME, but converted to fire cal. .44 Colt Cartridge. $850–$1,075.

SAME, but converted to fire cal. .44 Russian c.f. cartridge. $865–$1,095.

SAME, but Thuer conversion, cal. .44 c.f. $3,100–$3,925.

SAME, but converted to fire either the cal. .45 c.f. Government cartridge or the cal. .45 c.f. Colt cartridge. $850–$1,075.

COLT OLD MODEL POCKET PISTOL, also called Model of 1848 Pocket Pistol, etc., converted to cartridge, cal. .32 r.f. Conversion resembles that described above for the Colt Army Revolver, Model 1848. Values vary according to barrel length and other details but approximate those shown here. $300–$400.

SAME, but converted to cal. .32 c.f. cartridge. $375–$490.

COLT MODEL 1849 POCKET REVOLVER, also called Old Model Pocket Pistol, Model of 1849 Pocket Pistol, etc. Converted to cal. .32 r.f.; 5-shot; 4-inch octagon barrel marked "Address Sam'l Colt, New York City." Total length 9 inches. Straight round cylinders, engraved with usual stagecoach holdup scene, marked "Colt's Patent" with serial number, with rectangular slots. Hinged loading lever. Navy type latch. Brass trigger guard. Brass back strap. Regular frame marked "Colt's Patent" and serial number. Pin and hammer-notch sights. The cylinder was cut off forward of the nipples and the nipples were removed. A little spur was added to the hammer. The section removed from the cylinder was slotted and doweled with small pins. The extension fitted to the cylinder enters the slot. The two sections of the cylinder are inserted in the frame after the cartridges have been placed in the chambers, and the revolver is then ready to fire metallic cartridges. By removing the converted cylinder and using an ordinary percussion type cylinder, the revolver can be fired as a percussion arm. $245–$390.

SAME, but cal. .32 c.f. $245–$355.

COLT POCKET MODEL OF 1850, also called Improved Pocket Pistol and Old Model Pocket Pistol. When conversions of this so-called model appear, they are treated for appraisal purposes as though they were classified as Colt Model 1849 Pocket Revolver specimens. $275–$400.

COLT MODEL 1851 NAVY REVOLVER, also called Old Model Navy Pistol, etc., converted to cal. .38 r.f.; 6-shot; 7.5-inch octagon barrel marked "Address Sam'l Colt, Hartford, Connecticut." Straight round cylinder, engraved with scene of naval engagement, and marked "Colt's Patent" with the serial number. Rectangular slots. Loading lever is removed and a side ejector substituted. No latch. Iron trigger guard and back strap. The frame is marked "Patented July 25, 1871, July 2, 1872," and has a breechblock back of the cylinder with a loading gate. A firing pin was welded to the hammer. This was evidently a factory conversion accomplished in 1872 or shortly thereafter. The sights are the conventional ones for this model. Plate 25, Fig. 2. $325–$465.

SAME, marked "U. S. N." on butt with anchor and inspector's marks on bottom and on barrel. $400–$565.

SAME, but converted to cal. .38 c.f. $365–$535.

SAME, cal. .38, but Thuer conversion. $2,825–$3,575.

COLT POLICE POCKET PISTOL, also called Old Model Police Pistol, and erroneously called Wells Fargo Colt. As stated before, there is no true, distinct model of this name. This is actually a modification or variation of the Model 1849 Pocket Pistol, but we describe arms under this classification for the benefit of those who like to follow the old descriptions. Converted to cal. .32 c.f. $255–$350.

SAME, but converted to cal. .32 r.f. $255–$350.

COLT NEW MODEL POCKET PISTOL, also called Model of 1855 Pocket Pistol, Side-Hammer Colt, etc., converted to cal. .32 r.f. Values are for typical average specimens. $275–$350.

SAME, but converted to cal. .32 c.f. $250–$315.

COLT ARMY REVOLVER, MODEL 1860, also called New Model Army Pistol, etc., converted to cal. .44 c.f.; 6-shot; 5.5-inch round barrel marked "Address Sam'l Colt, New York, U.S. America." Rebated round cylinder engraved with naval engagement scene and words. Rectangular slots. Side ejector. Oval brass trigger guard marked ".44 Cal." Iron back strap. Knife-blade front sight with groove in breechblock for rear sight. Flat-face hammer. The frame is not cut for the shoulder stock on some specimens, but it is so cut on most of them. The cylinder was cut off, and a breechblock that includes a loading gate and a rebounding firing pin was inserted. $365–$600.

SAME, but with 8-inch barrel. Firing pin is in frame and not on hammer. $375–$625.

SAME, but converted to .44 r.f. $375–$625.

SAME, but converted to .44 c.f. Russian. $375–$625.

SAME, but converted to fire either .45 c.f. Government or .45 c.f. Colt cartridge. $370–$615.

SAME, but cal. .44 Colt c.f., 6-shot, 8-inch round barrel, with loading gate and side-rod ejector. Firing pin in frame. Plate 25, Fig. 8. $370–$615.

SAME, but cal. .44 Colt c.f., 6-shot, 8-inch round barrel, made with loading gate, side-rod ejector, and iron guard and straps. Plate 25, Fig. 9. $375–$605.

SAME, but Thuer conversion. Cal. .44, 6-shot; 8-inch round barrel marked "Address Sam'l Colt, New York, U.S. America." Total length 14 inches. Round rebated cylinder with naval engagement engraving and rectangular slots, marked "Colt's Patent" with the serial number and made with movable rear section which turns so that the hammer hits the ejecting pin and ejects forward of the chamber the fired cartridge case to the right of the one under the hammer. Creeping loading lever. Navy-type latch. Nickeled oval trigger guard. Nickeled back strap. Frame not cut for stock. Ordinary sight. Frame marked "Colt's Patent" with serial number. Conversion consists of steel plate containing firing pin and ejecting mechanism, fitting between cylinder and recoil plate. Chambers are tapered and loaded from the front. After firing, the plate is revolved to the letter E, opposite the hammer, which is then snapped 6 times, ejecting fired shells from front of cylinder. Plain grips. Plate 25, Fig. 7. $2,500–$3,665.

SAME, but with one-piece ivory grips, elaborately carved with an average amount of engraving. $3,100–$4,300.

COLT ARMY REVOLVER, MODEL 1872, but *not* a conversion. We list this type, or modification, or variation, or whatever it may be, because collectors and dealers sometimes erroneously list it as a conversion, and also because it conforms in general to the Colt Army Revolver, Model 1860, in its construction and design. However, none of the parts were apparently made for a percussion arm and none of them show any sign of having been altered

---

PLATE 25. Colt Percussion Revolvers Converted to Fire Metallic Cartridges

*Figure*

1. Army Revolver, Model 1848, cal. .44 long r.f., 6-shot, 8-inch round barrel. Loading lever retained.
2. Model 1851 Navy Revolver, cal. .38 long r.f., 6-shot, with loading gate and side-rod ejector.
3. New Model Pocket Pistol of Navy Caliber, cal. .38 c.f., 5-shot, 4.5-inch round barrel, with loading gate, side-rod ejector, and one-piece ivory grips, carved on right with Mexican eagle.
4. New Model Pocket Pistol of Navy Caliber, cal. .38 r.f., 5-shot, 4.5-inch octagon barrel, without loading gate or side-rod ejector, with all metal parts engraved, and silver-plated guard and straps.
5. New Model Pocket Pistol of Navy Caliber, cal. .38 r.f., 5-shot, 5.5-inch round barrel, with loading gate, side-rod ejector, and ivory grips.
6. New Model Pocket Pistol of Navy Caliber, cal. .38 long c.f., 5-shot, 3.5-inch barrel, with iron back strap, and made without loading gate or side-rod ejector.
7. Army Revolver, Model 1860, Thuer conversation, cal. .44 Thuer c.f., 6-shot, 8-inch round barrel. Iron back strap, brass guard, and strap.
8. Army Revolver, Model 1860, cal. .44 Colt c.f., 6-shot, 8-inch round barrel, with loading gate and side-rod ejector. The firing pin is in the frame and not on the hammer.
9. Army Revolver, Model 1860, cal. .44 Colt O.M., 6-shot, 8-inch round barrel, made with loading gate, side-rod ejector, and iron guard and straps.
10. Model 1861 Navy Revolver, cal. .38 c.f., 6-shot, 7.5-inch round barrel, made with loading gate, side-rod ejector, and brass guard and straps.
11. New Model Police Pistol, sometimes called Belt Model 1862, cal. .38 r.f., 5-shot, 4.5-inch round barrel, half-fluted cylinder, made with loading gate and side-rod ejector.

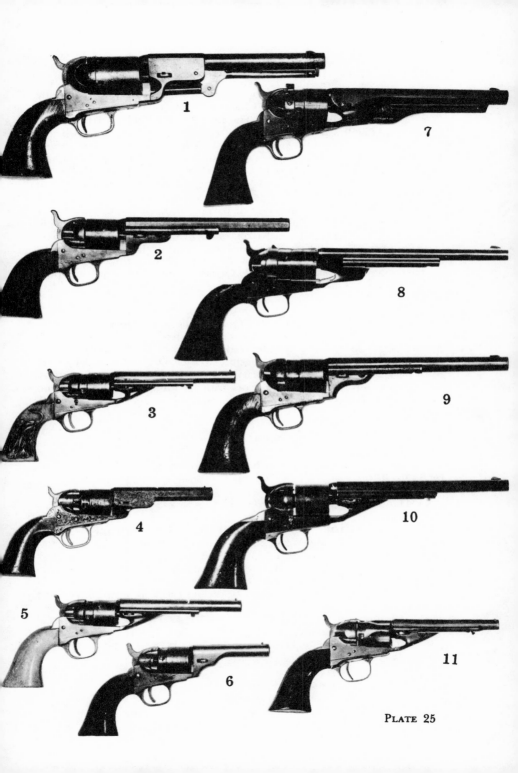

PLATE 25

from percussion to metallic-cartridge use. Instead, all parts were apparently made for metallic-cartridge fire. This model can be correctly called the first Colt Cartridge Revolver. Charles T. Haven and Frank Belden, in their text *A History of the Colt Revolver,* call it Model of 1872, Type of 1860 Army, which is probably the best possible classification, since it was probably made about 1872. We have seen only two specimens for sale. Cal. .44 r.f., 6-shot; 7.5-inch round barrel marked "Address Col. Sam'l Colt, New York, U.S. America." Straight round cylinder, 1.563 inches long, engraved with naval engagement scene and words, and marked "Colt's Patent" with a serial number. Rectangular slots. Side-rod ejector on right of barrel. No latch. Brass oval trigger guard. Brass back strap. Walnut grips. The frame does not have the groove in the standing breech portion which is on frames made for percussion fire to release the percussion primers. The rear sight is part of the barrel and raised above the surface; the front sight is a comparatively long ridge fastened on the barrel. Not cut for shoulder stock. Original finish was blue on one specimen examined. This is apparently a very rare weapon. Not illustrated. $1,300–$2,500.

COLT MODEL 1861 NAVY REVOLVER, also called New Model Navy Pistol, etc., converted to cal. .38 c.f.; 6-shot, 7.5-inch round barrel, total length 13 inches. Straight round cylinder with usual naval battle engraving and words. Rectangular slots. Side-rod ejector. No latch. Oval brass trigger guard. Brass back strap. Regular frame. Grooved hammer rear sight. Walnut grips. The nipples were cut off, a breechblock with a loading gate was added, and the regular hammer was provided with a center-fire pin. Plate 25, Fig. 10. $1,350–$2,200.

SAME, but cal. .38 r.f. $465–$700.

SAME, but marked "U.S.N." with anchor and inspector's marks under barrel. $485–$810.

SAME, but cal. 38 Thuer conversion. $2,475–$3,275.

COLT NEW MODEL POLICE PISTOL, also called Model of 1862 Pocket Pistol, etc., converted to cal. .38 r.f., with loading gate and a side-rod ejector, both on the right side; 5-shot; 4.5-inch round barrel marked "Address Sam'l Colt, N.Y., U.S. America." Half-fluted rebated cylinder, usually without engraving and often unmarked, with rectangular slots. Brass trigger guard and brass back strap. Total length 9.5 inches. Weight 1 lb. 7 oz. Firing pin welded to hammer, long enough to reach through breechblock. Frame marked "Colt's Patent." Trigger guard marked ".36 Cal." Walnut grips. External brass surfaces on some specimens are silver-plated. This is a typical factory job performed probably between 1870 and 1875. Plate 25, Fig. 11. $295–$450.

SAME, but converted to cal. .38 c.f. $295–$450.

SAME, but Thuer conversion, cal. .38 Thuer cartridge, 6-shot. $2,475–$3,275.

SAME, but ordinary conversion, not Thuer, and not a factory job. $150–$225.

SAME, ordinary conversion, with 6.5-inch round barrel, and not a factory job. $150–$225.

SAME, but ordinary conversion, 3.5-inch round barrel, made without a loading gate or a side-rod ejector. $200–$295.

SAME, but Thuer conversion with mixed models, consisting of cylinder and frame from two different models or modifications; cal. .38 Thuer cartridge; 6-shot; 4.5-inch round barrel marked "Address Sam'l Colt, New York, U.S. America"; total length 10 inches. Rebated round cylinder, engraved with stagecoach holdup scene, and marked "Colt's Patent" with serial number. Rectangular slots. Creeping loading lever. Navy-type latch. Brass oval trigger guard. Brass back strap. Ordinary frame marked "Colt's Patent." Pin and grooved hammer sights. Walnut grips. Probably factory conversion made shortly before or after 1870. $800–$1,350.

COLT NEW MODEL POCKET PISTOL OF NAVY CALIBER, also Pocket Navy Revolver, and Pocket Navy Pistol, converted to cal. .38 r.f.; 5-shot; 3.5-inch round barrel marked "Colt's Pt. F.A. Mfg. Co., Hartford, Ct., U.S.A." Round rebated cylinder, engraved with stagecoach holdup scene, marked "Colt's Patent" with serial number. Rectangular slots. Oval brass trigger guard marked ".36 Cal." No ejector. Brass back strap. Brass-pin and grooved-hammer sights. Ordinary frame marked "Pat. July 25, '71, July 2, '72." This conversion was accomplished about 1872 by cutting off the cylinder, providing a breechblock, joining a firing pin to the hammer, attaching a barrel without a loading lever, and cutting a cartridge groove on the right of the frame. Walnut grips. The exposed brass parts of some specimens have been silver-plated and on some specimens they have been nickel-plated, although a blued finish is not unusual. $330–$510.

SAME, but cal. .38 c.f. $325–$520.

SAME, but cal. .38 Thuer conversion. $1,325–$2,015.

SAME, but cal. .38 c.f., 5-shot, 4.5-inch round barrel, with loading gate and side-rod ejector. Plate 25, Fig. 3. $330–$555.

SAME, but cal. .38 r.f., 5-shot, 4.5-inch octagon barrel, without loading lever or side-rod ejector. All metal parts engraved. Silver-plated guard and straps. Plate 25, Fig. 4. $800–$1,065.

SAME, but cal. .38 r.f., 5-shot, 5.5-inch round barrel with loading gate, side-rod ejector, and ivory grips. Plate 25, Fig. 5. $440–$565.

SAME, but cal. .38 long c.f., 5-shot, 3.5-inch round barrel, with iron back strap, and made without loading gate or side-rod ejector. Plate 25, Fig. 6. $250–$445.

The greatest advance in values for Colt percussion revolvers converted to fire metallic cartridges, commonly referred to as "Colt conversions," has been in the group known as Thuer conversions, named for F. Alexander Thuer, one of Colt's most skilled artisans, who obtained a patent in 1868 for converting percussion arms to cartridge arms. Thuer's device made it possible to fire Colt percussion arms with either loose powder and ball or the newly marketed metallic cartridges, using a removable ring and cylinder. Comparatively few Thuer conversions were made. The general demand for Colt percussion revolvers, together with the scarcity of Thuer conversions, has caused the increase of values.

## Caution Regarding Thuer Conversions

Colt percussion revolvers converted to fire metallic cartridges according to the Thuer patent of 1868 always have been especially attractive to collectors, hence the values of such conversions have been comparatively high. Collectors and dealers sometimes innocently list their specimens as "Thuer conversions" when they are not.

This situation makes it necessary to examine Colt conversions carefully when ownership is transferred.

# Chapter 13

## COLT CARTRIDGE PISTOLS
## AND REVOLVERS

THIS chapter includes descriptions of all Colt cartridge revolvers, derringers, and automatic pistols generally recognized by gun collectors and dealers, including several that are essentially modern arms, sold principally on a basis of shooting condition.

The Colt weapons in this classification that are generally accepted as U.S. martial cartridge revolvers and automatic pistols are the following:

Single-Action Army Revolver, also called New Model Army Metallic Cartridge Revolving Pistol, Single-Action Army, Single-Action Frontier, Peacemaker, and Colt Army Revolver, Model 1872.

Double-Action Army, also called the Double-Action Frontier, and sometimes called the Colt Double-Action Army Revolver, Model 1878.

New Navy Double-Action, Self-cocking Revolver, Model 1889.

New Navy Double-Action, Self-cocking Revolver, Model 1892, which was really a modification of the Model 1889.

New Army Models 1892, 1894, 1896.

Army Model 1901, which was a modification of the New Army Models listed above.

Army Model 1903, which was a modification of the Model 1901.

Marine Corps Model 1905 (or Model 1907).

New Service Revolver, Model 1909.

Army Revolver, Model 1917.

Automatic Pistol, Model 1911.

Of the revolvers and automatic pistols made by Colt for the armed services during World War II, some are properly regarded as collectors' specimens at the present time.

It must be understood that Colt weapons, like those of other manufacturers, usually have several names. We cannot hope to give them all here, but have tried to present those most generally used. Also, it must be remembered that no weapon is truly a martial weapon unless it conforms to the exact specifications of the one used by the armed services. Such details as caliber, barrel length, finish, stock or grip material, sights, and the presence or absence of a lanyard ring are of vital importance.

## COLT CARTRIDGE DERRINGERS

The whole story of Henry Deringer, Jr., of Philadelphia, Pennsylvania, for whom all "deringers" and "derringers" are named, is found in the author's book, *Guns of the Old West.*

The late Arthur L. Ulrich, while he was the corporate secretary of Colt's Patent Fire Arms Manufacturing Co., also was its official historian. In discussing the manufacture of Colt firearms during the 1870-1912 period, he said:

"A unique type of gun introduced in this period was known as the Deringer. The first Deringers introduced by Colt's and National were short, all metal, single-barreled pistols using .41 caliber, rimfire cartridges. A second type known as the 'No. 2' Deringer using the same caliber cartridge and with wood stocks was later produced by both Colt's and National, which was followed later by the third Deringers, often referred to as the New Type Deringer. These third Deringers were introduced by Colt's in the late 'Seventies' and were furnished with two types of stocks. They used .41 caliber, rim-fire cartridges and were manufactured until about 1912 when the models were discontinued."

COLT NO. 1 DERRINGER, cal. .41 r.f., single-shot; 2.5-inch, oval, flat-top barrel with a button on the right for lock, and sometimes marked "Colt's P & F.A. Mfg. Co. No. 1 Hartford Ct. U.S.A." Knife-blade ejector. Curved all-metal butt. Engraved all-metal frame. Total length 4.25 inches. Weight 9 oz. Spur trigger. Barrels on some specimens are marked "Colt's Pt. F.A. Mfg. Co., Hartford Ct. U.S.A. No. 1." Originally made by the National Arms Co., but this model was made from 1870 to about 1890 by Colt. Plate 26, Fig. 1. $325–$620.

COLT NO. 2 DERRINGER, cal. .41 r.f., single-shot; 2.5-inch, oval, flat-top barrel with button on right for lock, and sometimes marked "Colt's P. &

F.A. Mfg. Co. Hartford, Ct. U.S.A. No. 2." or it may be marked "Colt's Pt. F.A. Mfg. Co. Hartford Ct. U.S.A. No. 2." Knife-blade ejector. Bird's-head-shaped walnut grips. Engraved iron frame, nickel-plated. Spur trigger. Total length 5.25 inches. Weight 9 oz. Originally made by National Arms Co., but made by Colt from 1870 to about 1890. Barrel swings left to load. Plate 26, Fig. 2. $325–$475.

SAME, but with English casing. $425–$725.

SAME, but with plain ivory grips. $350–$515.

COLT NO. 3 DERRINGER, TYPE NO. 1, cal. .41 r.f., single-shot; 2.5-inch round barrel with snap-type latch, marked simply "Colt's." Spring-type ejector. Bird's-head-shaped walnut grips. Nickel-plated brass frame. Spur trigger. Total length 4.5 inches. Weight 7 oz. Made only by Colt, from about 1875. Barrel swings right to load. The distinguishing feature of this type No. 1 is the very straight-up or high hammer spur. Plate 26, Fig. 3. $230–$345.

SAME, but with engraved frame and ivory grips. $390–$550.

SAME, but type No. 2, with walnut grips and nickel-plated frame. Production started sometime after 1875. The distinguishing feature is the tipped-back, or back-curving hammer spur. $195–$300.

SAME, but Type No. 3, with walnut grips and nickel-plated frame. Production started sometime after 1875. Discontinued in 1912. The distinguishing feature is the butt, which is larger and has a smaller curvature. $190–$300.

COLT OLD-LINE, .22 CALIBER, SINGLE-ACTION, POCKET REVOLVER, also known as the First Model .22 Caliber Colt Revolver; cal. .22, 7-shot; 2.5-inch round barrel marked "Colt's Pat. F. A. Mfg. Hartford, Conn. U.S.A." Total length 6.5 inches. Round unmarked cylinder. Made with side-rod ejector similar to that on Frontier Model when first produced. Bird's-head-shaped wood grips. Frame has low serial number, usually below 1,000 when made with side-rod ejector, but higher serial numbers may exist in this type. Barrel is removable by moving rotary catch to the side. No strap on frame over cylinder. High or straight-up hammer spur. Firing pin enters through a hole in frame and strikes cartridge at bottom. Made from about 1870 to about 1871, but not much later. Plate 26, Fig. 4. $525–$865.

SAME, but later version of the above, cal. .22, 7-shot; 2.5-inch round barrel marked as before, total length 6 inches. Unmarked round cylinder. Made without an ejector. Same grips. Frame may be marked ".22 Cal." or in a similar manner to show caliber, and serial numbers may or may not be found. Low hammer spur. Barrel is removable as on earlier version. No strap on frame over cylinder. Made from about 1871 to about 1885 or 1886, but dates are uncertain. Firing pin is set in left side of hammer and enters a slot in frame to left of center line. $200–$300.

SAME, but later version with 3-inch barrel. $200–$300.

SAME, but later version with 3.5-inch barrel. $200–$300.

*Note: We have no knowledge of 3-inch and 3.5-inch barrels on the early version, but they probably exist.*

COLT SINGLE-ACTION ARMY REVOLVER, originally called the New Model Army Metallic Cartridge Revolving Pistol, and also called the Colt Army Revolver, Model 1872, the Peacemaker, and the Frontier Model. Cal. .45, c.f., 6-shot, S.A., 7.5-inch round barrel, total length 12.5 inches, weight 2 lbs. 5 oz. Cylinder, half fluted, 1.56 inches long. Large, steel, blade front sight. V-notch frame rear sight. Steel frame and trigger guard. Blued barrel and cylinder. Casehardened hammer and frame. Oil-finished walnut stock (but also sold with rubber stock for extra charge). Rod-type hand ejector on right side of barrel. Setscrew holds cylinder pin at front end of frame. Safety, half, and full cock notches for hammer. Ordinary loading gate. Barrel marked "Colt's Pt. F.A. Mfg. Co. Hartford Ct. U.S.A." Frame marked "Pat. Sept. 18, 1871, July 2, 1872, Jan. 19, 1875, U.S." Cylinder not marked, except for serial number. Grips marked with initials of inspectors. Butt frame

---

## PLATE 26. Colt Cartridge Pistols and Revolvers

*Figure*

1. No. 1 Derringer.
2. No. 2 Derringer.
3. No. 3 Derringer.
4. Old-line, cal. .22, Single-Action, Pocket Revolver, also known as the First Model cal. .22, Colt Revolver.
5. Single-Action Army Revolver, originally called the New Model Army Metallic Cartridge Revolving Pistol, and also called the Colt Army Revolver, Model 1871. This one is the first .44 Army or Frontier Model.
6. Single-Action Army Revolver, Frontier Model, but cal. .38-40 W. c.f. with pearl grips and elaborate engraving.
7. House Pistol, also called Cloverleaf Colt, Jim Fisk Pistol, and Old Model Cloverleaf House Pistol, with 3-inch round barrel.
8. House Pistol, same as Fig. 7, but with 1.5-inch round barrel.
9. House Pistol, 5-shot, with round cylinder, 2.5-inch barrel.
10. New-Line Single-Action Pocket Revolver, cal. .41 r.f., 2.5-inch round barrel.
11. New-Line Single-Action Pocket Revolver, cal. .38 r.f. or c.f.
12. New-Line Single-Action Pocket Revolver, cal. .32 r.f. or c.f.
13. New-Line Single-Action Pocket Revolver, cal. .30 r.f.
14. New-Line Single-Action Pocket Revolver, cal. .22 r.f.

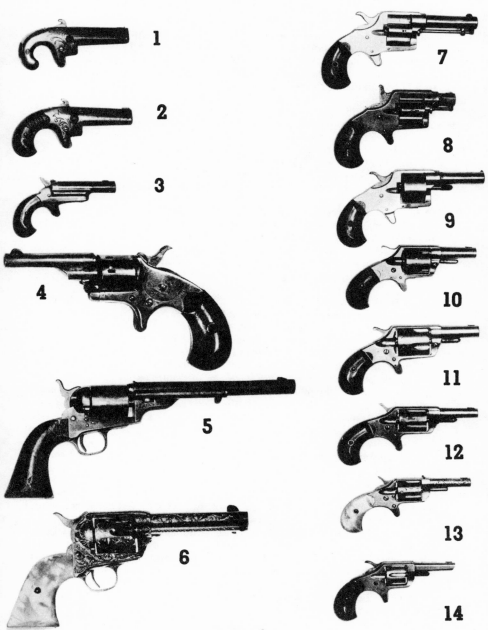

1

2

3

4

5

6

7

8

9

10

11

12

13

14

PLATE 26

and trigger guard marked with serial numbers. Its manufacture started in 1871, it was presented for test by the Army Ordnance Department in November 1872, and an initial order was placed by the Government for 8,000, to be issued to the Cavalry, in 1873. Made from 1873 to 1940. Numbered 1 to 357,859. This figure includes all calibers, barrel lengths, and variations. The standard barrel lengths were 7.5 inches, Cavalry Model or Peacemaker; 5.5 inches, Artillery Model; 4.75 inches, Civilian Model; and both 3 inches and 4 inches for the special-order pocket model without an ejector, but specimens have been found with a 3.5-inch barrel without an ejector.

Cavalry, or Peacemaker Model, with 7.5-inch barrel. $650–$1100.

Artillery Model, with 5.5-inch barrel, total length 11 inches. $575–$1000.

Civilian Model, with 4.75-inch barrel. $565–$1025.

Special Order, 3- or 4-inch barrel, without ejector. $565–$950.

SAME, but Frontier Model, chambered for .44-40 c.f. cartridge used in Winchester Model 1873 Repeating Rifle, with 7.5-inch barrel. Marked on barrel "Colt Frontier Six Shooter." Plate 26, Fig. 5. $450–$875.

SAME, but cal. .38-40 W.c.f., presentation model, elaborately engraved, with pearl grips. Plate 26, Fig. 6. $1100–$1,950.

SAME, but Spanish imitation, cal. .38 c.f., 6-inch round barrel, nickel-plated, rubber grips, usual markings. $30–$50.

*Note: The Cavalry (Peacemaker) and Artillery Models, described above, are definitely U.S. martial cartridge revolvers. The Frontier Model, in the caliber and barrel length described, may be regarded as a secondary U.S. martial arm in the broad sense of the term, but is not a martial weapon in the strict sense of the term. It has been chambered for the following cartridges in addition to those mentioned above: .22 r.f.; .32 Colt c.f.; .32 S & W; .32 Winchester c.f.; .38 Colt c.f., short, long, and special; .38 Winchester c.f.; .41 Colt c.f.; .44 Russian c.f.; .44 Colt c.f.; .44 Winchester c.f.; .44 S & W special c.f.; .45 Government; .45 Colt c.f.; .357 Magnum; and .45 auto cartridge, at the factory, and only Heaven knows in how many variations by gunsmiths and private individuals. The known barrel lengths are from 4.75 to 7.5 inches. Shooting qualities affect the value of collectors' specimens.*

COLT'S HOUSE PISTOL, also called Cloverleaf Colt, Jim Fisk Pistol, and Old Model Cloverleaf House Pistol, cal. .41 r.f., 4-shot; 3-inch round barrel marked "Colt's House Pistol, Hartford, Ct., U.S.A." Total length 7 inches. Cloverleaf-shaped cylinder. Rectangular slots. Ejector rod under barrel, with inside center pin. Straight-up or high hammer. Bird's-head-shaped walnut grips. Weight 14 oz. Brass frame. Spur trigger. Hammer may be low instead of high or straight-up, but high hammer is usually found on the earlier productions. Made from 1871 to 1875 with a few variations in the later years, but none of them are very important. From the mechanical viewpoint, this was the first revolver type to use the recessed chambers that Colt now calls the embedded-head cylinder, yet this important feature was neglected for more than half a century before Colt embodied it in modern cal. .22 target weapons. Plate 26, Fig. 7. $275–$425.

SAME, but 1.5-inch octagon barrel. $550–$850.

SAME, but 1.5-inch round barrel marked "Colt," total length 5.31 inches. Frame marked "Pat. Sept. 18, 1871," with serial number. Plate 26, Fig. 8. $350–$560.

COLT'S HOUSE PISTOL, 5-SHOT, WITH ROUND CYLINDER, cal. .41 r.f., 5-shot; 2.5-inch or 2.625-inch round barrel marked "Patent Sept. 19, 1871, Colt's House Pistol, Hartford, Ct., U.S.A." Rectangular slots. Round cylinder. No ejector. Center pin held by screw. Bird's-head-shaped walnut grips. Weight 15 oz. Total length about 6.5 inches. Frame marked "Pat. Sept. 19, 1871." Either low or high (straight-up) hammer. A few of these were made between 1871 and 1875. Plate 26, Fig. 9. $275–$440.

*Note: Colt's House Pistol was made with barrels from 1.5 to 3.5 inches long, but the above descriptions are representative of the usual, known specimens.*

COLT NEW-LINE SINGLE-ACTION POCKET REVOLVERS: These were made from about 1873 to about 1890, but dates are uncertain. The frames of some are marked with the caliber, while others lack this. All carry the words "Colt's Pt. F.A. Mfg. Co., Hartford, Ct." on the barrel, sometimes with patent numbers.

COLT NEW-LINE SINGLE-ACTION POCKET REVOLVER, cal. .41 r.f., 5-shot; 2.5-inch round barrel marked "Colt's Pt. F.A. Mfg. Co., Hartford, Ct., U.S.A., Colt New .41." Total length 6.25 inches. Unmarked, half fluted cylinder. No ejector. Bird's-head-shaped walnut grips. Frame marked ".41 Cal." Followed by serial number. Also made for .41 c.f. cartridges. Sometimes called the Big Colt because the largest caliber in this series was cal. .41, and the size depended upon the caliber in this group. Plate 26, Fig. 10. $210–$315.

SAME, but with plain ivory grips. $240–$365.

SAME, but cal. .38 r.f. or .38 c.f., with walnut grips. Sometimes called Pet Colt. Plate 26, Fig. 11. $185–$280.

SAME, but cal. .32 r.f., or c.f., 2.375-inch round barrel, 5-shot; fluted cylinder, cylinder slots on side, walnut bird's-head-shaped grips. Sometimes called Ladies' Colt. Total length 6 inches. Plate 26, Fig. 12. $130–$185.

SAME, but with ivory grips. $140–$195.

SAME, but cal. .30 r.f. (apparently there is no cal. .30 c.f.), 2.25-inch

188     GUN COLLECTOR'S HANDBOOK OF VALUES

round barrel, 5-shot, fluted cylinder with slots at end, bird's-head-shaped walnut grips, total length 5.75 inches. Sometimes called Pony Colt. Specimen shown has pearl grips. Plate 26, Fig. 13. $125–$200.

SAME, but with 1.75-inch barrel. $130–$200.

SAME, but cal. .22 r.f., 7-shot; 2.125-inch round barrel with flat sides; fluted cylinder with slots on end. Bird's-head-shaped walnut grips. Sometimes called Little Colt. Plate 26, Fig. 14. $125–$200.

SAME, but with plain ivory grips. $125–$215.

COLT NEW-LINE POLICE REVOLVER, also called New-Line Police Pistol, New Police Revolver, New York Police Pistol, and Police and Thug Model, cal. .38 r.f., S.A., 5-shot; 4.5-inch round barrel marked "Colt's Pat. F.A. Mfg. Co., Hartford, Ct., U.S.A. (New Police .38)." Unmarked, half fluted cylinder. Side-rod ejector and loading gate. Frame marked ".38 Cal." with serial number. Checkered, hard-rubber, square-end grips with embossed picture of policeman capturing a thug, hence the name Police and Thug Model. Total length 9 inches. Fundamentally it resembles the other New-Line Single-Action Pocket Revolver except for the square-end grips, the side-rod ejector, the loading gate, and the picture. It was manufactured from about 1874 or 1875 to about 1890. This specimen is the regular model. Plate 27, Fig. 1. $425–$670.

SAME, but with 6-inch barrel. $435–$680.

Note: Barrel lengths vary from 2.5 to 6 inches for above model.

COLT NEW-LINE POLICE PISTOL, or Short-barreled New-Line Police Pistol, cal. .38 c.f., cal. .38 r.f., cal. .41 r.f., or cal. .41 c.f., without much value variation for caliber difference. The 2.125-inch or 2.5-inch round barrel is marked "Colt's Pat. F.A. Mfg. Co., Hartford, Ct., U.S.A." on top and "Colt's House .38" on the side. Five-shot. Unmarked, half fluted cylinder. No ejector. Frame has serial number. Checkered, hard-rubber, square-end grips with embossed picture of policeman capturing thug. Similar to previously described model except for short barrel and absence of the ejector. Made from about 1874 to about 1890. $265–$470.

SAME, but with either plain walnut grips, or black hard-rubber grips marked with the word "Colt" in small letters at the top, but not with the policeman and thug picture. Made from about 1874 to about 1890, but the dates on this and the two previous descriptions are uncertain. $170–$230.

COLT SO-CALLED OPEN-TOP REVOLVERS, cal. .22. While the new-line models were being developed and manufactured one of the old-line models, a cal. .22 revolver without a top strap, commonly referred to by collectors as the Open-Top Revolver, was still being manufactured, and available with or without an ejector. It should be understood that this was not really a new model, but merely a modification or variation. There are slight variations of barrel length, and both low and high hammers are found, but none of these have much effect on values.

OPEN-TOP SIDE-EJECTOR, FIRST TYPE, cal. .22 r.f., 3-inch round barrel, 7-shot, spur trigger, brass frame, walnut grips. Firing pin enters through a hole in the frame, striking the cartridge at the bottom. Plate 27, Fig. 10. $285–$485.

SAME, but second type, 3-inch round barrel, 7-shot, spur trigger, brass frame, walnut grips. Firing pin is set in left side of hammer and enters a slot in the frame to the left of the center line. The ejector rod housing is integral with the barrel. Plate 27, Fig. 11. $270–$450.

OPEN-TOP, cal. .22 r.f., 2.375-inch round barrel, 7-shot, spur trigger, brass frame, nickel-plated, walnut grips. Plate 27, Fig. 2. $95–$150.

SAME, but with all-metal grips with lion's head in relief on right grip and floral design on left. Engraved frame and barrel. Grips are gold-plated, and the rest of the revolver is nickel-plated. Plate 27, Fig. 3. $175–$275.

SAME, but a presentation piece with pearl grips and more engraving. Plate 27, Fig. 4. $335–$485.

COLT NEW DOUBLE-ACTION, SELF-COCKING CENTRAL-FIRE 6-SHOT REVOLVER, also called Lightning Model, and New Model Double-Action Revolver, cal. .38 c.f., 6-shot; 3.5-inch round barrel marked "Colt's Pt. F.A. Mfg. Co., Hartford, Ct., U.S.A., Colt D.A. .38." Total length 8.5 inches. Unmarked, two-thirds fluted cylinder. No ejector, but it has a loading gate. Bird's-head-shaped, checkered, hard-rubber grips. Frame marked on left side "Pat. Sept. 19, '71, Sept. 15, '74, Jan. 19, '75." Trigger guard marked ".38 Cal." This was the first double-action revolver made by Colt and was manufactured from 1877 to 1912. Made in 2.5-, 3.5-, 4.5-, and 6-inch barrel lengths without apparent variation in values. Plate 28, Fig. 1. $130–$255.

SAME, but cal. .41 c.f., with various barrel lengths. $140–$215.

SAME, but cal. .38 c.f., made with side-rod ejector, and often found with 4.5-inch barrel and a total length of 8.75 inches. This was a first modification of the model described above without the side-rod ejector. Plate 28, Fig. 2. $140–$200.

SAME, but cal. .41, made with a side-rod ejector and usually with the 4.5-inch barrel and a total length of 8.75 inches, although the barrel length and the total length may vary. $170–$250.

COLT BISLEY MODEL REVOLVER, cal. .45 c.f., 6-shot; 7.5-inch round barrel, marked "Colt's Patent F.A. Mfg. Co., Hartford, Conn., U.S.A. Bisley Model .45 Colt's"; total length 13 inches. Half fluted cylinder without markings. Side-rod ejector. Frame marked on left "Pat. Sept. 19, 1871, July 2, 1872, Jan. 19, 1875," with rampant colt. Hard-rubber checkered grips. The Bisley was developed gradually from the original Single-Action Army or Frontier Model into a target arm by changing the trigger, hammer, and grips of the Frontier Model, and manufactured from 1896 or 1897 to 1912. Loading gate. Blued barrel. Frame and hammer are casehardened in natural colors. Plate 27, Fig. 5. $400–$675.

COLT BISLEY FLAT-TOP MODEL, cal. .38 special, 6-shot; 7.5-inch round barrel marked "Colt's Pat. F.A. Mfg. Co., Hartford, Conn., U.S.A. Bisley Model .38 Colt." Side-rod ejector. Half fluted cylinder. Total length 13 inches. Checkered hard-rubber grips. Blued finish. Flat-top frame marked "Pat. Sept. 19, 1871, July 2, 1872, Jan. 19, 1875." Special target sights, but specimens are sometimes found with ordinary sights. Plate 27, Fig. 6. $650–$950.

SAME, but cal. .38-40 W.c.f. $850–$1050.

SAME, but with carved ivory grips. Value varies greatly among speci-

---

PLATE 27. Colt Cartridge Pistols and Revolvers

*Figure*

1. New Police Revolver, also called New Line Police Pistol, New Police Revolver, New York Police Pistol, and often called the Police and Thug Model.
2. Open-Top, cal. .22 Revolver, 2.375-inch barrel, walnut grips.
3. Open-Top, cal. .22 Revolver, same as Fig. 2 but with all-metal grips having a lion's head in relief on right grip and a floral design on the left grip.
4. Open-Top, cal. .22 Revolver, same as Fig. 2 but with pearl grips and elaborately engraved metal parts.
5. Bisley Model Revolver, cal. .45 c.f., 6-shot, 7.5-inch round barrel.
6. Bisley Flat-Top Model, cal. .38 special, 6-shot, 7.5-inch round barrel.
7. Bisley Model, cal. .38-40 W.c.f. with 4.75-inch round barrel.

8. Double-Action Army or Frontier Revolver, Model 1878, cal. .45 c.f., 6-shot, 7.5-inch round barrel, made with hard-rubber grips.
9. Double-Action Army Revolver, Philippine Model.
10. Open-Top, cal. .22 r.f., Side-Ejector, First Type.
11. Open-Top, cal. .22 r.f., Side-Ejector, Second Type.
12. Pocket Model, .38 Automatic, Model of 1903, cal. .38 auto, 6-inch barrel, sporting type.
13. Military Model Automatic, cal. .45, sometimes called Model 1905 Automatic Pistol.
14. Government Model of 1911 Automatic Pistol, cal. .45, also called Model 1911 Automatic Pistol, cal. .45, auto-loading, marked "Model of 1911 U.S. Navy."

PLATE 27

mens, according to the quantity and quality of the carving, but the value indicated is for the usual specimen. $850–$1250.

SAME, but cal. .38-40 W.c.f., with checkered rubber grips and 4.75-inch round barrel. Plate 27, Fig. 7. $650–$825.

SAME, but so-called Pocket Size Bisley, cal. .45 c.f., 6-shot, 3-inch round barrel, total length 8.5 inches. Half fluted cylinder. Frame not fitted for side-rod ejector. Checkered hard-rubber grips. Barrel marked "Colt's Pt. F.A. Mfg. Co., Hartford, Ct., U.S.A." Frame marked "Pat. Sept. 19, 1871. July 2, 1872, January 19, 1875." Made from 1896 to 1912 in small quantities. Blued finish. $535–$750.

*Note on Bisley Models: Collectors often distinguish between the Bisley Model Revolver and the Bisley Target Model Revolver. They consider that the Bisley Model Revolver was made in barrel lengths of 4.75, 5.5, and 7.5 inches, and in calibers .45 Colt, .44-40 W.c.f., .44 S & W Russian, .41 long Colt c.f., .38-40 W.c.f., .38 long Colt c.f., .32-20 W.c.f., and .32 long c.f., and that this non-target or regular model was made until 1912, along with the target version.*

*Collectors believe that the Bisley Target Model was introduced after the regular model and that part of its popularity was due to its adjustable sights. They regard the 7.5-inch barrel as the only true Target Model barrel for the Bisley, and they recognize that it was made for calibers .455 Eley, .44-40 W.c.f., .44 S & W special, .44 S & W Russian, .41 long Colt c.f., .38-40 W.c.f., .38 long Colt c.f., .32-20 W.c.f., and .32 long Colt c.f.*

*In addition, collectors recognize the Pocket-Size or Special Short-Barrel Bisley as a distinct variation or modification.*

*The most popular from the collecting viewpoint is the Flat-Top Model with the flat-top strap over the cylinder and the old charcoal blue finish characteristic of only the early pieces made by the Colt factory. The demand, on the part of marksmen, for the target model, or the regular model with a long barrel and special sights, has raised the values higher than they would be if they were regarded only as collectors' specimens.*

COLT DOUBLE-ACTION ARMY OR FRONTIER REVOLVER, MODEL 1878, cal. .45 c.f., 6-shot; 7.5-inch round barrel marked on top "Colt's Pt. F.A. Mfg. Co., Hartford, Conn., U.S.A. .45 Colt's." Total length 12.5 inches. Weight 2 lbs. 7 oz. Cylinder, 1.56 inches long, two-thirds fluted, is unmarked. Large, steel-blade front sight. V-notch frame rear sight. Checked, bird's-head walnut grips. Lanyard ring in butt. Steel trigger guard and frame. Side-rod ejector on lower right side of barrel. There is a round disk on left side of frame, held in place by a hammer screw. The grips carry the Colt trademark of a rampant colt. The New Double-Action Revolver came out in January 1877, originally called the New Double-Action, Self-Cocking, Central-Fire, 6-shot Revolver, and later called the Lightning Model, made in cal. .38 and .41, c.f., in two types. In 1878 the Double-Action Army or Frontier Model appeared, similar to the previous model, but larger and cal. .45. The model described here was for the Army, as distinguished by the walnut grips. Made from 1877 to about 1905 in the various types described. $225–$360.

SAME, but with hard-rubber grip plates, for civilians. Plate 27, Fig. 8. $220–$375.

SAME, but with very large trigger and trigger guard, 6-inch barrel, full-fluted cylinder, iron back strap rounding to grips; originally intended for the Army in Alaska, but sent to the Philippines, hence called Philippine Model. Plate 27, Fig. 9. $195–$275.

*Note: This model was made in barrel lengths of 3.5 and 4 inches, without an ejector; and 4.75, 5.5, and 7.5 inches with an ejector. It was chambered for .38-40, .44-40, and .45 Colt cartridges; and also for .38 W.c.f., .44 W.c.f., and .44 S & W. Army models are strictly U.S. martial cartridge revolvers. This was the first large, heavy, double-action revolver made by Colt. This model and its variations were discontinued in 1910.*

COLT NEW NAVY, DOUBLE-ACTION, SELF-COCKING REVOLVER, MODEL 1889, 6-shot cal. .38 short and long Colt. Six-inch barrel, side-swing cylinder. Knife-blade and V-notch sights. Total length 11.25 inches. This is the first type of the swing-out cylinder, simultaneously ejecting Colt revolver. There are no cylinder-locking notches on the outside of the cylinder. Instead it is held in position by a double projection on the hand that grips the ratchet back of the cylinder. This was made from 1889 to 1892. It has the usual marks and resembles Colt Army Models 1892, 1894, and 1896. Butt frame marked "U.S.N. .38 D.A." with model year and serial number. Plate 28, Fig. 3. $150–$350.

SAME, but cal. .41 short and long Colt. $175–$365.

*Note: This model was also made with 3- and 4.5-inch barrels.*

COLT NEW NAVY, DOUBLE-ACTION, SELF-COCKING REVOLVER, MODEL 1892, cal. .41 short and long Colt, and cal. .38 short and long Colt. Six-shot, 6-inch barrel; knife-blade and V-notch sights. Same as the Model 1889, but this is really a second type of the Model 1889. The cylinder has two notches for the locking bolts. Beginning in 1892, this was applied to arms of the then new, solid-frame, swing-out-cylinder revolvers for several years. The barrel is marked on top "Colt's Pt. F.A. Mfg. Co., Hartford, Ct. U.S.A." The left side of the barrel is marked "Colt D.A. .38" or "Colt D.A. .41" as the case may be. This Model 1892 was made from 1892 to 1908. Plate 28, Fig. 4. $145–$225.

COLT NEW ARMY MODELS 1892, 1894, 1896, cal. .38 c.f., 6-shot, D.A.; 6-inch round barrel, total length 11.5 inches, weight 2 lbs. 1 oz. Solid frame, side-swing cylinder. Cylinder 1.5 inches long. Steel-blade front sight. Frame rear sight. Oval steel trigger guard. Steel grip frame. Blued finish. Oil-finished plain walnut grips. Similar to New Navy Models. First variation, or Model 1892, could not be securely locked with the cylinder and barrel in line. Second variation, or Model 1894, had locking lever which made it impossible to cock the piece until the cylinder was in line with the barrel and locked. In 1894, all available Model 1894 revolvers were altered to include the new locking device. The Model 1896 does not have any characteristics outstandingly different from the previous models. The barrel is marked on top "Colt's Pt. F.A. Mfg. Co. Hartford Ct. U.S.A. Patented Aug. 5, 1884, Nov. 6, '88, March 5, '95," and on the left "Colt D.A. 38." Grip frame marked "U.S. Army Model" with model year and serial number. The left grip bears date. Both sides of the grips bear the usual rampant-colt trademark. $145–$275.

COLT ARMY MODEL 1901. This is the same as the final form of the New Army Models previously described except for the addition of an oblong lanyard swivel. $150–$285.

COLT ARMY MODEL 1903. This is the same as the Model 1901, described above, except that the grip is smaller and shaped better for the hand, and the bore caliber is very slightly smaller to insure that the lands in the rifling bite into the bullet deeper, thus increasing accuracy in this particular revolver. $150–$250.

COLT MARINE CORPS MODEL 1905 (sometimes called Marine Corps

---

PLATE 28. Colt Cartridge Pistols and Revolvers

*Figure*

1. New Double-Action, Self-Cocking, Central-Fire, 6-shot Revolver, First Modification, without the side-rod ejector.
2. New Double-Action, Self-Cocking, Central-Fire, 6-shot Revolver, also called the Lightning Model and the New Model Double-Action Revolver, made with a side-rod ejector.
3. New Navy, Double-Action, Self-Cocking Revolver, Model 1889.
4. New Navy, Double-Action, Self-Cocking Revolver, Model 1892.
5. Marine Corps Model 1905, some-

times called Marine Corps Model 1907, with plain walnut grips.
6. Marine Corps Model 1905, with checked walnut grips.
7. New Service Revolver, Model 1909.
8. New Service Revolver, U.S. Marine Corps Model.
9. Automatic Pistol, cal. .38, Model of 1900.
10. Automatic Pistol, cal. .38. Military Model of 1902.
11. National Match Model Automatic, cal. .45.

PLATE 28

Model 1907), cal. .38 short and long Colt, 6-shot, D.A., 6-inch round barrel. Total length 10.5 inches. Weight 2 lbs. Checked walnut grips. Lanyard ring on butt. The grip is smaller and more rounded at the rear than that of the Army Model 1903 and the New Navy Model 1892, but otherwise this model resembles its Army and Navy predecessors. Barrel marked "Colt's Pt. F.A. Mfg. Co. Hartford, Ct., U.S.A. Patented Aug. 5, 1884, Nov. 6, '88, Mar. 5, '95." Butt frame marked "U.S.M.C." with a serial number. Left side of the barrel marked "Colt D.A. .38." The usual rampant colt appears on the frame. Knife-blade and V-notch sights. This model was made from 1905 to 1910. Plate 28, Fig. 6. $350–$675.

SAME, but butt not checked. Plate 28, Fig. 5. $350–$695.

COLT NEW SERVICE REVOLVER, MODEL 1909, cal. .45 c.f., 6-shot, D.A.; 5.5-inch round barrel, total length 10.625 inches. Weight 2 lbs. 8 oz. Fluted, side-swing cylinder 1.625 inches long. Blued barrel, cylinder, and frame. Bright steel hammer. Casehardened trigger. Steel-blade front sight. Frame rear sight. Oil-finished walnut grips. Lanyard swivel mounted in butt. Catch on left of frame operates side-swing action. Ejector rod slides through cylinder and pushes extractor plate which extracts all fired cartridge cases simultaneously. Barrel marked on top "Colt's Pt. F.A. Mfg. Co., Hartford Ct., U.S.A. Pt. Aug. 5, 1884, June 5, 1900, July 4, 1905," and marked on side "Colt D.A. 45." Butt frame marked "U.S. Army Model 1909" with serial number. Frame marked with rampant colt trademark. This model was originally presented in 1897 and has been made from that date until today without any substantial model changes. In the Colt catalogue of 1898 this model was listed as made with 4.5-, 5.5-, and 7.5-inch barrels, and with either a blued frame and barrel or a full nickel-plate finish. It has been chambered for a wide variety of cartridges, including the .45 Colt, .44 Russian, .44-40, and .38-40. At the beginning of World War I, the Colt New Service was chambered for the .45 automatic pistol cartridge and issued to the Army as the Model 1917 Revolver. In its original form it was adopted by the armed services of the United States in 1909 and discontinued only when the cal. .45 automatic pistol became the standard side arm. Plate 28, Fig. 7. $145–$225.

SAME, but U.S. Marine Corps Model, with checked walnut stock, a smaller grip, and a lanyard ring. Butt frame marked "U S.M.C." Plate 28, Fig. 8. $275–$450.

COLT ARMY REVOLVER MODEL 1917, cal. .45, 6-shot, D.A., 5.5-inch round barrel. Total length 10.75 inches. Weight 2 lbs. 8 oz. Fluted cylinder 1.53 inches long. Blued cylinder, barrel, and frame. Bright hammer. Steel-blade front sight. Frame rear sight. Oil-finished walnut grips. Resembles Model 1917 Smith & Wesson. Chambered for .45 automatic pistol cartridges, used in semi-circular clips of three because rimless case would not be handled by existing ejector. The cartridges could be loaded and fired without the clips, but it was then necessary to pry them out by hand. Later a cartridge was developed, called the .45 auto rim cartridge, which has a rimmed head and can be extracted by the revolver-type ejector, but the World War I Model 1917 did not have these new cartridges. Barrel marked on top "Colt's Pt. F.A. Mfg. Co., Hartford Ct., U.S.A., Patented Aug. 5, 1884, June 5, 1900, July 4, 1905" and marked on the side "Colt D.A. 45." Marked under barrel "United States Property." Frame has usual Colt trademark. Butt marked "U.S. Army Model 1917" with serial number. The United States bought 151,700 Colt Model 1917 Revolvers between April 6, 1917, and December 1918. $85–$140.

## COLT AUTOMATIC PISTOLS

COLT AUTOMATIC PISTOL, MODEL of 1900, cal. .38, cal. .38 auto, 7-shot magazine, 6-inch barrel, total length 9 inches. Two toggle lugs pinned to frame hold barrel to receiver. No slide lock. Sharp spur-type hammer. Knife-blade and V-notch sights. Slide marked on left "Colt's Pt. F.A. Mfg. Co., Hartford, Ct., U.S.A. Browning's Patent. Pat'd. April 20, 1897," and marked on right "Automatic Colt Caliber .38 Rimless Smokeless." This was either the first or one of the first automatic pistols made in the United States, and the first made by Colt. A combination safety and rear sight is pressed down to prevent hammer from hitting firing pin. Weight 37 oz. Manufactured from 1900 to 1902. Plate 28, Fig. 9. $200–$375.

COLT AUTOMATIC PISTOL, MILITARY MODEL OF 1902, cal. .38 auto, 6-inch barrel, 8-shot magazine, slide stop on left side. No safeties. Rounded back hammer. Knife-blade and V-notch sights. Slide marked on left "Patented April 20, 1897, Sept. 9, 1902, Colt's Patent F.A. Mfg. Co. Hartford, Ct. U.S.A." with Colt trademark on the right side "Automatic Colt Caliber .38 Rimless Smokeless Model 1902." Hammer rests on firing pin without the latter hitting the cartridge primer, since the firing pin is shorter than the distance from the hammer to the primer. Longer grip than sporting type of this model, and square at the bottom, with a lanyard ring. Total length 9 inches. Weight about 2 lbs. 5 oz. Stub trigger without spur. Checkered, hard-rubber grips. Plate 28, Fig. 10. $250–$410.

SAME, but Sporting Type, with shorter grip and without lanyard. $200–$360.

SAME, but Third Type, with modern, spur-type hammer, added in 1908. The original production started in 1902, and this Third Type was made until production stopped in 1928. $175–$215.

COLT POCKET MODEL OF 1903, cal. .38 auto, 4.5-inch barrel, 7-shot magazine; no slide lock, no safeties; spur-type hammer; knife-blade and V-notch sights; two-toggle-lug barrel attachment; total length 7.5 inches. Slide marked on left "Patented April 20, 1897, Sept. 9, 1902 Colt's Pt. F.A. Mfg. Co., Hartford, Ct., U.S.A." and on the right side "Automatic Colt Caliber .38 Rimless Smokeless." Rounded hammer like that on the 1902 Military Model was used from 1903, when production started, to 1908, but from 1908 until the end of production in 1928 it had a spur-type hammer of a more modern design. $175–$225.

SAME, but Sporting Model, with 6-inch barrel. Plate 27, Fig. 12. $175–$225.

COLT POCKET MODEL AUTOMATIC (1903), cal. .32 auto, 4-inch barrel, 8-shot magazine, total length 7 inches. Weight 23 oz. Thumb-operated slide-lock safety, and grip safety. Inside hammer, or so-called hammerless design. Knife-blade and V-notch sights. Slide marked on left "Patented April 20, 1897, Dec. 22, 1903, Colt's Pat. F.A. Mfg. Co., Hartford Conn., U.S.A." and on right side "Colt Automatic Caliber .32 Rimless Smokeless." Barrel held barrel-lock bushing at the muzzle. Production started in 1903; in 1908 it was chambered for the .380 cartridge, and it continued in its original form until 1911. Several changes made since 1911 have brought it up to date, hence it is now sold principally as a modern arm, according to shooting condition. Now fires .32 automatic Colt pistol cartridge. $150–$225.

COLT MILITARY MODEL AUTOMATIC, sometimes called Model 1905 Automatic Pistol, cal. .45 auto, 7-shot magazine, 5-inch barrel, total length 8 inches. Slide stop on left. No safeties. Rounded back hammer. Knife-blade and V-notch sights. Slide marked on left "Patented April 20, 1897, Sept. 9, 1902, Dec. 19, '05. Colt's Patent F.A. Mfg. Co., Hartford, Ct., U.S.A." and on right side "Automatic Colt Caliber .45 Rimless Smokeless." Checkered walnut grips. Blued finish. This was the first cal. .45 military automatic pistol made by Colt. Production started in 1905 and continued until 1911 when the U.S. Government Model of 1911, cal. .45, was introduced. Specimens made between 1908 and 1911 have a spur-type hammer. Some specimens are found with a short-grip safety, but these are regarded as experimental pieces and departures from the standard. Plate 27, Fig. 13. $250–$350.

SAME, but fitted for and equipped with a shoulder-stock holster especially made for this model from 1905 to 1911. $750–$1050.

COLT GOVERNMENT MODEL OF 1911 AUTOMATIC PISTOL, also called Model 1911 Automatic Pistol, cal. .45, auto-loading, 5-inch barrel, 7-shot magazine, total length 8.5 inches. Weight 2 lbs. 7 oz. with magazine empty. Has slide lock and slide stop on the left, and is equipped with slide lock and grip safeties. Flat-top and square-notch sights. Outside spur-type hammer. Muzzle bushing and breech-toggle-lug barrel attachment. Walnut stocks. Slide marked on left "Colt's Pat. F.A. Mfg. Co. Hartford Ct., U.S.A." with trademark and "Patented April 20, 1897, Sept. 9, 1902, Dec. 19, 1905, Feb. 14, 1911, Aug. 19, 1913." Government arms are marked on left side of frame "United States Property." Slide marked on right "Model of 1911 U.S. Army." Obviously this is a U.S. martial firearm. Production started in 1911 and has continued to date with several improvements. Value stated is for original model, disregarding shooting condition. $200–$275.

SAME, but factory-marked "Colt Automatic Caliber 45" and with Russian words. $225–$350.

SAME, but marked "Model of 1911 U.S. Navy." Plate 27, Fig. 14. $300–$450.

SAME, but manufactured and marked by Remington-UMC in World War I. $320-$475.

SAME, but marked "Model of 1911 U.S. Marine Corps." $350–$600.

SAME, but marked "Springfield Armory U.S.A." $400–$650.

*Note: The above values are for the earlier type, with the original markings, and not for some modern piece stolen from the United States and doctored up in a garage. When a weapon which may have belonged originally to the United States is bought, record all serial numbers and notify the nearest police department, the sheriff's office, and the nearest office of the Federal Bureau of Investigation, if you suspect that it was stolen. Otherwise you may later find yourself accused of stealing or receiving stolen property.*

SAME, but National Match Model Automatic, cal. .45. Modern, not a collector's piece. Plate 28, Fig. 11. Value not stated.

# Chapter 14

## U.S. MARTIAL SINGLE-SHOT CARTRIDGE PISTOLS

I T is a serious mistake to list the so-called U.S. Single-Shot Army Pistol, Model 1869, Springfield. There is no such model or type and it never existed except in the innocent imaginations of a few collectors, dealers, authors, and the museum curators who failed to give the subject serious thought. This dream gun is supposed to be cal. .50, c.f., with a 9-inch, round, rifle barrel, cut from a shoulder weapon, some parts from a U.S. Rifle, Model 1868, and other parts from a U.S. Rifled Musket, Model 1863. Two were made, tried, rejected and are now in the Springfield Armory Museum. Any offered to collectors are fakes.

U.S. NAVY MODEL 1866, REMINGTON SINGLE-SHOT PISTOL, cal. .50 r.f.; 8.5–inch round, blued, rifled barrel marked with an anchor. Total length 11.25 inches. Weight 2 lbs. 4 oz. Blade front sight. V-notch rear sight in breechblock. Casehardened breechblock, hammer, and trigger. Receiver marked "Remingtons Ilion N.Y. U.S.A. Pat. May 3d Nov. 15th 1864, April 17, 1866" on left, with initials on right. Walnut grips. Sheath trigger. Breechblock is locked and supported by the hammer when it is in the down position. Made from 1866 to 1875. Numbered 1 to over 1,000. Plate 29, Fig. 1. $600–$925.

U.S. NAVY MODEL 1867, REMINGTON SINGLE-SHOT PISTOL, cal. .50 c.f.; 7-inch round, blued, rifled barrel marked with an anchor and initials. Total length 11.75 inches. Weight 2 lbs. Blade front sight. V-shaped rear sight in breechblock. Sheath trigger of Model 1866 replaced by normal trigger and oval trigger guard. Walnut grips. Receiver marked "Remingtons Ilion N.Y. U.S.A. Pat. May 3d Nov 15th 1864. April 17th 1866" on left, with initials on right. In addition to the use of a normal trigger and trigger guard, this model differs from Model 1866 in having a shorter barrel and center fire. Made from 1867 to 1875. Numbered 1 to over 7,000. Plate 29, Fig. 2., $325–$625.

**U.S. ARMY MODEL 1871, REMINGTON SINGLE-SHOT PISTOL,** cal. .50 c.f.; 8-inch, round, rifled barrel. Knife-blade front sight. V-notch rear sight in breechblock. Total length 12 inches. Weight 2 lbs. Blued barrel and trigger. Frame casehardened in mottled colors. Breechblock and hammer finished bright. Receiver marked on left "Remingtons Ilion N.Y. U.S.A. Pat. May 3d Nov. 15th 1864. April 17th 1866," with initials. Rounded fishtail-shaped walnut grips. Resembles Navy Model 1867 except for grip, slight difference in front sight, and barrel length. Made from 1872 to 1888. Numbered from 1 to over 6,000. Plate 29, Fig. 3. $260–$565.

**SO-CALLED U.S. ARMY EXPERIMENTAL MODEL 1869, SPRING-FIELD PISTOL.** As late as 1961, in the museums of the U.S. Armory, Springfield, Massachusetts, and the U.S. Arsenal, Rock Island, Illinois, there were on display "pattern" or "experimental" single-shot pistols, which were never put into production and never issued for service use by the armed forces of the United States. One of these somewhat resembled the U.S. Pistol, Model 1842, as to mountings, but it was made to fire a special cadet cartridge, cal. .50, with a short cartridge case, 1.312 inches long. The pistol was marked "1869" on the breech, but this was merely the year the pistol was assembled and not a model year.

*Note: Collectors and dealers are warned against buying any pistol of this description. For further information on this pistol, see Chapter 8 of the author's book* U.S. Martial and Semi-Martial Single-Shot Pistols.

**SIGNAL PISTOL, 1882 MODEL,** 8 inches long, 4-inch barrel, spur trigger, all brass except minor iron parts; wood grips, 25 mm bore or 4 guage. Marked on left side of frame "Ord. Dept. U.S. N.Y.W., 1882." The year may vary, and it is possible that this model was used by both the Army and the Navy. The distinguishing feature of this gun is that the barrel revolves 360 degrees and can be loaded at either side. Plate 30, Fig. 5. $200–$325.

**U.S. NAVY SIGNAL PISTOL, 1882 MODEL,** 6 inches long, 4-inch brass barrel of 25mm, brass frame, spur trigger, lanyard ring in butt, two-piece wood grips. Barrel turns 360 degrees allowing unused flare to go in barrel which ejects the fired flare. Lieut. E. W. Very patented this pistol and flare on June 21, 1878, in Germany. He also patented his cartridge in the U.S. but not the gun. Usually marked "U.S.N.Y.W.–Ord. Dept." and dated 1882 or later. Plate 30, Fig. 1. $225–$325.

**U.S. NAVY SIGNAL PISTOL 1882 MODEL** of 10 gauge, 9-inch steel barrel inserted in the 25mm brass barrel; ejector is a sliding bar on the right side. Marked on the right side "Mfg. Ord. Dep. W.N.Y. 1895" followed by an anchor and "T.F.J." On the left side "Equip. Dep. No. 80 A.D." Purpose of this model was to reduce the size of flares previously used in 1882 model. Markings do vary. Plate 30, Fig. 2. $225–$350.

MARK II U.S. NAVY SIGNAL PISTOL, 10-gauge, 9-inch steel barrel, brass frame, wood grips. Marked "Mark II" and usually "Navy Yard N.Y." Some also marked "W.N.Y.," others "Model 96" with a date. Plate 30, Fig. 4. $170–$275.

MARK III U.S. ARMY SIGNAL PISTOL. Remington made about 25,000 of these for World War I. They are all marked Remington and are almost identical to the Mark II pistols. Plate 30, Fig. 3. $90–$150.

---

### PLATE 29. U.S. Martial Single-Shot Cartridge Pistols

*Figure*

1. U.S. Navy Model 1866, Remington Single-Shot Pistol.
2. U.S. Navy Model 1867, Remington Single-Shot Pistol.
3. U.S. Army Model 1871, Remington Single-Shot Pistol.

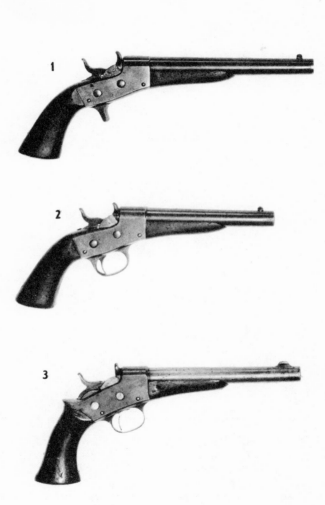

PLATE 29. U. S. Martial Single-Shot Cartridge Pistols

PLATE 30. U.S. Army and Navy Signal Pistols

*Figure*

1. U.S. Navy Signal Pistol, 1882.
2. U.S. Navy Signal Pistol, 10-gauge, 1894.
3. Mark III U.S. Army, Remington Model 10-gauge.
4. Mark II U.S. Navy, 10-gauge.
5. U.S. Signal Pistol, probably Army, 1883.

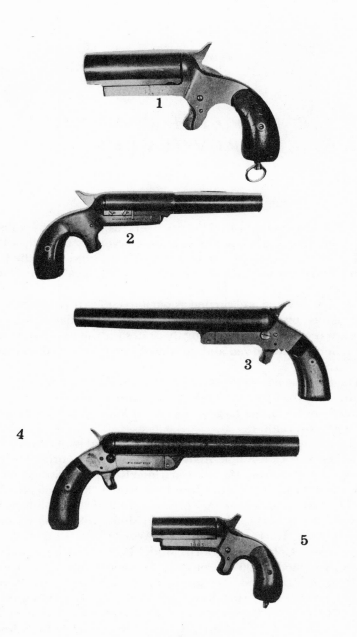

PLATE 30.

# Chapter 15

## *U.S. MARTIAL CARTRIDGE REVOLVERS*

THE U.S. martial cartridge revolvers, as classified by collectors, dealers, and historians, are those revolvers officially adopted by the U.S. Government for the armed services of the United States, and for issue to the organized militia, later called the National Guard.

Revolvers owned and carried as personal side arms, but not adopted or issued by the United States, are not U.S. martial weapons. Neither are revolvers purchased by the states for the use of state troops not federally recognized and not called into the federal service with such arms.

The fact that a revolver is called an Army, Navy, or military model by the manufacturer does not make it a martial revolver. It seems perfectly obvious that large calibers and long barrels are not determining factors either.

The revolvers that have been adopted by, and issued by, the United States are: Colt Single-Action Army Revolver, originally called the New Model Army Metallic Cartridge Revolving Pistol; Colt Double-Action Army or Frontier Revolver, Model 1878; Colt New Navy, Double-Action, Self-Cocking Revolver, Model 1889; Colt New Navy, Double-Action, Self-Cocking Revolver, Model 1892; Colt New Army Models 1892, 1894, and 1896; Colt Army Model 1901; Colt Army Model 1903; Colt Marine Corps Model 1905 (sometimes called Marine Corps Model 1907); Colt New Service Revolver, Model 1909; the Marine Corps modification of the Colt New Service Revolver, Model 1909; Colt Army Revolver, Model 1917; Remington New Model 1874 Army Revolver; Smith & Wesson Army Revolver, Model 1869; Smith & Wesson Army Revolver, Model 1875, Schoefield Patent; Smith & Wesson Army Revolver, Model 1899; Smith & Wesson Navy Revolver, Model 1899; and Smith & Wesson Army Revolver, Model 1917. Notice that all of these were made by either Colt or Smith & Wesson, except one made by Remington.

A revolver designed by a manufacturer for sale to the United States that was tested and rejected could be called a secondary U.S. martial cartridge revolver without much hesitation. However, this business of classifying weapons, particularly cartridge revolvers, as U.S. martial arms has been grossly abused. Because of the outright fraud associated with this practice, the author has decided to reject any phony and far-fetched system of secondary martial classification and place certain cartridge revolvers where they belong—with the ordinary American cartridge revolvers.

Why is it that certain revolvers which any informed person knows to be non-martial are given a martial classification? Ignorance might be pleaded, but the error, to put it mildly, has originated in the imagination of authors, collectors, and dealers who pride themselves on being authorities. If ignorance cannot be accepted, then what is the next alibi? If money is not the object, then perhaps a collector wants to "show off" by boasting about how many martial weapons he owns. But it does not start or stop there. If a dealer can classify a weapon as a martial arm, he can ask and often receive a higher price. It is like putting stale eggs in the same basket with fresh eggs.

The revolvers that are often erroneously classified as U.S. martial cartridge revolvers include among others the Bacon Mfg. Co. Navy Revolver; Forehand & Wadsworth Old Model Army Revolver; Forehand & Wadsworth New Model Army Revolver; Hopkins & Allen Navy Revolver; Merwin & Hulbert Model 1876 Army Revolver; Merwin & Hulbert Army Pocket Revolver; Plant Cup-Primer Army Cartridge Revolver; Pond Army Revolver; Prescott Navy Revolver; Smith & Wesson Revolver, Model No. 2; Smith & Wesson Navy Revolver, Model 1881; and the Smith & Wesson Army Revolver, Model 1881.

It must be remembered that not even all specimens of the revolvers approved in this chapter can be accepted as U.S. martial cartridge revolvers. For example, a Colt Single-Action Army Revolver with a 4.75-inch barrel is not a martial arm, because that was the civilian barrel length. It might be argued that it was originally a martial arm and that the barrel has been changed; if that is true, then the arm is worth slightly less. Likewise, if it is not of a military caliber, it is not a martial arm.

Jumping down to another example, Colt and Smith & Wesson

Model 1917 Army Revolvers, we find that these revolvers were being made and sold, with various modifications, long after the close of World War I. It is true that many were used in World War II, but if the modification is such that it is apparent that it was not issued to and used by the armed forces, then it is definitely not a martial arm, even though it is a member of the family. It would be just as sensible for Draft Dodger Dan to wear the honorable discharge button of his hero brother, Joe. In other words, a revolver is not a U.S. martial revolver unless it was officially used by the armed forces of the United States.

REMINGTON NEW MODEL 1874 ARMY REVOLVER, cal. .44, 6-shot, S.A.; 7.25-inch, rifled, round barrel marked "E. Remington & Sons, Ilion, N.Y., U.S.A." Total length 12.875 inches. Weight 2 lbs. 11 oz. German-silver blade front sight on barrel. Frame rear sight. Blued barrel, cylinder, frame, trigger, and trigger guard. Fluted cylinder. Casehardened hammer and loading gate. Walnut stocks. Lanyard ring on butt. Loading gate and side-rod ejector on right. This is a martial weapon. The Army received 3,000 in 1875, and 3,000 more, slightly modified, later. Made from 1875 to 1889. Numbered 1 to about 25,000. Plate 31, Fig. 1. $430–$690.

REMINGTON NEW MODEL 1874 ARMY REVOLVER, same as above with martial marks, $750–$1250.

SIMILAR, but 5.5-inch round barrel; and black, checkered, hard-rubber grips with Remington monogram at top. The under part of the rammer housing is quite different from that on the one described above. Total length 11.125 inches. Plate 31, Fig. 2. $405–$610.

SAME, but cal. .45. $375–$620.

Note: Since the Colt cartridge revolvers and the Smith & Wesson cartridge revolvers are described in their respective chapters, the Remington New Model 1874 Army Revolver and its variation are the only ones described and illustrated in this chapter.

---

PLATE 31. U.S. Martial Cartridge Revolvers

Figure

1. Remington New Model 1874 Army Revolver, cal. .44, 6-shot, S.A., 7.25-inch barrel.
2. Variation of the Remington New

Model 1874 Army Revolver with 5.5-inch barrel, hard-rubber grips, and different rammer housing.

Courtesy of James E. Serven

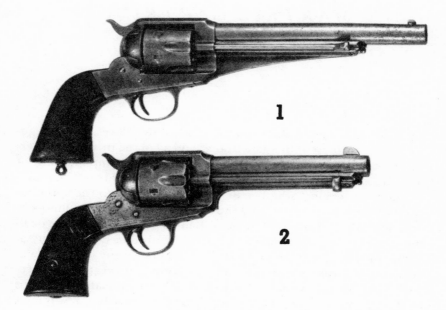

1

2

Remington New Model 1874 Army Revolver

PLATE 31.

# Chapter 16

## AMERICAN SECONDARY MARTIAL CARTRIDGE REVOLVERS

I N the early days of this republic, some of the officers of the regular forces, most of the state troops, and all of the privateers, guerrillas, sutlers, hustlers, feather merchants, and camp followers of all sexes and descriptions carried anything that would go "bang" and frighten the enemy, whether or not it conformed to the specifications of the United States for weapons. However, when the flintlocks and percussion arms began to go to Bannerman's, or to others dealing in war stores, cartridge arms could be produced in quantity at comparatively low prices and there was no longer any very good excuse for not arming everyone with the regulation weapons. Therefore, all weapons could be classified as either U.S. martial weapons or strictly civilian arms. There are a few exceptions, but they do not amount to much.

Of course, a cartridge arm manufactured in the hope of winning a government contract could be regarded as a trial model and classified as a U.S. secondary martial arm by anyone who wanted to do so, but it boils down to this: Either a cartridge weapon is a U.S. arm, and therefore in the martial classification, or it is not.

The firearms in this chapter have been described as "martial" by collectors, dealers, and historians for many years. The author classes them as "American Secondary Martial Cartridge Revolvers" in deference to the customs and traditions of gun collectors, but personally regards most of these weapons as purely civilian arms. Smith & Wesson weapons, which otherwise would be in this chapter, are described in the chapter on that company's products.

BACON MFG. CO. NAVY REVOLVER, cal. .38 r.f., 6-shot, S.A.; 7.5-inch, octagonal, rifled barrel marked "Bacon Mfg. Co. Norwich Conn." Total length 12.75 inches. Weight 2 lbs. 2 oz. Steel-blade front sight. Spur trigger. Engraved iron frame. Blued barrel and frame. Casehardened hammer. Walnut grips. Cylinder, 1.25 inches long, has stops at front and can be partly removed to use the cylinder pin as an ejector. There is no record of the adoption or use of this revolver which justifies classifying it as a martial arm of any description, but to avoid departing too far from the custom of the collectors we have classified it as an American secondary martial weapon. Plate 32, Fig. 1. $200–$300.

FOREHAND & WADSWORTH OLD MODEL ARMY REVOLVER, cal. .44 Russian c.f., 6-shot, S.A.; 7.5-inch, round, rifled barrel marked "Forehand & Wadsworth, Worcester, Mass. U.S. Pat'd Oct 22 '61, June 27 '71, Oct 28 '73." Total length 13.125 inches. Weight 2 lbs. 8 oz. Steel-blade front sight. Frame rear sight. Loading gate. Ejector pin, fastened to barrel, must move forward and then rotate to enter cylinder chambers. Cylinder pin is exposed by rotation of ejector. Iron frame. Walnut grips. Since this revolver was neither officially adopted nor used by the armed services, it is not a martial weapon and is only classed as a secondary martial arm because of the custom of many collectors. Plate 32, Fig. 2. $185–$300.

FOREHAND & WADSWORTH NEW MODEL ARMY REVOLVER, cal. .44 Russian c.f., 6-shot, S.A.; 6.5-inch, round, rifled barrel marked as above. Similar to Old Model except for barrel length, side ejector instead of former ejection system, exposed cylinder pin, and addition of a safety notch. Like the Old Model, it is not a martial weapon. Not illustrated. $185–$300.

HOPKINS & ALLEN NAVY REVOLVER, XL MODEL, cal. .38 r.f., 6-shot, S.A.; 6-inch, round, rifled barrel marked on top "Hopkins & Allen Mfg. Co., Pat. Mar. 28, '71, Apr. 27, '75," and on bottom "38-100 CA," with barrel strap marked "XL Navy." Total length 11 inches. Weight 1 lb. 10 oz. Brass-blade front sight. Frame rear sight. Fluted cylinder. Casehardened hammer and trigger. Other parts nickeled. This is not a martial weapon. Plate 32, Fig. 3. $185–$300.

MERWIN & HULBERT MODEL 1876 ARMY REVOLVER, sometimes called Automatic Ejecting Army Revolver, cal. .44 W.c.f., 6-shot, S.A.; 7-inch, round, rifled barrel marked on top "Merwin Hulbert & Co., New York, U.S.A. Pat Jan. 24, Apr. 21, Dec. 15, '74, Aug. 3, '75, July 11, '76, Apr. 17, '77, Pat's Mar. 6, '77," and on left "Hopkins & Allen Manufacturing Co., Norwich, Conn., U.S.A." Steel frame marked on left "Caliber Winchester 1873." Total length 12 inches. Weight 2 lbs. 9.5 oz. Blade front sight. Frame rear sight. Steel trigger guard. All parts nickeled except casehardened hammer and trigger. Fluted cylinder. Bird's-head handle. Hard-rubber checkered grips. Hole in butt for lanyard. No top strap. Loading gate. Tested and rejected by the U.S. Government in 1876. Not a martial weapon. $185–$300.

SAME, but with square butt. $200–$325.

SAME, but double-action, with bird's-head butt, as above. Plate 32, Fig. 4. $175–$275.

SAME, but double-action, with square butt. $200–$300.

MERWIN & HULBERT ARMY POCKET REVOLVER, sometimes called Automatic Ejecting Pocket Army Revolver, cal. .44 W.c.f., 6-shot, D.A.; 3.312-inch rifled barrel marked on left "Hopkins & Allen M'f'g Co., Norwich, Conn., U.S.A. Pat. Jan. 24, April 21, Dec. 15, '74, Aug. 3, '75, July 11, '76, Apr. 17, '77. Pats. Mar. 6, '77." Total length 8.625 inches. Weight 2 lbs. 5 oz. Blade front sight. Frame rear sight. Nickel-finished. Steel frame marked on right "Merwin Hulbert & Co., N.Y. Pocket Army," and marked on left "Caliber Winchester 1873." Steel trigger guard. Bird's-head handle. Hard-rubber checkered grips. Hole in butt for lanyard. Loading gate. Similar to Model 1876, but barrel is shorter and there is a top strap. Not a martial weapon. Plate 32, Fig. 5. $135–$225.

PLANT CUP-PRIMER ARMY REVOLVER, cal. .42, 6-shot, S.A.; 6-inch, octagonal, ribbed, rifled barrel marked "Merwin & Bray, New York" on the left and "Plant's Mfg. Co., New Haven Ct." on the rib. Total length 10.75 inches. Weight 2 lbs. White brass front sight in rib. Frame rear sight. Silver-plated bronze frame. Rosewood grips, or walnut grips. Sheath trigger. Cylinder, marked "Patented July 12, 1859 & July 21, 1863," can be exchanged for percussion cylinder with recessed primer cones, hence this revolver is also listed in this book as a percussion revolver. As a cartridge revolver, it fires hollow-base cup-primer cartridges, loaded from the front of the cylinder instead of the back. Side ejector rod on right of frame. This is not a martial weapon. Plate 32, Fig. 6 . $225–$325.

---

PLATE 32. American Secondary Martial Cartridge
Revolvers

*Figure*

1. Bacon Navy Revolver.
2. Forehand & Wadsworth Old Model Army Revolver.
3. Hopkins & Allen Navy Revolver, XL Model.
4. Merwin & Hulbert Model 1876 Army Revolver

5. Merwin & Hulbert Army Pocket Revolver, Double-Action, with Bird's-Head Butt.
6. Plant Cup-Primer Army Revolver, cal. .42.
7. Pond Army Revolver, cal. .44 r.f.
8. Prescott Navy Revolver.

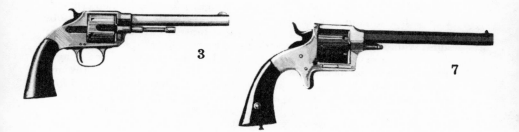

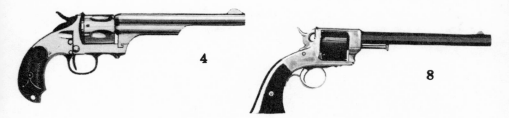

PLATE 32 American Secondary Martial Cartridge Revolvers

SAME, but cal. .28 cup-primer. $100–$150.

POND ARMY REVOLVER, cal. .44 r.f., 6-shot, S.A.; 7.25-inch, octagonal, rifled barrel marked "L.W. Pond, Worcester, Mass.," sometimes with patent date. Total length 12.75 inches. Weight 2 lbs. 8 oz. Steel-blade front sight. V-notch frame rear sight. Walnut grips. Sheath trigger. Barrel tips upward when two lugs on frame are pressed. Casehardened hammer and trigger; other parts silver-plated. Iron frame. This is not a martial weapon. Plate 32, Fig. 7. $800–$1,075.

SAME, but cal. .32 r.f., 6-shot, 6-inch barrel, total length 10.5 inches. $100–$200.

SAME, but cal. .32 r.f., 5-inch barrel. $100–$200.

SAME, but cal. .32 r.f., 4-inch barrel. $100–$175.

*Note: The smaller-caliber and shorter-barrel versions of the Pond Army Revolver must not be confused with the Pond Front-loading Cartridge Revolver, sometimes called the Pond Separate Chambers Revolver, which is much different.*

PRESCOTT NAVY REVOLVER, cal. .38 r.f., 6-shot, S.A.; 7.312-inch, octagon, rifled, blued barrel marked "E.A. Prescott, Worcester, Mass., Pat. Oct. 2, 1860." Total length 12.5 inches. Weight 1 lb. 13 oz. Blued cylinder, 1.25 inches long, may be removed, and fired cartridge cases picked out by hand. Brass-blade front sight. Silver-plated brass frame has V-notch rear sight. Walnut grips. Circular trigger guard forks at back. In some specimens there is a slot in the recoil shield for loading. Some frames are made of steel. The finish may be nickel. The grips may be rosewood. Barrel lengths, and consequently total lengths and weights, vary. Values vary slightly with differences. This is not a martial weapon. Plate 32, Fig. 8. $235–$375.

SAME, but 6.5-inch barrel. $235–$350.

# Chapter 17

# AMERICAN CARTRIDGE PISTOLS AND REVOLVERS

ALL cartridge pistols and revolvers manufactured in the United States of America, and generally regarded as collectors' specimens, are included in this chapter, except Colt, Smith & Wesson, Confederate, U.S. martial, and American secondary martial cartridge pistols and revolvers, all of which are described in other chapters. Obviously, some of the arms described in this chapter might belong in one of the special classifications, but our classification follows the majority view. It should be observed that Remington arms deserve a special chapter, but until we have a more complete knowledge of these important weapons, they will be retained in the general classification.

AETNA POCKET REVOLVER, cal. .32 short r.f.; 5-shot; 2.5-inch, round, rifled barrel. Fluted cylinder. All metal parts of nickel-plated steel. Frame marked "Aetna." Probably made by Harrington & Richardson but not so marked. $40–$70.

AETNA POCKET REVOLVER, cal. .22 r.f., 7-shot; 3-inch octagon barrel. Round cylinder. Square walnut grips. Sheathed trigger. Frame marked "Aetna." See above. $60–$100.

ALLEN SIDE-HAMMER REVOLVER, cal. .22 r.f., 7-shot; 2.375-inch octagon barrel marked "Ethan Allen & Co." with patent dates. Spur trigger. Nickel-plated. $45–$75.

SAME, but cal. .32 r.f., 6-shot, 3.75-inch octagon barrel. $45–$75.

ALLEN CARTRIDGE DERRINGER, cal. .41 r.f., single-shot; 2.5-inch round-octagon barrel marked "E. Allen & Co. Worcester Mass. Allen's Pat. Mch. 7, 1865." Resembles Colt No. 3 Derringer. Plate 33, Fig. 1. $150–$275.

SAME, but cal. .32 r.f., 3.25-inch round-octagon barrel. $150–$240.

ALLEN CARTRIDGE DERRINGER, cal. .41 r.f., single-shot, 2.5-inch octagon barrel marked as above. Spur trigger. Iron frame. Plate 33, Fig. 2. $150–$250.

ALLEN & WHEELOCK REVOLVERS using Allen lip cartridge, side hammer, barrel marked "Allen & Wheelock, Worcester, Ms" with patent dates. Barrel swings to right. Walnut grips. Trigger guard operates extractor:

Cal. .25, No. 50 Allen lip cartridge, 7-shot. $90–$140.
Cal. .32, No. 52 Allen lip cartridge, 6-shot. $90–$140.
Cal. .38 lip, 6-shot, 5-inch octagon barrel. Plate 33, Fig. 3. $125–$200.
Cal. .44, No. 58 Allen lip cartridge, 6-shot, 7.5-inch barrel. $125–$200.

ALLEN & WHEELOCK REVOLVERS using short rim-fire cartridge, side hammer. Barrel lengths vary for each piece:

Cal. .22 short r.f., 7-shot. $60–$100.
Cal. .32 short r.f., 6-shot. $60–$100.
Cal. .38 short r.f. $60–$100.
Cal. .44 short r.f. $60–$100.

---

PLATE 33. American Cartridge Pistols and Revolvers

*Figure*

1. Allen Cartridge Derringer.
2. Allen Cartridge Derringer.
3. Allen & Wheelock Revolver, cal. .38.
4. American Arms Co. Wheeler Double-Barrel Pistol.
5. Bacon Arms Co. Revolver.
6. Bacon Arms Co. Cartridge Pepperbox.
7. Bacon Mfg. Co. Pistol.
8. Bacon Mfg. Co. Revolver.
9. Brooklyn Arms Co. Slocum Revolver.
10. Chicago Fire Arms Co. Protector Palm Pistol.
11. D. D. Cone Revolver.
12. Connecticut Arms Co. Revolver.
13. Conn. Arms & Manf. Co. Hammond Bull Dog Pistol.
14. Continental Arms Co. Cartridge Pepperbox. Ladies' Companion.
15. Continental Single-Shot Pistol.
16. Copeland Revolver.
17. Cowles Single-Shot Pistol
18. Deringer Revolver, cal. .22.
19. Dickinson Pistol, cal. .32.
20. Bliss Revolver.
21. Dickinson Pistol, cal. .22.
22. Duplex 9-shot Revolver.
23. Grant Revolver, cal. .22.
24. Grant Revolver, cal. .32.
25. Harrington & Richardson Knife-Revolver, cal. .32.
26. Hopkins & Allen Police Revolver.
27. Hopkins & Allen Single-Shot Pistol.
28. Iver Johnson Revolver, cal. .38.
29. Lombard Single-Shot Pistol, cal. .22.
30. Lower Revolver, cal. .32.
31. Marlin Single-Shot Pistol.
32. Marlin XXX Standard Revolver.

PLATE 33

ALLEN & WHEELOCK SINGLE-SHOT CARTRIDGE PISTOLS:
Cal. .22 short r.f. $45–$60.
Cal. .32 short r.f. $60–$95.
Cal. .41 short r.f. $70–$125.

AMERICAN ARMS CO.—WHEELER DOUBLE-BARREL PISTOL, cal.
.41 r.f., 2.625-inch superposed barrels. Walnut grips. Spur trigger. Brass
frame. Rifled in solid block. Marked "American Arms Co. Boston Mass.
Wheeler's Pat Oct 31, 1865. June 19, 1866." Plate 33, Fig. 4. $170–$250.

AMERICAN ARMS CO. REVOLVER, cal. .38, both S.A. and D.A., 3.75-
inch barrel marked "American Arms Co. Boston Mass." Total length 8.5
inches. Brass-blade front sight. Changed from single to double action without dismounting. Also made in cal. .32 and cal. .41, and in both 5-shot and
6-shot variations, with some value changes. $115–$170.

AMERICAN ARMS CO. RING-EXTRACTING HINGE REVOLVER,
cal. .38 c.f., 5-shot; 3.25-inch, round, ribbed barrel marked as above.
$115–$170.

SAME, single-action, spur trigger. $115–$170.

AMERICAN ARMS CO. DOUBLE-BARREL PISTOL, cal. .32 r.f.; 2.5-
inch superposed barrels. Spur trigger. Bird's-head butt. Walnut grips. Brass
frame. Marked "American Arms Co., Boston, Mass. Pat. Oct. 31, 1865, June
19, 1866." $135–$225.

AMERICAN ARMS CO.—WHEELER DOUBLE-BARREL PISTOL, two
3-inch superposed barrels, one cal. .22 and one cal. .32 r.f., rifled in solid
block marked "American Arms Co. Boston Mass. Wheelers Pat Oct 31,
1865. June 19, 1866." $150–$275.

AMERICAN STANDARD TOOL CO. REVOLVER, cal. .22 r.f., 7-shot;
3.125-inch, octagon, ribbed barrel marked "American Standard Tool Co.
Newark, N.J." Weight 12 oz. Spur trigger. Walnut grips. Brass frame, nickel-plated. $60–$125.

BABCOCK PISTOL, cal. .32, single-shot, S.A.; 3.5-inch octagon barrel
marked "Babcock's Patent." Total length 8.5 inches. Stud trigger. Blued
finish. Large walnut handles. Resembles the Stafford Pocket Pistol. $45–$85.

BACON ARMS CO. REVOLVER, cal. .32 r.f., 5-shot; 4-inch, round barrel usually marked "Bacon Arms Co. Norwich, Conn." but may be marked
"Bacon Arms Co., Norwich, Ct. Cast-Steel." Total length 8.5 inches. Weight
1 lb. Half fluted cylinder. Spur trigger. Walnut grips. Plate 33, Fig. 5.
$100–$185.

BACON ARMS CO. CARTRIDGE PEPPERBOX, cal. .22 r.f., 6-shot; 2.5-inch, round, fluted barrels marked "Bacon Arms Co. Norwich Conn." Total length 5.5 inches. Weight 8 oz. Spur trigger. Iron frame. Walnut grips. Plate 33, Fig. 6. $165–$250.

BACON MFG. CO.—C. W. HOPKINS REVOLVER, cal. .32 r.f., 6-shot; 4-inch octagon barrel marked on top "Bacon Mfg. Co. Norwich Conn." and on side "C. W. Hopkins, Patented May 27, 1862." Spur trigger. Walnut grips. Cylinder swings right to load and eject. Ejector rod held under barrel by spring and removed to eject fired cases. Sometimes listed as C. W. Hopkins Revolver. $90–$140.

BACON MFG. CO. PISTOL, cal. .32 r.f., single-shot; 4-inch octagon barrel marked "Bacon Mfg. Co. Norwich, Conn." Barrel swings to right to load. Iron frame. Spur trigger. Walnut grips. Plate 33, Fig. 7. $55–$95.

SAME, but made without extractor. Barrel swings either right or left to load. $65–$125.

BACON MFG. CO. REVOLVER, cal. .32 r.f., 6-shot; 4-inch octagon barrel marked "Bacon Mfg. Co. Norwich, Conn." Total length 8.25 inches. Weight 18 oz. Trigger guard unscrews, allowing barrel to be pulled from base pin and cylinder to be removed for loading. Plate 33, Fig. 8. $75–$125.

SAME, but cal. .22 r.f., 2.5-inch octagon barrel. $60–$125.

BACON MFG. CO. NAVY REVOLVER—See Chapter 16.

BALLARD DERRINGER, cal. .41 r.f.; 2.75-inch round-octagon barrel usually marked "Ballard's" on top and "Ballard's Worcester Mass." or "C. H. Ballard & Co. Worcester Mass." with patent dates in either case; but "Ballard" is only mark on some. Total length 4.75 inches. Weight 8 oz. Barrel tips down to load. Spur trigger. Bronze frame. $225–$350.

SAME, with iron frame; reported, but not verified. $195–$275.

BILLINGS VEST-POCKET PISTOL, cal. .32 r.f., S.A.; 2.5-inch round barrel marked "Billings Vest Pocket Pistol Pat April 24, 1866." Total length 6 inches. Blued finish. Stud trigger. Large handles. Action resembles that of Remington-Rider breechblock. $100–$150.

BLISS REVOLVER, cal. .25 r.f., 6-shot; 3.25-inch octagon barrel marked "F.D. Bliss New Haven Ct." Total length 7 inches. Weight 8 oz. Iron frame. Spur trigger. Rear end of cylinder has a removable plate similar to a Remington conversion. Center-hung hammer. Either walnut or checkered hard-rubber grips. Illustration shows latter. Plate 33, Fig. 20. $85–$150.

BLISS AND GOODYEAR, cal. .22 and .32 r.f., round barrel and side plate. Spur trigger, 7-shot (both calibers). Numerous brand names. Bird's-head grips, walnut. Nickel finish. Patent date: April 23, 1878. $50–$90.

BROOKLYN ARMS CO.—SLOCUM FRONT-LOADING REVOLVER, cal. .32 r.f., 5-shot; 3-inch round barrel marked "B.A. Co. Patented April 14th 1863." Total length 7.5 inches. Weight 12 oz. Sometimes called Slocum Front-loading Revolver. Spur trigger. Engraved silver-plated frame. Blued barrel and cylinder. Chambers are sliding tubes fitted into troughs cut in cylinder proper. Tubes slide forward over a fixed ejector. Walnut grips. Plate 33, Fig. 9. $120–$220.

BROWN MFG. CO. SOUTHERNER DERRINGER, also called a pocket pistol, cal. .41 r.f., single-shot; 2.5-inch octagon barrel marked "Southerner." Left side of frame marked "Brown Mfg. Co. Newburyport, Mass. Pat. Apr. 9, 1867." Total length 5 inches. Weight 8 oz. Sheath trigger. Center hammer. Brass or iron frame. Side-swing. $150–$250.

CHICAGO ARMS CO. REVOLVER, cal. .38 c.f., D.A.; 2.25-inch round barrel marked "Chicago Arms Co." Nickel finish. Front blade sight. Notch in frame for rear sight. Checkered, hard-rubber handles. Total length 7.75 inches. Fired cartridge cases are automatically ejected when the revolver is "broken" open. Known as a hammerless type and has safety device on rear of handle which must be pressed before firing. Sometimes called a squeezer type. $100–$175.

CHICAGO FIRE ARMS CO. CREEDMORE REVOLVER, cal. .32 r.f., 5-shot, S.A.; 3-inch octagon barrel marked "Creedmore." Manufactured by the Chicago Fire Arms Co., of Chicago, Ill., and advertised in 1880 to retail through the mail for $1. It was guaranteed to "kill farther than an ordinary revolver will shoot." The late Dr. S. Traner Buck classed such models as "suicide guns." $45–$65.

CHICAGO FIRE ARMS CO. PROTECTOR PALM PISTOL, cal. .32 c.f., 7-shot; 1.75-inch, round, rifled barrel. So-called pistol is circular in shape to be concealed within the palm of the hand. Concealed trigger cocks, revolves, and fires at one action. Hard-rubber side plates. Meant to be fired by pressure of the palm against a lever. Marked "The Protector," with patent dates, and "Chicago Fire Arms Co., Chicago, Ill." Plate 33, Fig. 10. $265–$375.

CHICAGO FIRE ARMS CO. PROTECTOR PALM PISTOL, same as above, but factory "Cut-a-Way." $325–$450.

CHICAGO FIRE ARMS CO. PROTECTOR PALM PISTOL, same as above, but improved model with grip safety, and pearl inlays on the two large surfaces instead of rubber. $265–$375.

COLT CARTRIDGE REVOLVERS—See Chapter 13.

CONE REVOLVER, cal. .32 r.f., 6-shot, 5-inch octagon barrel. Total length 10 inches. Bronze frame marked "D. D. Cone; Washington, D.C." Ejector rod under barrel, held by spring plunger. Probably made by Sharp & Hankins, although the marks "D. D. Cone," "W. L. Grant," and "J. P. Lower" are often found on weapons that are otherwise identical. Plate 33, Fig. 11. $75–$125.

SAME, but cal. .22. $75–$125.

CONNECTICUT ARMS CO. REVOLVER, cal. .28, cup-primer, 6-shot; 3-inch, octagon, ribbed barrel marked "Conn. Arms Co., Norfolk, Conn." Total length 7 inches. Weight 12 oz. Brass frame. Spur trigger. Cylinder loads from front. Hook-shaped ejector on right side of frame. Cylinder bears patent date. Sometimes called Wood's Revolver. Plate 33, Fig. 12. $65–$125.

CONNECTICUT ARMS & MANF. CO.—HAMMOND BULL DOG PISTOL, cal. .44 r.f., 4-inch octagon barrel. Marked "Connecticut Arms & Manf. Co. Naubuc Conn. Patented Oct 25, 1864." Breechblock revolves left. Plate 33, Fig. 13. $160–$275.

SAME, but cal. .41, $135–$200.

CONTINENTAL ARMS CO. CARTRIDGE PEPPERBOX, sometimes called Ladies' Companion, cal. .22 r.f., 5-shot; 2.5-inch, round, fluted barrels. Total length 5.5 inches. Weight 8 oz. Iron frame, nickel-plated; spur trigger. Walnut grips. Cylinder marked "Continental Arms Co., Norwich, Ct," with patent date. Plate 33, Fig. 14. $200–$325.

CONTINENTAL SINGLE-SHOT PISTOL, cal. .22 r.f., 2-inch, part round, part octagon barrel. Hammer acts as breechblock. Spur trigger. Plate 33, Fig. 15. $60–$85.

CONTINENTAL REVOLVER, cal. .32 r.f., 5-shot, 2.5-inch round barrel marked "Continental 2." $50–$75.

CONTINENTAL REVOLVER, cal. .22, 7-shot, 2.5-inch barrel. Marked "Continental No. 1." $50–$75.

COPELAND REVOLVER cal. .22 r.f., 7-shot, 2.25-inch octagon barrel. Brass frame. Spur trigger. Walnut grips. Made by F. Copeland, Worcester, Mass., but usually not marked. Plate 33, Fig. 16. $60–$95.

COWLES SINGLE-SHOT PISTOL, cal. .22 r.f., S.A.; 3.25-inch round barrel marked "Cowles & Son, Chicopee, Mass." Brass frame. Walnut grips. Spur trigger. Barrel swings out to load. Plate 33, Fig. 17. $85–$125.

COWLES SINGLE-SHOT PISTOL, cal. .22 r.f.; 2.75-inch round barrel marked "W. A. Cowles, Dean & Co., Chicopee Falls, Mass." Polished hardwood handles. Bird's-head butt. Loading and extracting device under frame. $75–$125.

CRISPIN REVOLVER—See Smith Arms Co., below.

DERINGER REVOLVER, cal. .32 r.f., 5-shot; 3.5-inch, round, ribbed barrel marked "Deringer Philada." and also "Manuf'd at the Deringer Rifle and Pistol Works. Phila. Pa." Spur trigger. Engraved frame. Walnut grips. Nickel-plated. $150–$250.

SAME, but cal. .22 r.f. Plate 33, Fig. 18. $150–$285.

DERINGER REVOLVER, cal. .22 r.f., S.A., 7-shot; 3-inch, round, ribbed barrel marked "Deringer, Philadelphia" on top and on the left "Manuf'd at the Deringer Rifle and Pistol Works. Philadelphia." Stud-type trigger. Nickel finish. Fancy engraving. Total length 6.75 inches. Nickel front sight. Notched-frame rear sight. Bird's-head polished hardwood handles. Breaks upward to load. $150–$285.

DICKINSON PISTOL, cal. .32 r.f., single-shot; 3.75-inch, octagon, ribbed barrel marked "E.L. & J. Dickinson Springfield Mass." Hand extractor under barrel works on rack-and-pinion system. Plate 33, Fig. 19, $100–$125.

DICKINSON PISTOL, cal. .22 r.f., 3.75-inch, octagon, ribbed barrel marked as above. Brass frame. Spur trigger. Plate 33, Fig. 21. $100–$125.

DRISCOLE SINGLE-SHOT PISTOL, cal. .22 r.f.; 3.5-inch octagon barrel marked "J. B. Driscole: Springfield Mass." Bronze frame. Spur trigger. Walnut grips. Barrel drops down to load. $75–$125.

DUPLEX 9-SHOT REVOLVER, upper barrel cal. .22 r.f.; lower barrel cal. .32 r.f. Each barrel is round, ribbed, 2.5-inches long. Fires 8 shots cal. .22, and 1 shot cal. .32. The .32-cal. barrel serves as a base pin on which the cylinder revolves. Barrels tip up to load. Movable firing pin on hammer nose. Spur (stud) trigger. Walnut grips. Nickel-plated. Barrel marked "Pat'd. Dec. 7, 1880." Usually no other marks are found. Probably made by Osgood Gun Works, Norwich, Conn., but listed here because Duplex is the name by which it is known to most collectors and dealers. Plate 33, Fig. 22. $250–$475.

EAGLE ARMS CO.—See Plant, below.

EASTERN ARMS CO. REVOLVER, cal. .32 c.f., 5-shot; 3-inch round-octagon barrel marked "Eastern Arms Co." $35–$50.

ELLIS SINGLE-SHOT PISTOL, cal. .32 r.f., S.A.; 2.5-inch round barrel marked "Willard C. Ellis, Pat. April 1859." Total length 6.5 inches. Stud trigger. Blued barrel and hammer. Plain metal frame. Large, highly polished hardwood handles. $75–$100.

EMPIRE STATE ARMS CO. REVOLVER, cal. .32 c.f., 5-shot; 3-inch, round, ribbed barrel marked "Empire State Arms Co." $30–$40.

FOEHL AND WEEKS FIRE ARMS MFG. CO. cal. .32, 5-shot, concealed hammer, solid frame. Marked "Perfect." Double action. Patent date February 24, 1891. $75–$100.

FOREHAND & WADSWORTH SIDE-HAMMER RIM-FIRE CARTRIDGE REVOLVERS, usually marked "Forehand & Wadsworth Worcester Mass. Pat's. Sept. 24, Oct. 22, 1861" on barrel. Cal. .22 and .30. $45–$70.

SAME, but cal. .32 and .44. $45–$70.

FOREHAND & WADSWORTH REVOLVER, cal. .32 r.f., S.A., octagon barrel, 6-shot. Frame marked "Terror"; cal. .38 r.f., frame marked "Bull Dog"; and cal. .41 r.f., frame marked "Swamp Angel." $35–$65.

FOREHAND & WADSWORTH OLD MODEL ARMY REVOLVER, cal. .44 Russian c.f. See Chapter 16.

FOREHAND & WADSWORTH OLD MODEL, SOLID FRAME, D.A. REVOLVER, cal. .32 r.f., 6-shot, made with trigger guard; or cal. .38, 5-shot. $25–$45.

FOREHAND & WADSWORTH NEW MODEL, SOLID FRAME REVOLVER, frame straight on top, cal. .22 r.f.; or same as before with safety hammer; or same as before, cal. .38 without safety hammer; or cal. .38 with safety hammer. $25–$50.

FOREHAND & WADSWORTH HINGE-HAMMER REVOLVER, cal. .32, barrel 3.25, 4, or 5 inches long; or same, but cal. .38. $25–$50.

FOREHAND & WADSWORTH NEW HAMMERLESS MODEL REVOLVER (same as Hinge-Hammer model, but with safety hammer), cal. .32 or cal. .38; and either 3.25- or 5-inch barrel. $25–$50.

FOREHAND & WADSWORTH PERFECTION HAMMER REVOLVER, cal. .32, 3-inch barrel. $25–$50.

FOREHAND & WADSWORTH HAMMERLESS HINGE REVOLVER, cal. .32 or .38; and 4- or 5-inch barrel. $25–$55.

FOREHAND & WADSWORTH BRITISH BULL DOG REVOLVER, cal. .32, .38, or .44; 7-, 6-, or 5-shot; marked "British Bull Dog." $30–$55.

FYRBERG, ANDREW AND CO., cal. .32 and .38, hinged frame, self-ejector. Similar appearance to Iver Johnson models. Patent date August 4, 1903. $40–$75.

GRANT REVOLVER, cal. .22 r.f., 6-shot; 3-inch octagon barrel marked "W. L. Grant," but barrel may be marked "D. D. Cone" or "J. P. Lower," Total length 11 inches. Weight 1.5 lbs. Iron frame. Spur trigger. Rosewood grips, but also made with walnut grips without change in value. Also see revolvers listed under D. D. Cone and J. P. Lower. Plate 33, Fig. 23. $80–$125.

SAME, but cal. .32, 5-inch barrel, with loading gate and ejector rod under barrel, like Lower Revolver. Plate 33, Fig. 24. $80–$125.

SAME, but cal. .32, with 3-inch barrel. $80–$125.

GRANT HAMMOND AUTOMATIC PISTOL—See Chapter 19.

GREAT WESTERN, cal. .22, 7-shot, 2.5-inch octagon barrel, weight 8 oz. Walnut bird's-head grip. Plain cylinder. Blue barrel and cylinder, silver plate. Solid frame, spur trigger. $45–$90.

GROSS ARMS CO. REVOLVER, cal. .25 r.f., 7-shot, 6-inch barrel. Total length 9.5 inches. Marked "Gross Arms Co., Tiffin, Ohio." $90–$165.

SAME, but 4-inch barrel. Total length 7.25 inches. Weight 12 oz. Marked "Gross Patent 1861 Tiffin Ohio." $90–$165.

HARRINGTON & RICHARDSON KNIFE REVOLVER, cal. .32 c.f., 5-shot, D.A.; 4-inch, round, ribbed barrel. Top break; auto-ejection. Knife blade is 2.5 inches long, double edge, fixed to stud under barrel at muzzle. Blade swings out to form a dagger. Plate 33, Fig. 25. $175–$300.

SAME, but cal. .38 S&W short; barrel tips up to load. $200–$325.

*Note on Harrington & Richardson: The early cartridge revolvers of this make are sold disregarding shooting condition. The later models are sold according to shooting condition and are not generally regarded as collectors' pieces. The most popular H & R collectors' pieces are the knife revolver and the self-loading (automatic) pistols. The automatic pistols are listed in Chapter 19.*

HOOD FIRE ARMS CO. REVOLVER, cal. .32 r.f., 5-shot; 3.5-inch barrel marked "Hood Fire Arms Co., Norwich, Conn." Total length 7.5 inches. Weight 1 lb. Also made cal. .38 r.f., and cal. .41 r.f., without change of value. $35–$50.

C.W. HOPKINS PATENTED REVOLVER—See Bacon Mfg. Co., above.

HOOD FIRE ARMS CO. REVOLVER cal. .22, 7-shot, top of 2.125-inch octagon barrel marked "Hood F.A. Co. Patent April 6, 1875," length 5.5 inches, hard-rubber grips with anchor design. Cylinder pin release on frame front. $30–$50.

HOPKINS & ALLEN POLICE REVOLVER, cal. .38 r.f., S.A.; 4.5-inch round barrel, 6-shot, round butt. Ejector rod swings right. Frame marked "XL Police 38-100 Caliber." Plate 33, Fig. 26. $50–$75.

HOPKINS & ALLEN SAFETY POLICE REVOLVER, cal. .32 c.f., 5-shot; 3-inch round, ribbed barrel marked "Safety Police." $50–$75.

HOPKINS & ALLEN SIDE-SWING REVOLVER, cal. .41 r.f., 5-shot, spur trigger, 2.5-inch octagon barrel. Marked "XL NO. 6." $45–$70.

HOPKINS & ALLEN REVOLVER, cal. .38 c.f., D.A., 5-shot, 6-inch octagon barrel. Loading gate. Side ejector. Frame marked "XL 5 Double Action." $35–$50.

HOPKINS & ALLEN SINGLE-SHOT PISTOL, cal. .22 r.f., 1.75-inch barrel. Marked "Hopkins & Allen Arms Co., Norwich, Conn. U.S.A." Total length 3.375 inches. Barrel tips up to load. Folding trigger. Engraved frame. Plate 33, Fig. 27. $120–$185.

HOPKINS & ALLEN REVOLVER, cal. .32 c.f., D.A., 5-shot, 2.625-inch octagon barrel. Folding hammer spur. Frame marked "X.L. 3 Double Action." $30–$50.

HOPKINS & ALLEN NAVY REVOLVER, XL Model, cal. .38 r.f. See Chapter 16.

*Note on Hopkins & Allen Revolvers: Typical of this class are the following: Tramps Terror, cal. .22; Blue Jacket No. 1½, cal. .22, old and new models; Blue Jacket No. 2, cal. .32, old and new models; Dictator No. 2, cal. .32, old and new models; Ranger No. 2, cal. .32, with variations; Ranger No. 3, cal. .38; and Blue Jacket No. 2, cal. .32. These revolvers in various brand names and lighter calibers now constitute an accepted collector speciality.*

*These guns were originally sold by Chicago and New York mail-order houses at a* *rate of $1 to $2 per revolver. Collectors call these and similar revolvers "suicide spe-cials," "kill-and-run-guns," etc. When sold by antique dealers, the usual price today is from $15 to $30.*

IRVING REVOLVER, cal. .32 r.f., 7-shot, 3.5-inch octagon barrel. Brass frame, silver-plated; blued barrel. See Reid, below. $135–$275.

SAME, but cal. .22 r.f. See Reid, below. $125–$225.

IVER JOHNSON REVOLVERS. Collectors pay more for specimens marked with the names of banks, express companies, etc., especially if such organizations are now out of business. Notice that these had fancy names. Typical examples are:

FAVORITE REVOLVER, cal. .22 r.f., octagon barrel, bird's-head grips, fluted cylinder; also made in cal. .32, .38 and .41 r.f. $35–$55.

SMOKER REVOLVER, cal. .38, spur trigger, octagon barrel, fluted cylin-der. $30–$45.

TYCOON REVOLVER, cal. .22 r.f., 7-shot; cal. .32 r.f., 5-shot; cal. .38 r.f., 5-shot, and cal. .41 r.f., 5-shot. $30–$55.

DEFENDER REVOLVER, cal. .22 r.f., 7-shot, 2.25-inch octagon barrel, half fluted cylinder, spur trigger, saw handle; also made with round barrel, in various calibers and in various lengths. $25–$35.

AMERICAN BULL DOG REVOLVER, cal. .22 r.f.; .32 r.f. or c.f.; .38 r.f. or c.f.; and cal. .44 Webley. The usual barrel length is 4.5 or 6 inches. $30–$45.

IVER JOHNSON REVOLVER, cal. .38 c.f., 5-shot; 3.25-inch, round, ribbed barrel. Top break; auto-ejection. Rubber grips. Cylinder swings right on rod and pushes forward to eject fired cases. Plate 33, Fig. 28. $35–$45.

IVER JOHNSON POLICE REVOLVER, cal. .32 c.f., D.A., 5-shot; 3.25-inch, round ribbed barrel marked "Iver Johnson." Hard-rubber handles with knuckle-duster grip and a ring on the butt which permits a policeman to swing it on his finger while he uses other fingers in handcuffing a prison-er. Total length 8.5 inches. Made in 1902. Superior to other early Iver John-son revolvers. $125–$185.

KOLB HAMMERLESS REVOLVER, cal. .22 r.f., 6-shot; 1.5-inch, round, ribbed barrel marked "Henry M. Kolb, Phila. Pa." Also marked "Baby Ham-merless, Model 1910" with patent dates, although some specimens are un-marked. Total length 3.875 inches. Weight 4 oz. Concealed hammer, Folding trigger. Checkered, hard-rubber grip. Barrel and cylinder swing downward to eject. $115–$185.

LEE ARMS CO. REVOLVER, cal. .32 r.f., 2.5-inch octagon barrel. Spur trigger. Marked "The Lee Arms Co., Wilkesbarre, Pa." and "Red Jacket No. 3." Round wooden grips, or rubber or pearl grips. Value is about the same for all types of grips. $30–$45.

SAME, but with 3-inch barrel. $30–$45.

SAME, but cal. .22, marked "Red Jacket No. 1." $30–$45.

SAME, but marked "Red Jacket No. 4." $30–$45.

LESTER POCKET REVOLVER, cal. .36 r.f., S.A.; 4-inch octagon barrel marked "L.M. & G.H. Lester, N.Y." Frame marked "Lester Pat. Safety Lock." Total length 8.25 inches. Brass-blade front sight. Notched-frame rear sight. $85–$150.

LITTLE AND KEATING REVOLVER, cal. .32 r.f., S.A., 5-shot; 3.25-inch, engraved, octagon barrel marked "Little and Keating, San Francisco, Cal." Total length 8.5 inches. Stud trigger. Solid frame. Engraved hammer and cylinder. Bird's-head ivory handles. Center hammer. Blade front sight. Grooved rear sight. $100–$150.

LOMBARD SINGLE-SHOT PISTOL, cal. .22 r.f.; 3.5-inch octagon barrel marked "H. C. Lombard & Co. Springfield Mass." Total length 6.25 inches. Brass frame. Spur trigger. Walnut grips. Plate 33, Fig. 29. $70–$100.

SAME, but cal. .32 r.f. $60–$85.

LOWELL ARMS CO. REVOLVER, cal. .22 r.f., 7-shot; 3.125-inch blued barrel marked "Lowell Arms Co., Lowell, Mass." Nickel-plated. $70–$100.

LOWER REVOLVER, cal. .22 r.f., 6-shot; 3-inch octagon barrel marked "J. P. Lower," but the same revolver may be marked "D. D. Cone" or "W. L. Grant" instead. See arms so listed, above. Total length 7 inches $85–$125.

SAME, but cal. .32 r.f., 6-inch octagon barrel. Plate 33, Fig. 30. $85–$125.

MALTBY HENLEY REVOLVER, cal. .22 r.f., 7-shot, D.A.; 2.5-inch octagon barrel marked "Maltby, Henley & Co. New York U.S.A." with patent dates. Hammerless. Checkered rubber grips. Nickel-plated. Safety lock. $60–$100.

SAME, but cal. .32 S & W c.f. $60–$100.

SAME, but cal. .38 S & W c.f. $75–$125.

MANHATTAN SASH PISTOL, cal. .36, D.A., single-shot; 4-inch, half octagon barrel marked "Manhattan Arms Co." Bar hammer. Total length 7 inches. Bludgeon-type ivory handles. Very large trigger guard. No sights. $125–$165.

MANHATTAN FIREARMS MFG. CO. REVOLVER, copy of Smith & Wesson 1st Model, cal. .22 r.f., 7-shot; 3.125-inch, octagon, engraved, ribbed barrel marked on breech in semi-circle "Manhattan Firearms Manufg. Co. N.Y." $85–$140.

MANHATTAN FIRE ARMS MFG. CO. REVOLVER, cal. .22 r.f., 7-shot; 3-inch, octagon, engraved, ribbed barrel marked "Manhattan Fire Arms Mfg. Co. New York." $75–$125.

MANHATTAN ARMS MFG. CO. REVOLVER, cal. .32 r.f., S.A., 6-shot; 3.5-inch octagon barrel marked "Manhattan Arms Mfg. Co., New York." Total length 8.5 inches. Polished hardwood handles. Stud trigger. Brass-blade front sight. Adjustable notch rear sight. Rod under barrel ejects fired cases. Cylinder removed for loading. $75–$125.

MARLIN SINGLE-SHOT PISTOL, cal. .22 r.f.; 2.125-inch round barrel marked "J. M. Marlin New Haven Ct." Total length 4.125 inches. Spur trigger. Brass frame. Barrel swings right to load. Plate 33, Fig. 31. $75–$100.

MARLIN O.K. SINGLE-SHOT PISTOL, cal. .22 r.f.; 2.75-inch round-octagon barrel marked "O.K." on top and "J.M. Marlin, New Haven, Ct." on side. Total length 5 inches. Weight 8 oz. Brass frame. Spur trigger. $65–$100.

SAME, but cal. .30, 3-inch round barrel. $65–$100.

SAME, but cal. .32. $60–$115.

MARLIN VICTOR SINGLE-SHOT PISTOL, cal. .38 r.f.; 2.75-inch, round, ribbed barrel marked "Victor" on top and "J. M. Marlin, New Haven, Ct." with patent date on side. Sometimes called a "derringer." $85–$140.

MARLIN XL DERRINGER, cal. .41 r.f.; 2.5-inch, half octagon barrel. Total length 4.75 inches. Bird's-head grip. Nickel-plated frame. Marked "X.L. Derringer." $165–$225.

MARLIN XXX STANDARD REVOLVER, cal. .22 r.f., S.A., 5-shot; 3-inch barrel marked "J. M. Marlin, New Haven, Ct." with patent date, and "XXX Standard" with date. Total length 7 inches. Nickel-plated. $85–$125.

SAME, but cal. .30 r.f. $75–$110.

SAME, but cal. .32 r.f. $65–$95.

SAME, but engraved, with decorated metal grips. Plate 33, Fig. 32. $85–$125.

SAME, but cal. .38 r.f. $85–$125.

MARSTON 1ST MODEL 3-BARREL DAGGER OR KNIFE PISTOL, cal. .22 r.f., with 3 superposed, 3.125-inch, round barrels. Total length 6.125 inches. Engraved frame marked "Wm. W. Marston Patented May 26, 1857. New York City." Spur trigger. Walnut grips. Nickel-plated. A 3-inch dagger blade slides in groove cut in left side of barrels, held open or closed by a spring. Barrel tips down to load. Made without extractor. Plate 34, Fig. 1. $390–$600.

SAME, but cal. .22 r.f., with 3-inch dagger blade, and cased, with cleaning rod, in red-plush-lined mahogany case having a block for 50 cartridges. Plate 34, Fig. 2. $405–$700.

MARSTON MODEL 1864, 3-SHOT PISTOL, cal. .32 r.f., with 3 superposed, 4-inch, round barrels. Marked as above except for words "Improved 1864." A 3-pronged device on the right of the frame which serves as an extractor has been added. Made without knife blade. Indicator on right shows which barrels have been fired. The firing pin is changed from one barrel to another by operating a side stud. Plate 34, Fig. 3. $275–$425.

SAME, but with 3-inch round barrels. $275–$400.

SAME, but with 4-inch barrels and gold-plated frame. Plate 34, Fig. 4 shows left side view. $325–$440.

MERIDEN FIRE ARMS CO. REVOLVER, cal. .38 S & W, 5-shot, hammerless; 3.25-inch, round, ribbed barrel. Marked "Meriden Fire Arms Co., Meriden, Conn. U.S.A." Rubber grips. Top break. Auto-ejection. $30–$40.

MERIDIAN ARMS CO. VICTOR REVOLVER, cal. .32 r.f., 5-shot, 2.25-inch round barrel. Total length 6.75 inches. Frame marked "Victor No. 3, Patented May 23, 1875," or similarly with some other Victor number. J. M. Marlin, New Haven, Conn., made the Marlin Victor, which is different from this. $45–$60.

MERRIMACK ARMS & MFG. CO. SOUTHERNER DERRINGER, cal. .41 r.f., single-shot; 2.5-inch octagon barrel marked "Southerner." Total length 5 inches. Weight 8 oz. Some specimens marked on frame "Merrimack Arms & Mfg. Co., Newburyport, Mass. Patented April 9, 1867."

Side-swing. Sheath trigger. Square walnut grips. Frame may be either brass or iron. $175–$300.

MERWIN & BRAY REVOLVER, cal. .42, cup-primer, 6-shot; 5.25-inch, ribbed, octagon barrel marked "Merwin & Bray, New York." Brass frame. Spur trigger. Walnut grips. Ejector rod in rear of cylinder. Blued barrel and cylinder. $85–$125.

SAME, but with rounded iron frame. $100–$150.

SAME, but with 4.75-inch, octagon, ribbed barrel. Plate 34, Fig. 5. $90–$125.

SAME, but cal. .30, cup-primer; 3.5-inch, octagon, ribbed barrel marked "Merwin & Bray Fire Arms Co. N.Y." $60–$100.

SAME, but cal. .28, cup-primer; 3.5-inch, octagon, ribbed barrel; 5-shot. $60–$100.

MERWIN & BRAY REVOLVER, cal. .25 r.f., 5-shot, S.A.; 3-inch octagon barrel marked "Merwin and Bray F.A. Co. N.Y." Cylinder marked "Patented July 12, 1869 and July 21, 1863." Total length 7.5 inches. Stud trigger. Nickel finish. Polished rosewood handles. $60–$85.

---

PLATE 34. American Cartridge Pistols and Revolvers

*Figure*

1. Marston 1st Model 3-Barrel Dagger or Knife Pistol.
2. Marston 1st Model 3-Barrel Dagger or Knife Pistol.
3. Marston Model 1864, 3-Shot Pistol.
4. Marston Model 1864, 3-Shot Pistol.
5. Merwin & Bray Revolver.
6. Merwin & Bray Single-Shot Pistol.
7. Moore Revolver.
8. National Derringer.
9. Newbury Single-Shot Pistol.
10. Norwich Arms Co. Revolver.
11. Osgood Gun Works Duplex Revolver.
12. Peavey Knife Pistol.
13. Plant Revolver, cal. .22.
14. Pond Front-Loading Revolver, cal. .32.
15. Pond Front-Loading Revolver, cal. .22.
16. Prescott Revolver, cal. .32.
17. Reid Revolver, cal. .22.
18. Reid-Irving Revolver.
19. Reid Revolver, cal. .41, Marked "Reid's Derringer."
20. Reid Percussion-Cartridge Revolver.
21. Reid Ex'tr Revolver.
22. Reid My Friend Knuckle-Duster No. 1, cal. .22.
23. Reid My Friend Knuckle-Duster No. 2, cal. .32.
24. Reid My Friend Knuckle-Duster No. 2 with barrel.
25. Reid Derringer Knuckle-Duster.

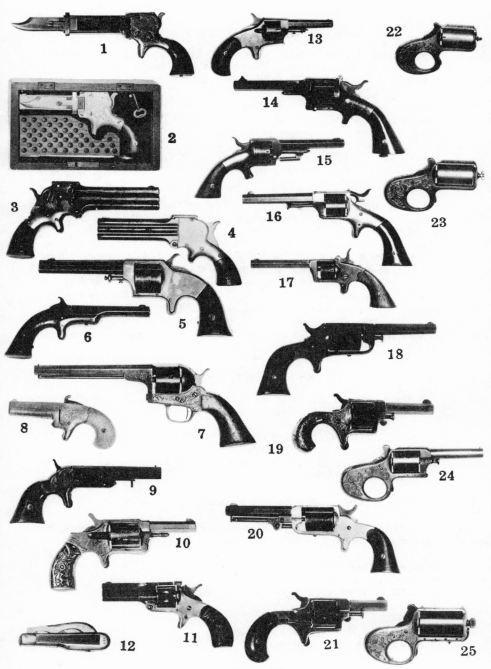

PLATE 34

MERWIN & BRAY SINGLE-SHOT PISTOL, cal. .32 r.f., 3.5-inch octagon barrel marked "Merwin & Bray New York." Bronze frame. Spur trigger. Walnut grips. Barrel swings right to load. Plate 34, Fig. 6. $60–$80.

*Note: Merwin & Bray were not manufacturers but distributors and financiers for manufacturers, including the makers of the Prescott and Plant Revolvers, hence Merwin & Bray arms are sometimes classified otherwise.*

MERWIN & HULBERT MODEL 1876 ARMY REVOLVER, sometimes called the Merwin & Hulbert Automatic Ejecting Army Revolver. See Chapter 16.

MERWIN & HULBERT ARMY POCKET REVOLVER, sometimes called the Merwin & Hulbert Automatic Ejecting Army Revolver. See Chapter 16.

MERWIN & HULBERT REVOLVER, cal. .38 c.f., D.A., 6-shot; 5.5-inch round barrel marked "Merwin Hulbert & Co., New York, U.S.A. Patented Jan. 24, April 21, Dec. 15, 1874" on top and marked on left "Hopkins Allen Mfg. Co. Norwich Conn." Total length 10 inches. Cartridges are loaded individually through side gate. Also made in cal. .44-40. $75–$95.

MERWIN & HULBERT REVOLVER, cal. .32 c.f., 7-shot, auto-ejecting. $40–$65.

SAME, but 5-shot, D.A., rubber grips, 3-inch barrel. $40–$55.

*Note: Merwin & Hulbert took over the business from Merwin & Bray, and were also promoters and distributors but not manufacturers.*

MINNEAPOLIS FIRE ARMS CO.—MINNEAPOLIS PROTECTOR PALM PISTOL, cal. .32 c.f., 7-shot; 1.75-inch, round, rifled barrel. Same as the Chicago Protector Palm Pistol but marked "The Protector. Minn. Fire Arms Co. Patented March 6, 1883." $250–$350.

SAME, but improved model with grip safety and pearl inlays. $265–$350.

MOHAWK ARMS CO. (1870's—Mohawk N. Y.), cal. .32, 5-shot, S.A., spur trigger, solid-frame cylinder stop in top strap (value not known).

MOORE DERRINGER, cal. .38; 2.25-inch, round, flat-top barrel marked "Moore's Pat. F.A. Co., Brooklyn, N.Y." on top and "D. Moore's Pat. Feb. 24, 1863" on under side. Brass frame. No ejector. $150–$260.

SAME, but cal. .41. $200–$350.

MOORE REVOLVER, cal. .30, "teat cartridge," S.A., 6-shot; 3.25-inch round barrel marked "Moore's Patent F.A. Co., Brooklyn, N.Y." Total length 7 inches. Cylinder marked "D. Williams Patent January 5, 1865." Stud trigger. Bird's-head handle. Polished hardwood grips. Unusual hammer. Brass-blade front sight. Notched-hammer rear sight. This revolver used a special cartridge with a projection called a teat, usually misspelled "tit," at the base. Very similar to a revolver made by National Arms Co., Brooklyn, N.Y. $100–$150.

MOORE REVOLVER, cal. .32 r.f., 7-shot; 6-inch octagon barrel marked "D. Moore Patent Sept 18, 1860." Total length 11 inches. Weight 1 lb. 10 oz. Brass guard, straps, and frame. Ejector rod under barrel. Barrel and cylinder swing right to load. Also made with 5-inch or 4-inch barrels, without value change. Illustration shows 6-inch barrel. Plate 34, Fig. 7. $150–$225.

MORGAN & CLAPP POCKET PISTOL, cal. .22 r.f., single-shot; 3.375-inch octagon barrel marked "Morgan & Clapp New Haven Ct." Brass frame. Spur trigger. Walnut grips. Barrel swings right to load. Also made in cal. .30 r.f. and cal. .32 r.f., without change in value. $65–$90.

MOUNTAIN EAGLE REVOLVER, cal. .32 r.f., S.A., 5-shot; 2.75-inch octagon barrel. Solid frame marked "Mountain Eagle," with serial number 8475 on specimen reported. $30–$45.

MY FRIEND—See Reid, below.

NAPOLEON—See Ryan, below.

NATIONAL DERRINGER, cal. .41 r.f.; 2.25-inch flat-top barrel marked "National Arms Co. Brooklyn N.Y." Spur trigger. Engraved brass frame. $225–$350.

SAME, silver-plated; ivory grips. Plate 34, Fig. 8. $400–$500.

*Note: National Arms Co. weapons are also found marked "D. Moore, Brooklyn, N.Y." or "Moore Fire Arms Co. N.Y." Likewise, the later model "D. Moore" is found with the marks of the National Arms Co. Apparently this switching of marks does not have much effect on values.*

NATIONAL FRONT-LOADING REVOLVER, cal. .42, teat-fire, 6-shot; 7.5-inch barrel marked "National Arms Co., Brooklyn, N.Y." $485–$875.

NATIONAL FRONT-LOADING REVOLVER, cal. .32, teat-fire, 6-shot; 3.25-inch round barrel marked as above. Also made in cal. .30, teat-fire, with ejector on right, without value change. $100–$150.

NEWBURY SINGLE-SHOT PISTOL, cal. .25 r.f.; 4-inch octagon barrel.

Walnut grips. Spur trigger. Brass frame. Barrel swings left to load. Hand extractor. Plate 34, Fig. 9. $175–$260.

NORWICH ARMS CO. REVOLVER, cal. .32 r.f., 5-shot; 2.5-inch octagon barrel marked "Norwich Arms Co., Norwich Ct." or "Norwich Arms Co. .32." Total length 6.5 inches. All-metal grips. Engraved frame. Spur trigger. Nickel-plated. Plate 34, Fig. 10. $45–$60.

NORWICH FALLS REVOLVER, cal. .38 r.f., 6-shot, S.A.; 8.5-inch octagon barrel marked "Norwich Falls, Conn." Total length 15.5 inches. Stud trigger. Polished hardwood handles. Brass-bead front sight. Grooved-frame rear sight. Pin under barrel for ejecting fired cases and also for use as ramrod. $45–$60.

OSGOOD GUN WORKS DUPLEX REVOLVER, cal. .22 and .32 r.f. Fires eight .22 and one .32 cal. rounds. Barrel tips down to unload. Hinged at bottom of frame. Barrel is 2.5 inches long, marked "Osgood Gun Works, Norwich, Conn. Patent 1880"; also marked "Duplex." Total length 6 inches. Weight 8 oz. Also see entry under Duplex, above. Plate 34, Fig. 11. $235–$350.

PEAVEY KNIFE PISTOL, cal. .22 r.f. Short iron barrel. Brass frame. Concealed trigger. Heavy knife blade. Hammer is outside and appears to be a knife blade. Firing pin is in barrel and is struck on top by the blade-like hammer. Marked "J. Peavey Pat. Sep. 5, 65 & Mar 27, 66." Plate 34, Fig. 12. $225–$350.

PERRY & GODDARD DERRINGER, cal. .32 r.f., S.A., 4-shot; 2 barrels, superposed, blued, 3.5 inches long, marked on top "Perry & Goddard New York City." Revolving firing-pin hammer-nose fires first one barrel and then the other. Stud trigger. Elaborately engraved brass frame. Brass-post front sight. Grooved rear sight. Polished carved rosewood handles. Action resembles Sharps 4-barrel pistol. $425–$615.

PLANT ARMY REVOLVER, cal. .42, cup-primer, etc.—See Chapter 16.

PLANT REVOLVER—EAGLE ARMS CO., cal. .42, cup-primer, marked "Eagle Arms Co., New York. Pat. July 12, 1859, July 21, 1863." $85–$135.

SAME, but cal. .36 cup-primer, cal. .30 cup-primer, or cal. .28 cup-primer. $75–$115.

PLANT REVOLVER, cal. .22 r.f., 7-shot; 2.5-inch, tapered, octagon barrel marked as above, but some specimens not marked. Rosewood grips. Spur trigger. Cylinder stops at front of cylinder. Iron frame. Plate 34, Fig. 13. $50–$80.

POINTER SINGLE-SHOT PISTOL, cal. .22 r.f., 2.75-inch, round, smoothbore barrel marked "Pointer" on top. Brass frame, nickel-plated. No ejector. Button under frame enables barrel to be broken to side. $35–$50.

POND ARMY REVOLVER—See Chapter 16.

POND FRONT-LOADING REVOLVER, cal. .32 r.f., 6-shot, S.A., made with 4-, 5- or 6-inch octagon barrel marked "L. W. Pond, Worcester, Mass. Pat'd Sept. 8, 1863." Plate 34, Fig. 14. $135–$200.

SAME, but cal. .22 r.f., S.A., 7-shot, 3.5-inch barrel. Total length 7 inches. Plate 34, Fig. 15. $135–$200.

*Note: The Pond Front-loading Revolver is also known as Pond's Separate-Chambers Revolver. Rear of cylinder is solid; each chamber contains withdrawable sleeve, bored to take a rim-fire, metallic cartridge. Firing pin strikes through slots in cylinder base. Ejector rod is attached to the base pin.*

PRESCOTT NAVY REVOLVER—See Chapter 16.

PRESCOTT REVOLVER, cal. .32 r.f., 6-shot, S.A.; 4-inch octagon barrel marked "E. A. Prescott Worcester Mass. Pat. Oct. 2, 1860." Total length 8.5 inches. Plate 34, Fig. 16. $75–$125.

SAME, but with 7.5-inch barrel. $75–$125.

PROTECTOR PALM PISTOLS—See earlier, listed under Chicago and also Minneapolis.

PROTECTOR REVOLVER, cal. .22 r.f., S.A., 7-shot; 3 5-inch round barrel marked "Protector Arms Co.—Phila. Pa." Total length 9 inches. Center hammer. Brass-bead front sight. Grooved-frame rear sight. Stud trigger. Engraved solid frame. Bird's-head bone handles. Engraved cylinder loaded from rear but removed for unloading. Cylinder pin serves as ramrod for unloading fired cases. $50–$95.

REID REVOLVER, cal. .22 r.f., 7-shot; 3.5-inch octagon barrel marked "J. Reid New York." Iron frame. Center hammer. Spur trigger. Plate 34, Fig. 17. $170–$300.

REID-IRVING REVOLVER, cal. .32 r.f., made by W. Irving and sometimes called the Irving Revolver. Marked either "Irving" or "J. Reid N.Y. City Patd. Apl. 28, 1863." Plate 34, Fig. 18. $135–$275.

REID REVOLVER, sometimes erroneously called a derringer, cal. .41

r.f., 5-shot; 2.75-inch octagon barrel marked "Reid's Derringer." All-metal frame and grips. Spur trigger. Engraved. Plate 34, Fig. 19. $285–$425.

REID PERCUSSION-CARTRIDGE REVOLVER, cal. .31 percussion or cal. .32 r.f., 6-shot; 4-inch octagon barrel marked "J. Reid N.Y. City Patd Apl. 28, 1863." Walnut grips. Spur trigger. Blued barrel and cylinder. Silver-plated frame. Loading lever under barrel. Upswing loading gate, right rear of cylinder on frame. Nipples unscrew. Cartridges fired with same hammer. Special wrench provided with this revolver. Plate 34, Fig. 20. $285–$425.

REID EX'TR REVOLVER, cal. .41 r.f., 5-shot; 2.375-inch octagon barrel marked "Reid's Ex'tr." Loading gate and extractor in one piece. Grip has peculiar shape. Plate 34, Fig. 21. $640–$890.

REID MY FRIEND KNUCKLE-DUSTER NO. 1, cal. .22 r.f., 7-shot; 1.5-inch round cylinder. Engraved brass frame marked "My Friend Pat'd Dec. 26, 1865." Nickel-plated. Plate 34, Fig. 22. $185–$255.

REID MY FRIEND KNUCKLE-DUSTER NO. 2, cal. .32 r.f., 5-shot. Otherwise like No. 1. Plate 34, Fig. 23. $200–$325.

REID MY FRIEND KNUCKLE-DUSTER NO. 2 with barrel, cal. .32 r.f., 5-shot, with 3-inch round barrel. Frame marked like No. 1. Plate 34, Fig. 24. $400–$650.

REID DERRINGER KNUCKLE-DUSTER, cal. .41 r.f., 5-shot, 2-inch round cylinder. Each chamber rifled and chambered. Engraved brass frame. Sliding safety lock under frame. Marked "My Friend Patd Dec. 26, 1865." Plate 34, Fig. 25. $1100–$1,500.

# REMINGTON CARTRIDGE REVOLVERS

REMINGTON SINGLE-SHOT MODEL 1866 NAVY PISTOL, MODEL 1867 NAVY PISTOL, AND MODEL 1871 ARMY PISTOL—See Chapter 14.

REMINGTON NEW MODEL 1874 ARMY REVOLVER—See Chapter 15.

REMINGTON ARMY SINGLE-ACTION REVOLVER, factory conversion from percussion, cal. .46 r.f., 5-shot; 8-inch octagon barrel. $200–$275.

SAME, but 6-shot, factory conversion. $200–$300.

SAME, but cal. .44 Colt Old Model, 5-shot. $190–$275.

REMINGTON DOUBLE-ACTION REVOLVER, conversion, cal. .38 r.f., 6-shot; 7.5-inch octagon barrel. $235—$350.

REMINGTON POCKET MODEL CONVERSION, cal. .38 r.f., 5-shot, 4.5-inch octagon barrel. Converted by using removable plate on rear of cylinder. $115–$165.

REMINGTON NAVY CONVERSION, cal. .38 r.f., 6-shot, S.A.; 6.5-inch octagon barrel. Removable plate at rear of cylinder. $210–$245.

REMINGTON ZIGZAG DERRINGER, cal. .22 r.f., 6-shot, D.A.; 3.25-inch fluted barrels, with rib in each flute. Ring trigger. Barrels revolved by stud engaging angular grooves in barrel, similar to principle of modern Webley-Fosbury automatic revolver. Loaded through hole in recoil plate. Frame marked "Manufactured by Remingtons. Ilion N.Y." Made from 1861 to 1862. Numbered 1 to about 1,000. Plate 35, Fig. 1. $535–$800.

REMINGTON VEST-POCKET DERRINGER, cal. .41 r.f.; 4-inch round-octagon barrel. Spur trigger. Rolling-block action but breech block is split and hammer rises in center. Marked "Remingtons Ilion N.Y. Patd Oct. 1, 1861 Nov. 15, 1862." Also made in cal. .38 r.f., .32 r.f., and .22 r.f., with barrels varying in length between 3.25 inches and 4 inches. About same value. Made from 1865 to 1888. Numbered 1 to over 25,000. Plate 35, Fig. 2. $200–$325.

REMINGTON FIRST MODEL, DOUBLE-BARREL DERRINGER, cal. .41 long r.f.; 3-inch, round, superposed barrels. All-metal grips. Spur trigger. High hammer spur. Extractors operated by two arms extending down sides of barrels. When barrels swing up, fired cases are extracted. Made from 1866 to 1935. Numbered 1 to over 150,000. Plate 35, Fig. 3. $150–$235.

REMINGTON PRESENTATION DOUBLE-BARREL DERRINGER, cal. .41 r.f., 3-inch, round, superposed barrels. Spur trigger. Barrels swing up to load. No provision made in this model for extractor. Elaborate engraving. Pearl grips. $250–$375.

REMINGTON-ELLIOT RING-TRIGGER DERRINGER, cal. .22 r.f., 5-shot, D.A.; 3-inch, round, fluted barrels. Nickel-plated. Barrels tip up to load. Made from 1863 to 1888. Numbered 1 to over 50,000. Plate 35, Fig. 4. $175–$250.

SAME, but cal. .30 r.f., 4-shot, D.A.; 3.5-inch, round, fluted barrels. $175–$250.

REMINGTON-ELLIOT SINGLE-SHOT DERRINGER, cal. .41 r.f., S.A.; 2.5-inch round barrel marked "Derringer." Spur trigger. Walnut grips. Iron frame. Total length 5 inches. Blued finish. Barrel unscrews for loading. Hammer acts as breechblock and falls past center so that force of case expanding when fired tends to hold block tighter. Brass-blade front sight. Notched rear sight. May have bone handles. Marked "Remingtons, Ilion, N.Y. Elliot Pat. Aug. 27, 1867." Made from 1867 to 1888. Numbered 1 to about 10,000. Plate 35, Fig. 5. $225–$350.

REMINGTON-RIDER MAGAZINE PISTOL, cal. .32 extra-short r.f., 5-shot; 3-inch octagon barrel marked "E. Remington & Sons, Ilion, N.Y. Riders Pat. Aug. 15th 1871." Spur trigger. Walnut grips. Tubular magazine. Blued barrel. Casehardened frame. Breechblock is depressed with thumb and drawn to rear, cocking hammer, raising magazine follower, and extracting fired case. On releasing block, it moves forward, placing cartridge in chamber and leaving hammer cocked. Made from 1871 to 1888. Numbered 1 to about 15,000. Plate 35, Fig. 6. $350–$450.

---

PLATE 35. American Cartridge Pistols and Revolvers

Figure

1. Remington Zigzag Derringer.
2. Remington Vest-Pocket Derringer.
3. Remington First Model Double-Barrel Derringer.
4. Remington-Elliot Ring-Trigger Derringer, cal. .22.
5. Remington-Elliot Single-Shot Derringer.
6. Remington-Rider Magazine Pistol.
7. Remington-Smoot Revolver, cal. .38.
8. Remington-Smoot Revolver, cal. .32.
9. Remington New Line Revolver.
10. Remington Frontier Model Revolver, cal. .44-40 W.c.f.
11. Shattuck Palm Pistol, cal. .22.
12. Rupertus Single-Shot Pistol, cal. .32.
13. Rupertus Double-Barreled Pistol.
14. Rupertus 8-Shot Pepperbox.
15. Rupertus 4-Barrel Derringer.
16. Rupertus Empire Revolver, cal. .41.
17. Rupertus Revolver, cal. .22.
18. Sharps Pepperbox No. 1.
19. Sharps Presentation Derringer.
20. Frank Wesson 2-Shot Vest-Pocket Pistol.
21. Frank Wesson Dagger Pistol, cal. .41.
22. Wesson & Harrington Revolver, cal. .32.
23. Springfield Arms Co. Revolver, cal. .25.
24. Stafford Single-Shot Pistol.
25. Rollin White Arms Co. Single-Shot Pistol.
26. Starr Derringer, Button Trigger, cal. .41.
27. Starr 4-Shot Button-Trigger Derringer, cal. .32.
28. Stevens Vest-Pocket Pistol, cal. .30.
29. Warner Revolver.
30. Frank Wesson Single-Shot Tip-Up Pistol.
31. Williamson Derringer.
32. Frank Wesson 2-Shot Superposed Pistol, cal. .22.
33. Rollin White Arms Co. Revolver.
34. Shattuck Signal Pistol.
35. Frank Wesson Pocket Rifle.
36. Xpert Single-Shot Pistol.

PLATE 35

REMINGTON-SMOOT REVOLVER, cal. .38 r.f., 5-shot; 3.75-inch octagon, ribbed barrel. Spur trigger. Nickel-plated. Side rod ejector. Checkered rubber grips. Made from 1875 to 1888. Numbered 1 to over 25,000. Plate 35, Fig. 7. $85–$135.

SAME, but cal. .32 r.f., 5-shot; 2.75-inch, octagon, ribbed barrel, otherwise like above except for ivory grips. Made from 1874 to 1888. Numbered 1 to over 20,000. Plate 35, Fig. 8. $100–$150.

SAME, but cal. .30 r.f. Made from 1873 to 1888. Numbered 1 to over 20,000. $80–$125.

REMINGTON NEW LINE REVOLVER, cal. .38 r.f., 5-shot; 2.5-inch round barrel. Checkered rubber grips. Spur trigger. Marked "E. Remington & Sons Ilion N.Y." Nickel-plated. Resembles the Remington-Smoot except that it is made without an ejector rod. Made from 1878 to 1888. Numbered 1 to about 50,000. Plate 35, Fig. 9. $100–$150.

REMINGTON, cal. .22, 7-shot, round 2¼-inch barrel, hard-rubber or pearl bird's-head grips, weight 7.5 ounces, length 5.5 inches, circular plate superposed on left side. Marked on side of barrel "E. Remington & Sons, Ilion N.Y." Some models marked "Iroquois" on barrel top. $125–$225.

REMINGTON NO. 2 POCKET REVOLVER, cal. .38 r.f., 5-shot 2.5-inch round barrel. Plain rubber grips. Spur trigger. Nickel-plated. Engraved frame, barrel, and cylinder. $80–$120.

REMINGTON SINGLE-SHOT TARGET PISTOL, cal. .22 r.f., 10-inch octagon barrel. Made from 1901 to 1909. Numbered 1 to about 700. $100–$150.

SAME, but 8-inch barrel. $150–$210.

SAME, but cal. .25, 10-inch barrel. $150–$225.

SAME, but cal. .44 S & W Russian c.f.; 10-inch barrel. $155–$215.

SAME, but cal. .50 c.f., 8-inch round barrel. $240–$300.

*Note: Remington target pistols, like some other semi-modern target pistols, are favored more by shooters than by collectors and are usually sold for shooting, hence the values vary greatly, depending principally on bore condition.*

REMINGTON FRONTIER MODEL REVOLVER, cal. .44-40 W.c.f., 6-shot; 7.5-inch round barrel. Walnut grips. Nickel-plated. Loading gate. Side rod ejector. Lanyard ring in butt. Made from 1891 to 1894. Numbered 1 to about 2,000. Plate 35, Fig. 10. $425–$625.

SAME, but cal. .45. Made from 1875 to 1889. Numbered 1 to about 25,000. $400–$625.

REMINGTON NEW MODEL REVOLVER, cal. .38 c.f., S.A., 5-shot; 3.25-inch round barrel marked "E. Remington Sons, Ilion, N.Y." Frame marked "New Model, Caliber .38." Stud trigger. Center hammer. Checkered, bird's-head, hard-rubber handles. Cylinder loads from gate on right. Fired cases ejected after removal of cylinder. Axis pin serves as ramrod for extraction. Resembles Remington-Smoot as to barrel, cylinder, and frame, but hammer, trigger, and handles resemble the Remington First Model Double-Barrel Derringer. $90–$200.

REMINGTON BELGIAN ARMY PISTOL, cal. .41 c.f., single-shot, S.A.; 7-inch round barrel, belled and banded muzzle, with Belgian proof marks. Frame marked on left "Remington, Ilion, U.S. America." Total length 12 inches. Trigger guard has projection for a finger rest. Butt has lanyard ring. $65–$100.

REMINGTON AUTO-LOADING PISTOL, cal. .380—See Chapter 19.

REMINGTON MODEL 1911 AUTOMATIC PISTOL—Same as Colt Model 1911.

REMINGTON MARK III SIGNAL PISTOL, 10-guage, single-shot, with 9-inch blued tip-up barrel marked "The Remington Arms—Union Metallic Cartridge Co., Inc. Mark III, Remington Bridgeport Works, Bridgeport, Connecticut, U.S.A." Brass frame, sheath trigger, and walnut grips. Made from 1915 to 1918 and serial numbered from 1 to about 24,500. $40–$70.

REYNOLDS REVOLVER, cal. .25 r.f., 5-shot, S.A.; 3-inch octagon barrel marked "Reynolds, Springfield, Mass." Cylinder marked "Pat. July 21, 1863, May 10, 1864." Stud trigger. Nickel finish. Brass-blade front sight. Grooved-frame rear sight. Polished rosewood handles. Total length 7.5 inches. Probably made by Plant. $60–$100.

RUPERTUS SINGLE-SHOT PISTOL, cal. .32 r.f., 4-inch round barrel marked "Rupertus Pat'd. Pistol Mfg. Co. Philadelphia." Walnut grips. Spur trigger. Iron frame. Barrel revolves left to load. Plate 35, Fig. 12. $125–$200.

SAME, cal. .22 r.f., 3-inch round barrel. $90–$135.

SAME, cal. .38 r.f., 5-inch round barrel. $90–$135.

RUPERTUS DOUBLE-BARRELED PISTOL, cal. .22 r.f., 3.125-inch round barrels. Walnut grips. Spur trigger. Blued. Hammer has movable firing pin to fire either barrel, the pin being moved by means of a knob. Barrels are side by side, and revolve left to load. Made without ejector. Marked "Rupertus Pat'd. Pistol Mfg. Co. Philadelphia." Plate 35, Fig. 13. $200–$275.

RUPERTUS 8-SHOT PEPPERBOX, cal. .22 r.f., 8-shot; 2.75-inch, round, fluted barrels. Walnut grips. Brass frame. Spur trigger. Recoil plate revolves, exposing loading gate. Butt marked "Rupertus Pat. Pistol Mfg. Co. Philadelphia." Plate 35, Fig. 14. $225–$375.

RUPERTUS 4-BARREL DERRINGER, cal. .30 r.f., 4-shot; 3-inch round barrels. Blued. Frame marked on side "Rupertus Patent Pistol Mfg. Co. Phila. 1863." Erroneously listed as a pepperbox in the first edition of this book. There is one specimen marked "R.S.V.P." on frame, but these letters were added by a Philadelphia collector who wanted to play a joke on another collector in the same city, this being regarded as a hilarious prank in sleepy old Philadelphia. Plate 35, Fig. 15. $175–$300.

RUPERTUS EMPIRE REVOLVER, cal. .41 r.f., 5-shot; 2.875-inch round barrel. Spur trigger. Walnut grips. Nickel-plated. Marked "J. Rupertus Phila. Pa." and "Empire 41." Plate 35, Fig. 16. $95–$150.

RUPERTUS REVOLVER, cal. .22 r.f., 7-shot; 2.75-inch round barrel marked "Empire Pat Nov 21. 71" on top and "J. Rupertus Phila." on side. Blued. Walnut grips. Spur trigger. Cylinder stops at front of cylinder. Plate 35, Fig. 17. $65–$100.

RYAN-NAPOLEON REVOLVER, cal. .22 r.f., 7-shot; 2.75-inch, octagon, rifled barrel. Engraved barrel, cylinder, and frame. Cylinder-pin unscrews for removing cylinder. Frame marked "Napoleon." Made by Thomas J. Ryan Pistol Mfg. Co., Norwich, Conn. $55–$65.

SAVAGE—See Chapter 19.

SHARPS PEPPERBOX NO. 1, cal. .22 r.f., 4-shot; 2.5-inch round barrels marked "C. Sharps Patent, 1859." Spur trigger. Hard-rubber grips. Plate 35, Fig. 18. $120–$225.

SHARPS PEPPERBOX NO. 2, cal. .30 r.f. $140–$225.

SHARPS PEPPERBOX NO. 3, cal. .32 r.f. $140–$225.

SHARPS PRESENTATION DERRINGER, cal. .30 r.f., 4-shot; 3-inch round barrels. Silver-plated frame marked "C. Sharps Patent 1859." Ivory grips with Roman soldier carved on left. Plate 35, Fig. 19. $375–$510.

SAME, but plain frame and wooden grips. $100–$165.

SHARPS & HANKINS PEPPERBOX, cal. .32, 4-shot, with four 3.5-inch round, blued barrels marked "Address Sharps & Hankins, Philadelphia, Penna." Engraved brass frame marked "C. Sharps Patent Jan. 25, 1859." Total length 6.5 inches. Weight 11 oz. Square grips. Stud trigger. Revolving firing pin on hammer. Brass-post front sight. Grooved rear sight. $165–$250.

SAME, but made with revolving firing pin inside frame. $165–$250.

SAME, but cal. .22 r.f. $105–$150.

SHARPS & HANKINS BULL DOG PISTOL, cal. .32 r.f., 4-shot; 3-inch round barrel. Total length 5 inches. Weight 10 oz. Frame marked "C. Sharps Patent Jan. 25, 1859." Originally called "Sharps Triumph No. 2½" $150–$250.

SHATTUCK PALM PISTOL, cal. .22 r.f., 4-shot, D.A.; 1.5-inch smooth-bore barrels. Total length 4 inches. Weight 10 oz. Barrels are bored in block which tips down to load. No trigger, but movable part of frame is squeezed to rotate firing pin and fire. Marked "Unique C.S. Shattuck Arms Co., Hatfield, Mass. Pat. Dec. 4, '06." Plate 35, Fig. 11. $200–$250.

SAME, but cal. .25 r.f. $240–$300.

SAME, but cal. .32 r.f. $240–$300.

SHATTUCK REVOLVER, cal. .32 r.f., 5-shot; 2.5-inch octagon barrel marked "C. S. Shattuck Hatfield Mass. Pat. Nov 4, 1879" and "Unique." Total length 7 inches. Weight 9 oz. Checkered rubber grips. Cylinder swings right. $45–$75.

SAME, but cal. .38 r.f. $45–$75.

SHATTUCK SIGNAL PISTOL, 12-guage, single-shot, 12-inch round barrel. Walnut grips. Spur trigger. Center-hung hammer. Barrel tips up to load. Marked "No. 1." Plate 35, Fig. 34. $65–$100.

SLOCUM FRONT-LOADING REVOLVER—See Brooklyn Arms Co., above.

OTIS A. SMITH REVOLVER, cal. .22 r.f., 7-shot; 2.375-inch round barrel. Frame marked "Smith's Patent Apr 15, 1873 No. 22." $55–$70.

SAME, but engraved, with pearl grips, in leather case. $75–$100.

SAME, similar marks, but cal. .32 r.f., 3-inch barrel. $60–$75.

SAME, similar marks, but cal. .38 r.f., 2.75-inch barrel. $60–$75.

SAME, similar marks, but cal. .41 r.f., 2.75-inch barrel. $70–$95.

OTIS A. SMITH'S NEW MODEL REVOLVER, cal. .32 r.f., 5-shot; 3-inch, round, ribbed barrel. Frame marked "Smith's New Model." Base pin released by cross plunger. $55–$80.

SAME, but engraved, with pearl grips and leather case. $175–$225.

SMITH ARMS CO.—CRISPIN REVOLVER, cal. .32, 5-inch octagon barrel. Total length 10.75 inches. Frame stamped "Smith Arms Co., New York City. Crispin's Pat. Oct. 3, 1865." Uses a peculiar cartridge with fulminate in a belted rim. This revolver is very dangerous to load, assuming that the correct cartridge is available. Based on Pat. No. 50,224 issued to Silas Crispin. $925–$1,350.

SMITH & WESSON—See Chapters 15 and 18.

SNEIDER REVOLVER, cal. .22 r.f., 14-shot; 2.75-inch, ribbed, octagon barrel. Walnut grips. Brass frame. Spur trigger. Engraved frame and barrel. Has two cylinders, each 7-shot, on same base pin. Unusual mechanism. Patented by Charles E. Sneider, Baltimore, Md., who was issued patents on Mar. 18, 1862, and Feb. 28, 1865. $1,250–$2,000.

SOUTHERNER—See Brown Mfg. Co., above.

SPRINGFIELD ARMS CO. REVOLVER, cal. .32 r.f., 5-shot; 3.125-inch, octagon, ribbed barrel marked "Springfield Arms Co. Mass." Spur trigger. Brass frame. Walnut grips. $90–$160.

SAME, but also marked "Mfg. for Smith & Wesson." $95–$150.

SAME, but cal. .25 r.f. Plate 35, Fig. 23. $75–$130.

STAFFORD SINGLE-SHOT PISTOL, cal. .22 r.f., 3.5-inch, octagon rifled barrel marked "T. J. Stafford New Haven Ct." Brass frame. Spur trigger. Walnut grips. Plate 35, Fig. 24. $90–$135.

STANDARD REVOLVER, cal. .22, 7-shot, 3.5-inch octagon barrel (resembles S & W No. 1-2nd issue). Weight 12 ounces. $70–$115.

STARR DERRINGER, cal. .41 r.f., single-shot, 2.875-inch round barrel. Brass frame. Button trigger. Side hammer. Frame marked "Starr's Pats. May 10, 1864." Plate 35, Fig. 26. $225–$325.

STARR 4-SHOT BUTTON-TRIGGER DERRINGER, cal. .41 r.f., 2.75-inch round barrel. Brass frame. Button trigger. Side hammer. Top-break action. Frame marked as above. $185–$275.

SAME, but cal. .32 r.f. Plate 35, Fig. 27. $185–$275.

STEVENS VEST-POCKET PISTOL, cal. .30 short r.f., 2.875-inch round-octagon barrel. Spur trigger. Iron frame. Walnut grips. Resembles Remington Vest-Pocket Derringer externally. Some specimens not marked. Plate 35, Fig. 28. $85–$135.

STEVENS GEM POCKET PISTOL, cal. .22 r.f., bird's-head grip. $125–$200.

SAME, but cal. .30 r.f. $125–$200.

STEVENS VEST-POCKET PISTOL, cal. .22 r.f., 3-inch, half-octagon barrel. Marked "J. Stevens & Co. Vest Pocket Pistol, Chicopee Falls, Mass." $75–$125.

STEVENS OLD MODEL POCKET PISTOL, cal. .22 r.f., 3.5-inch barrel. $65–$100.

SAME, but cal. .30 r.f. $60–$100.

STEVENS OLD MODEL POCKET RIFLE, cal. .22 r.f., 10-inch barrel. Spur trigger. Skeleton stock for holding pistol for shoulder fire. $100–$160.

SAME, but 8-inch barrel. $100–$160.

SAME, but 6-inch barrel. $100–$160.

STEVENS NEW MODEL POCKET OR BICYCLE RIFLE, cal. .22 r.f., with 10-, 12-, 15-, or 18-inch barrel. Spur trigger. Later made with trigger guard. Also made in calibers .25 Stevens, .32 and .22 W.r.f. Values run from $60–$100 for good, and from $100–$160 for fine condition, depending on caliber and barrel length.

TAYLOR SINGLE-SHOT POCKET PISTOL, cal. .32 r.f., 3.5-inch octagon barrel marked "L. B. Taylor & Co. Chicopee Mass." Total length 6.25 inches. Weight. 10 oz. Brass frame. Spur trigger. Walnut grips. $50–$70.

TERRY PISTOL, cal. .22 r.f., single-shot; 3.75-inch round barrel. Total length 4.75 inches. Brass frame. Hammer acts as breechblock. Walnut grips. Marked "J. C. Terry Patent Pending." $135–$225.

THAMES REVOLVER, cal. .38 c.f., 5-shot, D.A.; 3.25-inch, round, ribbed barrel. Rubber grips. Automatic ejection. Marked "Thames Arms Co. Norwich, Ct." with patent dates. $45–$55.

SAME, but cal. .32. $45–$55.

TURNER & ROSS REVOLVER, cal. .22 r.f., S.A., 7-shot; 5.5-inch, round, ribbed barrel. Rubber grips. Automatic ejection. Marked "T. & R. Patent Applied For." Center hammer. Solid frame. Brass-blade front sight. Grooved-frame rear sight. Bone handle. Cylinder loaded from rear but removed for extraction. Made for Turner & Ross, Boston, Mass. $35–$55.

SIMILAR, but octagon barrel, engraved frame, and marked "Czar" on cylinder strap. $60–$75.

UNION FIRE ARMS CO. REVOLVER, cal. .32 S & W c.f., semi-automatic 3-inch barrel. Total length 6.5 inches. Weight 1 lb. 2 oz. Marked "Union Fire Arms Co., Toledo, Ohio." $100–$140.

U.S. ARMS CO. KNIFE PISTOL, cal. .22 r.f., 1.25-inch barrel. Total length 6.5 inches, including knife blade 2.75 inches long. Weight 4 oz. $250–$425.

U.S. ARMS CO. REVOLVER, cal. .22 r.f., 7-shot; 2.25-inch, round, rifled barrel marked "U. S. Arms Co., N.Y." Also made as a 5-shot revolver in cal. .30 r.f., .32 r.f., and .38 r.f., without value change. $35–$45.

U.S. MARTIAL CARTRIDGE PISTOLS, U.S. MARTIAL CARTRIDGE REVOLVERS, AMERICAN SECONDARY MARTIAL CARTRIDGE REVOLVERS, etc.—See chapters having these titles.

VOLCANIC REPEATING PISTOLS. All have flat brass frames and flat butts. Made by Volcanic Repeating Arms Co. and New Haven Arms Co. between 1855 and 1858 and marketed soon after Smith & Wesson sold its patent and machinery to New Haven Arms Co. in July, 1855. Pistols could be bought silver-plated and engraved at factory at additional cost.
Cal. .30, 4-inch barrel pocket model, marked "Patent Feb. 14, 1854" on barrel. Specimen illustrated is serial No. 111. Plate 36, Fig. 5. $725–$925.
Cal. .30, 6-inch barrel target model, called "Target Model" by factory because of 6-inch barrel. Very few made. $875–$1,125.
Cal. .38, 8-inch barrel Navy model, called "8-inch barrel Navy." This pistol has magazine capacity of ten cartridges. Barrel marked "The Volcanic Repeating Arms Co. New Haven, Conn. Patent Feb. 14, 1854." Plate 36, Fig. 4. $1,025–$1,525.
Same, but made with non-detachable or detachable shoulder stock. Very rare. Specimens are in Milwaukee Public Museum. $1,525–$2,000.
Cal. .38, 16.5-inch barrel model made for detachable extension stock and called "Volcanic Pistol Carbine." Rare. Complete with stock. $1,400–$1,900. Pistol only, without stock. $1,195–$1,675.

*Note: A broadside released by New Haven Arms Co., October, 1859, listed three carbines as having been made; a 16-inch, a 20-inch, and a 24-inch barrel model, silver-plated and engraved on request at factory.*

WARNER AUTOMATIC PISTOL—See Chapter 19.

WARNER REVOLVER, cal. .30 r.f., S.A., 5-shot; 3-inch round barrel. Loading gate. Base pin serves as ejector rod. Marked "Warner's Patent 1857." Plate 35, Fig. 29. $135–$200.

SAME, but converted from percussion instead of being a factory-made cartridge revolver. $65–$100.

FRANK WESSON SINGLE-SHOT TIP-UP PISTOL, cal. .22 r.f., 3.5-inch round octagon barrel. Brass frame. Square grips. Total length 6 inches. Marked "F. Wesson. Patented Oct. 25, 1859." Plate 35, Fig. 30. $65–$100.

SAME, but marked "Frank Wesson, Worcester, Mass. Pat'd Oct. 25, 1859 & Nov. 11, 1862." $65–$100.

FRANK WESSON 2-SHOT VEST-POCKET PISTOL, cal. .22 r.f., 2-inch, round, superposed barrels marked "Frank Wesson Worcester Mass. Pt. Dec. 15/68." Total length 3.75 inches. Walnut grips. Spur trigger. Brass frame. Ring hammer. Barrels revolve by hand. Plate 35, Fig. 20. $225–$300.

FRANK WESSON 2-SHOT SUPERPOSED PISTOL, cal. .22 r.f., 2-shot; 2.5-inch octagon barrels marked "Frank Wesson, Worcester, Mass. Pat. Dec. 15, 1868." Spur trigger. Walnut grips. Plate 35, Fig. 32. $200–$300.

SAME, but cal. .32 r.f. $200–$275.

SAME, but cal. .41 r.f. $200–$275.

FRANK WESSON DAGGER PISTOL, cal. .41 r.f., 2-shot; 3-inch, octagon, superposed barrels marked "Frank Wesson Worcester. Mass. Pat. Dec. 15, 1868, July 20, 1869." Brass frame. Spur trigger. Plate 35, Fig. 21. $300–$505.

SAME, but cal. .32 r.f. $270–$400.

FRANK WESSON POCKET RIFLE, cal. .32 r.f., 20-octagon barrel. Walnut grips. Hand ejector. No rear sight. Pinhead, hooded front sight. Metal skeleton stock, detachable. Spur trigger. Instead of usual safety notch on hammer, there is a button on the frame that is pressed after the hammer has been lifted slightly. On fully cocking the hammer, this button springs out, allowing the hammer to fire the cartridge. Barrel revolves to right and is locked by a catch under the frame. This pocket rifle, sometimes called a bicycle rifle, was originally listed as the Sportsman's Jewel. Plate 35, Fig. 35. $165–$250.

*Note: Variations of the above pocket rifle were made in calibers .22 r.f. and .32 r.f., with 10-, 12-, 15-, 18-, and 20-inch barrels. On some the grips are walnut and on others they are rosewood. Some are side-swing and others are tip-up models.*

WESSON & HARRINGTON REVOLVER, cal. .32 r.f., 5-shot, 2.75-inch octagon barrel. Marked "Wesson & Harrington, Worcester, Mass. Pat. Feb. 7, June 1, '71." Plate 35, Fig. 22. $55–$75.

SAME, but cal. .22 r.f., 7-shot, 4-inch octagon barrel. Total length 6.25 inches. Wt. 8 oz. Marked as above. $55–$75.

SAME, but cal. .38 r.f., 5-shot, otherwise similar. $65–$100.

WESTERN ARMS CO. POCKET REVOLVER, cal. .32 r.f., 1.625-inch barrel. Total length 5.5 inches. Folding trigger. Marked "Western Arms Co. Patents Pending." $50–$65.

ROLLIN WHITE ARMS CO. SINGLE-SHOT PISTOL, cal. .32 r.f., 3-inch, octagon, ribbed barrel. Total length 7.25 inches. Weight 10 oz. Brass or steel frame. Spur trigger. Marked "Rollin White Arms Co. Lowell Mass. Patented April 13, 1858." Plate 35, Fig. 25. $150–$250.

ROLLIN WHITE ARMS CO. REVOLVER, cal. .22 r.f., 7-shot; 3.125-inch barrel marked "Made for Smith & Wesson By Rollin White Arms Co., Lowell, Mass." Brass body. Plate 35, Fig. 33. $150–$250.

WHITNEYVILLE ARMORY (WHITNEY ARMS CO.) POCKET RE-VOLVER, cal. .32 r.f., S.A., 5-shot; 2.5-inch octagon barrel marked "Whitneyville Armory, U.S.A. Pat. May 23, 1871." Total length 6.5 inches. Stud trigger. Nickel finish. Blade front sight. Notched-frame rear sight. Bird's-head ivory handles. $45–$75.

WHITNEYVILLE ARMORY (WHITNEY ARMS CO.) REVOLVER, cal. .22 r.f., 7-shot, 3-inch octagon barrel marked "Whitneyville Armory, Ct. U.S.A. Pat. May 23, 1871." Total length 6.5 inches. Weight 8 oz. Brass frame. $50–$90.

SAME, but 2.5-inch barrel. $50–$90.

SAME, but cal. .32 r.f., 3.25-inch barrel. $45–$85.

WHITNEYVILLE ARMORY (WHITNEY ARMS CO.) HOUSE PIS-TOL, cal. .38 r.f., 5-inch octagon barrel marked "Whitneyville." Brass frame. Spur trigger. Made to compete with Colt House Pistol. $60–$90.

WILLIAMSON DERRINGER, cal. .41 r.f., 2.5-inch, round, flat-top barrel marked "Williamson's Pat. Oct. 2, 1866, New York." Total length 5 inches. Weight 6 oz. Originally came with auxiliary chamber for percussion fire. Plate 35, Fig. 31. $225–$350.

WRIGHT ARMS CO. "LITTLE ALL RIGHT" REVOLVER, cal. .22 r.f., 1.75-inch barrel. Total length 5 inches. Weight 4 oz. Marked "Wright Arms Co., Lawrence, Mass." $350–$550.

WURFFLEIN TARGET PISTOL, cal. .22 r.f.; 10-inch round-octagon barrel. Iron guard with spur. Barrel tips to load. Marked "W. Wurfflein Philad'a Pa. U.S.A. Patented June 24th, 1884." $165–$250.

XL DERRINGER, cal. .41 r.f., single-shot; 2.25-inch octagon barrel. Marked "X.L. Derringer. Pat. Apl 5 1870." Probably made by Hopkins and Allen, but listed here because of lack of definite information. $165–$250.

XPERT PISTOL, cal. .30 r.f., single-shot; 7.5-inch round barrel marked "Xpert" with patent date of 1875. Spur trigger. Plate 35, Fig. 36. $75–$110.

# Chapter 18

## SMITH & WESSON REVOLVERS
## AND PISTOLS

A COMPLETE Smith & Wesson collection with associated items should include arms marked "Cast Steel, Smith & Wesson, Norwich, Ct. Patent Feb. 14, 1854," and those made at New Haven, Conn. marked "Pat. 14, 1854, New Haven, Ct." Each usually has an octagon barrel, bronze frame, walnut grips, lever action, and a tubular magazine made integral with the frame for magazine models. Norwich models are valued higher than those made at New Haven on some markets. The smallest caliber is often listed as cal. .30, although cal. .31 is probably correct.

All illustrations of arms described in this chapter were provided by Smith & Wesson. The descriptions of illustrated arms follow the information given by Smith & Wesson, supplemented by other information in the possession of the author. In general, the names of the arms and the descriptions are in accord with the Smith & Wesson terminology and also with that used by those collectors who specialize in this make.

In 1945, Roy C. McHenry and Walter F. Roper, authors of *Smith & Wesson Hand Guns,* published that year, supplied valuable information, which was in harmony with that obtained from the Smith & Wesson factory. In 1947, Harmon L. Remmel, master gunsmith, of Little Rock, Arkansas, went to the factory and checked the descriptions with Fred H. Miller, who was then the Smith & Wesson service and repair manager, and reported that they could find no errors.

Late in 1965, Fred H. Miller, who had advanced to sales manager of Smith & Wesson, said that this text is used by his office in answering questions about gun values. At the same time, Harmon L. Remmel said that collectors who specialize in Smith & Wesson firearms sometimes become involved in controversies regarding details. However, this is a normal situation.

Since 1970, Roy G. Jinks has been the handguns historian for Smith & Wesson, and while still retaining this position, also holds the job of product manager of the firm. Mr. Jinks, an S&W collector in his own right, is recognized as the foremost authority on Smith & Wesson and related items. He co-authored a book entitled *Smith & Wesson 1857–1945,* and in 1977, authored the book *History of Smith & Wesson* in conjunction with and to commemorate the company's 125th anniversary. He has also written many articles on the subject for several of the firearm publications.

## *LEVER-ACTION REPEATING PISTOLS*

The early Smith & Wesson pistols were a revolutionary design when first marketed, because of the self-contained cartridges. They marked the end of the old percussion days and were the forerunners of the famous lever-action Winchester rifle. They were awarded the Maryland Institute gold-medal of 1854.

The first pistols manufactured in 1854 and 1855 were stamped Smith & Wesson, Norwich, CT., patented February 14, 1854, Cast Steel, followed from 1855 to 1857 with Volcanic Repeating Arms Company, New Haven, Conn., patent Feb. 14, 1854, and finally, from 1857 until the end of production around 1860 were marked only New Haven, Conn., patent Feb. 14, 1854.

Descriptions of the pistols are as follows:

Cal. .30, 4-inch barrel, round butt, some made with spur on lever and some without spur, but no difference in value is noticed. Stamped on octagon part of barrel: "Smith & Wesson, Norwich, Ct." and on left side "Patent Feb. 14, 1854." Made between Feb., 1854 and July, 1855, when Smith & Wesson turned the patent on these magazine pistols over to the Volcanic Arms Co. Specimen illustrated bears serial number 17. Plate 36, Fig. 1. $1,020–$1,620.

Cal. .38, 6-inch barrel, flat butt, also made with or without spur on ring of lever. Marking similar to the small size, but without the patent date. Total length 12.5 inches. Very rare. $1,275–$1,895.

Cal. .38, 8-inch barrel, flat butt, made with or without spur on lever. Markings similar to above. Total length 14.5 inches. Very rare. $2,000–$3,200.

Cal. .41, 16.5-inch barrel, flat butt and made with spur on lever. Engraved iron frame and complete with shoulder stock like those on Volcanic Arms Co. brass frame pistols of similar size. Only two specimens of this size reported. $4,750–$6,950.

## REPEATING PISTOLS SOMETIMES LISTED AS VOLCANIC ARMS

SMITH & WESSON, cal. .38, 8-inch barrel, unfinished steel frame, square butt. Plate 36, Fig. 2. $2,000–$3,200.

SMITH & WESSON, cal. .41, 6-inch barrel, square butt, unfinished steel frame, no spur on lever of illustrated specimen although usual specimen has spur. Plate 36, Fig. 3. $1,400–$2,375.

CAL. .41, 8-inch blued barrel, square butt, brass frame; specimen illustrated has serial number 1920, but this was because of change of numbering system of New Haven Arms Co. to that of Volcanic Repeating Arms Co. Plate 36, Fig. 4. $1,250–$2,000.

Cal. 30. 3.5-inch barrel, square butt, stamped "New Haven, Conn., Patent Feb. 14, 1854." Plate 36, Fig. 5. $950–$1,625.

Although the magazine pistols belong in a Smith & Wesson collection, it must be understood that the Smith & Wesson line as we know it today started with what they called Model No. 1—First Model and continued through a series of model numbers and names that may confuse many beginners. Those referring to *Smith & Wesson Hand Guns* by Roy C. McHenry and Walter F. Roper should notice that the text lists the weapons in the order of caliber size, and not in the order of model numbers or in chronological order, in the back of the book.

In this chapter, we have listed all the principal models and types.

---

PLATE 36. Repeating Magazine Pistols

*Figure*

1. Cal. .30, 4-inch barrel with round butt and a spur on the lever.
2. Cal. .36, 8-inch barrel, square butt, and unfinished steel frame.
3. Cal. .41, 6-inch barrel, square butt, and unfinished steel frame.
4. Cal. .38, 8-inch blued barrel, square butt, and brass frame.
5. Cal. .30, 4-inch blued barrel, square butt, nickeled brass frame, and engraving.

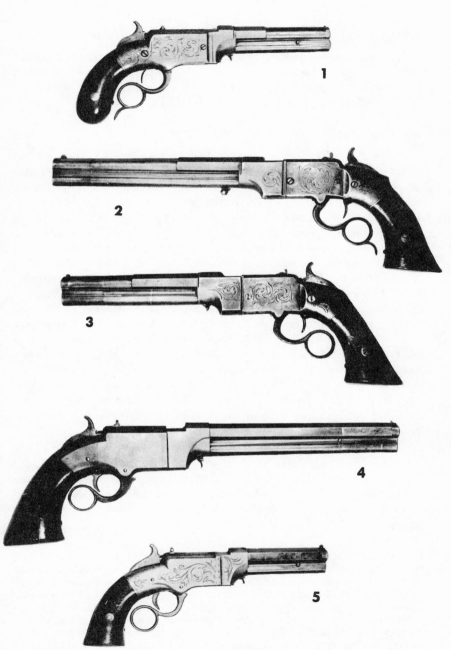

PLATE 36

There are some peculiar variations in existence, which a few collectors rave about, but the demand for such departures from standard models and types is so low that only a super-salesman with a high-pressure line can whoop up their values.

## CLASSIFICATION OF SMITH & WESSON HAND GUNS

In the standard text *Smith & Wesson Hand Guns,* McHenry and Roper have told the story of Smith and Wesson chronologically in the text, but in the appendix, called "Descriptions," they have listed the S & W hand guns by calibers, that is, in the order of caliber from small to large, going through .22, .32, .38, .44, and .45 calibers in that sequence, and they have listed arms in this manner: "Model No. 1—First Model; Model No. 1—Second Model; and Model No. 1—Third Model." This repetition of the word "model" causes confusion. The proper way to list a change in a model is to call it a modification, a mark, or an issue. For example, we could say "Model No. 1, Second Modification," or "Model No. 1, Mark 2," or "Model No. 1, Second Issue." All of these expressions mean the same thing as McHenry and Roper's "Model No. 1—Second Model," but they avoid the repeated use of the same word.

In this text, "Model No. 1, Second Issue" is the same as McHenry and Roper's "Model No. 1—Second Model." This conforms to the detailed information on these arms received by the author from the factory.

*Note: The terms Model No. 1, Model No. 1½, Model No. 2, and Model No. 3 refer to the four different frame sizes of the early Smith & Wesson handguns. They are: .22 Small Frame, .32 Small-Medium Frame, .38 Medium Frame, and .44 Large Frame, listed respectively to the model numbers above.*

MODEL NO. 1, FIRST ISSUE, cal. .22 S & W r.f., short, 7-shot; 3.187-inch, octagon, blued steel barrel jointed to frame at top strap stamped on rib "Smith & Wesson Springfield, Mass," rifled with 5 grooves and 5 lands. Blued cylinder, 7 chambers, not grooved, plain outside surface with patent dates stamped around cylinder, now worn off most specimens. Silver-plated brass frame with round side plate and square butt. Hammer has jointed thumbpiece to operate cylinder stop. Usual specimen has plain wood stock with piano finish, but some specimens have rosewood stock. Total length 7 inches. Weight 11 oz. Cylinder patent dates: April 3, 1855; July 5, 1859; Dec. 18, 1860. Manufactured from November 1857 to 1860, although some say a few were made in 1856. Serial numbers start with 1. This was the first breech-loading revolver using metallic ammunition as it is known today. Smith & Wesson held the patents for, and manufactured, both the revolver and the cartridge. To date, 11,671 is the highest number found. The author of this text prophesies that eventually this particular revolver will rise in value greatly. Plate 37, Fig. 1. $715–$1,885.

MODEL NO. 1, SECOND ISSUE, cal. .22 r.f. short. Specimen illustrated has silver-plated brass frame, nickel-plated steel barrel and cylinder, and bears serial number 118,368. This model was manufactured between 1860 and 1868, although some authorities in the past insisted that it began in 1863. About 114,700 of this issue were made, numbered consecutively with first issue from about No. 11,672, but no sales record is available. A total of 126,430 of the First and Second Issues were made. It is like the First Issue (3.187-inch, octagon blued steel barrel) except that the steel frame has a side plate of irregular shape and the hammer has a solid thumbpiece with a lug on top to operate the split-spring cylinder stop. Note that the usual specimen has a brass frame. Plate 37, Fig. 2. $110–$285.

MODEL NO. 1, THIRD ISSUE, cal. .22 S & W r.f. short. A total of 131,163 were manufactured from February 1868 to 1881 although some authorities believe that 1869 was the year of beginning. Serial numbers start with 1. Round 2.5-inch and 3-inch, blued or nickeled steel barrel, ribbed, jointed to frame at top strap. Blued or nickel-plated steel frame with round butt and irregular-shaped side plate. Hammer has solid thumbpiece with lug to operate split-spring cylinder stop. Piano-finished rosewood stock. Seven-chamber fluted cylinder. Total length 6.5 inches. Weight 9 oz. Specimen illustrated was nickel-plated and bears serial number 68702. Plate 37, Fig. 3. $85–$250.

MODEL NO. 2, OLD ISSUE, also called Smith & Wesson Army Revolver No. 2, cal. .32 r.f. long. Serial numbers start with 1, and 77,155 were made from June 1861 to 1874. Either 4-inch, 5-inch, or 6-inch, blued or nickeled, octagon steel barrel with rib, jointed to frame at top strap, latching to frame at bottom strap. Front sight driven into place and not pinned. Rammer pin-extractor. Steel frame; square butt plate, irregular-shaped side plate; solid straight trigger guard for single-action trigger; either blued or nickeled. Cylinder, 6 chambers, has plain exterior and has patent dates "April 31, 1855, July 5, 1859, December 18, 1860." Barrel rib marked "Smith & Wesson, Springfield, Mass." Hammer has a solid rectangular-shaped nose; straight side thumbpiece; lug at top for operating split-spring cylinder stop inserted in frame top strap; full-cock notch only. Highly polished rosewood stock. Total length with 6-inch barrel 11 inches. Weight with 6-inch barrel 26 oz. Army model has 6-inch barrel and walnut stock, usually. This revolver was never officially adopted, but it was carried as a personal side arm by officers of the United States during the Civil War, and possibly by some Confederates, and is therefore properly classed as a U.S. secondary martial revolver. Plate 37, Fig. 4. $125–$250.

*Note on Model 32 Rim-Fire Cartridge Revolvers made by others but sold by Smith & Wesson: As the result of a patent infringement suit won by Smith & Wesson in the United States Court for Massachusetts, Warner delivered 1,513 revolvers in 1863; Pond delivered 4,486 from 1863 to 1864; Moore delivered 3,376 in 1863; and Lowell delivered 6,682 revolvers from 1865 to 1872. These revolvers were die-stamped under the name of the manufacturer "Manufactured For Smith & Wesson." These revolvers are described elsewhere in this text. Those bearing the Smith & Wesson mark may be included in a large Smith & Wesson collection, or they may be grouped under the names of the actual manufacturers.*

MODEL NO. 1½, OLD ISSUE (sometimes called Model No. 1½, First Issue), cal. .32 r.f.; chambered for .32 r.f. short, but took .32 r.f. long, also; 3.5-inch and 4-inch, blued- or nickeled-steel, octagon-shaped barrel with rib, jointed to frame at top strap, latching to frame at bottom strap, with front sight driven into place, not pinned; rammer pin-extractor under the front end. Steel frame with square butt, blued or nickeled, irregularly shaped side plate, solid straight trigger guard for single-action trigger. Cylinder with plain exterior; 5 chambers. Hammer has straight side thumbpiece, solid rectangular-shaped nose, inserted pin to operated escapement-spring cylinder stop located in bottom of cylinder cut in frame; full notch only. Highly polished rosewood stock. Total length 8.125 inches Weight 15 oz. Specimen illustrated has nickel finish. Made from 1865 to 1868. Num-

---

PLATE 37. Smith & Wesson Revolvers and Pistols

*Figure*

1. Model No. 1, First Issue, cal. .22 S & W r.f., 7-shot.
2. Model No. 1, Second Issue, cal. .22 S & W r.f.7-shot.
3. Model No. 1, Third Issue, cal. .22 S & W r.f., 7-shot.
4. Model No. 2, Old Issue, also called Smith & Wesson Army Revolver No. 2, cal. .32 r.f., 6-shot.
5. Model No. 1½, Old Issue, sometimes called Model No. 1½, First Issue, cal. .32 r.f., 5-shot.
6. Model No. 1½, New Issue, sometimes called Model No. 1½, Second Issue, 5-shot.
7. Model No. 3, cal. .44 Single-Action American. First Issue; also called Smith & Wesson Army Revolver, Model 1869, and further known as the American Army Model, cal. .44 S & W American c.f., 6-shot, S.A.
8. Model No. 3. cal. .44 S & W Russian c.f. Single-Action New Model Russian, also called Third Model Russian. 6-shot.
9. Model cal. .45 S & W c.f. Single-Action, Second Model Schofield, also called Second Model Schofield Army Revolver, Model 1876 6-shot.
10. Model No. 2, First Issue, cal. .38 S&W c.f. Single-Action, also called Baby Russian Model 5-shot.
11. Model No. 1½ cal. .32 S & W c.f. Single-Action Revolver, 5-shot.

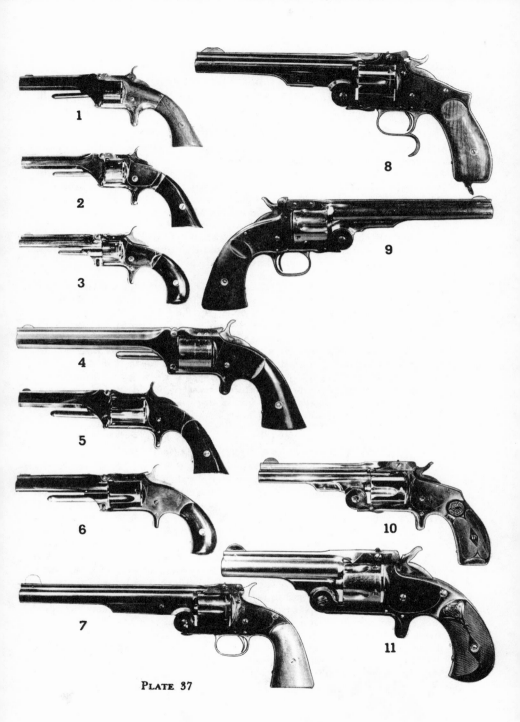

PLATE 37

bered 1 to about 26,300. Barrel rib marked "Smith & Wesson, Springfield, Mass. Pat'd. April 3, July 5, 1859, Nov. 21, 1865." Plate 37, Fig. 5. $100–$235.

MODEL NO. 1½, TRANSITION MODEL, cal. .32 S & W r.f. long. At the switch over from the Model 1½, Old Issue to the New Issue, the firm discovered that they had about 1,500 Old Issue barrel and cylinder units on hand without frames. So it was decided to fit the Old Issue barrels and cylinders to the New Issue frames. However, before this could be accomplished, the New Issue frames had to be milled wider at the base where the barrel catch was locked into place. The Transition Model was produced in the earlier part of 1869 only and was serial numbered in the range of about 27,200 to 28,800, this being in the same serial series of both the Model No. 1½, Old Issue and New Issue. It has been estimated that only 650 of this variation were produced. Thus, it is considered a scarce arm. $350–$715.

MODEL NO. 1½, NEW ISSUE (sometimes called Model No. 1½, Second Issue), cal. .32 S & W r.f. long. A total of 93,980 were made from 1868 to 1875. Serial numbers follow Model No. 1½, Old Model, and apparently start about 26,301 to about 127,100. Frame has round butt with irregularly shaped side plate, and straight trigger guard is made of steel, and nickeled or blued. Specimen illustrated is nickeled. Round 2.5-inch and 3.5-inch barrel, with rib marked "Smith & Wesson, Springfield, Mass., Pat. April 3 '55, July 5, '59 & Nov. 21, '65." Front sight driven, not pinned. Cylinder has 5 chambers and grooved exterior. Hammer has straight side thumbpiece, solid nose with lug to operate split-spring stop inserted in frame top strap. Highly polished rosewood stock. Total length 7.75 inches. Weight 13 oz. Plate 37, Fig. 6. $90–$175.

MODEL NO. 3, .44-CALIBER SINGLE-ACTION AMERICAN, FIRST ISSUE; also known as Smith & Wesson Army Revolver, Model 1869; and further known as the American Army Model, cal. .44 S & W American C.F., 6-shot, S.A.; 8-inch, round, blued, ribbed barrel marked "Smith & Wesson, Springfield, Mass., U.S.A., Pat. July 10, 1860, Jan. 17, Feb. 17, July 11, '65, Aug. 24, 1869." Made from 1870 to 1872. Caliber .44 S & W American and .44 r.f. Henry. Numbered 1 to about 8,000. Barrel jointed to frame at forward end of bottom strap. Total length 13.5 inches. Weight 42.5 oz. Fluted cylinder, 1.875 inches long, has straight-diameter chamber, counterbored to receive flanged-head extractor with ratchet. German-silver-blade front sight pinned in slot. Rear sight on latch. Blued or nickel finish for civilians but blued for Army. Oil-finished square butt, plain walnut stock. Latch in front of hammer operates top-break system. Rack and pinion mechanism operates ejector, which is on a square shaft and rises in rear of cylinder to eject fired cases. Army model has blued barrel, cylinder, frame, and trigger. Frame bears serial number. There are no records of the quantity made or the beginning and ending production dates. This model must not be confused with the Model No. 3, .44-caliber single-action Turkish Model, which is similar with the following exceptions: 6.5-inch barrel; rectangular hammer-nose hole in frame in position for rim-fire cartridge; no barrel catch locking slot as in American model. The U.S. Army ordered 1,000 of the American model, Dec. 29, 1870, and they were delivered in 1871, hence this is a U.S. martial cartridge revolver. This revolver represents one of the first steps toward real precision hand-gun manufacture. This model introduced interchangeability of parts and was among the famous guns of the western frontier days. Awarded a gold medal at the International Exhibition, Vienna, Austria, 1873. Plate 37, Fig. 7. $300–$610.

MODEL NO. 3, .44-CALIBER SINGLE-ACTION AMERICAN, SECOND ISSUE, is almost identical with first issue above. Made from 1872 to 1873. Cal. .44 S & W American and .44 r.f. Henry. Serial numbers about 8,001 to about 32,800. $285–$585.

MODEL NO. 3, .44-CALIBER SINGLE–ACTION RUSSIAN, FIRST ISSUE, Cal. .44 S & W Russian cartridge, manufactured from 1870 to 1875, and numbered from 1 to 215,704. Round, 6.5-inch, blued or nickeled barrel, jointed to frame at bottom strap forward of guard latching to frame at bolster interlocking frame post with jointed barrel catch. Patented July 10, 1860; Jan. 17, 1865; Feb. 17, 1865; July 11, 1865; Aug. 24, 1869. Service sights. Polished walnut stock with saw-handle grip. Six-shot. Blued or nickeled frame. Case-hardened hammer and guard. Carbon steel trigger, tempered. Spur or extension on trigger for second finger. Lanyard ring in butt. Adapted from the Model No. 3, First Issue, described above, at the request of Grand Duke Alexis of Russia; 250,000 were made for the Russian Imperial Army. As a target revolver, this Russian model was used to establish every record of its day. Gold medal awarded for this revolver at the Moscow International Exposition of 1872. Plate 37, Fig. 8. $250–$425.

When the barrel length is either 6.5 or 7 inches, the above revolver is called by collectors the Old Russian Model if it lacks a Russian inscription and coat of arms. $250–$375.

When the above revolver has a barrel length of 5.75 or 6.5 inches, a lanyard ring, a Russian inscription, and the Russian coat of arms, it is sometimes called the Russian Model made for the Russian Government. $325–$650.

(The service and repair manager of Smith & Wesson states that he has seen four entirely different Russian inscriptions on various revolvers which came back for repair. Harmon L. Remmel had an American Model, all numbers corresponding, cut for shoulder stock, with the usual markings on the barrel plus "Russian Model" toward the rear of the barrel. This gives rise to the idea that Smith & Wesson sent the Russians several thousand of the original Model No. 3, .44-Caliber Single-Action American, First Issue, in addition to those in the Russian contract. There is discrepancy in the numbering of the Russian Model, for it is known that the Russian Model numbers run from 1 to 215,704, and yet it is also known that Smith & Wesson made 250,000 for the Russians, plus more of the same for sale in the United States without the Russian inscription. In other words, this whole business of Russian markings is confused. The factory records are confused, and the author of this book is confused. This situation offers a golden opportunity for some fool to obtain a Doctor of Philosophy degree, or some arms dealer to get out a paper-bound pamphlet and charge too much for it.)

MODEL NO. 3, .44-CALIBER SINGLE-ACTION, TURKISH ISSUE, cal. .44 Turkish r.f. Resembles Model No. 3, First Issue (American Model), with the following few exceptions: The barrel is 6.5 inches long. The hammer-nose hole of the frame is rectangular and located to make use of rimfire cartridges. The nose shape is rectangular for rim fire, and the barrel-catch locking slot has been omitted. The dates of manufacture are from 1879 to 1883. Patented July 10, 1860; Jan. 17, 1865; Feb. 17, 1865; July 11, 1865; Aug. 24, 1869. A total of 5,461 were made in a caliber that was actually the same as .44 Henry rim fire. The inscription of the barrel should be in Turkish. This is a very rare piece. $400–$665.

MODEL .45-CALIBER SINGLE-ACTION, FIRST SCHOFIELD, also called Smith & Wesson Army Revolver, Model 1875, Schofield Patent. Made 1875 only, and serial numbered from 1 to 3,035. Caliber .45 S & W, 6-shot, single-action, 7-inch tapered round-ribbed barrel. Left barrel housing marked "Smith & Wesson, Springfield, Mass., U.S.A., Pat. Jan. 17th & 24th, '65, July 11th, '65, Aug. 24th, '69, July 25th, '71." Right barrel housing marked "Schofield's Pat. Apr. 22nd, 1873." Butt stamped "U.S." on the revolvers numbered from 1 to 3,000. Total length 12.5 inches. Weight 40 oz. Fluted cylinder, 1.437 inches long. Round blade front sight pinned in slot on barrel rib. Rear sight on latch. Blued or nickeled iron frame, cylinder, trigger, and casehardened hammer. Oil-finished square butt, plain walnut grips. Round ejector rises in rear of cylinder when revolver is broken open to eject empty shells. Generally resembles Model No. 3, American, First Issue (Model 1869) described earlier in this chapter, except for barrel length and fact that latch at rear of top frame tips back. The U.S. Army tested this revolver and, upon acceptance, contracted for 3,000 of the First Model Schofields that were sent to the Springfield Arsenal on July 12, 1875. Thus, this is a U.S. martial cartridge revolver that, with the exception of the last 35 revolvers made in this series, was not marked U.S. They were sold for commercial trade. $415–$815.

MODEL .45-CALIBER SINGLE-ACTION, SECOND SCHOFIELD, made 1876 to 1877, serial numbered consecutively in the same series as the First Schofield from 3,036 to about 8,969. Basically the same as the First Schofield except for a few improved changes, the most noticeable being the knurling and rounding off of the barrel latch, where the first model had a plain flat appearance. Other new features included the changing of the frame from iron to steel, thus eliminating the recoil plate found on the first model. The barrel latch screw was made thicker, the base pin was lengthened, and finally, the trigger was flatter. Of the 5,934 Second Model

Schofields manufactured, 5,285 were contracted by the U.S. Army and sent to the Springfield Arsenal on October 12, 1876. The last 649 revolvers made in this series were sold for commercial trade and not marked U.S. as were the military revolvers. Those marked as such are considered U.S. martial cartridge revolvers. Plate 37, Fig. 9. $410–$755.

*Note: Sometime during the 1880's, the government sold most, if not all, the Schofields to major dealers as surplus. Many of the First and Second Schofields were purchased by Wells Fargo & Co., the barrels were cut down from 7 inches to 5 inches, and the right barrel housing was stamped "W.F.& Co. Ex." followed by a stamped number, usually the same number as the serial number of the gun. WARNING!!! Beware of faked markings when buying Wells Fargo & Co. inscribed firearms. Because of the arms historical significance, the values of these revolvers vary. $375–$660.*

**MODEL NO. 2, FIRST ISSUE,** cal. .38 S & W c.f. cartridge; sometimes called the Baby Russian Model; and listed in the first edition of this text as Smith & Wesson Model No. 2½, First Issue. Single-action, 5-shot. Made with 3.25- and 4-inch, blued or nickeled, round barrel with top rib marked with patent dates, which are: Jan. 17-24, 1865; July 11, 1865; Aug. 24, 1869; Jan. 19, 1875; reissue July 25, 1871. Manufactured as a first issue from March 1876 to 1877. Numbered 1 to 25,548. Black, checked, hard-rubber stock with stamped S & W monograms. Blued or nickeled frame round butt. Service sights. Specimen illustrated was nickeled and has a 4-inch barrel. Plate 37, Fig. 10. $140–$265.

**MODEL NO. 2, SECOND ISSUE,** cal. .38 S & W c.f.: Second Issue and sometimes called Smith & Wesson Model 1880. Single-action. Resembles first model, described above, with a few changes. The joint edges of the frame are beveled. The extractor gear catch cut is omitted. The joint edges of the barrel at the counterbore are without raised flanges. An extractor cam is provided instead of the extractor gear catch. The Second Issue, numbered in its own series from 1 to 108,255, was made from 1877 to 1891. Sheathed trigger. Short barrel lug. Rebounding hammer. Usual specimen weighs about 16 oz., but weight depends upon barrel length. It is believed that in 1886, 8- and 10-inch barrels were provided in addition to the usual 3.25-, 4-, 5-, and 6-inch lengths. $100–$185.

**MODEL NO. 1½, SINGLE-ACTION,** 5-shot, cal. .32 short S & W c.f. Barrel made in 3-, 3.5-, and 6-inch lengths, also 8-inch and 10-inch barrel lengths, finished in either blue or nickel. Specimen illustrated has a 3-inch barrel and is finished in nickel. First made February 1878. Serial numbers from 1 to 97,574. Sales record books start with this model, discontinued in 1892, but McHenry & Roper do not give this production information, although it was obtained from Smith & Wesson by the author of this text several years ago. Round butt; bird's-head frame; solid stub trigger guard; inserted plate forward of trigger guard to cover cylinder-stop cut. Barrel made round, with a rib. Front sight inserted and pinned. Rib stamped "Smith & Wesson, Springfield, Mass. U.S.A. Pat'd Jan. 17 & 24 '65, July 11, '65, Aug. 24, '69, Feb. 20, 1877, Reissue July 25, 1871. Pat'd April 20, '75, Dec. 18, 1877." Cylinder exterior grooved. The stocks were at first plain, unchecked walnut, but later were made of checked, black, hard rubber stamped with S & W monograms, like the specimen illustrated. Total length 7 inches, with a 3-inch barrel. Weight with this barrel is 13 oz. Plate 37, Fig. 11. $80–$150.

MODEL NO. 3, .44-CALIBER, SINGLE-ACTION, FRONTIER, cal. .44-40 Winchester rifle cartridge, Model 1873. Manufactured from 1885 to 1908 and numbered from 1 to 2,072. Designed similar to Model No. 3, .44-Caliber, Single-Action, New Model, but the use of the rifle cartridge required a longer cylinder, measuring 1.56 inches, and long-strap barrel. Barrels were finished in either blue or nickel, equipped with target sights on order, and came in 4-, 5-, or 6.5-inch lengths. Either wooden or black hard-rubber stocks were furnished. Most of these revolvers were converted to use the cal. .44 S & W Russian cartridge; hence, this particular model is rare. $340–$650.

MODEL NO. 3, .44-CALIBER SINGLE-ACTION, but made for .38-Caliber Winchester rifle cartridge (.38-40 W.c.f.), but designed primarily like Model No. 3, .44-Caliber Single-Action, New Model, with a long strap, 6.5-inch barrel. Also made in 4-inch barrel length. Made from 1900 to 1907. It is said that only 75 of these were made, but information is meager. Some authorities claim that 275 were made. $600–$1,050.

MODEL NO. 3, .32-44-CALIBER SINGLE-ACTION, for .32-44 S & W gallery and .32-44 S & W target cartridges, like Model No. 3, .44-Cal., Single-Action, New Model, but with 6.5-inch barrel only, target sights, and either rubber or checked walnut stocks. Manufactured from 1887 to 1910. Most of these were made with a short-strap barrel and a cylinder 1.437 inches long, but a few were made with a long-strap barrel and a cylinder 1.56 inches long. Numbered in the same series from 1 to 4,333, of which 2,920 were cal. .32-44 and 1,413 were cal. .38-44. $275–$460.

MODEL NO. 3, .38-44-CALIBER SINGLE-ACTION, designed like Model No. 3, .44-Cal., Single-Action, New Model, but has 6.5-inch barrel only, target sights, and either rubber or checked walnut stocks. Manufactured from 1887 to 1910. Most of these had a short-strap barrel, and a cylinder 1.437 inches long, but a few had a long-strap barrel and a cylinder 1.56 inches long. $285–$460.

MODEL NO. 3, .44-CALIBER, SINGLE-ACTION, NEW MODEL, cal. .44 S & W Russian, cal. .44 S & W Russian gallery, and also made for cal. .450 Webley cartridges. Specimen illustrated made for cal. .44 S & W Russian. Barrels made in 3.5-, 4-, 5-, 6-, 6.5-, 7-, 7.5-, and 8-inch lengths. Specimen illustrated has 6.5-inch barrel. Finished in blue or nickel. Specimen illustrated is blued. Service sights. Round butt with checked walnut and rubber stock, and stamped S & W monograms. Numbered from 1 to 35,796 and made from 1878 to 1912. Patented Jan. 17, 1865; Jan. 24, 1865; July 11, 1865; Aug. 24, 1869; Apr. 20, 1875; Feb. 20, 1877; Dec. 18, 1877; reissued July 25, 1871. Front sight inserted and pinned in. Solid, bow-shaped trigger guard. This revolver is so popular with shooters that the collecting value is increased. Plate 38, Fig. 1. $325–$575.

MODEL .320-CALIBER REPEATING RIFLE, also called S&W .320 Revolver Rifle, and sometimes called S & W Revolving-Cylinder Rifle. Cal. .320 S & W rifle cartridge, conical ball, 11 grains of powder. Numbered from 1 to 977 and made from 1879 to 1887. Specimen illustrated is No. 540. Designed like Model No. 3, .44-Caliber, Single-Action, New Model Revolver, described above, with several exceptions. Blued frame with slotted butt and drilled rear tang for fastening extension stock. Barrel made in 2 sections, screwed together, and jointed about 2 inches in front of breech. Barrel lengths were 16 inches, 18 inches, and 20 inches. 239 were 16-inch barrels, 514 were 18-inch barrels, and 224 were 20-inch barrels. They were finished in blue. Specimen illustrated has 18-inch barrel. Cylinder is 1.43 inches long and has 6 straightbore chambers for the .320 S & W rifle cartridge. The hammer has a fly pivot on the hammer stud to avoid breaking the half-cock notch. There is an adjusting screw forward of the full-cock notch. The extension stock is made of Circassian walnut with a black rubber butt plate. There is a steel tang for joining the extension stock to the revolver butt. Open sights, but globe and peep sights were available. The stock proper is of mottled rubber. The forearm piece is made of mottled rubber, doweled and screwed to the barrel in front of the joint. Patented Jan. 17, 1865; Jan. 24, 1865; July 11, 1865; Aug. 24, 1869; Apr. 20, 1875; Feb. 20, 1877; Dec. 18, 1877. Reissue July 25, 1871. Specimen illustrated has a cross-hair drum front sight and an extension peep sight on the extension stock. There is a 2-position V-notch sight on the barrel. Fitted for stock but without stock. $900–$1,200. With stock attached. Plate 44, Fig. 5. $1,500–$2,200.

MODEL .32-CALIBER, DOUBLE-ACTION, FIRST ISSUE, cal. .32 S & W c.f. cartridge, 3-inch round barrel marked on top rib "Patented Jan. 17-24, 1865; July 11, 1865; Aug. 24, 1869; Feb. 20, 1877. Reissue July 25, 1871." Made only in 1880, serial numbered from 1 to 30. Round butt with plain black hard-rubber grips, pinned in front blade sight, irregular square-shaped side plate, concave back trigger guard, blue or nickel finish; and has a five-shot capacity, odd-shaped trigger. Plate 38, Fig. 2. $220–$530.

MODEL .32-CALIBER, DOUBLE-ACTION, SECOND ISSUE, designed like First Issue with changes as follows: 3-inch round barrel marked on top rib "Patented Jan. 17-24, 1865; July 11, 1865; Aug. 24, 1869; July 25, 1871; Dec. 2, 1879; May 11-25, 1880." Made from 1880 to 1882, serial numbered from 31 to 22,172. Round butt with checked or floral design, hard-rubber grips with S & W monograms in stocks circles, round-shaped side plate. $75–$145.

MODEL .32-CALIBER DOUBLE-ACTION, THIRD ISSUE, designed like Second Issue with changes as follows: 3-, 3½-, and 6-inch round barrels marked on top rib "Patented Jan. 24, 1865; July 11, 1865; Aug. 24, 1869. Reissue July 25, 1871; May 11, 1880; Jan. 3, 1882." Made from 1882 to 1883, serial numbered from 22,173 to 43,405. Round butt with checked hard-rubber grips with S & W monograms in stock circles, rocker style cylinder stop was dropped for a more favorable spring and hammer action, cylinder cut for a single set of stop notches rather than a double set on the cylinder of the previous two issues, and finally, the cylinder flutes were made longer on this issue. Plate 38, Fig. 3. $75–$145.

MODEL .32-CALIBER DOUBLE-ACTION, FOURTH ISSUE, designed like Third Issue, came in 3-, 3½-, 6-, 8-, and 10-inch barrel lengths. Made from 1883 to 1909, serial numbered from 43,406 to about 282,999. The cylinder stop and sear were reduced in size thus allowing them to be encased in the trigger well, the odd shaped trigger was changed to a more conventional type, and the trigger guard was made fully round from the previous concave-back trigger guard. $65–$120.

MODEL .32-CALIBER DOUBLE-ACTION, FIFTH ISSUE, designed like Fourth Issue with changes as follows: 3-, 3.5-, and 6-inch round barrels marked on top rib "Patented May 11, 1880; Jan. 3, 1882; Apr. 9, 1889" with Fourth Issue patent dates on some. Made from 1909 to 1919, serial numbered from about 283,000 to 327,641. The only basic difference in this issue is the front sight was forged on the barrel rib, where the previous four issues all had a round blade type front sight that was inserted into a slot on top of the barrel rib and held into place by a pin. $70–$125.

MODEL .44-CALIBER DOUBLE-ACTION, FIRST ISSUE, also called

---

PLATE 38. Smith & Wesson Revolvers and Pistols

*Figure*

1. Model No. 3, cal. .44 Single-Action, New Model, cal. .44 S & W Russian, also made for other cartridges.
2. Model cal. .32 Double-Action, First Issue.
3. Model cal. .32 Double-Action, Third Issue.
4. Model cal. .44 Double-Action, Frontier.
5. Model cal. .38 Safety, Fifth Issue.

6. Model cal. .38 Single-Action Mexican; also called Mexican Model; and actually a variation of Model No. 2, Third Issue, sometimes known as Model of 1891, Third Issue.
7. Model Single-Shot, First Issue, cal. .22 long rifle, S.A., Mod. 1891.
8. Model "I" Hand Ejector, First Issue, cal. .32 c.f., S & W long.

PLATE 38

New Model Navy No. 3 Revolver; and listed in first edition of this text as Smith & Wesson Model 1881 Navy Revolver. Cal. .44 S & W Russian cartridge, 6-shot, D.A.; 6.5-inch, round, ribbed barrel marked on top of rib "Smith & Wesson, Springfield, Mass., U.S.A., Pat. Jan. 17th & 24th, '65, July 11th, '65, Aug. 24th, '69, July 25th, '71, Dec. 2nd, '79, May 11th, 1880, May 25th, 1880," with the S & W trademark on right. Total length 11.5 inches. Weight 37 oz. Fluted cylinder, 1.56 inches long, has double series of stop notches with free grooves to receive action of double stop. Steel-blade front sight pinned to rib. Rear sight in latch. Blued or nickel-finished frame, barrel, and cylinder. Casehardened hammer and trigger. Checkered walnut or rubber stock. Rear of trigger guard is square. Top-break system operated by latch in receiver. Ejector on hexagonal shaft rises in rear of cylinder when revolver is broken. Also made with 4-, 5-, and 6-inch barrels. Numbered from 1 to 54,668, and manufactured from May 1881 to 1913. Of this total number, 275 were made for the .38-40 Winchester rifle cartridge, with 6.5-inch barrels and cylinders 1.56 inches long. This revolver was not officially adopted by the armed services of the United States, hence it is not a martial arm, and only by custom can it be called a U.S. secondary martial revolver. $135–$275.

SAME, but Smith & Wesson Army Revolver, Model 1881, also called New Model Army Revolver No. 3, similar to the above except that it is single-action and was made in 6- and 6.5-inch barrel lengths. It was not officially adopted and is customarily classed as a U.S. secondary martial revolver. $135–$275.

*Note: Most of the Model .44-Caliber Double-Action Revolvers using the cal. .44 S & W Russian cartridge were sold to Latin American countries, where they were, and still are, very popular.*

MODEL .44-CALIBER DOUBLE-ACTION, FRONTIER, cal. 44 Winchester rifle cartridge, 200-grain bullet, 40 grains of powder. Manufactured from August, 1886, to 1913, and numbered from 1 to 15,340. Designed like Model .44-Caliber Double-Action, First Issue, listed above, but made only on long-strap frame and with barrels having cylinders 1.56 inches long. Came in 4-, 5-, 6-, and 6.5 barrel lengths. Specimen illustrated has a 6.5-inch barrel, nickel finish, service sights, and hard-rubber grips. Plate 38, Fig. 4. $155–$355.

MODEL .44-CALIBER DOUBLE-ACTION, WESSON FAVORITE, cal. .44 S & W Russian cartridge, 5-inch barrel. Made from 1882 to 1883. Numbered 8,900 to 10,100. Designed like Model .44-Caliber Double-Action, First Issue, previously described, except for a few changes, as follows: Diameter of barrel decreased, with top strap grooved, and the bevel cut on the top strap extended to the sear. Grooves cut in sides of the bottom strap. Frame lockwork free cut is deeper. Inside tang cut is enlarged. A hole is drilled through the tang at the butt. The frame side-plate free cuts are deeper. The diameter of the cylinder is reduced. This modification is lighter in weight than the standard model. The serial numbers are included among those for Model .44-Caliber Double-Action, First Issue, and apparently the factory records are not clear on details. Therefore, it can be disregarded by most collectors as a separate model and left to the specialists. $735–$1,500.

MODEL HAND EJECTOR, NEW CENTURY, made for .44 S & W special; .450 Eley; .45 Colt; and .455 Mark II cartridges. Manufacture started 1908 and has continued since. Patented Mar. 27, 1894; May 21, 1895; Aug. 4, 1896; Dec. 22, 1896; and Oct. 8, 1901. Six-shot. Tapered round barrel made in 4-, 5-, 6.5-, and 7.5-inch lengths with patent dates on top and cartridge designation on left. Blued or nickeled square butt frame. Checked walnut stock with monogram insert. Value depends upon caliber and whether it is a plain or a target type. Made from 1908 to 1915. Serial numbered to 15,525. The values given here are an average of all. $140–$270.

*Note : The Model Hand Ejector, New Century, was popularly called the "Triple Lock." It was brought out in 1907. Twenty thousand were made, among which were 5,000 for the British Army, chambered for the .455-caliber British cartridge. The advantages of the triple lock feature were purely theoretical and actually only demonstrated the ability of Smith & Wesson to produce tremendously accurate machined parts.*

MODEL HAND EJECTOR, SECOND ISSUE. Serial number started with or near 15,376. Designed like the cal. .455 Mark II cartridge revolver but for either .44 cal. S & W special or the .44 cal. S & W Russian cartridge. Some were manufactured for cal. .45 Colt cartridge, in which case it has a 6.5-inch barrel. Patented Dec. 17, 1901; Feb. 6, 1906; and Sept. 14, 1908. Barrel marked "Smith & Wesson" on the left, stamped with cartridge designation on the right, and made in 4-, 5-, and 6-inch lengths. Checked walnut stock. Made from 1915 to 1950. Serial numbered from 15,376 to 50,000. The value given here disregards barrel condition. $120–$300.

MODEL .38-CALIBER SAFETY, FIRST ISSUE, catalogued as the Safety Hammerless, New Departure, cal. .38 S & W c.f. cartridge. Serial numbers from 1 to 5,250. Manufactured in January, 1887. Patented Feb. 20, 1877; Dec. 18, 1877; May 11, 1880; Sept. 11, 1883; Oct. 2, 1883; and Aug. 4, 1885. Round ribbed barrel made in 3.25-, 4-, 5-, and 6-inch lengths and marked "Smith & Wesson, Springfield, Mass. U.S.A." Five-shot. Externally grooved cylinder. Checked, hard-rubber stock with monogram. Cylinder stop is the "grasshopper" type, so called because of its length and shape. Casehardened trigger and hammer. $145–$275.

MODEL .38-CALIBER SAFETY, SECOND ISSUE, catalogued as the Safety Hammerless, New Departure. Serial numbers from 5,251 to 42,483. Patented Feb. 20, 1877; Dec. 18, 1877; May 11, 1880; Sept. 11, 1883; Oct. 2, 1833; Aug. 4, 1885; Feb. 14, 1886; Apr. 9, 1889; and June 3, 1890. Made from 1887 to 1890. Came in 3.25-, 4-, 5-, and 6-inch barrel lengths. Like the First Issue except for changes in the barrel, barrel catch, barrel catch lifter, stock, guard, trigger, and frame. Checked hard-rubber stock with monograms, or plain pearl stocks with gold-plated monograms. $100–$200.

MODEL .38-CALIBER SAFETY, THIRD ISSUE, catalogued as Safety Hammerless, New Departure. Serial numbers from 42,484 to 116,002. Made from 1890 to 1898. Like the Second Issue except for changes in the barrel, barrel catch, frame, and hammer stop. Barrel made in 3.25-, 4-, 5-, and 6-inch lengths. Hammer stop design changed to permit greater protection against accidental discharge. $100–$200.

MODEL .38-CALIBER SAFETY, FOURTH ISSUE. Serial numbers from 116,003 to about 220,000. Patented October 2, 1883; Aug. 4, 1885; and Apr. 9, 1889. Made from 1898 to 1907. Like the Third Issue except for changes in the barrel, cylinder, frame, barrel catch, and barrel catch cam. Barrel marked on left "38 S & W CTG.," with usual marks on top rib. Value depends on barrel length and barrel condition. $100 to $200.

MODEL .38-CALIBER SAFETY, FIFTH ISSUE, cal. .38 S & W regular cartridge, 3.25-inch barrel marked "Smith & Wesson, Springfield, Mass., U.S.A." on top rib, "Smith & Wesson" on left, and "38 S & W CTG." on right. Service sights. Checked walnut stocks without monogram. Blued finish. Designed like Fourth Model with a few changes. Numbered from about 220,001 to 261,493. Value depends on shooting condition, but if this is disregarded, as it should be for a collecting purpose only, the approximate value is that shown. Came in 2-, 3.25-, 4-, 5-, and 6-inch barrel lengths. Plate 38, Fig. 5. $100–$200.

*Note: Model .38-Caliber Safety has been discontinued by Smith & Wesson.*

MODEL NO. 2, THIRD ISSUE, also known as Model of 1891, Third Issue, and described in the first edition of this text as Smith & Wesson Model No. 2½, Third Issue, Single-Action Revolver. Cal. .38 S & W c.f. cartridge. Manufactured from February 1891 to 1911, and numbered from 1 to 28,107. Designed like Model No. 2, Second Issue, previously described, with several changes. Barrels made in 3.25-, 4-, 5-, and 6-inch lengths, marked "Smith & Wesson, Springfield, Mass. Model of 1891," with patent dates as follows: Apr. 20, 1875; Feb. 18-20, 1877; May 11, 1880. Hard-rubber stock with S & W monogram, or plain pearl with gold-plated S & W monograms inserted. $265–$405.

SAME, but so-called Mexican Model, listed according to the S & W system of nomenclature as Model .38-Caliber, Single-Action Mexican, and included in the first edition of this text under Smith & Wesson Model No. 2½, Third Issue. Only 2,000 or less were manufactured. The serial numbers are included among those for Model No. 2, Third Issue, described above. Designed like parent model with a few variations. Specimen illustrated has a 5-inch barrel, blued finish, and hard-rubber stocks. Plate 38, Fig. 6. $600–$925.

*Note: In the so-called Mexican Model, the trigger is a straight, checked finger piece, that is, it is a spur trigger; the trigger guard is straight, and not bow-shaped, and is held with a guard screw; the trigger spring is lighter in weight; there is no half-cock notch on the hammer; and the hammer thumbpiece is checked.*

MODEL SINGLE-SHOT, FIRST ISSUE, cal. .22 long rifle cartridge, S.A., with 6-, 8-, and 10-inch barrels. Made for cal. .32 S & W regular or gallery cartridge, and also made for cal. .38 S & W regular or gallery cartridges. Round barrel with ribbed top, jointed to frame at bottom strap. Hammer has flanged thumbpiece with a solid nose. Hard-rubber square buttstock, extra long. Made from May, 1893 to 1905. Numbered in the same series as Model No. 2, Third Issue. Manufactured as an interchangeable, combined revolver and single-shot target pistol. Specimen illustrated has a 10-inch barrel, blued finish, and an adjustable target rear sight. Plate 38, Fig. 7. $190–$330.

MODEL SINGLE-SHOT, SECOND ISSUE, made from 1905 to 1909, numbered 1 to 4,617, made as a single-shot pistol only, and not as a combination. Designed like the above First Model, with a few variations. Like the First Model, it has a .38 single-action frame, but without hand and stop slots; bolster flanges were removed and relief grooves cut in the sides. Came in 6-, 8-, and 10-inch barrel lengths. The windage adjustment screws were made adjustable from the sides of the catch against the round body of the sight leaf. In blue or nickel finish. Came .22 only. $170–$285.

MODEL SINGLE-SHOT, THIRD ISSUE, originally catalogued as the Perfected Target Pistol. This modification began with serial number 4,618. Made from 1909 to 1923, serial numbers 4,618 to 11,641. Caliber .22 long rifle. 10-inch barrel and blued finish only. This arm sells primarily for its shooting value. $170–$280.

## SMITH & WESSON REVOLVERS MADE FOR WINCHESTER .32-20 CARTRIDGES.

When the Winchester Repeating Arms Company produced the .32 Winchester cartridge, also known as the .32-20, with its 115-grain .32-caliber bullet and its 20-grain powder charge, suitable for killing small animals, Smith & Wesson began to manufacture revolvers for this cartridge. The names of these revolvers are rather puzzling to the beginner, but they are not of great importance as collectors' pieces and are sold partly according to their shooting condition.

MODEL .32-20 HAND EJECTOR, WINCHESTER FIRST ISSUE. Made from Mar. 24, 1899, to 1902. Patented July 1, 1884; Apr. 9, 1889; May 21, 1895; July 16, 1895; Aug. 4, 1896; Dec. 22, 1896; and Oct. 4, 1898. Tapered round barrel made in 4-, 5-, 6-, and 6.5-inch lengths. with threads for screwing to frame, solid front sight, marked with patent dates on top and cartridge designation on left. Six-shot. Externally grooved cylinder, chambered for this cartridge. Blued or nickeled frame with round butt, and irregularly shaped side plate held with four screws, with monogram. Hammer has straight sides, checked thumbpiece. Decarbonized, casehardened hammer and trigger. Serial numbered from 1 to 5,311. $155-$235.

MODEL .32-20 HAND EJECTOR, WINCHESTER SECOND ISSUE, OF 1902. Like above with comparatively minor changes in the barrel, extractor rod, hammer, cylinder, and yoke. Came in 4-, 5-, and 6.5-inch barrel lengths. Made from 1902 to 1903. Numbered 5,312 to 9,811. Patented July 1, 1884, Apr. 9, 1889; May 21, 1895; July 16, 1895; Aug. 4, 1896; Dec. 22, 1896; and Oct. 4, 1898. Sold largely on shooting condition. $180–$235.

MODEL .32-20 HAND EJECTOR, WINCHESTER ISSUE OF 1902, FIRST CHANGE, Oct. 27, 1903. Made from 1903 to 1905. Numbered 9,812 to 18,125. Similar to previous model with small changes in the barrel, frame, yoke, and stock. The square buttstock has checked wood construction only, while the round buttstock has checked wood and hard-rubber construction. Came in 4-, 5-, and 6.5-inch barrel lengths. Sold largely according to shooting condition. $145–$230.

MODEL .32-20 HAND EJECTOR, WINCHESTER ISSUE OF 1905, May, 1905. Serial numbers from 18,126 to 22,426. Patented Apr. 9, 1889; Mar. 27, 1894; May 21, 1895; July 16, 1895; Aug. 4, 1896; Dec. 22, 1896; Oct. 4, 1898; Oct. 8, 1901; and Dec. 17, 1901. Made from 1905 to 1906. Resembles previous revolver with minor changes in the cylinder, frame, and extractor. Came in 4-, 5-, and 6.5-inch barrel lengths. Sold largely according to shooting condition. $155–$235.

MODEL .32-20 HAND EJECTOR, WINCHESTER ISSUE OF 1905, FIRST CHANGE. Resembles previous revolver with minor changes in the frame, hammer, and rebound slide. Serial numbers from 22,427 to 45,200. Patented Apr. 9, 1889; Mar. 27, 1894; May 21, 1895; July 16, 1895; Aug. 4, 1896; Dec. 22, 1896; Oct. 4, 1898; Oct. 8, 1901; Dec. 17, 1901; and Feb. 6, 1906. Made from 1906 to 1909. Came in 4-, 5-, 6-, and 6.5-inch barrel lengths. Sold largely according to shooting condition. $150–$230.

MODEL .32-20 HAND EJECTOR, WINCHESTER ISSUE OF 1905, SECOND CHANGE. Exactly like the previous one except that minor changes were made in the frame, hammer, extractor, and rebound slide of certain revolvers of the Model .32-20 Hand Ejector, Winchester Issue of 1905, First Change. Made from 1906 to 1909. The records of the S & W factory do not show which ones were modified, or how many, hence specimens of this Second Change bear numbers somewhere between 22,427 and 45,200. Came in 4-, 5-, 6-, and 6.5-inch barrel lengths. Sold largely according to shooting condition. $150–$230.

MODEL .32-20 HAND EJECTOR, WINCHESTER ISSUE OF 1905, THIRD CHANGE. Like the previous one except for changes in the bolt, hammer, trigger, sear, and rebound slide. Made from 1909 to 1915. Came in 4-inch and 6-inch barrel lengths. Serial numbers from 45,201 to 65,700. Patented Mar. 27, 1894; May 21, 1895; Aug. 4, 1896; Dec. 22, 1896; Oct. 8, 1901; Dec. 17, 1901; Feb. 6, 1906; and Sept. 14, 1909. Sold largely on a basis of shooting condition. $150–$235.

MODEL .32-20 HAND EJECTOR, WINCHESTER ISSUE OF 1905, FOURTH CHANGE. Like the previous one except for changes in the cylinder, extractor, hammer, sight, hammer block, trigger, hand, and side plate. Made from May, 1915, to 1940. Serial numbered from 65,701 to 144,084. Patented Oct. 8, 1901; Dec. 17, 1901; Feb. 6, 1906; Sept. 14, 1909; and Dec. 29, 1914. The cylinder was heat-treated, beginning with No. 81,287, in 1919. Changes were made in the sights in 1922 and 1923. Came in 4-, 5-, and 6-inch barrel lengths. The target type was made with a square butt, blued finish, and a 6-inch barrel. Sold principally according to shooting condition. $140–$210.

MODEL "I" HAND EJECTOR, FIRST ISSUE, cal. .32 c.f. S & W long cartridge, 6-shot. Made from 1896 to 1903. Serial numbers from 1 to 19,712. Patented July 1, 1884; Apr. 9, 1889; Mar. 27, 1894; May 29, 1894; May 21, 1895; July 16, 1895. Specimen illustrated has 4.5-inch barrel, service sights, nickel finish, and round-butt, checkered, black rubber stocks bearing stamped S & W monograms. Made in 3.25-, 4.25-, and 6-inch barrel lengths. Sold largely according to shooting condition. Plate 38, Fig. 8. $100–$185.

MODEL .38-CALIBER DOUBLE-ACTION, FIRST ISSUE, cal. .38 S & W c.f. Numbered 1 to about 4,000. Manufacture started February, 1880. Patented Jan. 17-24, 1865; July 11, 1865; Aug. 24, 1869; Jan. 19, 1875; reissue of July 25, 1871. Five-shot. Externally grooved cylinder. Blued or nickeled frame with round steel butt having curved front and straight edge. Blued or nickeled, round ribbed barrel, 3.25 and 4 inches long, marked on top "Smith & Wesson, Springfield, Mass. U.S.A.," with patent dates. Checked, hard-rubber stock with monogram. The side plates have a square shape. $115–$245.

*Note: All 4,000 of the Model .38-Caliber Double-Action, First Issue, had the straight-cut or "square" side plates, but this weakened the frame and caused repair work, hence the factory reverted to the irregular shape that had been used before in all models.*

MODEL .38-CALIBER DOUBLE-ACTION, SECOND ISSUE. Same as First Issue except for minor changes in side plate and the side plate cut in the frame. Serial numbers from 4,001 to 119,000. Came in 3.25-, 4-, 5-, and 6-inch barrel lengths. Made from 1880 to 1884. The side plates have an irregular shape. $75–$115.

MODEL .38-CALIBER DOUBLE-ACTION, THIRD ISSUE. Same as Second Issue, with small changes in the hammer and rear sear. Made from 1884 to 1885. Came in 3.25-, 4-, 5-, 6-, 8-, and 10-inch barrel lengths. Serial numbers from 119,001 to 322,700. $65–$95.

*Note: There is a variation which has side plates which the collectors describe as square.*

MODEL.38-CALIBER DOUBLE-ACTION, FOURTH ISSUE, cal. .38 S & W c.f. cartridges. Made from 1885 to 1909. Specimen illustrated has 5-inch barrel; blued finish; black, hard-rubber grips, stamped with S & W monogram; and reverse-curve trigger guard, as used on First, Second, and Third Issues. Serial numbers from 322,701 to 539,000. Patented May 11, 1880; Jan. 3, 1882; Apr. 9, 1889. Designed like the Third Issue with several changes. Barrels made in 3.25-, 4-, 5-, and 6-inch lengths, and marked "Smith & Wesson, Springfield, Mass., U.S.A.," with patent dates on top rib. Shape of trigger guard bow changed to conform to trigger finger piece, and side walls at trigger cut extended to cover exposed action of rear sear. Plate 39, Fig. 1. $60–$95.

MODEL. .38-CALIBER DOUBLE-ACTION, FIFTH ISSUE. Same as Fourth Issue with changes in the barrel, barrel catch, and barrel catch cam. Serial numbers from 539,001 to 554,077. Made from 1909 to 1911. The barrel is marked on its top rib "Smith & Wesson, Springfield, Mass. U.S.A." $75–$115.

---

PLATE 39. Smith & Wesson Revolvers and Pistols

*Figure*

1. Model cal. .38 Double-Action, Fourth Issue.
2. Model cal. .38 Hand Ejector, Military and Police, First Issue; also known as the Model of 1899; and sometimes called the Smith & Wesson Model 1899 Army-Navy Revolver, 6-shot, D.A.
3. Model cal. .32 Safety, Third Issue.
4. Model "M" Hand Ejector, First Issue. cal. .22 r.f.
5. Model cal. .38 Hand Ejector, Military and Police, Second Issue.
6. Model cal. .45 Hand Ejector, U.S. Service, sometimes called Smith & Wesson Model 1917 Army Revolver.
7. Model "I" Hand Ejector, Issue of 1903, Fifth Change.
8. Model cal. .32 Automatic Pistol, Model 1925.
9. Model cal. .35 Automatic Pistol, Model 1913, cal. .35 S & W automatic.

PLATE 39

MODEL .38-CALIBER DOUBLE-ACTION, PERFECTED, cal. .38 S & W c.f. cartridge. Manufactured from January, 1909, to 1920. Serial numbers from 1 to 59,400. Patented Aug. 4, 1896; Dec. 22, 1896; Oct. 8, 1901; Feb. 6, 1906; Sept. 14, 1909. Blued or nickeled, round, ribbed barrel, made in 3.25-, 4-, 5-, and 6-inch lengths, and marked "Smith & Wesson, Springfield, Mass., U.S.A." with patent dates on top rib and "38 S & W CTG." on left. Five-shot. Nickel steel cylinder, externally grooved. Blued or nickeled frame with round butt, solid trigger guard, and checked hard-rubber stock with S & W monogram. $135–$230.

MODEL .32-CALIBER SAFETY, FIRST ISSUE, catalogued as Safety Hammerless, New Departure, cal. .32 c.f. Made from February 1888 to September 1902. Patented Feb. 20, 1877; Dec. 18, 1877; May 11, 1880; Sept. 11, 1883; Oct. 2, 1883; and Aug. 4, 1885. Round, ribbed, blued or nickeled barrel, made in 2-, 3-, and 3.5-inch barrel lengths, with patent dates on top rib and front sight inserted and pinned. Five-shot. Externally grooved cylinder with internal square threaded section for base pin. Round butt. Cylinder stop usually called a grasshopper stop because of its length and shape. Checked hard-rubber stock with monogram. Serial numbered from 1 to 91,417. $75–$125.

MODEL .32-CALIBER SAFETY, SECOND ISSUE, cal. .32 c.f. Resembles the First Issue except for comparatively minor changes in the barrel, barrel catch, frame, and latch spring. Came in 2-, 3-, 3.5-, and 6-inch barrel. Made from 1902 to 1909. Numbered 91,418 to about 170,000. $75–$135.

MODEL .38-CALIBER HAND EJECTOR MILITARY AND POLICE FIRST ISSUE; listed in the first edition of this text as Smith & Wesson Model 1899 Army-Navy Revolver, cal. .38, 6-shot, D.A., also commonly called Model 1899. Cal. .38 long Colt U.S. service cartridge. Serial numbers from 1 to 20,975 manufactured from Mar. 24, 1899. Two thousand were made for the U.S. Navy and 1,000 for the U.S. Army. In the Army or Navy form, this is a U.S. martial revolver. The Army version has a 6.5-inch, tapered, round, blued barrel marked on top "Smith & Wesson, Springfield, Mass., U.S.A., Pat'd. July 1, '84, April 9, '89, May 21, '95, Jul. 16, '95, Aug. 4, '96, Dec. 22, '96 Oct. 4, '98" and on the side "S. & W. 38 Mil." Frame marked on right with S & W trademark. Grip frame marked "U.S. Army Model 1899." Total length 11.5 inches. Fluted cylinder 1.56 inches long. Steelblade front sight in rib. Rear sight in frame. Blued or nickeled frame and cylinder. Casehardened hammer and trigger. Walnut stock, checked without monogram, or hard-rubber stock, checked with monogram at stock circle. Also made in 4-, 5-, and 6-inch barrel lengths. Left swing cylinder. Lanyard swivel in butt. Made from 1899 to 1902. Specimen illustrated is neither the Army nor the Navy version, but has a 5-inch barrel and is the police type. Plate 39, Fig. 2. $120–$200.

SAME, but Army type as described above. Numbered 13,001 to 14,000. $130–$260.

SAME, but Navy version, with butt marked "S. & W. Navy 1899 U.S.N." with an anchor, "38 D.A.," and arrow and the serial number, as well as the inspector's initials. Numbered 5,001 to 6,000. Collectors argue about whether a true Army model has a 6.5-inch barrel and a Navy model has a 6-inch barrel, or the reverse, but this does not seem to affect values. Also, they argue about which has a front latch, but neither has a front latch. $125–$205.

MODEL .32-CALIBER SAFETY, THIRD ISSUE. Specimen illustrated is cal. .32 S &W short, with 3-inch barrel, service sights, checkered hard-rubber stocks with stamped S & W monograms, and a blued finish. Since it is a modern arm, it is sold principally on a basis of shooting condition. Came in 2-, 3-, 3.5-inch barrel lengths. Made from 1909 to 1937. Numbered from about 17,001 to 242,981. Plate 39, Fig. 3. $60–$105.

MODEL "M" HAND EJECTOR, FIRST ISSUE, also called First Model Ladysmith, cal. .22 r.f., short, long, or long rifle. Serial numbers from 1 to 4,575. Made from 1902 to 1906. Specimen illustrated is chambered for the cal. .22 long rifle cartridge, has a 3.5-inch round barrel, 7-shot cylinder, hard-rubber stocks, and a blued finish. Barrel lengths of 2.25-, 3-, and 3.5-inches. Barrel is threaded and screwed to frame. Frame has a side-wing yoke, hand ejector, round butt, and an irregularly shaped side plate. Fluted cylinder. Hammer has a flanged finger piece with spring insert to operate stop. Trigger has a flanged finger piece insert to operate stop. There is no locking lug under the barrel. The cylinder release catch is round, knurled button on the left side of the frame, in the same position as the cylinder catch release on modern models. Plate 39, Fig. 4. $250–$460.

MODEL "M" HAND EJECTOR, SECOND ISSUE, also called Second Model Ladysmith, cal. .22 r.f., short, long, and long rifle. Serial numbers from 4,576 to 13,950. Made from 1906 to 1910. Resembles the First Issue except that the barrel was made only in 3- and 3.5-inch lengths, and was made with the locking bolt in the lug with a knob to draw the bolt from the extractor rod at the front end, with a slight change in the centerpin spring; and the frame was made without a bolt for the rear-end cylinder lock. $270–$435.

MODEL "M" HAND EJECTOR, THIRD ISSUE, also called Third Model Ladysmith, catalogued and known as the 22 Perfected Hand Ejector. Cal. .22 r.f., short, long, and long rifle. Made from 1910 to 1921. Numbered 13,951 to 26,154. Tapered round barrel with a solid front sight and a front locking bolt. Square-butt frame, without bolt, with plain walnut stock having a piano finish and gold monograms. Regular and target sights, with sight leaf and slide adjustable for elevation and windage. Seven-chamber, externally grooved cylinder, with solid gas ring, elongated stop slots and an extractor dowel pin. Flanged thumbpiece, chafing pins, and full double-action throw seat for rebound slide on hammer. Trigger has flanged fingerpiece which is slotted for hand and trigger levers, and notched for the full-throw double action. The rebound slide has a rebounding and blocking hammer which encases a coiled trigger spring. There is an elongated stud slot to permit the trigger to catch on recovery, which is held in the normal position by the coiled-wire trigger spring. Came in 2.5-, 3-, 3.5-, and 6-inch barrel lengths. $240–$425.

MODEL .22-32 HAND EJECTOR, also known as .22-32 Heavy Frame Target Revolver, cal. .22 r.f. short, long, and long rifle. Manufacture started June, 1911. Serial numbers run in the same series with the Model .32-20 Hand Ejector, Winchester Issue of 1902, First Change, Oct. 27, 1903. This is a target revolver only and is sold largely on a basis of shooting condition. Made only with a 6-inch barrel. Six-shot. Checked, walnut, square buttstock of extended length or with the .22 Single-Shot Perfected Model Target Stock. Blued finish only. $145–$230.

MODEL. 38-CALIBER HAND EJECTOR, MILITARY AND POLICE, SECOND ISSUE, 1902, cal. .38 S & W special cartridge, or U.S. service cartridge (cal. .38 long Colt). Specimen illustrated has 5-inch barrel; service sights; round-butt, checkered, black-rubber stocks with stamped S & W monograms; and a blued finish. Made from 1902 to 1903. Numbered 20,976 to 33,803. Notice that the serial numbers follow those of the Model .38 Hand Ejector, Military and Police, First Issue, otherwise known as the Model 1899 Army and Navy Revolver. Patented Apr. 9, 1889; Mar. 27, 1894; May 21, 1895; July 16, 1895; Aug. 4, 1896; Dec. 22, 1896; Oct. 4, 1898; Oct. 8, 1901; Dec. 17, 1901. Designed like its predecessor, the First Issue, with a few changes. The cylinder has stop notches lined with hardened-steel shims to prevent upsetting. The hammer has two pins drawn through and protruding beyond the surface of the sides as bearings to prevent chafing the finish. The barrel has a round lug raised from the body of the barrel forward of the extractor rod. There are slight changes in the design of the extractor rod and the yoke. Came in barrel lengths of 4-, 5-, 6-, and 6.5-inches. Plate 39, Fig. 5. $140–$210.

MODEL.38-CALIBER HAND EJECTOR, MILITARY AND POLICE, SECOND ISSUE, 1902, FIRST CHANGE, October 27, 1903; like Second Issue (1902), previously described, except for comparatively minor changes in the barrel, frame, stock, and yoke. Made from 1903 to 1905. Numbered 33,804 to 62,449. Made for .38 S & W special cartridge. Came in 4-, 5-, and 6.5-inch barrel lengths. $135–$210.

MODEL .38-CALIBER HAND EJECTOR, MILITARY AND POLICE, THIRD ISSUE, 1905, Modification, May, 1905, made like Second Issue (1902), First Change, except for comparatively minor changes in the cylinder, frame, trigger, and extractor. Made from 1905 to 1906. Numbered 62,450 to 73,250. Made for .38 S & W special cartridge. Patented Apr. 9, 1889; Mar. 27, 1894; May 21, 1895; July 16, 1895; Aug. 4, 1898; Oct. 8, 1901; and Dec. 17, 1901. Came in 4-, 5-, and 6.5-inch barrel lengths. Value depends mostly on shooting condition. $135–$215.

MODEL .38-CALIBER HAND EJECTOR, MILITARY AND POLICE, THIRD ISSUE, 1905, FIRST CHANGE, February 1906; made from 1906 to 1909. Designed like Third Issue (1905) with comparatively minor changes in the frame, hammer, and rebound slide. Made for .38 S & W special cartridge. Patented Apr. 9, 1889; Mar. 27, 1894; May 21, 1895; July 16, 1895; Aug. 4, 1896; Dec. 22, 1896: Oct. 4, 1898; Oct. 8, 1901; Dec. 17, 1901; and Feb. 6, 1906. Serial numbers from 73,251 to 146,899. This revolver included both the First and Second Changes. Value depends principally on shooting condition. Came in 4-, 5-, 6-, and 6.5-inch barrel lengths. $100–$185.

MODEL .38–CALIBER HAND EJECTOR, MILITARY AND POLICE, THIRD ISSUE, 1905, SECOND CHANGE, made for .38 S & W special cartridge, like Third Issue (1905), First Change, with comparatively minor changes in the frame, hammer, extractor, and rebound slide. Patented Mar. 27, 1894; May 21, 1895; Aug. 4, 1896; Dec. 22, 1896; Oct. 8, 1901; Dec. 17, 1901; and Feb. 6, 1906. Made from 1909 to 1915. Apparently no exact record of serial numbers exists. Came in 4-, 5-, 6-, and 6.5-inch barrel lengths. Value depends principally on shooting condition. $100–$180.

MODEL .38-CALIBER HAND EJECTOR, MILITARY AND POLICE, THIRD ISSUE, 1905, THIRD CHANGE, made for .38 S & W special cartridge, like Third Issue (1905), Second Change, with comparatively minor changes in the extractor, hammer, sear, and rebound slide. Serial numbers from 146,900 to 241,703. Patented Mar. 27, 1894; May 21, 1895; Aug. 4, 1896; Dec. 22, 1896; Oct. 8, 1901; Dec. 17, 1901; Feb. 6, 1906; and Sept. 14, 1909. Came in 4- and 6-inch barrel lengths only. Value depends principally on shooting condition. $100–$180.

MODEL .38-CALIBER HAND EJECTOR, MILITARY AND POLICE, THIRD ISSUE, 1905, FOURTH CHANGE, made for .38 S & W special cartridge, like Third Issue. Made from 1915 to 1942. Third Change, with changes in cylinder, sight, target version, extractor, hammer, trigger, hammer block, hand, and side plate. Serial numbers start with No. 241,704 and Dec. 29, 1914. Value depends principally on shooting condition. Made in 2-, 4-, 5-, and 6-inch barrel lengths. $100–$180.

MODEL .38-CALIBER HAND EJECTOR, REGULATION POLICE, FIRST ISSUE. According to Smith and Wesson, this model is still being manufactured today, but with numerous modern changes throughout the revolver over the old model. Made in 2-, 4-, 5-, and 6-inch barrel lengths. Made for .38 S & W and .38 S & W gallery. Manufacture started Feb. 6, 1917. Serial numbers start with No. 1. Patented Feb. 6, 1908; Sept. 14, 1909; and Dec. 29, 1914. Made like Model "I" Hand Ejector, cal. .32 Regulation Police (eighth entry below this) except for changes in the barrel, which was made for .38 caliber in 4-inch length only, and in the cylinder, frame, yoke, extractor, center pin, stock, extractor rod, and sight. Checked walnut square buttstock only. Five-shot. Shooting condition affects value. $100–$175.

MODEL "I" HAND EJECTOR, ISSUE OF 1903, cal. .32 c.f. S & W long cartridge. Serial numbers from 1 to 19,425. Manufacture started January, 1903. Patented Apr. 9, 1869; Mar. 27, 1894; May 21, 1895; Aug. 4, 1896; Dec. 22, 1896; Oct. 4, 1898; Oct. 8, 1901; and Sept. 2, 1902. Made from 1903 to 1904. Tapered round barrel made in 3.5-, 4.25-, and 6-inch lengths. Six-shot. Externally grooved cylinder. Blued or nickeled frame with round butt and irregularly shaped side plate held with four plate screws. Frame threaded to take barrel at top strap. Solid trigger guard. Straight-sided hammer with checked thumbpiece, and casehardened finish. Principally sold as a collector's item. $105–$180.

MODEL "I" HAND EJECTOR, ISSUE OF 1903, FIRST CHANGE, like previous one with comparatively minor changes in cylinder, extractor, trigger, stop, and rebound catch. Came in 3.25-, 4.25-, and 6-inch barrel lengths. Made from 1904 to 1906. Numbered 19,426 to 51,126. Principally sold as a collector's item. $75–$105.

MODEL "I" HAND EJECTOR, ISSUE OF 1903, SECOND CHANGE, same as before except for comparatively minor changes in the hammer, rebound slide, and trigger. Came in 3.25-, 4.25-, and 6-inch barrel lengths. Made from 1906 to 1909. Numbered 51,127 to 95,500. Shooting condition influences value. $75–$105

MODEL "I" HAND EJECTOR, ISSUE OF 1903, THIRD CHANGE, same as before with comparatively minor changes in the hammer, rebound slide, and trigger. Came in 3.25-, 4.25-, and 6-inch barrel lengths. Made from 1909 to 1910. Numbered 95,501 to 96,125. Shooting condition influences value. $120–$190.

MODEL "I" HAND EJECTOR, ISSUE OF 1903, FOURTH CHANGE, same as before with comparatively minor changes in the hand. Came in 3.25-, 4.25-, and 6-inch barrel lengths. Made in 1910. Numbered 96,126 to 102,500. Shooting condition influences value. $120–$170.

MODEL "I" HAND EJECTOR, ISSUE OF 1903, FIFTH CHANGE; cal. .32 c.f. Made from 1910 to 1917. Numbered 102,501 to 263,000. Specimen illustrated has a 3.25-inch barrel, blued finish, old extractor-rod knob, round butt, and checkered walnut stocks, without monograms, but frame has monogram on left side. Designed like the Model "I" Hand Ejector, Model of 1903, Fourth Change, with a few exceptions. Barrel lengths of 3.25, 4.25, and 6 inches. Barrel has patent dates stamped on top. Solid front sight. The hammer shape at foot, forward of the rebound seat, engages notch in trigger for double-action throw. The chafing bushings have been removed from the hammer. The trigger is notched below the full-cock lip, engaging the hammer foot after the sear action, thus extending the double-action throw. There are other small changes. Shooting condition influences value. Plate 39, Fig. 7. $75–$110.

MODEL "I" HAND EJECTOR, ISSUE OF 1903, SIXTH CHANGE, same as before with comparatively minor changes in the hand, hammer block, trigger, and side plate. Made from 1917 to about 1920. Numbered about 263,001 to 331,319. Shooting condition influences value. $75–$110.

MODEL "I" HAND EJECTOR, THIRD ISSUE, also known as the Model "I" Hand Ejector, Third Model, and catalogued as the Regulation Police Model, cal. .32. Came in 3.25-, 4.25-, and 6-inch barrel lengths. This is like the Model "I" Hand Ejector, Issue of 1903, Sixth Change, except that the tang of the frame has a shoulder at the back strap to provide a joint for the extended, square-butt, wood stock. Made from 1911 to 1942. The serial numbers started with No. 331,320, to about 534,532, hence this arm is sold principally according to its shooting condition. $75–$120.

MODEL.45-CALIBER HAND EJECTOR, U.S. SERVICE, listed in the first edition of this text as Smith & Wesson Model 1917 Army Revolver. Caliber .45 automatic Colt cartridge. The Army model is 6-shot, D.A., with 5.5-inch round barrel marked on top "Smith & Wesson, Springfield, Mass., U.S.A., Patented Dec. 17, 1901, Feb. 6, 1906, Sept. 14, 1908"; on side "S. & W. D. A. 45," and on the bottom "United States Property"; frame marked "U. S. Army Model 1917" with serial number. Total length 10.75 inches. Weight 2 lbs. 4 oz. Fluted cylinder, 1.53 inches long with square shoulder, for .45 cal. automatic ammunition. Steel-blade front sight. U-notch rear sight in frame. Blued barrel, frame, and cylinder. Casehardened hammer and trigger. Oil-finished plain walnut stock with rounded shape at stock circle and lanyard loop in base of butt. Side-swing. The cal. .45 rimless automatic cartridges are loaded in two crescent-shaped clips, 3 rounds to a clip, and are slotted, made of thin steel. The ejector removes the fired cases and the clips in one motion. The revolver can be loaded and fired without these clips, but then extraction is manual. Made from 1917 to 1946. Numbered 1 to 210,320. The U. S. bought 153,311 between Apr. 6, 1917, and December, 1918; many were sold by the Government after World War I, but during World War II this old faithful saw service again. Since this is a valuable shooting arm as well as a collector's piece, value depends upon demand and shooting condition. The specimen illustrated is the commercial version, and not the Army version. Plate 39, fig. 6. $80–$120.

SAME, but Army version. Numbered 1 to 175,000. $50–$75.

SINGLE-SHOT, STRAIGHT-LINE MODEL PISTOL, cal. .22, 10-inch barrel. Made from 1925 to 1936. Numbered 1 to 1,870. The stock is a slanted parallelogram, resembling somewhat the Model .35-Caliber Automatic Pistol, Model 1913. Action opened by half-cocking and swinging the barrel to the right on a pivot. Hammer strikes cartridge with a plunger-like motion. Total weight 34 ounces. The catalogue described it in part as follows: ". . . we adapted the type of handle typical of the Auto Pistol, as when shot with the arm *extended* this shape makes the pistol point naturally without any bending of the wrist . . . we have used a straight pull trigger and a hammer that moves in a straight line parallel to the bore." This pistol was finished only in blue. It was usually sold in a felt-lined metal box with a cleaning rod and a screw driver. $170–$260.

# SMITH & WESSON AUTOMATIC ARMS

MODEL .35-CALIBER AUTOMATIC PISTOL, MODEL 1913, using cal. .35 S & W automatic cartridge. From May 6, 1913, to Jan. 27, 1921, 8,350 were made. Patented Sept. 24, 1910; Dec. 13, 1910; Feb. 28, 1911; July 30, 1912; Sept. 24, 1912. Finished in blue or nickel. Specimen illustrated has 3.5-inch round barrel, service sights, blue finish, and polished walnut stocks with gold-plated S & W monograms. This pistol has what is technically described as a straight blowback action, similar to that of the Belgian Clement pistol, but improved. The breechblock has a disconnector, enabling it to be drawn back without the force otherwise required to compress the mainspring. This was intended to appeal to women and men with weak hands. The grip safety is on the forward side of the grip, and is squeezed with the second finger, instead of being located at the rear, as on most American automatic pistols. Since the barrel and frame top are stationary, the sights are on a solid and stationary surface, thus providing a better aim and more accuracy than on usual types. Releasing the trigger guard permits the barrel and the top of the frame to swing up from a pivot to the top and rear. The breechblock is then removed and the pistol can be cleaned easily. The mainspring is above the barrel and ordinarily is not removed. The cartridge is listed as cal. .35 but it is actually cal. .32, with a metal-jacketed bullet having an enlarged rear end with the lead core (that is, without the jacket) exposed to receive the rifling of the barrel. The purpose of the special bullet was to reduce barrel wear, but not enough stores stocked this special ammunition to make the pistol popular. Plate 39, Fig. 9. $195–$310.

MODEL-CALIBER .32 AUTOMATIC PISTOL, MODEL 1925, cal. .32 a.c.p. Made from February 1924 to July 9, 1936. Numbered 1 to 957. The barrel is not hinged to the frame, as it is in the Model 1913, but is inside a two-part slide, the rear of which contains the firing mechanism and can be retracted separately from the forward portion. This makes it possible to load a cartridge without compressing the recoil spring. Like the Model 1913, this model resembles the Belgian Clement pistol. The mechanical features are similar to the Model 1913, but the appearance is more streamlined. The firearms laws passed in 1926 greatly reduced the sale of automatic pistols just at the time that this model was being marketed, hence it never attained the popularity it deserved. Also, anyone wanting an automatic pistol usually desires a caliber greater than .32. The specimen illustrated has a 3.5-inch barrel, service sight, blued finish, and smooth walnut stocks with gold-plated S & W monograms. Plate 39, Fig. 8. $365–$575.

SMITH & WESSON LIGHT RIFLE, cal. 9 mm Luger cartridge; 20-shot, staggered, double-column box magazine; weight 8 lbs. 4 oz.; total length 32.375 inches. Blowback action. Cocked with bolt open. Ejects cartridges downward through ejection tube, which is part of the magazine housing. Magazine is inserted from the front of the magazine housing and is locked in position below the barrel. Came in 9.75-inch barrel length only. Made in 1940. Numbered 1 to 1,010. This does *not* belong to a private collection for obvious reasons. It is described here merely for information. $845–$1,350.

# WORLD WAR II MODELS

MODEL .38-CALIBER HAND EJECTOR, MILITARY AND POLICE, THIRD ISSUE, 1905, FOURTH CHANGE, in all modifications and varieties, was produced in great quantities during World War II, with a variety of finishes, except that nickel plating was dropped. Made from 1915 to 1942. These revolvers were primarily intended for civilian use, including law-enforcement bodies, but their use by the armed forces in certain cases might bring them into the "U. S. Secondary Martial Revolver" classification. Came in 2-, 4-, 5-, and 6-inch barrel lengths. $65–$90.

.38-CALIBER SPECIAL VICTORY MODEL, almost identical to the square-butt commercial Military and Police Revolver, chambered for .38 S & W special cartridges, with standard 4-inch barrels for the armed services and 2-inch barrels for the U. S. Department of Justice. Butt swivels. Blued finish. Checkered stocks with monograms. Issued to and used by the U. S. Navy, particularly aviation forces, and by the U. S. Coast Guard which serves under the Navy in time of war. Also issued to the U. S. Maritime Commission, and to various federal and quasi-federal defense and law enforcement organizations. Made from 1942 to 1945. $65–$90.

BRITISH S & W .38–200 SERVICE REVOLVER; also called the .38 Military and Police Model; and further known as the K-200. Resembles the square-butt Military and Police Revolver, but chambered for the S & W .38 regular cartridge instead of the .38 S & W special. Blued finish. Five-inch barrel. Butt swivel. Came in 4-, 5-, 6-inch barrel lengths. Made from 1940 to 1945. Smith & Wesson believe that this has been the most extensively used military revolver ever issued to and used by the armed services of any nation. It was especially popular with the British Commandos. $65–$85.

## Caution on War Relics

The values given for Smith & Wesson World War II revolvers disregard shooting condition. Thousands of these Smith & Wesson revolvers of World War II have been sold as war surplus. Some are in almost "factory new" condition and many are assembled from parts picked up on battlefields. In buying these and all other weapons which are sold by dealers who specialize in getting rid of quantities of relics, instead of items primarily for collectors, the buyer must exercise great caution. Weapons sold by war surplus dealers may or may not be desirable specimens for a collection, but many of them are extremely dangerous to fire.

## Miscellaneous Smith & Wesson Item

WESSON BREECH-LOADING SHOTGUN, 12-gauge, hammer type with 30-inch double barrels. Marked on top of the barrel rib "Wesson Fire Arms Co., Springfield, Mass." Weight from 7 to 7.25 lbs. Manufactured from 1867 to about 1870. Numbered 1 to about 219. It is believed that each shotgun was sold with its own case and accessories. Shotgun alone $675–$925, with case and accessories $1,000–$1,475.

Note: The Wesson Fire Arms Company was a subsidiary of Smith & Wesson, as Daniel B. Wesson was company president and Horace Smith listed as a director.

## Error in Previous Editions

In previous editions of this text, on page 202, in describing MODEL NO. 3, 44-CALIBER SINGLE-ACTION AMERICAN, SECOND ISSUE, it was described as "exactly like the First Issue except that the cut across the face above the hammer nose for the barrel-catch lock was eliminated," etc. Actually, the First Model, First Issue, did not have the slot across the hammer. The slot was put on the Second Issue and on into the Russian and the Model No. 3, Single-Action, New Model.

# Chapter 19

## AMERICAN AUTOMATIC PISTOLS

THIS chapter describes those American-made handguns that are generally described as automatic pistols, even though the term "automatic" usually means "semi-automatic." We also have included a few that are automatic only in their feeding action and require manual operation for loading and ejecting. Colt and Smith & Wesson automatic pistols are described in the chapters on those makes.

Prior to the development of the modern automatic pistol there were many weapons that were multi-shot. In the flintlock era there were several makes and types of repeating pistols. In the percussion period, and especially at the beginning of the cartridge era, there were repeating pistols that had several barrels, which could be fired in turn without moving them. Then there were multi-barrel pistols, such as those of the harmonica type, that had a row of barrels which moved laterally into position for firing. In addition, the pepperbox principle is well known to collectors.

The volcanic pistols described in Chapter 18 on Smith & Wesson arms, the Chicago Fire Arms Company's Protector Palm Pistol, and the Remington-Rider Magazine Pistol patented in 1871 are all examples of early efforts to produce an automatic pistol.

When a so-called "automatic" pistol requires a new squeeze (pull) of the trigger to fire each shot, it is correctly described as semi-automatic, auto-loading, or self-loading. However, even the manufacturers insist upon calling their semi-automatic pistols "automatic," hence this term is used by collectors. If a pistol were truly automatic, it would continue to fire as long as the trigger was held back and until the ammunition was expended. Almost all "automatic" pistols ever made are semi-automatic.

FIALA REPEATING TARGET PISTOL, cal. .22; made by Fiala Outfitters, Inc., New York City, with an action similar to that of the Colt Woodsman, and sold as part of a set with 3 interchangeable barrels and an extension shoulder stock. Magazine-fed. Manually operated by pulling breechblock back and forth for ejecting, cocking, and loading. There is a short barrel, 3 or 4 inches long, a 6-inch barrel, and a rifle-length barrel. Marketed for a short time after World War I. The value indicated is for the complete set. $245–$325.

GRANT HAMMOND AUTOMATIC PISTOL, cal. .45 automatic, 6.75-inch barrel. Total length 11.25 inches. Weight 2 lbs. 10 oz. Eight-round magazine. Walnut stocks. Slide marked on right "Grant Hammond Mfg. Corp. New Haven Conn. U.S.A.," on top "Hammond," and on right side "Patented May 4, 1915 Other Patents Pending." Only 11 were reported made and these for tests only. Resembles the Luger in shape, but the Japanese Nambu in operation. An unusual feature is that the magazine ejects automatically when empty. This feature alone was enough to damn it in the eyes of the U.S. Army. $625–$1,150.

HARRINGTON & RICHARDSON SELF-LOADING (AUTOMATIC) PISTOL, cal. .25, auto, 2-inch barrel. Total length 4.5 inches. Weight 12.5 oz. Six-round magazine. Closely resembles the English Webley & Scott automatic pistol, the principal difference being that this H & R pistol uses a coil mainspring instead of the V-type spring and has an inside straight-drive coil-spring-driven firing pin and a grip safety instead of the outside hammer found on the Webley & Scott pistol. $170–$250.

SAME, but cal. .32, auto, 3.5-inch barrel. Total length 6.5 inches, with 8-shot magazine. $210–$280.

HARTFORD ARMS AND EQUIPMENT CO. SEMI-AUTOMATIC TARGET PISTOL, cal. .22; made from about 1929 to 1930, similar to the Colt Woodsman and the corresponding High Standard Arms Co. pistol. Apparently discontinued after a few were made. Further details not available. $180–$270.

SAME, but automatic repeating pistol, cal. .22; cartridges fed automatically from a box magazine in the butt, but manually operated for each shot. A variation of this pistol was sold without the magazine as a single-shot. Discontinued about 1930. $145–$185.

HIGH STANDARD ARMS CO. AUTOMATIC PISTOLS. These are very modern, excellent pistols, which are sold entirely on the basis of their shooting condition. They are not regarded as collectors' specimens, hence there is no point in describing them in detail or assigning values.

PHOENIX AUTOMATIC PISTOL, cal. .25, auto, similar to the Belgian

Melior Automatic Pistol, which in turn was copied from the Fabrique Nationale Browning Model 1900. Blowback action. Retractor spring on top of barrel. Made in Lowell, Mass., about 1920, in small numbers and rarely found in collections. $175–$230.

SAME, but cal. .32 auto. $175–$230.

REMINGTON AUTOMATIC PISTOL, MILITARY TYPE, cal. .45, similar in appearance to the Remington Model 51 Pocket Automatic Pistol described below, but smaller. This pistol was offered to the United States during World War I. It was tested by the Navy in 1918, and by the Infantry of the U. S. Army in 1920, and although the Navy was about to accept it as a standard side arm, the final decision was that the armed services should all use the same weapon, namely, the Colt Model 1911; hence the only specimens of this pistol in existence are experimental models whose value is difficult to assign. $850–$1,200.

REMINGTON MODEL 51 POCKET AUTOMATIC PISTOL, cal. .32, introduced in 1918. Carefully designed slide and grip. Low sights. Classified by ordnance experts as having a rocker-action, friction-delayed blowback action. Discontinued in 1934. Numbered 1 to about 65,000. $145–$195.

SAME, but cal. .38. $165–$260.

SAVAGE AUTOMATIC PISTOL, MODEL 1905, MILITARY TYPE, cal. .45; auto, 5.25-inch barrel marked "Manufactured by Savage Arms Co. In Utica, N.Y. U.S.A., Nov. 21, 1905 Cal. .45," but the first five pistols had no marks. A total of 200 were made. Total length 9 inches. Weight 2 lbs. 3.5 oz. with empty magazine. Eight-round magazine. Blued finish except hammer, which is casehardened. Checkered walnut grips. A turning barrel unlocks the slide and breechblock on recoil, hence this pistol is classified as a retarded blowback type and not as a true locked-breech type. Grip safety. Small, rounded, external hammer at rear of slide. $600–$925.

SAVAGE POCKET AUTOMATIC PISTOL, MODEL 1907, cal. .32 ACP; similar in all respects to the above described Model 1905, with 3.5-inch barrel and 10-round magazine. Total length 6.5 inches. Weight 19 oz. Discontinued in 1917. $165–$240.

SAME, but chambered in 1913 for the cal. .380 ACP cartridge. Discontinued in 1917. $130–$200.

SAVAGE HAMMERLESS AUTOMATIC PISTOL, MODEL 1915, cal. .32, auto-loading, 3.75-inch barrel. Total length 6.5 inches. Weight 21 oz. Hammerless feature is merely a reduction of the size of the small rounded hammer at the rear of the slide on the earlier model and the closing of the slot in which the hammer traveled by means of a small piece of metal. The operation and design are similar to those of the earlier models. Discontinued in 1917. $95–$145.

SAME, but cal. .380, auto-loading, or 9 mm. Browning short. Discontinued in 1917. $180–$290.

SAVAGE AUTOMATIC PISTOL, MODEL 1917, cal. .380. This model has a larger hammer than the Model 1907 and an addition to the material at the back and rear slope of the grip, instead of having the grip nearly at right angles to the barrel as is the case in the Model 1907. Adopted by the Portuguese Army and Navy after World War I. Manufactured in comparatively large quantities until 1928. $100–$145.

SAME, but cal. .32. $130–$205.

SMITH & WESSON AUTOMATIC PISTOLS—See Chapter 18.

UNION FIRE ARMS CO. SEMI-AUTOMATIC REVOLVER, cal. .32 S & W, 3-inch barrel. Total length 6.5 inches. Weight 1 lb. 2 oz. Marked "Union Fire Arms Co., Toledo, Ohio." This description is a repetition of the one given in Chapter 17 on American cartridge pistols and revolvers, presented here for emphasis and to distinguish it from the weapon described below. Operates by recoil of the barrel and cylinder. $125–$180.

UNION FIRE ARMS CO. AUTOMATIC PISTOL, POCKET-SIZE, cal. .32. Resembles the Luger military model in appearance and size. $150–$210.

WARNER ARMS CORPORATION SCHWARZLOSE GERMAN POCKET AUTOMATIC PISTOL, cal. .32; marked "The Warner Arms Corporation, Brooklyn, New York, U.S.A. 2" and also "W.A.C." in addition to the marks originally applied in Germany, where this pistol was made. Since this is not an American arm, we present only a few details. It is listed here to clear up doubt in the minds of some collectors. Blow-forward action. Grip safety on front side of the grip. Retractor spring under barrel. Hammerless type. $130–$175.

# Chapter 20

## WINCHESTER RIFLES AND CARBINES

I N any discussion of the value of Winchester arms, immediate consideration of course must be given to the condition of the firearms, that is "fine" or "good," as defined earlier in this book. This is especially true of Winchesters because, since the inception of the company, their product has been almost wholly a working weapon, one that was used on a daily basis rather than, for instance, a revolver stored in a drawer, as were many of the earlier six-shooters.

As much as almost any other American firearm, the Winchester deserves the title of "the gun that won the West." This despite the fact that many laymen believe the West was conquered by the Civil War. By the mid-1800's poverty in the East drove hordes of settlers west, lured by the promise of cheap land and golden opportunity.

And these settlers who went west most often chose the Winchester as their most valuable tool, using it for defense, for protection of their flocks and herds from predators, and for hunting meat for the table. For this reason alone, there are few "mint" early-model Winchesters. Whether rifle or carbine, the Winchester spent most of its time on active duty, and active duty has a habit of wearing even the finest firearm.

Although tested several times for the government, Winchester never really succeeded in selling to the United States, although many models were ordered by European and Central and South American countries. Most of these are not on today's market and will not be dealt with in this chapter.

This chapter will concentrate on models produced from 1866 to 1895, disregarding various slide-action shotguns, bolt-action rifles, and other miscellaneous weapons produced by Winchester in more than a hundred years.

One word of caution. A point that has fascinated collectors of Winchesters from the beginning is their extreme variety. A large number of factory options have been available including, but not limited to, longer or shorter barrels, heavier or lighter barrels, factory engraving, special stocks and buttplates, octagon, round, or "half and half" barrels, set triggers, and many more varieties of increasing rarity.

A complete list of all of the Winchester variations with their mathematical permutations would fill a book of this length by itself, therefore the author has confined himself to listing the standard model of each with its value, assuming a collector may, by reference to any of the expert books on the Winchester, determine for himself the relative rarity of any variation.

The Winchester repeater traces its lineage from the Hunt repeater of 1848, through the Smith-Jennings, Smith & Wesson and the Volcanic Repeating Arms Co., of which Oliver F. Winchester was elected a director in 1855. Through a series of circumstances, Winchester became involved with the New Haven Arms Co., later the producer of the Henry rifle.

In 1866, the name of the company was changed to the Winchester Repeating Arms Co., and the first Winchesters were produced. Their manufacture, incidentally, overlapped production of the later Henrys.

Somewhere over 155,000 Winchesters of the 1866 Model were manufactured for domestic consumption from 1866 to the end of production in 1898. Approximately 75% of production was carbines and 25% rifles. Standard carbine barrel length was 20 inches and standard barrel length for rifle was 24 inches in all four major submodels as catalogued below. Model 1866 was not designated as such by Winchester until the introduction of Model 1873, and no model markings appear on any Model 1866. All lever action, cal. .44.

FIRST MODEL 1866. Originally termed "The Improved Henry" by Winchester, this weapon is identical in many ways to its predecessor and probably used many of the same dies. It has the abrupt Henry drop at the receiver ahead of the hammer. Serial numbers are on the inside portion of upper tang. $600–$1,550.

SECOND MODEL 1866, an improved version with a frame change and less of a drop ahead of the hammer. Many outside serial numbers on lower tang. $710–$1,525.

THIRD MODEL 1866. Drop ahead of hammer now is even less pronounced and serial numbers are in block between adjusting screw and trigger on lower tang. $625–$1,425.

FOURTH MODEL 1866. In final version, the Henry drop rifle almost disappeared and script serial numbers are now located between lower tang screw and lever latch. $620–$1,375.

WINCHESTER MODEL 1873. This model was put into production in 1873, overlapping Model 1866, and was produced until 1924, ending with serial number 720610. Calibers available included the standard .44, but Winchester now added models in cal. .38, .32, and .22. The 1873 is today one of the most popular of the collectibles and is noted for its wide range of variations, many the same as noted for Model 1866. All have a model designation on the tang; the lower tang in early versions and on the upper tang in later versions. Assembly numbers were used intermittently, and the 24-inch barrel continued to be standard in the rifle and the 20-inch in the carbine. All lever action.

FIRST MODEL 1873. Sometimes classified into early and late models, with the primary difference being different dust covers. Later models also had a pinned trigger and trigger block safeties are also found. Cal. .44 rifle. $495–$910.

SECOND MODEL 1873. These have an improved dust cover with a center guide fixed to the receiver with screws. Cal. .44 rifle. $460–$860.

THIRD MODEL 1873. Center dust-cover guide is integral with the receiver, hammer and trigger are fixed with new internal pins, and lower tang screws are even farther back. Cal. .44 rifle. $450–$825.

SAME, but cal. .38 rifle. $405–$790.

SAME, but cal. .32 rifle. $405–$790.

SAME, but cal. .22 rifle. $600–$1,175.

SAME, but cal. .44 carbine. $485–$885.

SAME, but cal. .32 carbine. $425–$825.

SAME, but cal. .38 carbine. $440–$830.

WINCHESTER MODEL 1876, introduced in that year during the Philadelphia Centennial Exposition and aptly named "The Centennial Model."

The Centennial was very much like its forerunner the 1873 except for a larger and stronger receiver and action to handle larger caliber and more powerful cartridges. It was available, by and large only in this size and with a 350-grain bullet, until 1879, when the 45–60 and the 50–95 express were introduced, almost simultaneously, followed by the 40–60 W.c.f. in 1884.

As is usual with Winchester, a large number of modifications to such items as dust covers, extractors, and unusual tang designs were made as production continued. Short, long, and part octagon, part round barrels were also noted. Also to be encountered are the usual special engravings, special stocks, and grips.

But perhaps more common were the standard rifles, accounting for the absolute majority of manufacture, and the octagon barrel, accounting for perhaps two out of three rifles produced.

At least 1,000 carbines were furnished the Canadian North West Mounted Police as part of that country's campaign to keep Sitting Bull and his Sioux tribes out of Canada and in the United States. Later orders from the "Mounties" were in the 44,000 range. Model 1876 served as the standard weapon with the North West Mounted Police until just after the turn of the century. Production actually was halted in 1886, although the last Winchester 1876 left the plant after 1897.

NWMP MODEL 1876, furnished carbines chambered for 45–75 Winchester cartridge. Rear sights vary with date of manufacture and stock marking "NWMP" may be all but illegible on many samples. Marking "APP" for Alberta Province Police may also be noted on models later transferred to that department. $835–$1,790.

STANDARD MODEL 1876 RIFLE, but with octagon barrel. $425–$820.

STANDARD MODEL 1876 CARBINE. $525–$865.

STANDARD MODEL 1876 RIFLE, chambered for 45–60. $495–$895.

STANDARD MODEL 1876 RIFLE, chambered for 50–95 express. $610–$1,120.

Special modifications include heavier barrels, set triggers, and special butt plates and sights, most optional or special order from the manufacturer.

# COMPONENT PARTS

OF THE

## WINCHESTER REPEATING RIFLES.

### MODELS OF 1873 AND 1876.

MORTISE COVER

M. COVER STOP

RECEIVER

SPRING COVER

BREECH PIN BASE

EXTRACTOR

LEFT HAND LINK

BREECH PIN COMPLETE

RIGHT HAND LINK

FIRING PIN

FINGER LEVER

CARRIER BLOCK

HAMMER

CARRIER LEVER

MAIN SPRING

FINGER LEVER SPRING

CARRIER LEVER SPRING

SAFETY CATCH

RETRACTOR

CATCH HOOK SPRING

SEAR SPRING PLAIN

SEAR SPRING SET

SAFETY CATCH SPRING

KNOCK OFF SPRING

SET SEAR

PLAIN SEAR

RIGHT HAND SIDE PLATE

CATCH HOOK

KNOCK OFF

SET TRIGGER

PLAIN TRIGGER

PLATE 40. Component Parts of Winchester Repeating Rifles

WINCHESTER MODEL 1886. Model 1886 combined the early Winchester lever action with the cam and bolt lock of the single shot, while retaining the standard repeating action. And through the years of manufacture of the 1886, it was offered in a wide variety of calibers and cartridges.

This Winchester remained in production in the wide variety of forms and models of carbines and rifles until final assembly of the last few remaining 1886's, in 1935. Approximately 160,000 were made.

Standard rifle length is 26 inches; for the carbines it is 22 inches, round. In the 1886, it can be noted, all barrels are exactly one-eighth inch shorter than specified.

Standard guns had caliber marks atop the barrel just a bit forward of the breech, and may be found in the following calibers:

|  | First Listed |  |
|---|---|---|
| STANDARD MODEL 1886 RIFLE, 38–70 | April, 1884 | $190–$375 |
| STANDARD MODEL 1886 RIFLE, 40–70 | April, 1884 | $190–$385 |
| STANDARD MODEL 1886 RIFLE, 45–70 | October, 1886 | $325–$550 |
| STANDARD MODEL 1886 RIFLE, 40–82 | October, 1886 | $235–$450 |
| STANDARD MODEL 1886 RIFLE, 40–65 | June, 1887 | $230–$395 |
| STANDARD MODEL 1886 RIFLE, 38–56 | June, 1887 | $230–$395 |
| STANDARD MODEL 1886 RIFLE, 50–110 express | August, 1895 | $300–$575 |
| STANDARD MODEL 1886 RIFLE, 45–90 | October, 1886 | $280–$470 |
| STANDARD MODEL 1886 RIFLE, cal. .33 | March, 1903 | $200–$385 |
| MODEL 1886 CARBINE |  | $450–$845 |

*Note: 1886 carbines are very scarce, hence the price rise over rifles.*

The variety and combinations of variations available with Model 1886 is apparently endless. Included are the standard options such as checkering, plating (gold, silver, nickel), and sights. There have been recorded such unusual variations as Lyman receiver sights, a three-bladed "express" sight, double set triggers (available on special order), and extra-heavy barrels.

Also to be noted are such "standard" Winchester variations as pistol grips, octagon barrels, shotgun butts, half- and three-quarter capacity magazines, and many others.

---

PLATE 41. Winchester Rifles

*Figure*

1. Winchester Rifle Model 1866.
2. Winchester Rifle Model 1873.

3. Winchester Rifle Model 1876.

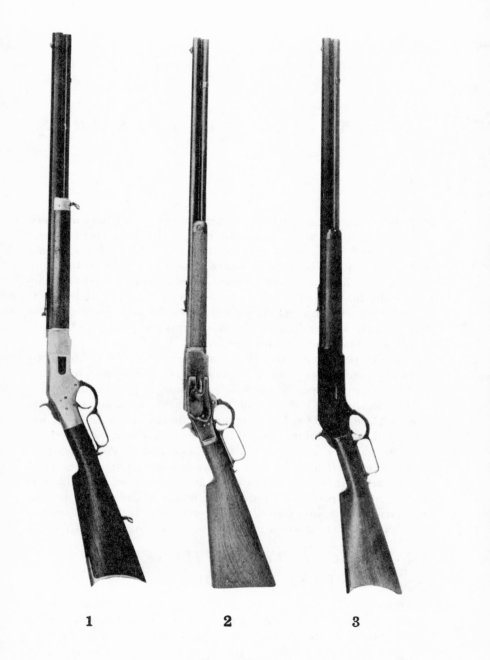

1            2            3

PLATE 41

# Chapter 21

## U.S. MARTIAL SHOULDER ARMS

THE United States martial shoulder arms are all those muskets, musketoons, rifles, and carbines made by the armories of the United States, or bought by the United States from private contractors, issued to United States armed forces or to the state forces called into the service of the United States, and actually carried in the field by such forces. Weapons that were issued experimentally for trial and test do not belong in this classification in the strict sense of the term. Such shoulder arms are properly classified as U.S. secondary martial shoulder arms.

Kentucky (Pennsylvania) rifles and other types of shoulder arms that were used by our armed forces but not officially purchased according to definite specifications do not belong in this classification.

Any and all of the U.S. martial shoulder arms made and issued before the close of the Civil War, including flintlocks, can be regarded as Confederate shoulder arms if it can be established by something more than family tradition or a fond hope that they were actually used by the Confederates in the field against the United States. How this can be done to the satisfaction of any unemotional individual is often a difficult problem. Confederate marks in themselves are not necessarily proof, or even admissible evidence, unless it is certain that such marks are genuine and were made during the Civil War.

## ARMS ASSOCIATED WITH EARLY UNITED STATES HISTORY

Before turning our attention to the U.S. martial shoulder arms, we must first consider certain arms associated with the early history of the United States. These are the Committee of Safety muskets, the Jäger rifles, and the British Brown Bess muskets. The Kentucky

(Pennsylvania) rifles and the French flintlock martial shoulder arms also belong in this group but they are described in other chapters.

## Committee of Safety Muskets

Committee of Safety muskets were those purchased by the "Committees of Safety" in the various American colonies for the arming of the people in preparation for the coming Revolution. There is no one, definite, individual type, make, or model that can be placed in this classification to the exclusion of all other flintlock shoulder arms. Each committee appointed agents to obtain arms already made, and gunsmiths were chosen to make new arms, some of which followed the British Brown Bess of that period while others copied the French martial shoulder arms of the same era. Many of these arms were not marked. Some were assembled from parts made by different men; thus, a lock plate might have one name, and the barrel another; parts from foreign-made arms were freely used.

Collectors and dealers often consult a list of makers who were supposed to have made arms for the committees. If one of these names appears on a martial-type flintlock, it is then called a Committee of Safety piece, if that is what the collector or dealer wants to call it, but in spite of a great deal of research there is still too much guesswork about the whole affair. Values vary greatly. A genuine Committee of Safety musket is probably worth from $750 to $1,500 in good condition, and worth from $1,500 to $2,000 in fine condition, but the uncertainty of identification and the scarcity of reports of sales of genuine pieces of this type make it difficult to give accurate values.

## Jäger Rifles

Jäger rifles were those central European flintlock rifles used during the first quarter of the eighteenth century by the men known as "jägers" or "chasseurs" in the region occupied by Germany, Austria, the dependent provinces governed by those countries, and Switzerland, prior to World War II. The present changes in national boundaries make it necessary to present this definition.

The typical specimen has a short barrel, thick stock, clumsy lines, a big bore, and a large, fragile trigger guard. Those made in Germany seldom had rear sights, but those made in Switzerland often had elaborate adjustable rear sights.

Jäger-type rifles were used to a limited extent during the Revolutionary War by both the British and the Americans, but they are important to us principally because they were ancestors of the Kentucky (Pennsylvania) rifle and somewhat influenced the design of some of the early U.S. martial shoulder arms, although this statement must not be taken too seriously.

It must be understood that not all Jägers are alike; hence the condition and the quality of the original workmanship are very important in assessing values. A genuine specimen is worth from $600 to $850 in good condition, and from $1,000 to $1,350 in fine condition. Be sure it is genuine.

## British Brown Bess Muskets

"British Brown Bess" was a general term applied to British muskets from the time of Queen Elizabeth until well into the nineteenth century, but the British Brown Bess used by both sides during the Revolutionary War was a smoothbore, muzzle-loading, flintlock musket, varying in caliber from .684 to .758, the average being .753. A distinguishing feature is that the barrel is fixed to the stock by lugs under the barrel, held by sliding pins through the stock and not by bands. There are many variations. Obviously there should be British proof marks. A genuine specimen is worth from $450 to $1,250 in good condition, and from $725 to $2,000 in fine condition. Be sure it is genuine.

## Books on U.S. Martial Shoulder Arms

The early reference works on this subject are: *Springfield Muzzle-loading Shoulder Arms*, by Claude E. Fuller, Francis Bannerman Sons, New York, 1930; *The Breech-Loader in the Service*, by Claude E. Fuller, Arms Reference Club, Topeka, Kansas, 1933; *Notes on United States Ordnance, Vol. II*, by James E. Hicks, published by the author, Mount Vernon, N.Y., 1940; *Firearms in American History, Vol. I, All Kinds, 1600–1800*, by Charles Winthrop Sawyer, published by the author, Boston, Mass., 1910; *Firearms in American History, Vol. III, Our Rifles*, by Charles Winthrop Sawyer, published by the author, Boston, Mass., 1920. At this writing, all of these books are out of print, but they can be found in the larger public libraries and purchased from dealers in rare gunbooks. Most antique-arms dealers carry a line of such books when they are available. However, these texts are principally for the advanced collector and the man interested in the fine technical points of gunlock construction, etc.

U.S. MUSKET, MODEL 1795, cal. .69, flintlock, smoothbore, 44.75-inch barrel, 56.5-inch stock. Total length 59.5 inches. Lock plate 6.625 inches long and 1.28 inches wide. Trigger guard 13 inches long with pointed ends. Three bands. Stamped "Springfield" in a curve at the rear of the lock plate. Marked "U.S." in script over an eagle on the lock plate in front of the cock. The year of manufacture was marked in shallow script on the tang of the butt plate. Head of the eagle faced to the rear. Iron pan with a fence at the rear. Beginning in 1802, the word "Springfield" ran straight on the lock plate, but in 1804 the word was placed in front of the cock, and the "U.S." was placed over the eagle. The rear end of the lock plate was then marked with the year of manufacture. This model was copied from the French flintlock musket, model 1763, known as the "Charleville Pattern" to collectors. Butt plates were dated from 1799. $1,450–$2,600.

U.S. MUSKET MODEL 1795, short, same as the U.S. Musket Model 1795, except for a shorter barrel and a few minor changes which cannot be accurately classified. In general the barrels were made by cutting 12 inches off the 1795 Model barrels, which would reduce them to 32.75 inches in length, but for some unaccountable reason the Springfield Armory did not cut all to the same length. It is interesting to learn that the superintendent of the Springfield Armory officially reported, "I think they might answer some purpose for the Navy." $800–$1,375.

U.S. MUSKET MODEL 1795, regular model with 44.75-inch barrel but made and marked by early contractors, such as Gilbert or McCormick. $865–$1,525.

U.S. MUSKET MODEL 1795, altered to percussion. $650–$900.

U.S. MUSKET MODEL 1795, flintlock, made under contract of 1798 (mostly made later) by any of the following contractors: Amasa Allen; Samuel Grant and Joseph Bernard; Thomas Brickness; Elisha Brown; William Henry; Stephen Jenks and Hosea Humphreys; Adam Kinsley and James Perkins; William Rhodes and William Tyler; Amos Stillman & Co.; Eli Whitney; Alexander Clagett; Darius Chipman; Royal Crafts; Thomas Hooker and John Smith; Joseph Clark; Nathan and Henry Cobb; Owen Evans; Mathew and Nathan Eliot; Richard Falley; Daniel Gilbert; Gurdon Huntington; John Livingston; Josiah Bellow and David Stone; Jonathan Nichols, Jr.; Abijah Peck; Mathias Shroyer; Thomas Towsey and Samuel Chipman; Elie Williams; Nicholas White; Thomas Crabb; Jacob Metzger and Christopher Barnhizle. $850–$1,550.

SAME, but known as the Commonwealth of Pennsylvania (C.P.) Flintlock Musket. Same as U.S. Musket, Model 1795, but made under the Pennsylvania contract of 1797, from 1797 to 1801, and sometimes marked by one of the private contractors with the letters "C.P." or without the contractor's mark and with only "C.P." Those made for the U.S. and then issued to Pennsylvania may have "US" on the barrel, followed by "C.P.," while those made for Pennsylvania and not taken over by the U.S. may have only "C.P." The contractors for this weapon are supposed to have been the following: Peter Brong; Henry Dehuff; Jacob Dickert; Mathew Llewellin; Edward Evans; James Evans; Owen Evans; John Fondersmith, Lancaster; John Fondersmith, Strasburg; Albert Gallatin; Jack Haeffer; Abraham Henry & John Graeff; William Henry; John Kerlin, Jr., & Samuel Kerlin; Thomas & John Ketland, of Philadelphia; Jacob Laether & Kunrat Welhanze; John Miles (2 contracts to this name); Robert McCormick & Richard B. Johnston; Conrad Welhanze; Jacob Doll & Henry Pickel. The names of gunmakers were often omitted for fear of British reprisals, and the names, when found, are often spelled differently because the early gunsmiths were by no means educated men in most instances. The quality of the original workmanship has an important bearing on value. Muskets by these makers of excellent quality of materials and workmanship are worth at least $650 in good condition and $1,050 in fine condition; but when the materials and workmanship are mediocre, the value is $530 in good condition and $850 in fine condition. The same applies to U.S. MUSKET MODEL 1795, above.

U.S. BLUNDERBUSS OR WALL PIECE, HARPERS FERRY, flintlock; part octagonal barrel measures 3 inches vertically and 2 inches horizontally at muzzle, and is 27.75 inches long and measures 1.75 inches across the almost square breech. Total length 43 inches. Weight 9.5 lbs. Iron-mounted except for 2 brass ramrod thimbles and the brass plate for the lock screws. Iron butt plate marked "U.S." Rear sling swivel screwed to stock near butt plate and forward sling swivel attached to stock about one-half the distance between the trigger and the muzzle. Lock marked "Harpers Ferry," "U.S.," with a spread eagle and the year, which is 1808, on some specimens, although this type of weapon was used before the Revolution and was definitely made at Harpers Ferry shortly after that armory was established. Blunderbusses were used by federal land and sea forces, aboard ships, on boats, on the ramparts of forts, and in every conceivable place where a scatter-gun was needed. They were also used by the privateers. $2,875–$3,865.

SAME, but made under contract by T. French, Canton, Mass., in 1811, with a shorter barrel and a round muzzle. $2,100–$3,025.

U.S. ELI WHITNEY MUSKET MODEL 1798, cal. .69, flintlock, smoothbore, 43-inch barrel, 55-inch stock. Total length, 58 inches. Lock plate 6.5 inches long and 1.375 inches wide. Trigger guard 10.5 inches long with rear end round. Three bands. Lock plate marked "New Haven" under eagle, and "U. States" in curve to rear of hammer. Marked "CP" with letters run together on barrel. This model was an improvment on the French Model 1763, being based upon the French Model 1777. There is a brass pan without a fence and mounted at an angle, a frizzen with a flared head and shortened toe, and a round-faced cock. $675–$975.

SAME, but a copy of the Model 1763 French Charleville musket, made by Eli Whitney before he produced the above improvement. Whitney made a total of 10,000 arms under the 1798 contract, some of which were copied from the French, while the later ones were as described above. Including Whitney, there were 27 contractors who copied the French 1763 musket, but most of their arms were so poor that the inspectors recommended that they be sold abroad. $825–$1,180.

U.S. RIFLE MODEL 1803, HARPERS FERRY (also called Model 1800 and Model 1804), flintlock, rifled, cal. .54. Barrel is variously listed as 32, 32.813, 33.375, or 36 inches long, but 33 inches is probably approximately correct. The total length is usually between 48 and 49.5 inches. The walnut half-stock is usually about 26 inches long. The lock plate is usually 5.25 inches long and 1 inch wide. The trigger guard is usually 5.75 inches long with round ends. Polished brass furniture. Steel lock, trigger, and ramrod. Lock plate marked "Harpers Ferry" with the year, in 3 lines behind the cock, and with a spread eagle and "U.S." No bayonet. Weight about 9.25 lbs. with steel ramrod, but weight varies with length of rifle. The ramrod is held by thimbles attached to a rib under the barrel. A brass key holds the barrel to the stock. This weapon resembles the U.S. Rifle, Model 1814, described below.

Marked before 1808. $1,200–$1,950.

Marked after 1808. $950–$1,675.

MODEL 1807 SMALL MUSKET OR CARBINE FOR INDIAN DEPARTMENT (Springfield), cal. .54, flintlock, smoothbore, 33.75-inch barrel, 45.75-inch stock. Total length 48.25 inches. Lock plate 5.75 inches long and 1.15 inches wide. Trigger guard 8.75 inches long with round ends. Brass front sight and furniture. Pin-fastened stock without bands or slides. Brass hoop at muzzle end of stock to prevent splitting. Wooden ramrod. Intended for issue to friendly Indians but apparently never distributed to them. A few were issued to U.S. Military Academy, West Point, N.Y., with bayonet stud added and stock fore end shortened, but this cannot be considered as a cadet arm or as a U.S. Carbine. Made at the Springfield Armory. Lock plate, in front of cock, marked "U.S." in script over eagle with "Springfield" in curved line under eagle. Rear of lock plate marked with year. $1,400–$2,350.

U.S. MUSKET MODEL 1809 (sometimes called Model 1808), cal. .69, flintlock, smoothbore, barrel 44.5 inches long, stock 56 inches long. Lock plate 6.31 inches long and 1.31 inches wide. Trigger guard 10.75 inches long with round ends. Three bands. It is not possible to assign definitely the year 1808 to a model, but collectors for years have assumed that there is such a model. In 1808, parts from the Model 1795 were still being used to make muskets, but in 1809 the Springfield Armory began to make muskets which remained the same until the U.S. Musket, Model 1812, began to be assembled late in 1815; hence we should not speak of a Model 1808, but instead we should list a Model 1809, already described. Some specimens marked on lockplate in front of cock with "U.S." in script over eagle, with "Springfield" in curved line under eagle. Rear of lock plate marked with year. This model closely follows the Model 1795 except for a change in the lock, the turning lug on the barrel, and the barrel tang lug. $540–$925.

U.S. MUSKET CONTRACT OF 1808, cal. .69, flintlock, smoothbore, 42-inch barrel, 54.25-inch stock. Total length very slightly more than 57 inches. Lock plate 6.5 inches long and from 1.188 inches to 1.25 inches wide. Trigger guard 11.25 inches long with pointed ends. Three bands. Copied from muskets furnished as samples by the Springfield Armory and the Harpers Ferry Armory, and possibly the French Model 1763, Charleville Pattern muskets. Made by the following contractors: J. & C. Barstow; A. & P. Bartlett; Oliver Bidwell; J.J. and N. Brooke; O. & E. Jr. Evans; French, Blake & Kinsley; F. Goetz & Westphale; Daniel Gilbert; Wm. & J.J. Henry; S.A. & Geo. 2nd Jenks; R. & C. Leonard; John Miles; Rufus Perkins; W. & H. Shannon; Ethan Stillman; E. & A. Walters & N. Whitmore; Wheeler & Morrison; Winner, Nippes & Steinman. There was a vast amount of deviation from the dimensions given above because of muskets being made by contractors lacking experience, the shortage of competent inspectors, etc. Therefore, collectors will always argue about this model. $540–$915.

U.S. FLINTLOCK "CARBINE" MODEL 1809-10, cal. .56; 33.5-inch barrel attached to stock with under pin fastenings in place of usual bands. Stock extends to end of barrel; not made to take bayonet. Springfield marks. Historians doubt the authenticity of this weapon as a distinct, official type, but arms of this description exist in several collections. $1,025–$1,750.

U.S. MUSKET MODEL 1812, cal. .69, flintlock, smoothbore, 42-inch barrel, 54-inch stock. Total length 57 inches. Lock plate 6.375 inches long and 1.31 inches wide. Trigger guard 11 inches long with round ends. Three bands. The grip does not extend into the stock as it did on previous models. The left side of the stock has a cheek recess if made at Springfield, which characterizes this model as distinguished from that made at Harpers Ferry. Some collectors divide this model into 3 patterns. There were 3 arrangements of band springs: The first had them to the rear, the second type had spring studs, and the third type had the band springs to the front. Since this was the period of the War of 1812, parts from various models were mixed in the field, to the confusion of collectors. Lock plate marked with "U.S." in script over eagle and "Springfield" in curved line under eagle, in front of cock. Year marked to rear of lock plate behind cock. First pattern. Bottom band retained by band spring 3 inches long to rear of band with usual lug on spring fitting into a hole in band. $510–$725.

Second pattern. Bottom band retained by stud spring forward of band. $475–$675.

Third pattern. Bottom band retained by string 2.5 inches long, forward of band. $475–$660.

SAME, but made by Henry Deringer and also by Robert Johnson, in 1814, under contract. $565–$750.

U.S. MUSKET MODEL 1812, ELI WHITNEY CONTRACT, cal. .69, flintlock, smoothbore, 41.875-inch barrel, 54.25-inch stock. Total length 57.25 inches. Lock plate 6.5 inches long and 1.375 inches wide. Trigger guard 10.5 inches long with rear end round. Three bands. Brass pan. Stock resembles that of U.S. Musket, Model 1816, sometimes called Model 1822. This 1812 Whitney Model is sometimes confused with the weapons made under the contract of 1808, but it is actually a later production. Lock plate, in front of cock, marked "N. Haven" in curved scroll near bottom. $505–$700.

U.S. RIFLE MODEL 1814, cal. .54; flintlock, rifled, lock plate 5.25 inches long and 1 inch wide, trigger guard 8 inches long with round ends, keyed instead of having bands. This was made at Harpers Ferry in 2 lengths as follows:
   Barrel 33 inches, stock 29.125 inches, total length 49.31 inches.
   Barrel 36 inches, stock 30.25 inches, total length 52 inches.

This is the same as the U.S. Rifle, Model 1803, also made at Harpers Ferry, except for the barrel length and a few small changes. Lock plate marked "Harpers Ferry 1814" behind the cock and with an eagle forward of the cock. $925–$1,625.

U.S. RIFLE CONTRACT MODEL 1814, cal. .54, flintlock; rifled, 33.312-inch, part round, part octagonal barrel; marked on top flat at breech "J.D. Johnson" and "Middletown"; marked on left flat at breech "P" and "Conn." Stud band retainers and finger grips in rear of trigger guard. Oval iron patch box in stock, which was carried over to Model 1817 Common Rifle. Equipped with brass head, steel ramrod. Made by Robert Johnson of Middletown, Conn., under contract dated Nov. 23, 1814. Very rare. $790–$1,300.

SAME, but made by Henry Deringer, of Philadelphia, under contract dated Mar. 17, 1814. Extremely rare. $870–$1,425.

U.S. MUSKET MODEL 1816, cal. .69, flintlock, smoothbore, 42-inch barrel, 54.375-inch stock. Total length 57.5 inches. Lock plate 6.875 inches long and 1.34 inches wide. Trigger guard 9.75 inches long with round ends. Three bands. This model is sometimes mistakenly listed Model 1821 or Model 1822. Inclined brass pan. Collectors divide this model into 3 types as follows: (1) muskets made to 1822, with the lower sling swivel fastened to a stud in front of the trigger bow, and with some parts bright and others browned; (2) muskets made from 1822 to 1831, parts browned, lower sling swivel riveted to the trigger bow; and (3) muskets made after 1831, parts finished bright, and ball-shaped trigger bow section at the point of drilling the hole for the sling swivel rivet. Lock plate marked in front of cock with eagle over "U.S.," and behind cock with either "Harpers Ferry" or "Springfield" and year in 3 lines. $495–$670.

U.S. RIFLE MODEL 1817, "THE COMMON RIFLE," cal. .54, flintlock, rifled 36-inch barrel, 48-inch stock. Total length 51.5 inches. Lock plate 5.5 inches long and 1.18 inches wide. Trigger guard 9 inches long with round ends. Weight with bayonet 10.25 lbs. Three bands. The lock is like that of the Model 1816 Musket but smaller. All iron parts except brass pan. Oval-shaped patch box in right of butt with iron cover. Harpers Ferry model differs from those made by contractors in having bayonet lug on barrel and front sight on top band. Lock plate marked "Harpers Ferry 1817," with large spread eagle, "US," etc. $825–$1,235.

SAME, but made by Johnson, marked on lock plate, in front of cock, "R. Johnson" in a curved line over the eagle. "U" is to the left of the eagle and "S" to the right. In a curved line under the eagle are the abbreviations "Middn Conn." The year is behind the cock. $675–$1,050.

SAME, but marked by Henry Deringer, Philadelphia. $700–$1,075.

SAME, but marked by S. North, Middletown, Conn. $700–$1,075.

SAME, but marked by N. Starr, Middletown, Conn. $700–$1,075.

SAME, average value for any of the above converted to percussion, but without special marks. $390–$840.

SAME, average value for any of the above converted to percussion, with Confederate marks. $750–$1,100.

U.S. MUSKET MODEL 1817, ARTILLERY, CADET, SHORT, OR SPECIAL, cal. .69; flintlock, smoothbore, 36-inch barrel marked "V.P." with eagle head, year (sometimes 1819), serial number, and inspector's initial or initials. Somewhat resembles U.S. Musket, Model 1816, except for length of barrel, length of stock, total length, and spacing of the 3 bands. Stock is 48.375 inches long. Total length 51.5 inches. Lock plate 6.875 inches long and 1.34 inches wide, marked "Harpers Ferry," "US," with spread eagle and year, sometimes 1819. Trigger guard, 9.75 inches long with round ends, is separate part from trigger plate. Rear swivel held by stud in front of guard. Band springs in front of bands. The spacing of the 3 bands shows that this was not the Model 1816 Musket cut down. The distance measured from the breech to the lower band is 10.375 inches, to the middle band 20.375 inches, and to the upper band 30.625 inches, on a typical specimen. Historians believe that this was prepared for the cadets at the U.S. Military Academy, but it was called an artillery musket in some official correspondence, and a short musket in other official correspondence. $565–$850.

**U.S. RIFLE MODEL 1819, JOHN H. HALL BREECHLOADER**, cal. .52, flintlock, 32.7-inch barrel. Black walnut stock 49.625 inches long. Total length without bayonet 52.6 inches, with bayonet 68.6 inches. Trigger guard 8.12 inches long with square ends. Three bands. Polished steel ramrod 32 inches long. Polished steel bayonet with 16.5-inch blade. Barrel and all other iron and steel parts are finished in brown lacquer, except that screw heads are blued. At the muzzle the lands are reamed out for 1.5 inches to the rear, giving the appearance of a smoothbore on a casual inspection. The barrel bore increases gradually in size toward the breech until it becomes 0.545-inch in the receiver. Fixed sights, offset to avoid sighting through pan and hammer, on the original flintlock version. The receiver of this rifle is interchangeable with the later percussion receiver. Before buying one in supposedly original flintlock condition, try to aim. If the pan and hammer obstruct the aim, the receiver is not one made for flintlock ignition. Likewise, the socket bayonet for this arm has an offset stud to facilitate aiming. Adjustable hair trigger. Three bands held by pins in early version, but in later versions bands are held by band springs. Made at Harpers Ferry from 1824 to 1841. Receiver marked "J.H. Hall, U.S.," followed by the year and with the other conventional marks. This was the first breechloading weapon officially adopted by the United States and the first weapon manufactured on the interchangeable parts system in an armory of the United States. $650–$1,265.

**U.S. RIFLE MODEL 1819, SIMEON NORTH BREECHLOADER**, identical to Harpers Ferry production except for North breechblock marking and barrel band fastening. $700–$1,300.

**U.S. MUSKET MODEL 1821** (also called Model 1822), cal. .69; flintlock, smoothbore, barrel 42 inches long, with bayonet lug on top. Black walnut stock 54 inches long, made without a comb. All iron mountings. Double top band carries knife-blade front sight. Total length from muzzle to butt 57.64 inches, with fixed bayonet 73.64 inches. Weight without bayonet 10 lbs. ¼ oz.

In addition to the description given above, collectors describe this model as having a brass pan without a fence and without a swivel lug. Weapons of this description were made in vast quantities by the national armories at Harpers Ferry and Springfield, and in large numbers by private contractors.

On Dec. 31, 1821, the active contractors were recorded as Adam Carruth, Greenville, S.C.; Alexander McRae, Richmond, Va.; Eli Whitney, New Haven, Conn.; Asa Waters, Millbury, Mass.; Lemuel Pomeroy, Pittsfield, Mass.; and Marine T. Wickham, Philadelphia, Pa. In addition P. & E.W. Blake, W. L. Evans, B. Evans, Henry Deringer, John Rogers, N. Starr, and P. & J.D. Johnson were recognized as contractors of this period who made weapons for the U.S. Government. Approximate average value, flintlock. $450–$645.

SAME, but altered to percussion. $250–$375.

SAME, altered to percussion, with Confederate marks. $600–$850.

U. S. MUSKET, CADET, MODEL 1830, cal. .54, flintlock, smoothbore, 40.5-inch barrel, 43-inch stock. Total length 55.75 inches. Lock plate 5.4 inches long and 1.2 inches wide. Trigger guard 9.35 inches long with round ends. Three bands. Marked on lock plate between cock and hammer with a small eagle looking to the rear and "U.S." Marked behind the cock "Spring Field" in 2 lines, with the year of manufacture underneath in a third line. Marked on barrel with a "P," an eagle head and "V," and the year. Butt plate tang marked "U.S." The more important parts of this musket were not made at Springfield but came from previous models made either at Harpers Ferry or by contractors. $450–$705.

SAME, but 36-inch barrel, 48-inch stock, and total length 51 inches. $400–$625.

U.S. CARBINE MODEL 1833, HALL BREECHLOADER, SIMEON NORTH, MAKER, cal. .69, percussion, breechloader, smoothbore, 26.5-inch barrel, 36-inch stock. Total length 51 inches. Trigger guard 19.62 inches long with square ends. Two bands. Receiver marked in 4 lines "U.S. S. NORTH MIDLtn CONN 1833." This weapon was based on the John H. Hall patent of 1811 for a breech-loading flintlock rifle. Hall was paid a small salary plus a royalty on each weapon made at a public armory, hence he objected to the award of a contract to make arms according to his breechloading system to another contractor, but Simeon North, nevertheless, made this carbine at Middletown, Conn. $465–$665.

U.S. SMOOTHBORE CARBINE MODEL 1833, HARPERS FERRY, HALL'S PATENT, cal. .69 flintlock, 23-inch smoothbore barrel. Black walnut stock. Total length 43 inches. Length with bayonet 61.25 inches. Sling swivel attached to eyebolt in stock, instead of swivel. Receiver marked "J.H. Hall, H. Ferry, U.S." with the year. The bore diameter of the barrel is 0.64 inch, and the bore diameter of the receiver is 0.69 inch. This weapon is seldom listed, but it exists as a distinct model. $725–$975.

U.S. MUSKET MODEL 1840, cal. .69, flintlock, smoothbore, 42-inch barrel, 55-inch stock. Total length 57.75 inches. Lock plate 6.312 inches long and 1.25 inches wide. Trigger guard 9.625 inches long with round ends. Three bands. The first patterns or models were copied from the French Flintlock Musket, Model 1822, at Harpers Ferry, and marked "Model 1835" on the barrel. In an adapted version, barrel length was reduced in 1840 from that of the French musket by 0.68 inch, and the finger grooves of the French musket were eliminated. This was the last of the flintlock muskets made for the armed services. It was manufactured at the Springfield Armory from 1840 to 1844, and by private contractors until 1848. Lock plate marked in front of cock with eagle over "U.S." and "Springfield" with the year, in 3 lines behind the cock. Most of these were converted to percussion. They are rare in the original condition. Some bear marks of Daniel Nippes, Mill Creek, Pa.; and others are marked by Lemuel Pomeroy, Pittsfield, Mass. $1,075–$2,050.

U.S. RIFLED CARBINE MODEL 1836, MADE BY SIMEON NORTH, HALL'S PATENT, cal. .54, percussion, rifled, breechloader, 21-inch barrel, 36-inch stock. Total length, 39.75 inches. Trigger guard 13 inches long with square ends. Two bands. Marked on receiver "U.S. S. NORTH MIDLtn CONN. 1840," in 5 lines. This is substantially the same as the Simeon North U.S. Carbine, Model 1833, but the barrel is shorter and it is rifled. $575–$875.

U.S. MUSKETOON MODEL 1839 (1840), cal. .69, flintlock, smoothbore, 26-inch barrel with a bayonet stud 2 inches from the end of the barrel at its bottom, taking Model 1839 (1840) bayonet. Marked "V.P." and eagle head at breech. Breech tang 2 inches long. Walnut stock 38 inches long with a 0.75-inch comb 8 inches from the butt. Total length 41 inches without bayonet, 59 inches with bayonet. Weight without bayonet 7 lbs. 3 oz. Lock plate is from 5.5 to 6.25 inches long and from 1.25 inches to 1.375 inches wide, with the rear end more pointed and rounded than previous models. Trigger-guard plate is 8.5 to 9.5 inches long and 1.25 to 1.375 inches wide, with the trigger guard a separate part. Lock plate marked between cock and hammer with small spread eagle looking to the rear, "U.S." under the eagle, and "Harpers Ferry" with the year, in 3 lines behind the cock. Two bands. Top band is shaped like that on U.S. Musket, Model 1821 (1822). Beware of fakes. $910–$1,250.

SAME, but made and marked at Springfield, with the top band shaped like that of the U.S. Musket Model 1835 (usually called Model 1840). This was the standard issue of the Model 1839 Musketoon, while the Harpers Ferry issue is regarded as being limited to model or pattern pieces. $825–$1,150.

U.S. CARBINE MODEL 1840, SIMEON NORTH, HALL'S PATENT, cal. .54, percussion, smoothbore, 21-inch barrel, 36.188-inch walnut stock. Total length 40 inches. Bore diameter of barrel is 0.52 inch, and bore diameter of receiver is 0.56 inch. Ramrod 19.5 inches long. Trigger guard 11.5 inches long with square ends. Two bands. Outstanding characteristic is the "fishtail" lever for operating the breechlock, that is, for moving the receiver. Marked "U.S. S. NORTH MIDLtn. CONN." with the year on the receiver. Commodore Perry presented several John H. Hall firearms to the Emperor of Japan. General John C. Fremont bought a quantity of these Hall carbines for the United States during the Civil War, thereby playing an innocent part in what developed into a scandal involving civilians who were making a fortune by buying arms from one branch of the government and selling them to another at a big profit. $425–$800.

U.S. MUSKET, CADET, MODEL 1841 (1842), cal. .54, percussion, smoothbore, 40-inch barrel. Walnut stock 52.25 inches long. Total length 54.5 inches. Lock plate 5.25 inches long and 1.25 inches wide. Trigger guard 9 inches long with round ends. Weight 8.5 lbs. Two bands. Browned barrel and mountings. Bayonet 14 inches long. Marked on lock plate forward of cock with small eagle looking to the left over "U.S.," with "Springfield" and the year in 3 lines behind the cock. Made by the Springfield Armory in 1844 and 1845. $400–$590.

SAME, with Confederate marks. $550–$850.

U.S. RIFLE MODEL 1841 (1842), cal. .54, percussion, 33-inch barrel, 43-inch stock. Total length 55.25 inches. Lock plate 5.25 inches long and 1.25 inches wide. Trigger guard 9 inches long with round ends. Two bands. Marked with an eagle with raised wings facing to the rear on the lock plate in front of the cock, and over the "U.S.," and in the rear of the cock "Harpers Ferry" with the year in 3 lines. This rifle has more aliases than a fellow traveler. It is called the Mississippi Rifle, Mississippi Model, Harpers Ferry Rifle, Harpers Ferry Yager, Windsor Rifle, Model 1841, and Model 1842.

Marked "Springfield." $800–$1,160.
Marked "Harpers Ferry." $560–$875.

SAME, bored to cal. .58, with long-range rear sight for elongated (Minié-type) ammunition. $400–$675.

SAME, cal. .54, with ordinary sights and Confederate marks. $750–$1,000.

SAME, but cal. .58, long-range sights and Confederate marks. $750–$1,000.

*Note: This rifle was made at both the Springfield and Harpers Ferry armories, and by the following contractors: Remington; Robbins & Lawrence; Robbins, Kendall & Lawrence; Tryon; and Whitney. Contractor-made.*

U.S. MUSKET MODEL 1842, cal. .69, percussion, smoothbore, 42-inch barrel, 55-inch stock. Total length 57.75 inches. Lock plate 6.25 inches long and 1.28 inches wide. Trigger guard 9.625 inches long with round ends. Three bands. Marked in front of cock on lock plate with usual eagle (wings down) over "U.S." and marked behind the cock in 3 lines "Springfield" and the year. $400–$525.

SAME, but marked "Harpers Ferry" on lock plate, with date. $400–$575.

SAME, but with Confederate marks. $425–$625.

*Note: Some specimens are cal. .69. Value is the same.*

U.S. RIFLED MUSKET MODEL 1842, same as U. S. Musket Model 1842, but bored and rifled to cal. .69, with long-range rear sight for Model 1855 elongated (Minié-type) ammunition. Strictly speaking, this is not a separate official model but a modification or variation. Marked "Springfield," with other details as described for 1842 Musket. $300–$390.

SAME, but marked "Harpers Ferry." $425–$600.

SAME, but with Confederate marks. $650–$800.

*Note: The U.S. Musket Model 1842 and the U.S. Rifled Musket Model 1842 were made principally at the Springfield and Harpers Ferry armories from 1843 to 1855, but a very few are reported to have been made by G. Flagg & Co., Millbury, Mass., and some by the Palmetto Armory. Specimens marked by the last 2 named markers are worth $475–$785.*


# PERCUSSION MUSKETS CONVERTED FROM FLINTLOCK MUSKETS, 1842 TO CIVIL WAR

In 1842 the War Department decided to inspect and classify all muskets made before 1832 as well as those made later. Those in serviceable condition made after 1831 were to be retained without examination. Those in serviceable condition made from 1821 to 1831 were to be issued when needed and otherwise retained for alteration from flintlock to percussion. Those made from 1812 to 1820 were not to be considered satisfactory for issue or for alteration but were to be held in reserve for any emergency. Those made before 1812 and all damaged or unserviceable arms not worth repairing were to be set aside for sale. In practice this last class of arms was found to contain many weapons made from 1828 to 1831. The following are typical specimens.

FLINTLOCK MUSKET CONVERTED TO PERCUSSION, SPRINGFIELD MARKS. $275–$375.

SAME, but converted and marked by Remington. $400–$525.

SAME, but rifled and equipped with long-range, folding-leaf, rear sight. $400–$575.

SAME, but converted to Maynard tape primer system with new lock. $450–$625.

SAME, but U.S. Model 1816 converted by Remington Arms Co., Ilion, N.Y., under contract of 1854, to Maynard System with new lock. $425–$600.

SAME, but U.S. MODEL 1840, converted by Pomeroy from flintlock to ordinary percussion by inserting a new breech in a cutoff barrel, marked "H & P" on the bolster face. $450–$725.

## Morse Alteration

A typical specimen of the Morse alteration is a U.S. flintlock musket, cal. .69, converted to a breechloader by cutting the top of the barrel and hinging a breech action in the rear, with the original hammer cut down to form a cocking piece, and a redesigned firing pin. A typical specimen of a carbine converted by the Morse alteration has a 20-inch barrel, a total length of 40 inches, and a weight of 6.5 lbs. There is usually a butternut or walnut stock and a full-length forepiece. The breech action resembles that of the altered flintlock musket, but the hammer is swung in the middle. The ramrod is held in place by a lug on the bottom of the barrel and brass ramrod ferrules. The Morse alteration was patented in 1856, there were a few made for Army trial boards, and in 1859 it was reported that there were 20 arms converted according to the Morse system; but it was never officially adopted. This explanation is presented because many collectors seem to think that the Morse alteration belongs in a U.S. martial shoulder arm collection, whereas it is at the best only a trial or experimental arm. It was never used in the armed services.

## Typical Methods of Altering Flintlocks to Percussion

Briefly, the methods of altering flintlock shoulder arms to percussion were as follows: (1) using the old hammer with a side lug; (2) using a new hammer with a side lug; (3) providing a bolster lug with a clean-out screw; (4) providing a bolster lug as part of a new barrel breech; and (5) screwing a cone into the top of the barrel. An example of the bolster-type alteration was the Pomeroy contract conversion of the Model 1835, accomplished by inserting a new breech into the old barrel which had been cut off. Another type of alteration was the Remington Arms Co. contract of 1854, wherein U.S. Musket, Model 1816, was altered to the Maynard system by providing an entirely new lock.

U.S. CARBINE, MODEL 1843, "NORTH'S IMPROVEMENT" (HALL PATENT), cal. .52, percussion, smoothbore, 21-inch barrel, 36-inch stock. Total length 39.75 inches. Trigger guard 11.75 inches long with square ends. Two bands. The slide-lever action, called "North's Improvement" by historians and collectors, was added to actuate the raising and closing of the breechblock in accordance with the suggestions of Simeon North. Receiver marked "U.S.S. NORTH MIDLtn CONN. 1843" in 5 lines. $450–$725.

U.S. MUSKETOON MODEL 1847 (commonly called Model 1842), for Artillery, Cavalry, and Sappers, cal. .69, percussion, smoothbore, 26-inch barrel, 38.25-inch stock. Total length 41 inches. Lock plate 5.1875 inches long and 1.25 inches wide. Trigger guard with round ends, 8.75 inches long for Artillery and Cavalry and 8.5 inches long for Sappers. Usual eagle and "U.S." on lock plate. Lock plate marked "Springfield 1842" in 3 lines behind cock, but this model was not made in quantity until officially authorized in 1847. The manufacture ceased in 1856. There were various alterations, modifications, and interchange of parts, with the result that specimens are found with all iron furniture, all brass furniture, and mixed iron and brass furniture. In 1851 the ramrod was altered. This model should not be confused with sawed-off rifles and muskets of earlier models.

Average value, without bayonet $575–$860.

ARTILLERY MODEL, with Artillery bayonet, total length 59 inches, weight 7.7 lbs. Scarcer than the Cavalry Model. (Including bayonet.) $625–$1,025.

SAPPERS AND MINERS MODEL, same as Artillery, but there are lugs on barrel and top band for fixing 22-inch, Roman-type, double-edge bayonet, which weighs 2.33 lbs. by itself. Total length with bayonet 62.1 inches. Weight with bayonet 9.35 lbs. Extremely rare. With bayonet. $685–$1,015.

CAVALRY MODEL, brass mountings instead of iron, top band shaped differently, ramrod shaped differently to use swivel attachment, ring and bar replace the ordinary swivels. Not supplied with bayonet. $525–$840.

*Note: Artillery bayonet is worth from $100 to $150. The Sappers' bayonet, with 22-inch Roman blade, is worth from $325 to $525.*

U.S. MUSKET, CADET, MODEL 1851, cal. .57, percussion, smoothbore, 40-inch barrel, 52.25-inch stock. Total length 55.25 inches. Lock plate 5.25 inches long and 1.25 inches wide. Trigger guard 9 inches long with round ends. Three bands. This is a bastard model. The lock of the Model 1847 Musketoon was placed on the Model 1841 Cadet Musket after the tang had been enlarged and the barrel diameter increased. About 4,000 of these muskets were made in 1852 and 1853, hence it is obvious that it was not intended solely for the cadets at the U.S. Military Academy, since there was no need for this quantity. In 1857 this model was rifled and equipped with sights. Apparently made only at the Springfield Armory and so marked. Sometimes called a Special Model Musketoon. $475–$610.

U.S. FENCING MUSKET, like regular 1842 Model muskets but with rough stock, without lock cut, and with the barrel vent closed. It has been reported that 60 were made in 1858. The demand is poor.$100–$200.

U.S. RIFLED CARBINE MODEL 1855 (MODEL 1854), cal. .58 or cal. .54, percussion, 22-inch barrel, 29.438-inch stock. Total length 36.75 inches. Lock plate 5.25 inches long and 1.203 inches wide. Trigger guard 8.75 inches long with round ends. One band. More than 1,000 of these rifled carbines were made at the Springfield Armory. Lock plate marked "U.S. SPRINGFIELD" with date and usual eagle. Barrel marked with eagle head and "V.P.," with date on tang of barrel. Apparently made originally as cal. .54. $1100–$1,150.

U.S. RIFLED MUSKET MODEL 1855 (MAYNARD), cal. .58, Maynard tape lock, 40-inch barrel, 52.85-inch stock. Total length 56 inches. Weight 9.18 lbs. Lock plate 5.5 inches long and 1.875 inches wide. Trigger guard 7.5 inches long with round ends. Three bands. A smaller rear sight was adopted in 1858. A patch box was added to the stock in 1859. Marked either "Springfield" or "Harpers Ferry," and the date, but it is believed most government-made arms were made at Springfield. $550–$850.

SAME, but made by the following contractors: A. M. Burt; J. T. Hodge; A. Jenks & Son; J. Mulholland; J. D. Mowry; and E. Whitney. $350–$540.

SAME, any of the above armory or contractor makes, with Confederate marks. $625–$850.

U.S. RIFLE MODEL 1855 (MAYNARD), cal. .58, Maynard tape lock, 33-inch barrel, 44-inch stock. Total length 49 inches. Lock plate 5.5 inches long and 1.875 inches wide. Trigger guard 7.5 inches long with round ends. Two bands. Marked "U.S. Harpers Ferry, 1859" on lock plate. Large spread eagle on tape box cover. This was the first military rifle to be fitted with the Maynard primer. Specimens are found with Springfield locks, but it was probably made entirely at Harpers Ferry. $575–$950.

SAME, but with Confederate marks. $1,000–$1,350.

U.S. PISTOL-CARBINE MODEL 1855, cal. .58, rifled, percussion, Maynard tape lock, 12-inch barrel, 26.5-inch stock. Total length 28.25 inches. Trigger guard 5.25 inches long with round ends. One band. The pistol weighs about 3½ pounds without the stock and slightly more than 5 pounds with the stock. The stock is detachable. Dragoons carried it in 2 pieces on the saddle; when they dismounted to fight, they used it as a carbine. It was made at the Springfield Armory and so marked. For obvious reasons this weapon is listed in Chapter 6 on U.S. martial percussion pistols. Primer cover marked with eagle with upraised wings in front of hammer. Forward of eagle and below, marked "U.S." over "SPRINGFIELD." Pistol without stock. $590–$860.

SAME, but with detachable stock. $1,155–$2,000.

U.S. CADET MUSKET MODEL 1858, RIFLED, cal. .58, percussion, Maynard tape lock, 38-inch barrel, 50-inch stock. Total length 53 inches. Lock plate 5.45 inches long and 1.9 inches wide. Trigger guard 7.5 inches long with round ends. Three bands. This was identical with the U.S. Rifled Musket, Model 1855, except for the barrel, the stock, the rammer, and the bayonet. Made at the Springfield Armory. $700–$995.

U.S. RIFLED MUSKET MODEL 1861, cal. .58, percussion, 40-inch barrel, 40-inch stock. Total length 58.5 inches. Lock plate 5.375 inches long, 1.25 inches wide. Trigger guard 7.5 inches long with round ends. Three bands. This was the principal infantry weapon of the Civil War. It was adopted because of dissatisfaction with the Maynard tape lock model of 1855. There is no magazine for the Maynard primer, and the stock is not cut to admit the lock plate which has the magazine. The mainspring is longer. Otherwise, it conforms to the model of 1855. Weight with 18-inch socket bayonet 9.75 lbs. $325–$660.

SAME, but cadet size, total length 53 inches. If not faked, $350–$625.

SAME, but with Confederate marks, regular length. $575–$800.

**U.S. RIFLED MUSKET MODEL 1861, COLT.** Same as previous model but marked on lock plate "U.S. Colt's Pt. F.A. Mfg. Co. Hartford, Ct." $525–$850.

SAME, but with Confederate marks. $650–$975.

**U.S. RIFLED MUSKET MODEL 1861, AMOSKEAG.** Same as previous model but marked on lock plate "Amoskeag Mfg. Co., Manchester, N.H.," with the date and an eagle between the "U" and the "S." $525–$850.

SAME, but with Confederate marks. $525–$900.

**U.S. RIFLED MUSKET MODEL 1861, LAMSON, GOODNOW & YALE.** Same as previous model but marked "L. G. & Y., Windsor, Vt.", with "U.S." under the eagle and the date behind the hammer. $425–$575.

SAME, but with Confederate marks. $375–$650.

*Civil War Contractors:* In addition to those mentioned above, Civil War contractors included the following: Wm. Mason, Wm. Muir & Co., Parker Snow & Co., E. Robinson, Norwich Arms Co., R. W. Savage, C. D. Shubarth, E. Remington, New York Arms Co., Providence Tool Co., Sarson & Roberts, and others. Some made Model 1861 shoulder arms, while others made later models.

**U.S. RIFLED MUSKET MODEL 1863, FIRST TYPE,** cal. .58, percussion, 40-inch barrel, 52.5-inch stock. Total length 56 inches. Lock plate 5.375 inches long, 1.25 inches wide. Trigger guard 7.5 inches long with round ends. Three bands. The stock is not cut for band springs and otherwise conforms to the model of 1861. The lock plate is the same as in the model of 1861 except that it is casehardened. The barrel cone seat is shorter than in the model of 1855 and lacks a vent screw. The hammer has an S shape but differs from previous models in shape and also in color, since it is casehardened. The ramrod is straight. There is a ramrod spring but no band springs. The bands are oval and open, with band screws. Marked "Springfield" with an eagle and the date behind the hammer. $375–$650.

SAME, but made and marked by contractors. Value varies. $395–$750.

**U.S. RIFLED MUSKET MODEL 1863, SECOND TYPE** (sometimes called Model 1864), cal. .58, percussion, 40-inch barrel, 52.5-inch stock. Total length 56 inches. Lock plate 5.448 inches long and 1.313 inches wide. Trigger guard 7.5 inches long with round ends. Three bands. This model was approved by the War Department on Dec. 17, 1863; hence it may be correctly designated as the Model of 1863 although it is obvious that production could not start successfully before 1864. Marked "Springfield" with eagle and date behind hammer. Band springs and solid bands. The rearsight mortise in the barrel was eliminated, and the method of attaching the rear sight to the barrel was changed. $400–$645.

U.S. RIFLE MODEL 1863, REMINGTON ARMS CO. CONTRACT, cal. .54, percussion, rifled, 33-inch barrel, 44-inch stock. Trigger guard 7.5 inches long with round ends. Three bands. Barrel and lock are those of the model 1841 Rifle. Bands and ramrod are copied from the Model 1863 Rifled Musket, Second Type. Butt plate, trigger guard, stock, and stock tip are copied from the Model 1855 Rifle. The brass patch box is almost identical with that of the Model 1855 Rifle. Marked "Remington's, Ilion, N.Y. 1863" with an eagle. Lock, lock plate, and hammer casehardened in mottled colors. Blue-black barrel. Trigger, band springs, and all screws heat-blued. Other furniture was polished brass. $750–$1,250.

U.S. RIFLE MODEL 1863, NAVY, cal. .69; 34.25-inch, round, rifled barrel. Muzzle-loading. Lock marked "US" under eagle and "Whitney-Ville 1863." Finger spur rear of guard. Large ramrod tip. Known to collectors as the "Navy Plymouth Model" or the "Whitney-Ville Model." Not usually recognized as a distinct model by historians, but so recognized by most advanced collectors. $750–$1,350.

U.S. DOUBLE MUSKET (LINDSAY) MODEL 1863, cal. .58, percussion, 41.375-inch barrel, 53-inch stock. Total length 56 inches. Trigger guard 7.5 inches long with round ends. Three bands. Marked "Lindsay Patent Oct. 9, 1860." A single trigger operates 2 hammers centrally hung side by side, each of which ignites a percussion cap on one of the 2 nipples. Two charges are loaded into the barrel, one on top of the other. The fire from the cone of the right hammer ignites the forward charge, and the rear charge of powder is fired from the left hammer. This was an experimental model, hence it is not a U.S. martial shoulder arm in the very strict sense of the term. $640–$1,100.

*Note: The following models are all breechloaders:*

U.S. RIFLE MODEL 1865 (Allin Alteration), cal. .58, breechloader, rimfire, 40-inch barrel. 52.2-inch stock. Total length 56 inches. Lock plate 5.375 inches long and 1.25 inches wide. Trigger guard 7.5 inches long with round ends. Three bands. This rifle was the first to use metallic cartridges. Muzzle-loading muskets were converted into breechloaders by milling open the breech section of the barrel and inserting a hinged bolt fastened to the top of the barrel, forward of the opening, by 2 screws. Lock plate marked with eagle with upraised wings in front of hammer, "U.S. Springfield" in 2 straight lines forward of eagle and low, with the year behind the hammer. $500–$875.

U.S. RIFLE MODEL 1866, cal. .50 breechloader, 40-inch barrel, center-fire, 52.5-inch stock. Total length 56 inches. Lock plate 5.375 inches long and 1.25 inches wide with round ends. Three bands. This was another conversion from muzzle-loading to breech-loading. The caliber was reduced from .58 to .50 by brazing a tube inside the barrel. The ratchet-action extractor of the Model 1865 was replaced by a U-shaped spring. Half of those issued were ordered varnished, and the other half were to be issued unvarnished. Marked "Model 1866" on breechblock. $325–$600.

MIXED MODELS OF CIVIL WAR RIFLED MUSKETS were composed of parts from 2 or more makes or models, either government-made or contract-made or both, assembled in government arsenals, armories, and depots, or by organization armorers in the field, sometimes by the Union Army but more often by the Confederates. During the intervening years collectors and dealers have acquired separate parts and assembled them. These bastards are not popular with collectors, who naturally mistrust the parentage, and the values are low regardless of condition. $190–$245.

SPECIAL MODELS OF CIVIL WAR MUSKETS were generally assembled from parts from models of the years 1855, 1861, and 1863, provided with either originally short or sawed-off barrels, and issued to artillerymen, foraging parties of mounted infantry, and others who were not expected to need the best quality of shoulder arms. Collectors and dealers have duplicated these "bar sinister" special models by assembling junk so much that the value is poor regardless of condition. $190–$275.

CIVIL WAR SHOULDER ARMS used by Confederates were everything known to man. They included flintlock, percussion, cartridge, muzzle-loading, breech-loading, single-shot, repeating, long-barrel, short-barrel, rifled, and smoothbore arms made in United States armories by United States contractors, in Confederate armories by Confederate contractors, by Europeans, and by anyone else who could deliver to them. Even shotguns and spears were used. If a shoulder arm in genuine, original condition can be proved to be of distinctly Confederate origin, it should be worth a great deal more then the regular specimen, but old grandfathers' tales, family tradition, and accompanying love letters are worth nothing in valuing such arms. Confederate marks are usually easy to fake on either wood or metal.

U.S. RIFLE, CADET, MODEL 1866, cal. .50, breechloader, 34.625-inch barrel, center-fire, 42.375-inch stock. Total length 54.813 inches. Lock plate 5.375 inches long and 1.25 inches wide. Trigger guard 7.5 inches long with round ends. Marked "U.S. Springfield" on lock plate, with eagle and "Model 1866" on breechblock. New barrel but lock plate from percussion arms. New stock with 2 bands. Breech action same as Model 1866 Rifle. Not cut down. Beware of fakes. $200–$375.

U.S. RIFLE MODEL 1868, cal. .50, breechloader, 32.625-inch barrel, center-fire, 48.75-inch stock. Total length 52 inches. Lock plate 5.375 inches long and 1.25 inches wide. Trigger guard 7.5 inches long with round ends. This model, unlike the previous model, has a receiver which is a separate unit with a new barrel screwed into it. The breechblock swings upward and forward, as in the U.S. Rifle, Model 1866. The ramrod is shorter and secured in its bed by a shoulder about 4 inches from the heard, which rests against a stop inserted in the stock below the tip. The middle band is omitted. The swivel is attached to the upper band. The bands are held by springs. A long-range sliding sight replaces the short-range leaf sight and is secured to the barrel by a dovetail mortise and screw. The cupping of the hammer was removed. The mainspring swivel was shortened. Marked "Model 1868" on breechblock. $360–$650.

U.S. RIFLE, CADET, MODEL 1869, cal. .50, breechloader, 29.5-inch barrel, center-fire, 48.75-inch stock. Total length 51.875 inches. Lock plate 5.375 inches long and 1.25 inches wide. Trigger guard 7.5 inches long with round ends. Two bands. This model is similar to the U.S. Rifle, Model 1868, except for a shorter barrel and a corresponding reduction in certain other dimensions. Not a cut-down rifle. $350–$610.

U.S. RIFLE MODEL 1870, cal. .50, breechloader, 32.6-inch barrel, center-fire. Total length 51.75 inches. Lock plate 5.5 inches long and 1.375 inches wide. Trigger guard 5.75 inches long with round ends. Two bands. The receiver in front of the hinge was shortened 0.7 inch. The sight notches were made smaller, the front sight was silver-plated, and the rear sight leaf was not casehardened. The pull of the trigger was adjusted to a range of 6 to 8 pounds. The ramrod has a double shoulder for the stop. Marked as previous models and "MODEL 1870" on the breechblock. $300–$525.

U.S. RIFLE MODEL 1870, NAVY, cal. .50, breechloader, 31.125-inch barrel, 43.875-inch stock. Total length 48.625 inches. Trigger guard 7.25 inches long with a square front. Two bands. This model used the Remington rolling block action. The barrel was that of the U.S. Model 1868, Springfield. The U.S. government sold 10,000, manufactured at the Springfield Armory, to Poultney & Trimble, Baltimore, Md., for shipment to France for use in the Franco-Prussian War, at a price that permitted 12,000 more to be made for the U.S. Navy. Those sold to France had the rear sight too near the breech for U.S. Navy use, but were serviceable. Marked with eagle with upraised wings, and "U.S.N. Springfield" with the year, in 3 lines. $375–$540.

U.S. RIFLE MODEL 1870, ARMY, cal. .50, breechloader, 34.375-inch barrel, center-fire, 48.448-inch stock. Total length 51.75 inches. Trigger guard 7.5 inches long with square front. Two bands. Of this model 1,008 were made and issued to troops for field testing. Like the Model 1870, Navy, it used the Remington rolling block action. $425–$610.

U.S. RIFLE MODEL 1871, Army, same as the U.S. Rifle, Model 1870, Navy, except that it has a longer barrel. Cal. .50, breechloader, 36-inch barrel, total length 51.75 inches. Two bands. Marked on frame "Model 1871" and "U.S. SPRINGFIELD 1872." Marked on tang of receiver "REMINGTON'S PATENT. PAT. MAY 3RD, NOV. 15, 1864, APRIL 17TH, 1868." $400–$600.

U.S. RIFLE MODEL 1871, WARD BURTON, cal. .50, breechloader, 32.625-inch barrel, center-fire, 48.875-inch stock, bolt action. Total length 51.875 inches. Trigger guard 7.5 inches long with round ends. Two bands. This was an experimental rifle issued to troops for testing. $650–$850.

U.S. CARBINE MODEL 1871, WARD BURTON, cal. .50, breechloader, bolt action, hammerless, 27.75-inch barrel, 30-inch stock. Total length 41.25 inches. Similar to above Ward Burton Rifle, but shorter. Of this model 313 were made at the Springfield Armory in 1871 and issued to cavalry for tests in 1872. Marked "U.S. Springfield 1871" and "Ward Burton Patent Dec. 20, 1859. Feb. 21, 1871." There is only 1 band. Usual lock plate. $750–$1,000.

U.S. RIFLE MODEL 1873, cal. .45, breechloader, 32.375-inch barrel, center-fire, 48.7-inch stock. Total length 51.92 inches. Lock plate 5.375 inches long and 1.312 inches wide. Trigger guard 7.5 inches long with round ends. Two bands. Marked "Springfield" on the lock plate, with a large eagle and a year. Breechblock stamped "Model 1873" with an eagle head, arrows, and "U.S." This rifle is similar to the U.S. Rifle Model 1870, except for the caliber and improvements in construction. The barrel was made of steel instead of iron, which had been used before. The lock plate was thinner with no beveled edge. The hammer was rounded. The stock was rounded near the lock plate and also on its upper edges as far as the lower band. A screw was used instead of the rivet on the guard bow swivel. The heads of the tumbler screw, tang screw, and side screws were rounded, and the side screws were shortened. The ramrod was improved in various details, such as cannelures cut near the small end to give a better grip. $275–$495.

U.S. RIFLE MODEL 1873, CADET, cal. .45, breechloader, 29.5-inch barrel, center-fire, 45.75-inch stock. Total length 48.92 inches. Lock plate 5.375 inches long and 1.312 inches wide. Trigger guard 7.5 inches long with round ends. Two bands. The upper band has no sling swivel. The stacking swivel lug has a different size and shape. There is no sling swivel on the guard bow. The barrel has the same muzzle diameter as the rifle. $275–$425.

**U.S. CARBINE MODEL** 1873, cal. .45, breechloader, 21.875-inch barrel, center-fire, 30-inch stock. Total length 41.313 inches. Lock plate of usual dimensions. Trigger guard as before. One band. Plain butt plate without trap for cleaning rods. $375–$650.

**U.S. RIFLE, SPECIAL MODEL** 1873, same as U.S. Rifle, Model 1873, except that it has a 28-inch barrel for cavalry, using rifle instead of carbine cartridge; special rear sight; upper swivel on top band; lower swivel on trigger guard. Some are without swivels and have an 1879 carbine sight. $900–$1,350.

**U.S. RIFLE, MARKSMAN OR MATCH MODEL** 1873, same as U.S. Rifle Model 1873, except that it has 28.5-inch, heavy octagon barrel; target sights; regular stock cut down and checkered. Total length 49 inches. Weight 10 lbs. Not recognized as an official, distinct model by some authorities. $950–$1,425.

**U.S. RIFLE OFFICERS' MODEL** 1875 (sometimes called Officers' Model 1873), cal. .45, breechloader, center-fire, 26-inch barrel, 33.625-inch stock. Total length 47.375 inches. Usual lock plate and trigger guard dimensions. One band. Stock checked forward and behind the breech, and tipped with white metal. Plain buckhorn sight on barrel, graduated like service issue sight. Also has peep and globe sights. Single set trigger set by pushing thumb forward after cocking. Wood ramrod with ends ferruled with nickel-plated brass. Plain engraving on hammer, breechblock, receiver, lock, band, and heel of butt plate. After April 1877, equipped with detachable pistol-grip handle. $2,000–$2,950.

**U.S. RIFLE MODEL** 1878, HOTCHKISS, cal. .45, breechloader, center-fire, 28.688-inch barrel, 45.5-inch stock. Total length 48.625 inches. Bolt action. Usual trigger guard dimensions. Manufactured by the Springfield Armory, except for the actions, and also manufactured by the Winchester Arms Co. The U.S. Navy received 3,500 from 1879 to 1881. Apparently the U.S. Army received slightly more than 500 from 1879 to 1880. This arm is sometimes known as the Hotchkiss Military Magazine Rifle, Model 1879. The tubular magazine located in the butt of the stock, loaded through a trap in the butt plate, has a capacity of 5 cartridges. With one in the chamber, the weapon has a total capacity of 6 cartridges. $325–$600.

**U.S. RIFLE MODEL** 1879, HOTCHKISS, NAVY. Same as U.S. Rifle Model 1878, Hotchkiss, described above, but with Navy marks. $350–$625.

**U.S. RIFLE MODEL** 1879, cal. .45, center-fire, 32.375-inch barrel, 48.625-inch stock. Total length 51.75 inches. Usual lock plate and trigger guard dimensions. Two bands. Similar to U.S. Rifle Model 1873, except for a few details. The rear sight is the buckhorn type, made in different forms. $275–$400.

SAME, but made for rod instead of triangular bayonet. $275–$400.

U.S. RIFLE CADET, MODEL 1879, (sometimes called Model 1877 Carbine), same as above but 29.5-inch barrel, 45.75-inch stock, and total length 48.92 inches. $285–$425.

U.S. CARBINE MODEL 1879, same as above, but 21.875-inch barrel, 30-inch stock, and total length 41.313 inches. One band. Butt plate has a trap to contain a jointed cleaning rod. Band with stacking swivel eliminated. Lower band of rifle substituted. $425–$575.

U.S. EXPERIMENTAL CARBINE MODEL 1882, First Variation, cal. .45, breechloader, center-fire, 27.75-inch barrel, 43.5-inch stock. Total length 47.375 inches. Usual lock plate and trigger guard dimensions. Two bands. This carbine or "short rifle" was an attempt to design a weapon halfway between the carbine of the cavalry and the regular service rifle of the foot troops. The sling was to be used in the customary manner, but the swivels were to be bent to conform to the round of the stock for mounted use, so that the rifle could be jerked out of the saddle boot quickly. The Second Variation has the same dimensions except that the stock length is 44.25 inches. The Third Variation has a 23.75-inch barrel, a 39.75-inch stock, and a total length of 43.188 inches. Lock plate marked with eagle with upraised wings in front of hammer, and "U.S. Springfield" in 2 lines forward of eagle. $650–$850.

Note: In 1881 the crimp, or renewable, primer was developed and used in all cartridges manufactured for the armed services.

U.S. RIFLE MODEL 1882, CHAFFEE-REECE, cal. .45, breechloader, center-fire, 27.875-inch barrel, 46-inch stock. Total length 49 inches. Bolt action. Two bands. Trigger guard 10 inches long with round ends. Made at Springfield Armory. Marked on breech "U.S. Springfield 1884." The magazine is in the butt. A fixed chamber is closed by a movable breech bolt sliding and rotating. Two ratchet bars, one fixed and one sliding, hold the cartridges in the magazine; these bars are operated when the bolt is turned back and closed. The magazine being loaded, the bolt is thrown open and backward, and each tooth of the sliding bar moves behind the base of the cartridge in its rear. Closing the bolt moves the ratchet forward, driving each cartridge to the front. This rifle can be used as a single-loader by means of a cutoff that disengages the rack action. $450–$600.

U.S. RIFLE MODEL 1884, with Buffington wind-guage sight, cal. .45, breechloader, center-fire, 32.375-inch barrel, 48.625-inch stock. Total length 51.75 inches. Lock plate 5.375 inches long and 1.312 inches wide. Trigger guard 7.5 inches long with round ends. Two bands. Like the Model 1879 with a few differences, the most important being the Buffington wind-gauge sight, which was the first military sight on U.S. weapons that provided for corrections for the drift of bullets caused by the wind. $300–$425.

U.S. RIFLE MODEL 1884, with round rod bayonet. Same as the other Model 1884 except for minor variations, the principal one being the round ramrod-type bayonet. Equipped with the Buffington wind-gauge sight. Very small differences in dimensions are found. The model had the same barrel length, a 48.7-inch stock, and a total length of 51.92 inches. Marked on lock plate "U.S. Springfield" with an eagle. Marked on breechblock "U.S. Model 1884." $300–$425.

U.S. RIFLE, CADET, MODEL 1884, cal. .45, breechloader, center-fire, 29.5-inch barrel, 44.75-inch stock. Total length 48.75 inches. Other dimensions and marks resemble the two Model 1884 rifles. Two bands. $310–$475.

U.S. CARBINE MODEL 1884, 21.875-inch barrel, 30-inch stock, total length 41.313 inches. One band. Other dimensions like the other Model 1884 rifles. $300–$550.

U.S. RIFLE MODEL 1889 (sometimes called Model 1888), cal. .45, breech-loader, center-fire, 32.375-inch barrel, 48.625-inch stock. Total length 51.75 inches. Usual lock plate and trigger guard dimensions. Two bands. Rod bayonet. This was the last of the cal. .45 single-shot rifles used by U.S. forces. It is sometimes called Model 1888, but it was not officially approved as a model until 1889. $310–$475.

U.S. MAGAZINE RIFLE, MODEL 1892, KRAG-JORGENSEN, cal. .30, magazine rifle, 30-inch barrel, 46-inch stock. Total length 49.14 inches. Bolt action. Trigger guard 3.625 inches long with round ends. Two bands. Knife bayonet. This was an improvement on the original Danish Krag-Jorgensen Rifle. The magazine holds 5 cartridges and is under the receiver, to the left. A cutoff makes it possible to fire it as a single-loader. This was the first U.S. rifle with the top of the barrel covered with wood to serve as a hand guard. A carbine of this model was discussed but not made. All 1892 Model rifles were eventually converted to Model 1896. The magazine cutoff was then altered to indicate that the magazine was functioning when the cutoff was in the upright position, and out of use when the cutoff was down. This was the first rifle of the armed services to use smokeless powder and a reduced caliber cartridge. Rare in genuine, original condition. $450–$750.

U.S. MAGAZINE RIFLE MODEL 1896, cal. .30, 30-inch barrel, 46.05-inch stock, total length 48.9 inches. Bolt action. Trigger guard 3.625 inches long with round ends. Two bands. Similar to the Model 1892 rifle, but the length and weight were slightly reduced. The butt plate was thickened and supplied with a hinged trap for inserting and removing the ramrod, which was unjointed and kept in a hole in the butt when not used. The toe of the butt was rounded. The model date is stamped on the stock. The rear sight differs slightly from the previous model. The upper band was made so that the barrel was encircled by 2 rings. $125–$210.

U.S. MAGAZINE CARBINE MODEL 1896, ca. .30. Similar to Model 1896 rifle, but with a 22-inch barrel, a 30.05-inch stock, and a total length of 40.9 inches. One band with an elevated section over the barrel to serve as a rear-sight protector. $135–$225.

SAME, but so-called Cadet Model, doubtful official sanction. $60–$90.

U.S. MAGAZINE RIFLE MODEL 1898, cal. .30, 30-inch barrel, 46.06-inch stock, total length 49.188 inches. Bolt action. Trigger guard as before. Two bands. In this model, and in later models, the bolt-handle seat was cut off flush with the receiver, and the seat for the bolt handle in the stock made correspondingly smaller. A new leaf-type rear sight, like the Model 1902 rear sight except that there was no milling on the leaf edges, was provided. $165–$230.

U.S. MAGAZINE CARBINE MODEL 1898, cal. .30, 22-inch barrel, 30.05-inch stock, total length 40.9 inches. Bolt action. Same trigger guard dimensions. One band. Otherwise similar to U.S. Magazine Rifle, Model 1898. $175–$275.

U.S. MAGAZINE CARBINE MODEL 1899, same dimensions as Model 1898 carbine except that the stock was 32 inches long, whereas the length of the stock of the former was 30.05 inches. A band is held by a pin piercing the stock. There are a few other small differences. Most collectors and dealers treat this as a Model 1898 carbine, but there are enough who regard it as a separate model to justify this listing. $150–$250.

U.S. EXPERIMENTAL MAGAZINE RIFLE MODEL 1900, cal. .30, 30.75-inch barrel, 47-inch stock, total length 49.5 inches. Bolt action. Trigger guard 8.25 inches long with round ends. Two bands. The board of officers convened at the Springfield Armory described this entirely experimental rifle as embodying features of both the Mauser and the then existing U.S. magazine rifles, but it is also described by some authorities as having an action resembling the Mannlicher. It will be noticed that we do not list this as a model, because even an experimental model should have a record of use, preferably by troops in the field, sufficient to regard it as more than a sample. $500–$600.

U.S. MAGAZINE RIFLE MODEL 1901, cal. .30, 29.5-inch barrel, 48-inch stock, total length 50.25 inches. Bolt action. Two bands. This differed from the Krag-Jorgensen in having the magazine in the stock, under the receiver, instead of projecting to one side. Two lugs, instead of one, hold the bolt against the force of recoil. A cleaning rod under the barrel was supposed to be pulled into place and function as a bayonet. This rifle is an actual model and not merely an experimental rifle. Very rare. $750–$1,000.

U.S. MAGAZINE RIFLE MODEL 1903, cal. .30, 23.5-inch barrel, 41.5-inch stock, total length 43.5 inches. Bolt action. Two bands. The first barrels were marked on top with the bursting bomb of the Ordnance Department, the initials for the arsenal (either R.I.A. for Rock Island Arsenal or S.A. for Springfield Arsenal), and the year. The month in which the rifle was made was later added, such as "12–09" to show that it was manufactured in December, 1909. This rifle was first equipped with a rod bayonet, and then in 1905 when the great President Theodore Roosevelt objected to the worthlessness of the rod bayonet, the knife bayonet was adopted. The change in bayonet models and the various changes in ammunition caused slight changes in the rifle. From the time of its adoption to the present, the Model 1903 has been one of the "Guns of Glory," for it was carried into action by soldiers, sailors, and marines in campaigns, expeditions, and 2 world wars. It will be used again in World War III. After alteration in 1905, the new dimensions were: 23.79-inch barrel, 40.166-inch stock, total length 43.212 inches. Since this is an excellent big-game hunting rifle, shooting condition affects value. $125–$225.

U.S. RIFLE MODEL 1903, GALLERY PRACTICE, cal. .22. This rifle is exactly the same as the U.S. Rifle Model 1903, cal. .30, except that the barrel is cal. .22; the mainspring was made weaker; and the rear sight leaf is graduated for .22-cal. ammunition. It was assembled from parts made for the service rifle, which were below standard but still strong enough for the reduced pressure of the .22-cal. cartridge. A cartridge was loaded into a holder that resembled a dummy cartridge. Five dummy-like holders could be loaded in the chamber like .30-cal. cartridges. The author was personally trained in marksmanship with this model in 1919. Most of these rifles were eventually scrapped. $185–$265.

Bullets for cal. .30 rifles: The German-type "spitzer" bullet was adopted for the armed services in 1906. This bullet had a pointed nose and a flat base and weighed 150 grains. It was used until the adoption of the 172-grain bullet with boattail base in 1924.

U.S. RIFLE MODEL 1903 NM, cal. .30. Same as Model 1903, cal. .30, but manufactured at the Springfiled Armory especially for use in the National Matches, held annually at Camp Perry, Ohio. Some of these were issued to various organizations of the Army, Navy, and Marine Corps for teams to use in practice; hence they found their way into combat organizations and have been fired in action. The barrel is especially selected and star-gauged. The bolt is usually finished bright. The stock is the pistol-grip type. Many of the parts are specially finished. Since this is an excellent hunting rifle, shooting condition affects value. $275–$425.

U.S. RIFLE MODEL 1903 A-1, cal. .30. This is the Model 1903, standard issue service rifle, made with the type-C pistol grip of the National Match rifle, authorized for service use in 1930. Shooting condition affects value. $75–$135.

U.S. RIFLE MODEL 1917, cal. .30 (Enfield), 26-inch barrel, 42.875-inch stock, total length 46.5 inches. Bolt action. Two bands. The British Enfield Rifle Model 1914, then being manufactured in the United States for the British government, was modified by reducing the caliber from .303 to .30; the face of the bolt was changed to take the headless case of the Model 1906 cartridge; and the magazine was altered to provide for the difference between the length of the British and the American cartridges. This rifle was manufactured, under contract with the U. S. Government, by the Winchester Repeating Arms Co., New Haven, Conn.; the Remington Arms, U.M.C. Co., Ilion, N.Y.; and by the Eddystone Rifle Plant of Pa., which was owned by the Remington Arms Co. of Del. This rifle was used in World War I and carried by troops for several years after that war. Shooting condition affects value. $100–$165.

U.S. RIFLE MODEL 1922, cal. .22, long rifle, 24-inch barrel, 31.25-inch stock. Total length 43.625 inches. Bolt action. Trigger guard 8.5 inches long with round ends. One band. Clip-fed, 5 rounds to the clip. Shotgun-type butt plate. Sporting-type half-stock. Lyman No. 48 rear sight. Used for gallery practice. Shooting condition affects value. $175–$225.

U.S. RIFLE MODEL 1922 M-1, cal. 22, long rifle, issued 1927. Same as Model 1922, cal. .22, long rifle, but clip flush with floor plate; service-type butt plate; bolt has single striker, new type firing-pin rod and ejector; but differences in bolt assembly are not necessarily found on all of the rifles of this model if bolt was changed. Shooting condition affects value. $175–$225.

U.S. RIFLE MODEL 1922 M-2, cal. .22, long rifle. Same as preceding model, but bolt assembly made to provide for head-space adjustment in the post or regimental armorer's shop, instead of requiring adjustment at a manufacturing arsenal or ordnance depot. Shooting condition affects value. $175–$225.

U.S. RIFLE MODEL 1936 M-1, cal. .30 (Garand), 22-inch barrel, 29.75-inch stock. Total length 43 inches. Bolt action (automatic). Trigger guard 6.75 inches long with square ends. Two bands. This is a self-loading shoulder weapon, gas-operated, clip-fed, and air-cooled. It weighs approximately

9 pounds, and the bayonet weighs an additional pound. The ammunition is loaded in clips of 8 rounds. Bandoleers of ammunition for this rifle have 6 pockets with a total of 40 rounds and weigh 3¼ pounds each. The 3 wooden parts are the stock, the front hand guard, and the rear hand guard. $250–$385.

# Chapter 22

## U.S. SECONDARY MARTIAL SHOULDER ARMS

THE United States secondary martial shoulder arms include, in the strict sense of the term, only those that were not officially adopted by the United States for its armed forces, or were not purchased by the states for troops mustered into the federal service in time of war, but were tested by the United States or used in a restricted sense for experimental purposes only. However, it is an old established custom of collectors and dealers to include in this group many arms that should be classified as U.S. martial shoulder arms, and others that are not known to have been martially used in any manner.

This is the only chapter for which the author offers an apology. Bowing to the old custom, he has described here arms that in future editions of this text may be included in the chapter on U.S. martial shoulder arms, and arms that belong in chapters on civilian arms, although he has included several that are properly classified here.

Several arms that were tested, and hence belong in this secondary group, are not described here because they are not usually found in collections or on the shelves of dealers. It would be foolish to identify and evaluate arms that very rarely enter the arms trade and that are of little interest to the majority of collectors.

BALL & LAMSON REPEATING CARBINE, sometimes called Ball Magazine Carbine, using .56-56 Spencer r.f. cartridge. Seven-shot. Barrel 21 inches, marked "U.S. Ball's Patent, June 23, 1863, Mar. 15, 1864." U.S. Government received 1,002 May 14, 1865, under the contract of 1864. Total length 37.5 inches. Weight 7 lbs. 6 oz. Tubular magazine. Lever action. The actual martial use of this weapon has been questioned. $425–$750.

SAME, but cal. .44, long r.f., with a smaller hammer. $325–$590.

BALLARD BREECHLOADING CARBINE, cal. .54, using No. 56 Ballard r.f. cartridge, and later the Spencer .56-56, which did not fit properly. Round barrel 22 inches, marked "Ballard's Patent, Nov. 5, 1861" and "Merwin & Bray, Agents." Total length 38 inches. Weight 7 lbs. This was the earlier military carbine, and we have no knowledge of its martial use. $180–$310.

BALLARD BREECHLOADING CARBINE, cal. 44, r.f., lever action. Round barrel 22 inches. Total length 37.25 inches. Weight 6.375 lbs. Frame marked "Ball & Williams, Worcester, Mass." and "Merwin & Bray, Agents, New York," and "Ballard's Patent, Nov. 5, 1861." All parts are marked with the serial number. The U.S. bought 1,509 during the Civil War. Solid breechblocks on early specimens. $165–$280.

BALLARD BREECHLOADING MILITARY RIFLE, also called Ballard Military Rifle, cal. .54, using No. 56 Ballard r.f. cartridge, with 30-inch round barrel, like the Ballard Breechloading Carbine, cal. .54, except for the barrel length. $225–$375.

BALLARD "KENTUCKY STATE" MILITARY RIFLE. Same marks as on other Ballards, except that it is also stamped on the top of the frame "Kentucky," supposedly because the State of Kentucky bought it for its Home Guard, but this story has not been verified by the author. Round barrel, 30 inches, total length 45.25 inches, weight 8 lbs. $240–$370.

BURNSIDE BREECHLOADING RIFLED CARBINE, FIRST MODEL, cal. .54 c.f., metallic cartridge fired with a percussion cap. Lever action. A movable chamber is pivoted in front, under the barrel. When the breechblock is closed, a forward movement pushes the tapered cartridge into the barrel. This is the first model and lacks the Foster trigger-guard lock. $525–$850.

BURNSIDE BREECHLOADING RIFLED CARBINE, SECOND MODEL. Barrel marked on top "Cast Steel 1861." Lock plate marked "Burnside Rifle Co., Providence, R.I." Breech marked on top "Burnside's Patent, Mar. 25, 1856" with a serial number. This second model does not have a wooden fore stock and has a single-hinge breechblock requiring a long hammer. A latch and catch patented by Geo. P. Foster are arranged so that the latch extends under the trigger and moves with it, and has its fulcrum carried by the guard lever to operate the charge holder or movable breech. $265–$500.

BURNSIDE BREECHLOADING RIFLED CARBINE, THIRD MODEL. Barrel marked "Cast Steel 1862." This third model resembles the second, but the hammer has a different shape, and there is a wooden fore stock. $285–$445.

BURNSIDE BREECHLOADING RIFLED CARBINE, FOURTH MODEL. Breech frame marked on top "Burnside's Patent Model of 1864" with the serial number. The barrel is blued and the frame casehardened. Navy models are tinned. Instead of a screw there is a removable hinge pin. The breechblock has a double hinge action. $245–$440.

*Note: The U.S. Government bought 55,567 Burnside carbines during the Civil War, all models of which were in service.*

COLT—See Chapter 26.

COSMOPOLITAN LEVER–ACTION, BREECHLOADING, PERCUSSION CARBINE, cal. .50, paper cartridge. Barrel 19 inches, total length 39 inches, weight 6.5 lbs. Marked "Gwyn & Campbell, Hamilton, Ohio" on the lock plate, and "Union Rifle" on the frame. This carbine is sometimes called the Gross, the Grapevine, or the Gwyn & Campbell carbine, and occasionally the Union carbine. $275–$505.

GALLAGHER BREECHLOADING CARTRIDGE CARBINE, cal. .50, using the Spencer .56-50 r.f. cartridge, 22-inch barrel, total length 38 inches, weight 7.5 lbs. The War Department bought 5,000 in 1865. $250–$450.

GALLAGHER BREECHLOADING PERCUSSION CARBINE, cal. .50, percussion using Poultney foil cartridge sometimes called a metallic cartridge. Lock plate marked "Manufactured by Richardson & Overman, Philadelphia" with the serial number and "Gallagher's Patent, July 17, 1860." Barrel 22 inches, total length 38 inches, weight 7.5 lbs. The U.S. Government bought 22,728 of these carbines during the Civil War. Falling block. Lever action slides barrel forward and tips it up for loading. $290–$495.

GIBBS BREECHLOADING, RIFLED, PERCUSSION CARBINE, cal. .54, paper cartridge. Barrel 22 inches, total length 38.25 inches, weight 7.375 lbs. Barrel moves forward and the rear tilts up to load, hence this is sometimes called a sliding-barrel type. Lock plate marked "William F. Brooks Mfg. Co., New York." Breech marked "L.H. Gibbs, Pat'd Jan. 8, 1856." The U.S. Government bought 1,052 of these carbines in 1863. $440–$600.

GREENE'S BREECHLOADING, RIFLED, PERCUSSION CARBINE, cal. .53, paper cartridge. Barrel 18 inches, marked on tang "Greene's Patent, June 17, 1854." Lock plate marked "Mass. Arms Co., Chicopee Falls, Mass., U.S.A., 1856." Tape-box cover marked "Maynard's Patent, Sept. 22, 1845."

Lock plate marked with British crown, "V.R.," and British proof marks, as have all other parts too. Barrel also stamped with double arrow and "S," which were British marks to show that a weapon was no longer used. Prior to Nov. 5, 1857, 170 of these were supposedly issued to the army. It has been said that the British bought 2,000 in 1858, that they were not actually accepted, and that they were sold to the U.S. Government during the Civil War. Total length 34.5 inches. Rotating-barrel type. $290–$600.

GREENE'S UNDERHAMMER, BOLT–ACTION, PERCUSSION RI-FLE, cal. .53, oval bore, paper cartridge, 36-inch barrel. Total length 52.5 inches. Weight 10 lbs. Marked "Greene's Patent Nov. 17, 1857." The caliber of the bore before cutting was .53, and the cut was 0.008 inch deep on each side; hence the caliber is sometimes shown as .546. Made at Millbury, Mass., in the Waters shops, with machinery bought from Charles Lancaster, of London, England, who had made oval-bore rifles in England previously. The U.S. War Department bought 900 of these rifles during the Civil War. It is assumed that some were used at the Battle of Antietam, since bullets fired through this type of rifling were found afterward on the battlefield. $385–$635.

HENRY LEVER–ACTION CARTRIDGE, MAGAZINE RIFLE, cal. .44 Henry r.f. (bored cal. .42, with grooves about 0.005-inch deep, making actual cal. .43 for a .44 bullet), 24-inch barrel. Total length 43.5 inches. Weight 9.25 lbs. The War Department bought 1,731 Henry rifles, and several of the states bought them for their troops. It is reported that about 10,000 were made. It is known that they were carried by United States soldiers on Sherman's march through Georgia. Marked "Henry's Patent Oct. 16, 1860. Manufact'd by the New Haven Arms Co., New Haven, Ct." Brass frame. This was described by the Confederates as "that damned Yankee rifle that is loaded on Sunday and fired all week." $1,915–$3,785.

SAME, but made with iron frame instead of brass frame. $3,265–$5,165.

SAME, but with martial marks. $2,535–$4,715.

SAME, but engraved. $3,115–$6,100.

HOTCHKISS—See Winchester, below.

*Note on Jenks shoulder arms: The Jenks martial-type shoulder arms described below might belong in the "U.S. Martial" classification, but because we are not certain of their official status we have classified them as U.S. secondary martial.*

JENKS BREECHLOADING FLINTLOCK CARBINE, cal. .69, but also reported as cal. 64, 19.5-inch barrel, total length 36 inches, weight 6 lbs. 4 oz. Barrel marked on top of breech "1839, Wm. Jenks, U.S.N.W.P.,P." and marked on lock plate "Chicopee Falls Co., M.S." Breech action consists of a sliding bolt linked to a hinged lever. To retract the bolt, the lever is raised and swung backward, thus making it possible to load the powder and ball from the breech. Brass pan with high fence. Two flat, pin-held bands. Sling swivel at rear of trigger-guard plate. Ramrod and hammer resemble those on the U.S. muskets manufactured about 1835. Beware of percussion carbines altered back to flintlock. Values indicated are for genuine, original flintlock. $2,500–$3,365.

JENKS BREECHLOADING, NAVY, PERCUSSION CARBINE, cal. .52, 24.5-inch barrel, total length 41.5 inches, weight 6 lbs. Barrel marked "N.P. Ames, Springfield, Mass." and "U.S.N.," although some specimens are marked "Wm. Jenks, U.S.N." with initials and "1846" on the barrel, marked "N.P. Ames, Springfield, Mass." on the lock plate. Whether this was used by the Navy or by the Revenue Service (predecessor of the U.S. Coast Guard) is apparently uncertain. $325–$535.

SAME, but made with a tape lock and a change in the hammer to cut the tape. Barrel marked "Wm. Jenks, U.S.N.,R.P.," and "P," and "1847." Made of cast steel. $350–$585.

JENKS BREECHLOADING, NAVY, PERCUSSION CARBINE. Same, but made by Remington, marked on barrel "Wm. Jenks, U.S.N.,R.P.," "P," and "1847," and "Cast Steel." Lock plate marked "Remington's Herkimer, N.Y." Made as originally, with tape primer. $400–$620.

JENKS BREECHLOADING, NAVY, PERCUSSION RIFLE, cal. .54, 36-inch browned barrel marked "Wm. Jenks, U.S.N.,R.P. 1844 P." Total length 52.5-inches. Weight with bayonet 7.5 lbs. Three screw-held flat bands. Brass butt plate, bands, and trigger guard. Bright steel "mule-ear" lock. Side hammer. No ramrod. Supposedly bought by the Navy. $400–$640.

JENKS BREECHLOADING, ARMY, PERCUSSION CARBINE, cal. .52, barrel about 25 inches long, and total length about 41 inches. This carbine was tested by the Army in 1842, and there is a record of its being issued to 2 companies of dragoons in 1844, but there is no certainty about its being more than a trial weapon. $690–$1,025.

JOSLYN BREECHLOADING PERCUSSION CARBINE, cal. .50, paper cartridge, 22-inch barrel, total length 38 inches, weight 7.25 lbs. Top lever marked "Pat'd by B.F. Joslyn, Aug. 23, 1855." Lock marked "A.H. Waters & Co., Milbury, Mass." The U.S. War Department bought 200 in 1861. It is reported that 40 were sent to Kansas in the slavery war of 1856. $430–$600.

SAME, but cal. .56, with small changes. Marked "B.F. Joslyn Fire Arms Co. Stonington, Conn." The War Department bought 660 in 1862. $375–$570.

SAME, but later model, with firing pin protected by circular shield, heavier locking device for breech, and knob for breech operation. $340–$505.

JOSLYN BREECHLOADING CARTRIDGE CARBINE, cal. .54, Spencer r.f. cartridge. Swinging block. It is reported that 2,200 of these were bought by the War Department in 1863. $270–$580.

SAME, but later model, cal. .52, using the Spencer .56-56 r.f. cartridge, 22-inch barrel. Total length 38.75 inches, weight 6.625 lbs. Breechblock marked "B.F. Joslyn's Patent October 8, 1861," and lock plate marked "Joslyn Fire Arms Co., Stonington, Conn. 1864." The War Department bought 8,000 from 1864 to 1865. $265–$400.

JOSLYN BREECHLOADING ARMY RIFLE, cal. .50-70 Govt., 35.5-inch barrel, total length 52 inches, weight 9.25 lbs. Lock plate marked "U.S. Springfield 1864," and breechblock marked "B. F. Joslyn's Patent Oct 6, 1861, June 24, 1862." Supposedly made at the U.S. Armory, Springfield, Mass., for experimental firing. Originally made for rim-fire but changed for center-fire in 1871. The exact martial status of this weapon is unknown. Apparently all pieces were sold by the War Department to civilians who later exported them. $475–$690.

LEE BREECHLOADING CARTRIDGE CARBINE, cal. .44, long r.f., 21.5-inch barrel, total length 36.5 inches, weight 5.5 lbs. Marked "Lee Arms Co., Milwaukee, Wis." Patented by James Lee, Stevens Point, Wis., July 27, 1862. Lee had a contract, but his carbines were apparently not accepted by the War Department, and there is no record of martial use. Their chief interest is the fact that they were made in the Middle West during the Civil War by a man born in Scotland, who spent almost every cent he had in an effort to make arms for those who were giving their lives to save this United States. $300–$450.

LINDNER RISING-BLOCK, BREECHLOADING, PERCUSSION CARBINE, cal. .58 paper cartridge, 23-inch barrel, total length 39 inches, weight 6 lbs. Lock plate marked "Amoskeag Mfg. Co., Manchester, N.H." with eagle and "1864." $465–$675.

SAME, but later model, breech marked "Edward Lindner's Patent, March 29, 1859." A total of 892 Lindner carbines were bought by the War Department during the Civil War, probably including both models described here. $475–$710.

SAME, but marked "Ed. Lindner's Patent 1858. S. Meyer A. Zurich." $240–$420.

MAYNARD BREECHLOADING PERCUSSION CARBINE, cal. .50, metallic cartridge fired with a percussion primer. Frame marked "Maynard

Arms Co., Washington" and "Manufactured by Mass. Arms Co., Chicopee Falls." The cartridge has a wide large base, with a small hole admitting the spark from the primer when ignited. Made with Maynard tape lock, patch box with Maynard patent markings, adjustable rear sight on tang, sling swivel. Barrel 20 inches, total length 36.75 inches, weight about 6.5 lbs. The War Department issued 143 in 1859, 100 in 1860, and probably many more later. This carbine was also bought at the beginning of the Civil War by the Confederates and used against the United States during that rebellion. $240–$375.

SIMILAR, but made without tape priming system. Marked "Edward Maynard, Patented May 27, 1851, Dec. 6, 1859. Manufactured by Mass. Arms Co., Chicopee Falls." Tilt-up 20-inch barrel, total length 36.75 inches, and weight about 6 lbs. The War Department bought 20,002 during 1864 and 1865. This is sometimes called the Maynard Carbine, Model 1863. $215–$360.

MERRILL, LATROBE & THOMAS BREECHLOADING PERCUSSION CARBINE, cal. .54 or cal. .58 paper cartridge, usually the latter. Probably made by Remington but unmarked throughout except a few presentation specimens whose markings are of little identification value as to the maker. Made with Maynard priming system for loose ball and powder, or ball and paper cartridge. Outside lock. One variation has a friction spring and pin holding the lever in place when open, and another has a side lever instead of the usual top lever, together with an improved Maynard mechanism. The martial use of this weapon has not been verified. It is presented here for the record only. Details vary. $340–$520.

MERRILL BREECHLOADING PERCUSSION CARBINE, cal. .54, 20-inch barrel, total length 38 inches, weight 6.5 lbs. Lock plate marked "J. H. Merrill, Balto. Pat. July, 1858, April 9, May 21–28, '61." Top lever marked "J.H. Merrill, Balto, Pat. July, 1858." The War Department bought 14,255 from 1861 to 1864. $260–$340.

*Note regarding Merrill weapons: The Merrill patents essentially cover conversion methods which were applied to several makes and models of rifles and carbines of the older vintage. For this reason there are many specimens which can be described as Merrill, yet these same weapons also include Maynard priming features and were actually made by manufacturers other than Merrill or Maynard. In arms listings they should be listed first according to the manufacturer, and then according to the various features added to the basic weapon. We have tried to follow this method in this text, but in some cases we have had to deviate in order to adhere fairly closely to the old established custom of the collectors and dealers, many of whom list weapons according to the name of the inventor of some attached feature.*

MERRILL BREECHLOADING, NAVY, PERCUSSION RIFLE, cal. .54,

Merrill foil or paper cartridge. Lock plate marked "J.H. Merrill Balto. Pat. July, 1858. Apl. 9, May 21-28, '61." Top lever marked "J.H. Merrill, Balto. Pat. July, 1858." Browned barrel 34 inches, total length 48.5 inches, weight 9 lbs. Brass bands. Brass patch box. Saber-bayonet stud. The United States bought 770 in 1862 and 1863. Some specimens have tinned finish for Navy use. $385–$565.

PALMER BREECHLOADING CARTRIDGE CARBINE, cal. .50, r.f., using Spencer .56-50 r.f. cartridge, and also the .56-52. Bolt action, single-shot. Breech marked on top "Wm. Palmer Patent Dec. 22, 1863." Lock plate marked "U.S. E. G. Lamson & Co. Windsor, Vt. 1865." The United States bought 1,001, but apparently there is no record of the number actually issued and used. $365–$605.

PEABODY BREECHLOADING CARBINE, cal. .50 r.f., metallic cartridge. Frame marked "Peabody Pat. July 22, 1862. Manfd. by Providence Tool Co., Prov. R.I. U.S.A." Single-shot. Some were made with an internal hammer, but later ones had external hammer. Further details not available. Apparently not officially used in Civil War. $225–$390.

PEABODY BREECHLOADING RIFLE, cal. .50–60 r.f., although made in other calibers. Usual specimen may have 33-inch barrel, total length of 51.5 inches, and weight of 9.5 lbs. with a triangular bayonet. Marked like the carbine on most specimens. It is emphasized that there is apparently no record of U.S. martial use, and that there are a variety of Peabody rifles and Peabody-Martini rifles, most of which were sold abroad. These Peabody arms are included here only because of the old custom of collectors who classify them in this group for some strange reason no one understands. $215–$315.

PERRY PERCUSSION CARBINE, sometimes called Perry Lever-Action, Navy, Percussion Carbine, cal. .54, paper or linen cartridge. Copper primers fed from tubular magazine in stock. Breechblock marked on top "Perry's Patent Arms Co., Newark, N.J.," or with similar words. Barrel may be marked "Cast Steel Hitchcock & Muzzey." Octagon rifled barrel 26 inches. Total length 45 inches. The breechblock, which is hung "like a cartwheel," to use Charles Winthrop Sawyer's description, swings up by the leverage of the trigger guard. This carbine was apparently used by the Navy to some extent, but its status as a U.S. martial arm is open for verification. $485–$850.

REMINGTON-KEENE BOLT-ACTION, NAVY, MAGAZINE RIFLE, cal. .45-70 Govt., 9-shot magazine, 30-inch barrel, made for U.S. Navy, and about 250 delivered about 1880. Accurate details unknown. The prototype was the Remington-Keene Sporting Magazine Rifle, with 8-shot tubular magazine, made for either .45-70 Govt. or .44–40 Winchester, with 24-inch octagonal barrel. Value shown is for Navy model if identified as such. $375–$690.

## REMINGTON-KEENE BOLT-ACTION, MILITARY, MAGAZINE CARBINE. $440–$660.

REMINGTON-LEE NAVY MAGAZINE RIFLE, MODEL 1880, cal. .45-70 Govt., 6-shot, 32-inch round barrel, total length 52 inches, weight about 9 lbs. Blued finish. Full stock, walnut. Breech marked on top "Remington Arms Co., Ilion, N.Y., U.S.A. Sole Manufacturers & Agents," followed by serial number. Breech marked on side "Pat. Nov. 4, 1879." Bought by Navy in 1880. $340–$425.

SHARPS BREECHLOADING PERCUSSION CARBINE, cal. .56, 21.5-inch barrel marked "Sharps Rifle Manufg. Co., Hartford, Conn." Total length 37.5 inches. Lock plate marked "Sharps Patent 1852." Breech tang marked "Sharps Patent 1848" followed by serial number. Brass-mounted. Brass patch box in stock. Sling-ring bar extends from band and sling ring to breech frame. This is the sloping-breech type. Made with pellet-priming device. Elevating rear sight with single leaf. Tested by Army. $440–$750.

SAME, but made with fixed rear sight, slightly different sling-ring bar, and Maynard priming device marked "Edward Maynard Patentee, 1845." Probably tested by Army. $440–$750.

SIMILAR, but with lock plate having hammer inside the lock plate, special Maynard priming device marked like the previous one, rear sight without graduating slide on the single elevating leaf, sling-ring bar like the first model described, butt plate tang marked "U.S. 1852." Probably tested by Army. $500–$950.

SHARPS & HANKINS, NAVY RIFLE, cal. .56 Sharps & Hankins, using cal. .52 r.f. cartridge, 32.75-inch barrel marked "Sharps & Hankins, Philadelphia" and "Sharps Pat. 1859." Total length 47.5 inches, weight 8.5 lbs. Sliding-barrel type. A few were bought by the Navy, and it is known that they were test-fired by the U.S. Marine Corps. Values are for specimens with Navy marks. $350–$550.

SAME, but carbine with 24-inch barrel, total length 38.625 inches, weight 7.5 lbs. Some barrels were supposedly covered with leather for Navy and Marine Corps use aboard ship. Values are for specimens with Navy marks. If barrel has original leather covering, add 25%. $375–$500.

*Note on Sharps values: The model brought out in 1859 is worth less than the one produced in 1865. There is so much variation among the Sharps arms, which affects value, that it requires an experienced collector or dealer, making a careful visual inspection, to determine identification and value.*

SMITH BREECHLOADING PERCUSSION CARBINE, cal. .52, rubber cartridge, or foil cartridge covered with paper, 22-inch barrel marked "Manufactured by Am'n. M'ch'n. Wks., Springfield, Mass." and "Address Poultney & Trimble, Baltimore, U.S.A." Also marked "Smith's Patent Ju. 23, 1857." Total length 39.5 inches. Weight 7.5 lbs. Tested by the Army in 1857. $360–$575.

SAME, but marked "Manufactured by Mass. Arms Co., Chicopee Falls." The War Department bought 300 in 1860, and 30,062 from 1862 to 1865. Which ones were bought is not certain but apparently practically all Smith Carbines can be regarded as secondary material. $360–$575.

SPENCER REPEATING RIFLE, ARMY MODEL, cal. .52, using Spencer No. 56 r.f. cartridge, sometimes called the .56-56. Barrel 30 inches, marked "Spencer Repeating Rifle Co. Boston, Mass. Pat'd. March 6, 1860." The War Department accepted 7,500 in 1862 and 1863, and they were used by the Michigan Cavalry Brigade at the Battle of Gettysburg, and by Wilder's Lightning Brigade in other battles. Total length 47 inches, weight 10 lbs. Seven-shot. Falling block. $315–$490.

SAME, but made with 32-inch barrel and provided with cleaning rod. Frame marked "Spencer Repeating Rifle, Pat'd. March 6, 1860, Manuf'd at Prov. R.I., by Burnside Rifle Co., Model 1865," followed by a serial number. Made with the Stabler cutoff which was patented in 1865. May have been used in Indian campaigns. $350–$555.

SPENCER BREECHLOADING, REPEATING CARBINE, cal. .54 r.f., 22-inch round barrel, 7-shot. Total length 39 inches. Weight 8.25 lbs. Marked like first model of Spencer Rifle. The War Department accepted 61,685 from 1863 to 1865, of which number all but 15,500 were delivered before the surrender of General Robert E. Lee. These carbines were issued to the Michigan Cavalry Brigade and Wilder's Lightning Brigade to replace the Spencer rifles previously issued. Falling block. $285–$415.

SAME, but cal. .52, with 19-inch round barrel and Stabler cutoff. The War Department accepted these near the end of and shortly after the Civil War. Used in Indian campaigns. $315–$485.

SAME, but cal. .50, 22-inch barrel, with Stabler cutoff. Used in Indian campaigns. About 5,000 were accepted in 1865 and 1866. $315–$490.

SAME, but 20-inch barrel, using Spencer .56-50 r.f. cartridge. Marked "Spencer Repeating Rifle Model 1865, Pat'd. Mar. 6, 1860. Manufactured at Prov. R.I. by Burnside Rifle Co." These are called the Indian Model because they were made too late for the Civil War and were used in the Indian campaigns. It is known that Custer's Seventh Cavalry carried these carbines at the Battle of the Washita, Nov. 27, 1868, and that other troops in the Indian campaigns carried this and other Spencer carbines. Total length 37 inches. Weight 8.75 lbs. $315–$530.

STARR BREECHLOADING PERCUSSION CARBINE, cal. .54, Starr's linen or paper cartridge, 21-inch barrel. Serial number stamped on the side of the right breechblock extension. Total length 38.625 inches. Weight 7.375 lbs. Back strap marked "Starr's Patent Set. 14, 1858." The War Department bought and accepted 20,601 in 1863 and 1864. $400–$570.

STARR BREECHLOADING CARTRIDGE CARBINE, cal. .52 r.f., using a Starr copper cartridge or the Spencer .56-56. In 1865, 5,001 of these carbines were delivered to the U.S. Government. Very similar in appearance and markings to the percussion model. $440–$600.

SYMMES BREECHLOADING PERCUSSION CARBINE, cal. .54, paper cartridge. Breechblock rotates upward by lever action, around an axis at the rear, bringing the hole in the breechblock in line with the bore to insert the cartridge which is fired by a priming system similar to the Maynard. Patented by John C. Symmes, Watertown Arsenal, Mass., Nov. 16, 1858, Patent No. 22,094. In 1856 the War Department ordered 200, and in 1857 correspondence showed that 20 had been delivered. Apparently there is no record of further deliveries or of martial use. Descriptive details are lacking. $1,235–$1,785.

TRIPLETT & SCOTT MAGAZINE CARBINE, cal. .50, using Spencer .56-50 cartridge. Receiver marked on upper tang "Triplett & Scott Patent Dec 6, 1864." Frame marked "Meriden Man'f'g. Co., Meriden, Conn." and "Kentucky." Barrel 20 inches, total length 38 inches, weight 7.25 lbs. Also made with a 30-inch barrel without change of value. Rotating barrel. Seven-shot magazine in stock. Barrel and forearm make a half turn to feed cartridges from the magazine in the stock to the barrel. It is reported that this carbine was made for the Kentucky Home Guard during the Civil War. $325–$490.

VIRGINIA MANUFACTORY FLINTLOCK MUSKET, cal. .69, 41.5-inch smoothbore barrel. Total length 56.5 inches. Weight 9 lbs. 8 oz. Brass pan. Band springs of lower and middle bands are in front of bands. Lower sling swivel on trigger-guard retaining stud. Lock plate marked "Virginia Manufactory," with the word "Manufactory" in script, and "Richmond" in a curved line, with the date, but the word "Richmond" is arranged differently from the way it is on the rifle described below. The rare model is dated from 1802 to 1809 and has a gooseneck cock. $1,000–$1,450.

SAME, made before 1809, but converted to percussion. $550–$675.

SAME, but made and marked after 1809, with double-neck hammer; but flintlock. $800–$1,250.

SAME, but made after 1809, converted to percussion. $550–$675.

VIRGINIA MANUFACTORY FLINTLOCK RIFLE, cal. .54, 39-inch octagon barrel. Total length 54.5 inches. Weight 9 lbs. 14 oz. Full-length walnut stock to end of barrel with brass tip. Brass butt plate, patch-box cover, and trigger guard. Patch-box-cover spring catch at bottom of stock. Wooden ramrod held by 3 brass ramrod ferrules. Lock plate marked "Virginia" between cock and pan, and "Richmond," which is arranged differently from that on Virginia Manufactory Flintlock Musket. $1,250–$1,875.

SAME, but converted to percussion. $950–$1,350.

SAME, but cal. about .44, 44-inch octagon barrel. Total length is 58 inches. Marked with Virginia State marks. $750–$1,450.

*Note: Ornamental patch box, bearing some legend or motto, may be found on Civil War models.*

WARNER CARTRIDGE CARBINE, cal. .50 r.f. Warner metallic cartridge, although chamber diameter is 0.52 inch. Also chambered for the Spencer .56-50 cartridge. Marked "James Warner, Springfield, Mass., Warner's Patent." The War Department bought 2,500 in 1865. James Warner, who was the inventor, also did business as the Springfield Arms Co. Swinging block. Brass frame. Manually operated extractor. $500–$685.

WESSON BREECHLOADING CARTRIDGE CARBINE, cal. .44, long r.f., metallic cartridge. Barrel 24 inches, total length 39.25 inches, weight 5.75 lbs. Double trigger. Marked "F. Wesson's Patent Oct. 25, 1859 & Nov. 11, 1862" and also marked "B. Kittredge & Co., Cincinnati, O." The War Department bought 151 of these carbines. The states of Indiana, Kansas, Kentucky, and Missouri bought these carbines for troops they sent into the Union Army, and possibly they were also bought by other states. $240–$500.

# Chapter 23

## *CONFEDERATE SHOULDER ARMS*

CONFEDERATE shoulder arms include all shoulder arms used by the Confederate States of America during the Civil War. This is an extremely broad classification because it includes all United States martial shoulder arms made before the end of the Civil War, many of the United States secondary martial shoulder arms, all of the shoulder arms of martial size made in the Confederacy during the Civil War, all of the martial-type shoulder arms made in the Southern states before the Civil War, and many European arms, especially English models. The Confederates fired at the United States Army everything that would shoot, including flintlock, percussion, and cartridge arms, not forgetting shotguns.

When is a shoulder arm a Confederate weapon? Must it have Confederate or Southern state marks to place it in this classification? How is it possible to distinguish between a genuine Confederate-marked weapon and one that someone has marked with counterfeit words or letters? Exactly what are the values of Confederate weapons? All of these questions must be left in the air until more information is in the possession of collectors and dealers. Meanwhile the collector of Confederate arms should first study all U.S. martial shoulder arms made before 1865, and then he should read the outstanding text on the subject: *Firearms of the Confederacy*, by Claude E. Fuller and Richard D. Steuart, published 1944 by Standard Publications, Inc., Huntington, W. Va. Even then, there will be many questions which cannot be answered accurately.

In this chapter we have included those Confederate shoulder arms that we consider to be typical and characteristic. In general we have not included arms that are described in the chapters on U.S. martial and U.S. secondary martial shoulder arms, even though many of those arms were used by the Confederacy.

336

ASHEVILLE ARMORY, N.C.-ENFIELD RIFLE, cal. .58, 32.625-inch barrel with a saber-bayonet lug near the muzzle. Total length 48.625 inches. Brass butt plate, stock tip, and trigger guard. Iron bands without springs. Fixed rear sight. Weight without bayonet 8 lbs. 6 oz. Lock plate marked "Asheville, N.C." This resembles the Enfield Short Pattern Rifle imported from England and widely used by Confederate Infantry. The Asheville Armory made arms principally for the North Carolina forces. $550–$790.

M. A. BAKER RIFLE, converted from U.S. Rifle Model 1817, "The Common Rifle," flintlock to percussion. Cal. .52, 36-inch barrel marked "N. Carolina" and the date on the tang. Total length 51 inches. Lug for sword bayonet. Lock plate marked "M. A. Baker, Fayetteville, N.C." Butt plate tang marked "U.S." $475–$600.

BLUNT (OR OTHER MAKE) RIFLED MUSKET, cal. .58, 39-inch barrel. Total length 55 inches. Weight 8.75 lbs. Brass trigger guard and butt plate. Iron bands. Closely resembles British Enfield Rifled Musket. Black walnut stock. Supposedly made by Orison Blunt, New York City, but some authorities think that perhaps it was made by the Marshall Manufacturing Co., Holly Spring, Miss., who operated the Holly Spring Armory, and who were also known as W. S. McElwaine & Co., and as Jones, McElwaine & Co. Whoever made this weapon apparently used a British barrel and British sights but copied the bands, trigger guard, butt plate, and stock in their own plant. The year of manufacture, usually 1862, is marked forward of the hammer. A shield with the letter "M" under a spread eagle is marked in the rear of the hammer. $350–$450.

COOK & BROTHER, ATHENS, GA. INFANTRY RIFLE, cal. .58, 33-inch barrel marked with serial number and date. Total length 49 inches. Lock plate 5.375 inches long, marked "Cook & Brother, Athens, Ga." with the date and serial number forward of the hammer and the Confederate flag to the rear of the hammer. Cherry stock. Iron with cup-shaped brass end. Resembles British Enfield Rifle. All brass mountings. $455–$725.

COOK & BROTHER, ATHENS, GA. ARTILLERY RIFLE, cal. .58, 24-inch barrel marked "Athens" with the date and the word "Proved." Total length 40 inches. Lock plate marked like Cook Infantry Rifle above. Black walnut stock. British Enfield type made short. $435–$690.

COOK & BROTHER, ATHENS, GA. MUSKETOON, cal. .58, 21-inch barrel marked with a serial number. Total length 36.5 inches. Lock plate marked like Cook Infantry rifle above. British Enfield type made short. $550–$705.

DAVIS & BOZEMAN, ALABAMA RIFLE, cal. .58, 33-inch barrel marked "Ala. 1864." Total length 48 inches. Lock plate marked "D & B Ala., 1864." Brass butt plate, trigger guard, and double upper band. Davis &

Bozeman made rifles for Alabama near Central, in Cousa County. Date may be 1863 on some specimens. $625–$815.

DICKSON, NELSON & CO., ALABAMA CARBINE OR MUSKETOON, cal. .58, 24-inch barrel. Total length 40 inches. Lock plate marked "Dickson, Nelson & Company, Ala., 1864." Brass butt plate, trigger guard, band, and fore-end tip. Fixed rear sight. Swivel ramrod. $560–$815.

DICKSON, NELSON & CO. RIFLE, cal. .58, 33-inch barrel marked "Ala" and "1863." Total length 49 inches. The lock and cone seat are like those on the U.S. Rifle, Model 1841 (1842), but otherwise it resembles the U.S. Rifle, Model 1855. Flat bands with springs. All brass mountings. No lug for saber bayonet. Two-leaf rear sight. Lock plate marked "Dickson, Nelson & Co., C.S." forward of hammer, and marked "Ala 1863" behind hammer. Cherry stock. $600–$800.

SAME, but black walnut stock, fixed rear sight, longer trigger guard, oval clamping-type bands, and 1865 for the date. $540–$700.

FAYETTEVILLE RIFLE, cal. .58, 33-inch barrel marked "V," and "P," with eagle head and year. Total length 49 inches. Weight 8 lbs. 14 oz. Two bands. Brass bands, butt plate, stock tip, and trigger guard. Butt plate tang marked "C.S." Lock plate marked "Fayetteville" with spread eagle over "C.S.A." Model 1861 sights. This rifle was probably assembled from parts of existing rifles plus parts made with tools and equipment taken from Harpers Ferry. $650–$850.

J. & F. GARRETT & CO.—J.H. TARPLEY BREECHLOADING CARBINE, cal. .52, paper cartridge, 23-inch barrel. Tang marked "J.H. Tarpley's Patent Feb. 14, 1863." Stock marked "Manufactured by J & F Garrett & Co., Greensboro, N.C." and "C.S.A." Brass breech. Iron butt plate. Breechblock swings left when catch spring is opened. The Confederate Patent Office issued a patent on this weapon to Jere H. Tarpley, Feb. 14, 1863. $1,950–$3,200.

GEORGIA ARMORY RIFLE, cal. .58, 33-inch barrel. Total length 49 inches. Lock plate marked "Ga. Armory, 1862" in rear of hammer. All brass mountings. Some specimens have saber-bayonet lug. $575–$795.

GLAZE, WILLIAM & CO.—See Palmetto Armory below.

D. C. HODGKINS & CO.—U.S. RIFLED CARBINE, MODEL 1855, cal. .58, 22-inch barrel marked "P. C.S.A." Total length 36.75 inches. Stock 29.438 inches. Swivel ramrod. All iron mountings except brass fore-end tip. Lock marked on inside "C," followed by a number. Made at Macon, Ga. Probably not more than 100 were made. $1,450–$1,850.

HOLLY SPRINGS ARMORY, also known as Marshall Manufacturing Co., W. S. McElwaine & Co., and Jones, McElwaine & Co., of Holly Springs, Miss., is believed to have manufactured for the Confederacy a rifled musket of the same pattern and size as the British Enfield Rifled Musket, cal. .58, 39-inch barrel, with brass guard and brass butt plate. The lack of information makes it impossible to quote accurate values.

H. C. LAMB & CO., NORTH CAROLINA RIFLE, cal. .58, 33-inch barrel, octagon-shaped at breech. Total length 49.25 inches. Brass trigger guard, butt plate, and fore-end tip. Notched rear sight. Lug for saber bayonet. Two flat bands. Stock marked "H. C. Lamb & Co. N.C." with serial number. Made at Jamestown, N.C., for State of North Carolina. Yellow oak stock. Inferior workmanship. $590–$745.

MORSE BREECHLOADING CARBINE, altered from U.S. Model, Cadet, Model 1830 (1831), cal. .69, altered to a breechloader with the top of the barrel cut away and a breech action hinged in the rear. The firing pin is in the bolt connected to the hinge cover of the action. The original hammer was cut down and used as a cocking piece, with the firing pin attached to the tumbler inside the lock. Lock plate on some Confederate specimens is marked "U.S." with the spread eagle, "Springfield," and "1839" Barrel 40.5 inches, 43-inch stock, total length 55.75 inches. With Confederate or Southern state marks. $710–$955.

SAME, but with 36-inch barrel, 48-inch stock, total length 51 inches. With Confederate or Southern state marks. $500–$715.

PALMETTO ARMORY RIFLED MUSKET, cal. .58, percussion, rifled, 32-inch barrel, 55-inch stock. Total length 57.75 inches. Provided with long-range rear sight. Lock plate marked "Palmetto Armory, S.C." in a circle around a palmetto tree, and "Columbia, S.C." with the date behind the hammer. The butt plate tang is marked "S.C." This weapon resembles the U.S. Rifled Musket Model 1842, which, in turn, resembes the U.S. Musket Model 1842, except for the larger caliber, and the long-range rear sight. $565–$750.

PALMETTO ARMORY RIFLE, cal. .54, percussion, rifled, 33-inch barrel. Total length 48.5 inches, although greater total lengths are reported. Weight 9.75 lbs. Resembles U.S. Rifle Model 1841 (Model 1842), variously called the Mississippi Rifle, Mississippi Model, Harpers Ferry Rifle, Harpers Ferry Yager, and Windsor Rifle. Lock plate marked "Palmetto Armory, S.C." in a circle around the palmetto tree, and "Columbia, S.C." behind the hammer. $615–$835.

PALMETTO ARMORY RIFLED MUSKET, cal. .69, 42-inch barrel, total length 57.5 inches. Has long-range rear sight. Lock plate marked "Palmetto

Armory, S.C." in a circle around a palmetto tree. Marked "Columbia, S.C." and the date behind the hammer. Butt plate tang marked "S.C." Generally resembles U.S. Rifled Musket, Model 1841 (1842). $545–$790.

PALMETTO ARMORY RIFLE, cal. .58, 33-inch barrel, total length 48.5 inches. Generally resembles U.S. Rifle Model 1841 (1842), often called the Mississippi Rifle, Harper's Ferry Yager, etc. Lock plate marked "Palmetto Armory, S.C." in a circle around a palmetto tree. Marked "Columbia, S.C." behind hammer. $610–$850.

REPUBLIC OF TEXAS (TRYON) RIFLE, cal. .54, rifled with one turn in 6 feet, using round ball. Barrel 33 inches. No bayonet. Total length 48.5 inches. Weight about 9.75 lbs. Resembles U.S. Rifle, Model 1841 (Model 1842), known by many other names. Made under a contract dated Apr. 3, 1840, between Tryon Son & Co., Philadelphia, Pa., and the Republic of Texas, but after the annexation of Texas to the United States delivery of remaining arms was made to the United States. Lock plate marked "Republic of Texas" in a circle surrounding a 5-pointed star, forward of the hammer. Marked "Tryon" with a date behind the hammer. Most specimens found in collections are cal. .58, but the original was cal. .54. There is no definite record that this rifle was officially used by the Confederates, but it is logical to assume that such was the case. $1,200–$2,000.

RICHMOND RIFLED MUSKET, cal. .58, 40-inch barrel. Total length 56 inches. Weight 9.18 lbs. Resembles the U.S. Rifled Musket, Model 1855, except it has a brass butt plate; it does not have the device for cutting primer tape found on the Model 1855; it has the rear sight found on the U.S. Rifled Musket Model 1861; and it has the same type of hammer as the Model 1861. It is marked "C.S. Richmond, Va." on the front end of the lock plate, together with the year. The same year is also marked near the breech end of the barrel. $435–$575.

RICHMOND NAVY MUSKETOON, cal. .62, 30-inch smoothbore barrel. Total length 46 inches. Weight 7 lbs. 8 oz. Lock plate marked "C. S. Richmond, Va." and the year. With the exception of these details, it resembles the U.S. Rifled Musket Model 1855. Evidently the original barrel was cut down and bored smooth to the larger caliber for ease in loading. $415–$545.

RICHMOND CARBINE, cal. .58, 25-inch barrel. Total length 40.75 inches. Weight 7 lbs. 6 oz. Two bands. High front sight on barrel. Bronze butt plate and stock tip. Maynard tape lock plate, but with a new hammer and no cutting device. Sling swivels on butt, trigger guard, and top band. Lock plate marked "C.S. Richmond, Va." with the year. Barrel marked "C.S." and the year. Butt plate tang marked "C.S." $485–$600.

*Note: Lock plates on the Confederate shoulder arms made at the Richmond Armo-*

*ry may be dated 1861, 1862, 1863, 1864, or 1865. On Apr. 4, 1865, Richmond was captured by the United States Army.*

**S. C. ROBINSON ARMS MFG. CO. SHARPS CARBINE**, cal. .52, 21.5-inch barrel. Total length 37.5 inches. Barrel and lock plate marked "S. C. Robinson Arms Mfg. Co., Richmond, Va., 1862" with serial number. This was an imitation of the Sharps Carbine, but made without the priming magazine. Fixed rear sight. Brass band and butt plate. Block moves perpendicular to barrel. These carbines often burst when fired. The Confederate Government terminated the contract and used the factory to make muzzle-loaders. $525–$775.

**L.G. STURDIVANT RIFLE**, cal. .54, 32-inch barrel, total length 47 inches. All brass mountings. No marks except serial number. Made by L.G. Sturdivant for State of Alabama at Talladega, Ala. $225–$300.

**TALLAHASSEE MUZZLE-LOADING CARBINE**, cal. .58, 25-inch barrel, total length 40.75 inches. Enfield-type lock plate marked forward of hammer "C.S. Tallahassee, Ala." in 3 lines. Date marked in rear of hammer. Brass trigger guard, butt plate, and 2 clamping-type brass bands. Sling swivels. Maple stock. $650–$775.

**TALLAHASSEE BREECHLOADING CARBINE**, cal. .52, 22.5-inch barrel, total length 40 inches. Generally not marked except for "P" on barrel and breechblock and sometimes serial numbers. Bronze frame. Iron breechblock with bronze lining. Breechblock actuated by toggle lever. Often called Perry Confederate Breechloading Rifled Carbine and sometimes called Maynard Confederate Breechloading Rifled Carbine; but although it resembles both the Perry and the Maynard superficially, it differs from both. $800–$1,100.

**TARPLEY CARBINE**—See J. & F. Garrett & Co., above.

**TYLER, TEXAS-AUSTRIAN RIFLE**, cal. .54, 37.25-inch barrel. Total length 53 inches. Iron mountings. Two bands. Sling swivels attached to top band and trigger guard. Lock attached to stock with 1 screw. Lock plate marked forward of hammer "Austrian Rifle, Tyler, Tex. Cal. .54," and "C.S." with the date behind the hammer. $610–$815.

**TYLER, TEXAS-ENFIELD RIFLE**, cal. .57, 33-inch barrel marked "C.S." Total length 48.5 inches. Lock plate marked "Texas Rifle, Tyler, Cal. .57" in 3 lines in front of hammer, and "C.S." behind hammer. All brass mountings. Trigger guard shaped like Enfield. Flat bands retained by band springs. Lock attached to stock by 1 screw forward of hammer. Lug for saber bayonet. $605–$775.

*Note on Tyler, Texas, Rifles: The lock plates show a variety of markings which have puzzled collectors and historians. Also, some rifles resemble the British Enfield, some are like the Austrian Rifle, and others are like the U.S. Rifle Model 1841 (1842) Rifle, but the characteristics may be mixed in the same rifle.*

WHITNEY ENFIELD, STATE OF MISSISSIPPI RIFLE, cal. .61, percussion, 33-inch rifled barrel. Total length 49 inches. Weight 7.25 pounds. Rifled with 7 grooves. Walnut stock 44 inches long, extending to within 5 inches of muzzle. Sling-strap swivels on front band and trigger guard. Knife-blade front sight. Single-leaf adjustable rear sight. Lock plate marked "E. Whitney." No other marks. Brass trigger guard with iron trigger-guard plate. Iron butt plate. Saber-bayonet lug on barrel. This rifle was assembled as the result of a contract executed on June 6, 1860, between Eli Whitney and the State of Mississippi to manufacture rifles of the U.S. Model 1841 type. Whitney delivered 60 as samples, like the one described here, but they were assembled from old parts from various arms, including the British Enfield; hence the State of Mississippi refused to accept more and kept the samples.

WHITNEY CONFEDERATE RIFLED MUSKET, U.S. Model 1885 type, cal. .58, percussion, 40-inch barrel; almost exactly like the U.S. Rifled Musket, Model 1855, but there are no marks except "E. Whitney" faintly inscribed on the lock, which resembles other Confederate locks made in Richmond during the early days of the Civil War. Experts on Confederate arms do not know whether the whole arm was made by Whitney, or only the lock, and the official records of the Confederacy do not definitely indicate the existence of this weapon as an official model.

WYTHEVILLE, HALL MUZZLE-LOADING RIFLE, cal. .54, made from U.S. Rifle, Model 1819, Hall Breechloader, except lock and stock. A one-piece brass casting replaces the original breechblock frame and supports the entire action with the center-hung hammer. The original offset sights of the Hall flintlock are retained. Made at Wytheville, Va., from parts and with tools and machinery taken from Harpers Ferry. $850–$1,250.

## General Comments on Confederate Shoulder Arms

In addition to reading *Firearms of the Confederacy* mentioned at the beginning of this chapter, another excellent text is *Confederate Arms*, by William A. Albaugh, III, and Edward N. Simmons, published in 1957 by the Stackpole Co. The author's own book, *U.S. Martial and Semi-Martial Single-Shot Pistols*, not only includes a chapter on Confederate pistols but discusses in detail many Confederate shoulder arms and their makers because many Confederate pistols were made by those who produced shoulder arms. In *Guns of the Old West*, Confederate shoulder arms are included because, at the close of the

Civil War, many veterans of the Confederate Army went to the wild Western states and territories and took their firearms with them. Finally, the values in this chapter are the result of exhaustive correspondence and traveling. They do not necessarily reflect the scarcity of the arms, but they do result from the demand. Once more, the author cautions collectors to beware of fakes!

# Chapter 24

## COLT LONG ARMS AND REVOLVING SHOULDER ARMS OTHER THAN COLTS

COLT long arms were made first at the Paterson, New Jersey, factory and then at the Hartford factory. Since the demand by collectors is primarily for pistols and revolvers and only secondarily for long arms, even though some of the Paterson Colt shoulder arms are more rare than their counterparts among the percussion revolvers, their value is considerably less.

It must be emphasized that the above statement applies equally to all makes of firearms, not merely to the Colts in this chapter.

.Since some of the Colt shoulder arms were used by the United States forces in campaigns before the Civil War and during the suppression of that rebellion, they can be classified as U.S. martial shoulder arms. However; the historical information about these arms is so meager and so lacking in accuracy that it is difficult to state exactly which models and types were martially used.

Collectors who are interested in Colt revolving shoulder arms often collect the revolving shoulder arms of other manufacturers, hence such weapons are described later in this chapter.

Typical Paterson-made specimens are shown by Figs. 3, 4, and 5 of Plate 42. Fig. 3 is the Ring-Trigger Revolving Rifle; Fig. 4 is the Ring-Trigger Revolving Carbine with a loading lever; and Fig. 5 is the Revolving Carbine with loading lever but without the ring trigger. Incidentally, these particular illustrations are furnished by the experts at the Colt factory as representative.

344

# PATERSON COLT REVOLVING-CYLINDER PERCUSSION RIFLES

Some collectors recognize only Model 1837 and Model 1839, while others recognize a Model 1836. In each model classification there are two or more types or variations recognized by the specialists; but they do not agree with each other, and there are so few who speak with any authority that all we can do is to present what seems certain.

MODEL 1836, cal. .34, 8-shot, 32-inch barrel, total length 50 inches, weight 12.5 lbs. Fluted cylinder. Made without loading lever. Barrel usually marked "Patent Arms Mfg. Co. Paterson N.J.," but there are variations from this marking. Hammerless. $2,875–$4,375.

SAME, but made with a loading lever. $2,975–$4,450.

SAME, but cal. .44, 30-inch barrel, made without loading lever. $2,975–$4,450.

SAME, but cal. .44, and made with loading lever. $2,975–$4,390.

SAME, but cal. .69, 7-shot, hammerless. Cocked and revolved by ring in front of trigger. The first 12 of this type and model made had the shields and a locking device to the rear of the cylinder. This is the type of which 100 were supposedly made, 20 lost in a river, and 50 sold to the United States for use in the Seminole War. $3,250–$4,610.

MODEL 1837, cal. .44, 6-shot, 32-inch barrel, total length 51 inches, weight 10.5 lbs. Type A is hammerless, with a shield over the nipples and another over the front of the cylinder, but this would probably place it as a Model 1836. Type B has no shields. Hammerless. Cocking lever in front of trigger in the form of a ringed lever outside and in front of the trigger guard. Blued steel. Polished walnut stock. Some specimens have jointed lever ramrod added at the Colt factory after 1839. Apparently made in various calibers and definitely made with from 5 to 8 chambers in cylinder. Value is for Type B. $3,250–$4,675.

MODEL 1839, cal. .56, 5-shot, 32-inch barrel, total length 50 inches. Center-hung hammer. Blued steel. Polished walnut stock. Ramrod on side of frame, although some specimens have ramrod under the frame. Various specimens are found with from 5 to 8 chambers in the cylinder. Also made in other calibers and barrel lengths. Barrel marked "Pat. Arms Mfg. Co. Paterson N.J. Colt's Pat." The original company failed financially in 1841 and ceased manufacturing in 1842, hence the Model 1839 rifles, carbines, and shotguns were the last made at Paterson. Patent No. 1,304, issued Aug. 29, 1839, described the improved loading lever found on this model. Other minor improvements were made in the mechanism. $3,250–$3,650.

## PATERSON COLT REVOLVING-CYLINDER PERCUSSION CARBINES

Like the Paterson Colt rifles, the Paterson Colt carbines are classified as Model 1837 or Model 1839 and further subclassified according to details of construction. They were made in various calibers and barrel lengths and with from 5 to 8 chambers in the cylinder. The ones described below are typical of those found in the better collections. Paterson is sometimes spelled "Patterson."

Cal. .56; 6-shot; 24.5-inch, part round smoothbore barrel marked "Patent Arms M'g Co., Paterson N.J. Colt's Pt." on right side. Browned barrel. Blued cylinder and frame. Iron trigger guard, the tang forming a pistol grip. Center-hung hammer. Cone front sight. Open rear sight. Walnut buttstock. Sling swivels. Plate 43, Fig. 5. $2,800–$4,025.

Cal. .53; 6-shot; 21-inch, round, smoothbore barrel marked on left "Patent Arms Mfg. Co. Paterson N.J. Colt's Pt." Cylinder engraved with sailing ship, lion, and other figures, and marked "Patent Arms Man'y Patterson Jer-

---

### PLATE 42. Colt Rifles and Carbines

*Figure*

1. Paterson-Colt Revolving-Cylinder Percussion Carbine, cal. .44.
2. Paterson-Colt Revolving-Cylinder Percussion Shotgun, 30-gauge.
3. Paterson-Colt Revolving-Cylinder Percussion Rifle.
4. Paterson-Colt Revolving-Cylinder Percussion Carbine with Loading Lever.
5. Paterson-Colt Revolving-Cylinder Percussion Carbine with Loading Lever.
6. Colt Model 1855 Revolving-Cylinder Percussion Rifle, cal. .36.
7. Colt Model 1855 Revolving-Cylinder Percussion Shotgun, cal. .75.
8. Colt Model 1855 Revolving-Cylinder Percussion Musket, U.S. Army Model, with Bayonet.
9. Colt Model 1855 Revolving-Cylinder Percussion Rifle, cal. 56.
10. Colt Berdan Russian Single-Shot, Breechloading Cartridge Rifle.
11. Colt Berdan Russian Single-Shot, Breechloading Cartridge Carbine.

PLATE 42

sey." Center-hung hammer. Loading lever and rammer on right side of barrel. Iron trigger guard, the tang forming the pistol grip. Walnut stock made without forearm and having a metal patch box in right side. Browned barrel. This is a Model 1839. $2,800–$4,060.

Cal. .47, 6-shot, 24.5-inch barrel, total length 42.5 inches, weight 8.5 lbs. Made with loading lever. Cylinder marked "Colt's Pat." Frame marked "Patent Arms Mfg. Co., Paterson, N.J. Colt's Pt." This is the Model 1839, of which 100 were bought by the U.S. War Department in March, 1841, and 60 were bought in June, 1841, for trial by the school for Dragoons at Carlisle, Pa. $2,975–$3,975.

Cal. .44, 8-shot, 24-inch octagon barrel marked on top near the breech "Patent Arms M'g. Co. Paterson, N.J. Colt's Pt.," and held to base pin by wedge with 2 wedge screws, as in Paterson shotgun described below. Originally issued without loading lever, but recalled and fitted with loading lever at the factory. Two-inch cylinder with 2 grooves 1 inch apart, between which is engraved a hunting scene similar to that found on Paterson shotguns. Cylinder is revolved and inside hammer cocked at the same time by pulling downward and rearward on a ring trigger located in front of the trigger guard. Semi-pistol-grip. Curved butt plate. Walnut stock. All serial numbers the same. This is probably a Model 1837, hammerless. Plate 42, Fig. 1. $3,250–$4,550.

## PATERSON MODEL SHOTGUNS

Revolving-cylinder percussion shotguns made by Colt at Paterson, New Jersey, are rarer than Paterson rifles, carbines, or smoothbore shoulder arms, but the demand is weak, and hence the values are not as high as the rarity would seem to indicate. The specimens usually found in collections are 20-gauge, and the barrel lengths are 30.75, 35.25, and 38 inches, although other gauges and barrel lengths are occasionally discovered. Barrel length does not seem to affect value very much, and also the gauge has little effect. The small number of reported sales makes it very difficult to indicate values accurately. Two specimens are described below, but it is not intended that they should be regarded as typical in all details.

TWENTY-GAUGE, 35.25-inch round barrel, 6-shot. Cylinder is 3.5 inches long. Center-hung hammer. Iron guard, the tang forming a pistol grip. Steel butt plate. Walnut stock made without forearm. Bead front sight. Open rear sight. Bright finish. Barrel marked "Patent Arms Mg. Co. Paterson N.J." on right side near breech. All serial numbers the same. $2,100–$2,950.

THIRTY-GAUGE, 30.75-inch round, twist-steel barrel, 6-shot. Bead front sight. Wide grooved rear sight. Barrel held to base pin by usual wedge and 2 wedge screws. Side of barrel marked "Patent Arms Mfg. Co. Paterson N.J. Colt's Pt." Cylinder is 3.25 inches long with 2 grooves 1.25 inches apart, running circumferentially. Between these grooves and the front of the cylinder are engraved a centaur firing a rifle at a running deer and a horseman jumping a hurdle with 2 others following. Between the cylinder grooves is engraved a naval battle scene with frigates in an oval. The cylinder is marked "Patent Arms Man'y Patterson, Jersey Colt's Patent" and the name of the engraver, "W.L. Ormsby." Iron fore stock, also iron trigger guard and pistol grip. Curved iron butt plate. Walnut stock. Plate 42, Fig. 2. $2,150–$2,650.

## COLT MODEL 1855, REVOLVING-CYLINDER PERCUSSION CARBINES

All Model 1855, revolving-cylinder, percussion long arms made at Hartford had frames which were basically copied from that of the Model 1855 Pocket Pistol. Rifles, carbines, muskets, and shotguns were made in this model. Shotguns are described later in this chapter.

5-SHOT, 21-INCH ROUND BARREL. Cal. .56. Full-fluted cylinder. Walnut buttstock. Made without forearm. Blade front sight. Open-leaf rear sight. Sling swivels. Weight 9 lbs. 8 oz. Brass butt plate and trigger guard. Some specimens have ring on left side of receiver for carrying when mounted. Blued. Plate 42, Fig. 9. $1,000–$1,540.

SAME, but made at Hartford with special sights, loading lever under barrel, and British proof marks. Plate 43, Fig. 7. $1,060–$1,595.

Cal. .56, 5-shot, 18-inch barrel. $1,010–$1,460.

Cal. .56, 5-shot, 15-inch barrel. $975–$1,560.

Cal. .44, 6-shot, 21-inch barrel, weight 8 lbs. 12 oz. $965–$1,460.

Cal. .44, 6-shot, 18-inch barrel. $965–$1,455.

Cal. .44, 6-shot, 15-inch barrel. $965–$1,525.

Cal. .36, 6-shot, 21-inch barrel, weight 8 lbs. 8 oz. $985–$1,540.

Cal. .36, 6-shot, 18-inch barrel. $925–$1,470.

Cal. .36, 6-shot, 15-inch barrel. $980–$1,350.

# COLT MODEL 1855, REVOLVING-CYLINDER PERCUSSION RIFLES

Specimens of the Model 1855 arms are found either with or without wooden (usually walnut) forearms (fore ends), and with either round or octagonal barrels, although round barrels seem to be in the majority. The presence of a patent oiling device adds to the value. This device, patented March 3, 1857, supplied one or two drops of oil from a little tank to the front of a ball seated in the chamber or to the chamber surface forward of the ball, which amounts to the same thing. Military arms were finished in blue except that the lever and hammer were casehardened in natural colors. Military stocks were plain walnut finished with linseed oil. The finish of sporting rifles was dependent upon the taste of the purchaser, since many were made on special order. The presence of English proof marks in addition to the usual Hartford Colt marks raises the value slightly in some cases. In general the longer barrels and larger calibers are worth slightly more than the shorter barrels and smaller calibers. The presence of special sights also increases the value somewhat.

These model 1855 rifles, as well as the Model 1855 carbines, are "Guns of Glory." They should be classified as U.S. martial shoulder arms in some cases, and practically all of them can be classified as U.S. secondary martial shoulder arms. For example, the First and Second Regiments of U.S. Army Sharpshooters, often called "Berdan's Sharpshooters" or "Berdan's Brigade," were armed with Colt Model 1855, cal. .56 rifles with the 31.312-inch barrels before they received Sharps Rifles. Many other famous regiments also carried these arms or similar ones, and although they were not popular with enlisted men, about 7,000 Colt revolving long arms of all types were actually used in the Civil War. The short-barrel cal. .56 carbines were often carried by officers as personal side arms.

Cal. .56, 5-shot, barrel 24 inches. Weight 8 lbs. 14 oz. $1,015–$1,575.

Barrel 27 inches. Weight 9 lbs. 11 oz. $1,025–$1,575. Round barrel 31.312 inches. Walnut buttstock and forearm, the latter extending nearly to the muzzle. Button-tip steel ramrod. Sling swivels and leather sling. Full-fluted cylinder. Side hammer. Blade front sight. Open folding-leaf, rear sight. Tang in rear of guard. Weight 9 lbs. 15 oz. This is the Army pattern. $950–$1,650.

Cal. .50, 6-shot, barrel 24 inches. Weight 8 lbs. 11 oz. $1,245–$1,805.
Barrel 27 inches. Weight 8 lbs. 14 oz. $1,270–$1,865.
Barrel 31.312 inches. Weight 9 lbs. 6 oz. Full stock. $1,300–$1,815.

Cal. .44, 6-shot, barrel 24 inches. Weight 8 lbs. 15 oz. $975–$1,565.
Barrel 27 inches. Weight 8 lbs. 14 oz. $1,015–$1,650.
Barrel 27 inches. Weight 9 lbs. 2 oz. $975–$1,560.
Barrel 31.312 inches. Weight 9 lbs. 6 oz. Full stock. $1,125–$1,775.

Cal. .40, 6-shot, barrel 24 inches. Weight 8 lbs. 12 oz. $1,190–$1,675.
Barrel 27 inches. Weight 9 lbs. 12 oz. $1,225–$1,690
Barrel 31.312 inches. Weight 10 lbs. 4 oz. Full stock. $1,225–$1,775.

Cal. .36, 6-shot, round barrel 24 inches. Walnut buttstock without forearm. Low blade front sight. Open-quadrant rear sight. Cleaning rod screwed into thimbles on left side of frame and barrel. On the left side of frame in front of cylinder there may be an oiling device. Loading lever under barrel. Cylinder marked "Colt's Patent Sporting Rifle." Barrel marked "Colt's Pt. 1856. Address Col. Colt Hartford Ct. U.S.A." Weight 9 lbs. $1,375–$1,925.
Barrel 27 inches. Weight 10 lbs. Plate 43, Fig. 6. $1,340–$1,910.
Barrel 30 inches. Weight 10 lbs. 8 oz. $1,350–$1,950.

SAME, but 21-inch round barrel. Plate 42, Fig. 6. $1,350–$1,950.

SAME, but presentation model. Fine walnut stock. Steel rifle butt plate. Loading lever under barrel. Oiling device on side of frame in front of cylinder. Full-length cleaning rod on left side extending from point near rear end of cylinder to the muzzle. Low blade front sight. Leaf rear sight. Round cylinder. Side hammer. Cylinder marked "Colt's Patent Sporting Rifle" with serial number. Upper tang engraved with name of person to whom rifle was given, followed by the words "Compliments of the Inventor, Col. Colt." Blued finish. This piece is typical of those which Colt gave to people who could help him to obtain business. $3,000–$4,400.

# COLT MODEL 1855, REVOLVING-CYLINDER PERCUSSION MUSKETS

The only specimens that we have examined are cal. .56, 5-shot, made in 24-, 27-, and 31.312-inch barrel lengths. They are usually provided with a walnut stock and forearm, the latter extending nearly to the muzzle on most specimens, full-fluted cylinders, cleaning rod under barrel, loading lever under forearm, side hammer, brass-blade front sight, 3-leaf rear sight, 2 stock bands, brass patch box in buttstock, and trap in butt for a cleaning rod. The frame is usually marked "Col. Colt Hartford Ct. U.S.A." on top and "Colt's Patent Nov. 24th, 1857," with the serial number, on the side. Sling swivels. $1,275–$1,900.

Note: The one illustrated by Fig. 8 of Plate 42 is the U.S. Army Model and is shown with bayonet attached.

## COLT MODEL 1855, REVOLVING-CYLINDER PERCUSSION SHOTGUNS

Among the Model 1855 Colt long arms, all with frames patterned after that of the Model 1855 Pocket Pistol, were revolving-cylinder, percussion, side-hammer shotguns, made in calibers .60 and .75, with barrels, 27, 30, 33, and 36 inches long, and usually weighing from 9 lbs. 9 oz. to 10 lbs. 4 oz., although one weighed only 8 lbs. 12 oz. The cylinders may be either round or fluted, as on the other long arms of this model period, and some specimens have a finger rest for the left hand in front of the trigger guard. Walnut buttstock and fore end. The top of the frame may be marked "Col. Colt Hartford Ct., U.S.A.," and the side of the frame may be marked "Colt's Patent Nov. 24, 1857." The trigger guard and butt plate are brass on some specimens and steel on others. There is a loading lever under the fore end, that is, it is under the barrel. The fore end may be tipped with German silver. The trigger guard forms a semi-pistol-grip on some specimens. Both 5-shot and 6-shot specimens are found, although the 5-shot examples seem to be more common. All of these were made at Hartford.

---

PLATE 43. Colt and Other Revolving Shoulder Arms.

Figure

1. Revolving Matchlock Shoulder Arm with Four Chambers.
2. North & Skinner Revolving Percussion Rifle Marked "H. S. North Pat. 1852."
3. C. B. Allen-Cochran's Patent Percussion Turret Rifle.
4. B. Bigelow Revolving Pill-Lock Rifle.
5. Paterson-Colt Revolving-Cylinder Percussion Carbine, cal. .56.
6. Colt Model 1855 Revolving-Cylinder Percussion Sporting Rifle.
7. Colt Model 1855 Revolving-Cylinder Percussion Carbine, cal. .56.
8. Colt Double-Barrel Cartridge Sporting Rifle.

1

2

3

4

5

6

7

8

PLATE 43

Cal. .75, 27-inch barrel, 5-shot. Plate 42, Fig. 7. $750–$1,025.

Cal. .75, 30-inch barrel, 5-shot. $950–$1,400.

Cal. .75, 33-inch barrel, 5-shot. $950–$1,400.

Cal. .75, 36-inch barrel, 5-shot. $950–$1,450.

Cal. .60, 27-inch barrel, 5-shot. $950–$1,475.

Cal. .60, 30-inch barrel. $975–$1,485.

Cal. .60, 33-inch barrel. $985–$1,495.

Cal. .60, 36-inch barrel. $995–$1,500.

U.S. RIFLED MUSKET MODEL 1861, COLT, cal. .58, percussion, 40-inch barrel. Lock plate marked "U.S. Colt's Pt. F.A. Mfg. Co. Hartford, Ct." and the year. The Colt Company obtained a contract in 1861 and delivered 99,000 from Sept. 26, 1862 to Dec. 27, 1864. This is also described in Chapter 20 entitled "U.S. Martial Shoulder Arms," but is repeated here to make this Colt list complete. Some specimens equipped with 3-leaf rear sight, 100-300-500 yards. Barrel sometimes marked "Steel." $275–$650.

BERDAN RUSSIAN SINGLE-SHOT, BREECHLOADING, CARTRIDGE RIFLE (1870), cal. .42-77-370, bottlenecked, center-fire cartridge using the Berdan Primer and a charge of 77 grains of black powder with a cal. .42 bullet weighing 370 grains. Barrel 30 inches. Total length 50 inches. Tip-up breech action hinged at the level of the cartridge head and moved by a knob catch on the right. Superficially this weapon appears to have a center-hung hammer, but the striker is a straight pin cocked by an external spur at the rear of the action and driven by a spiral spring. The patent for this system was granted to General Hiram Berdan, U.S. Army, on Mar. 30, 1869. The Colt Company obtained a contract with the Russian Government in 1870 to deliver 40,000 of these rifles, which was accomplished between 1870 and 1872. A target version of this rifle was made in a very small quantity for a rifle club at the Colt factory, having a heavier barrel, a special stock, and target sights; but there is apparently no record of sales among collectors. Plate 42, Fig. 10. $340–$675.

SAME, but carbine. Plate 42, Fig. 11. $340–$675.

## SHOTGUNS OF THE CARTRIDGE PERIOD, WITH HAMMERS

DOUBLE-BARRELED HAMMER-TYPE SHOTGUN, introduced in

1878 and discontinued in 1890. Numbered 1 to about 22,690. In several grades of imported twist-type barrels. Barrel 28 inches, 10-gauge. $125–$175.

SAME, but 30-inch barrel, 10-gauge. $195–$265.

SAME, but 32-inch barrel, 10-gauge. $195–$275.

SAME, but 28-inch barrel, 12-gauge. $200–$285.

SAME, but 30-inch barrel, 12-gauge. $200–$285.

SAME, but 32-inch barrel, 12-gauge. $200–$300.

# HAMMERLESS SHOTGUNS OF THE CARTRIDGE PERIOD

DOUBLE-BARRELED, HAMMERLESS-TYPE SHOTGUN introduced in 1883, in the same lengths and with the same range of barrel qualities as the hammer type described above, and discontinued in 1900. When the engraved word "Safe" on the breech action is exposed, the gun cannot be fired, and when it is covered by pushing forward the slide, either or both barrels can be fired. Stocks made of English or Circassian walnut at option of buyer. Barrels brazed and soldered by machinery. Rebounding locks. Opening the breech withdraws the firing pins by a positive motion, without springs, preventing premature explosion in closing the breech. Metal parts were elaborately engraved on request. Barrels could be of "twist," "fine twist," "laminated," or "Damascus" construction at the option of the purchaser. Retail prices in 1888 ranged from $50 to $125, according to various details, and special ornamentation was extra. The typical stock dimensions were: drop at butt, 2.75 to 3.5 inches; drop at comb, 2 inches; from front trigger to center of butt plate, 13.875 to 14.375 inches. Made in 10-gauge and 12-gauge, and with 28-, 30-, and 32-inch barrels. $325-$550.

DOUBLE-BARREL CARTRIDGE SPORTING RIFLE (1880), cal. .45-70 Govt. cartridge, with 2, 28.25-inch, round, Damascus steel barrels, side by side. Two hammers and 2 triggers. Walnut stock, checkered walnut forearm and pistol grip. Checkered hard-rubber butt plate. Top-break action as in double-barrel Colt shotgun. Plain ejectors. The movement of the top lever to the right to open the barrels also retracts the firing pins so that they are free of the chambers. Silver-bead front sight with folding, porcelain-bead night sight in rear. British-type, folding-leaf, express rear sight having 3 leaves, one of which is stationary. Matted rib extends from breech to muzzle. Rib marked "Colt's Pt. F. A. Mfg. Co., Hartford, Ct. U.S.A." Locks marked "Colt's Pt. F. A. Mfg. Co." Silver-plated oval name plate inlaid in underside of stock in rear of pistol grip. Browned barrels. Blued trigger guard and fore end iron. Weight 9 lbs. 10 oz. Not more than 20 of these Colt Double-Barrel Sporting Rifles were made. The small number in existence and the few recorded sales make it very difficult to assign values accurately. Plate 43, Fig. 8. $3,600–$5,750.

LEVER-ACTION MAGAZINE RIFLE (1883), sometimes called the Burgess-Colt Repeating Rifle, the Burgess Rifle, or erroneously called the Winchester-Colt. Cal. .44-40 W.c.f. cartridge; 25-inch barrel, round, half-octagon, or octagon; total length 42.75 inches. Lever, repeating breech action. Fifteen-shot. Manufactured under patents issued to Andrew Burgess and assigned to Colt Company, one of which was issued Dec. 13, 1881. This was the first repeating rifle for metallic cartridges made by Colt, and it superficially resembled the Winchester Model 1873. Introduced in 1883 and discontinued in 1884. A total of 6,043 arms of this general type were made, including all variations. Weight 8.5 lbs. with round barrel and 8.75 lbs. with octagon barrel. Barrel marked "Colt's Pt. F. A. Mfg. Co., Hartford, Ct., U.S.A. Pat. Jan. 7 '73, Oct. 19, '75, Apr. 1, '79, Dec. 7, '80, Dec. 13, '81, Jan 3, '82." Full-length tubular magazine. Walnut buttstock and forearm. Trap in butt. Blade front sight. Open rear sight. Blued finish. Sliding door on right side of receiver for loading the magazine. The Colt advertisements said, "If longer barrels and magazines are required, $1.00 for each additional inch will be charged"; and they also stated that this rifle used the same cartridges as those used in their "Frontier" Model Revolvers, that is, cal. .44 c.f., with 40 grains of powder and a 200-grain bullet. $500–$1,000.

SAME, but carbine, with 20-inch round barrel, 12-shot, weight 7.25 lbs. $465–$910.

SAME, but sporting rifle, 15-shot; 25.5-inch round, half-octagon, or full-octagon barrel; weight 8.25 to 8.5 lbs. $350–$695.

## NEW LIGHTNING MAGAZINE RIFLE (1885)

This was a slide-action or pump-action type, which should not be confused with the lever-action type. It was manufactured under the patents issued to Dr. William H. Elliott in 1883, and made in a variety of calibers, barrel lengths, and frame types. The first series consisted of medium-weight rifles of .32-20, .38-40, and .44-40 calibers. The cartridge used in the .44-cal. rifle and carbine was the same as that used in the "Frontier" .44-cal. revolvers, that is, 40 grains of powder with a 200-grain bullet; the cartridge used in the .38-cal. rifle had 40 grains of powder and a 180-grain bullet; the cartridge used in the .32-cal. rifle had 20 grains of powder and a 100-grain bullet. The sporting rifle with a 26-inch round barrel weighs 6.75

lbs., and with an octagonal barrel of the same length weighs 7.25 lbs. A carbine with 20-inch round barrel weighs 6.25 lbs.; and the "Baby Carbine" model weighs 5.5 lbs. The rifles have 15-shot tubular magazines, and the carbines have 12-shot tubular magazines. The buttstock and fore end are walnut and may be checkered. The front sight may be either a bead or a blade, and the rear sight may be either an open-leaf or a semi-buckthorn type. Carbines may have a special ring for mounted use.

### First or Medium-Weight Series (Discontinued 1900)

RIFLE, cal. .32-20 W.c.f. $200–$350.
RIFLE, cal. .38-40 W.c.f. $200–$350.
RIFLE, cal. .44-40 W.c.f. $200–$375.
CARBINE, cal. .32-20 W.c.f. $210–$400.
CARBINE, cal. .38-40 W.c.f. $210–$425.
CARBINE, cal. .44-40 W.c.f. $225–$475.

### New or Small-Caliber Series

RIFLE, cal. .22 short and .22 long r.f., 24-inch round or octagon barrel, firing either 15 long or 16 short cartridges or mixed short and long. Weight with round barrel 6 lbs., and weight with octagon barrel 6.25 lbs. Barrel marked "Colt's Lightning .22 Cal." on right side. The slide handle or forearm is checkered but not the stock. The left side of the barrel is marked ".22 Cal." Discontinued in 1903. The design of this rifle differs from that of the other Lightning Models. $175–$200.

RIFLE, cal. .25-50, with 36-inch barrel. This type is reported but unknown personally to the author. If it exists, the value is as stated. $185–$295.

RIFLE, cal. .25-50, with 20-inch barrel. This type is reported but unknown personally to the author. If it exists, the value is as stated. $185–$295.

## NEW LIGHTNING MAGAZINE EXPRESS RIFLES AND CARBINES (1888)

An "Express" series of rifles was announced in 1888 and discontinued in 1895. These were made for the black-powder cartridges of that era, in calibers .38-56, .40-60, .45-60, .45-85, and .50-95, in rifle, carbine, and baby carbine sizes, and with round and octagonal barrels. With a 28-inch round barrel, a rifle weighed 9.75 lbs., with an octagonal barrel of the same length it weighed 10 lbs. The carbine with a 22-inch barrel weighed 9 lbs., and the baby carbine with a 22-inch barrel weighed 8 lbs. These were the last sporting arms made by the Colt Company. A typical piece has a walnut stock and a checkered walnut forearm which may be made in one or two pieces. There is a blade front sight and an open rear sight, but the tang may be drilled, tapped, and fitted with a peep sight. The barrel is marked "Colt's Pt. F. A. Mfg. Co., Hartford, Ct. U.S.A." with the patent dates below. The receiver is marked with a rampant colt.

RIFLE, cal. .38-56, 28-inch barrel, 10-shot, weight 10 lbs. or 9.75 lbs. $250–$475.
CARBINE, cal. .38-56, 22-inch barrel, 8-shot, weight 9 lbs. $190–$340.
BABY CARBINE, cal. .38-56, 22-inch barrel, 8-shot, weight 8 lbs. $410–$700.

*Note: Barrel lengths, number of shots, and weight are approximately the same for the remaining calibers, except cal. .50-95, which was made with a 26-inch barrel only, except on special order.*

RIFLE, cal. .40-60. $300–$475.
CARBINE, cal. .40-60. $325–$495.
BABY CARBINE, cal. .40-60. $425–$700.
RIFLE, cal. .45-60. $275–$610.
CARBINE, cal. .45-60. $275–$650.
BABY CARBINE, cal. .45-60. $325–$675.
RIFLE, cal. .45-85. $340–$575.
CARBINE, cal. .45-85. $325–$625.
BABY CARBINE, cal. .45-85. $410–$750.
RIFLE, cal. .50-95. $565–$850.

## REVOLVING SHOULDER ARMS OTHER THAN COLTS

Collectors interested in Colt revolving-cylinder shoulder arms often also collect revolving rifles and shotguns made by other manufacturers. It is interesting to know that the C. B. Allen-Cochran's Patent Percussion Turret Rifle and its almost identical counterpart, the Cochran Percussion Revolving Rifle, are the only arms in this group which are in great demand. Second in popularity in this group are the Billinghurst revolving shoulder arms, with the other makes trailing behind.

We do not pretend to list all of the American-made arms in this classification, but we have included all the best-known makes and models, and, in addition, we have described the *Le Mat*, which was made in France and imported to the United States. Like some of the *Le Mat* hand arms, it became so well known that many Americans think that it must have been made here.

The revolving matchblock shoulder arm with four chambers is illustrated by Fig. 1 on Plate 43. It is presented here to emphasize the fact that revolving arms are by no means a modern invention. This weapon was in the collection of Dr. S. Traner Buck, which was sold through the Kimball Arms Co. It was probably made in the seventeenth century in Indo-China. It is 63 inches overall with a 34-inch steel barrel flaring at the muzzle. (Only part of the arm is shown in the picture.) The revolving cylinder itself is 6.5 inches long. Each chamber has its own flash pan. The hammer is a typical serpentine matchlock hammer. This type of weapon is extremely rare, but the demand is not great; hence the value on the present market is about $2,000 in good condition and about $2,750 in fine condition.

C. B. ALLEN–COCHRAN'S PATENT PERCUSSION TURRET RIFLE, cal. .44, 7-shot, 30.5-inch octagon barrel. Frame marked on top strap "Cochran's Patent. C. B. Allen Springfield Mass." Similar to Cochran Percussion Revolving Rifle described below. Plate 43, Fig. 3, $2,015–$2,950.

ALLEN & WHEELOCK PERCUSSION REVOLVING CARBINE, cal. .44, 20-inch barrel, total length 34 inches. $1,310–$2,015.

B. BIGELOW REVOLVING PILL-LOCK RIFLE, cal. .44, 7-shot, 25.5-inch octagon barrel marked "B. Bigelow, Marysville, Cal." Plate 43, Fig. 4. $1,160–$1,515.

BILLINGHURST REVOLVING PILL-LOCK RIFLE, cal. 44, 7-shot, 27-inch octagon barrel marked "W. Billinghurst, Rochester, N.Y." $1,175–$1,600.

BILLINGHURST PERCUSSION REVOLVING CARBINE, cal. .40, 7-shot, 24.375-inch octagon barrel marked "W. Billinghurst." Walnut stock. Back-action lock engraved. Brass patch box. $1,050–$1,625.

BILLINGHURST PERCUSSION REVOLVING RIFLE, cal. .40, 30-inch octagon barrel. Otherwise the same as the carbine. $1,175–$1,800.

COCHRAN PERCUSSION REVOLVING RIFLE, cal. .44, 8-shot, 31-

inch octagon barrel marked only "Cochran's Patent." Similar to the C. B. Allen-Cochran's Patent Rifle described above. $2,050–$2,850.

ALEXANDER HALL PERCUSSION REVOLVING RIFLE, cal. .36, 15-shot, 30-inch round barrel. Cylinder marked "Alexander Hall, Pat. 1856." Curly maple stock. Cylinder released by pulling a drop hook, and turned by hand. Cocked by pulling front trigger to rear. Hammer operates internally, inside brass frame. According to tradition, there are five known specimens. $2,425–$3,740.

LE MAT REVOLVING PERCUSSION RIFLE AND SHOTGUN, cal. .43, 9-shot, 23.25-inch round rifle barrel; single-shot, 28-gauge shotgun barrel under the rifle barrel. $1,250–$1,950.

NORTH & SKINNER REVOLVING PERCUSSION RIFLE, marked "H. S. North Pat 1852." Plate 43, Fig. 2. $1,185–$1,900.

H. S. NORTH REVOLVING PERCUSSION SHOTGUN, cal. .60, 6-shot, 27-inch barrel marked "H.S. North, Middletown, Conn." This was based on the North & Skinner Patent No. 8982, dated June 1, 1852. $1,115–$1,600.

E. S. ORMSBY PILL-LOCK REVOLVING-CYLINDER RIFLE, cal. 44, 7-shot, 32-inch round barrel marked "E.S. Ormsby." Ormsby was the man who engraved the Colt percussion cylinders bearing his name. Plate 44, Fig. 1. $1,065–$1,515.

PORTER PERCUSSION TURRET RIFLE, cal. .50, pill-lock, 9-shot, 26-inch octagon barrel marked "Address P. W. Porter, New York. P. W. Porter's Patent 1851." Total length 47 inches. Weight about 9 lbs. 12 oz. Walnut stock. Iron butt plate. Steel frame. Browned. Plate 44, Fig. 2. $835–$1,210.

SAME, but cal. .44, 28-inch octagon barrel. Made with loading lever on top of barrel. Marked as above. Walnut stock. Iron butt plate. Steel frame, right side hinged at front. $850–$1,275.

---

PLATE 44. Revolving Shoulder Arms Other Than Colts

Figure

1. E. S. Ormsby Pill-Lock Revolving-Cylinder Rifle.
2. Porter Percussion Turret Rifle.
3. Remington Revolving Percussion Carbine.
4. Roper 4-Shot Revolving Shotgun.
5. Smith & Wesson Revolving-Cylinder Rifle.
6. James Warner Revolving Percussion Rifle.
7. J. L. Wyler Revolving Percussion Rifle.

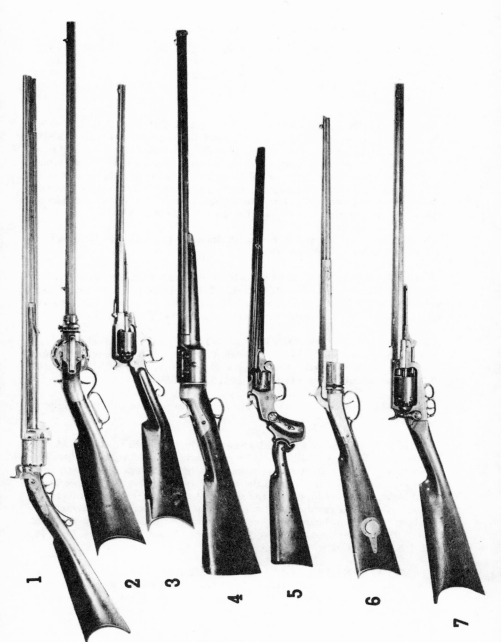

PLATE 44

**REMINGTON PERCUSSION AND CARTRIDGE REVOLVING RIFLE,** with 2 cylinders, cal. .36, percussion, and cal. .38, short or long rim-fire cartridge. Apparently extremely rare. Weight 7 lbs. Made from 1866 to 1879. This rifle and the two listed below were numbered 1 to about 3,000. $985–$1,531.

**REMINGTON REVOLVING PERCUSSION RIFLE,** cal. .44, 6-shot, 28.5-inch octagon barrel. Walnut buttstock made without forearm. Blade front sight, open and peep folding-leaf rear sight. Brass butt plate and trigger guard. German silver disk inlaid in each side of small of stock. Browned finish. Some specimens have a 26-inch, part round, part octagon barrel without value change. Remington revolving-cylinder rifles and carbines of this type were made with barrels of various lengths and either octagon or round-octagon, without much variation in value. $1,031–$1,415.

SAME, but carbine, cal. .44, 6-shot; 22-inch, part round, part octagon barrel. Plate 44, Fig. 3. $985–$1,300.

**ROPER 4-SHOT REVOLVING RIFLE AND SHOTGUN,** with 2 interchangeable barrels, cal. .41 rifle barrel and cal. .64 shotgun barrel, each barrel being marked "Roper Repeating Rifle Co., Amherst, Mass." Each barrel 27 inches long. Total length 48 inches. Walnut stock. $915–$1,415.

**ROPER 4-SHOT REVOLVING SHOTGUN,** cal. .64, steel cartridge cases with percussion primers, 27-inch barrel marked "Roper Repeating Rifle Co., Amherst, Mass." Total length 48 inches. Weight 6.75 lbs. Detachable choke. Walnut stock. Plate 44, Fig. 4. $525–$950.

SAME, but cylinder throws to right for loading. Made with two triggers. $775–$1,165.

**SMITH & WESSON REVOLVING-CYLINDER RIFLE,** cal. 32-44 S & W, 6-shot; 16-inch, round, ribbed barrel. Checkered red rubber grips. Single-action. Top-break. Auto-ejection. Detachable walnut stock with iron yoke and screw for attaching to the butt of the revolver. Detachable blade front sight. Open folding-leaf rear sight. Blued finish. This weapon can be classed as either a revolving-cylinder rifle or a revolver with a detachable stock. Usually found in original case. Also made with 20-inch barrel, total length 25.5 inches, and total length with stock affixed 36.5 inches. Plate 44, Fig. 5. $1,100–$2,025.

**JAMES WARNER REVOLVING PERCUSSION RIFLE,** cal. .44, 6-shot, 27-inch octagon or round-octagon barrel marked "James Warner, Springfield, Mass." Total length 46 inches. Weight 10 lbs. Frame marked "James Warner." Frames of some specimens marked "Warner's Patent." Plate 44, Fig. 6. $765–$1,025.

SAME, but cal. .40, 27.75-inch octagon barrel. $765–$1,035.

SAME, but cal. .31, 24-inch round-octagon barrel, total length 43 inches, weight 7.75 lbs. Notice that there is considerable variation as to caliber and barrel length in specimens of these James Warner revolving rifles. Caliber and barrel length have a slight effect on value. $875–$1,260.

WESSON & LEAVITT'S REVOLVING PERCUSSION RIFLE, cal. 44, 6-shot, 27.5-inch octagon barrel. Heavy cylinder. Lock marked "Wesson & Leavitt's Patent." Brass trigger guard and mountings. $1,140–$1,740.

O. W. WHITTIER PERCUSSION REVOLVING RIFLE, patented in 1837, by O. W. Whittier, of Enfield, N.H. Cylinder turned by a stud sliding in external grooves. One known specimen has a curly maple stock similar to that on Kentucky rifles. Further details not available. $1,650–$2,475.

J. L. WYLER REVOLVING PERCUSSION RIFLE, cal. .41, 6-shot, 26-inch octagon barrel marked "J.L. Wyler." Walnut stock. Made without forearm. Iron butt plate and patch box. Iron trigger guard with another guard in front. Loading lever under barrel resembles Colt's. Solid frame with top strap over cylinder. Side hammer as in Colt. Base pin unscrews and is removed through rear of frame. Cylinder revolved by hand as in a revolver. Blade front sight. V-notch rear sight. Plate 44, Fig. 7. $1,030–$1,390.

# Chapter 25

## KENTUCKY (PENNSYLVANIA) RIFLES

THE Kentucky rifle originated as a distinct type in the vicinity of Lancaster, Pennsylvania, and many of the early makers of this outstandingly important American shoulder arm lived in Pennsylvania. The name "Kentucky" was not applied until long after this weapon evolved as an arm entirely different from anything previously made in any other part of the world. The whole weight of history supports the statement that we should cease calling it the Kentucky and rightfully term it the Pennsylvania rifle.

No two Kentucky rifles were ever made exactly alike, even when they were made by the same man. Also, the Kentucky rifle evolved gradually, in both design and construction, to meet the needs of the men and boys who carried this unique American weapon on hunting trails and in battles against their enemies, both foreign and domestic. Since this text is a handbook of values, the author must, of necessity, refer the reader to the more extensive descriptions, explanations, and illustrations in *Guns of the Old West,* and *The Complete Book of Gun Collecting.* The rifling of barrels, the design and construction of stocks, etc., is explained in *The Complete Guide to Gunsmithing.*

The Pennsylvania rifle became a fully developed type sometime between 1725 and 1728. The oldest specimen of which the author has knowledge is marked 1728. Flintlock long arms were made prior to that date, but they retain characteristics of the European weapons from which they were copied.

An examination of more than 200 early Pennsylvania rifles shows that the average bore diameter is 0.45 inch, the average weight is 9 pounds, and the average barrel length is 40 inches, although many of the rifles were apparently shortened years ago. Of this large group of representative pieces, one-third were rifled with 7 grooves, one-fourth were rifled with 8 grooves, 5% were rifled with 6 grooves, 2% were cut octagon, 2.5% were straight cut, and 30% were smoothbore although a number of these were obviously rebored rifles. The average stock of these rifles has a drop at the heel of 4 inches, is made of curly maple, and has a butt of the shotgun type. The butt plate, trigger guard, patch box and other fittings are almost always made of brass.

The only European influence on the earliest Pennsylvania rifles is found in the incised carving and the raised carving sometimes executed in panels, often for the full length of the stock in the better grade pieces. Those made after about 1790 generally lack the beautiful carving, but have metal inlays, usually silver, if they were made for wealthy men, although those carried by the frontiersmen were often decorated with brass. These inlays include an 8-pointed star, which is one of the oldest decorations found on the Kentucky rifle; a crescent moon with or without a star; a crooked heart with the point turned to one side to "hex" an enemy; the Chinese yin-yang emblem; various fraternal symbols, such as the square and compass of Free and Accepted Masonry; animals, birds, fish, leaves, acorns, etc. The barrel is sometimes found with "X" marks, usually on the underside, to protect the owner from evil spirits, witches, and demons.

Those made after 1800 usually have a thinner buttstock, the butt plate is more crescent-shaped, carving is rarely found, and there are usually more inlays; because by that time rifles had become more of a sporting arm than an absolute necessity for the average man.

The author once examined carefully a very representative collection of 43 Pennsylvania rifles and found that the average caliber was .439, the average barrel length was 44.31 inches, the average total length was 58.14 inches, and the average weight was 9.546 pounds. All of these were authentic flintlock pieces in their original condition, probably made before 1800. A rifle of caliber .439 would fire bullets whose weight was such that about 57 balls could be made from one pound of lead, depending upon how tightly the ball fitted the rifling and whether or not a greased patch was used. These were the average figures only. In reality, of the 43 rifles, 16 used 60 balls to the pound, 4 used 80 to the pound, 4 used 52 balls to the pound, and 4 fired 120 balls to the pound. The number of balls to the pound for the remainder of the group varied greatly, hence an average figure does not mean a great deal.

In 1807 an event took place in the British Isles which eventually spelled the doom of the Pennsylvania rifle. In that year the Reverend Alexander Forsyth, a Scotch Presbyterian minister, received a patent for a percussion ignition system. In 1812 he founded his own company in London. By 1816 percussion ignition firearms were becoming fairly well known in the United States. About 1828, one hundred years after the Pennsylvania rifle was developed as a distinct type of weapon, its makers began to use percussion ignition on most of their arms, and by 1830 the original flintlock pattern was considered obsolete. However, we must remember that the percussion system was not generally adopted for other types of arms until after 1842 and that flintlock arms were used in battle, although to a small degree, by the Confederates in the Civil War.

The value of genuine Kentucky rifles, otherwise known as Pennsylvania rifles, has increased faster than most other weapons. Genuine flintlock specimens in original condition are worth more than others. Percussion specimens are worth less. Those that were originally made as flintlock rifles and then converted to percussion are worth more than those made originally as percussion arms. However, those that were originally percussion arms and then converted back to flintlock by some collector or dealer are under suspicion and are lowest in value for obvious reasons. Let the buyer beware!

---

## PLATE 45. Kentucky (Pennsylvania) Arms

*Figure*

1. H. Leman, Lancaster, Pa., Kentucky Rifle.
2. H. Leman, Lancaster, Pa., Kentucky Rifle.
3. M. Fordney, Lancaster, Pa., Kentucky Rifle.
4. M. Fordney, Lancaster, Pa., Kentucky Rifle.
5. J.H. Johnson Kentucky Rifle.
6. Eichholtz & Bros., Lancaster, Pa., Kentucky Rifle.
7. A. Gumph, Lancaster, Pa., Kentucky Rifle.
8. H. Gibbs, Lancaster, Pa., Kentucky Rifle.
9. C. Isch, Lancaster, Pa., Kentucky Pistol.
10. John Settle, Pa., Boy's Kentucky Rifle.

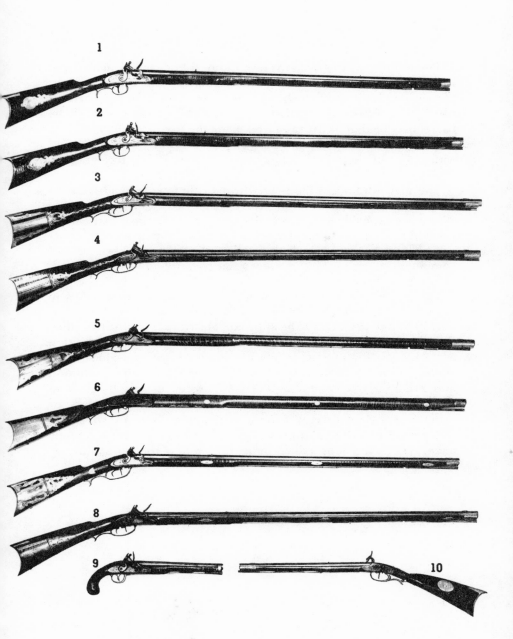

PLATE 45

The identity of the maker is important, if known, but many were not marked during Colonial and Revolutionary days because of fear of reprisals from the British. The name on the top of the barrel is usually that of the rifle maker; the name on the underside of the barrel may be that of the man who made the barrel, or the man who repaired the rifle; and the name on the lock may not correspond with either of the other names and may be that of a foreign lock-maker.

The men who made the Pennsylvania rifle were individualists of the front rank, and their products varied as widely as they did. There are probably many exceptions to every statement made here. All that we can do in this chapter is to explain the principal characteristics, warn the beginner to obtain the advice of honest and competent specialists, and present a few representative specimens illustrated on Plate 45.

The approximate average value of genuine Kentucky rifles in their original flintlock condition is $2,375 in good condition and $6,250 in fine condition. The approximate average value of genuine flintlock specimens altered to percussion is $1,400 in good condition and $4,200 in fine condition. The approximate average value of specimens originally made as percussion rifles is $800 in good condition and $1,500 in fine condition. These values represent the statement of men who specialize in Kentucky rifles as collectors, dealers, or museum curators. Like all general statements, these are subject to many valid exceptions. No two Kentucky rifles were made exactly alike, even by the same maker, hence no two have the same value.

# Chapter 26

## *AMERICAN GUNMAKERS OF THE FLINTLOCK PERIOD*

THE value of a flintlock is often greater if it was made in America during the flintlock period, and the value is still greater if the maker can be identified as one who supplied arms to a Committee of Safety or to the federal and state governments. For this reason, a list of some of the leading makers is given here.

The authors of various books list gunmakers, but no two books agree exactly because any conscientious author hates to list makers of whom he has no knowledge. Every flintlock maker in this list produced at least one flintlock firearm, usually a Kentucky rifle, which either has been inspected by the author or by one or more competent specialists.

There is a story behind every name on this list. For example, Joseph Andrew, Detroit, Michigan, was a volunteer soldier who fought Indians in that region; Russell Bean, of Tennessee, was the first white child born in that state; Samuel Boone was a nephew of Daniel Boone; Squire Boone was a brother of Daniel Boone; Thomas Boone was a cousin of Daniel Boone. Thomas Crockett came from Virginia, worked in Kentucky, and made rifles for the soldiers of General Harrison for a campaign against the Indians. (Remember "Tippecanoe and Tyler, Too"?) Henry Deringer's son made the Deringer ("derringer") pistol used to murder the saintly Lincoln. John Dickenson, of Russell County, Virginia, left his gun factory to his Negro slave, who made several fine rifles now proudly displayed by some of the leading families of Norfolk and Richmond, which the author has seen. Henry Drepperd, of Lancaster, Pennsylvania, always put his name on his lock plates, which was unusual, and he is also famous as the only known gunmaker whose name can be spelled backwards or forwards. William Foulks, of Pennsylvania, was more famous for his penmanship than his gunmaking, proving that once the pen was really mightier than the sword; and John Hall, of Yarmouth, Maine, invented the Hall Breechloading Flintlock Rifle.

John Joseph Henry followed Benedict Arnold on the expedition to Quebec and came back to found the Boulton Gun Works. John Henry, of Lancaster, Pennsylvania, left his business to his wife, Eliza, and she is said to have made better rifles than he did. William Henry I fought under Braddock at Fort Duquesne. His son and his grandson continued in the gun business, and a whole book could be written about this one family.

J. Honaker, of Pennsylvania, was famous for his turkey rifles. His relatives in Virginia and West Virginia also made rifles. Abner Klase, of Ringtown, Pennsylvania, made long-barreled rifles, but his wife made all the stocks. John Roop, of Allentown, Pennsylvania, made rifles before and after the Revolution and took great delight in decorating them with emblems of the Masonic fraternity, including not only the usual ones but also some that only a careful student of Masonic symbolism would recognize, such as the golf club with the balls.

C. Stahl, of Pennsylvania, wins the prize for the longest known American rifles, one of them being 81 inches overall. G. Weiker, of Pennsylvania, was the first gunmaker in America who put his catalogue on his products, one of them being marked on the patch box: "G. Weiker, gunsmith, has his price, $16.48 for manufacturing." Yes, it's just a list of names!

The family name is followed by the initials and Christian names, where known; then by the colony or state in which the person worked; and finally, by the letter "K" if he is known to have made Kentucky rifles, and by the letter "C" if he is known to have supplied arms to a Committee of Safety, but the omission of these letters does not mean that such arms were not made. The spelling of names varied greatly in flintlock days; the same man often spelled his name in different ways, and it was the exception rather than the rule for pieces to be marked at all.

The names of gunmakers of the flintlock period who are mentioned in this text, or whose arms are described in detail, are followed by the number of the chapter. Some of the people listed here made only barrels, some made stocks, some made locks, and others made entire guns. In some instances, these people were contractors and sublet their contracts to others.

It is ethical to restore antique firearms if repairs are required to preserve them from deterioration. Before any restoration is begun, review Chapter 2, "Condition," in this book. Any restoration which is too extensive or poorly accomplished can greatly reduce the value of any antique firearm, especially flintlocks.

If restoration or repair is contemplated, whether the owner of a firearm intends to do the work himself, or hire a competent gunsmith, he should examine those portions of any book on gunsmithing which explains the selection of woods and metals, and the construction of stocks and other wooden parts, as well as the rifling of barrels and the fabrication of metal parts. These subjects, along with others, are in the author's text, *The Complete Guide to Gunsmithing*, a revision of an earlier book, *Gun Care and Repair*.

The gunmakers of the flintlock period listed on the following pages all made various types of firearms during the flintlock period. Some are followed by an abbreviation for the state in which they made weapons; the letter "K" indicates that they make Kentucky rifles and possible Kentucky pistols, and the letter "C" means that they probably make firearms for the Committees of Safety established in the original Thirteen American Colonies shortly before the American Revolution. Chapter designations serve as a cross-reference to chapters of this book describing arms made by these gunmakers.

In using the list of American gunmakers of the flintlock period, it should be understood that all did not make a complete rifle, a complete musket, a complete carbine, a complete musketoon, or a complete shotgun. Some were barrel makers, some were stock makers, and others were lock makers, but all were regarded then as gunmakers.

Adam, Daniel; K.
Adams, Samuel; N.Y.; K.
Adams, W.; K.
Adams, Wm.; W. Va.; K.
Ager, A.; O.; K.
Agy; Pa.; K.

Albrecht, Andrew; Pa.
Albrecht, Heinrich; Pa.
Albright, Israel; Pa., K.
Aldenderfer, J.M.; Pa.; K.
Aldenderfer, Metschl; Pa.; K.
Allbright, Henry; Pa.; K.

Allen, Amasa; Mass.; Chap. 21
Allen, Silas; Mass.; K.
Allen, Wm.; N.Y.
Allison, T.; Pa.; K.
Andrew, J.; Mich.; K.
Angstad, Adam; Pa.; K.
Angstadt, Peter; Pa.; K.
Angush, J.; Pa.
Annely, Edw.; N.J.
Annely, Thomas; N.J.
Ansted, A. & J.; Chaps. 3,4
Antis, Wm.; Pa.; C.
Armstrong, John; Md.; K.
Babbit, L. W.; O.
Backhouse, Richard; Pa.; K.
Baer, J.; Pa.; K.
Bailey, Nathan; Conn.; C.
Baker, J. S.; Pa.; K.
Baker, John; Pa.; K.C.
Ball, Elisha; N. C.; K.
Barlow, J.; Ind.; K.
Barnhardt, Wm.; Pa. & O.; K.
Barnhart, Geo.; Pa.
Barnhart, N.; Pa.; K.
Barnhart, S.; Pa.; K.
Barnhart, W.; Pa.; K.
Barnhizle, Christopher; Chap. 21
Barrett, Samuel; Mass.; C.
Barstow, J. & C. C.; N.H.; Chap. 21
Bartlett, A.P.; Chap. 21
Bartlett; Pa.; K.
Bates, R.; N. C.; K.
Bauer, George; Pa.
Bauer, J.; Pa.
Baum, S.; Pa.; K.
Baur, George; Pa.; K.
Baxter, A. T.; Md.; K.
Bean, Baxter; Tenn.; K.
Bean, Charles; Tenn.; K.
Bean, James; Tenn.; K.
Bean, Russell; Tenn.; K.
Bechtler, C.; N. C.; K.
Beck, C.; Pa.; K.
Beck, Isasc; Pa.; K.
Beck, J.; K.
Beck, J. P.; Pa.; K.

Becker, J.; Pa.; K.
Beerstecher, F.; Pa.; K.
Beig, S.; Pa.; K.
Bell, Conder; K.
Bell, Elias; Pa.; K.
Bellis; Pa.; K.
Bellow, Josiah; Chap. 21
Beman; Mass.; C.
Bemis, Edmund; Mass.
Bender, J.; Pa.; K.
Benfer, Amos; Pa.; K.
Benfer, Arnig; Pa.; K.
Berlin, Abraham; Pa.; K.
Berlin, Isaac; Pa.; K.
Bernard, Joseph; Chap. 21
Berry, A. P.; K.
Berry, B.; N. Y.; K.
Berry, W.; N. Y.
Berstrow, H. T.; N. Y.; K.
Bery, T. B.; K.
Best, M.; Pa.; K.
Beyer, N.; Pa.; K.
Bidwell, Oliver; Chap. 21
Bingham, Henry; Pa.; C.
Bird, C.; Pa.; K.
Bird, C. & Co.; Chap. 4
Bishop, A.; Pa.; K.
Blackwood, Marmaduke; Pa.; C.
Blaisdell, David Jr.; Mass.; C.
Blake, P. & E. W.; Chap. 21
Bloodgood; N. C.; K.
Bloom, Jacob; Pa.; K.
Blymyre, Geo.; Pa.; K.
Bodenheimer; Pa.; K.
Boenzli, A.; Pa.; K.
Boone, E.; Pa.; K. C.
Boone, Samuel; Pa.; K. C.
Boone, Squire; N. C.; K.
Boone, Thomas; Pa.; K.
Booth; Chap. 4
Bosler, J.; Pa.; K.
Bossworth; Pa.; K.
Boyd, James; Md.; C.
Boyd, Robert; N. Y.
Boyer, D.; Pa.; K.
Boyer, M.; Pa.; K.

Boyer, N.; Pa.; K.
Brandageez; N. Y.; K.
Breidenhart, Chris; Pa.;
    (C. repairs)
Brey, Elids; K.
Brickness, Thomas; Chap. 21
Brigh, S.; Pa.; K.
Brong, J.; Pa.; K.
Brong, Peter; Pa.; K.; Chap. 21
Brooke, I. I. & N.; Pa.
Brooke, J. J. & N.; Pa.; Chap. 21
Brown, Elisha; Chap. 21
Brown, F. B.; Pa.; K.
Bryan, Dan; N. C.; K.
Buck, Dan.; Pa.; K.
Buell, Elisha; Conn.
Bull, Elisha; N. C.; K.
Burd, C.; Pa.; K.
Busch, F. L.; Pa.; K.
Busler, J.; Pa.; K.
Butler, John; Pa.; K. C.
Butler, Thomas; Pa.
Byers, N.; Pa.; K.
Bynes, Michael; Pa.
Calderwood, Wm.; Chaps. 3,4
Call, G.; Pa.; K.
Camel & Co.; N. Y.; K.
Carlisle, H.; Pa.; K.
Carruth, Adam; Chap. 21
Caswell, J. M.; N. Y.; K.
Caup, Levi; Pa; K.
Chapman, James; Pa.; C.
Charlottesville Rifle Works;
    N. C.; K.
Cherington, Thomas P., Sr.; Pa.;
    K. Chap. 4
Cherington, Thomas P., Jr.; Pa.;
    K. Chap. 4
Chipman, Darius; Chap. 21
Chipman, Samuel; Chap. 21
Chnader, J.; Pa.; K.
Chrisky, L.; Pa.; K.
Christ, D.; Pa.; K.
Christ, Jacob
Clagett, Alexander; Chap. 21
Clallch, H. M.; Pa.; K.

Clapham, Josiah; Va.
Clark, Andrew; Mich.; K.
Clark, Joseph; Chap. 21
Clause, Nathan; Pa.; K.
Clewfin, W.
Cline, C.; Pa.; K.
Cobb, Nathan & Henry; Chap. 21
Coell, Ebenezer; Pa.; K. C.
Colderwood; Pa.; K.
Collier, Elisha H.; Mass.; Chap. 4
Constable, R.; Chap. 4
Cooke, Jacob; Chap. 3
Cooley, D.
Coons, E.; Pa.; K.
Coster, Abraham; Pa.
Coutty; Chap. 4
Cowell, E.; Pa.; K.
Cowell, J.; Mass.
Cowell, P.; Pa.; K.
Crabb, Thomas; Chap. 21
Crabtree, A.; Tenn.; K.
Crafts, Royal; Chap. 21
Craig, Robert; Pa.; C.
Cramer, P.; Pa.; K.
Crandall, M. F.; N. Y.; K.
Cravalty & Dugan; Md.; C.
Crockett, T.; Ky.; C.
Cryth, John; Pa.; K.
Cushing, A. D.; N.Y.; K.
Dallam, Richard; Md.; C.
Daub, J.; Pa.; K.
Davis, A.; N. Y.; K.
Davis, Isaac; Mass.; C.
Deckhard, Jacob, alias Dechert,
    Dechart, and Dickhart; Pa.; K.
Deeds, W.; Pa.
De Haven, Hugh; Pa.; C.
De Haven, Peter; Pa.; C.
De Huff, Gonter & Dichert;
    Chap. 3
De Huff, Henry; Pa.; K.; Chap. 21
Delaney, N.; Pa.; K.
De Reiner; Pa.; K. C.
Deringer, Henry; Pa.; K.;
    Chaps. 4, 21
Derr, John; Pa.; K.

Deterer, Adam; Pa.; K. C.
Detwiler, C.; Pa.; K.
Devane, J. & J.; N. C.
Dewey, Samuel; C.
Dickenson, J.; Va.; K.
Dickert, J.; Pa.; K.; Chap. 21
Diets; Pa.
Diffendorf, L.; N.Y.; K.
Diffendorf; Md.; K.
Dike, Anthony; Mass.; C.
Dimmick, H.E.; Mo.; K.
Disboch; Pa.; K.
Doll, Jacob; Chap. 21
Dooley; K.
Dopler, Robert; W. Va.; K.
Dorman, R.; Pa.; K.
Dorn, alias Lorn; Pa.; K.
Douglass, John; Pa.; K.
Doyle, John; Pa.; K.
Drepperd, Henry; Pa.; K.
Dresbach, J.; Pa.; K.
Dresbach, J., Jr.; Pa.; K.
Drippard, alias Drepperd; Pa.; K.
Dull, alias Doll; Pa.
Dunkle, G.; Pa.; K.
Dunseth, A.; Mo.; K.
Dunwicke; Pa.; C.
Earle, Thomas; Mass.; C.
Eberly; Pa.; K.C.
Eckles, H.; Pa.; K.
Ehlers
Ehrmon, H.; Pa.; K.
Eicholtz & Bro.; Pa.; K.; Chap. 25
Eliot, Matthew & Nathan; Chap. 21
Elwell, H.; Pa.; K.
Ely, Martin; Mass.; C.
Ernst, J.; Md.; K.
Evans, B.; Chap. 21
Evans, Edward; Chap. 21
Evans, James; Chap. 21
Evans, Owen; Chap. 21
Evans, O. & E.; Chaps. 3, 4, 21
Evans, Stephen; Pa.
Evans, W. L.; Chap. 3
Evatt; Md.; K.
Fainot, G. F.; Pa.; K.

Falley, Richard; Mass.; C.; Chap. 21
Farnot, Frank; Pa.; K.
Farnot, Jacob; Pa.; K.
Faulk, A.; Pa.; K.
Feder, G.; K.
Fehr, J.; Pa.; K.
Ferguson, C.; N.Y.
Ferree, Geo.; Pa.; K.
Ferree, Isaac; Pa.; K.
Ferree, Jacob; Pa.; K.
Ferree, Joel; Pa.; K.C.
Fitch, John; N.J.
Flagg, G. & Co.; Chap. 21
Fleek; Pa.; K.
Follecht; Pa.; K.
Fondergrift; Pa.; K.
Fondersmith, John; Chap. 21
Fondersmith & Son; Pa.; K.
Ford, J.; Va.
Fordney, C.; Md.
Fordney, I.
Fordney, Melchior; Pa.; K.
Foster, J.; Pa.
Foster, Joseph; Pa.; C.
Foulks, Wm.; Pa.; K.
Fox, R.; Pa.; K.
Francis & Tillingham; Pa.; C.
Franck; Pa.; K.
French, T.; Mass.; Chaps. 4, 21
French, Blake, & Kinsley; Chap. 21
Frock, J.; Pa.; K.
Froher, Ludwig; Pa.; C.
Frost, Gideon; Mass.; C.
Frye, Martin; Chap. 3
Gable & Son; Pa.
Galenbeck, J.; Pa.
Gallatin, Albert; Chap. 21
Gardner, G.; N.Y.
Garrett, Amos; Md.
Gaspard; Pa.
Gauyter, G.; Pa.; K.
Gehrett, J.F.; Pa.
Georg, Jacob; Pa.; K.
Geotz, F. & Westphall; Chap. 21
Gibbs, H.; Pa.; K.; Chap. 25
Gibson, S.; Tenn.; K.

Gilbert, Daniel; Chap. 21
Gill, B. D.; Pa.
Gillespie, M.; N. C.; K.
Gingerich, Henry; Pa.; K.C.
Glassbremer, G.; Pa.; K.
Glaze; Pa.
Golcher, George
Golcher, James; Pa.; Chap. 4
Golcher, John; Pa.; Chap. 4
Golcher, Joseph; Pa.; Chap. 4
Golcher, Manuel; Pa.; Chap. 4
Gontec, Peter, alias Gonter; Pa.; K.
Gonter, Peter, alias Gontec; Pa.; K.
Gonter, Peter, Jr., alias Gonder,
    Gontee; Pa.
Good, P.; Pa.
Goodling, P.
Gorsarge, Thomas; O.
Gouger; Pa.; C.
Goulcher, John; Pa.; C.
Graeff, Abraham; Chap. 21
Graeff, John; Pa.; K.; Chap. 21
Graeff, Wm.; Pa.; K.
Graham, J.; Pa.
Grandstatt, J.; K.
Grant, Samuel; Chap. 21
Green; Ga.
Gresheim; Pa.; K.
Grimes, Dan.; Pa.
Groce, H.; Pa.
Groff, H.S.
Grove, S.; Pa.
Grubb, T.; Pa.; K.; Chap. 4
Guest, I.; Pa.; Chap. 3
Guger, J. P.; Pa.
Gullam, Benjamin; Mass.; C.
Gumpf, Christopher; Pa.; K.
Gumpf, James; Pa.; K.
Gumph; Chap. 25
Gurn, A.; Pa.
Guyer, J.; Pa.
Haeffer, J.; Pa.; K.; Chap. 21
Haeffer, P. B.; K.
Hagi, J.; Pa.
Hain, P. L.; Pa.
Haines, Isaac; Pa.; K

Halbach & Sons; Chap. 4
Halburn, Caspar; Pa.; C.
Haldeman, F.; Pa.
Halk, I.
Hall, Charles; Pa.
Hall, John; Me.; Chap. 4
Hamilton, J.; N.C.
Hanks, Uriah; Conn.; C.
Harpers Ferry; see U.S. Armories
Harris, Isaac; Md.; C.
Harris, Jason; Pa.; K.
Harter; Pa.
Haslett, James; Md.
Hawk, Nicholas; Pa.
Hawken, W.; Pa.
Hawkins; Pa.
Heckert, P.; Pa.; K.
Hell, Thomas; Vt.; C.
Hench; Pa.; K.
Hennefelt, N.S.; Pa.
Henry, Abraham; Pa.; Chaps. 3, 21
Henry, James
Henry, John; Pa.
Henry, John Joseph; Pa.; K.;
    Chaps. 3, 4, 5
Henry, Joseph; Chaps. 3, 4
Henry, Mrs. John; Pa.
Henry, Wm. 1st; Pa.; Chap. 21
Henry, Wm. 2nd; Pa.
Henry, Wm. 3rd; Pa.
Hep, Philip, Jr.; K.
Herthe, August; Pa.
Hertzog, Andrew; Pa.; C.
Hess, J.; Pa.
Hillegas, J.; K.
Hoake, J.; K.
Holburn, Caspar L.
Honaker, J.; Pa.
Hooker, Thomas; Chap. 21
Horn, Conrad; Pa.
Horn, Stephen; Pa.; K.
Horn, William; Pa.; K.
Humble, Michael; Ky.
Humphreys, Hosea; Chap. 21
Hunter, David; Va.; C.
Huntington; Pa.

Huntington, Gurdon; Chap. 21
Hutchinson, R. J.; Pa.
Hutz; Pa.
Isch, Christian; Pa.; K.; Chap. 25
James, M.; Pa.; K.
Jenks, Geo. II; Chap. 21
Jenks, Stephen; Chap. 21
Johnson, J. H., Sr.; Chap. 25
Johnson, P. & D.; Chap. 21
Johnson, Robert; Chaps. 3, 21
Johnson, Seth; Mass.; C.
Johnston, Richard B.; Chap. 21
Jones, Amos; Conn.; C.
Jones, Charles; Pa.; K.
Jones, Robert; Pa.; K.
Josan; Pa.
Jost (Yost); Pa.; C.
Kantz; K.
Kascheline, Peter; Pa.; C.
Kaup, Levi; Pa.
Keely, Matthias; Pa.; C.
Keely, Sebastian; Pa.; C.
Keener, Samuel; Md.; C.
Keffer, Jacob; Pa.; K.
Keller, I.; Pa.; K.
Kelly, Samuel
Kemmerer; K.
Kennedy, E. M.
Kerlin, John; Pa.; C.; Chap. 21
Kerlin, Samuel; Chap. 21
Kern, Dan; Pa.; K.
Ketland, J. & T.; Chap. 21
Ketland, T. & Co.; Chap. 5
Key, R.; Pa.; K.
Kile, Nathan; O.; K.
Kinder; Pa.; C.
Kinsley, Adam; Chap. 21
Kiser, A.; K.
Kitchen, Wheeler; Pa.
Klase, A.; Pa.
Kleist, Daniel; Pa.; K.
Kline, C.; Pa.; Chap. 4
Koesler
Kolcher, P.; Pa.; K.
Koons, Frank; Pa.; K.
Kornman, A. D.; Pa.; K.
Krider, John; Pa.; K.

Kunkle; Pa.
Kuntz, Dan; Pa.
Kuntz, J.; Chap. 4
Laether, Jacob; Chap. 21
Lagunbra; Pa.
Lawrence, Capt.; Mass.; C.
Lawrence; Pa.; Chap. 4
Layendecker; Pa.
Lechiler; Pa.
Lefevre, Philip; Pa.
Legler; Tenn.
Leitner, Adam; Chap. 3
Leman, Henry E.; Pa.; K.
Leman, Peter; Pa.; K.
Lennard; Pa.
Leonard, Charles; Mass.
Leonard, R. & C.; Chap. 21
Lether & Co.; Pa.
Little, D.; Pa.; K.
Livingston, John; Chap. 21
Llewellin, Matthew; Chap. 21
Lloyd, Wm.; Pa.
Loder; Pa.; K.
Lodge Bros.; Pa.
Lodge, J.; Pa.
Long, James; Pa.
Lorney, M.; Pa.
Lowery, David; Conn.; C.
Luddington; Pa.
Ludwig, Paul; Pa.; K.
Lutes, Wm.; Ky.
Lydick, Peter; Md.; C.
Mange, H.
Marker, Daniel; Pa.; K.
Marshall, Job; Pa.
Martin, M.; K.
Martin, T.
Mauger, H.; K.
Maus, P.; Pa.; K.
Mause, D. E.; Pa.
Mayesch; Pa.
McCavery; N.Y.; C.
McCormick, James; Pa.; C.
McCormick, Robert; Pa.; Chaps. 4, 21
McK. & Bro.; Md.; Chap. 4
McNaught; Chap. 4

McRae, Alexander; Chap. 21
Meacham & Pond
Melchoir, M.
Messersmith, John; Pa.; K. C.
Messersmith, Samuel; Md.
Metzger, J.; Pa.; K.; Chap. 21
Meylan, Martin; Pa.
"W.G.M.," unknown; K.
Miles, John; N.J.; C.; Chaps. 3, 4
    21
Miles, Thomas; Pa.
Miller, I.
Miller, John; Pa.; K.
Miller, Mathias; Pa.; K.
Miller, Simon; Pa.; K.; Chap. 5
Mills, Ben; Ky.; K.
Milnor, I.; Pa.; K.
Moll, I.
Moll, John; Pa.
Moll, J. & W. H.; Pa.
Moll, N.; Pa.
Moll, Peter & David; Pa.; K.; Chap.
    4
Moore, Abraham; Pa.; C.
Morgan, J.; Pa.; K.
Morgan, James; N.Y.; K.
Morrison, Milton; Pa.
Morrison, S.; Pa.; K.
Mower, P.; Pa.; K.
Munro, Nathaniel; Pa.; C.
Musser, H.; Pa.
Myer, Henry; Pa.; K.
Newbaker; Pa.; K.
Newhardt, Jacob; Pa.
Newhardt, Peter; Pa.
Nichols, Jonathan, Jr.; Chap. 21
Nicholson, John; Pa.; C.
Nippes, D.; Pa.; K.; Chap. 21
North, S.; Chaps. 3, 4
North & Cheney; Chap. 3
Oakes, Sam; Pa.
Oberholtzer; Pa.; K. C.
Ogden, alias Odgen; N.Y.
Osborn, Lot; Conn.; C.
Page, John; Conn.; C.
Palm, Jacob; Pa.; K.
Palm, John; Pa.; K.

Palmer, Thos.; Pa.; C.
Palmetto Armory; Chap. 21
Pannabecker, Jeff; Pa.; K.
Pannabecker, John; Pa.
Pannabecker, Jesse; Pa.
Pannabecker, S.; Pa.
Pannabecker, Wm. Sr.; Pa.; K.
Pannabecker, Wm. Jr.
Parrish, W. A.; Pa.; K.
Paul, Andrew; Pa.
Pearson, James; Pa.; C.
Peck, Abijah; Chap. 21
Perkin, I.; Chap. 4
Perkins, J.; Pa.; Chap. 21
Perkins, Rufus; Chap. 21
Phelps, Silas; Conn.; C.
Philipy, J.
Pickel or Pickle, Henry; Pa.; K.;
    Chaps. 3, 21
Pomeroy, Lemuel; Chap. 21
Pomeroy, Seth; Mass.; C.
Pond & Co.; Chap. 4
Prahl, Lewis; Pa.; C.
Pringle, John; Pa.; C.
Puling, J.
Putnam, Enoch; Mass.; C.
Radfang, Geo.; Pa.; C.
Rappahannock Forge; Chaps. 3, 4,
    10
Rathfong, George; Pa.; K.
Reasor, David; Pa.
Razor, Jacob; Md.; C.
Reading; Pa.; K.
Reddick; Md.; C.
Redfan, alias Rathfong; Pa.
Read, Wm.; Md.; C.
Reed, J.; N. H.; K.
Reed, J.; Pa.; K.
Reed, Robert; Md.; C.
Reid, Templeton; Ga.
Remmerer, David
Resor, J.
Reynolds; Pa.; K.
Rhodes, Wm.; Chap. 21
Richmond, Va., Armory; Chap. 4
Riddle, Pa.; K.
Rigert, alias Reigart; Pa.; K.

Righter, J. G.; Ohio
Riner, Michael; Pa.
Rittenhouse, Benj.; Pa.; C.
Robbins; Tenn.; K.
Robinson; Pa.
Robertson; Pa.
Roesser, Mat.; Pa.; K.
Roesser, Peter; Pa.; K.
Rogers, John; Chap. 21
Rogers & Bros.; Chap. 4
Roop, John; Pa.; K.
Roth, Henry; Pa.
Rupp, John; Chap. 4
Ruppert, Wm.; Pa.
Russily, Jacob; Pa.
Rynes, Michael; Pa.
St. Clair, S. H.; Pa.
Scho'b, I.; Pa.; K.
Schorer, Andrew; Pa.
Schridt, John; Pa.
Schriver, J.; Pa.
Schroyer, Mathias; Chap. 21
Schuler, John; Pa.
Schull, M.
Schultz, C.; Pa.
Scott; Pa.; K.
Sell, Fred; Md.
Selvidge, John; Tenn.; K.
Senseny, J.; Pa.
Serles, D.; Pa.; K.
Settle, F.; Ky.; K.
Settle, J.; Pa.; K.; Chap. 25
Settle, W.; Ky.; K.
Sever, Joseph; Mass.; C.
Sever, Shubabel; Mass.; C.
Shafer, Joseph
Shannon, Wm. & Hugh; Chap. 3
Shaw; Mass.; C.
Sheesley, George; Pa.
Sheets, M.; Va.
Sheffield, Jeremiah; R. I.; C.
Shell, John; Ky.; K.
Shell, M.; Pa.
Shell, Samuel; Ky.
Shennefelt; Pa.; K.
Sherry, J.; Pa.; K.
Sherwood, T.; W. Va.; K.

Shule, J.; Pa.; K.
Shuler, John; Chaps. 3, 4
Shuler, S.; Pa.; K.
Shultz, H.; Pa.
Sibert, G.; Pa.; K.
Slocumb, Samuel D.; La.
Smith, Abbe
Smith, Adam; C.
Smith, Adam; O.
Smith, Anthony; Pa.; K.
Smith, J. F.; Pa.; K.
Smith, John; Chap. 21
Smith, Johnson; Pa.; K.
Smith, P.; Pa.; K.
Smith, Stoeffel; Pa.; K.
Smith & Hyslop; Chap. 4
Sneider, Anthony; Pa.
Sneider, T.
Snyder, Adam, George, Henry, and
    John; Pa.
Snyder, Ira; Pa.
Spang & Wallace; Pa.
Spangler, S.; Pa.; K.
Sparling, L. D.; N. Y.
Specht, Eley; Pa.
Spitzer, Sr.; Va.; C.
Springfield; see U.S. Armories
Stahl, C.; Pa.; K.
Stapelton, J.; Pa.
Starr; Pa.; K.
Starr, N.; Chap. 21
Stenzel, alias Stengel; Pa.
Stillman, Amos & Co.; Chap. 21
Stillman, Ethan; Chap. 21
Stinger, Thomas; Pa.
Stone, David; Chap. 21
Sunderland; Pa.
Sweitzer & Co.; Chap. 4
Sweitzer, A.; Pa.
Sweitzer, Daniel; Pa.; C.
Switzer & Co.
Switzer, Dan; Pa.; K.
Taylor, Geo.; Pa.
Teaff, Nimrod; O.
Teff, Geo.; R. I.; C.
Tell, Fred; Md. & Pa.
Tomlinson, Joshua; Pa.; C.

Town, Ben.; Pa.; C.
Towsey, Thomas; Chap. 21
Trout, John; Pa.
Tryon, Geo. W.; Pa.; K.; Chap. 4
Tyler, John; Pa.
Tyler, Wm.; Chap. 21
Unseld, John; Md.; C.
Updegraph, Jacob; Pa.
U.S. Armories: Harpers Ferry,
  Chaps. 3, 21; Springfield, Chaps.
  3, 21
Vanderslice, T.; Pa.
Velee; Pa.
Virginia Manufactory; Chaps. 4, 5,
  10, 22
Vogler, C.; N. C.
Vogler, N.; Pa.; K.
Vogler, P.; N. C.; K.
Volght, Henry; Pa.; C.
Volvert, alias Volkert; Pa.; K.
Vondergrift, John; Pa.; C.
Vondersmith; Pa.
Wagonhorst
Wally, Sam; Pa.; K.
Walsh, James; Pa.; C.; Chap. 4
Walters, E. & A.; Chap. 21
Waters, Andrus; Mass.; C.
Waters, Asa; Mass.; C.; Chaps. 3, 21
Waters; Duchess Co., N.Y.; C.
Waters, Nippes & Steinman; Chap.
  4
Watkeys, Henry; N.Y.; C.
Watt; Pa.; K.
Weaver, Crypret; Pa.; K.
Weiker, G.; Pa.; K.
Weiser, G. W.; Pa.
Weishens, J.
Welhanze, Conrad; Chap. 21
Wellhance, Kunrat; Chap. 21
Welshantz, Conrad; Pa.; K.
Welshantz, Jacob; Pa.; K.
Welshantz, Joseph; Pa.; K.
Welton, Ard, Lt.; Conn.; C.
Westfall; Chap. 21
Wetzel, J.; Pa.
Wheeler & Morrison; Chap. 21

Whetcroft, Wm.; Md.; C.
White, Horace; Mass.; C.
White, J.; Pa.; K.
White, Nicholas; Chap. 21
White, Peter; K.
Whitesides, John M.; Tenn.
Whitmore, N.; Chap. 21
Whitney, Eli; Chap. 21
Whittemore, Amos; Mass.; C.
Wickham, Marine T.; Chap. 21
Wickham, T.; Pa.; C.
Wigfal, Sam; Pa.; C.
Williams, Elie; Chap. 21
Williams, Nicholas; Chap. 21
Willis, John; Pa.; C.
Winger, Richard; Pa.; C.
Wingert, W.; Mich.
Winner, Nippes & Steinman,
  Chaps. 3, 21
Winters, Elisha; Md.; C.
Withers, Michael; Pa.; C.
Wofheimer, Philip
Wood, E. C.; N. Y.; K.
Wood, John; Mass.; C.
Wood, Josiah; Pa.; C.
Woods, Robert; Pa.; K.
Workman, J.; Pa.
Worl, H.; Pa.
Worley, J.
Wurfflein, Andrew; Pa.; K.
Wurfflein, J.; Pa.
Yeomans, Daniel; Pa.
Yeomans, David; N. C.; K.
Yocum, D.; Pa.; K.
Yomens; N. C.
Yost, Caspar; Pa.; C.
Yost, John; Md.; C.
Youmans; N. C.; K.
Young, D.; Pa.
Young, Henry; Pa.
Young, Jacob
Young, John; Md.
Young, John; Pa.; K. C.
Young, Joseph; W. Va.
Zarger, Fred; Pa.; C.
Zimmerman; Pa.

# Chapter 27

## CASED SETS

A CASED set is appraised by starting with the value of the gun itself. Knowing the value of the gun with standard wooden grips, add not less than $40 if it has plain ivory grips, and about $60 if the grips are plain but the quality of the ivory is superior. If it has well-carved ivory grips, add not less than $60 and possibly from $90 up, depending, of course, on the quality of the carving. This applies to the usual collector's item, but in dealing with a piece that is in great demand, such as a Colt percussion revolver, start with $50 for plain ivory grips, and $100 for ivory grips with simple carving, and go on up according to the quantity and quality of the carving. Elephant ivory is better than walrus ivory, and either is better than the ordinary bone that passes for ivory in some shops. Deep carving is considered more valuable than shallow carving, and it should be obvious that ivory grips carved with a cameo-like bust of a beautiful woman are worth more than those decorated with an eagle or bull's head.

The quantity and quality of the metal engraving of the gun are also important. Deep engraving executed in fine, intricate figures is greatly desired. Gold inlay is also a factor in appraising value. If the gold is inlaid in several colors or different degrees of gold hardness, the value is increased greatly, especially if different colors of gold are combined to form a picture. Examine the method of inlaying to be sure that vibration and shocks will not jar the gold loose.

If there is a perfectly matched pair of arms, do not simply multiply the value of a single piece by 2, but multiply by 2 and add 50%, since a matched pair is rarer and more in demand than unmatched single pieces.

380

Next, examine the accessories. There may be a bullet mold, a powder-and-ball flask, a priming device ("capper"), a nipple wrench, a cleaning rod, and other tools. There may be bullets already cast, and a box of primers. Each of these has some value, but the bullet mold and the powder-and-ball flask are the most important. A mold or flask for an ordinary piece may be worth from $50 to $75, depending upon type, model, make, condition, etc., or it may be worth only from $40 to $60. A bullet mold or a flask for a Colt percussion revolver may be worth from $50 to $150.

Occasionally a cased set is found with an extra barrel, especially in the case of Paterson Colt revolvers. The value of the barrel hinges upon the value of the gun it accompanies, as well as on its own condition, for condition is just as important in appraising accessories as in fixing the value of guns. If the accompanying spare barrel has the same serial number as the gun, the value jumps again, for this is rare. An extra cylinder is appraised in a similar manner.

An original, factory-made case is more desirable than one made for the owner after the gun left the factory, but an exception exists if there is something about the case that gives it value as a case, that is, if it is made of rare or inlaid wood, has gold or silver inlays, and bears an engraved presentation notice of historical importance, or has some other feature that gives it value independent of the contents.

Factory-made cases often have illustrated directions pasted inside the lid. This adds to the value. However, in some instances the label inside the cover was pasted there by the owner of a retail shop, hence the collector may confuse the name of the owner with the maker of the gun, especially if the latter is not clearly marked.

A gun that was a presentation piece may have the name of the donor and the donee engraved on the frame or barrel, and the same or similar engraving may appear on metal plates affixed to the inside or outside of the box, or both. These add to value, especially if either the donor or the donee was famous. On the other hand, the engraved plates may bear the name of the owner of the gun, and this, too, enhances the appraisal, but do not be deceived. It is an old trick to engrave someone's name on a plate to boost the price. Engraving is comparatively cheap if it will make a handsome profit on the sale of otherwise low-value arms. Buy guns. Do not buy the dealer's yarns. Fiction of the pulp variety is sold at rates from two to three cents a word, except in the gun business where it commands a much higher rate.

The original owners of cased arms prized their guns highly or they would not have purchased them cased in the first place. Consequently, cased sets have often come down to us in practically factory-new condition in every respect.

Appraising a cased set is much like estimating the value of a woman. If she has an ugly face, no figure, bad breath, athlete's foot, no brains, and no sense of humor, her value is low even if she wears the finest dress on the market and spends half of her life in a so-called beauty parlor. Likewise, if a gun has no value in itself, the fact that it is cased with accessories should not deceive the collector. In other words, the value of the case and the accessories rises and falls with the value of the gun.

The majority of the experienced, ethical arms-dealers in the United States read remarks similar to these in the first edition of this text, and they all agreed with the author; and yet it is interesting to find that they sometimes forget the factors involved in appraising a cased set and sell it for little more than the value of the gun by itself. This does not happen often, but it occurs frequently enough for the careful buyer occasionally to acquire a bargain. Beginners should leave bargains strictly alone, for what appears to be a bargain to them is often merely a fool trap for suckers.

Appraising the value of a cased set that is alleged by the owner to have historical significance requires a high degree of courage, experience, and diplomacy. For example, the author of this text was asked to appraise the value of a cased set of pistols that the owner believed was used during a San Francisco duel. There was nothing about the case or the contents that connected the cased set of pistols with any historical event, least of all the duel, which was not a duel at all but a common murder. Furthermore, the pistols were not dueling pistols by any stretch of imagination. The author stated the facts, much to the displeasure of the owner, who promptly engaged another firearms appraiser because the cased set had been insured for a fantastically high amount. Let all insurance companies and their agents beware of sentimental owners of cased sets.

# Chapter 28

## FREAKS AND ODDITIES

FREAKS and oddities are sometimes described as "special purpose" or "combination arms," depending upon their function and construction. The present chapter indicates the types of weapons in this classification found in the usual collection.

ALARM GUN. Strictly speaking, this should not discharge a bullet but only powder, although some so-called alarm guns are actually trap or spring guns and do fire bullets. A representative specimen is the S. Coon Alarm Pistol, about cal. .25, percussion, 2.5-inch round barrel, with a heavy spring on top of the barrel which acts as a hammer to fire the primer. A long screw attached to the barrel is fastened to the door or window so that when it is opened it will cause the pistol to fire.

SAME, but an unmarked, American-made, cartridge alarm pistol with a rectangular steel frame, 2 inches by three-fourths inch, attached to the window or doorjamb with a screw at one end, similar to the S. Coon Pistol; and at the opposite side is a spring-driven arm with a firing pin in its end. A blank .22 r.f. cartridge is placed in the chamber after the arm has been pulled out at right angles to the frame. When the door or window opens, the arm springs in and fires the blank, hence this is a real alarm gun and not a trap gun. Marked "R.F. Pat'd. May 12, 1874."

APACHE PISTOL. This may be a combination of a revolver with brass or steel knuckles or with a dagger or knife, or it may have both the knuckles and the blade. Many have been made and sold in Belgium and France, and they acquired their name from their use by the "Apaches" in the slums of Paris, which is a gross libel on American Apache Indians. A typical specimen is cal. .32 r.f., D.A., 6-shot; with a 1.5-inch, fluted, round cylinder; an iron frame marked "L. Dolne Invor."; iron knuckles, for grips, that fold under the piece; a folding trigger; and a folding wavy-blade dagger on the left side of the frame.

SAME, but 8 mm, pin-fire, D.A., 6-shot; 1.625-inch, round, fluted cylinder; white metal frame marked "L. Dolne Invor."; brass knuckles form the pistol grip and fold under the piece; a folding dagger 3.625 inches long is on the left side of the frame. Like the specimen described above, this is double-action with an outside hammer spring. There is a Liege proof mark on the cylinder.

BAR PISTOL. This type has 2 or more chambers cut out of a rectangular, solid metal bar. A typical example is the German Bar Pistol, which has 4 chambers in the bar and 2 barrels. The 2 cartridges in the top chambers are fired first; then the bar is unlatched and revolved through a complete circle to expose the other 2 chambers for firing. It was designed to lie flat in the hand for concealment. The specimen described here is cal. .25, auto, 4-shot, 2.5-inch round barrels superposed, D.A., hammerless, marked "Patent" with patent numbers for various countries.

BATTLE-AX PISTOL. Genuine specimens of battle-ax pistols usually date back to the sixteenth century and sometimes to the seventeenth century, but a few were apparently made as late as the eighteenth century. The method of ignition ranges from wheel lock to flintlock, and the value varies not only with the value of the firearm but also with the workmanship of the ax and the ornamentation of the whole piece.

BLUDGEON PISTOL. This is a pistol with a handle constructed to be used as a club after the pistol is fired, usually a single-shot pistol. This type is found as late as the percussion era but is more common when made with a flintlock.

BOOTLEG PISTOL. This type was usually made for target practice, dueling, and plain murder. It was generally made without a trigger guard and often with an underhammer. Several examples are described in Chapter 9. A good example is the Gibbs, Tiffany & Co. Percussion Bootleg Pistol, cal. .34; 6-inch, round-octagon, rifled barrel marked "Cast Steel"; total length 10 inches; made without a trigger guard, but with an underhammer. It has a blade front sight and a peep rear sight. The frame is marked "Gibbs Tiffany & Co. Sturbridge Mass."

CANE GUN. This type was formerly made in great quantities in France, England, and Belgium, for naturalists, gamekeepers, and poachers. A concealed trigger is characteristic. Also, the piece may be made so that it can be separated into 3 parts for ease in carrying or concealment. In the better specimens only a close inspection will reveal the presence of the gun inside the cane. The ignition system may be either percussion or cartridge. The value varies greatly.

CUTLASS PISTOL. Typical specimens are the Elgin Cutlass Pistols made by C. B. Allen and by Morrill, Mosman & Blair, described in Chapters 6 and 7. There are several variations in size and construction.

DAGGER PISTOL. This means exactly the same as Knife Pistol, but it sounds better to the customer. An ordinary, unidentified, American cartridge pistol, cal. .22 r.f., all-metal, nickel-plated, with a short barrel and a heavy knife blade marked only "Patented," is satisfactory to represent the type.

SAME, but Peavey Knife Pistol, cal. .22 r.f., short iron barrel, brass frame, wooden inlaid grips, concealed trigger, a heavy knife blade, outside hammer built to resemble a knife blade, firing pin contained in barrel and struck on top by the hammer, and marked only "A.J.Peavy" with patent dates.

SIMILAR, but English James Rodgers Percussion Knife Pistol, cal. .32, 3.5-inch, hexagonal German silver barrel. Entire knife frame made of German silver covered with horn. Two blades, 3.5 and 2.5 inches long. Folding trigger. Center-hung hammer. Primer box in butt. Bullet mold in recess in frame of pistol. British proof marks. Blade marked "James Rodgers Sheffield, Protector" and etched with the figure of an eagle.

SAME, but Belgian Mariette Dagger Pepperbox, cal. .33, 8-shot; 3.25-inch, round, Damascus barrels. Ring trigger. Underhammer. Engraved iron frame marked "Mariette Brevete." The dagger has a 2.625-inch concealed blade that must be unscrewed and fixed before using. Carved and fluted walnut grips.

DUCK FOOT. A duck foot is a multi-barrel pistol with the barrels radiating from the handle at angles like the fingers of the hand when spread out, or like the toes of a duck's foot. The inventor's intention was probably to provide a weapon that could be fired into a crowd without changing the position of the shooter's hand. An example is an English flintlock pistol of this type. It has four 2.75-inch, round barrels, laid horizontally, that unscrew to load and are mounted with their muzzles one-fourth inch apart. The caliber is .42 smoothbore, there is a center-hung hammer with a safety lock, and a walnut grip. The frame is engraved with a stand of arms and the words "Forth York," but the breech has the French fleur-de-lis on the upper side and British proof marks below.

SIMILAR, but cal. .31 smoothbore, with three 2.5-inch, round barrels that unscrew to load and are marked "Cast St. O:K.X." Barrels radiate from the same breech, their muzzles are three-fourths inch apart, and all 3 fire at the same time. Center-hung hammer with safety lock. Walnut stock. Apparently English.

HARMONICA PISTOL. This weapon gets its name from its shape. There are usually a number of rifled barrels drilled through a solid block. Behind the barrels are an equal number of cartridges, usually pin-fire, which are held in a perforated frame. As the trigger is pulled, the barrels automatically travel across the face of the cartridge frame, the direction of travel being either sideways or up and down, depending on whether the barrels are mounted horizontally or vertically. A typical example is the Belgian Jarre Harmonica Pistol, cal. 7 mm, pin-fire, 10-shot, D.A., 2-inch barrels. Iron frame. Nickel-plated. Solid block through which barrels are bored is 3.25 inches long with flutes between the barrels. A hinged strap is fixed to the top rear of the barrel block and serves to hold the cartridges in place and protect the pins. The barrels move horizontally as the trigger is pulled for each shot. The ejector rod screws into the top of the grip. Marked "A.Jarre Bvt. S.C.D.G." with Liege, Belgium, proof marks.

KNIFE PISTOL—Same as Dagger Pistol.

KNUCKLE–DUSTER. The true knuckle-duster pistol or revolver has a large, flat, metal butt with a hole in the center for grasping with the fingers in using it like brass knuckles. This is not to be confused with the so-called Apache Pistols, which may have brass or steel knuckles and a dagger combined with the gun. The outstanding example is found in the group of knuckle-dusters made by J.Reid, and described in Chapter 17 on American cartridge pistols and revolvers. There are several types and sizes with a corresponding range of values.

LADIES' OR MUFF PISTOLS. These are any small-caliber tiny pistols that can be carried in a lady's purse or handbag, although they were sometimes carried in muffs back in the days when those objects were in style. The classification is so broad that it is impossible to give any intelligent range of values.

PALM PISTOLS. These are firearms that can be concealed in the palm of the hand, such as the Chicago Protector Palm Pistol, described in detail in Chapter 17. The Minneapolis Protector Palm Pistol is very similar.

PENCIL OR FOUNTAIN PEN PISTOL. This is any single-shot pistol constructed to look like a pencil or a fountain pen. A few years ago fountain pen pistols were made and advertised to fire gas cartridges, but a cartridge with a bullet could be loaded, and then they were as dangerous to the shooter as to his target. A good example of a pencil cartridge pistol is cal. .32 c.f., 1.75-inch round barrel, nickel-plated, with a soft rubber knob on the end to act as cushion in the hand. A ring around the barrel is squeezed to the rear to cock and fire. It is marked only "Pat. Apld. For."

POWDER TESTER, sometimes called an Eprouvette. There are many types, makes, and models. Most of them are flintlock, although percussion specimens are found. In a typical flintlock specimen, a measured charge of powder is placed in a vertical tube connected at its bottom with the pan. The priming powder is placed in the pan and the dial set at zero. On firing, the explosion acts through the tube to move a graduated dial that thus measures the strength of the powder.

SIMILAR, but Percussion Powder Tester. In one form, a pair of arms extended downward from the muzzle. At the bottom of the arms is a wheel under spring tension, which is graduated. The lip on the rim of the wheel fits over the muzzle of the barrel. The piece is fired by igniting the charge through a hole in the top of the barrel.

SIMILAR, but another form of Percussion Powder Tester. There is an iron frame, a center-hung hammer, and a pointer on the frame that indicates the force of the explosion on a dial numbered from 1 to 15, held under spring tension. Made without a trigger guard.

SALON OR SALOON PISTOL. This does not mean a pistol carried into a cocktail lounge but a "parlor pistol," that is, any very light small-caliber pistol which in theory could be shot indoors safely. It means the same as a Lady's Pistol or a Muff Pistol, hence it does not mean anything very definite except as to size. It is a quaint custom of ignorant dealers to call any piece of junk for which they have no other name a saloon pistol, with the result that all kinds of trash from a watch-charm toy pistol to a sawed-off shotgun may bob up under this heading.

SIGNAL PISTOL. Other names that mean the same thing are Flare, Rocket, Parachute, and Very Pistol, the latter term coming from the inventor, Lieutenant Very, U.S. Navy. It has a very large bore and fires into the air a missile which lights up the surrounding area. There is usually a choice of several colors and one kind has a slowly descending parachute that carries the fireworks. When used by the armed forces of the United States, it may be classified as a U.S. martial pistol.

SAME, U.S. ARMY SIGNAL PISTOL, CIVIL WAR PERCUSSION TYPE, cal. .75, percussion, 1.625-inch brass barrel. Spur trigger. Center-hung hammer. Iron lever extends down from barrel along frame to hold flare in barrel. Brass frame. Butt marked "U.S. Army Signal Pistol 1862."

SAME, but C. S. Shattuck Signal Pistol, 12-gauge, 12-inch round barrel, single-shot, walnut grips, spur trigger, and center-hung hammer. Barrel tips up to load.

SPRING GUN OR TRAP GUN. Typical examples are the North & Couch Percussion Trap Pistol and Reuthe's American Percussion Trap Gun, described in Chapter 9.

SWORD PISTOL. This is similar in design to a dagger or knife pistol. A good example is a Japanese Percussion Sword Pistol, cal. .48; 10.5-inch, round, ribbed barrel with a grip like that of a Japanese sword, copper-bound at the ends and covered with leather painted in floral patterns. The hammer resembles the American underhammer type. The trigger is hook-shaped. The scabbard is copper and painted leather, like a Japanese sword scabbard of that period. There is a button-tip ramrod inside the scabbard.

TINDER LIGHTER. Before friction matches were invented, people had to save glowing coals to start a fire, or use flint and steel. The flintlock on an unloaded gun served the same purpose, but a more convenient device was the "tinder lighter," which resembles the lock on a flintlock arm but has a metal receptacle, instead of a barrel, to hold the tinder (which may be any highly inflammable substance) to catch the sparks.

## Why No Values Are Stated in This Chapter

In some previous editions of this book, values were given for the items in this chapter, but for several reasons, no values are given in this edition. Some of the reasons are as follows:

1. The possession of several of the items is a violation of federal and state laws.

2. Some are dangerous to fire.

3. Most of the items are described and assigned values in other chapters.

4. In previous editions approximate values were stated, but this caused some collectors to pay too much for some items and sell others at prices which were too low.

5. Some of the items are not firearms. An example is a tinder lighter.

6. Experts who specialize in certain types of firearms object to calling their items freaks and oddities.

# Chapter 29

## *BRITISH FIREARMS*

BRITISH firearms, particularly those used in Colonial and Revolutionary America, have always been collected by serious students of our early history, especially by native-born Americans whose ancestors bled and died to make and preserve us a nation. Those who have come to our shores during the last seventy-five years, and their descendants, usually have been descended from people who were jealous of the British and hated anything British, including firearms. However, in the World Wars recently fought, our armed forces have become interested in British arms. Hence, no book on appraising values would be complete without some discussion of these weapons.

The British flintlock pistols and revolvers are generally examples of fine craftsmanship. Many were made in pairs and cased. That explains why they are often found in fine condition and are worth comparatively large sums of money. The British did not produce percussion arms of the same variety and quality as American percussion arms, collectively speaking, hence such arms are found in smaller numbers in the usual collection. The British laws restricting the use and possession of firearms came during the cartridge period, hence there are very few interesting and desirable specimens in that group.

The firearms described and illustrated in this chapter are what many collectors in the United States of America describe as "British." These are all handguns and especially selected for their quality of design and construction. A truly British collection would include handguns and shoulder arms made in England, Scotland, Ireland, Wales, or any spot on earth where the Union Jack still flies, and where the people still sing "God Save the Queen."

There is no text on British arms which the author can recommend wholeheartedly. *English Pistols and Revolvers* by J. N. George is written in such vague general terms, as though it were ungentlemanly to be precise in describing arms, that its value is limited to anyone except an experienced collector of these weapons. *A History of Firearms* by H. B. C. Pollard is written in the same casual style and is out of print.

ANNLIY BRASS-BARREL FLINTLOCK PISTOL, cal. .62, 7-inch, round, brass barrel. Full-length walnut stock. All brass mountings with a lion mask on the butt. Gooseneck hammer. Iron pan. Lock marked "E. & Tho. Annliy." No proof marks. Horn-tipped ramrod. Plate 46, Fig. 2. $500–$785.

ARCHER FLINTLOCK PISTOL, cal. .62; 9-inch, round, pin-fastened, steel barrel with early English proof marks. Total length 14.5 inches. Full-length walnut stock. Brass butt cap, thimbles, lock plate, pan, and trigger guard. Ivory-tipped oak ramrod. Safety lock in rear of hammer. Lock marked "Archer." Plate 46, Fig. 4. $400–$525.

ARCHER FLINTLOCK PISTOL, cal. .42, 2.225-inch round barrel which unscrews to load. Frame engraved and marked "Archer London." Center-hung hammer. Frizzen spring inletted into barrel and not attached to frizzen. Sterling silver butt cap carved in likeness of a man's face. Plate 46, Fig. 5. $385–$500.

BENNETT FLINTLOCK PISTOL, cal. .61; 10-inch round-octagon barrel marked "Royal Exchange London." Lock marked "Bennett" in raised letters on gold plate. Full-length walnut stock. Iron guard, pan, and thimbles. Sliding safety lock in rear of gooseneck hammer. Horn-tipped mahogany ramrod. Plate 46, Fig. 6. $450–$600.

SAME, but cal. .58, 9-inch round barrel, and otherwise the same as the above. Plate 46, Fig. 7. $450–$600.

BIRCHETT BREECHLOADING FLINTLOCK PISTOL, military type, made in London during the Queen Anne period. The entire barrel unscrews by moving back the trigger guard which acts as a lock. Where most screw barrels are joined in front of the pan, this one has the joint back of the pan. The cannon barrel is 8 inches long, and the total length is 13.5 inches. The butt is silver-masked, and there is a silver medallion back of the walnut grip. The specimen illustrated is one of a matched pair. The value shown is for the pair. Plate 48, Fig. 9. $1,650–$2,500.

BLAKE FLINTLOCK HOLSTER PISTOL, cal. .62; 14.25-inch round-octagon barrel. Total length 19.25 inches. Full-length walnut stock. Brass guard, thimbles, and butt cap, the latter being carved in relief. Iron pan. Safety lock. Marked "Ann Blake Gun Maker 95 Wapping Old Stairs London." Plate 46, Fig. 11. $350–$450.

BRITISH MARTIAL WHEEL-LOCK PISTOL, cal. .54; 19.75-inch, part round, part octagon, pin-fastened barrel. Full-length walnut stock. Iron butt cap. Iron-tipped hardwood ramrod. Outside wheel. Total length 27 inches. This is larger than the usual genuine wheel-lock pistol found in collections but it is authentic in all respects. Plate 46, Fig. 1. $1,650–$2,600.

BRITISH CAVALRY FLINTLOCK PISTOL, GEORGE III PERIOD, cal. .69; smoothbore, 9.25-inch, round, slightly belled muzzle. Made without sights. Full-length walnut stock. Brass thimble, trigger guard, and butt cap. Flat lock plate and hammer, as distinguished from the other type of British Cavalry pistol which was almost identical except that it had a gooseneck hammer and a round-face lock plate. Lock marked "Tower." In front of hammer is a large crown above the letters "G.R." Forward on the crown is the broad arrow, the symbol of the British Government ownership. Plate 46, Fig. 3. $450–$600.

BRITISH MILITARY HEAVY DRAGOON FLINTLOCK PISTOL. Walnut full stock. 12-inch barrel, heavy brass furniture. Lockplate marked in front of hammer with "Crown and Gr" and broad arrow, behind the hammer "Grice 1759." Length 19.5 inches. Brass escutcheon plate on grip with regimental markings. $1,200–$2,200.

BRITISH NAVY FLINTLOCK PISTOL, GEORGE III PERIOD, WITH BELT HOOK. The standard military horse pistol was brass-mounted, with a 12-inch barrel of No. 24 bore, adopted in the reign of George II for cavalry, and used until the close of the American Revolution. Officers used a lighter weapon of similar bore but with a barrel length of 10 inches or less. The pistols used by the Navy were similar to the cavalry pistol but of larger bore, and usually with 9-inch barrels, and sometimes fitted with a steel belt hook on the left side of the stock, to be carried on the seaman's belt. The specimen illustrated is typical of the Navy issue. The lock plate is marked with a crown over "G.R." forward of the hammer, and "Tower" on the rear portion of the lock plate. There are the usual proof marks in addition. Plate 51. Fig. 1. $550–$800.

BUNNEY FLINTLOCK PISTOL, cal. .55; 5.25-inch, round, brass, cannon-muzzle barrel marked "Bunney London", with Birmingham proof marks. Walnut stock heavily inlaid with silver wire. Engraved brass frame. Iron guard. Gooseneck hammer. Frizzen spring inlaid in barrel. Plate 46, Fig. 8. $525–$675.

CARTMELL-DONCASTER BRASS-BARREL, FLINTLOCK, BLUN-

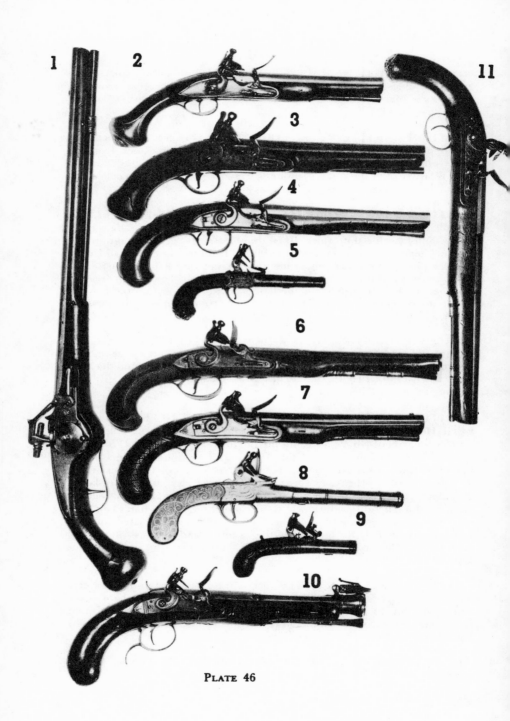

PLATE 46

DERBUSS PISTOL, cal. about 0.875 inch at muzzle; 8-inch, round-octagon, brass barrel marked "Doncaster," with a cannon-shaped muzzle. Total length 13 inches. Nearly full-length walnut stock. Brass mounted with spur on trigger guard. Ebony-tip, hickory ramrod. Iron pan with water gutters. Flat lock plate. Flat gooseneck hammer. Triangular-bladed 5.5-inch bayonet or dagger on top of barrel, hinged near muzzle, and held closed by a catch on the barrel tang. Lock marked "Cartmell." Birmingham proof marks. Plate 46, Fig. 10. $875–$1,200.

CARTMELL–DONCASTER FLINTLOCK PISTOL, cal. 46, smooth-bore, 1.75-inch round barrel with engraved muzzle. Center-hung hammer. Brass frame engraved with 2 stands of flags and words "Cartmell Doncaster." Folding trigger. Sliding safety lock. Walnut grip inlaid with silver wire in scroll design. Silver diamond on stock. The maker was active about 1832. Plate 46, Fig. 9. $265–$375.

CLARKSON, FERGUSON-TYPE, BREECHLOADING, RIFLED, FLINTLOCK PISTOL, made by Clarkson, who was in business from 1680 to 1740, which may indicate that Ferguson did not invent this system but only adapted it to the needs of the British Army in his Ferguson rifle. Barrel 7.5 inches, signed by Clarkson under the early-type pan spring. Breech pin has double screw which opens up completely with one turn. Silver butt plate and silver medallion on back of grip. Square-back trigger guard. Plate 51, Fig. 8. $4,500–$6,000.

CLARKSON FLINTLOCK PISTOL, cal. .58; 5.125-inch round, cannon-muzzle barrel, unscrews to load. Center-hung hammer. Iron trigger guard. Engraved frame marked "Clarkson, London." Walnut grip with silver inlay. Plate 47, Fig. 1. $475–$650.

CONSTABLE, ENGLISH-AMERICAN, DOUBLE-BARREL, FLINT-LOCK PISTOL, cal. .48, 2.25-inch round barrels. Engraved brass frame

---

PLATE 46. British Wheel-Lock and Flintlock Pistols.

*Figure*

1. British Martial Wheel-Lock Pistol.
2. Annliy Brass-Barrel Flintlock Pistol.
3. British Cavalry Flintlock Pistol, George III Period.
4. Archer Flintlock Pistol, cal. .62, 9-inch Barrel.
5. Archer Flintlock Pistol, cal. .42, 2.225-inch Barrel.
6. Bennett Flintlock Pistol, cal. .61, 10-inch Barrel.
7. Bennett Flintlock Pistol, cal. .58, 9-inch Barrel.
8. Bunney Flintlock Pistol with Brass Barrel.
9. Cartmell-Doncaster Flintlock Pistol, cal. .46, 1.75-inch Barrel.
10. Cartmell-Doncaster, Brass-Barrel, Flintlock, Blunderbuss Pistol.
11. Blake Flintlock Holster Pistol.

marked "Constable Philadelphia" with British proof marks. Engraved iron trigger guard. Double-neck center-hung hammer. Rotating drum changes fire from one barrel to the other. Walnut grips. This piece was probably made in the British Isles for export to Constable of Philadelphia, and is listed here because it was undoubtedly British made. Plate 47, Fig. 2. $700–$950.

COLLIER FLINTLOCK REVOLVER, PATENTED 1818. Manufactured in London by Elisha Haydon Collier, an American citizen living there. Hand-turning cylinder. Five-shot. The barrel is smoothbore on all known specimens and may be from 4 to 6 inches long, with a revolver total length of from 11.5 to 14 inches. The caliber is usually given as a bore number and may be No. 44 or No. 60 bore, or somewhere between. The exact place and date of manufacture is not known. Collier also invented and manufactured, or caused to be manufactured, revolving-cylinder sporting arms, both rifles and shotguns. The value is about the same for all Collier revolving-cylinder arms, contrary to the usual rule that pistols and revolvers are worth more than shoulder arms. The late Dr. S. Traner Buck, of Philadelphia, first brought this type to the author's attention in 1938. The specimen illustrated was in Dr. Buck's collection until it was sold to Mr. W. G. C. Kimball, of Woburn, Mass. Plate 51, Fig. 2. $8,500–$12,000.

SAME, but from the James E. Serven collection. Plate 47, Fig. 13. $8,500–$12,000.

COOKSON-TYPE, GLASS, FLINTLOCK, REPEATING PISTOLS, A PAIR. Although usually attributed to Cookson, this type of flintlock repeating pistol was probably invented about 1660 by Lorenzoni of Florence, Italy. The specimens illustrated were made by Glass in England about 1775. A magazine opening on the left side contains powder and round balls. The pistol is pointed downward, the lever is turned, and a ball drops into the barrel, followed by the powder. Turning the lever the whole distance of its travel cocks and primes the pistol. Returning the lever to the original position closes the breech. Plate 51, Fig. 3. $9,000–$14,500.

COOKSON-TYPE, WILSON, FLINTLOCK, REPEATING PISTOL, 6-inch chiseled cannon barrel. Engraved frame. Self-priming lock signed by Wilson. Heavy silver-masked butt with silver inlay. Plate 51, Fig. 4. $7,500–$9,500.

D. EGG FLINTLOCK DUELING PISTOL (not a pair), cal. .51; 9.75-inch, smoothbore, octagon barrel inlaid with "D.Egg London." Lock marked "D.Egg." Walnut half-stock, checkered grip, engraved steel tip. Iron rib under barrel with one iron thimble. Ivory-tip ramrod. Engraved steel butt cap and trigger guard. Single set trigger. Flat lock plate. Iron pan with fence. Flat gooseneck hammer. Safety lock. Gold-lined vent and pan. Plate 47, Fig. 3. Each $600–$800.

D. EGG OFFICER'S FLINTLOCK PISTOL, cal. .64; 9.5-inch, wedge-fastened, round, flat-top, twist-steel barrel marked "D. Egg London" with gold inlay. Walnut stock with checkered grip. One iron thimble. Swivel ramrod. Engraved iron guard with pineapple tip. Single-neck hammer. Sliding safety lock at rear of lock plate. Roller on frizzen spring. Lock marked "D. Egg." Plate 47, Fig. 4. $600–$800.

D. EGG DOUBLE-BARREL FLINTLOCK PISTOLS, CASED PAIR, cal. .70, smoothbore, 7.5-inch octagon barrels superposed. Total length 13 inches. Weight 3 lbs. 7 oz. each. Walnut stock, checkered grip. Iron-mounted. Engraved. Safety lock serves both hammer and frizzen. Platinum-lined vents. Gold bands inlaid across rear end of barrels. Gold oval on grip, engraved with picture of sitting woman. Top of each barrel inlaid in gold with maker's name, "D. Egg London." Frizzens marked "D. Egg Patent." Iron-tipped wooden ramrod, 2 iron thimbles. Roller on frizzen spring. Mahogany case with powder flask, oiler, mold, and loading and cleaning rod with worm. Plate 47, Fig. 5. $450–$600 for one. Cased pair: $2,500–$3,500.

D. EGG DOUBLE-BARREL FLINTLOCK PISTOL, cal. .40, with two 2.5-inch, round, superposed barrels. Center-hung hammer with sliding safety lock. Frame engraved with stand of arms and marked "D. Egg London." Bottom of flashpan is a drum which, when revolved by a small lever on side of frame, changes the vent from one barrel to another. Plate 47, Fig. 6. $350–$475.

DURS EGG DOUBLE-BARREL FLINTLOCK PISTOL, over-and-under type, cal. .76; smoothbore, 8.5-inch octagon barrels with platinum vents. Equipped with belt hook. Two triggers. Two locks. Checkered walnut grip. Marked "D. Egg London." Plate 51, Fig. 13. $650–$800.

JAMES FREEMAN DOUBLE-LOADING FLINTLOCK PISTOL, SCREW-BARREL TYPE. This type of pistol was designed for a double load, so that the pan moves to provide for firing the forward charge first. Made about 1710 and sometimes called a Queen Anne Pistol, because this type became famous during her reign. Freeman, who often marked his pistols "J. Freeman" in such a manner that the "J" appeared as an "I," also made pistols for officers between 1725 and 1750. Plate 51, Fig. 5. $2,150–$3,000.

GOFF FLINTLOCK PISTOLS, A PAIR, cal. .50, smoothbore, 4.25-inch round barrel. Equipped with 2 extra barrels, each 1.375-inches long, which can be screwed onto frame to give additional barrel length. Walnut grip. Bird's-head butt. Center-hung hammer. Folding concealed trigger. Frame, hammer, and frizzen chased around edges. British proof marks. Frame marked on side "D. Goff, London." This maker worked from 1804 to 1832. All metal polished bright. This was the original finish. Plate 47, Fig. 7. $1,100–$1,400 for the pair.

HARMAN FLINTLOCK PISTOL, cal. .66; 5.75-inch, round, cannon-muzzle barrel unscrews to load. Round gooseneck hammer. Iron pan. Frizzen spring is flat and follows the contour of the lower side of the pan. Walnut grip with silver inlay. Silver butt cap made to resemble a man's face. Marked "Harman Londini" with London proof marks, and made about 1730. Plate 47, Fig. 8. $975–$1,200.

ROBERT HARVEY SCREW-BARREL FLINTLOCK HOLSTER PISTOL, made in London about 1690. Cannon screw barrel 5 inches. Total length 11.5 inches. Early frizzen spring. Silver-masked butt. Silver medallion and some silver wire decoration on the carved stock. The specimen illustrated is one of a matched pair. The value indicated is for the pair. Plate 48, Fig. 11. $850–$1,200.

INNES & WALLACE SCOTCH-TYPE FLINTLOCK PISTOL, cal. .65; 9-inch, octagon, wedge-fastened, browned barrel marked "Innes & Wallace Gunmakers to His Majesty Edinr." Engraved iron guard with pineapple tip. Two iron thimbles. Gooseneck hammer. Iron pan. Horn-tipped mahogany ramrod. Roller on frizzen spring. Lock marked "Innes & Wallace." Full-length highly polished stock. All metal parts except barrel polished bright. Made about 1800. Not illustrated. $750–$900.

KENT & CO. FLINTLOCK DERRINGERS, CASED PAIR, cal. .46, 2.5-inch octagon barrel marked "63 New Bond Street." Lock marked "Kent & Co., London." Lock plate 2.375 inches long, fitted with safety lock. Platinum-lined vent. Full-length rosewood stock with checkered grip. Walnut ramrod. Engraved iron trigger guard. Small, silver, blade front sight. V-notch rear sight on tang. Mahogany case, green fleece-lined, containing following accessories: ball mold, loading rod, and powder flask, but the flask is not shown in the illustration. Two covered compartments for powder and

---

PLATE 47. British Flintlock Pistols and Revolvers

*Figure*

1. Clarkson Flintlock Pistol.
2. Constable, English-American, Double-Barrel, Flintlock Pistol.
3. D. Egg Flintlock Dueling Pistol.
4. D. Egg Officer's Flintlock Pistol.
5. D. Egg Double-Barrel Flintlock Pistols, Cased Pair.
6. D. Egg Double-Barrel Flintlock Pistol.
7. Goff Flintlock Pistols, a Pair with Extra Barrels.
8. Harman Flintlock Pistol, Cannon-Muzzle Barrel.
9. Kent & Co. Flintlock Derringers, Cased Pair.
10. H. New Double-Barrel Flintlock Pistol.
11. R. Wilson Scotch-Type Flintlock Pistol.
12. Nicholson 7-Barrel, Revolving, Flintlock Revolver.
13. Collier Flintlock Revolver.

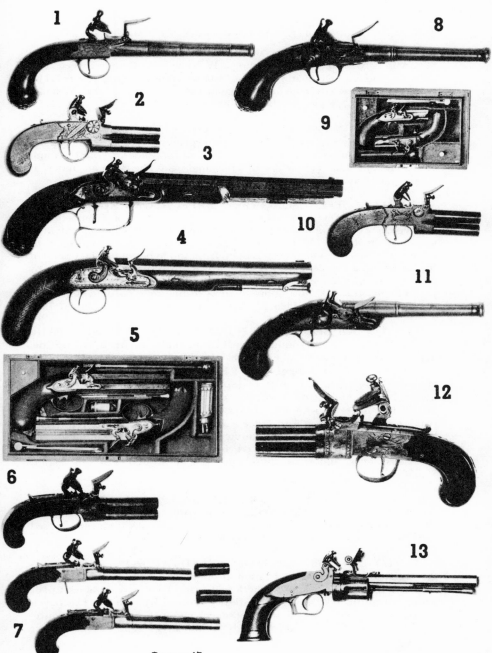

PLATE 47

balls. On the inside of the case cover is a label reading "Collins Successor to Mr. Wilson. Gun & Pistol Repository, 12 Viov Lane Regent Street. The Greatest Choice of Detonating & Flint Guns by all the London Makers." The brass plate on the cover of this particular case is engraved with the name "Lanely." Plate 47, Fig. 9. $1,100–$1,400.

RICHARD KING FLINTLOCK PISTOL, 5.5-inch cannon-type screw barrel, total length 12 inches. Early frizzen springs. Silver-masked butt. Silver medallion on back of grip. Silver lock strap. Made in London about 1690. The one illustrated is one of a matched pair. The value given here is for the pair. Plate 48, Fig. 10. $1,200–$1,450.

KNUBLEY, FERGUSON-TYPE, BREECHLOADING, RIFLED, FLINTLOCK PISTOL. Although Ferguson's name is usually attached to this type, since he had it adopted by the British Army to a limited extent, it was invented about 1730 in France by either or both of 2 gunsmiths, Chaumette and Chauvin. The breech is open from top to bottom and is operated for loading by a double-threaded screw which opens the breech at the top by making one complete turn. This pistol was made by Knubley, a British subject. The illustrations show different views of the same pistol to emphasize the peculiar construction. Plate 51, Figs. 6 and 7 (two views). $5,000–$7,750.

MANTON DOUBLE-BARREL FLINTLOCK PISTOLS, CASED PAIR, cal. .58; 2-shot; 10-inch, round, twist-steel, smoothbore barrels, side by side, marked "Manton. London." Flat bevel-edged locks marked "Manton. London." Each pistol has 2 triggers and 2 hammers. Walnut half-stock. Checkered saw-handle grip with projecting spur. Iron thimble in stock top and one under barrel. Mahogany ramrod, horn-tipped. Engraved iron trigger guard. Pineapple tip with spur. Gooseneck hammers with a safety lock in rear of each. Iron pans with fence. Gold band over barrel breech. Gold-lined vents. Velvet-lined, brass-mounted, mahogany case including the following accessories: oak cleaning rod, rosewood loading rod. Sykes copper flask, steel oiler, and spare flints. Only one illustrated. Plate 48, Fig. 1. $3,650–$5,250.

JOSEPH MANTON FLINTLOCK DUELING PISTOLS, CASED PAIR, cal. .50, smoothbore. Typical Manton quality workmanship is shown in the locks with rainproof pans, the safety catches, and the platinum vents. Cased with the usual accessories. Plate 51, Fig. 9. $2,200–$4,500.

MANTON FLINTLOCK PISTOLS, CASED PAIR, cal. .55; 8-inch, octagon, twist-steel barrel marked "Manton London." Lock marked "Manton." Full-length walnut stock with checkered grip. Two iron thimbles under stock. Horn-tipped mahogany ramrod. Engraved iron guard. Flat bevel-edged lock. Safety lock in rear of gooseneck hammer. Iron pan with fence. Gold-lined vent. Silver-bead front sight. V-notch rear sight. Engraved silver oval inlaid in back of grip. Felt-lined mahogany case with the following accessories: copper flask with 2 compartments, iron ball mold, mahogany loading rod, and key. Aside from condition, the value depends on whether the pair were made by John Manton or Joseph Manton, and signed accordingly. Only one illustrated. Plate 48, Fig. 2. $2,150–$3,750 for cased pair.

### J. A. MITCHIE SCOTTISH HIGHLANDER FLINTLOCK PISTOL.
This pistol, made about 1750 by J. A. Mitchie, of Doune, Scotland, has a ram's-horn butt and a great deal of carving and chiseling. Plate 51, Fig. 11. $2,000–$3,000.

### MORTIMER FLINTLOCK HOLSTER PISTOLS, CASED PAIR, cal.
.60; 6-inch, round, flat-top, wedge-fastened barrel with silver escutcheons. Full-length mahogany stock with checkered grip. Brass-tipped ebony ramrod. Iron trigger guard with pineapple tip and iron thimble, both blued. Iron pan with gutters. Roller on frizzen spring. Lock marked "T. Mortimer & Son" and "T. Mortimer & Son, 44 Ludgate Hill. London Gunmakers to His Majesty." Engraved lock and hammer. Safety lock in rear of hammer on lock plate. Mahogany case with green felt lining and the following accessories: wad cutter, screw driver, Dixon powder flask, bullet mold, cleaning rod, extra flints, and key to the case. Not illustrated. $1,850–$2,750 for the cased pair.

### MORTIMER FLINTLOCK OFFICER'S PISTOLS, CASED PAIR, cal.
.74, smoothbore, 6-inch octagon barrel marked "T. Mortimer & Son, 44 Ludgate Hill, London. Gun Makers to His Majesty." Lock marked "T. Mortimer." Walnut stock, checkered grip. Iron-mounted. Trigger guard, breech, and lock are engraved. Horn-tipped wooden ramrod. Two iron thimbles. Safety lock serves hammer and frizzen. Roller on frizzen spring. Brass-bound mahogany case includes powder flask, oiler, mold, cleaning rod, and worm. Plate 48, Fig. 8. $1,850–$2,750 for the cased pair.

### MORTIMER FLINTLOCK DUELING PISTOLS, CASED PAIR, cal.
.48; 10-inch, octagon, twist-steel, smoothbore, browned barrel, marked "London. Gunmaker to His Majesty." Walnut stock with checkered saw-handle grip. Silver tip and silver wedge escutcheons. Iron rib under barrel with 2 iron thimbles. Brass-tipped ebony ramrod. Engraved iron guard with spur. Single set trigger. Engraved flat lock plate. Flat gooseneck hammer with safety lock in rear of hammer on lock plate. Iron pan with fence and water gutter. Oval silver coat of arms inlaid in left side of stock. Felt-lined mahogany case with following accessories: mold, loading rod, powder flask, spare flints, linen patches, and key. The label in the cover of the case reads "H. W. Mortimer" and gives his address. The cover has a brass plate on the outside, engraved with the name of the original owner. Only one illustrated. Plate 48, Fig. 4, $2,150–$3,000 for the pair.

MURDOCH, ALL-METAL, SCOTTISH HIGHLANDER, FLINT-LOCK PISTOLS, A PAIR. This pair of pistols, with ram's-horn butts, was made about 1780 by John Murdoch of Doune. Plate 51, Fig. 12. $5,000–$7,500 for the pair.

H. NEW DOUBLE-BARREL FLINTLOCK PISTOL, cal. .40, with 2 su-perposed, 2.225-inch, browned, round barrels. Plain walnut grips. Center-hung hammer with sliding safety. Revolving drum changes vent from one barrel to another. Marked "H. New London." Plate 47, Fig. 10. $365–$475.

NICHOLSON 7-BARREL, REVOLVING, FLINTLOCK REVOLVER, made by Nicholson, London, with center hammer and pan, safety catch, and engraved steel frame. This is actually a pepperbox and not a revolver in the modern technical sense, but it is often listed as such. The specimen illustrat-ed was in the Buck collection. The value would be much higher than that shown here if this particular arm were better known. Plate 47, Fig. 12. $2,500–$3,500.

PARKER DOUBLE-BARREL FLINTLOCK PISTOL, cal. .65, smooth-bore; with 2 side-by-side, 8-inch, round barrels, twist-steel, wedge-fastened, browned, with silver-lined vents and rib marked "W. Parker, Maker to His Majesty, Holborn, London." Locks marked "W. Parker." Walnut stock, checkered grip. Engraved locks, guard, and other metal parts. Safety locks. Rollers on frizzen springs. U-notch rear sight. Bead front sight. Parker was famous as a maker of police pistols from 1800 to 1840. Plate 48, Fig. 3. $950–$1,250.

POLINSON'S PATENT FLINTLOCK REVOLVER. This is a very rare weapon. The design is more conventional than that of the Collier described above, and there are a smaller number of recognized specimens, but this make is not as well known as the Collier in the United States. Plate 51, Fig. 14. $7,500–$9,500.

---

## PLATE 48. British Flintlock Pistols

*Figure*

1. Manton Double-Barrel Flintlock Pistol, Side-by-Side Barrels.
2. Manton Flintlock Pistol, cal. .55, 8-inch Barrel.
3. Parker Double-Barrel Flintlock Pis-tol.
4. Mortimer Flintlock Dueling Pistol.
5. Prosser Flintlock Pistol.
6. Scotch-Type, Double-Barrel, All-Metal, Flintlock Pistol.
7. Wheeler Flintlock Pistol.
8. Mortimer Flintlock Officer's Pistols, Cased Pair.
9. Birchett Breech-loading Flintlock Pistol, Queen Anne Period.
10. R. King Flintlock Pistol, about 1690.
11. R. Harvey Flintlock Pistol, about 1690.

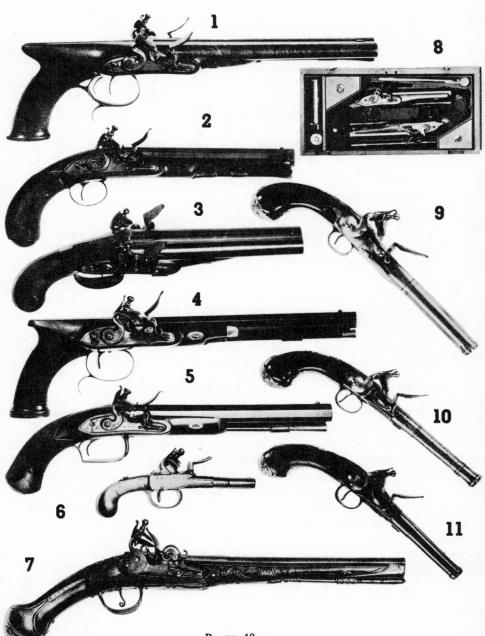

PLATE 48

PROSSER FLINTLOCK PISTOL, cal. .60; 9.75-inch, octagon, twist-steel barrel marked "Prosser Charing Cross London, EC 1150," but 1150 is not the date, since Prosser worked in the last quarter of the eighteenth century. Lock marked "Prosser." Walnut half-stock. Engraved, square-back, iron trigger guard. Stock tip is engraved steel. Iron thimble on rib under barrel. Steel-tipped ebony ramrod. Engraved steel butt cap. Gooseneck hammer. Iron spring. Plate 48, Fig. 5. $425–$585.

SCOTCH-TYPE, DOUBLE-BARREL, ALL-METAL, FLINTLOCK PISTOL, cal. .39, with two 2-inch, round cannon-muzzle barrels. All parts are made of iron. There is no other material used. Line engravings. Not marked. Early Scotch type with frizzen springs inlaid in the barrel. Finished bright. Plate 48, Fig. 6. $400–$600.

WHEELER FLINTLOCK PISTOL, cal. .60; 12-inch, pin-fastened, round-octagon barrel marked "London." Lock marked "Wheeler." Full-length walnut stock. Engraved brass trigger guard. Brass thimbles. Horn-tipped ebony ramrod. Gooseneck hammer. Iron pan. Roller on frizzen spring. Plate 48, Fig. 7. $1,200–$1,500.

R. WILSON SCOTCH-TYPE FLINTLOCK PISTOL, cal. .59; 7-inch, round, cannon-muzzle barrel with early proof marks and letters "R.W." under a crown. Also marked "Edinboro" and "D. Scott, Edinboro 1745." Total length 12 inches. Walnut stock. Round gooseneck hammer. Brass trigger guard and butt cap, the latter in the likeness of a man's face. Brass inlay on grip with initials "D.M." in script. Iron pan. Plate 47, Fig. 11. $750–$900.

## PERCUSSION PISTOLS AND REVOLVERS

The British-made percussion pistols and revolvers constitute an interesting and valuable field for the advanced American collector or for the British beginner. They range in value from comparatively low-priced pieces to the very expensive cased pairs and the early Forsyth specimens, whether made by the inventor himself or not.

The American collectors have largely concentrated on British flintlock pieces and have neglected the percussions. As the years roll by, the percussion pieces should go up in value.

BEATTIE 4-BARREL PERCUSSION PISTOL, cal. .49, smoothbore, 4-shot; four 5-inch, round barrels marked "J. Beattie, 205 Regent St., London." Checkered walnut grips. Primer box in butt. Iron guard and engraved frame. Safety locks in rear of hammers. Barrels revolve by hand. Belt hook fastened to barrels. Made about 1851. Plate 49, Fig. 1. $385–$475.

BENTLEY PERCUSSION PISTOL, cal. .42, 4.625-inch octagon barrel marked "Bentley," with German silver rib underneath, with 1 thimble. German silver, all-metal, saw-handle grip and trigger guard. Primer box in butt. Side hammer. Plate 49, Fig. 2. $225–$325.

BERRY PERCUSSION PEPPERBOX, cal. .35, 6-shot; D.A., 2.75-inch, round, fluted barrels. Iron guard. Marked "Berry Woodbridge." English proof marks. Primer box in butt. Checkered walnut grips. Engraved German silver frame. $250–$325.

SIMILAR, but unmarked, cal. .36, 6-shot; 2.75-inch, round, fluted barrels. Walnut grips. Iron guard. German silver engraved frame and barrels. British proof marks. $240–$310.

SIMILAR, but unmarked, cal. .36, 6-shot, 2.5-inch, round, fluted barrels. $240–$310.

J. BLISSETT PERCUSSION BELT PISTOL, cal. .75, smoothbore, 4.25-inch octagon barrel. Checkered walnut grips. Swivel rammer. Engraved hammer, lock, and top tang. Primer box in butt. Silver inlay on back of grip. Belt hook on left side. Marked "J. Blissett, Liverpool." Plate 50, Fig. 13. $150–$195.

BOND DOUBLE-BARREL PERCUSSION PISTOLS, CASED PAIR, cal. .65, smoothbore, with two 7.125-inch, round, browned, twist-steel barrels, side by side, with barrel rib marked "E. & W. Bond, 45 Cornhill. London." Walnut stock extending nearly to muzzle. Swivel ramrod with button tip. Iron guard with engraved pineapple tip. Checkered grip. Back-action locks with safety lock in rear of hammers. Lock plates and hammers engraved. Bead front sight. Patent breech. Silver oval inlay on back of grip with engraved initials. Belt hook attached to left lock extends along side of stock. All parts except barrels either blued or casehardened. Mahogany case, lined with green felt, contains following accessories: iron ball mold, spring vise, copper flask, with shell design in relief, marked "G & J W. H. Fire Proof," loading and cleaning rod, nipple wrench and pick, ivory box containing nipples, chamois bag containing primers, and key to case. Label inside case states that E. & W. Bond are gunmakers and swordsmiths to the Ordnance Department and the East India Co. Only one pistol, and not the cased set, is illustrated. Plate 49, Fig. 3. $850–$1,250 for the pair.

BRITISH NAVY PERCUSSION PISTOL, cal. .57, smoothbore, 6-inch round barrel with British proof marks. Walnut stock extending nearly to the muzzle with a brass plate on the tip. All brass mountings. Button-tip swivel rammer. Lanyard ring on butt. Lock marked "VR" under a crown and "Tower 1849." Belt hook on left side of stock. Stock marked on left side "Holland & Son. G. Harris." Finished bright. Plate 49, Fig. 4. $250–$350.

CONWAY PERCUSSION REVOLVER, CASED, cal. .44, D.A., 5-shot, 6-

inch barrel marked "T. Conway Blackfriars St. Manchester." Cylinder marked "Tranter's Patent Combination Revolver." Walnut case with usual accessories. Plate 49, Fig. 5. $295–$385.

C. & H. EGG PERCUSSION PEPPERBOX, cal. .36, 6-shot; 3.5-inch, round, fluted barrels. Polished walnut grips. Engraved German silver frame. Marked "C. & H. Egg" with English proof marks. Plate 50, Fig. 14. $195–$265.

EVANS PERCUSSION POCKET PISTOL, cal. .43; 1.5-inch round barrel, unscrews for loading. Finely checkered walnut grip. Silver lion head on butt. Engraved brass frame marked "J. Evans Carmarthen." Concealed trigger. Center-hung hammer with sliding safety. Blued steel parts. Made about 1832 by converting from flintlock by removing frizzen and installing safety arranged so that when it is down the hammer cannot hit the primer. Plate 49, Fig. 6. $125–$195.

FORSYTH ORIGINAL MODEL PERCUSSION PISTOL, made with the Scent Bottle magazine. A typical genuine Forsyth pistol; has a 5.5-inch, rifled, octagonal barrel, and may be No. 38 bore, rifled with 24 fine grooves. The lock is usually "Forsyth & Co. Patent." Plate 49, Fig. 7. $5,000–$6,500.

HARPER PERCUSSION PEPPERBOX, cal. .58, smoothbore, 5-shot; 5.25-inch round barrels with fluted ribs numbered from 1 to 5, with proof marks. Checkered walnut grips. Steel frame, trigger guard, and butt cap. Primer box in butt. Elaborately engraved frame and trigger guard. Hammer is that of typical English pepperbox with sliding safety on frame in rear. Nipple shield around front of frame. Hammer engraved "James Harper, 85 Weaman St." Silver name plate on back of grip. Total length 10.75 inches. Weight 3 lbs. 4 oz. Plate 49, Fig. 8. $240–$295.

HOLLIS PERCUSSION REVOLVER, CASED, cal. .41, 5-shot, D.A.,

---

PLATE 49. British Percussion Pistols and Revolvers

*Figure*

1. Beattie 4-Barrel Percussion Pistol.
2. Bentley Percussion Pistol.
3. Bond Double-Barrel Percussion Pistol.
4. British Navy Percussion Pistol.
5. Conway Percussion Revolver, Cased.
6. Evans Percussion Pocket Pistol.
7. Forsyth Original Model Percussion Pistol with Scent Bottle Magazine.
8. Harper Percussion Pepperbox.
9. Hollis Percussion Revolver, Cased.
10. "Improved" Percussion Revolver.
11. J. Lang Percussion Dueling Pistols, Cased Pair.
12. Le Mat English-made Percussion Revolver.

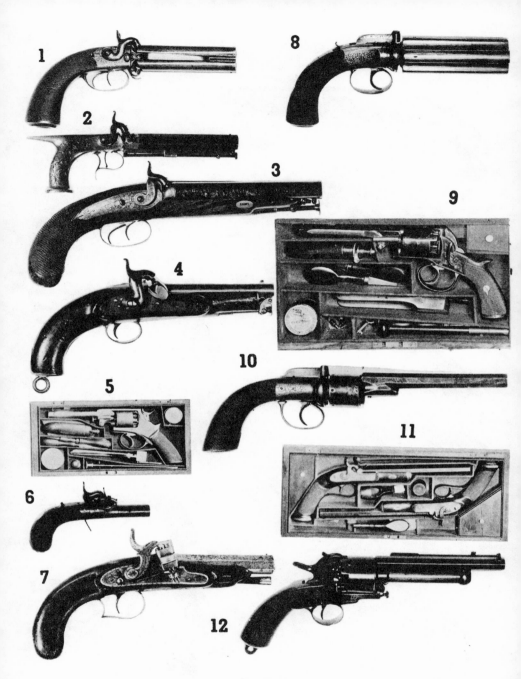

PLATE 49

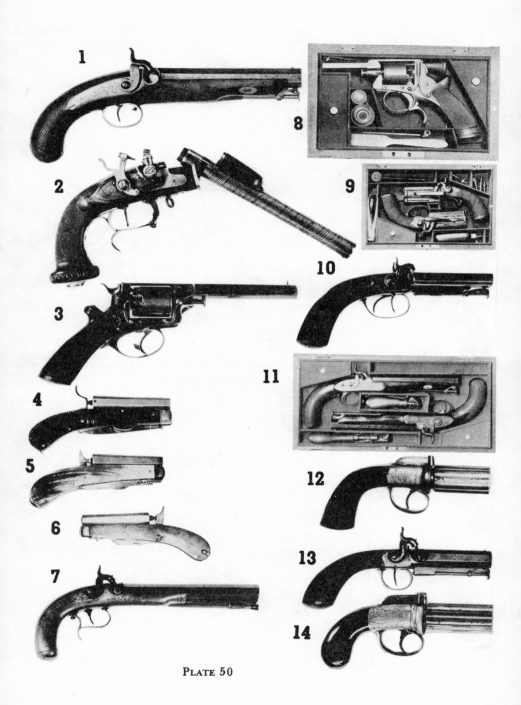

PLATE 50

4.875-inch octagon barrel, with loading lever on left side of barrel. Engraved frame. Blued finish. Checkered walnut grips. Oak case, lined with green felt, containing the following accessories: brass-tipped mahogany cleaning rod; nipple wrench; spare nipples; 2 screw drivers of different sizes; brass bullet mold; lacquered powder flask, 4.5 by 1.25 inches; and a can of Eley primers ("caps"). Inside the cover of the case is a label bearing the name of the manufacturer, Isaac Hollis & Sons, and their address, together with a brief list of their products. Plate 49, Fig. 9. $385–$475.

"IMPROVED" PERCUSSION REVOLVER, cal. .43, 6-shot, 6.75-inch octagon barrel marked "Improved" and with British proof marks. Checkered walnut grips. Iron guard and frame engraved. Hammer resembles that on pepperboxes. Plate 49, Fig. 10. $250–$350.

J. LANG PERCUSSION DUELING PISTOLS, CASED PAIR, cal. .50; 9.5-inch, octagon, twist-steel barrels engraved "J. Lang, Haymarket, London." Safety lock. Walnut stocks, checkered grips. Triggers have screw for adjusting pull. Locks marked "J. Lang." Engraved accessories include wad-cutting die, primer box, nipple wrench, cleaning rod, and nipple box. Label in case cover reads "Joseph Lang, No. 7 Haymarket, London, Gun Manufacturer." It should be noticed that the letter "J" is often mistaken for an "I" on the early guns. Plate 49, Fig. 11. $1,000–$1,350.

LE MAT ENGLISH-MADE PERCUSSION REVOLVER, cal. .40, 9-shot, S.A., 6.5-inch octagon barrel marked "Le Mat and Girard's Patent London," with British proof marks. Under this revolver barrel is a 20-gauge shotgun barrel which serves as the base pin on which the cylinder revolves. A movable nose on the hammer can be changed to fire either the revolver or the shotgun barrel. Loading lever on left side. Sometimes found with a heavy leather holster. Le Mat was a French inventor who had arms made in

---

PLATE 50. British Percussion Pistols and Revolvers

*Figure*

1. Manton Percussion Pistol.
2. Paulette, Forsyth-Type, Breech-loading, Percussion Pistol.
3. Rigby-Tranter Percussion Revolver.
4. James Rodgers Percussion Knife Pistol, cal. .28.
5. James Rodgers Percussion Knife Pistol, cal. .25.
6. James Rogers Percussion Knife Pistol, cal. .31.
7. H. Smith All-Metal Percussion Pistol.
8. Tranter Percussion Revolver, Cased.
9. Swinburn & Son Over-Under Percussion Pistols, Cased Pair.
10. G. C. Warden Double-Barrel Percussion Pistol.
11. Westley Richards Percussion Pistols, Cased Pair.
12. Berry Woodbridge Percussion Pepperbox, 6-Shot.
13. J. Blissett Percussion Belt Pistol.
14. C. & H. Egg Percussion Pepperbox.

France, Belgium, and England. He sold many to the Confederates during the American Civil War. Plate 49, Fig. 12. $1,100–$1,450.

MANTON PERCUSSION PISTOLS, CASED PAIR, cal. .65, smooth-bore; 7-inch, octagon, wedge-fastened, twist-steel barrel marked "London." Light walnut stock, horn-tipped, extending nearly to muzzle, with check-ered grip. One iron thimble and swivel ramrod. Lock-action percussion lock engraved. Patent breech. Lock marked "Manton." Mahogany case, lined with blue velvet, containing following accessories: lacquered copper powder flask, iron ball mold, screw driver, spring vise, can of primers. Only one of the pistols, and not the case, is shown. Plate 50, Fig. 1. $1,200–$1,800.

JOSEPH MANTON TUBE-LOCK DUELING PISTOLS, A PAIR, cal. .50, smoothbore. The tube lock was an early form of percussion ignition. The fulminate was enclosed in small copper tubes which were pushed into the vents that were the same as vents on a flintlock. When the hammer struck the tube about in the center, it caused a flash to ignite the powder. Plate 51. Fig. 10. $2,750–$4,000.

PAULETTE, FORSYTH-TYPE, BREECHLOADING, PERCUSSION PISTOL. Made about 1810 by Paulette of Paris, using the Forsyth ignition system. This piece was in the Dr. S. Traner Buck collection and then passed into the hands of Mr. W. G. C. Kimball. Cal. .50; 9-inch, round, twist barrel. Total length 15 inches. Lock signed by Paulette. Half-walnut stock with checkered grip and some carving. When cocked, the pill compartment auto-matically comes to an upright position and falls away when the trigger is pulled, so that the hammer falls on the pill left in the tube. Plate 50, Fig. 2. $1,000–$1,350.

WESTLEY RICHARDS PERCUSSION PISTOLS, CASED PAIR, cal. .72, smoothbore; 8-inch, octagon, twist-steel barrel. Total length 13.25 inches. Full-length walnut stock, checkered grip. Swivel ramrod. Front-action lock with sliding safety. Steel trigger guard and ramrod thimble. Nip-ple seat has platinum-lined vent. Lock marked "Westley Richards." Barrel marked "Westley Richards, 170 New Bond St., London." Paper label inside cover of case reads: "Westley Richards Gun Manufacturer to His Royal Highness Prince Albert, 170 New Bond St., London." Mahogany case with the usual accessories. Plate 50, Fig. 11. $1,275–$1,450.

RIGBY-TRANTER PERCUSSION REVOLVER, cal. .44, 5-shot, D.A., 6-inch octagon barrel, with loading lever on left side. Checkered walnut grips. Blued and engraved. Safety lock on right side of frame. Cylinder finished bright. Frame marked "Tranter's Patent" and "Wm. & Jno. Rigby 24 Suffolk St. Dublin." Plate 50, Fig. 3. $265–$375.

JAMES RODGERS PERCUSSION KNIFE PISTOL, cal. .28, 3.5-inch oc-tagon barrel. German silver finish. Both sides of knife are covered with dark brown horn. The grip at the rear is checkered. Center-hung hammer. Folding trigger. In the butt of the grip is a primer box with a German silver cover. Fitted under the left grip is a bullet mold to cast one ball. In the right grip is a place for a loading rod. Single knife blade, 3.75 inches long, marked "Self Protector." The base of the blade is marked "James Rodgers & Co., Sheffield." Plate 50, Fig. 4. $225–$325.

JAMES RODGERS PERCUSSION KNIFE PISTOL, cal. .25; 2.375-inch, hexagonal, German silver barrel. Entire frame is made of German silver covered with horn. Two knife blades, 2.75 and 2 inches long respectively. Longer blade is etched with American eagle and the words "Self Protector." Folding trigger. British proof marks. Primer box in butt. Alongside primer box is a German silver bullet mold casting one ball. Nipple pick is in grip. Center-hung hammer. Frame marked "James Rodgers Sheffield." Plate 50, Fig. 5. $225–$325.

SAME, but cal. .31, percussion, smoothbore, 3.375-inch German silver barrel. Horn handles. Two knife blades. Folding trigger. Center-hung hammer. Primer box in butt, together with nipple pick. English proof marks on barrel. Both blades marked "James Rogers Sheffield." Note difference in spelling of "Rogers." This is sometimes listed as the "Unwin & Rogers Knife Pistol." Plate 50, Fig. 6. $225–$325.

H. SMITH ALL-METAL PERCUSSION PISTOL, cal. .43, smoothbore, 7-inch octagon barrel. Primer box in butt. German silver half-stock engraved, and German silver guard, ramrod rib, and thimble. Copper-tipped German silver ramrod. Marked "H. Smith London." Plate 50, Fig. 7. $250–$360.

SWINBURN & SON OVER-UNDER PERCUSSION PISTOLS, CASED PAIR, cal. .46, smoothbore, 2.75-inch round barrel. Frame marked "Swinburn & Son, Makers." Checkered walnut grip. Swivel ramrod. Primer box in butt. All metal engraved except barrels. Nose of right hammer is longer than left and fires lower barrel. Mahogany case with the usual accessories. Plate 50, Fig. 9. $1,200–$1,500.

TRANTER PERCUSSION REVOLVER, CASED, cal. .31, 5-shot, D.A., 3-inch octagon barrel. Two triggers, one extending through the trigger guard with the firing trigger fixed to it inside the guard. Engraved and blued metal parts. Marked "Tranter's Patent." Checkered walnut grips. Mahogany case assembled with brass screws, lined with blue felt, and containing the following accessories: brass bullet mold, nipple wrench, ebony patch box, powder measure, cleaning rod, nipple pick in bone case, oil can, and cleaning brush. Plate 50, Fig. 8. $500–$700.

G. C. WARDEN DOUBLE-BARREL PERCUSSION PISTOLS, CASED PAIR, cal. .50, smoothbore, 2-shot, with two 4-inch, round barrels, side by side, casehardened in natural colors. Walnut grips checkered. Steel butt cap with primer box. Iron rib under barrel with swivel rammer. Iron trigger guard. Outside hammers with safety locks in frame. Frame and butt cap are elaborately engraved. Barrels, frame, hammers, and butt caps are all casehardened in natural colors. Trigger guard and rib under barrels are blued. Marked "G. C. Warden" with British proof marks. Mahogany case, brassbound, green-felt-lined, containing lacquered powder flask with top and bottom compartments, blued iron bullet mold, hardwood loading rod, nipple wrench, and cleaning tip for loading rod. Plate 50, Fig. 10. $750–$900.

BERRY WOODBRIDGE PERCUSSION PEPPERBOX, cal. .35, 6-shot, D.A.; 2.75-inch, round, fluted barrels. Checkered walnut grips. Engraved German silver frame. Iron trigger guard. Primer box in butt. English proof marks. Marked "Berry Woodbridge." Plate 50, Fig. 12. $210–275.

---

### PLATE 51. Outstanding British Pistols and Revolvers

*Figure*

1. British Navy Flintlock Pistol, George III Period, with Belt Hook.
2. Collier Flintlock Revolver.
3. Cookson-Type, Glass, Flintlock, Repeating Pistol.
4. Cookson-Type, Wilson, Flintlock, Repeating Pistol.
5. James Freeman Double-Loading Flintlock Pistol, Screw-Barrel Type.
6. Knubley, Ferguson-Type, Breechloading, Rifled, Flintlock Pistol.
7. Knubley, Ferguson-Type, Same as Fig. 6, but Another View.
8. Clarkson, Ferguson-Type, Breechloading, Rifled, Flintlock Pistol.
9. Joseph Manton Flintlock Dueling Pistol.
10. Joseph Manton Tube-Lock Dueling Pistol.
11. J. A. Mitchie Scottish Highlander Flintlock Pistol.
12. Murdoch, All-Metal, Scottish Highlander, Flintlock Pistols, a Pair.
13. Durs Egg Double-Barrel Flintlock Pistol.
14. Polinson's Patent Flintlock Revolver.

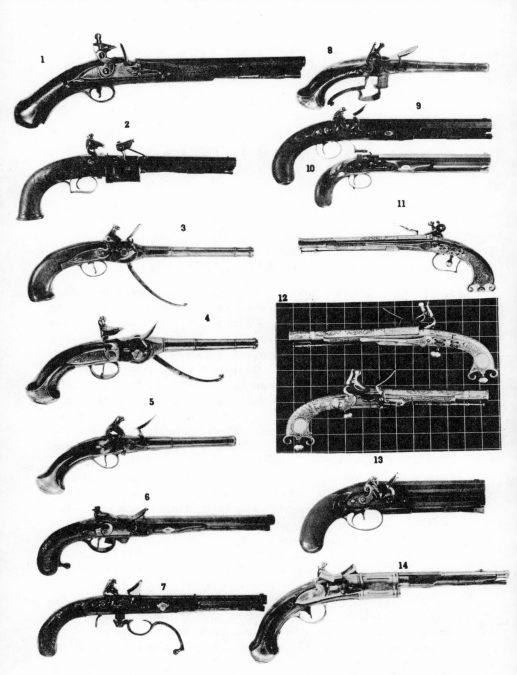

PLATE 51

# Chapter 30

## FRENCH FIREARMS

### FRENCH MARTIAL ARMS

FRENCH martial firearms are of interest to collectors who specialize in the martial arms of the United States, and to those who specialize in the better type of early European weapons. During our colonial period Americans were loyal subjects of the king and fought against the French in several wars or campaigns in which French arms were captured. During the American Revolution France supplied the United States with arms and later sent troops. Our earliest flintlock shoulder and hand arms were patterned largely after certain French models. In the War of 1812 French arms and United States arms patterned after French models were still in use. In our Civil War both the United States and the Confederate States obtained French arms, particularly revolvers. In World War I French small arms were used by the United States to a limited extent, but they were not officially adopted as United States weapons and are not generally regarded today as collectors' specimens. Those used or copied during the American Revolutionary War are the ones in demand in the United States.

The best text on French martial firearms is *Notes on French Ordnance, 1717–1936*, written and published by James Hicks, Mount Vernon, N.Y., in 1938.

Initials representing Armée Nationale, Armée Republicaine, République Française, Empire Français, and Manufacture Royale indicate the date of manufacture of flintlock arms because of the changes in the form of government in France. The House of Bourbon reigned from 1717 to 1774; the First Republic existed from 1792 to 1804; the First Empire under Napoleon Bonaparte lasted from 1804 to 1814. The Bourbons were restored and reigned from 1814 to 1830. This period of French history covers the most important years of the flintlock era. Before 1717 the flintlock was already a distinct type, but other, earlier types, such as the matchlock, were still in use. After 1830 the flintlock began to give way to the percussion era.

Flintlock arms made at Charleville (Ardennes), France, are important to American collectors because they exerted a greater influence on the design of our first United States martial flintlock shoulder and hand arms than any other weapons. Such arms may be marked "Manufacture de Charleville," or they may be marked "Manufacture de Libreville," because the name "Charleville" was changed to "Libreville" on Nov. 13, 1793, known to the French as "23 Brumaire of the Year II" (1793–1794), according to the French Republican calendar, which started on the day of the Proclamation of the Republic, Sept. 22, 1792, and continued until Dec. 22, 1805, when the Gregorian calendar was restored. This covered a period of approximately fourteen Republican calendar years.

Before 1792 the symbol of the manufacturer was marked on the barrels, lock plates, and stocks. The National Guard was ordered to mark the right side of the butt with the letters "AN" representing Armée Nationale, Arme Nationale, or Garde Nationale, in 1791, and the order was repeated in 1792. The letters "AR," which look like "AP" on some specimens, were placed on the barrel and stock to represent the words Armée Républicaine, prior to the Year IX (1800–1801).

Acceptance marks were not officially used before the Year IX, but in that year it was ordered that the letters "RF" for République Francaise be stamped in front of the touchhole of the barrel, and on the right side of the butt. The steel die used for this mark sometimes split the wood, hence the butt of a shoulder arm was drilled and a hard wood plug was inserted to receive the blow of the die. This process was not applied to pistol stocks because of the danger of splitting them. The butt was stamped "EF" for Empire Française during the days of the Empire, and also the barrel. These letters were usually surrounded by a wreath that included the year, month, and initials of the inspectors and at least one other official, usually the First Controller.

The acceptance marks of the inspectors and other officials who examined martial arms prior to delivery to the armed forces appear in greater numbers on the later weapons. Barrels were marked with such stamps before 1809. The Manufacturing İnspector, the First Controller, the Barrel Controller, and other officials, in a characteristically French love of ceremony and decoration, fell over one another in an effort to place their initials on firearms, like the children and morons who write on washroom walls. There was even a Controller of Lock Plates who was entitled to place his initials on the lock plate in front of the hammer. The Controller-in-Charge could place his initials on any part of the weapon, and he usually did.

## The Metric System

The caliber, barrel length, and total length of French arms are given by the French according to the metric system, which is universally used by scientists and should be adopted by the British and Americans to replace the awkward English system of measurement. The unit of length is the meter, which equals 39.37 inches. There are 100 centimeters in a meter, hence 1 centimeter equals 0.3937 inch. There are 1,000 millimeters in a meter, hence 1 millimeter equals 0.03937 inch. Therefore, to change millimeters to inches, multiply by 0.03937. One inch equals 2.54 centimeters, or 25.4 millimeters. Therefore, to change inches back to millimeters, multiply by 25.4. In this text the English system of measurement is used.

*Note: When "U.S." is stamped on locks and "U. States" is branded on buttstocks, the value increases from 10% to 25% above that stated here, but only if such marks are genuine. Beware of fakes. If you are a beginner, trust only honest, experienced collectors and dealers, and even then keep your eyes open.*

# FRENCH MARTIAL FLINTLOCK SHOULDER ARMS

These shoulder arms were made during the reign of the House of Bourbon (Louis XV and Louis XVI) and used by the French in America during the French and Indian Wars.

MODEL 1717 MUSKET, cal. .69 (17.5 mm); 46.89-inch round barrel fastened to stock with pins and 4 tenons brazed on bottom. Total length 62.5 inches. Flat lock plate comes to point at the rear. Iron pan with fence. Gooseneck hammer. Three ramrod thimbles. $650–$950.

MODEL 1728 MUSKET, resembles Model 1717 Musket, but barrel held to stock by 3 bands, the upper of which has 2 rings and a ramrod funnel. Wooden ramrod resembles that of Model 1717, but it has an iron reinforcing ring at the end. No ramrod thimbles. $575–$875.

MODEL 1746 MUSKET, cal. .69 (17.5 mm). Total length 62.5 inches. Three bands. Upper band is short. Middle and lower bands are held by friction. Swan-neck hammer. Iron ramrod with buttonhead. $575–$875.

MODEL 1754 MUSKET, resembles Model 1746, except that swivels are under the barrel instead of being on the left side as before. The upper band is shorter than before. This model has a tang from the pan to the frizzen screw, unlike the previous model. $525–$825.

MODEL 1754 OFFICERS' MUSKET, same as previous model except that workmanship is superior, the furniture is engraved, and both the musket and its bayonet are shorter. $525–$825.

MODEL 1763 MUSKET, cal. .69. Barrel 44.7 inches long. Total length 60 inches. Brass front sight. Flat lock plate. Iron pan with fence. Flat-faced hammer and pierced hammer jaw screen. Frizzen curls at foot and upper back. $750–$1,375.

MODEL 1763 MUSKETOON, cal. .67. Barrel 31 inches long. Total length 45 inches. Flat lock plate. Flat-faced hammer with pierced hammer jaw screw. Brass furniture except that swivel rod is iron. Stocked to end of barrel. Front sight is on lower ring of upper band. $750–$1,185.

MODEL 1766 MUSKET, resembles Model 1763 Musket, except that it is of lighter construction and somewhat better workmanship. The hammer is reinforced. Steel ramrod with buttonhead. The ramrod retaining spring is fastened to the bottom of the barrel. $750–$1,150.

MODEL 1766 MUSKETOON, resembles Model 1763 Musketoon, but the iron sight is on top of the barrel, and the stock extends only to within about 14 inches from the muzzle. The swivel bar is on a bracelet-shaped iron band. $675–$985.

MODEL 1768 MUSKET, cal. .69. Total length 59 inches. Two oval swivels, one welded to the middle band and the other welded to the trigger bow, replace the former flat swivels; otherwise this musket resembles previous model. $675–$985.

MODEL 1770 MUSKET, cal. .69. Total length 59 inches. The 3 bands have a more substantial appearance than those on previous models. The lower band holds a ramrod retaining spring. Roundfaced lock plate. The ramrod stop is an integral part of the trigger plate. $450–$710.

MODEL 1771 MUSKET, cal. .69. Total length 60 inches. The barrel and bands are reinforced. Iron pan. Lock plate has rounded face. Bayonet stud fastened to lower side of barrel. The stock swells and has a small comb. No ramrod stop. $410–$650.

MODEL 1773 MUSKET, resembles Model 1771, with a few differences. The ramrod retaining spring is in the lower band. The end of the frizzen branch is cut square. The bayonet lacks a locking ring but has a ferrule for locking the bayonet by means of a spring on the barrel. Steel ramrod with pear-shaped head. $375–$585.

MODEL 1777 MUSKET, INFANTRY, cal. .69. Total length 60 inches. This is sometimes listed as "Model 1776 Infantry Musket," but the usual date on the arm is 1777. The brass pan slopes downward and lacks a fence. The frizzen curls at the top and in the lower branches. The middle band is held by a screw, and also the upper band; and the lower band is held by a front band spring. The brass front sight and the ramrod retaining spring are on the upper band. The hammer has a straight head. The touchhole slopes forward. The trigger bow is a separate part. There is a ramrod stop on the escutcheon. $425–$700.

MODEL 1777 MUSKET, ARTILLERY, resembles the Model 1777, Infantry, except that the barrel is slightly over 36 inches long, and the total length is 51.5 inches. Brass furniture. Iron swivels. $410–$585.

MODEL 1777 MUSKET, DRAGOONS, resembles Model 1777, Infantry, but the total length is 57.5 inches, and the barrel is 42.5 inches long. There are 3 bands: the upper and lower bands are brass, and the middle band is iron, with 2 rings. The side plate and trigger bow are brass. $410–$585.

MODEL 1777 MUSKET, NAVY, similar to Model 1777, Infantry, but the total length is 57.5 inches, and all furniture is brass. $400–$600.

MODEL 1777 MUSKETOON, HEAVY CAVALRY, resembles Model 1766 Musketoon, but total length is 46 inches, and the barrel is 33.3 inches long. The bands and swivel bar are brass. The steel ramrod has a pear-shaped head. The stock has a cheekpiece. $375–$615.

MODEL 1786 MUSKETOON, LIGHT CAVALRY, cal. .69, 27.7-inch barrel, total length 42 inches. The stock is short and has no cheekpiece. The front sight is mounted on the upper of the 2 rings on the upper band. Brass furniture. Steel ramrod extends the entire length of the stock. $310–$425.

The following are shoulder arms made during the period of the First Republic.

MODEL NO. 1, RÉPUBLIQUE MUSKET, cal. .69. Total length 60 inches. Resembles Model 1777 Infantry Musket, but the breech tang is marked "Modele No. 1, Republique." There is a cheekpiece. The upper band has a retaining catch instead of a screw. The tenon is not on the barrel. $390–$525.

FUSIL DEPAREILLE. This is a mixed or assembled m gg and not a distinct, separate type or model. It is usually composed of     s from several models, such as the 1763, 1774, and 1777 models. $390–$510.

MODEL 1793 CARBINE, INFANTRY, cal. .53 (sometimes called cal. .54, but it is very slightly more than cal. .53). Hexagonal barrel, 25.6 inches, fastened with pins to the stock which extends to the muzzle. Total length 40.5 inches. Swan-neck hammer resembles that of Model 1777 Musketoon. No side plate. Ramrod held by 3 brass thimbles. Marked "Manufacture de Versailles." $250–$385.

MODEL 1793 CARBINE, CAVALRY, resembles infantry carbine, but barrel is only 16 inches long, and the total length is 31 inches. $250–$400.

MODEL 1793 CARBINE, OFFICERS AND NONCOMISSIONED OFFICERS. This modification was made for the officers and N.C.O.'s of the Light Infantry. The inscription is in capital letters instead of the italics used on the regular model, but there are exceptions to this statement, and so many minor variations that the only general statement that can can be made is that it is a 1793 carbine of better workmanship than the regular issue. $245–$475.

MODEL 1777 MUSKET, MODIFIED IN YEAR IX (1800–1801), cal. .69, 44.7-inch barrel, total length 60 inches. Brass pan without fence. Reinforced hammer. Stock swells slightly. Body of lock plate and hammer slightly convex. No curl to frizzen. Steel ramrod with pear-shaped head. Ramrod retaining spring fastened to stock by pin. $250–$465.

MODEL YEAR IX (1800–1801) MUSKET, DRAGOONS, cal. .69, 40.5-inch barrel, total length 55.75 inches; otherwise similar to previous model. Brass furniture except that middle bank and swivels are iron. $250–$465.

MODEL YEAR IX (1800–1801) MUSKET, NAVY, same as Dragoon model above, but all furniture is brass. $250–$465.

MODEL YEAR IX (1800–1801) MUSKETOON, CAVALRY, cal. .69, 30-inch barrel, total length 43.9 inches. Two bands, with upper swivel attached to lower band. Lower swivel attached to rear end of trigger guard. Trigger bow is separate part. No cheekpiece. Stock has slight swell. Brass furniture. $275–$420.

## FRENCH GUARD WEAPONS

MODEL 1777, MODIFIED YEAR IX (1800–1801), MUSKET, INFANTRY, GRENADIER, similar to Model 1777, with few variations. It has brass furniture and square brass swivels. Lock plate marked "Manufacture de Versailles" in capital letters in a straight line. Lower swivel attached to stud forward of trigger bow, similar to that of Model 1793 Carbine. Total length 59.5 inches. $250–$395.

MODEL 1777 MUSKET, SHORT, INFANTRY, same as previous model, but the total length is only 54.5 inches, and the barrel is correspondingly shorter. $250–$390.

DRAGOON GUARD MUSKETOON, RIFLED, 29.5-inch rifled barrel, total length 43.3 inches. Stocked to within 11.8 inches from muzzle. Side plate of previous model replaced by brass rosette. Two rings on upper band. Stock and furniture especially made for Guards, and whole weapon is of superior workmanship for that era and for an enlisted man's weapon. Pear-shaped ramrod. $250–$395.

GUARD MODEL BLUNDERBUSS (TROMBLON DE MAMELUK). Bell muzzle. Barrel is fastened to stock with pins and is 5-sided from breech to within 15.8 inches from muzzle. Brass trigger guard. Short stock. Swan-neck hammer. Lock plate closely resembles that of Model 1793 Carbine, and the ramrod is the same as that for the Model 1793 Carbine. $475–$585.

## FRENCH MARTIAL FLINTLOCK PISTOLS

MODEL 1763 CAVALRY PISTOL, cal. .673, 9-inch round barrel, total length 16.14 inches. Iron pan with high fence. Long straight stock with iron furniture. Band spring holds 2 rings. Lock resembles that on Model 1763 Musket. Ramrod retaining spring under barrel. Plain butt cap. $610–$820.

SIMILAR to above but all brass furniture. $575–$815.

MODEL 1763, GENDARMERIE PISTOL, cal. .598, 5.04-inch barrel. Full-length walnut stock. Iron pan with fence, wedge-shaped on bottom. Lock marked "Maubeuge Manuf. Rle" on some pieces. Resembles 1763 Cavalry Pistol but, in general, is one-third smaller. Iron upper band with 2 barrel straps. Iron butt cap, guard, and button-tip ramrod. Flat lock plate. Flat hammer with reinforced neck. $300–$415.

MODEL 1777 NAVY PISTOL, cal. .673, 7.44-inch round barrel, total length 13.78 inches. Brass pan without fence. Made either with or without an iron belt hook fastened by a screw under the trigger bow. Oval-faced hammer. Trigger bow is a separate part held in front by a screw and hinged at the rear by another screw. Frizzen spring is in the opposite of the usual direction. Fore-end cap and housing for lock are integral. The name of the manufacturing arsenal is marked in script in a curve under the hammer. This French pistol has the greatest interest to American collectors, for it was used as a model for the first United States Government contract pistol made by North and Cheney at Berlin, Connecticut. These were made at three French arsenals—Charleville, Maubeuge, and St. Etienne. $500–$775.

MODEL YEAR IX (1800–1801) CAVALRY PISTOL, cal. .69, 7.9-inch barrel, total length 14.567 inches. Round-faced reinforced hammer. Brass pan without fence. Brass band, butt cap, side plate, and separate trigger bow. Lock plate has rounded face at rear end. $385–$525.

MODEL YEAR IX (1800–1801) GENDARMERIE OR INFANTRY OF-FICERS' PISTOL, cal. .60, 5.04-inch barrel, total length 10.24 inches. Resembles Model Year IX Cavalry Pistol except for iron furniture. $275–$370.

MODEL YEAR XIII (1804–1805) CAVALRY PISTOL, cal. .673, 7.9-inch barrel, total length 14.57 inches. Resembles Model Year IX Gendarmerie or Infantry Officers' Pistol, described above, except that the fore-end band has only 1 ring and is shaped differently. The fore-end band is held in place by a lock plate retaining screw which passes through a pierced tang. $275–$370.

MODEL 1816 CAVALRY OR GENDARMERIE PISTOL, resembles previous pistol except that the fore-end band is rounded toward the rear on the lower side. There is a lanyard ring on the butt cap. $260–$360.

MODEL 1822 CAVALRY OR GENDARMERIE PISTOL, resembles the Model 1816 Cavalry or Gendarmerie Pistol, except for brass fore-end band, trigger bow, side plate, and butt cap shapes. Buttonhead ramrod. $260–$340.

## FRENCH REVOLVERS USED IN AMERICAN CIVIL WAR

LEFAUCHEUX FRENCH NAVY REVOLVER, cal. .41 (sometimes listed as cal. .42), pin-fire cartridge, 6-shot, D.A., 7-inch octagon barrel marked "Lefaucheux Arms Co., Paris, France." Total length 12 inches. Round hardwood handles, with ring for lanyard. Brass-bead front sight. Notched-hammer rear sight. The cartridge case has a pin attached at right angles to the main axis of the case. This weapon was used in the early days of the Civil War until discarded in favor of American hand arms. It might be classed as a U.S. secondary martial revolver. There are many minor variations which do not affect value materially. $150–$200.

LEFAUCHEUX FRENCH DRAGOON REVOLVER, cal. .4725, pin-fire, 6-shot, 7.5-inch round-octagon barrel. Weight 4 lbs. 14.5 oz. Walnut grips. Steel butt cap. Lanyard swivel. Loading gate. Side-rod ejector. Center-hung hammer. Extension lug on underside of barrel forms frame bottom to which straps are screwed. Marked "Invor. F. Lefaucheux Brevete S.G.D.G. Paris." Used in the American Civil War and classifiable as a U.S. secondary martial revolver. $290–$375.

LE MAT FRENCH ARMY AND NAVY REVOLVER, cal. .44, 12-gauge, 10-shot, pin-fire, 6.75-inch barrel. The upper barrel is rifled, and 9 rounds can be fired through it. The lower barrel serves as an axis on which the cylinder turns, and buckshot can be fired through it. The nose of the hammer is hinged for adjustment to either barrel. Made in France and used during the American Civil War, hence it might be classed as a U.S. secondary martial revolver. Some specimens are marked "Col. Le Mat Br'e SGDC." Some are marked "Syst. Le Mat, Bté, s.g.d.g. Paris." Total length 13.25 inches. The inventor was Doctor (and Colonel) Alexandre François Le Mat, of New Orleans, Louisiana, and Paris, France. Originally made for percussion cartridges and later altered to use center-fire cartridges. $800–$1,350.

SAME, but cal. .38, 10-shot, 3-inch octagon barrel. Under barrel is 28-gauge shotgun barrel, 3 inches long, which serves as base pin for cylinder. Loaded through swinging breech under hammer. Movable pin on hammer for firing either shot gun or revolver barrel. Walnut grips. Iron guard. Single action. Loading gate. Side-rod ejector. Practically the same as the Le Mat described above. Notice that it was the percussion, and not the pin-fire type, that was officially used during the Civil War. $950–$1,500.

PERRIN FRENCH ARMY REVOLVER, cal. .45, r.f., D.A., 6-shot, originally made for pin-fire cartridges. The hammer, made without a cocking piece, has no full-cock action. Hardwood handles with lanyard ring. Brass-post front sight. Notched-hammer rear sight. Made in Paris, France, by Perrin et Cie. (Perrin & Co.), under the Perrin patent, sold to the United States for use during the Civil War, and converted from pin-fire to normal rim-fire in U.S. armories. Classed as a U.S. secondary martial revolver. $290–$440.

RAPHAEL FRENCH ARMY REVOLVER, cal. .41 c.f., D.A., 6-shot, 5.5-inch barrel marked "Raphael, Paris," total length 10.5 inches. Brass-post front sight. Raised-notch rear sight in front of cylinder. Hardwood handles with lanyard ring. Two-part cylinder removed for loading and extracting. Bought by U.S. for use during Civil War, hence classed as a U.S. secondary martial revolver. $325–$450.

# MISCELLANEOUS FRENCH FLINTLOCK PISTOLS

MARTIAL FLINTLOCK PISTOL, MODEL 1777, cal. .69, 7.5-inch round barrel. Total length 13.5 inches. Cast brass frame marked "Charleville" and "P 80." Flashpan made integral with frame. Brass trigger guard and butt cap. Straight trigger. Tang marked "1777." Walnut grip stamped "385." $500–$775.

GENDARME FLINTLOCK PISTOL, cal. .60, 5-inch round barrel marked "1812." Full-length walnut stock. Iron trigger guard, butt cap, and muzzle band, latter being spring-fastened. Double-neck hammer. Brass pan. Brass-tipped ramrod. Used as a pocket pistol by officers of the French Army, as well as a side arm for gendarmes and others. $225–$310.

GENDARME FLINTLOCK PISTOL, cal. .60, 5-inch round barrel. Total length 9.5 inches. Full-length walnut stock. Iron upper band with 2 barrel straps. Iron guard and butt cap. Button-tip iron ramrod. Flat lock plate. Iron pan with fence, wedge-shaped on bottom. Flat hammer with reinforced neck. Lock marked "Maubeuge Manuf. Fle." $225–$310.

DOUBLE-BARREL FLINTLOCK PISTOL, cal. .54, smoothbore; 6.625-inch, round, wedge-fastened barrels. Total length 12.5 inches. Walnut stock with checkered grip. Butt carved in leaf design and finished with engraved steel cap. Engraved steel trigger guard, hammers, and locks. Silver-lined pans. Floral design in gold around breech end of the barrels. On the rib the name "Canon A. Rubans" is inlaid in gold. Gold band around muzzles, and gold name plate on grip. Swell-tipped ramrod. Bead front sight. $450–$640.

A. MAICHE FLINTLOCK PISTOL, cal. .56, 9-inch round barrel marked "A. Maiche en Franche Conte," with raised flat rib on top which has been chiseled from the barrel itself. Leaf chiseled in relief in rear of rib. Full-length walnut stock. Straight trigger. Brass mountings and silver plating. Horn-tipped ramrod. Flat, gooseneck hammer. Brass pan. $275–$380.

FLINTLOCK POCKET PISTOL, cal. .36; 1.25-inch round barrel, with cannon muzzle, unscrews to load. Walnut half-stock. Iron butt cap. Iron guard. Gooseneck hammer. Iron pan. French proof marks. $195–$280.

FLINTLOCK DAGGER PISTOL, cal. .40; 4-inch, round superposed barrels. Center-hung hammer. Bottom of frizzen is a drum which, when revolved by outside lever on frame, changes vent from one barrel to the other. Sliding trigger guard acts as catch for folding spring dagger under barrel. Guard engraved with wild boar or with bull. This was one of a pair. One had the bull picture, and the other pistol the boar. Marked "Bontoms Au Me'-nil." $475–$600.

# MISCELLANEOUS FRENCH PERCUSSION PISTOLS AND REVOLVERS

LE PAGE PERCUSSION 2-SHOT PISTOL, cal. .64, 2 shots from same barrel; 7.625-inch, octagon, Damascus steel, express-type, rifled barrel etched on underside "Bis in idem." Designed according to the American Lindsay principle. Two hammers. One trigger. Circassian walnut grip. Steel guard with trigger operating in rear of guard similar to spur trigger. Back-action locks. Back and front straps, locks, hammers, guard, breech, and muzzle of barrel etched in deep foliated design. One each lock and on back strap are gargoyles. Inlaid in gold on top of barrel are words "Le Page Moutier arqrr. du Roi à Paris." Left lock marked "Le Page," and right lock marked "arqrr. du roi." One charge is loaded on top of the other. Both hammers are cocked and right hammer falls on first pull of trigger, as in the Lindsay. $525–$750.

TIZERAY PERCUSSION, DOUBLE-BARREL, DAGGER PISTOL, cal. .41, 3.75-inch round barrels, in groove down center of blade, one in each side of the blade, etched with words "Tizeray Bté à Paris" in Old English lettering. Dagger blade 9.5 inches long, elaborately etched. Quillions, or guard, form hammers for pistols, the 2 on upper edge of blade being the hammers. One concealed trigger in grip fires barrels, singly or simultaneously. Ivory grips grooved. Engraved pommel. Fire-gilded etched quillions, pommel, and barrels. Metal scabbard covered with black velvet. Total length of whole weapon in scabbard 15 inches. $500–$650.

HOULLIER-BLANCHAR PERCUSSION PEPPERBOX, cal. .48, 6-shot; 5.875-inch, round, Damascus steel barrels numbered in rotation. Burl walnut grips fluted. Engraved iron frame. Ring trigger with adjusting screw for hammer release. Scoop-shaped underhammer. French proof marks. Marked "Fni. Par Houllier-Blanchar à Paris." The maker was famous in Paris from 1845 to 1851, and in 1847 invented the pin-fire cartridge. $280–$365.

PILL-LOCK TURRET PISTOL, cal. .30, 10-shot, D.A., 3.5-inch octagon barrel. Walnut grips. Folding trigger. Turret is vertical and housed in frame, which is cylindrical at point of housing. Left side of frame has hinged cover which, when opened, allows removal of turret. Horizontal mule-ear-type hammer on right of frame. Swinging safety lock on frame under hammer. High rib on barrel. Very high pointed front sight. Frame, barrel, and rib engraved. Serial number but no name. $490–$750.

LE PAGE 20-SHOT PIN-FIRE REVOLVER, 7mm., 20-shot; 4.75-inch, round, superposed barrels marked "Le Page Freres a Paris. Rue d'Enchein." Total length 9.625 inches. Ebony grips. Folding trigger. Loading gate. Side-rod ejector. Cylinder has 2 rows of chambers, 1 within the other, each row has 10 chambers. Hammer has 2 firing pins, 1 for each row of chambers, the inner set firing through the lower barrel and the outer through the upper barrel. $600–$775.

# MISCELLANEOUS FRENCH PISTOLS AND REVOLVERS

SALOON PISTOL, MAGAZINE TYPE, cal. .40 c.f., 1.5-inch octagon barrel. Checkered and carved walnut grip. Engraved steel frame, butt cap, and trigger guard. Center-hung hammer with sliding safety. Magazine on top of barrel, gravity-fed and tubular-shaped with open sides. As the hammer is cocked, breechblock containing chamber is raised vertically until chamber is in line with magazine. When hammer is brought to full cock, breechblock drops shut, ready for firing. Bullet contains powder and primer, hence no cartridge case is used. Blued finish. $250–$400.

L. DOLNE APACHE-TYPE KNUCKLE-DUSTER REVOLVER, cal. .32 r.f., 6-shot, D.A.; 1.5-inch, round, fluted cylinder. Iron frame marked "L. Dolne Invor." Grip of pistol constitutes the iron knuckles that fold under the piece. Folding trigger. On left side of frame is a folding wavy-blade dagger 3.5 inches long. Outside hammer spring. $475–$625.

MITRAILLEUSE PALM PISTOL, cal. 8 mm, c.f., 6-shot; 2.25-inch, round, ribbed barrel with rib marked "Mitrailleuse." Frame is 2 inches long, 2.5 inches high, and 0.625 inch thick. Nickel-plated. Mauser-type magazine, loaded by removing right side of frame, exposing mechanism. Sliding cover on top of frame similar to Model 73 Winchester. Breechblock and housing for grip spring project from back of frame and are joined by a crosspiece covered with hard rubber, checkered. Safety lock. Marked "Manufacture Française D'Armes St. Etienne. Déchargement et Démontage." $375–$485.

# Chapter 31

## *FOREIGN FIREARMS OTHER THAN BRITISH AND FRENCH*

T HE comments in this chapter apply in general to all firearms, regardless of their origin, but special attention is paid to those firearms made outside the United States by nationalities other than the British and French.

In flintlock days and before, no two gunmakers could produce arms that were more than approximately alike, even when they had a pattern to follow, and no two weapons made by the same man were identical. This situation continued to exist well into the percussion period, but with the introduction of cartridge arms came an increased use of machinery that did much to cut down the number of models, modifications, and variations that delight the collector but make the cataloguing of arms an endless task.

However, it must not be thought that firearms are perfectly standardized even today, for there are still many operations in the manufacture of firearms which require handwork. Then, too, the manufacturers are constantly experimenting with what they hope will be improvements, and they are always ready to make special types for those who have the money to pay for their orders. Consequently it is fairly simple to ascertain values for arms made in great quantities with little variation, but it is difficult to appraise the rarities and the beautifully executed and ornamented presentation pieces, such as, for example, the cased pair of presentation flintlock pistols made by Boutet and given to the Admiral of Spain by Napoleon, while he was First Consul in the tenth year of the French Republic, which corresponded to 1802-1803.

In considering the values of all firearms suitable for collections, the law of supply and demand prevails. This becomes complicated in appraising the values of firearms made outside the United States, whether such weapons are British, French, German, Italian, African, Asiatic, or of any other origin.

The citizens of each nation prefer to collect the firearms made in their own country, hence values may be higher than they would be for the same weapons in another land, but this is only a strong tendency, and by no means an economic law.

For example, while serving in the Fourth Regiment, U.S. Marine Corps, in China, the author saw beautiful examples of the art and skill of Chinese gunmakers in private collections and in museums. Those same firearms, which were rightfully valued very highly by their Chinese owners, would not have been appraised very highly in the United States at that time because few American collectors knew anything about Chinese firearms. The demand was low in the United States, hence the value was low.

The same Chinese collectors of firearms knew nothing about the revolving shoulder arms and handguns made by Samuel Colt at his Paterson, New Jersey, factory and would not have offered anything for them if they did know about them. However, a few of the Chinese who had been educated in England also collected English flintlock pistols, which they correctly regarded as having high values.

The author's service in China was during the years 1933, 1934, and 1935. Shortly after 1935, the Japanese armies swept down from their staging area north of the Great Wall of China, their airplanes bombed the cities of China, and their Imperial Japanese Navy flattened most of the great seaport of Shanghai. Years passed, the Russian hordes drove out the Japanese. All of the Chinese gentlemen whose gun collections I examined were killed without mercy. Their collections are gone forever.

Wars, revolutions, fires, and floods constantly destroy gun collections. The supply gradually but surely decreases, but the demand increases with the population. The values indicated in this chapter reflect the world market as well as the American market.

## VALUES ACCORDING TO IGNITION PERIODS

### Hand Cannon

Practically all hand-cannon specimens priced within the reach of the average collector are Chinese and Japanese pieces, made long after the end of the hand-cannon period. Many of them are made today for tourists and collectors and certainly not for use. A genuine European hand cannon of the hand-cannon period is very rare, very high priced, and should be bought only on the advice of honest experts. A substitute, to illustrate the type, exists. This is the Malay Lantaka, ranging in value from $60 to $90 for a small specimen, and from $300 to $450 for one four or five feet long. It is *not* a true hand cannon and never was, but it will impress visitors.

## Matchlocks

A matchlock pistol can be bought for $250 if one chooses a Japanese specimen of a late period in good condition. The same piece in fine condition would cost $450, but these values are for plain Japanese matchlock pistols, with little or no decoration. A specimen of a late period in good condition with a fair amount of decoration is worth at least $300; one in fine condition is worth about $550. If a piece made in an early period is desired, the cost will be from $400 to $500 for a plain piece, and from $500 to $750 for a well-decorated weapon.

European matchlock pistols are exceedingly rare and costly. European matchlock muskets and rifles are usually sold for at least $800 in plain, good condition and for at least $1,500 in plain, fine condition, but these values are for good specimens made during the matchlock period and still in their original condition, not converted to percussion or flintlock and then converted back again. If highly engraved, carved, and inlaid, the matchlocks are worth much more. However, the general rule is that a matchlock rifle or musket can be bought for at least 25% less than a matchlock pistol of the same period, condition, and quality of ornamentation. This applies beyond doubt to Japanese matchlocks and has general force in regard to other makes.

## Wheel Locks

Wheel-lock arms are also found in many grades and values. Wheel-lock pistols are sometimes sold as low as $300 for very plain, small specimens in good condition, but in 1940 an elaborately decorated, well-made pair of wheel-lock arms was sold for $5,000 to an experienced collector who knew values, and the pair was worth at least $12,000 in 1965. These are extremes, of course. A plain, military-type, wheel-lock pistol in good condition is worth $400, in fine condition it is worth $600, but advanced collectors think nothing of paying from $600 to $900 for well-made, martial, wheel-lock pistols. Like other ignition types, wheel-lock shoulder arms are usually worth from 25% to 33⅓% less than pistols of the same period and condition.

Beware of fakes!

## Pyrites-Lock Firearms

The pyrites lock is a disputed ignition type, usually considered to have been a transition between the wheel lock and the true flintlock, but some experts say there is no such thing as a pyrites lock. The questionable status of this type, and the danger of being fooled, combine to make this a poor purchase for a beginner. Our advice is to judge a so-called pyrites lock on the same basis as you would appraise a flintlock and pay accordingly, disregarding any fiction prepared by some imaginative collector or collector-dealer. On the other hand, if you have become rich on the black market while your neighbor and his son were in the armed service, the author hopes that you will buy a truckload.

## Snaphance Alias Snaphaunce

The snaphance, also spelled "snaphaunce," "snapharmce," and "snaphaan," and several other things in low and high Dutch and German, has the battery (frizzen) and the pan cover made in separate pieces, as distinguished from the typical flintlock, which has the battery and cover in one piece, attached to the pan by a hinge. The separate pan cover of the snaphance was copied from the wheel lock; it is merely a sliding plate, but it is connected to the cock by a rod so that when the piece is cocked, the pan cover is pulled to the rear to expose the priming powder.

Although the function of this book is to describe individual pieces and state values, we explain the snaphance lock because ordinary flintlocks are sometimes sold to suckers as snaphances. A plain European snaphance pistol is worth from $350 to $525 in good condition and from $600 to $900 in fine condition.

Beware of fakes!

## Miquelet Locks

The miquelet lock has the frizzen and pan cover in one piece, but it is easily recognized by the presence of a safety catch which consists of a bolt at right angles to the lock plate, and a nose on the front of the cock that rests on the bolt at the half-cock position. The first part of the pull on the trigger releases the bolt and leaves the cock free to strike the frizzen.

Like other arms, the period of manufacture, the craftsmanship of the maker, and the amount of ornamentation, as well as the size of the piece, are determining factors in appraising values. A small Oriental miquelet pistol can be bought occasionally for $100 in good condition and for $150 in fine condition, while a large one is worth from $200 to $300 at least and sometimes more. Likewise, the value of a European miquelet pistol extends from $150 to $225 for plain, small good ones, and from $250 to $375 for large ones, but ornamentation increases the value, and some collectors will pay more for a larger specimen.

Beware of fakes!

## Flintlocks

The flintlock values are well shown by the pieces described throughout the book. American collectors prefer American-made flintlocks, preferably of the Colonial and Revolutionary War periods. Secondly, they like English military and naval flintlocks of the same period. Third, they seek the French martial flintlocks of the same period. Since demand is the most important cause of value, the values of flintlocks range in that order, condition being the same.

## Percussion Firearms

Percussion arms made abroad are of interest to American collectors for one of the following reasons: (1) They illustrate an ignition type or sub-type, such as the pin-fire, for example; (2) They have an unusual mechanism, such as a 20-shot revolver, for example; (3) The arms are associated with the martial history of the United States or of the nation where they are made; (4) The arms are beautifully engraved, carved, or cased, such as presentation pieces or cased dueling pistols in matched pairs.

*Cartridge Firearms*

Cartridge arms made abroad are of less general interest to American collectors than any other ignition type for many reasons. When they are collected, it is usually for one of the four reasons given above for collecting percussion arms.

## *JAPANESE MATCHLOCK PISTOLS*

Cal. .36; 5.75-inch round, cannon-muzzle barrel, inlaid with gold and silver dragon. Total length 10.5 inches. Light-colored hardwood stock. All metal parts are brass except barrel and serpentine. Serpentine has to jaw with screw to hold the match, which is unusual. $300–$500.

Cal. .54; 4.625-inch octagon, cannon-muzzle barrel, inlaid with gold and silver in dragon design and family crest. All metal parts are brass except the barrel. Black lacquered stock with floral design and family crest, consisting of 3 heart-shaped segments within an oval. Black lacquered ramrod. $300–$500.

Cal. .30; 4.375-inch octagon barrel, inlaid in silver with dragon and floral design. Total length 9 inches. Hardwood stock. All metal parts are brass except barrel. Button trigger. Small calibers and sizes are apparently less common than larger arms. $300–$500.

Cal. .56; 6-inch, flat-topped, round barrel. Total length 10.25 inches. Hardwood stock with peculiar butt. All metal parts are brass except the barrel. $300–$500.

Cal. .46; 3.875-inch, octagon, cannon-muzzle barrel, inlaid with gold and silver in dragon design and family crest. Hardwood stock, lacquered black with floral design and family crest in gold lacquer. Brass lock, pan cover, band, and serpentine. Front and rear sights. Wooden ramrod. Total length 7.25 inches. $350–$600.

Cal. .35; 4.5-inch, octagon, cannon-muzzle, bronze barrel, with dragon in high relief covering the top. Total length 8.125 inches. Hardwood stock. Serpentine spring on outside of lock. U-shaped spring inside lock. Button trigger. $300–$500.

Cal. .22; 3.125-inch, round, flat-top, cannon-muzzle barrel, with 2 very small brass butterflies in relief, and a brass band. Total length 6 inches. Cherry-wood stock nearly to muzzle. Brass lock plate, trigger, and serpentine. Swinging brass pan cover. Front and rear sights. Ramrod. $300–$500.

Cal. .59; 10.75-inch, round, flat-top, cannon-muzzle barrel. Hardwood stock extends nearly to muzzle. Two brass barrel bands. Brass lock plate, serpentine, and pan cover. $300–$500.

Cal. .35; 17-inch, octagon, cannon-muzzle barrel. Total length 26.75 inches. Light-colored hardwood stock, inlaid with brass designs. All metal parts are brass except the barrel. U-shaped serpentine spring outside lock plate. Family crest of 2 crossed leaves within a circle inlaid on barrel. $300–$500.

Cal. .48; 14.25-inch, octagon, cannon-muzzle barrel, inlaid with design of tree with 3 branches and a flower on each branch. All metal parts are brass except the barrel. Made with a trigger guard. Black lacquered stock with gold floral design. The quality of the workmanship increases the value of this piece. $300–$750.

Cal. .50; 14.5-inch, octagon, cannon-muzzle barrel. Total length 23.25 inches.Light-colored hardwood stock. All metal parts are brass except the barrel. Folding trigger. Signed with the name of the maker, in Japanese characters naturally. $300–$750.

## JAPANESE MATCHLOCK RIFLES

Cal. .48; 28.5-inch, octagon, peg-fastened barrel with tulip muzzle. Dark oak stock almost to muzzle. Wooden ramrod. Front and rear sights. Barrel inlaid with silver flowers near breech. Brass trigger guard, lock plate, and serpentine, all polished bright. Careful workmanship. $150–$250.

Cal. .62; 27.5-inch, octagon, cannon-muzzle barrel, inlaid with silver dragon for 16.5 inches of the length, and inlaid in silver near breech with crest having 2 parallel lines within a circle. Brass lock plate. Iron hammer. All lock mechanism inside the lock plate. Total length 39 inches. Weight 10 lbs. 8 oz. $150–$250.

Cal. .50; 39.25-inch round barrel, with wide brass band around the breech, engraved; a dragon inlaid in silver; and the cannon muzzle inlaid with a silver scroll. Full-length, dark, hardwood stock with a brass tree trunk entwined with flowers on the underside. Brass lock. Butt stock inlaid with brass flowers and a band along the comb. Total length 51 inches. Front and rear sights. $170–$250.

Cal. .48, 39.75-inch octagon barrel with a cannon muzzle, and the breech inlaid with silver and brass horses and flowers. Full-length, dark, hardwood stock with brass flowers and wheel-like inlays on the butt. Brass lock and mechanism. Brass trigger guard and pan cover. Total length 51.25 inches. $225–$300.

# TYPICAL WHEEL-LOCK PISTOLS

ITALIAN ALL-METAL RIGHT-ANGLE, WHEEL-LOCK PISTOL, 16TH CENTURY. The stock approaches a right angle to the barrel, which is rare in a wheel-lock pistol. Rectangular trigger guard. Ball butt. $3,000–$5,000.

COMBINATION WHEEL-LOCK PISTOL, BATTLE-AX, AND HAMMER, ALL-METAL, 16TH CENTURY. Barrel 15 inches, with a muzzle which ends in a battle-ax and a long-pointed fighting hammer. Total length 26 inches. There is a steel rope handle and a heavy steel, ball butt. There is a belt hook and a steel ramrod on the right side of the frame. The steel is beautifully chased throughout. This specimen was bought from the Hearst collection by Dr. S. Traner Buck and sold by his estate to Mr. W. G. C. Kimball. $5,000–$10,000.

SAXON BALL-BUTT, MILITARY, WHEEL-LOCK PISTOL, DATED 1591. Barrel 13 inches, half-octagon, dated 1591. Total length 22 inches. Full-length dark wood stock with ivory inlays and plain military lock. $2,500–$4,500.

SAXON WHEEL-LOCK DAG, 17TH CENTURY. This piece is distinguished by its quantity and quality of ivory inlays and has a matching ivory inlaid flask. The total length is about 26 inches. Flask $350–$500. Pistol $4,500–$7,500.

SAXON ALL-METAL SELF-SPANNING WHEEL-LOCK PISTOL. This piece is about 23 inches long. The rectangular trigger guard is lighter in construction than many of this type. The self-spanning feature is its most interesting characteristic. $1,500–$2,200.

ITALIAN MILITARY WHEEL-LOCK PISTOL, LATE 17TH CENTURY. The total length is about 24 inches. The construction is rugged throughout, with a plain military lock. The butt is flatter and thinner than the more ornate types. $1,500–$3,500.

WHEEL-LOCK HAND CANNON AND GRENADE-THROWER, COMBINED, 16TH CENTURY. About 19 inches long. Stock elaborately decorated with ivory inlays. This may have been a pure-type hand-cannon pistol originally and then converted to wheel lock. It also has a grenade-throwing device attached. If its background were traced beyond the wheel-lock period and it could be established definitely that it was originally a hand-cannon pistol, the value would be several times the one we have assigned, but collectors and dealers are cautious about the hand-cannon designation, hence this piece is classed and valued as a wheel lock only. $5,000–$7,500.

ITALIAN BALL-BUTT WHEEL-LOCK PISTOL, LATE 17TH CENTURY. This pistol is remarkable principally for its beauty. The stock and the ball butt are inlaid with ivory in delicate designs. $3,000–$6,000.

ITALIAN MILITARY WHEEL-LOCK PISTOL, 17TH CENTURY, cal. .51, smoothbore, 14-inch octagon barrel. Light-colored hardwood stock. Steel stock tip, ramrod thimble, butt cap, and pierced trigger guard. Wooden ramrod. Lock has wheel on outside of plate. Wheel marked "S." $2,000–$5,000.

## WHEEL-LOCK SHOULDER ARMS

GERMAN WHEEL-LOCK RIFLE, MADE ABOUT 1675, cal. .50; 33-inch, octagon, wedge-fastened, rifled barrel. Full-length walnut stock with horn tip. Typical wheel-lock, buttstock with wide, sloping cheekpiece. Long wooden-covered patch box on right side of stock. The stock is elaborately carved in leaf design. The forearm is checkered. Three brass ramrod thimbles. Horn-tipped wooden ramrod. Large brass trigger guard with finger holds for right hand. Double set triggers. Steel lock with wheel inside the lock plate. Made without pan cover. Jaws for holding pyrites are forward of the pan and turn down to the rear. The lock is engraved "G. Kaiser in Kremsmunster." Low blade front sight. V-notch rear sight. Peep sight with windage on tang. Brass escutcheons. Brass-bound butt with brass inlays. $1,500–$3,500.

SAXON WHEEL-LOCK RIFLED ARQUEBUS, 17TH CENTURY, cal. .73, 27-inch octagon barrel with 8 deep grooves. Total length 38 inches. Full-length pinned stock with carved ivory tip and 2 elaborately carved ramrod pipes. The butt stock is carved and has a large ivory lion inlaid on the left side and 2 ivory inlays as lockscrew washers. Sliding patch-box cover of ivory with running deer and foliated design. Ivory-tipped ramrod. Plain lock with set trigger. Made about 1630. $1,500–$3,500.

AUSTRIAN WHEEL-LOCK RIFLED ARQUEBUS, MADE IN THE LATE 17TH CENTURY, cal. .60; 32-inch, heavy, octagon, rifled barrel with gold inlays at the muzzle and breech, and the name of the maker, Joseph Hamerl, Wien (Vienna). Total length 43 inches. Finely chiseled wheel lock with elaborate brass lock strap. Finely carved stock with spanner compartment having a sliding cover with a brass inlay. Set trigger. $1,500–$3,500.

AUSTRIAN—MATHEUS MATL WHEEL-LOCK RIFLE, MID-17TH CENTURY, cal. .47; 31.625-inch, octagon, rifled barrel marked "Matheus Matl 1668" and "2." The lock is 7.75 inches long and 2.125 inches wide, and is engraved with floral patterns and seated woman pointing to a scroll reading "Lorenz Lipert Eferdi NG." Full-length walnut stock, brass-tipped.

Three brass thimbles. Brass butt plate. Brass trigger guard. Patch box covered on ends with heavy brass. All brass is elaborately engraved with hunting scenes and floral designs. Hardwood ramrod with brass tip. Trigger guard made with fingerholds. Double set triggers. Stock carved in floral design. Blade front sight. Open rear sight. Peep sight on tang. $1,500–$3,500.

SAXON WHEEL-LOCK RIFLED ARQUEBUS, LATE 17TH CENTURY, cal. .58, 35-inch octagon barrel. Total length 47 inches. Finely chased and engraved wheel lock, showing 4 horsemen and a castle. The lock is signed "Hine Aver," who worked in Salzburg. Beautifully carved, full-length, ivory-covered stock, completely carved from muzzle to butt with carefully executed scenes of camps, forests, battles, mounted men, stands of arms, coaches, hunting a stag with a dog, castles, etc. $2,000–$4,500.

GERMAN WHEEL-LOCK CARBINE, MADE ABOUT 1700, cal. .69; 23-inch, part round, part octagon barrel with one brass band. Walnut half-stock carved on sides and bottom. Carved wooden-covered patch box. Brass thimble, trigger guard, side plate, and butt plate. Front of guard engraved with hunting scene showing a wild boar. Lock plate and other lock parts engraved with hunting scenes. Sliding pan cover. Single trigger. Blade front sight. No rear sight. Brass-tipped ramrod. There is a spanner for winding the lock in the patch box. Lock marked "Lost." $2,000–$4,500.

SAXON WHEEL-LOCK, SHORT, MILITARY, RIFLED ARQUEBUS, cal. .65; 27-inch, heavy, octagon barrel, having a countersunk hallmark showing the number 1724R. Full-length, dark, walnut stock with ivory tip. Plain wheel lock. Double set trigger. Very thick carved stock with coat of arms in gold and silver back of the grip. Compartment for spanner. $2,000–$4,500.

SAXON COMBINED WHEEL-LOCK AND MATCHLOCK WALL PIECE. The 34-inch octagon barrel has a diameter of 1.5 inches at the muzzle and 1.75 inches at the breech, with a caliber of about .70, and is rifled with seven deep grooves. The total length is 63 inches. Full-length walnut stock, completely inlaid with ivory and bone carved in many grotesque designs. This is a combination matchlock and wheel lock. Weight about 40 pounds. There is a wide flare at the butt. The butt measurement across the butt cap is 9.5 inches long and nearly 3 inches wide. $3,500–$6,500.

# SNAPHANCE ARMS

ITALIAN SNAPHANCE PISTOL, ABOUT 1690, cal. .48; 7-inch, part round, part octagon barrel. Full-length, burled, walnut stock, carved on both sides almost completely. Two steel thimbles. Horn-tipped hardwood ramrod, with a steel jag. Steel trigger guard with scalloped edge, with a figure of a head in relief underneath, and a tip which is pierced and chased in relief in the shape of a head. Ball butt with steel cap, held in place by a screw chiseled into a human face. Rounded lock plate with a face in high relief on the tail. Gooseneck hammer, with its screw in the shape of a face. Horizontal pan with fence and sliding pan cover. Striking face of frizzen is rectangular-shaped and in the form of a woman. There are 10 human heads or busts chiseled or engraved in the steel parts alone. It is impossible to describe this piece adequately in detail. $2,500–$5,000.

BRESCIAN SNAPHANCE PISTOLS, A PAIR. These pistols have an elaborate amount of chiseling and a great quantity of cut-steel work. They are generally reputed to be one of the finest pairs of pistols in existence. They have been in excellent condition for centuries, hence the lower value merely indicates what they would be worth if they were in only good condition. $5,000–$10,000.

BRESCIAN SNAPHANCE COURT PISTOL, 17TH CENTURY. This pistol is from the St. Louis Museum and is a highly ornamented piece, although not in the same grade as the ones described above. $2,500–$5,000.

NORTH AFRICAN SNAPHANCE MUSKET, cal. .59, smooth bore; 46.5-inch, part round, part octagon barrel, tulip muzzle. Black hardwood stock almost to muzzle. Barrel fastened to stock with eight 4-inch brass bands, engraved. Blade front sight. Open rear sight. Circular brass trigger guard. Sliding pan cover. The small of the stock is very short and narrow and swells rapidly into the extremely high, narrow butt, which is made of ivory, 8.375 inches high, 1.75 inches wide, and 0.5 inch thick. Elaborate silver wire inlay in Arabian designs in both the stock and in the metal. This piece was probably the weapon of a wealthy merchant or tribal chief among the Berbers of Morocco or Algeria. $200–$300.

# MIQUELET-LOCK PISTOLS

Cal. .50, smoothbore; 3.375-inch, part round, part octagon, cannon-muzzle barrel, with 3 copper inlays at the breech. Full-length walnut stock. Brass trigger guard, butt cap, thimble, and ornamentation on back of grip. All brass engraved except butt cap, which is face-hammered in relief. Outside hammer spring, sear, and sear notch. Unmarked. $250–$450.

Cal. .50, 4-inch, part round, part octagon barrel, thin at muzzle, heavy at breech. Lock has heavy hammer and powerful spring. Frizzen is short and wide. Walnut stock with heavy brass butt cap and tangs running up each side. Brass trigger guard, thimbles, and stock tip. Brass-tipped ramrod. Made about 1700. Unmarked. $250–$450.

SPANISH, cal. .54; 5.25-inch, half round, half octagon barrel with the armorer's seal on top at the breech. Full-length walnut stock. Engraved brass butt cap, trigger guard, inlay on top of grip, and inlay around ramrod hole. Belt hook on left side of stock. $250–$450.

SPANISH, cal. .70; 9-inch, part round, part octagon barrel, cannon muzzle. Full-length walnut stock, finely carved. Floral design is raised on barrel and inlaid with gold forward of octagon part. The octagon part has silver inlaid in a floral design. Silver trigger guard, thimbles, and butt cap, with creased borders. Hammer spring on outside of lock plate, as well as the sear and the sear notch. Lock plate marked "Torrento." Breech of barrel has marks of the maker. Silver plate on stock for lock-plate screws, with engraved border. Silver ramrod tip. Made about 1700. $300–$450.

CAUCASUS MOUNTAINS, cal. .63, smoothbore, 11.25-inch round barrel with face of a man chiseled in relief on the breech, and an inscription that is not legible. Large ivory ball on butt. Button trigger. Large silver strap on back of grip. Leather-covered wooden stock. Silver mountings with floral design in relief, oxidized black. $180–$270.

Cal. .50, 5.625-inch round barrel, octagon breech. Full-length stock, silver-tipped. Engraved silver trigger guard, butt cap, and inlays in grip and along stock. Ivory-tipped wooden ramrod in silver thimbles. Outside lock mechanism. Belt hook on left of stock. Not marked. $175–$275.

ARABIAN OR MOORISH, cal. .63, 11.75-inch round barrel, octagon breech, with 2 brass bands. Full-length brass stock, engraved. Iron ramrod. Rattail grip. Iron lock mechanism, all on outside of lock plate. $175–$275.

CAUCASUS MOUNTAINS, cal. .50, 13.25-inch, round, Damascus steel barrel, with silver band at muzzle, and breech inlaid with gold. Lock inlaid with gold. Grip covered with silver in raised design and oxidized. Large ivory ball on butt. Leather-covered wooden stock almost to muzzle. Straight trigger. $175–$275.

CAUCASUS MOUNTAINS, cal. .60, 13.75-inch,round, steel barrel with people and horses elaborately engraved on the top and tang. Leather-covered wooden stock extends nearly to muzzle. Ivory ball butt. Button trigger. Lanyard ring. Outside lock mechanism. Finished bright steel. $175–$275.

PERSIAN ALL-METAL, cal. .62, 11.5-inch round barrel with 2 brass bands. Total length 19 inches. All brass stock. Rattail grip. Iron guard. Outside lock mechanism. Steel is chased and engraved. $200–$350.

EUROPEAN, cal. .72, smoothbore, 9-inch round barrel, octagon breech marked "1813." Nearly full-length walnut stock, brass tip. Brass butt cap, lock-plate screw escutcheons, pan, thimbles, and trigger guard. Swivel rammer. Outside lock mechanism marked "B" under a crown on a plate, and "Aran Buru" inside. $150–$225.

## MIQUELET-LOCK SHOULDER ARMS

The miquelet-lock shoulder arms in this group are in the Nunnemacher Collection of the Milwaukee Public Museum. Individual values are not assigned because these particular pieces have not been on the market for many years.

Cal. .58, 54.25-inch damascened barrel. Lock has sliding cover characteristic of the wheel lock, and the steel or frizzen is not combined with the cover but is independent; thus the lock might be termed a snaphance, which was a transition between the wheel lock and the flintlock. Ornamented with numerous brass bands. Leather-covered stock. The origin was probably Turkish or Arabian.

Cal. .45, 48.75-inch, octagon, smoothbore barrel with thin walls, without sights. Spanish-type lock. Wooden stock nearly covered with richly engraved or etched iron. Lock plate marked "Bavbuti." The origin may be Arabian.

Cal. .60; 39-inch, half octagon, smoothbore barrel with a flared muzzle, marked "M.K." Front sight missing. Butt consists of alternate bands of ivory and ebony. Bone and colored ivory inlaid in stock. Possibly Arabian origin.

Cal. .68; 50.5-inch octagon, smoothbore barrel with bell-shaped muzzle, marked with Arabic inscription. Wooden stock covered with engraved or etched iron, embellished with brass and mother-of pearl. Arabian.

Cal. .58; 45.5-inch, octagon, smoothbore barrel with thin walls. Rear sight missing. Engraved lock. Stock ornamented with punched metal. Ferrule for ramrod in form of double-headed eagle. Fleur-de-lis inlaid in breech. Top of stock has plate marked "I.H.S.," surmounted by a cross.

Cal. .48; 45.25-inch, octagon, smoothbore barrel. Eight plain brass bands hold the barrel to the stock. Iron trigger guard. Flat leaf-shaped bayonet is shown with this weapon. The origin may be African.

Cal. .59; 41.5-inch, smoothbore barrel with bell-shaped muzzle. Ball trigger. Top of barrel inlaid with gold and silver arabesques; stock inlaid with diamond-shaped designs of mother-of-pearl and small patterns in brass. There was once a carrying strap on the left. The origin was probably Moroccan.

Cal. .68; 42.5-inch, round, smoothbore barrel with bell-shaped muzzle. Forward part of barrel has fish-scale design; rear inlaid with conventionalized silver patterns. Has 3 sights and large miquelet lock. Stock inlaid with many small designs of mother-of-pearl and with large carved disks of the same material. Persian origin.

Cal. .72; 35.25-inch, half octagon barrel, rear part deeply engraved, partly inlaid with gold. Fore stock has 2 silver bands and is inlaid with the figure of a fish. Trigger guard engraved. Gold-lined flashpan. Hallmarks and fleur-de-lis stamped on breech. Lock plate marked with what appears to be "Fernz. Maxua." This weapon was probably used as a shotgun. The origin might be Spanish.

Cal. .54; 33-inch, rifled, damascened barrel with bell-shaped muzzle. Three holes in rear peep sight. Lock and barrel inlaid with gold. Rear of stock covered with embossed silver ornamented with coral-like beads. Plush-covered butt. Barrel held to stock by broad pins originally, but now replaced with numerous punched and embosed silver bands. Persian origin possibly.

Cal. .64; 34.5-inch, octagon, rifled, damascened barrel, top inlaid with designs in silver. Engraved miquelet lock, ball trigger, and rear peep sight. Pentagonal-shaped stock, elaborately inlaid with minute designs in brass and ivory. Barrel formerly held to stock with flat pins, since replaced with 4 engraved silver bands. Origin unknown.

# Chapter 32

## HOW TO MAKE A PROFIT FROM GUN COLLECTING

THE collecting of antique and semi-antique firearms can be both a happy and a profitable hobby if a person follows a few time-tested procedures. Since gun collectors are individualists, each man who collects weapons evolves his own methods.

All collectors have duplicates, which they must either trade or sell. When a collector has enough on hand to make it worth while, he may insert an advertisement in the few magazines that cater to gun collectors and then send a list to those who reply with stamped, addressed envelopes. He should throw in the wastebasket letters from those who expect you to provide both stamps and list, because it has been found from long experience that serious collectors always send either stamps or an addressed, stamped envelope. The others will not buy and are merely childish or broke.

The list should include detailed descriptions of every gun offered for sale and a very careful statement regarding the condition of each gun. Descriptions such as those in this text are used by the successful dealers, and the definitions given in this book for "good" and "fine" condition are followed by all ethical collectors and dealers.

Guns should be shipped only upon receipt of payment, or C.O.D., unless the seller is absolutely certain of the credit status of the buyer and his promptness in paying for merchandise. If the gun has been carefully described and the condition is exactly as stated, the buyer will seldom complain, but if he does complain, the seller should refund his money promptly, and there should be no "service charge" or "packing fee" unless the nature and amount of such charges are agreed upon in advance by both parties.

When the collector has sold his duplicates, he may wish to advertise for more arms. This raises a question of what he should pay. Collectors who are buying for their own collection and not for resale generally pay the amounts shown in this text for values, although it must be remembered that condition is extremely important. A gun may be in a condition between good and fine, better than fine, etc., and it should be valued accordingly.

If a collector has been successful in disposing of his duplicates, he may decide to buy and sell arms as a part-time occupation, especially if he wants to continue to add to his private collection without receiving complaints from his wife about dipping into the family budget. He must then decide how much to pay in his new status as a collector-dealer. This is a difficult question and there is no fixed answer.

When arms can be resold quickly, the profit may be small on each gun, but the profit at the end of the year may be great. For example, we know of one very successful dealer who averages paying about 75% of the retail value. He is usually able to resell his guns within sixty days after purchase, and hence he makes a gross profit of 25% in that period of time. By turning over his money six times during the year, total gross profit on his working capital is 150%, if he neither adds to nor subtracts from the amount set aside for that purpose at the beginning of the year, and further if all guns are actually sold.

On the other hand, if a dealer has his guns on hand for a year before he sells them, he cannot operate on a 25% gross profit, and he may not be able to pay more than 50% of the retail value for the arms he buys. Obviously, he is in competition with the man who only tries to make 25% profit, hence he can buy fewer arms over a period of time.

A department store, a sporting goods store, or a large antique shop, doing business in the high-rent district of a big city and paying the union scale of wages to their employees, obviously has a big overhead. Another factor in their cost of operation is the payroll for the executives and supervisory personnel. On top of that, if it is a corporation, the stockholders expect dividends, the comptroller advises setting aside funds for depreciation, etc. For this reason some of the large department stores that have sold antique arms, either for themselves or on a concession basis, have charged and are now charging prices which are often more than 100% above the correct retail values quoted in this text, and they surprisingly often receive amounts which are two and three times as much as they should be. They "get by" with these fantastic prices principally because they sell to people who know nothing whatever about guns, and still less about the value of guns. This is not true of all large shops by any means, but it is true of enough to warrant these comments.

A well-established antique shop, operated by people who know something about guns, will usually charge prices that are somewhere near the true values, but the little shops beside the road, run by tired old widows, maiden aunts, cripples, sick people, and those who are just plain lazy, are very erratic in their pricing. They pay as little as possible on the ground that, since they know nothing about values, they might suffer a loss. When they sell, they watch the buyer and guess how much he will pay. They can be spotted instantly because they do not place price tags on their merchandise and they are very vague in using firearms terminology. You can never obtain a fair price in selling to such stands, and yet you may be able to obtain some bargains if you wear old clothes, do not act anxious, and pretend that you do not know a muzzle from a hammer.

Pawnshops were once a good source of bargains, but hundreds of "loan brokers" bought the first edition of this text, and now they are surprisingly accurate in their ability to appraise firearms. However, those who have not heard of this handbook are still basing their prices on what they loaned, hence they are fertile fields for the collector and the dealer looking for more stock.

Having discussed retail prices, we can now turn to the problem of the man who decides to become a full-time dealer in antique arms. He does not need a place of business in the commercial district. Some of the most successful arms dealers in America run all their affairs from one room in their home, or from their garage, but it is apparent that if they make enough profit they are justified in adding a wing to the house, or erecting another structure in the back yard, which is exactly what many of them have done.

Some dealers own an antique shop, hardware store, sporting goods emporium, or other retail business where the addition of the antique arms department increases the revenue without adding to the overhead. Soon they find that the tail wags the dog and their original vocation becomes a sideline.

In selecting his stock, the collector-dealer or the full-time dealer should emphasize condition. Do not lay in a big stock of junk, especially during a period of inflation, for there lies the road to insolvency. Avoid the purchase of any gun that is not in "good condition," as defined in this book, and do not earn a reputation among your customers for dealing in poor-quality arms. They will be sold, certainly, but the turnover is slow, the profit is low, and the danger of having defective arms on your shelf is ever present.

Accessories for muzzle-loading shooters are always salable. Many men start as collectors of the old flintlock and percussion arms and then become members of clubs that fire the old relics on the range. Ramrods, molds, bullets, powder, primers, flints, gun grease, oil, cleaning rags, targets, and similar items can be sold profitably in any community where this fast-growing sport is popular.

Firearms books are always a source of profit. There are several thousand books that were written about guns during the past century, and every one of these books appeals to some gun fan sooner or later. However, those books that describe firearms in detail are more salable than long-winded accounts of how some game hog shot a record number of quail back in the days when the grass grew as high as the wheels of a wagon.

Most gun books increase in value a few years after they are published because only a few thousand, and sometimes only a few hundred, are printed by the average publisher. When the edition is exhausted, he does not want to risk the cost of a second printing, with the result that the book is out of print, there are more buyers than sellers, and the price skyrockets. It is surprising to many dealers to learn that some of their competitors make more profit from the sale of books than they do from guns, although when their shops are visited, the guns are more in evidence than the books.

No business can succeed unless it remains in the mind of the public. This is an age of advertising. All of the financially successful dealers advertise in every manner possible. They have an advertisement in each issue of all the magazines appealing to gun collectors, they maintain mailing lists and circularize their prospects, they give lectures at luncheon clubs, they talk about guns on radio programs, and they write, or get someone else to write, articles for magazines and newspapers about gun collecting and muzzle-loading marksmanship.

There is profit in the antique-gun business if it is run right. Buy when others are selling, and sell when others are buying, if possible.

This means that you should try to build up your stock during a depression and avoid buying much during a boom; but your stock is soon exhausted during a boom, and then you must continue to buy or go out of business. Under such conditions, examine the condition of each gun carefully before buying it, compare the price asked with the probable resale price, using this text as a guide, and then advertise widely to unload rapidly.

If you buy only the guns you love, the ones you would like to retain in your private collection, you can combine fun with business, and it is probable that you will not suffer any serious loss, that you will make a profit.

Every successful dealer in antique firearms either has the services of a gunsmith at his disposal, or eventually becomes a gunsmith to some extent. The author of this text had this problem in mind when he wrote *The Complete Guide to Gunsmithing—Gun Care and Repair.* That book was written for the man of only average skill who has only a limited amount of capital and equipment. No book can do your work for you, but it can give you ideas. When properly applied, ideas may mean profits from gun collecting.

# BIBLIOGRAPHY

THERE are more than two thousand books in the English language on firearms, not including paper-bound pamphlets, military manuals, and similar publications. The ones listed here are those that the author considers most interesting for the average firearms collector.

Albaugh, William A., III, and Simmons, Edward N., *Confederate Arms.* Harrisburg, Penna.: The Stackpole Co., 1957

Baker, Ezekiel, *Remarks on Rifle Guns,* also titled *Baker's Remarks on the Rifle.* London: Joseph Mallett, 1835

Bartholomew, Ed, *The Biographical Album of Western Gunfighters.* Houston: The Frontier Press, 1958

Bosworth, N., *A Treatise on the Rifle, Musket, Pistol and Fowling Piece.* New York: J. S. Redfield, 1846

Braverman, Shelley, *The Firearms Encyclopedia.* Athens, New York, 1960

Burrard, Gerald, *The Modern Shotgun* (in two volumes). New York: Charles Scribner's Sons, 1931

Chapel, Charles Edward, *The Art of Shooting.* New York: A. S. Barnes & Co., Inc., 1960

——— *The Boy's Book of Rifles.* New York : Coward-McCann, Inc., 1948

——— *The Complete Book of Gun Collecting.* New York: Coward-McCann, Inc., 1960

——— *The Complete Guide to Gunsmithing—Gun Care and Repair.* New York: A. S. Barnes & Co., Inc., 1962

——— *Field, Skeet, and Trap Shooting.* New York: Coward-McCann, Inc., 1949

——— *Forensic Ballistics.* Chicago: Institute of Applied Science, 1933

——— *Guns of the Old West,* New York: Coward-McCann, Inc., 1960

——— *Simplified Pistol and Revolver Shooting.* New York: Coward-McCann, Inc., 1950

———— *Simplified Rifle Shooting.* New York: Coward-McCann, Inc., 1950

———— *U.S. Martial and Semi-Martial Single-Shot Pistols.* New York: Coward-McCann, Inc., 1962

Clephan, Robert Coltman, *An Outline of the History and Development of Hand Firearms, Etc.* London: The Walter Scott Publishing Co., 1906

Cline, Walter M., *The Muzzle-Loading Rifle, Then and Now.* Huntington, West Virginia: Standard Printing and Publishing Co., 1942

Connecticut Historical Society, *Samuel Colt's Own Record of Transactions With Captain Walker and Eli Whitney, Jr., in 1847.* Hartford, Conn.: The Connecticut Historical Society, 1949

Deane, *Deane's Manual of the History and Science of Fire-Arms.* London: Longman, Brown, Green, Longman's & Roberts, 1858

Dillin, John G. W., *The Kentucky Rifle.* Wilmington, Delaware: George N. Hyatt, 1959

Dougall, James Dalziel, *Shooting: Its Appliances, Practice, and Purpose.* London: Sampson Low, Marston, Searle & Rivington, 1881

Edwards, William B., *The Story of Colt's Revolver.* Harrisburg, Penna.: The Stackpole Co., 1957

Freidel, Frank, *The Splendid Little War.* Boston: Little, Brown & Co., 1958

Fuller, Claude E., *The Breech-Loader in the Service.* Topeka, Kansas: F. Theodore Dexter, 1933

———— *The Rifled Musket.* Harrisburg, Penna.: The Stackpole Co., 1958

———— *Springfield Muzzle-loading Shoulder Arms.* New York: Francis Bannerman Sons, 1930

———— *The Whitney Firearms.* Huntington, West Virginia: Standard Publications, Inc., 1946

Fuller, Claude E., and Steuart, Richard D., *Firearms of the Confederacy.* Huntington, West Virginia: Standard Publications, Inc., 1944

Gardner, Robert E., *American Arms and Arms Makers.* Columbus, Ohio: The F. J. Heer Printing Printing Co., 1938

George, J. N., *English Guns and Rifles.* Plantersville, S. C.: Small-Arms Technical Publishing Co., 1947

———— *English Pistòls and Revolvers.* Onslow County, N.C.: Small-Arms Technical Publishing Co., 1938

Gluckman, Arcadi, *Catalogue of United States Martial Pistols*. Buffalo: Otto Ulbrich Co., 1939

―――― *United States Martial Pistols and Revolvers*. Buffalo: Otto Ulbrich Co., 1939

―――― *United States Muskets, Rifles and Carbines*. Buffalo: Otto Ulbrich Co., Inc., 1948

Gluckman, Arcadi, and Satterlee, L. D., *American Gun Makers*. Harrisburg, Penna.: The Stackpole Co., 1953

Grant, James, *More Single-Shot Rifles*. New York: William Morrow & Co., 1959

―――― *Single-Shot Rifles*. New York: William Morrow & Co., 1947

Gunther, Jack Disbrow, and Gunther, Charles O., *The Identification of Firearms*. New York: John Wiley & Sons, Inc., 1935

Hardee, W. J., *Rifle and Light Infantry Tactics* (two or more volumes). Philadelphia: Lippincott, Grambo & Co., 1835

Hatch, Alden, *Remington Arms in American History*. New York: Rinehart & Co., Inc., 1956

Hatcher, Julian S., *Hatcher's Notebook*. Harrisburg, Penna.: Military Service Publishing Co., 1947

―――― *Textbook of Firearms Investigation, Identification and Evidence*. Marines, Onslow County, N.C.: Small-Arms Technical Publishing Co., 1935

Haven, Charles T., and Belden, Frank A., *A History of the Colt Revolver*. New York: William Morrow & Co., 1940

Held, Robert, *The Age of Firearms*. New York: Harper & Brothers, 1957

Hicks, James E.

(Author's Notice: The books by James E. Hicks were published by him at Mt. Vernon, N.Y., thus:)

*Notes on United States Ordnance*, Vol. I, *Small Arms*, 1940

*Notes on United States Ordnance*, Vol. II, *Ordnance Correspondence*, 1940

*Notes on United States Ordnance*, Vol. III, *Ordnance Correspondence*, 1940

*Notes on German Ordnance*, 1937

*Notes on French Ordnance*, 1937

*Notes on French Ordnance* (Translation of Mémoires d'Artillerie) 1939

*U.S. Firearms* (Revision of Vol. I, above), 1946

Hunter, J. Marvin, and Rose, Noah H., *The Album of Gun-Fighters.* San Antonio, Texas: Published by the Authors, 1951

Johnson, Melvin M., Jr., and Haven, Charles T., *Automatic Weapons of the World.* New York: William Morrow & Co., 1945

Kalman, James M., and Patterson, C. Meade, *Pictorial History of U.S. Single-Shot Martial Pistols.* New York: Charles Scribner's Sons, 1957

Karr, Charles Lee, Jr., and Robbins, Carroll, *Remington Handguns.* Harrisburg, Penna.: The Stackpole Co., 1951

Leffingwell, William Bruce, *The Art of Wing Shooting.* Chicago: Rand, McNally & Co., 1894

Lenz, Ellis Christian, *Muzzle Flashers.* Huntington, West Virginia: Standard Publications, Inc., 1944

———— *Rifleman's Progress.* Huntington, West Virginia: Standard Publications, Inc., 1946

Lindsay, Merrill, *One Hundred Great Guns.* New York: Walker & Co., 1967

Logan, Herschel C., *Cartridges—A Pictorial Digest of Small Arms Ammunition.* Huntington, West Virginia: Standard Publications, Inc., 1948

———— *Hand Cannon to Automatic.* Huntington, West Virginia: Standard Publications, Inc., 1944

McClellan, George B., *Manual of Bayonet Exercises, Prepared for the Use of the United States Army.* Philadelphia: J. B. Lippincott & Co., 1852

McConnell, Duncan, *Grandpappy's Pistol.* New York: Coward-McCann, Inc., 1956

McGivern, Ed, *Ed McGivern's Book on Fast and Fancy Revolver Shooting and Police Training.* Springfield, Mass.: King Richardson Co., 1938

McHenry, Roy C., and Roper, Walter F., *Smith & Wesson Hand Guns.* Harrisburg, Penna.: The Stackpole Co., 1958

Madis, George, *The Winchester Book.* Dallas, Texas: Taylor Publishing Company, 1961

Mayer, Dr. Joseph R., *Five Centuries of Gunsmiths, Swordsmiths and Armourers, 1400-1900.* Columbus, Ohio: Walter F. Heer, 1948

Metschl, John, *The Rudolph J. Nunnemacher Collection of Projectile Arms.* Milwaukee: The Milwaukee Public Museum, 1928

Neal, Robert J. and Jinks, Roy G., *Smith & Wesson, 1857-1945*. South Brunswick, N. J.: A. S. Barnes and Co., 1966

Nutter, Waldo E., *Manhattan Firearms*. Harrisburg, Penna.: The Stackpole Co., 1958

Parsons, John E., *Henry Deringer's Pocket Pistol*. New York: William Morrow & Co., 1952

_____ *The Peacemaker and Its Rivals*. New York: William Morrow & Co., 1957

_____ *Smith & Wesson Revolvers: The Pioneer Single-Action Models*. New York: William Morrow & Co., 1957

Parsons, John E., and DuMont, John S., *Firearms In the Custer Battle*. Harrisburg, Penna.: The Stackpole Co., 1954

Pollard, H. B. C., *A History of Firearms*. London: Geoffrey Bles, 1931. Boston: Houghton Mifflin Co., 1931

Rohan, Jack, *Yankee Arms Maker*. New York: Harper & Brothers, 1948

Rosebush, Waldo E., *Frontier Steel, The Men and Their Weapons*. Appleton, Wisconsin: C. C. Nelson Publishing Co., 1958

Russell, Carl P., *Guns of the Early Frontiers*. Berkeley, Calif.: University of California Press, 1957

Rywell, Martin, *Samuel Colt, A Man and an Epoch*. Harriman, Tenn.: Pioneer Press, 1952

Sandoz, Mari, *The Buffalo Hunters*. New York: Hasting House Publishers, 1954

Satterlee, L. D., *A Catalog of Firearms for the Collector*. Detroit: Published by the Author, 1939

Sawyer, Charles Winthrop, "The Firearms In American History Series." Vol. I, *Firearms in American History, 1600-1800*, 1910, out of print. Vol. II, *The Revolver, 1800-1911*, 1911, out of print. *Note: The second printing of this book was a limited, numbered edition of 1,100 copies, published in 1939 by Charles Edward Chapel and clearly marked as a new printing, but it is also out of print. Firearms in American History*, Vol. III, *Our Rifles*, 1920. Out of print. *Note: The second printing of this book was a trade edition published in 1941 by Williams Book Store, Boston, Mass.* Vol.IV, *United States Single-Shot Martial Pistols*, 1913 (paper-bound only). Out of print. *Note: The only book in the above series of four which carried the so-called volume number on the cover was the one on the revolver, marked "Volume Two."*

*although it was a distinctly separate book from the others. Also, notice that the book on single-shot pistols was published between the date of the so-called Volume II and the so-called Volume III. The first editions are extremely rare, and the reprint of Volume II is already a collector's item.*

Scott, Winfield, *Abstract of Infantry Tactics.* Boston: Hilliard, Gray, Little & Wikins, 1830

————— *Infantry Tactics in Three Volumes.* New York: Harper & Brothers, 1858

Sellers, Frank, and Smith, Samuel, *The American Percussion Revolver.* Ottawa, Canada: The Museum Restoration Service, 1971

Serven, James E., *Colt Firearms.* Santa Ana, Calif.: James E. Serven, 1965

Sharpe, Philip B., *The Rifle in America.* New York: Funk & Wagnalls Co., 1938

Sherlock, Herbert Arment, *Black Powder Snapshots.* Huntington, West Virginia: Standard Publications, Inc., 1946

Shields, Joseph W., *From Flintlock to M-1.* New York: Coward-McCann, Inc., 1954

Smith, Lawrence B., *Shotgun Psychology.* New York: Charles Scribner's Sons, 1938

Smith & Wesson, Inc., *Burning Powder.* Springfield, Mass.: Smith & Wesson, Inc., 1921, *et seq.*

Stevens, Captain C.A., *Berdan's United States Sharpshooters in the Army of the Potomac, 1861–65.* St. Paul, Minnesota: Price-McGill Co., 1892

Ulrich, Arthur L., *A Century of Achievement, 1836–1936, Colt's 100th Anniversary Fire Arms Manual.* Hartford, Conn.: Colt's Patent Fire Arms Manufacturing Co., 1936

Van Rensselaer, Stephen, *An Histology of American Gunsmiths, Arms Manufacturers, and Patentees with Detailed Description of Their Arms.* Morristown, N.J.: Mrs. Stephen Van Rensselaer, 1947

Williamson, Harold F., *Winchester, The Gun That Won the West.* Washington, D.C.: Combat Force Press, 1952

Winant, Lewis, *Early Percussion Firearms.* New York: William Morrow & Co., 1959

————— *Firearms Curiosa.* New York: Greenberg, 1955

————— *Pepperbox Firearms.* New York: Greenberg, 1952

# ACKNOWLEDGMENTS

## Acknowledgments for Photographs

The author acknowledges with thanks the generosity of the following who photographed firearms in their collections for illustrations in this book:

Colt's Inc., Firearms Division; Colt Industries, Inc., formerly known as Colt's Patent Fire Arms Manufacturing Co., Hartford, Connecticut, especially Thomas J. Turner, Manager, Advertising and Public Relations.

Smith & Wesson, Springfield, Massachusetts, especially F. H. Miller, Sales Manager.

Winchester Repeating Arms Company, New Haven, Connecticut, especially Mr. Thomas Hall, Curator.

Calvin Hetrick, New Enterprise, Pennsylvania.

Herman P. Dean, Huntington, West Virginia.

Frank Russell, Fort Lauderdale, Florida.

James E. Serven, Santa Ana, California.

Samuel E. Smith, Markesan, Wisconsin.

Those listed in the Acknowledgments section of previous editions of this book as having contributed photographs from their collections who are not listed here are either unaccounted for or among the honored dead.

All of the arms illustrated were separately photographed and then grouped on the plates, with the result that all firearms and accessories are not necessarily illustrated according to a common scale. The reader is urged to consult the descriptions in the text in order to obtain an accurate idea of the relative sizes.

## Acknowledgments for Editorial and Technical Assistance

The author also thanks the following gentlemen, most of whom devoted long hours of their valuable time to research, correspondence, and proofreading this and previous editions of *The Gun Collector's Handbook of Values:*

Robert Abels, New York City; Ed Agramonte, Yonkers, New York; Langdon Albright, Portageville, New York; Shelley Braverman, Athens, New York; Frank Royce ("Bob") Brownell, Montezuma, Iowa; Edward R. Clark, Silver Springs, Maryland; Cuddy De Marco, Jr., McKeesport, Pennsylvania; Herman P. Dean, Huntington, West Virginia; William B. Edwards, San Francisco, California; Robert Ellithorpe, Encino, California; Robert G. Elz, Orange, California; Robert A. Erlandson, Baltimore, Maryland; Colonel Charles W. Fritz, U.S.A., Ret., Madeira, Ohio; Herbert Glass, Bullville, New York; J. Garnand Hamilton, Canton, Ohio; Gil Hebard, Knoxville, Illinois; Calvin Hetrick, New Enterprise, Pennsylvania; Major James E. Hicks, La Canada, California; Marvin E. Hoffman, Miami Beach, Florida; E. Howe, Coopers Mills, Maine; Leon C. Jackson, Dallas, Texas; Wesley L. Kindig, Lodi, Ohio; Lt. Col. R. C. Kuhn, U.S.A.F., Ret., Chicago, Illinois; Robert Lawrence, Santa Ana, California; Gilbert G. Levy, Hialeah, Florida; Colonel B. R. Lewis, U.S.A., Ret., Vista, California; Herschel C. Logan, Santa Ana, California; Ralph A. Millermaster, Milwaukee, Wisconsin; Charles W. Moore, Schenevus, New York; C. Meade Patterson, Hyattsville, Maryland; Milton F. Perry, Independence, Missouri; Harmon L. Remmel, Fayetteville, Arkansas; Ray Riling, Philadelphia, Pennsylvania; James E. Serven, Tucson, Arizona; Major Hugh Smiley, Henniker, New Hampshire; Samuel E. Smith, Markesan, Wisconsin; and Frank Wheeler, Osborne, Kansas.

The revisor assumes all responsibility for this, the Thirteenth Revised Edition, and actually the Fourteenth Edition. All of those who have worked with the author through the years disagree with one another about the values of some items, but collectively agree that if condition is strictly interpreted according to the author's definitions of "good" and "fine" condition, the descriptions and values are sound.

MRS. CHARLES EDWARD CHAPEL

# INDEX

Stevens pocket pistols, 245
Stillman, A., & Co., musket, 297
Stillman, Ethan, musket, 300
Stocking & Co. pistols, 127
Sturdivant, L.G., rifle, 341
Sutherland pistols, 127, 139
Sweitzer pistol, 56
Swinburn & Son pistols, 409
Swiss firearms, 295
Sword pistol, 387–88
Symmes carbine, 334

Tallahassee carbines, 341
Target pistols, 94, 97, 131, 192, 240, 246, 269, 276, 284, 384
Tarpley carbine, 338
Taylor pocket pistol, 245
Terry pistol, 245
Texas, Republic of, Tryon Rifle, 340
Texas Paterson Colt pistol, 143
Texas war with Mexico, pistols and revolvers in, 77
Thames revolvers, 245
Thuer's conversion, 173–80
Tinder lighter, 388
Tizeray dagger pistol, 422
Towsey & Chipman musket, 297
Tranter revolver, 409
Trap guns, 117–18, 122, 387
Triple-lock model (S&W), 267
Triplett & Scott carbine, 334
Tryon: derringers and pistols, 57, 75, 127–28; rifles, 306, 340
Tucker & Sherrod revolver, 139–40
Turkish model (S&W), 258–59
Turner & Ross revolvers, 246
Turret pistol, Cochran patent, 79–80
Tyler, Texas rifles, 341–42

Ulrich, Arthur, 182
Union Arms Co. handguns, 86–88, 128–30
Union Fire Arms Co. handguns, 246, 286
U.S. Arms Co. knife pistol and revolver, 246
U.S. cartridge handguns, 200–5, and see Army models and Navy models under Colt cartridge handguns and under Smith & Wesson
U.S. cartridge shoulder arms, 313–23
U.S. flintlock pistols, 35–42
U.S. flintlock shoulder arms, 294–305

U.S. Martial and Semi-Martial Single-Shot Pistols, 13, 15, 26, 132, 135, 143, 201, 342
U.S. musket model 1795, 297–98
U.S. musket model 1821 (1822), 303–4
U.S. musket of 1808, 300
U.S. muskets, various models listed chronologically, 297–314
United States Ordnance, Notes on (Hicks), 296
U.S. percussion handguns, 65–69, and see Army models and Navy models under Colt percussion revolvers
U.S. percussion shoulder arms, 304–14, 345–54
U.S. pistol model 1799, 35–36
U.S. pistol model 1805 Harpers Ferry, 36
U.S. pistol model 1807 Springfield, 36
U.S. pistol model 1807–1808, contractor-made, 36–37, 43, 52, 56
U.S. pistol model 1817 Springfield, 38
U.S. pistol (Army, signal) 1862, 69
U.S. pistol (Navy, signal) 1861, 69
U.S. pistol (Navy, signal) 1882, 201–2
U.S. pistol (Navy, signal) 10 gauge 1882, 201–2
U.S. pistol (Navy and Army, signal) 4 gauge 1882, 201–2
U.S. rifle model 1819 Hall breechloader, 48–51, 303
U.S. rifles, various models listed chronologically, 35–42, 65–69, 200–5, 297–323

Values (general comments): 17–28; of cased sets, 380–82; condition a factor in, of Confederate arms, 134–37, 140; of flintlock arms, 369; of foreign arms, 402, 424–30; of freaks and oddities, 388; of Kentucky pistols and rifles, 26, 60, 366
Victory model (S&W), 281
Virginia Manufactory: muskets and rifles, 334–35; pistols, 57, 140
Volcanic arms, 246, 251, 252, 283

Walch revolvers, 88, 130
Walker pistol (Whitneyville, Colt), 146–49
Walking Beam Whitney revolvers, 131
Walsh, J., pistol, 57